PENGUIN BOOKS

Don't Tell Mama!
The Penguin Book of
Italian American Writing

Professor of English literature and feminist theory at the University of Connecticut, Regina Barreca grew up in Brooklyn and on Long Island, and received a B.A. from Dartmouth College, an M.A. from Cambridge University (where she was a Reynolds Fellow), and a Ph.D. from the City University of New York. She has served as an advisor to the Library of Congress for work on humor and the American character, and has been called a "feminist humor maven" by *Ms.* magazine. An award-winning weekly columnist for the *Hartford Courant,* Barreca has published articles in the *New York Times* and the *Chicago Tribune,* and has created, along with columnist Gene Weingarten of the *Washington Post,* a monthly humor "debate" for the *Post's* Sunday magazine upon which an upcoming book about women, men, and humor is based. She is a popular media expert who has appeared on scores of radio and television programs, including *20/20, 48 Hours, Today,* and *The Oprah Winfrey Show.*

Barreca's works, which have been translated into Chinese, German, Spanish, Italian, Japanese, and Czech, include the best-selling *They Used to Call Me Snow White, but I Drifted; Perfect Husbands (and Other Fairy Tales); Sweet Revenge: The Wicked Delights of Getting Even; Untamed and Unabashed: Essays on Women and Humor in British Literature; Too Much of a Good Thing Is Wonderful;* and (as editor) *The Penguin Book of Women's Humor; The Signet Book of American Humor; The Erotics of Instruction;* and *A Sit-Down with the Sopranos: Watching Italian American Culture on TV's Most Talked-About Series.* Barreca lives with her husband, also a professor of English, in Connecticut. Her Web site address is: www.gina barreca.com.

Don't Tell Mama!

The Penguin Book of Italian American Writing

Edited with an Introduction by

Regina Barreca

Penguin Books

PENGUIN BOOKS

Published by the Penguin Group
Penguin Putnam Inc., 375 Hudson Street,
New York, New York 10014, U.S.A.
Penguin Books Ltd, 80 Strand, London WC2R 0RL, England
Penguin Books Australia Ltd, 250 Camberwell Road,
Camberwell, Victoria 3124, Australia
Penguin Books Canada Ltd, 10 Alcorn Avenue,
Toronto, Ontario, Canada M4V 3B2
Penguin Books India (P) Ltd, 11 Community Centre,
Panchsheel Park, New Delhi - 110 017, India
Penguin Books (N.Z.) Ltd, Cnr Rosedale and Airborne Roads,
Albany, Auckland, New Zealand
Penguin Books (South Africa) (Pty) Ltd, 24 Sturdee Avenue,
Rosebank, Johannesburg 2196, South Africa

Penguin Books Ltd, Registered Offices:
Harmondsworth, Middlesex, England

First published in Penguin Books 2002

1 3 5 7 9 10 8 6 4 2

Copyright © Regina Barreca, 2002
All rights reserved

Pages 537–545 constitute an extension of this copyright page.

LIBRARY OF CONGRESS CATALOGING-IN-PUBLICATION DATA

Don't tell mama! : the Penguin book of Italian American writing / edited
with an introduction by Regina Barreca.
p. cm.
ISBN 0-14-200247-X
1. American literature—Italian American authors. 2. Italian Americans—
Literary collections.   I. Barreca, Regina.
PS508.I73 D66 2002
810.8'0851—dc21   2002028996

PRINTED IN THE UNITED STATES OF AMERICA
Set in Bembo
Designed by Ellen Cipriano

This is one for the tribe: my father, Hugo Barreca, my brother Hugo Barreca, Jr., my nephew Hugo Ben Barreca (notice a pattern?), and my nieces Laura and Anne, my uncles and aunts (here and gone), and my cousins—especially Rosemarie and John Rutigliano. And the voices collected here also sing to the ones we've adopted, persuaded, seduced, loved, and kidded into being honorary Italian Americans, especially Michael, Matthew, Tim, and Erica, as well as Wendy and the whole Schlemm crew.
Grazie.

Acknowledgments

Without Michael Millman and Claire Hunsaker at Penguin Putnam in New York, this book would have remained merely a good idea discussed over bottles of Chianti and glasses of sambuca. Michael Millman's swift support and intelligent good humor guided the project from an idea into a publication; Claire kept us on track and on time—she worked incredibly hard while remaining patient and funny, and for that I am enormously grateful. In my office at the University of Connecticut, graduate assistants—both now honorary Italian Americans—Barbara Campbell and Mara Reisman (a.ka. "The Angels of Grace") did all the really demanding work required to put together a volume of this size. They found copies of obscure books and addresses of famous authors. They read and evaluated and helped me decide which pieces to include. They even did the legwork in securing the copyrights and permissions, which is in some cases like finding the owner of an umbrella left on a train—you don't even know where to begin. Margaret E. Mitchell, who has kept me sane (or close to it) through a number of books, not only did her share of sleuthing for the author biographies, which she wrote brilliantly, but did the much more complex job of copyediting the entire manuscript when it was assembled by the press. Many of the writers did me the great personal honor of permitting me to reprint their work gratis, and for this I am also unspeakably grateful, as I am to those writers who prepared new manuscripts particularly for this collection (among these are Wally Lamb, Carole DeSanti, John Glavin, Rose Quiello, Joe Cuomo, Josephine Hendin, Joanna Herman, Mary Saracino, and Mary Ann Mannino). My husband, Michael Meyer, who knows a few things about the process of preparing a hefty literature anthology, reminded me during the toughest moments that being Italian American is worthy of hard work and celebration. He joins me, every day, in doing both.

Contents

Introduction

Why *Don't Tell Mama! The Penguin Book of Italian American Writing*?

Let's start with a cliché: Italian Americans have more fun during a Sunday dinner than many other ethnic groups have in two or three years. Protest all you want that I'm invoking a stereotype, but please understand that your argument in no way undermines my claim. I've not only attended these dinners, I've *cooked* them. Few Italian Americans would dispute the axiomatic portrait of the tribe as a family-centered, conversation-loving, food-appreciating, spirited group. Certain cultural clichés have power because they essentialize and illuminate a portion of the truth and this is one. Trust me.

Another stereotype about Italian Americans, however, is worth fighting over: that of Italian Americans as deliberately dense, badly educated, and culturally unsophisticated. The idea of Italian Americans as a people who would never choose to read a book, let alone write one, is welded into American culture. Such a set of hazardous concepts cannot simply be outlived; it must be dismantled. Here we go.

From where does this stereotype emerge?

Rumor. Rumor has it that Italian Americans don't read very much, buy many books, or produce any authors. Italian Americans, Rumor argues, can't boast of flamboyant storytellers like those offered by Irish Americans, nor of the witty satirists offered by the immigrants from Russia, Poland, and Hungary, nor of the lyrical tragedians drawing from the deep, magical wells of South and Central American culture. "There simply are no young, sophisticated contemporary Italian American writers," Rumor shrugs. "Not like those cutting-edge kids we read in *The New Yorker.*"

"Indeed," acknowledges Rumor, with a patronizing little smile,

"Italian Americans have made some good flicks." And "they've given us some really terrific sports figures." And pizza. And landscaping. ("They're so good with their hands," Rumor gushes.) But Italian Americans writing literature? Rumor raises thin eyebrows, purses thin lips, and drawls, "I don't think so . . . none that I've heard of."

Pull up a chair, sit down, put on your glasses, and get ready to read. Maybe you want a nice cup of coffee, too, because you're going to be reading for a long time.

Why These Selections?

The next 524 pages offer readers an unprecedented collection of the best Italian American writing from the 1800s to the present. Many of the selections will be familiar but, happily, a great many new pieces by well-known Italian American writers are being published for the first time in this volume. Those who expect a uniformity of expression, a picture of life that is as simple and violent as a child's drawing, will be surprised.

Encompassing all forms of style, topic, and genre, this volume includes a more extensive range of voices than such collections generally admit. *Don't Tell Mama! The Penguin Book of Italian American Writing* explores the complex relationship between ethnicity and writing. Mapping our culture's significant Italian American written work is the goal of this volume. Yet, by bringing together close to a hundred voices from well over a hundred years, I have not attempted to homogenize the diversity of Italian American culture . . . but to celebrate it.

Not that I could have homogenized these voices even if I'd wanted to.

Erasing, or even blurring, differences between us would prove useless, were it not impossible. You would no more mistake a Neapolitan for a Calabrese or a Venetian for a Sicilian than you would mistake a diamond for a heart: same deck but an entirely different suit. One of my uncle's favorite jokes illustrates the point: "A nice boy goes off to college and he wants to bring home a girl for Sunday dinner. He warns his mother, 'Ma, I should tell you, she's Swedish, not Italian.' 'So what?' says his mother, 'I'm sure she's a good girl, bring her.' Next month, he's got a new date. 'Ma, I should tell you, she's Jewish, not Italian.' 'I'm sure she's lovely, bring her.' A couple of months later, he shows up with a girl from Hong Kong. 'What a beauty!' his mother says, and welcomes her. A couple of months later, the son walks into the kitchen, hugs his mother, and announces proudly, 'Ma! Guess what? Next Sunday I'm finally bringing home an Italian girl to dinner!' 'No you don't,' yells his mother, waving a wooden spoon in protest, 'not until I know what part of Italy her family is from.' "

The selections gathered in this collection illustrate how Italian American writing has chronicled the process of forming and entering communities. Many of the pieces do not suppress their outrage at the barriers erected by non–Italian Americans against the new arrivals. Next to such works are others persuasively, infectiously, and joyfully reveling in "making America." Even after decades of citizenship, we see contemporary writers struggling still with the concept of Italian American identity. And Italian Americans, accustomed historically to regard ourselves as perpetual outsiders, have had to adjust and recalibrate our written work to adapt to our changing place in the American landscape.

Although most of the writers included in this collection are more concerned with the nuances of personal existence than with the vicissitudes of public life, they nevertheless establish a political and social context for understanding Italian American literature. And while familiar, standard, and mainstream names might lead the way, there are also works by new writers. This is not a collection offering merely the perspective of the dominant Italian American literary group.

Don't Tell Mama! The Penguin Book of Italian American Writing gathers, under one aegis, a complex chorus emphasizing the fact that Italian Americans live (and have always lived) a life not inherited, but invented. Aware of their own process of transformation from citizens of another country to residents of a new land (however long ago the journey was made), the writers here yet again lead us to new paths of understanding the Italian American experience, offering insights into the past as well as providing witness to how we live now. Insight into a sort of collective immigrant history continues to offer fresh material for the construction of even a contemporary writer's sense of identity.

A family's reasons for leaving Italy, for example, are part of a complex narrative that is both personal and historical. If precise details are unknowable, the range of possibilities is clear: escape from noxious poverty or unbearable personal or political persecution; the need to shake off a suffocating social position or economic class; a sense of imaginative unease coupled with a fascination with the very idea of "America"; antagonism from military or religious authorities; untenable family or personal duties; a hunger for education or social betterment. All are described in the pages that follow. There were souls who set off for America under the banner of blessings, with ambition tucked under one arm and self-determination under the other, vowing to return to their villages and cities in triumph; others who left under cover of darkness, sliding out of lives straitjacketed by feudal poverty and despair, grateful for the New World's promise of anonymity and hopeful of shedding the handcuffs of the past. Their stories shape and influence the works printed here.

One of the striking patterns in Italian American writing is the implication that individual identity is attached to a particularly American idea: nobody was born with the right to operate this country. Somebody has to accept responsibility for making sure it all runs smoothly—the Van Burens, the Roosevelts, the Kennedys, or Bushes, for instance—but the privilege should not be taken too seriously. There must be a manager, or a CEO, or a senator, or a minister, just as somebody has to be the cook, or the mason, or the tailor. So you end up playing one position instead of another. But so what? "Nobody is better than you," many Italian children have been counseled. Anybody who thinks he is better is a self-righteous, self-deluded boor, a *cafone*. The converse is also true: if you believe you're worse than everybody, then you deserve what you get because you're a self-righteous, self-pitying chump, a *scimunita*.

Italian Americans write, first and foremost, not to deliver polemics or impart dogma, but to offer the heady and complex mix of pleasure and brutality inherent in art. The writers in this collection should not be expected to be champions or record-keepers for the Italian American community any more than they should be expected to be anthropologists or, for that matter, apologists. Keeping close to life, the writer nevertheless must offer what life does not: the expression of a single moment, an instant that invokes timelessness, and the finely wrought depiction of an unknown soul that we instantly recognize as familiar.

In other words, the vocation of an artist bears little resemblance to the task of cheerleader. Their roles should not be confused. It's not the business of an author to shed a flattering light on everything, but instead to illuminate the real. The result is that we, in our privileged position as readers, can recognize and understand the full range of the Italian American experience. The unease and trepidation our grandparents felt in the presence of the noble and the haughty we might now feel in the presence of the vulgar and the violent. But that offers no more reason to pretend the vulgar doesn't exist than to pretend the noble is not part of the world: each group, however small, has made a significant impact on our world. From their extraordinary positions at the edges of life, they have created and defined the ordinary world in which most of us live. To the extraordinary lives, too, some of the writers here bear witness, portraying such lives not as representative, but as powerful.

Why Me?

Since I was about four years old, I spent summer evenings overhearing my relatives mutter, "She has a real mouth on her, that one. Makes a story out of everything." The women who said it nodded slowly and looked at me as if I were a foreign object, talking about me as if I were out of the room when I was hula-hooping right next to them. Ages twenty-five to ninety-two (the younger ones scooped and packed into ice-cream-colored dresses, the older ones swathed in black), these women sat on folding chairs in front of open garage doors (cooler air, relief from the concrete heat) exchanging knowing looks from under raised eyebrows. They fanned themselves and smoked while their men washed already gleaming cars or weeded the cramped, perfect garden shaded by the fig tree behind my grandmother's house in Brooklyn.

What my grandmother, aunts, and cousins said about me wasn't meant to flatter and it didn't. The description stung and, like a vaccination, it also took. Their words were prophetic. Nerve. A Mouth. Making a story, a "big deal" out of everything: it's what I am, what I do.

I thought it was only me. Turns out it's what Italian Americans do— especially the ones who make it their business to put words on paper. When I learned this, it made me feel better about the uncle who, by way of urging me to be brief whenever I was just getting into the important details of a story, would say, "Sweetheart, remember the meter is running."

I come from a family of accomplished storytellers. I don't say this by way of apology or warning; I say it as a preface the way somebody else might say, "I come from a family of bankers" or "I come from New Jersey." It's a fact. "Never give them your real name" could have been the family motto, carved in granite, translated from the Latin. After all, who really cared if our clan's legend was handed down through generations or made up last Tuesday? "Making a story out of it" was the cornerstone, the bedrock, the shaky but nevertheless enduring foundation upon which the life of my family was built. And here's the tricky part: I'm not sure I'd want to make an argument against it. Why settle for fact? Why offer up prose when you can produce poetry? Why not make a story out of ordinary, found incidents, the way certain artists make sculptures out of wrecked cars or fabricate fabulous images out of dirt, blood, and rust? So it's different from how you found it; so you changed it. So who cares, as long as you made it better?

Despite all this, I look for promises and I make people swear that they are telling me the truth. I need the words.

And I discovered, much later than I should have, that the words I was looking for were out there.

This book grew out of my discovery, about ten years ago, that almost every Italian American writer emerged from pretty much the same backyard—and from a world full of storytellers with a need for words. It wasn't until I was in my mid-thirties that I started to see myself as part of this larger group of writers who shared a heritage. It was then that I started to read everybody I should have been reading all along and rereading the ones I had read all along in the context of Italian American culture: Ciardi, Grizzuti Harrison, Perillo, DeLillo, Parini, di Donato, Fante, Barolini, Gardaphé, di Prima, DeSalvo, Gilbert, and the others. Okay, maybe not absolutely every single one came from the same place. Some had elegant, elaborately educated families, while still others came from households bloodied and shredded by extreme poverty and injustice. Nevertheless, we shared habits and perspectives. Traditions, stories, beliefs, ties, hardships, backyards, and perspectives are what we shared; the range and diversity of Italian American literature demanded to be explored and recorded. And, in many respects, this enormous task was already far along; it was now our business, those of us who handled words for a living, to get books into the hands of readers who also wanted to be a part of this particularly ethnic reading group.

Fred Gardaphé explains at the beginning of his groundbreaking treatment of the stages of the development of Italian American written culture, *Italian Signs, American Streets,* that "the only books that entered my home were those we [he and his siblings] smuggled in from public institutions. Reading anything beyond newspapers and the mail required escaping from my family. [. . .] It betrayed my willingness to enter mainstream American culture, and while my family tolerated this, they did little to make that move an easy one." Sketching for his readers the portrait of four children all sitting around the kitchen table doing homework while life continues to whirl and shout around them, Gardaphé invokes one of the difficulties faced by Italian Americans who have been drawn to books.

Because reading is an act made simpler by solitude and demanding intellectual privacy (meaning that it is more easily accomplished when a person is not, as Gardaphé points out, "subjected to countless interruptions from the family and friends who passed through the house regularly"), reading does not fit neatly into the bustling routine of most working-class households. Italian Americans are subject to additional cultural ambivalence about reading. Catholicism, at least the grassroots variety found in many immigrant communities, did not encourage its followers to go to the Bible itself for instruction, but instead to go to the priest as mediator. Only a man of the cloth could understand and interpret the words on the page correctly. Reading it on your own would only "mix you up." Getting "all mixed up" was considered a great danger in my family, and I believe this applied to other families as well, because it meant you were trying to take on more than you could handle intellectually.

And while there was a respect for learning—a phrase my grandmother used to recite can be loosely translated as "What you carry in your head, you don't have to carry on your back"—there was a competing sense of regard and esteem for the practical applications of one's talents. My family, for example, is still suspicious about how I make a living. My father, whom I adore, would still secretly like to see me go to law school, like my brother. Being tenured and promoted to full professor by forty did not impress. They think because I now teach two days a week, I'm working part-time and should waitress on the other days.

My family carries a not unwarranted prejudice against the usual booklists and best-seller lineups. The worlds portrayed in many traditional works are unfamiliar and uninteresting to them. In few places are their own experiences mirrored; in few works are their own perspectives employed or explored. As a scholar who has studied women's humor, I am comfortable with the process of revealing, not inventing, traditions—especially traditions that have existed without much public exposure outside a select group.

This is not to say, however, that I didn't have my own vast and previously buried prejudices to overcome.

I came to some of the selections for this book with my hat in my hand and a tentative air, with a touch of nostalgia worn as lightly as a veil because I had the nerve to assume that the writings recommended to me by other scholars might be of more sentimental than aesthetic value. I was prepared to be noble; what I was, instead, was humbled. If I approached some works as, so to speak, an "Italian American writer," as a "paisan," rather than as a professor of literature, it was only to discover that my sense of caution should have been applied to my own misconceptions and limited vision. I was entranced by what I read, hungry for more, amazed that it had taken me so long to come to these works and that so many of them had been difficult to find.

I want to make it easier to find these writers; I want them to be as well known as the strength of their writing is obvious. In this quest, I find myself in good company: several writers, critics, and even a few anthologizers have set themselves the same task. As far as I am concerned, the same applies to books as applies to food: the more the better.

It's good for you. You'll like it. Enjoy. And *grazie.*

Explanatory Notes and
Caveats to the Introduction

Hugo Barreca, J.D., M.B.A.

My sister, the editor of this book, will put this at the end of the introduction. She's going to do this because she'll be afraid to offer it as a preamble. This is because I might ruin half her stories by telling you the truth. Well, "truth" is too strong. Let's call it "the other side" of the stories, the unspoken sides of the stories. No one in the family ever told my sister the whole story about anything.

My sister perceives these missing sides of stories with some kind of looking-over-the-shoulder sixth sense. If she were on a subway platform and felt this way, police specialists would advise her to trust her instincts and move along to another spot. She knows these sides to the stories are there, the way you know the other sides of coins are there, even though you can only look at one side at a time.

Oh, I know what you're thinking. This is a setup. The brother in the sister's book, give me a break, they're both in on something. But, nope. Nah-ah. I heard she's editing a book about Italian American writers. Well, I'm as Italian American as she is, so what can she do? Hear it from me for the next fifty Thanksgivings, or put it up front and the hell with it?

Let me explain about Gina and the stories told by the family.

My sister, the big-shot editor with the Ph.D.? When she discovers some tiny particle of a tale that she, by some clever research and deductive reasoning, can prove is not true, she's outraged. Outraged. You should hear her on the telephone. "Hugo, did you know that Tony and Josie were never really married! That the whole wedding was phony, with printed invitations to a nonexistent address? Can you believe it?" So, that's one reason why you can't tell her anything. She doesn't get it: it doesn't matter if they were married or not. No one cares. Well, certainly the men didn't care. We were all putting on this show so no one bothered us, that's all. So "they," the outside world with the so-called reality, will leave us under the radar. It defeats the purpose when someone in your own family blows the cover. We look at each other and roll our eyes: there she goes again! Who let her know?

In order to remain versatile in your ability to dissimulate, you had to stay in practice. For example, I can still remember leaving my Uncle Bill's house and hearing him admonish as I went through the doorway, "Don't give them your real name!" It was kind of a joke, but kind of not, either. He said the same thing every time I left, as a kind of ritual blessing. The liberating thing about his saying this was the assumption that it was somehow "us" versus "them," and almost anyone else was "them." Particularly if they belonged to any sort of institution (church, school, police, federal or state government agencies, medicine, law, corporations, municipalities, museums, racetracks, and the military, to name a few).

The stories we told were not questioned, and not to be questioned. They were to be taken at face value—prima facie, "first face." You see the front of the house and you don't go poking around the back unless invited. It would be insulting to cross-examine your Aunt Rose in order to demonstrate, for example, that her story about shopping for five hours on Nostrand Avenue, yet coming home without any bags, was a tissue of lies. It didn't mean she was doing anything bad. Maybe she was playing Bingo and didn't want to explain to Uncle Phil where she got the ten bucks in the first place. No one cared. It wasn't that we didn't care for each other—quite the opposite—it was that our feelings about Rosie remained unchanged no matter what she did for five hours. Of course, no one checked anything much. Until my sister joined us, that is. As soon as she was about old enough to breathe, everyone had to be on their toes.

As I said, it was considered to be telling close to the truth, certainly not lying (not really), if what you reported as your own actions had actually happened to somebody at one time or another. Therefore, an efficient technique was to borrow from the lives of historical figures. Our family was not real familiar with historical figures from written history; however, our past was rich with oral tradition that could serve as an alternative source. The result was that members of the family sometimes "borrowed" pieces of other people's lives. One had to be careful that these stories didn't slop out of the trough in the wrong places. Then there were these puzzled looks that would come across the listeners' faces—didn't that same thing happen to your brother in 1944? What a coincidence! And in the same leg, too.

The best moments came when you could watch a master in action from the sidelines while being in on the trick. For example, my immediate family, my sister and father and mother and I, often crossed the Canadian border to visit my mother's relatives in Montreal and Quebec. Of course, you had to provide a story to the border guard. The point was, what story? My father considered the border to be a challenge to his imagination, but also an exercise in control. You wanted a story that would be convincing but completely ordinary. However, an alibi devoid of detail could be equally suspicious. A home run was to elicit a bored wave of the hand from the guard as he ushered you past, already focusing on the next car. Telling the truth was, of course, out of the question.

The time I remember the best was the hot day in August when only three of us were going across the border as a group for the first time, due to the fact that Mom was going over as a box of ashes en route to her final resting place, a cemetery in Quebec City. Mom was tucked into a smallish rosewood box, which in turn was wrapped in a black garbage bag and nestled under the tools in the trunk. Up we pull to the border. Now, this is where years of practice at telling a believable story can really pay off. My dad rolls down the window of the Buick.

"What is your name, please?" They type your license plate into the computer, so they know the name they're looking for. The days of giving another name are gone, at least here. Out comes the real name. "Where were you born?" the guard continues. They always ask this in this way. It's supposed to throw you into betraying your real nationality. Dad always joked about answering, "In a hospital," but he never did. It was looking for trouble, and, besides, he wasn't born in a hospital, he was born in a three-room flat on East Houston Street.

"New York City," was the reply, said with a congenial smile.

"Your destination?"

"Montreal." Actually, we were going to Quebec City.

"The purpose of your visit?"

"Holiday."

"Where are you staying?"

"We don't know," said my dad with an easygoing shrug. "We'll just find a place when we get there." Actually, we had confirmed reservations at a nice hotel.

"Are you bringing any gifts with you?"

"Yes, some things for my niece." We weren't going to visit any niece. We had nothing for a niece.

"What's the most expensive gift you're bringing?" Another trick question to catch you off guard.

My father hesitated just the time it would take to mentally rummage through a pile of gifts. Then, the perfect answer.

"A photograph album."

A photograph album! Brilliant! Fabulous! Unbeatable! I watched him the way people watch champion golfers make difficult putts. Just the right touch, just the right spin. He had chosen, without a doubt, the most dead-boring yet plausible gift you could possibly bring to your niece. Then it came, that wonderful, nonchalant wave of the hand from the guard, his eyes looking up to type in the license plate number of the following car. Off we went, smoothly accelerating, my dad rolling up the window. Years of improvisation at his command, yet only a small smile to himself providing a visible measure of his satisfaction.

I won't go on to the details of how we settled my mother in her chosen spot because I don't want to reveal anything to the authorities, no matter how long ago the incident. If I actually had a mother, that is, and if she's buried in Canada, which may or may not be the case.

In the end, it's not surprising that my sister turned to literature as a livelihood. She has been swimming in a sea of fiction since the day she was born.

Don't Tell Mama!

Flavia Alaya

From *Under the Rose: A Confession*

So it was that after about three weeks with my cousins I had been rather glad to come away to Perugia, where new Fulbright grantees had been invited to be prepped for what was, *sub rosa,* really a year's duty as paradiplomats for the Eisenhower State Department. And so it was that on this strangely sublime October day I had already been in the hilly Umbrian city a week—time enough to know I would always be late for afternoon lectures, time enough to have learned to sprint up those last few marble steps and, with my aerobic heart still pounding, let the blinding shade of the portico chill the sweat off me before I made my red-faced entrance through the front door of the lecture hall.

But even as the familiar cool grabbed my hair, I could hear from deep inside an echoing riff of American laughter, unmistakable as bebop. In the frame of the great door, space and time collapse. My face abruptly meets his face shining above the thick black pillar of his cassock. Somebody shouts, *"Canceled!"* and he fractures the news back at us like some bad archangel: *"Barzini has died! Barzini is risen! Barzini will come again!"* Laughing, laughing with relief—for I have not missed the lecture after all—I let the momentum pivot me into reverse again. Somebody says, "Meet Father Browne." Our eyes join in a sudden clearing of haze.

I did not know I would love him. I thought I still loved someone I had left behind me. That day meant nothing more to me then than a reclaimed afternoon, a few sunny hours to sip vermouth under a yellow umbrella, to sail like an American fleet out to the Corso and into the bay of the piazza, Father Browne and the three of us: a young California composer named Paul Glass going to Milan, Anna McGill, a weaver from Milwaukee going to Florence—and me, a master's year in English and comp lit at Columbia behind me, taking my Fulbright to Padua to read literature and politics at the university.

This Cagney Irish priest named Browne was Father Henry J., a Catholic University professor on a research grant in immigration history, just arrived from New York. Paul had staked a personal and instant claim to him. I could see why: the movie star presence, the face a miracle of cunningless animal brightness like a feral child's, the electric violence in his wonderful hair. He had a bristly military brush cut, black sketched with gray—more fur than hair, really—jump-starting from a sharp widow's peak and surging back over that splendid head, which was set as squarely on his thick shoulders as a prizefighter's. And he was funny. Before we'd even ordered our drinks he was off the runway like a Cessna in an updraft, everything Ful- or half-bright, the underbelly of every American careerist in Italy in his gunsights, soaring away as the laughter crashed. The timing infallible, one resistless jolt after another. My brain spun. I laughed as if he'd invented it, as if a depth charge were rupturing some deep archeology of Italian-woman seriousness crusted down in me like a buried sea of Sicilian salt.

He asked me if I was from New York, and still daubing my eyes with a fingertip, I nodded yes. "Well, actually from New Rochelle," I corrected. His burst of laughter was ruthless—the stab-laugh of a comic with a ready punchline. His face came at me in a pitch of forehead that stopped at a pair of black eyebrows like skidmarks, tiny hairs at the tips seeming to sway like antennas. He croons: "Forty-five minutes from Broadway. . . . And oh what a difference it makes." I hear myself say that I still go to the dentist in East Harlem. I hear him roar again. Everybody roars. He is on to me. When he asks, *"Di dove?"* in Italian, I know he means it just as Italians would: from where have my people come, from what inhospitable bony piece of southern mother-soil did they tear their roots? Mine is a New York story and he obviously loves it. And yet he seems also to love having me feel safe in his laughter, unraveling that old familiar worm of Italian girl-child shame like a knot. I notice that his eyes under that jagged fringe of eyelash break light to pieces. I beam him a reassuring smile. *I see what a difference it makes,* it says. *I see what a difference it makes to know the difference.*

He grins back. "Great teeth," he says.

———

I started awake in the night, staring up into the dreary stretch of pregnancy as if I lay at the bottom of a well. So many plans—so thwarted now. Another child, another infant child, needing me, *needing* me, a fetal parasite to consume me down the years again, draining me, its host animal, of every other creation.

I couldn't believe my own thoughts. Hadn't I loved my children, didn't I love them now? Didn't I still cherish their gift of days? I cursed myself—the unspeakable pridefulness of wanting to smother this nascent life to give *me* room to grow! And yet I had loved their infancies, *their* needs, done so much for them—with them. Only now I was exhausted with birthing: children, college, new life. I couldn't go through with it. I wanted to *work*. To make something immortal.

I prayed like a child, like my mother: *Mother Mary*— But St. Ann came to me, in that image of my girlhood saints, wagging her admonishing finger, in her acid-green gown.

I was forty, not a threshold a woman ever crosses without a certain awful fear that this is all there is, all there will ever be. Not even now, a year before the great new millennium, though they tell us now that forty is quite young enough to beat a woman's unforgiving clock—if she wants to. We used to think—can it be only twenty years ago?—that childbirth at forty put mother and child at risk. So wise ones told me then, so I told myself. Was it unreasonable to rationalize an abortion this way? The cool English surgeon who finally agreed to perform it rationalized it this way. He could possibly see what I might do if he hadn't.

The agony of that choice is still as alive as it was—so vivid that I can still find it in myself to think sometimes how little it would have mattered in the scheme of things to spare that germ of life—for what great achievement, in the end, offset the pity of its loss? To see myself the Scarlet Woman after all, sick with the arrogance of ambition. To wonder if even the three I nurtured without an instant's regret might think harshly of me, remembering perhaps what I've forgotten of their pain as I withdrew from them in the anguish of my fear, fleeing like a victim, insane, savage, hysterical, down the corridors of my little time, stinking with death. To imagine how I may have crushed Harry—once, always a priest—with my certainty, with all the transparent certainty of my hysteria, that this was what I needed to do, this was all I wanted. I will punish myself with father thoughts, with mother thoughts, forever, here and hereafter. But I will never let myself forget I had to do it.

And I will never forget that this has happened to millions of women. It will undo nothing to ruminate my own private suffering, and I will still always die that little death. But I will never forget, because it is good to remember, *this:* that when I first went to English doctors, for whom abortion was then an entirely legal procedure, and sought their help and counsel, they offered me none. The U.S. Supreme Court, with *Roe v. Wade* the year before in America, had thrown our own puritan system into confusion, but it had not yet made abortion easy. These English doctors knew this, and treated me like a fugitive whose sole motive was child-murder. How I remember envying this invisible embryo they wanted so ferociously to save without a passing thought to saving the woman it came in.

It is not an English attitude, though I thought it was then. Just a cruel one, a narrow one, without nationality, and without boundaries of time.

———

His hands are palsied now. He can hardly sign his own name. It is enough to make me cry to think of him suffering the slow agony of this loss. It has often been enough, I have watched him time and again struggle against his shaking wrist to put the quivering pen to paper. Yet it no longer seems to trouble him. Nothing does, now that my mother's adoring pity has ceased to be the theater of his meaning. Perhaps he has come too close to dying too many times, even while she lived. *She* could sign his name then, while he still managed by TV remote and princess telephone to gamble his heart out, terrorizing her with his investment brinksmanship as she pictured him annihilating their life savings in a single day's shoot-out on the options exchange. Sandy and I still laugh about the ambulance night we hurried to his side in the hospital, when all he could say in a hoarse, pleading sputter, as I leaned into his white face for his last words, was: *"Close . . . all . . . my . . . positions."*

Of course these were not his last words, which he has yet to utter, though he has reminded us more than once of his own mother's ancestral Italian wisdom, that life, after all—even a life as long as his—is only *un'affacciata alla finestra*—a glance out of the window. He still sleeps in his own bed, hired women performing all the necessary caring offices Maria did when she was alive. His television window still opens onto Italian opera videos and masses from the Vatican or St. Patrick's Cathedral. And his real window is still there to glance out of, literally and otherwise, with its incomparable view of hillsides as rockbound and spiny, and skies as nearly unchangeably blue, as those that look immemorially down on his mother's grave in the Vesuvian foothills of Sperone, along the Appian Way.

We thought he was dying of pneumonia last year, just before his ninety-ninth birthday. Even as he fought through he seemed finally, hopelessly old, old beyond old. I sat beside his hospital bed, drawing him again and again in pencil and chalk, trying to capture that queer mix of granite and grace that had carried him so far. He has only begun to admit his hearing is failing. Lou and I, tired of shouting, finally bought him a little chest-hung amplifier with earphones, and I would sit there, beyond any fear of him now, holding his smooth hand, talking, listening. For knowing somehow that I had been writing of him, *he* would talk, mostly, about his childhood, his family, his boyhood in Libya, his near-drowning once on the African shore where he'd stopped for a dip in the sea, his stint with D'Annunzio's *Arditi* in the Great War. I ask how he translates *ardito* and he instantly snaps back: *foolhardy*. He tells me of his immigration, his businesses, his mother. He seems to want to tell me everything—everything—before he goes. For memory, he seems to know at last, is all he will take with him.

Something confessional clung to this moment, inspiring me to want to help him go shriven and clean, if it was what he wanted. And yet, in a strangely guilty reversal, it was my own shriving that spoke almost unbidden from my heart when I spoke, needing to know if he could forgive me the hurts I had done him, that perhaps I was still to do. And unhesitatingly he shook his head and sighed and said, "I should sooner ask that of you."

For moments after, I couldn't speak. When I found my voice again and asked if there were anything he had still to tell me, he replied with such imperious finality, "I have said what I needed to say," that I was forced to laugh. And understanding I meant, "No secrets?" he smiled at me with a sad irony, as he does now. "My life is my life," he said. "Nothing about it is secret. Only things . . . at a certain point . . . no longer spoken of."

Well, evasive to the end, I thought. And yet it flashed on me, like a swift glance of light off a mirror, that he *knew* I knew.

But he did not go then. He rallied beautifully. We celebrated his ninety-ninth birthday in the hospital. Ann followed me to California, but he said no more to her. Then he returned home. Months passed. We lamented, at intervals, that after all he would take his story to the grave.

In September he was sick again, and again I arrived in Temecula, just as he was declared out of danger and back in his own bed, to find him looking pale and weary, his spotty pinkness the skin-deep flush of cartridged oxygen. I dug the amplifier out of a dresser drawer and placed it around his neck like an amulet.

It was as though our conversation had never been interrupted. He continued the saga of his young life, bringing me to New York City now, to Yorkville, where he had roomed in the 1920s, to the young German couple who'd taken him in as a boarder. She was a very good cook, he said—and then, abruptly, as if he must blurt it out or never say it: "You have a brother." I took his meaning without ambiguity. He looked straight into the unstartled look on my face. But I think at that moment no look of mine could have stayed him.

It had happened just before he was married, he said. In her husband's benighted innocent affection for him, the child had actually been named

Mario. He told me his surname, when and where he'd been born. The odd but significant fact that the doctor who'd delivered him had been the same who later delivered my brothers and me—but not Ann.

Ah, but this, for him, was an emotional old country. He had left it behind him. He would not venture back—not now, not any more. He let me go alone, imagining my guess true, that she had come to know while she was pregnant with Ann and had wanted to die. Maria's venerated ashes sit there on his bureau in a beautiful bronze and silver box, their double portrait beside it, smiling—still lovers.

Time has been merciful to my father's face, its wrinklelessness a wonder of the world. I marvel that it can still tell his emotions like a boy's, show such changeful sweeps of inner sorrow. Only there is this terrible thing: his tear ducts have dried—he can no longer cry. Even after this confession he seemed unrelieved, shutting his eyes as if in pain, opening them again and again, blinking dryly.

At last he resumed in a rough whisper, taking gulping breaths, staring straight ahead of him: "A few years later—we arranged to meet— an uptown subway station—on the West Side." He paused. "I had not seen her since my marriage," he went on. "It was the worst of the Depression—her husband out of work." Again he paused. "She had come to me—desperate—begging for help—" his voice broke and he squeezed his eyes helplessly shut. "I refused her," he whispered.

Suddenly, uncannily, I could see her—the young mother standing before us both in that cold tunnel, her child clinging to her hand.

His chest heaved. "I turned her away." I knew he had entered the purgatory of those who can no longer weep. My heart caved with pity as he repeated: *"I turned her away."*

I wept for him. I wept for her. I wept for me.

Carol Bonomo Albright and Elvira Di Fabio

Introduction to Rocchietti's
Lorenzo and Oonalaska

As a grandchild of Italian immigrants, I wanted to be fully a part of America, and so in grammar school history class, I waited for some mention of an Italian presence in early American history. To no avail. By high school, I had given up this early hope, but became reanimated in college European history classes at any mention of Italian history.

After grad school, having joined the American Italian Historical Association, I finally learned about the Italian architects and artists responsible for many government buildings in Washington, D.C., about Italian American soldiers and generals in the Revolutionary and Civil wars, about the stone cutters and carvers of Barre, Vermont, and many similarly interesting facts. With my background in literary studies, though, I knew that literature often acts as a means of "fleshing out" history and putting a "face" on people and events, and so I was eager to find some early Italian American novelists who could put an historical face on my experience.

One morning in 1999, I received a catalogue of rare books and noticed a listing for an 1835 novel, *Lorenzo and Oonalaska,* published in Virginia and written by a certain Joseph Rocchietti of Casale Monferrato, a small town outside of Turin. Was this the historical link I was looking for?

The novel consists of a series of letters—some are love letters between the title characters, and others expound political ideals and experiences exchanged between the protagonist and his brother and friends. Through Oonalaska's letters we learn of a young woman who clearly engages her maidenly assertiveness to persuade Lorenzo to stop speaking to her about his political ideals, since such "pursuits, delightful as they may be, are not all-sufficient," and instead to sing her songs of love.

Of equal importance to this love story, Rocchietti, through his presumably autobiographical character, Lorenzo, voices principles resonant of the American experience. Despite his different circumstances, Lorenzo expresses feelings similar to our ancestors of the great migration. On first arriving in America, he, as they, feels like an outsider, "[a] man . . . abandoned, unknown, poor, and friendless in a strange country." In crying for Italy to be free of the tyranny of Austria, Lorenzo, like Patrick Henry, calls for "liberty or death." Furthermore, he reveres the republican principles of George Washington and shares Washington's esteem of *Cato,* Joseph Addison's play against tyranny. And like our ancestors, Rocchietti celebrates the same creativity and inventiveness that marked the Italian American entrepreneurial experience. At one point, for example, Lorenzo theorizes about inventing a vessel "in the shape of a fish" for "swimming in the air."

I had finally found what I was looking for. In many respects— through Lorenzo's cry for liberty and against tyranny, Rocchietti's celebrations of creativity and the entrepreneurial spirit—this novel brought together the two strains that existed in me, the Italian and the American ones. Did it satisfy me? Partly. My colleague, Elvira Di Fabio of Harvard University, and I are bringing out an annotated edition of Rocchietti's novel for others to use as a guide to their American experience, and our selections that follow will, we hope, give a taste of what's to be savored. But since this book existed on overlooked bookshelves for some 165 years, there must be, we reason, other books by Italian American authors of this and earlier periods yet to be discovered. And, so, the search goes on.

Carol Bonomo Albright
Elvira Di Fabio

J. Rocchietti

From *Lorenzo and Oonalaska (1835)*

Oonalaska writes to Lorenzo from Bern, Switzerland: A heart and feelings in perfect unison with ours, are most difficult to be met with. Education and custom oblige us to suppress natural feeling, and appear in the world the thing we are not; and, if by chance, supposing ourselves friends, nature asserting her rights, we show ourselves as we are and as we ought to be, malice and envy immediately set to work to make us every thing we are not. . . . Miserable is that being whose heart is formed with every kind feeling towards his fellow-creatures; yet, looks around in vain for one congenial mind, into whose bosom it may pour the rich treasure of its affection: it fears to love, lest it meets with coldness and contempt: it fears to place confidence, lest it be betrayed: thus, the heart which possesses every requisite to make others happy, cannot be so in itself: its best feelings are chilled, its best affections are nipped in the bud: thus the mind, having no external object on which it can repose itself, is obliged to have recourse to those intellectual pursuits, which can then alone render life desirable, by diverting its thoughts from its unoccupied feelings. But, there are moments, when even these pursuits, delightful as they may be, are not all-sufficient.

If, in our pilgrimage through life, we chance to find one being who seems capable of understanding us, who thinks and feels as we do, to whom it is not necessary to explain our feelings, with what pleasure do we look on, and converse with that being. The soul seems to have found its better half, unto which it expands with delight; all is instantly seen through another medium; to the heartlessness of the world we are no longer sensible; our pains are mitigated, and our pleasures heightened.

Narrator recounts a meeting between Oonalaska and Lorenzo: Oonalaska was playing on the harp, when Lorenzo entered her room.

"Why do you not proceed, Oonalaska."

"I shall; but, after so long an absence, I want to tell you a great many things."

They sat down near a window, from whence the lake of Geneva presented a beautiful landscape.

"How fine is now that lake, Lorenzo!"

"Very much so."

"Do you see the steamboat?"

"I see it reflected in your eyes."

She smiled and blushed; and after a rapturous moment of interchanged looks, with her innocent manners, Oonalaska related all the little adventures of their [her family's] voyage. Afterward she took the *Vicar of Wakefield;* and, in presenting it to Lorenzo, she asked if he had ever read that fine tale.

"I have, Oonalaska; but every time I open it, it seems always new to me."

"Well, Lorenzo, read it now to me, whilst I am sewing this handkerchief for my father."

He read; but the fine descriptions of that little book could not prevent our reader from stopping, when he saw a tear rolling down the cheek of Oonalaska.

"Well, Lorenzo, to-morrow we will proceed from this touching passage: for the moment I will fulfill my promise."

She took her harp, and with an expressive voice, she sung [*sic*]: "Di piacer mi balza il cor" ["My heart flutters from pleasure"].

The sunset was giving his last ray to the horizon of the lake of Geneva, when Lorenzo took leave of Oonalaska. In going home, which was about two miles from that of Mr. Ethelbert, the full moon was enlightening the walk, which his lovely thoughts rendered still more delightful; and whilst he saw no obstacles before his future happiness, his imagination was in extacy [*sic*]. But did the sky ever shine [for such] a long time for a worthy man of this earth!

Oonalaska writes to Lorenzo from Lausanne, Switzerland: Thou thoughtest of me! Every time I walked through these delightful fields, I did the same, and thy memory endeared my life. My heart embraced all nature, and nature smiled on me. How many times I sent my heart to thee on the wings of my thought, and then I felt the ambrosia exhaling from the plants, and a zephyr caressing my forehead. If our souls were not immortal would I have felt such sympathy? When on the mountains of Swizerland [sic] thou feltest an inebriate pleasure of divinity, it was thy soul, which flying to me made me feel the joy thou wishedest [to] impart to me.

Lorenzo writes to Oonalaska from America: Excuse me, my love, if I do not write to thee on the manners and customs of this nation: excuse me, if I do not describe to thee these fine mountains: every thing is sublime because I am thinking of thee. Yes, this beautiful nature should be a desert without the thought of thy love: every time I am occupied in something, I see only thy inspiring image: and how could I be able to write were it not about thy amiability. Very often, absorbed in the fine ideal which surrounds thee, my pen falls, believing thou are in my presence. . . .

Who would have believed, before the invention of vessels, that man would have sailed around the globe? And now, who would believe our age or posterity will find the means of swimming in the air? Till now the attempts of going against the wind have failed: but, if I were a mechanic, I would construe a balloon in the shape of a fish; and by means of a machine, I would move the fins in several directions. It seems to me it would not be difficult to swim against the airy elements as the fishes do against the most rapid waterfalls.

Lorenzo writes to his friend Charles from Turin, Italy: [A] great many of my friends left Piedmont; Austria invades Italy; and the sound of liberty repeated every where is now silent. My mother and sister, with tears rolling down their cheeks, wish me in Switzerland, fearing the government might cast me into prison. Indeed, if they will not doom me like G . . . , who [was executed], a perpetual confinement might be my end. Now I never go out without two pistols in my pocket; but what can these avail against the strongest? I, who wanted nothing but the rights of man, and sacrificed the whole of my property for my country, am now obliged to live as an outlaw. Dear mother, dear sisters! How can I leave you, now destitute of every thing? The infamous tyrants, not satisfied to see us deprived of our whole property on earth, took from your mouth your daily support. But now, what can I do? I cannot stay longer in the land of my nativity. My dear father fell on the field of honor; my brother Henry was hanged for having been another Gracchus; and my brother-in-law Jacopo, and brother Hippolitus, are now fighting in Spain for the same cause of liberty.

★ ★ ★

Charles writes to Lorenzo from Paris, France: Come with me to England. The days of our sports are past, my dear Lorenzo. How often I recollect the university in which we received an education so contradictory to the iron government of thy country! Who would have believed the sentiments of Cicero, Cato, Plato, Dante, Petrarch, and Machiavel, could have made unhappy my best friend Lorenzo? I will remember all my life when thou, in reading Bruto Secondo of Alfieri, spokest with such sublime eloquence against the oppressors of thy country. I feel yet a chill. If the Italian people had been present at thy oration, thou wouldst not now be obliged to flee from thy tyrants.

Lorenzo writes to Charles from Missolonghi, Greece: The state of Greece is in great danger; they have a great many intestine divisions: however I am determined to be either conqueror or conquered for the good cause. A man must operate according to his own sentiments. The greater part of Greece is for freedom. I shall do all a man ought to do against the tyrants of an oppressed people. And when shall we see our rights established among men? The Pope, not feeling the interest his predecessor felt in the time of the crusades, does not impart his holy blessings in favor of his own christianity [sic], against the believers of Mahomet, because he prefers to sustain his temporal holiness with the diabolical alliance of kings, than to be crowned in heaven by the hand of Jesus: and now he is silent as a convict before judges. . . .

From my window I see the Turks surrounding the city of the most brave Greeks. Will men always be in contradiction with themselves? Behold, Charles, within the walls of this city, men struggling against tyranny, and a greater number without ready to slay the former, because they took arms to defend their own rights. And for whom are those Turks now fighting against us? For the Sultan! for a man swimming in a harem of pleasures: for a man who shuts up their daughters in golden rooms, because they were the prettiest of the country: and after having shed their blood on the field, they present willingly their heads to the executioner, if the freak should pass through their master's brain of seeing their heads on the ground. And do you believe, Charles, they would be so blind, if they were not under the creed of Mahomet? So Lucretius: "Bantum [sic] religio, potuit suadere malorum" ["Too much religion is apt to sway us into evils"]. . . .

Write to my mother to tell my sister, Carlotta, not to be alarmed about my situation. From the very moment that we, poor creatures of clay, breathe the breath of life, we are doomed to make the first step towards the occident, among a thousand dangers, which very often put an end to us before the short period of 75 years of age. And, does this life of calamities deserve an attachment? My life is nothing else but a little spark, losing itself in infinity of atoms; and when the molecules will be dissipated, it shall be the same as it was, obscurity around its little circle. Before the end of it, I am told, by my dear father, to act with honor and integrity towards the sufferers: I feel his own soul in my heart: and if I have a son, I would teach him the same principles: liberty, or death. . . .

And why do not all nations shake hands with each other, and crush to death the few tyrants of this planet? Shall we always be obliged to exclaim with Campbell: "Shall crimes and tyrants cease but with the world?" . . .

And from Switzerland: Here I am neither obliged to speak haughtily to the clown, nor affectionately to those of exalted birth. I may now linger on objects agreeable to me, without losing time in insignificant attentions and ceremonies which people bestow one up another.

Charles writes to Lorenzo from London, England: Yes, Lorenzo, I heard many clergymen, who excited in me the very loathful sensations which you describe in your last letter. As we find a great many, following professions for which they have no vocation, so, we find spouting orators of the church, who believe the true source of rhetoric is nothing else but speaking loud, and inveighing against writers, whom they could not, or would not understand.

Oonalaska writes to Lorenzo from Neuchâtel, Switzerland: Last night I went to a ball, at which, instead of enjoying the society of each other, I found a great many strangers wanting only to show a consciousness of superiority over their fellow beings. It would seem that such aristocratic creatures go into society with no other purpose than as candidates for king and queen, to secure the favor of their inferiors. I would not give an hour of your society, Lorenzo, for all the balls of this universe.

Exchange between Mr. Ethelbert, Oonalaska's father, and Lorenzo: Mr. Ethelbert, finding his daughter in love with Lorenzo, one day he called the latter in his private room.

"Lorenzo," said he, "your sincerity leads me to perceive your love toward my daughter. I would have no objection if your political sentiments were like mine: however, after having been disappointed in your noble struggles, I find no reason why you should not renounce your democracy. I am a rich man in England, and I have this only daughter:

should you coincide with me, not only Oonalaska is your wife; but, with my means and your talents, I promise you an eminent place in London."

"Dear sir," replied Lorenzo, "I love Oonalaska, and could not be happy had I all the world without her. But, sir, you are not bound as I am in behalf of my sentiments towards a Republic. I admire your politeness and hospitality, Mr. Ethelbert, in not having opposed my sentiments: but, permit me only to tell you, that the cause I advocate is but the progress of education, which will bring all nations to banish any other government but that in favor of plurality. But, from this moment, in paying homage to your gentility, I will always be silent on this subject."

"No, Lorenzo, it cannot be, unless you abandon your principles."

"It is impossible, Mr. Ethelbert; a few days before my dear father expired on the field of honour, he made me swear against every other principle of politic but those of Brutus, Cato, and Washington."

"It is with a breaking heart I must tell you, Lorenzo, you cannot be my son-in-law." . . .

So that, without uttering a single word to Oonalaska, with a heartbreak, Lorenzo took leave from the object of all his hopes.

Lorenzo writes to Oonalaska from Ingouville, France: The original sin, Oonalaska, is the want of education. . . .

I prove a very singular sensation every time I present myself in a hotel in which hospitality is given with more, or less kindness according to the extensiveness of your purse. They measure all travellers from foot to cap; and elevate them towards heaven, according to the exterior appearances of their travelling expenses. Such is their acuteness, that they are seldom found putting a Lord on the seventh, or a Burgess on the first floor; so that, from the first floor to the garret, where all pedestrians are confounded, you would know the standing of each traveller in society by the several degrees of their rooms: and the landlord is more or less cheerful with you, according to the quantity of money you spend. If in the New-world I shall not find better people, I will go on the top of a mountain to breathe the air embalmed with flowers. . . .

After my solitary reflections on the top of a hill, I do not like to see at the table, fops fond of distinguishing themselves by causing the servants to feel their inferiority before them. It seems they sit at the table of four francs, not to satisfy their want; but, to play the gentlemen. . . .

Now from New York, Lorenzo writes: It is with sorrow of mind I find among Americans too much anxiety of money. If this wise government

were encouraging superior men on every side of the United States
to deliver public lectures on history, showing to the people the evil of
the times which are past, America would become the polestar of a true
Republic.

Lorenzo writes to Charles from New York: I am one of those cosmopolites,
who believe, that a person has no right to disregard a nation, because he
observes in it, particular instances of depravity, for, he should reflect,
that man is always man with more, or less modification, according to the
age in which he lives. We cannot find a single nation which is not
adorned by men of virtue, and my impression is, that we are prejudiced
in favour of our native country, because we there received the first ca-
resses of our parents.

Lorenzo writes to his brother, Hippolitus, from Philadelphia: Do not yet attempt to emulate the splendid style of any author, who had dazzled you:
your tender age is not fit to follow the eagle in his flight. No strong passion if you do not feel it: write according to your own heart. Your age
is not fit for an ingenious sensibility, which is always agreeable when you
exhibit it in its natural simplicity: no exclamations; no tropes, no figures:
write as if you were explaining your feeling with the sincerity of a soul
before the Great Judge of human secrets; and your writing will be eloquent.

   If you wish to run the difficult career of learning, form your heart,
and nothing will be wanting: but, if we do not feel in ourselves nobility, and sublimity of mind, the attempt will be always a disgraceful one:
it is the fire of heaven alone, which can purify the mind of man. Europe, my dear brother, swarms now too much with pretensions to learning: but, if the writer's aim is not that of being useful to society, this
noble art is nothing but a profane prattle. . . .

   Do not bewail our situation, dear Hippolitus: man is born to un-
dergo inconveniences: misfortune is a great school for those, who are
wise to learn from it: a life spent among books in all the comforts of the
closet, may fit a man for becoming an astronomer, or artist: but, he will
be always ignorant of himself, and of the human heart. . . .

   See, even among republics, the many are attached to the richest
party, because they fear to lose their direct interest with the wealthy
people. Ignorance is deceived by want of knowing a gentleman among
cunning rascals. . . .

   This little globe turning around, the very inconsistent Being called
Man improving, must feel the noble sentiment of becoming a true citizen of the world.

George Anastasia

Sinatra's "Associations" with the Mob

Shortly before the first casino opened in Atlantic City back in 1978, a local mobster went into the bar business.

The guy was named Saul Kane. He had been a bail bondsman and later he went to jail for dealing drugs. But when he was on top of his game, he was known in certain circles as the Meyer Lansky of the Boardwalk, a major money-maker and confidant of soon-to-be mob boss Nicodemo "Little Nicky" Scarfo.

Kane opened a joint on Pacific Avenue a few blocks from the Resorts International Casino-Hotel. He called the place the My Way Lounge—had the interior plastered with photos of Frank Sinatra, had the jukebox jammed with Sinatra tunes. Soon all the local wiseguys and wannabes started hanging out there.

Kane would run ads in the paper touting his bar and tweaking the cops. "Come meet the Mob at the My Way," the ads screamed.

Frank Sinatra never set foot inside the place, but what did it matter? It was another link, however tenuous, between the greatest saloon singer of all time and one of the most exclusive men's clubs in America.

Sinatra and the mob.

Fact or fiction?

Probably a little of both.

First, a disclaimer. There are those who get upset at any discussion of the "associations" Frank Sinatra had during his career as a singer and movie star. Just because his name ends in a vowel, they say, people want to claim he's a mobster, a Mafioso, a wiseguy.

That's not what it says here. What it says here is that over the course of his long and storied career, Frank Sinatra crossed paths with guys who never had to work a 9-to-5 job, guys who cheated and stole and lied to get ahead, guys who knew where the bodies were buried.

And they weren't all politicians.

Sinatra, on the public record at least, never said much about this. But his associations were fairly well-documented and frequently attracted law-enforcement attention.

Where to start?

How about the trip he took to Havana in 1947 with one Joseph "Joey Fish" Fischetti? Sinatra apparently was just along for the ride, but Fischetti and nearly a dozen other top American mobsters had business in Cuba. They met there with Charles "Lucky" Luciano, who had been deported to Italy and was angling to get back into the United States to solidify his control of the American La Cosa Nostra.

Or how about Sinatra's partnership interest in the Berkshire Downs Racetrack with, among others, New England mob boss Raymond Patriarca? Or how about how he decided to give up his Nevada gaming license rather than fight charges that might have exposed his ties to Chicago Mafia don Sam (Momo) Giancana?

The Giancana incident, perhaps more than any other, epitomizes the complex and titillating nature of Sinatra's oft-cited "connections." And while some in law enforcement say it was just the tip of the iceberg, a glimpse of a more sinister association, for those in the entertainer's camp it demonstrated the price Sinatra was willing to pay when it came to friendship and loyalty.

So it was that in 1963, Sinatra gave up his interest in the Cal-Neva gaming lodge in Lake Tahoe, where he had allowed Giancana to stay as a guest even though Giancana was on the state gaming authority's "black list" and banned from all Nevada casinos. Giancana was reportedly visiting his girlfriend, Phyllis McGuire, who was performing with her sister at the casino.

The affair, which attracted a lot of media attention, was one of a series of incidents that led to a split with President John F. Kennedy, for whom Sinatra had raised serious campaign money in 1960. But while the president and his attorney-general brother, Robert, decided they had to sever all ties with Sinatra, goodfellas such as Giancana never forgot.

Giancana, according to a book co-authored by his brother and nephew, used to complain about the entertainers who got a leg up in the business from a "family member," then forgot about it when they made it big. Sinatra, said Giancana in the book *Double Cross,* wasn't that way.

"He's too good for those bums in Hollywood," Giancana told his brother. Sinatra, he said in what is the highest form of underworld praise, was "a real stand-up guy."

Giancana, who himself moved in many circles, went on to share a mistress with President Kennedy, a woman named Judith Exner who had met the president through Sinatra. Sinatra had also had a brief fling with the flashy brunette.

Strange bedfellows indeed.

Several years later, Sinatra again found himself in the middle of a big Mafia media flap when he performed at a fund-raiser at the Westchester Premier Dinner Theater in Tarrytown, N.Y. The feds eventually charged that the theater was the target of a mob operation in which New York boss of bosses Carlo Gambino and several of his top associates pocketed in excess of $400,000.

The fund-raiser was just one of several alleged mob scams that had the theater as a backdrop. It's mentioned only because of an infamous photo taken backstage after Sinatra's performance.

Ol' Blue Eyes is in the center of the picture surrounded by eight serious fans, all of whom showed up on organizational charts in the FBI's New York office. Among them were Paul Castellano, Vincent "Jimmy the Weasel" Fratianno and, smiling benevolently with his eyes closed as the camera flashed, Carlo Gambino.

The boss of bosses. Just one of the guys. Rubbing elbows with the star.

Go figure.

That Sinatra had a special place in the hearts of certain nefarious underworld characters is without dispute. Those who knew him and those who wanted to—like the guys down at the My Way Lounge—apparently held the skinny kid from Hoboken in the highest regard.

He epitomized what these guys wanted to be. Think of the image: a cigarette dangling from his lips in some smoky bar, suit jacket thrown over the back of his chair, tie loosened, a scotch in one hand, a beautiful woman in the other.

The existential macho man.

Sinatra's mob associations have been detailed in dozens of organized-crime books, from *Double Cross* and Fratianno's tell-all, *The Last Mafioso,* to Stephen Fox's *Blood and Power* and Jay R. Nash's *World Encyclopedia of Organized Crime.*

Everybody who writes about the mob, it seems, has a Sinatra story to tell.

The post-performance party at the Westchester Dinner Theater is one of the most repeated.

Another, told in several versions, deals with Willie Moretti, the North Jersey gangster who either discovered Sinatra or gave the young singer's career a boost when he really needed it.

Moretti, the story goes, was the guy who helped Sinatra get out of what was thought to be an iron-clad contract with bandleader Tommy Dorsey. Sinatra wanted out so he could pursue a career on his own, but Dorsey wasn't about to give up control over the crooner.

Enter Moretti, who "negotiated" a deal with Dorsey one night in the dressing room of a club where the band was performing. Moretti put a gun in Dorsey's mouth, according to various accounts of the incident, and told the bandleader he had two choices. Either he, Dorsey, would sign an agreement releasing Sinatra from his contract, or he, Moretti, would pull the trigger.

It was an offer that Dorsey "couldn't refuse."

Later Mario Puzo in *The Godfather* would borrow some of the details, add a horse's head, and create the signature phrase of perhaps the most widely read piece of Mafia fiction ever written.

Over the course of nearly 70 years in the spotlight, Frank Sinatra, wittingly or unwittingly, provided wiseguys, politicians and writers with a piece of himself. The attraction is obvious. He was the best at what he did, a one-of-a-kind. No one interpreted a lyric in quite the same way. And when he stood on stage or sat in a recording studio, no one was his equal.

Sine qua non, said the Romans long ago.

That's what they were going for in the My Way Lounge down on Pacific Avenue. Even wiseguys have heroes.

Tony Ardizzone

Holy Cards

The Milk Bottles

"Children," the Sister of Christian Charity called out. "Children, who made us?"

From his fifth-row desk, Dominic stared dreamily out the classroom window. The sky behind the bare trees on Armitage Avenue appeared to be breaking apart. Little pieces of it drifted lazily to the sidewalk. Snow. A bad window, it showed only the sides of things. Dominic lived in the second-floor flat in the corner building on Fullerton and Southport, and from its high bay windows enjoyed a more expansive view. He enjoyed looking down at all the traffic moving out from the busy stop below. He liked watching the different people on the street. He was small and dark, with a swoop of straight black hair that fell across his forehead like a comma. Here in class, he had to look up to see anything.

"Once again, children. Louder. Who made us?"

This one was easy. "God made us," the children singsonged.

At home a service flag hung in the center window, blocking Dominic's way. He'd have to crouch to see under it, or else he'd push it aside. His ma would yell when she caught him pulling on the flag's fringe. It was something special or holy. Sometimes when there were no buses or delivery trucks to look at, his fingertips would trace the outline of the flag's star. Sitting at his desk watching the snow, Dominic reached forward and traced the figure of his father's star.

Sister rapped her wooden yardstick across her desk. An old woman, perhaps in her late sixties, she wore thick glasses and had a large mole on the right side of her nose and a gold front tooth. "And who is God?"

Dominic pictured the blue cover of his *Baltimore Catechism*. When he sat studying in the red stuffed chair across the room from the windows, he'd try to keep his eyes on the letters in the book and away from the sky and the streets. Sometimes when his Aunt Rose came over to visit, she'd help him out and pretend to be his teacher, Sister Mary Justine. Aunt Rose would ask each question and give him hints whenever he got stuck. After he finished his homework and had thoroughly dusted the front room and the dining room, he could look out the corner windows and play.

"God is the Supreme Being," the children were reciting, "who is infinitely perfect and who made all things and keeps them in existence."

"And why did God make us?" Sister Justine asked.

The snow outside grew thick and furious, swirling and dashing itself against the panes of glass. "God made us to know, love, and serve him and to be happy with him forever in Heaven," the children chanted. Sister then told the class to open their catechisms to the next chapter. Dominic looked in his book, thinking of Heaven and happiness. But there he saw depicted three milk bottles.

The first bottle was dark, as if full of chocolate milk. Sister Justine explained that actually the bottle was empty, symbolizing the soul before baptism, with its absence of sanctifying grace. With the holy sacrament of baptism, Sister explained, the bottle became filled. The second bottle was white, full of milk, and topped by a glowing halo. The third bottle had spots. Sister explained that the spots in its milk were sins.

"Children," she said, "there is nothing more evil than sin. There is no ink on earth black enough to portray its darkness and horror. Not even Satan himself, the Prince of Evil and enemy of baby Jesus, could make an ink so black as to show you how loathsome sin really is."

Dominic stared out the windows into the raging snow. A milk truck was making its daily delivery to the convent across the street. All the nuns who taught at Saint Stephen's lived in the convent. Dominic tried to see if any of the bottles the milkman was carrying were chocolate. Sister Justine asked the class if sin was dreadful and if they would each renounce it for the remainder of their lives. All the children, particularly the girls of row three, shouted out, nodding. The class grew as rowdy as a birthday party. "Yes, Sister!" the children cried. "Oh, yes! Yes!" Dominic wanted to raise his hand to warn Sister about the milkman, but he couldn't see. The snow was too fast and thick. So he turned away from the window and shouted along with the others.

Then Sister told them to be quiet and to take out their number books and pencils, and Dominic forgot about milk bottles and the Prince of Evil and chocolate and spots. Next to a drawing of seven shiny baseballs he wrote a large 7 and then gave each baseball a pair of eyes and a happy smile and a curly handlebar moustache.

The Holy Ghost

Dominic learned more things about God. He learned that there was only one God, and that Heaven lay just above the clouds. For some weeks then while at the bay windows Dominic ignored the buses and trucks and gazed up at the Chicago sky. He did this until his mother yelled at him to stop before he deformed his neck.

Then Sister Justine confused his picture of things by informing her class about the existence of the Holy Trinity. Try as she would to explain it, even by offering analogies to shamrocks and isosceles triangles and 3-In-One Oil, the children simply couldn't fathom how one person could really be three persons at the same time. No matter how you looked at it, Dominic reasoned, it didn't make any sense. From the lessons in his number book he knew that one plus one plus one could never equal anything but three. Finally he gave up trying to understand, thinking he'd wait until he died in the state of sanctifying grace and his eternal soul drifted up just behind the clouds. Then he'd see God's arithmetic for himself.

Heaven gave Dominic problems too. Sister told the class that Heaven consisted mainly of the beatific vision, which was being able to look upon the face, or faces, of God. Dominic understood that looking at a pretty face was pleasurable—he did like to look at Aunt Rose's face and one evening as a test did for as long as he could until she told him to cut it out because he was making her extremely uncomfortable—but he wondered if he could do it for all of eternity. Eternity was a very long time.

He had pictures of God in his missal and on holy cards, which Sister gave the children occasionally as a special reward for doing some difficult thing perfectly, like cleaning the erasers and not getting chalk dust on everything. Each holy card depicted a special moment in a holy person's life, sort of like snapshots in God's family album. Already Dominic had collected Saint Francis of Assisi talking to several chipmunks, a doe, and two doves. He had one of Saint Christopher giving baby Jesus a piggyback ride. He had Christ pointing to his immense and bloody Sacred Heart. He had Our Lady of Fatima standing on a cloud before three children and their lambs. He had Saint Joseph holding his carpenter's tools and a white lily. Dominic cherished his holy cards but didn't think he could look at them or at God forever. Did anyone ever look away? he thought. What happened to them when they did? What if they had to go to the bathroom? Or had to sneeze? Wriggling in his seat, Dominic was tempted to ask Sister these questions but was too frightened. He went back to staring at the sky and the bare, intricate branches of trees.

Sister told the children that when they had questions of faith they should pray to the Holy Ghost for strength. He was in charge of all of God's grace, Sister said. She showed the class a picture of the Holy Ghost hovering over the Virgin Mary's head, shooting out tiny rays of grace.

Dominic prayed then to the Holy Ghost. He felt sort of sorry for him because he was just a bird. It seemed unfair since God the Father, with his long white beard and fancy gold chair up in Heaven, and God the Son, with his crown of thorns and crucifix, got to be actual people. Dominic wondered if the Holy Ghost ever felt jealous. Dominic knew he'd be jealous if he were the Holy Ghost.

While at Mass the next Sunday morning with his mother and Aunt Rose, with the priest singing "Dominus vobiscum," and the people singing in response, "Et cum spiritu tuo," Dominic spied a pigeon flying just below the high, arched ceiling of the church.

"There's the Holy Ghost!" he cried.

Aunt Rose laughed. His ma told him to hush. But Dominic became so excited that he cried out once more. Aunt Rose then leaned over to him and very seriously whispered, "Look, when he flies near the lights, you can see his halo, can't you?" That silenced Dominic for a while. Sure enough it was true, if you squinted your eyes just right. When Mass was over Dominic pulled away from the two women to kneel and wave good-bye.

The next day at morning Mass with his classmates he kept an eye on the ceiling, and then again just after the Offertory everyone in church saw him as he fluttered off the top of one of the lights and swooped down low over the children's heads, and each of the children looked up. Then for a while he flew back and forth, kind of showing off, while the priest offered the bread and wine. Then everyone saw him fly straight as an arrow into one of the stained-glass windows and, with a smash, break his holy neck. Several of the children screamed. A few of the smaller kids began to cry, undoubtedly overwhelmed by all of the grace invisibly exploding out of the feebly flapping body as it twirled down through the air and then landed with a soft thump on the church's marble floor.

Dominic smiled and prayed feverishly. He knew that the Holy Ghost had been finally fed up with being just a bird and had decided to die like his big brother Jesus. Dominic knew that after three days the Holy Ghost would rise up and be alive again, and that later he'd ascend into Heaven. And, sure enough, three days later when Dominic checked the pews beneath the stained-glass window, the Holy Ghost was no longer there. Dominic was filled with joy because he knew that the Holy Ghost had risen.

"Alleluia, alleluia," Dominic cried. "Alleluia."

Martyrs

The Chicago sky was as gray as lint clogging a drain. Dominic sat at his desk, head resting on his arms, eyes staring out the windows. He was counting the pink bricks of the convent across the street, grouping them in tens, then twenties. Before him stood Sister Justine, her arms folded beneath the outer robes of her black habit.

"Children," she was saying, "we learn through example." Her gold front tooth glistened wetly in the room's fluorescent light.

She was telling them the story of Saint Stephen, their patron saint. He had been the Church's first martyr. Stoned by the Church's enemies because they were envious of his knowledge and power, Stephen had gained the immediate reward of Heaven. Sister told the children that they must learn to suffer for their faith.

Before Stephen died, he said two things. Sister had asked the class to memorize these last sacred words, as they were recorded in the Acts of the Apostles by one of the apostles who had witnessed Stephen's death.

Dominic was counting the bricks around the hedges. He was up to sixteen. Four more would make another twenty. He stopped, surveyed the back of the kid's head in front of him, shivered in the suddenly chilly classroom, and then slowly raised his hand.

"Yes, Dominic?" Sister said.

He was nervous as he stood in the aisle. He could feel everyone in class looking at him. It was no small thing interrupting a lesson, but if your question was a good one, one that showed attention and thought, you earned extra points toward your next holy card. Slowly he asked, "Sister, why didn't the apostle try to help Saint Stephen?"

"I don't know what you mean," Sister said.

Maybe it was a dumb question, Dominic thought. He looked out the windows at the convent, then rubbed his chin. "I mean, if he was there too when the heathens were killing him, why didn't he fight too?"

Sister Justine gave him the forced smile that meant she was running out of patience. "I still don't understand you," she said. "Why don't you sit back down and allow the class to continue with today's lesson?"

Dominic started to sit, then hesitated. No, he thought, it was a good question. He cleared his throat. "Didn't Saint Stephen fight, Sister?"

"Fight whom?" said the nun.

"The Church's evil heathen enemies, Sister," replied Dominic.

"Good. Now what were the heathens doing to Stephen?"

Dominic thought for a moment. It was yesterday's new word. Finally he said, "Stoning him, Sister."

"Very good. Now what is your question?"

"I'm asking why the apostle didn't help Saint Stephen fight back." Dominic could feel his back beginning to sweat.

"Saint Stephen didn't fight," Sister said. She turned and drew her yardstick from the top of her desk, then brandished it in the air. "Does anyone else here think that Saint Stephen fought?"

When she said "fought," she sounded as if she were spitting. No one in class raised a hand. The girls of row three stared at Dominic with wide eyes, wagging their astonished heads.

"Well, Dominic," Sister said, "as you can see you're the only one in the room who thinks Saint Stephen fought. Now, children, why didn't he?"

The room erupted with raised hands. "Because fighting's wrong," the girls of row three singsonged.

"Yes, girls," Sister said, "that's very good. And why else?"

No one could think of another reason.

"Because it was the will of God," Sister said. The children nodded their heads. Dominic was confused.

"You mean Saint Stephen just let them kill him, Sister?"

A rush of blood colored Sister's face, leaving a pale halo around the mole on the side of her nose. "Yes, Dominic," she said. "Because it was the will of God."

"But Sister, what about the apostle who was watching, who wrote it all down?"

"Dominic," Sister said sharply, "I think you're deliberately trying to waste the class's time by asking these ridiculous questions. You know that time is invaluable and can never be replaced. Very well then, we'll begin our lesson with you. What did Stephen cry out as he was stoned?"

Dominic was flustered. He was trying to figure out how Stephen and the apostle knew it was the will of God. What if they had tried to fight? he thought. Would God have struck them down right then and there because their actions were against his will? The boy thought of Lot's wife, how God had turned her into a pillar of salt. He thought of how God had banned Moses from entering the land of milk and honey. "Sit down," Sister Justine said, "and write out twenty times the last holy words of Saint Stephen." Dominic held back his tears, and she continued the lesson.

Stephen was buried by a man named Gamaliel in the year A.D. 36. Then, decades later, a pious old priest named Lucien discovered Stephen's body, which was miraculously preserved, still warm to the touch, and as white as the purest of snows.

Dominic wasn't listening. He sat sadly at his desk, his left hand pressed down hard against his writing tablet, his tongue sticking out of the corner of his mouth, writing over and over, *"Lord Jesus, receive my spirit."* And just below that: *"Lord, lay not this sin to their charge."*

God's All-Stars

Dominic's mother sat in the red stuffed chair near the old cathedral radio. The chair had been her husband's favorite. Against the wall was the matching sofa, worn and pink at its edges, a pair of end tables, and a lamp. Across from her stood the oil heater. That morning she'd filled it carefully, not spilling a drop. She was good at not spilling things. She was good at numbers, at keeping them straight. In a notebook she figured the month's expenses, drawing her wool sweater more tightly around herself. It was a Wednesday, her day off from the Dixie Diner, where she worked.

Dominic whistled as he washed in the bathroom. He'd just come home from school and had given his mom a big kiss and his day's papers. His cheeks were flushed. He was wearing his new blue Cubs jacket, purchased the night before.

At the busy department store near Lincoln and Belmont, Dominic had made faces in the mirrors and claimed both his arms were broken until his mom consented to the young salesman to let her son try the Cubs jacket on. It was loose, but Dominic pleaded with her to buy it.

"But honey," she said, "it's the wrong size."

"He's sure to grow into it," the salesman said brightly.

"Please," Dominic said. "Pretty please."

"We've got White Sox jackets too," offered the salesman.

Dominic shook his head. He hated the White Sox even though they were the better team. He was a North Sider, and the Cubs were the North Side team. It was that simple.

She heard him open the icebox, then the silverware drawer. He was making his usual after-school snack, peanut-butter Holy Communions. By working the bread with his hands the boy would form the Hosts, which he then topped with peanut butter, or, sometimes, marmalade.

"Dominic," she called.

He walked into the front room, the cuffs of his new jacket hanging over his hands and wet from when he'd washed.

"Dominic," she asked, "what's this?"

She held up his religion test. He'd received a 70. Marked with large red checks were the answers DEE FONDY, HANK SAUER, and ERNIE BANKS.

"Dominic," she said again.

His mouth was full of Communion. He chewed slowly and raised one finger to ask her to wait. Then he ran into his bedroom and returned with his cigar box. He opened it before her, sitting by her legs on the floor.

"Look, Ma," he said proudly. Bound neatly with green rubber bands were his holy cards depicting the bloody deaths of martyrs, the miracles of the Virgin and the many saints, and the various faces of God. Mixed with them were his baseball cards. On several Dominic had drawn halos or put crosses on the bats.

"The Cubs are the martyrs," he said, "see?" showing her the various cards listing previous years' National League standings. On nearly all of them the Cubs were listed seventh or eighth, in last place. "And this guy here, Saint Tarcissus, he was a ballplayer too." Dominic showed his mother his Saint Tarcissus holy card. On its back was the story of how the young Roman martyr had played a crude form of baseball with his friends until the afternoon he agreed to secretly carry the Eucharist beneath his cloak to the catacombs to help the early Christians celebrate Mass and was stoned to death because he refused to stop and play a ball game. He died in the arms of a beautiful maiden. Dominic adored Saint Tarcissus because the card said that he fought back viciously.

"But this test," his mother said.

"Sister don't know nothing," Dominic said.

"But she's there to teach you," his mother began, but then stopped when he took her hand and led her into his bedroom.

Smiling, he pointed to the wall above his dresser. There hung his Cubs pennant and his glow-in-the-dark crucifix. Behind the crucifix and a sheaf of palms was a sheet of his writing paper.

THE ALL-STARS

1. GOD THE FATHER FIRST PERSON 1st base
2. GOD THE SON SECOND PERSON 2nd
3. GOD THE HOLY GHOST THIRD PERSON 3rd
4. ERNIE BANKS I DON'T CARE IF HE'S CHOCOLATE shortstop
5. HANK SAUER right field A HOLY MARTYR CUB
6. RALPH KINER left field A HOLY MARTYR CUB
7. SAINT TARCISSUS catcher BUT HE DOESN'T HAVE TO PLAY IF HE DON'T WANT TO
8. FRANK BAUMHOLTZ center ANOTHER HOLY MARTYR CUB
9. OUR LADY OF PERPETUAL HELP the pitcher BECAUSE OF HER BIG GOOD ARMS

Laughing, his mother suggested they move his lineup from behind the crucifix to just beneath the Cubs pennant. Dominic nodded and then ran to the kitchen for a thumbtack.

The Bleeding Bureau

He was certain his nickel was somewhere. Dominic plunged his hands into his pockets, stretching nearly horizontal at his desk. Around him, the other kids who'd received Communion at morning Mass were finishing their breakfasts, their fingernails idly scraping the sides of their waxed milk cartons. The girls of row three were chewing silently, thirty times before swallowing, as Sister Justine instructed. In five bites Dominic had wolfed down his flat egg on toast, always soggy by the time he ate it.

He checked his back pockets. Each was empty, save for lint. Then he remembered that he'd put his nickel in his shirt pocket, for good luck, in the hope that it would put his row over the five-dollar mark and thus allow them this Friday morning to buy and name a pagan baby.

Kenneth, the tall row captain, had already left his seat and stood waiting before the row. He held his hands at his sides, as if at military attention. Dominic smiled at his nickel, then spat on it. Now it was even more lucky. He dropped his lint into his inkwell and looked back at the pagan baby mission board tallies.

ROW ONE	ROW TWO	ROW THREE	ROW FOUR	ROW FIVE	ROW SIX
Gabriel	Pius X	Stephen	Cosmas	Daria	Hippolytus
Achilleus		Justina	Damian	Agapitus	
		Praxedes		Valentine	
		Clare			
		Madeleine			
		Sophie			
		Barat			
		Scholastica			
		Gertrude			
		Bridget			
		Mary			
		Euphrasia			
		Pelletier			

Sister usually helped out with suggestions for the names, but the children of each row voted, democratically, the majority ruling. This year they were buying their pagan babies from an orphanage in a place called Siam. Dominic liked Siam because he knew it was where Siamese cats and twins came from. Every time the good missionary priests received another five dollars, they took an unnamed boy or girl out of its crib and baptized and named it. Then for all eternity the kid owed the everlasting salvation of its soul to the generosity of the good Catholic children in Chicago whose pennies and nickels and dimes enabled the pagan child to be saved.

Something whizzed past Dominic's face. It was a spitball, likely from someone in row two. Dominic turned in his seat and looked for the culprit. Row two made the room's best spitballs: neither too dry nor too wet. A good spitball smacked but wasn't sloppy. It stuck but didn't stay. Row two was famous for shooting spitballs at the classroom's ceiling, where they'd hang for ten or more tantalizing minutes—so long that maybe even the spitball's creator had forgotten he'd shot it up there—until it fell in the middle of the aisle or on some kid's desk or head, disrupting everything, and nobody was the wiser. Dominic tore a scrap of paper off his tablet and worked up some saliva and wet the paper carefully on his tongue, then chewed it into shape. A guy couldn't not defend himself or else he'd become everybody's target. He squeezed the spitball gently between his fingertips. As Sister turned toward the blackboard, Dominic crouched in the aisle and fired. It hit Willie Berger in row one right on the ear.

"Have your money ready now, children," Sister called out.

Kenneth marched down the aisle, firmly gripping the shoulder of each fifth rower until the kid contributed something—at least a penny or two—to his box. He was a good row captain. Running for election earlier that year, Kenneth told the class that his dad was the alderman's right-hand man, so he knew how to make government work. That was the city's slogan: Chicago was the city that worked. Dominic understood enough to know that only a fool didn't drop a couple of coins on an open palm backed up by a hand squeezing your shoulder.

Suddenly, from the middle of row two, Eddie Dymkowycz stood in his seat and made a noise like a stepped-on horse. Out from his mouth shot a stream of vomit so solid it splashed the back of Angela Donofrio's long brunette hair. She grasped her barrettes and shrieked. The first three rows emptied faster than a fire drill, fleeing the sight and surprisingly horrible smell: a cross between old cheese and the wettest corner of a flooded basement. They took refuge by the front blackboard as Eddie let loose a second column of vomit that bounced off his desk top and rained on the floor. Rows four, five, and six darted to the side windows.

Sister Justine rapped her yardstick on her desk for order. With the exception of Angela Donofrio, the kids quieted down to a reasonable roar. Sister then ordered one of the girls of row three to fetch the janitor and told gasping Eddie and hysterical Angela to report immediately to Mother Superior's office. The boys of row six jerked open the windows without her having to ask.

Dominic shivered from the sudden cold. He wanted to throw up too. He was sympathetic that way. When people around him cried, he felt like crying too. When others vomited, he too had to vomit. He swallowed back down a mouthful of his egg-and-toast sandwich and tried to get his mind to change the subject. He tried to get his nose to smell the cold, fresh air. Sister started in on something. Dominic focused on her gold tooth.

"As we wait for the custodian, children, let's continue our unit on the Holy Eucharist and perhaps use this event as a lesson. Let me tell you a true story. There once was a boy who received Holy Communion in the state of mortal sin. Too weak to defend his faith, he ate meat one Friday with his Protestant friends. Then he committed the grave sin of pride and thought it didn't matter. Well, it did! After leaving the Communion rail, just like our Edward he vomited. You see, children, Jesus does not like entering an unclean soul, just as you or I would not like going into a dirty house."

The janitor came to the classroom door wheeling before him a bucket and a mop, and carrying a broom and a bag of sawdust.

"Children," Sister continued, "here's another true story I know, about a bad boy who purposely bit into the Host. He was angry at Jesus for some petty reason. Well, his mouth immediately filled with Christ's blood, and in his shame he swallowed much of it. Then he fell sick and vomited, and only after the blessed sacrament of confession was the boy well again."

As the janitor mopped up what he could, the children shuffled back to their seats.

"A very curious child once walked to the back of the church and spat the Eucharist into his handkerchief and foolishly took it home, then further desecrated it by hiding it in his dresser drawer. What could this boy have been thinking? Did he think he could contain Christ? By dawn the next morning, his bureau drawer overflowed with blood! It got on his hands and face, and when the boy tried to wipe it off it couldn't be removed! The little sinner then tried to staunch its flow, but no tourniquet save the prayers of an anointed priest could stem the flood of blood gushing from the drawer."

The janitor slowly spread the sawdust.

"Now children, I certainly don't intend to say that either Edward or Angela did any of these things, but I do want to impress upon each of you that God is supremely powerful, and that he works in many strange and mysterious ways!"

Dominic swallowed hard as he stared at a spot on his desk top. He pictured his own bureau gushing with blood, his mother's disappointment, the monsignor's angry face, Aunt Rose's sadness. During the next moment, as a spitball plopped on his desk, he imagined the crucified Christ's extraordinary pain and Satan's simultaneous glee. Dominic shuddered. His pants flowed hot and wet.

As soon as he realized what he'd done, he began crying. No one yet noticed the puddle beneath his desk, so he slowly raised his hand.

When Sister moved on to another story—this one about a bad boy who impaled a stolen Host upon a nail—Dominic stood and covered the front of his pants with his hands and made his way down his row, past a kid picking his nose, a girl copying her spelling words in neat Palmer cursive, a boy playing paper-puck hockey with his pencil and inkwell, Kenneth counting the row's nickels and dimes.

"Dominic," Sister called, "return to your seat at once."

He knew that she'd discover his accident in another minute, so he made his way to Mother Superior's office without waiting to be told. He didn't turn. Peeing was bad enough. He didn't want the whole class to see his tears too.

Nativity

The cathedral radio played a medley of church songs.

"Wear two pairs of socks," his mother called. She was untangling a string of Christmas tree lights at the table in the dining room. Around her were the cardboard boxes in which she stored their holiday things. Already she'd unpacked the wooden manger and a few of their glass ornaments. The figure of the lame shepherd boy carrying a lamb across his shoulders lay in a loose fold of tissue paper. The other figures were still in their boxes, waiting for Dominic to unwrap them and put them in place. Since he was old enough to understand Christmas, she let the boy set up their manger. It was a tradition. She believed in traditions. She could hear her son in his bedroom singing along with the radio. Then the boy's singing stopped.

"Everything stinks," he shouted.

"What?" she said. She walked to the radio and turned it down, then tucked her hands under her arms.

Dominic was trying to open his bedroom window. Beyond the glass it was snowing so thickly that he couldn't make out the lights of the tavern directly across the street. On his bed were his good winter clothes.

"Poison gas," Dominic said. He held his neck and coughed.

His mother laughed. "Take the mothballs out of your pockets, smart guy," she said. Dominic laughed too, then carried the heavy jacket into the front room.

"I'll do it out here with the music," he said.

His mother gathered the lights from the table and sat across from him on the sofa. Dominic took his father's chair.

"When I was a girl," his mother said, "we waited and bought our tree on Christmas Eve. We were poor, and trees were cheaper then." She held up the string of multicolored lights.

Dominic held several mothballs. "Ma," he said, "are we poor?"

The woman smiled. "Well," she said, "are you ever hungry? Or cold? Or do you have to wear rags to school?"

"No," he said.

"Do you have a warm place at night to sleep?"

He nodded.

"Then we're not poor."

"Well," he said, "are we rich then?"

"We don't have money to burn, if that's what you mean," his mother said. She was staring at the radio that was between them.

Dominic laughed. He thought that was pretty funny. "You can't burn nickels or dimes," he said. He put the mothballs on the floor in front of the radio and faced his mother and wiped his hands.

His mother laughed too, then gazed down at the rug. "You know, when I was a little girl, once on Christmas day my father gave me three pennies." She turned and plugged in the string of lights. Dominic gasped. The soft glowing lights made her appear so beautiful. "My pa said that one penny was for the old year, one for the new, and the third"—she stared at him for a moment—"the third penny was for something very special." She smiled, brushing back from her face her long auburn hair. "It was a joke, honey. We were very poor. But you and me, we're a different story. Don't we have enough?" She unplugged the lights and stood.

"Sure," Dominic said. "Three cents is enough."

Outside, the large snowflakes veiled even the streetlights. Mounds of snow grew on window ledges and in doorways, gathered heavily on the tops of awnings, covering the green metal hoods over the traffic lights and the street side of the parking meters. The traffic on Fullerton Avenue moved slowly, muffled into near silence by the thick snow. Dominic's mother took big steps. The boy's heart raced in his chest.

They walked west up Fullerton Avenue past Tartaglia's grocery and fresh meats to the vacant lot between the Jewish bakery and Zileski's shoe store. Bright lights were strung from wooden poles. The lot resembled a pine forest. Knots of people warmed themselves around fires in oil-drum garbage cans. Orange sparks flew eagerly into the air. An old man with a cane and a large black dog sat silently inside a dark shed.

"Stay close by me now," Dominic's mother told him.

He held her arm as they looked at the trees and helped her when she pulled one out and inspected it. Most of them, she said, were too expensive or not full enough or had the wrong kind of needles. Dominic filled his nose with their exciting smell.

"We used to get a tree for twenty cents," she said, shaking her head. "And look, they want three dollars."

"Why don't we wait until next week?" Dominic asked. He remembered the story she'd told him. Next week was Christmas Eve.

"Because we don't have to," she said. She shook her head, then led her son to one of the fires. Dominic spread his hands over the warm flames.

"They'd send me because I was the littlest," she said. "You don't remember them, do you?"

Dominic said no. He didn't realize he had grandparents.

"Of course your Aunt Rose would come with me too, to help me carry the tree home, but I had to go into the lot all by myself. You see, Dominic, the men sold them the cheapest to the smallest children."

His mother's face glowed in the fire.

"The children would gather outside the lot, and then, just after midnight, after the church bells rang out, the men would throw them all the leftover trees. You could get hurt if you weren't careful. We did that for a few years, Rose and me, when we didn't have any money, but when we had a few pennies they'd send me into the lot."

"I can do that this year," Dominic said. He really wanted to.

"Oh no," his mother said. She stared at the flames in the can. "Once I saw a boy robbed by three bigger boys after he let on that he had some money. And once a little girl was trampled because she went for the first tree." She looked at her son. "Besides," she winked, "we've got money."

She turned and walked to the shed. The black dog stood and sniffed the hem of her coat.

"I'll give you a dollar for that tree, take it or leave it," she said to the old man inside. She pointed to the three-dollar tree.

The old man spat on the ground. Dominic watched his mother.

"That's a three-dollar tree," the old man said.

"And I'm a Rockefeller," Dominic's mother said. "I'll give you a dollar fifty."

The old man rubbed the big dog's neck. "Two and a half and it's yours, lady. Come on, I gotta make a buck."

"Not off me."

"Merry Christmas to you, lady."

"You're going to sell all these trees by next week?" She gestured to the scores of trees that filled the lot. "A very merry Christmas to you, sir." She pulled Dominic's hand and turned.

"OK, lady, two dollars even."

"Let's split the difference. A dollar seventy-five."

The old man nodded.

"A dollar seventy-five then," she said. She was smiling.

The old man stood and hobbled to the tree. The dark tip of his cane sunk deep into the snow. The dog followed him, panting a white cloud. The old man tore the tag from the tree and said, "All right, lady, take it."

Dominic's mother handed him a dollar and three quarters. Snowflakes sparkled in her hair. Dominic helped her carry the green tree.

The two were silent as they began the walk home. Then Dominic grinned and began the song he'd heard earlier on the radio. "O little town of Bethlehem," he sang, "how still we see thee lie." His mother joined him singing as they carried the tree between them through the falling snow.

The Clock

Sleet fell as if without end.

Dominic stood at his front windows. When he looked toward the city's horizon, all he could see were streaks. Above the horizon the sky was dirty white, like an old T-shirt. His hand touched the windowpane. He was glad his mom had finally taken down the service flag. The cold rain fell in broad straight lines and splashed upon the street and its slow traffic.

Below, from the left window, lay Fullerton Avenue, a bright and nearly always crowded street. The file of autos from the east cut through the late-afternoon rain with its headlights. They made the rain and ice on his windows glisten. As the cars passed under the streetlights, their roofs gleamed with a clean, shiny splendor. The tires made a sleepy shushing sound.

The tavern at the opposite corner had dark windows lit by neon beer signs. They flashed off and on, night and day. The tavern door was made of strong wood and had a dark little window shaped like a diamond set so high that you had to be tall—grown up—to see through it.

On the sidewalk in front of the tavern was a bearded Jew. He didn't have an umbrella. Dominic could tell that the man was a Jew because the man wore a Jew's skullcap and walked patiently in his long overcoat. Even when it wasn't sleeting, the Jews on Fullerton walked like that.

The Germans had blond hair. Italians had dark, flashing eyes. The Polish looked like Germans but were skinnier. The Irish had big ears and freckles.

The Jew on the street below walked past the currency exchange and then turned north to walk up Southport Avenue. A passing bread truck pulled close to the curb and splashed him.

By turning to his right and looking out the center window, Dominic could see east down Fullerton toward the lake. Now that he was taller, the cars and buses didn't disappear behind the currency exchange. They disappeared behind the big gray building farther down the block. The currency exchange had a green window, in the center of which hung a huge electric clock. Around its edges were orange lights that rolled word by word on and then flashed off for several seconds and started over. The lights said NOW IS THE TIME TO SAVE.

He could walk north up Southport when he went to see his mother at the restaurant. He could walk down Southport when he went to school or to play with his friends. He was not allowed to walk west, up

Fullerton, or east, down Fullerton. He could look at Fullerton from his hallway door, but then he had to turn the corner. He could look into the window of the candy store, but only for a minute and never as if he were begging. The woman in the store always wore the same pink dress.

Once, on Fullerton, he saw a man sleeping on the sidewalk. Once he saw three men drink from a paper bag. Once he saw two women in a parked car kissing. Once he saw a gang of older boys throwing matches at an alley cat. Once, a drunken man on their landing pounded on their door shouting over and over, "Let me in there!" They had to call the police. Once, someone threw up on their hallway staircase, and more than once someone urinated. Each time his mother cleaned it up.

Once, on Southport, he saw a rat as big as a cat run across the sidewalk and into a shady gangway. Dominic ran the rest of the way home to tell his mom about that. She told him rats carried polio and rabies. So did squirrels and dogs. If you got rabies you had to get painful shots with a long needle right in the belly button every day for three months. In first grade in Sister Augustine's class there was a girl who had polio. She sat in a wheelchair in the first row by the side blackboard. She stayed at the school for a month and then left.

Once Dominic dreamed that he had polio and couldn't walk. Once he dreamed that he forgot his address and couldn't find his house. Then his mother taught him about Chicago, and a nurse came to school and gave everybody polio shots.

Fullerton was 2400 North. The way you said it was twenty-four hundred. Diversey was 2800. Belmont was 3200, and Armitage was 2000. Saint Stephen's was on Armitage. Southport was 1400 West. His address was 1401 West Fullerton, Chicago, Illinois, USA.

One of the kids at school said that on Clybourn Avenue there were people who owned goats. He said that the goats ate a million tin cans every day, and that if you parked your car near them they'd eat that too.

Aunt Rose said that was no lie, what with all of the city's thieves. She said it was a changing neighborhood. She said that nearly every time she came over to visit. That was why she'd moved north, to Addison Street. Dominic didn't know what number Addison was, but he did know that it was by the ball park. At her house every time they visited, he gazed out her front windows to see it. It was bigger than Saint Stephen's Church, and if you looked up at it from the sidewalk on Waveland Avenue it said CHICAGO CUBS inside a big bright flag.

Sometimes he'd listen to the ball game on the radio. He'd sit in the big armchair with his head down, concentrating, praying for a Chicago Cubs hit. Once he was sitting there when his mother came in the room from the kitchen. She was folding her apron. He could see her out of the corner of his eye, but he didn't look up because there were two strikes on Ransom Jackson and Dominic was afraid he'd jinx him.

Then he heard his mother say, "You're just like your father."

And she was crying. Ransom Jackson took strike three. Dominic felt bad and wondered if he had done something wrong.

Below, by a fire hydrant, he saw several pigeons. He wondered how they felt when they got wet. Why didn't they fly somewhere out of the rain? They pecked the garbage floating past them in the gutter.

Behind him, wind whistled in the oil heater. The sound startled him. He turned and stared at the silent heater until he again felt safe and then turned back to his window, shivering.

Two Poles were crossing Fullerton, holding newspapers up over their heads. His mother had taught him it was wrong to call them polacks. It was wrong to say krauts or micks or spics or dagos. Nearly everybody in the whole world had a bad name. He nearly wished that the devil had never been invented. Dominic looked at a patrol car double-parked in front of the currency exchange. Its dome light flashed in circles.

NOW, the sign said.

A moment later it said NOW IS THE TIME.

He wondered what currency was. He wondered what exchange meant. He wondered why he didn't have a father. Was it because of something he had done? he thought. The patrol car drove away, siren blaring, and the two Poles huddled inside a doorway.

Dominic stared at the clock's rolling message. NOW it said. NOW IS THE TIME TO SAVE.

It was seven-eighteen. He turned to watch the tavern corner. His father was dead, that's all. His fingers tapped the windowsill. Soon, the boy thought, at seven-thirty, his ma would be finished working her shift at the restaurant, and he'd be here to watch her walk home.

David Baldacci

From *Wish You Well*

They all peered over the edge of the well's opening. It was black, seemingly without bottom; they could have been staring at the other side of the world. All sorts of things could have been peering back.

"Why do you say it's haunted?" Oz asked breathlessly.

Diamond sprawled in the grass next to the well and they joined him.

"'Bout a thousand million years ago," he began in a thick and thrilling voice that made Oz's eyes widen, fast-blink, and water all at the same time, "they was a man and woman live up here. Now, they was in love, ain't no denying that. And so's they wanted to get hitched o'course. But they's family hated each other, wouldn't let 'em do it. No sir. So they come up with a plan to run off. Only somethin' went bad and the feller thought the woman had done got herself kilt. He was so broke up, he came to this here well and jumped in. It's way deep, shoot, you seed that. And he drowned hisself. Now the girl found out what was what, and she come and jumped in herself too. Never found 'em 'cause it was like they was plopped on the sun. Not a durn thing left."

Lou was completely unmoved by this sad tale. "That sounds a lot like Romeo and Juliet."

Diamond looked puzzled. "That kin of yours?"

"You're making this up," she said.

All around them sounds of peculiar quality started up, like millions of tiny voices all trying to jabber at once, as though ants had suddenly acquired larynxes.

"What's that?" Oz said, clinging to Lou.

"Don't be doubting my words, Lou," Diamond hissed, his face the color of cream. "You riling the spirits."

"Yeah, Lou," said Oz, who was looking everywhere for demons of hell coming for them. "Don't be riling the spirits."

The noises finally died down, and Diamond, regaining his confidence, stared triumphantly at Lou. "Shoot, any fool can see this well's magic. You see a house anywhere round? No, and I tell you why. This well growed up right out of the earth, that's why. And it ain't just a haunted well. It what you call a wishing well."

Oz said, "A wishing well? How?"

"Them two people lost each other, but they's still in love. Now, people die, but love don't never die. Made the well magic. Anybody done got a wish, they come here, wish for it, and it'll happen. Ever time. Rain or shine."

Oz clutched his arm. "Any wish? You're sure?"

"Yep. 'Cept they's one little catch."

Lou spoke up, "I thought so. What is it?"

"'Cause them folks died to make this here a wishing well, anybody want a wish, they's got to give up somethin' too."

"Give up what?" This came from Oz, who was so excited the boy seemed to float above the supple grass like a tethered bubble.

Diamond lifted his arms to the dark sky. "Like just the most grand-est, importantest thing they got in the whole dang world."

I am sure if your father were here he would tell you that there is no shame in repeating the words of others. That it's a show of respect, in fact.

Helen Barolini

Buried Alive by Language

I remembered two seemingly incongruous things when I first heard about the racial murder of the Black youth Yusuf Hawkins in August 1989 in the Bensonhurst section of Brooklyn by a gang of mostly Ital-ian American young men. I remembered a friend telling me of being in Louisiana and finding "Wop Salad" featured on a menu. What was that? I asked. He laughed and said, salad with Italian dressing. "Didn't anyone care about the language?" I wondered. No, he said, it was a joke. But language is no joke. And racial murder starts with racial intolerance that arises and spreads from such apparently innocuous jokes.

The second thing I remembered was hearing Lynn Samuels' talk show on radio WOR when a listener called in and said, "How come I'm called anti-Semitic if I make a remark, but Jews can get away with calling the rest of us goyim, schwartzer, wop, or whatever it is?"

Samuels, who is Jewish herself, answered unhesitatingly, "They're politically organized."

And that, I told myself, is why there'll never be a kike salad on any menu.

I think that Italian Americans are too easily used as objects of ridicule and scorn. It has been said that anti-Catholicism is the prejudice of choice of the liberal intellectual. That could be expanded to include Italian Americans, as reflected in the reportage of the Bensonhurst affair in the *New York Times*. What happened was a tragedy of far greater ram-ifications than reported in the news media. What also is tragic is the insularity and backwardness of the Italian Americans. "Niggers, stay out of our neighborhoods!" they shouted to Black marchers protesting the Hawkins murder. Their language was shocking, arresting. Worse, it was uninformed and unformed. Listen to their voices, as quoted on the murder in their neighborhood, by the *Times* reporter: "This wasn't racial and I've never been racial in my life. But white people should stick together for ourselves," says a young woman. And an old woman in a Bensonhurst candy store, speaking of the murdering gang, adds, "These were good boys . . . they were defending the neighborhood."

"We don't go to Harlem; the kids were in the wrong spot," says an eighteen-year-old youth. "This is Bensonhurst. It's all Italian. We don't need these niggers."

These Americans of Italian descent spoke haltingly when interviewed on television; they groped for words to express themselves, their constructions were ear-grating, their words defamatory, racist, pathetically ignorant. They were people imprisoned by being closed off from education, from wide social interaction, from knowledge of broader values than those of their Old World village. As their pastor, Father Fermeglia of St. Dominic's Church in Bensonhurst, explains, "This is a very provincial neighborhood . . . everyone knows each other. . . . People get the meaning of their lives from their relationships."

What they also get is an inbred, self-perpetuating inability to think, and hence to speak in an informed way; they are buried alive in the low language of insularity.

Like illiterates using picture language, they hold up emblems of their intolerance, watermelons are raised as a racial taunt against the Blacks marching in protest of the Yusuf Hawkins murder. Ludicrously, they hold up an Italian flag. What they can't express verbally, they show. Show and Tell: that is the level of a people in a linguistic backwater, in a backwater of old outdated attitudes; of a people uneducated in values beyond the blatant materialistic one that seduces so many newcomers to America: get rich and make good, defend your property values.

"It is an old truth that if we do not have mastery over our language, language itself will master us . . . it is through language that we control and create the world. We discover life through language, and that—as all great writers have told us—is why we must master it," Malcolm Bradbury wrote in another context.

Language *is* relevant. The racial outbursts that have taken place in Howard Beach, Staten Island, Bensonhurst are committed by young white men who are both poorly educated and socially marginal. They are feeling what it is to be outcasts in a society which promised them that if they made it materially, that would be what mattered. They are outraged because society lied; they are looking for scapegoats to take their rage out on, they are responsible for the reprehensible attacks on Blacks (and more recently, Jews). As the anthropologist and writer Thomas Belmonte has said, "We ignore their yearning and waste their fierce energies at our peril."

Along with the tragedy of the murdered Yusuf Hawkins is the tragedy of a whole community locked in extreme xenophobia and doing, wrongfully, to others what was done to them. It is useful to review the discrimination perpetrated against Italian Americans themselves in order to put into context some of the motivation for their current antisocial behavior. They, too, were once victimized by those who got here before they did and so "owned" their neighborhoods and didn't want the wops in them. Did Italian Americans learn another American lesson as well as materialism—that violence is a means of expression, and the last one in gets it? They got it, now they'll give it to the Blacks who move into "the Italian neighborhood."

In an ironic synchronization, Black filmmaker Spike Lee's film *Do the Right Thing,* about Blacks in Brooklyn hanging out at Sal's pizza parlor, came out just at the time of the Bensonhurst murders, and addressed racial violence. What, in fact, is the right thing to do? Is it, as in the film, for Blacks to take out resentments and rage on white society by attacking and destroying their pizza parlor? Is it, as the last scene of the film shows, for the Black pillagers to remove from Sal's ruined walls the photographic totems of his Italian American allegiance—Sinatra, DiMaggio, Perry Como, et al.—and to replace them with photos of Martin Luther King, Jr., and Malcolm X?

Symbolically that is a masterful statement. The leaders of the Black movement, who have powerfully and eloquently spoken for their people and have had broad social influence, will in the end replace the meager idols of Italian Americans, for whom the inadequate message has been: make a pile, keep it in the family, aim for material satisfactions. What do the "famous" Italian Americans stand for? Money and celebrity status. Not much uplift there, not much for the soul of an alienated and ambivalent people to feed on. No gut nourishment.

Take this exchange between Sal's son Vinnie and Moukie, the Black youth who works as a delivery boy at the pizza parlor. When Moukie says, "Hey Vinnie, how come you're always talking of Black baseball stars and singers? I think you want to be Black," Vinnie, who is imprisoned as much by inadequate language (the reflection of inadequate thought) as by his restrictive social attitudes, gropes to express what he has never thought out. "They're not Black," he finally mumbles, "they're famous."

Vinnie thus not only unconsciously identifies the unillustrious (including himself) with the to him demeaning connotation of Black, but must painfully grasp for words and meaning in order to speak at all. The scene is a graphic illustration of what it is to be without articulation because the language of thought has never been fully absorbed or respected, only the language of money.

Thus, "Black" is code for poor, deprived, ignorant, the dregs; it's nigger and wop all over again. And that includes all who have believed only in the commercial opportunities of this country and haven't educated themselves in the language of other values or in what America most hopefully signifies.

It's the triumph of materialist views and Sal's narrow sense of property rights (not exclusively an Italian American attitude, as we recall the actions of Southern Anglo-Americans) that contribute to racial tensions. Rather than recognize the interdependence between his business and the exclusively Black clientele who eat his pizza, Sal insists on making his place a fortress of his Italian background. And the Blacks, too, like Moukie, look for the differences, not the commonality between them. Just as the Power Structure intends.

"Break the Power" is the theme song of the film which is dedicated to the Black or Hispanic victims of police brutality. It is powerful music, and the words are aimed at the structure of a society that abuses people, makes them violent and filled with rage, makes them drown each other out with shouts and curses and shrieking radio music, and ultimately causes them to turn on each other in their frustration.

The police in their patrol car who go up and down the streets of the Black neighborhood where Sal's pizza parlor is located look malevolent as they view the scene through cold, suspicious slit-eyes. Their counterpart is the striking arrangement of three Black men under a bright umbrella against a red wall who are laid-back, benevolent, and the wise commentators on what they observe. They spurn a boycott against Sal, as do others in the neighborhood ("I was born and brought up on Sal's pizza," says a Black girl). And yet in the anguish of their powerlessness, the Blacks will, reacting to police violence, vent their fury against Sal rather than against the societal attitudes that keep them *all* down.

With two eloquent and effective metaphors, *Do the Right Thing* depicts the futility of racial war. One is the wall of photos that provokes one Black youth to ask why, since all of Sal's customers are Black, he doesn't have Martin Luther King and Malcolm X up there, too. Sal says it's his place and he's Italian and he'll have who he wants, showing remarkable insensitivity and stupidity all at once.

The other symbolic device used by director Spike Lee is the shrieking radio music that prevents spoken communication between people as talk becomes a duel of shouts and curses, each attempting to drown the other out. The blaring music is the final provocation that incites Sal to throw a Black kid and his radio out of his place. This precipitates a police action that ends in the youth's death at the hands of the police. Moukie then leads a riot destroying not only Sal's place but his own livelihood and something of value to the neighborhood. The Blacks will be as much kept down by their more overt and mindless violence as Sal and sons by their impoverished social attitudes and lack of self-knowledge.

Blindly, not even noticing the friction between them, Sal had extolled to his sons the money that can be made in a business when families are in it together. He tells them (to their horror) that he'll pass the business on to them. Feeling trapped in the alien territory of a Black neighborhood, all the sons want to do is get out.

But what will get them out? Sal is blind in his defense of a lost cause: his family, his business, his property rights, his pathetic Italian pride, as manifested on his wall by Sinatra & Co., none of whom has the stature of the Black leaders. Sal has not awakened to reality, he lives in a time warp of old, played-out, irrelevant allegiances and chauvinism. He's a decent, hardworking guy, and his sense of responsibility and kindness are well contrasted with the recklessness of Moukie who has fathered a son and left him, and seems to have no aim in life. But Sal has not evolved with the times. He is harboring a narrow, limited mentality in a time and place that urgently call for more expansiveness. Are the Koreans across the street, whose place is spared by the rioting Blacks, meant to be Sal's smart counterpart? At least they understand the reality of their situation and are not spinning pipe dreams based on spurious values.

Chauvinistically, Sal has defended a wall of false images. In the end, the photos of Martin Luther King, Jr., and Malcolm X, with their two different messages, get pinned to Sal's burned-out wall which no longer can mark the bounds of narrow territoriality. That, Spike Lee's film seems to say, is the right thing to do. It's a lesson, like language, still to be learned in some insular Italian American city enclaves.

A young man in Bensonhurst, again quoted in the *Times,* spoke an American fact of life that many harbor, few speak: "No one likes no one if they don't look the same. Everybody's prejudiced. And that's the way it is."

He is confirmed, sadly, by Adele Dutton Terrell, program director of the National Institute against Prejudice and Violence, who adds, "Every day we have incidents . . . the sad lesson is that in America we have neighborhoods where people do and don't belong."

But *Do the Right Thing* tells clearly that such narrow territoriality is doomed.

"Go home," call the Italian American taunters of Bensonhurst to the protestors who march through their blocks. "We are home," the Black marchers call back.

From *Umbertina*

From the first Umbertina had kept her marriage bedspread on the one bed of that room. It not only kept them warm in winter, it was her one thing of beauty in all that squalor; it was her remembrance of leaves and flowers and the sun overhead, just as it was the image of what they had come for—something better than they had known.

During their first summer, when babies in the tenements dropped like flies, the city's summer doctors came with free advice and medicine; following them came nurses from the Board of Health's Italian department. The visiting nurse who came to Umbertina's block was an Italian woman named Anna Giordani. Her family had arrived in the earlier, political immigration of 1848 when Garibaldi himself had arrived in America after defeat in the siege of Rome. The Giordanis were northern Italians of the Protestant Waldensian sect; they were educated and had some money. Anna Giordani was a middle-aged spinster who was devoting her life to work among the new Italian immigrants, the southerners, who were as removed from her experience as the Negroes of New York were from the whites. She felt in conflict about these people, who, politically, she had to consider her countrymen, and spiritually her brothers. She never managed to like them, but she did her duty unflinchingly, as a kind of penance and discipline for her soul. She was tall, lean, fair-skinned, with watery light eyes and graying brown hair. She was fastidious; she wore white gloves and every bit of her person was clean and orderly when she came to work in the slum tenements.

It astonished Umbertina to see such a lady in her attic room the first day Anna Giordani came to call on her. From the start, Anna respected Umbertina. She saw in her the stubbornness of not wanting to succumb to the tenements, of being determined to leave them behind.

"*Brava, signora,*" she said encouragingly. "Things will get better for you because you want them to." And she admired the bedspread from Castagna, which shone like an ensign of hope in the dingy room.

It was Anna Giordani who helped Umbertina get Paolo through that critical first summer. She showed Umbertina how to get to the East River with the baby and children so they'd get a breath of moving air to fill their deprived and pinched bodies. Umbertina was still nursing Paolo, but she would buy milk for the other boys and take them all to the river, where they would watch the boats with their cargoes of garbage being picked over by Italian ragpickers for what they could scavenge; or they would see the unmarked coffins of the poor being taken on barges to Potter's Field, where they would be dumped in a trench at city expense, crowded in death as they had been in life to save space that had more value for the city than their lives; or, from the new piers on the East River, they'd watch the naked boys who swam from them until the police came to chase them away.

Once she saw tramps and vagrants and a group of lunatics being taken by guards out to the penal workhouses and asylums on the islands in the East River, which looked green and inviting with their trees and which her eyes strained toward. In Calabria the harshness of life had made people sick in body; here, she saw, the life sickened the heart and soul.

She was learning the American story—money was the key to everything. If you were fortunate enough to keep your health and reason in the midst of the purgatorial tenements you were forced to pass through in the New York sojourn, you might be able to get to some other place with the money you saved.

But the tenement got and kept most lives; it made people into its own image, lower than when they had arrived. Anna Giordani was always exclaiming, "Why do you Italians put up with the worst conditions, take the worst jobs, and then either send your money back to Italy or let yourself be robbed of it by a *padrone!*"

"*My* money won't go back," Umbertina told her fiercely. "It's to get us out of here. We are not like the *napoletani* on Mulberry Street. They came from the slums of Naples and are happy in the slums of New York. But we are country people. We don't live like this."

That winter and the next they froze, trying to keep warm in the attic room with whatever coal or wood Umbertina and the boys were able to scavenge from the streets. Serafino's gang work stopped when the snow came, so that all he could earn during the winter was whatever he got from shoveling snow. The children loved the sight of snow falling out of the sky, and Umbertina, too, found peace in its softness and the quiet it brought. It seemed right that Christmas should come in such softness. She learned from her neighbors to make a *granita de caffè* with the freshly fallen snow, some coffee, and sugar. But soon the white blanket turned to black slush, making the streets worse than ever and clinging to her skirts.

It was in winter that the city's Sanitary Police came around at night, banging on doors and calling *"Apri porta!"* to gather evidence of illegal overcrowding in the tenements. For when work was scarce and people kept arriving in the city, the only solution was for the jobless to take in lodgers at night and for the homeless to pay their nickel a spot to lie on someone's floor or to sleep, sitting up squeezed in an alcove or someone's doorway. One night, in the room below them, Umbertina saw the police evict twelve people and send them off to a police station probably as overcrowded and as filthy as the hole they had been driven from. And she wondered what kind of country it was that tried to do good by recognizing evil, but whose remedies were as bad as the original evil. It strengthened her resolution that they had to take care of themselves and be their own salvation.

But the summers were the worst, with the cooking, sleeping, working, living all together in the sweltering tenements and streets, unable to breathe. In the newer tenements, the Barracks, those who could moved to the roofs and fire escapes to sleep, but those in the old frame houses were trapped there in rooms heavy with sweat and stale, fetid air. This was the time of year when babies slipped from windows and adults rolled off rooftops in their sleep. And in the the streets the Americanized children chanted at their games, "July, July, go to Hell and die!"

People who had worked all their lives in open fields became tubercular. Almost every front doorway on every block bore the grimy white bow with streamers that announced an infant's death in the building.

Despite Umbertina's constant wish to get away, they slipped into the rhythm of the place. Serafino stopped nightly in the saloon downstairs to pay 2¢ for a mug of stale beer and talk to his comrades; Giacomo and Benedetto had begun to go to the American school and speak English and wanted to be called Jake and Ben; Umbertina found some solace in the company of other Calabrian women, with whom she sat out on the sidewalk and chatted while she mended or shelled beans or picked over the greens for their meal.

She learned from them a dozen ways to cook escarole. And she heard with a feeling of shock how they derided the American teachers of their children.

"Uh-ei!" said one of the tough *comari*. "These American *femmine* know nothing. My Vito comes home and says his teacher told the class

they should have meat, potatoes, and a vegetable on their plates every night, all together. Like pigs eating from a trough, I tell him. In my house I have a *minestra,* a second dish, and a third dish. And beans if I want to! Madonna, that skinny American telling us what to eat!"

"These teachers are not good," said another. "They make the kids cry because they can't pronounce Italian names and make them ashamed. Annunziata says her teacher makes a face like she's vomiting when she calls her name. *Miserabile!*"

Umbertina's great frustration was that her hands weren't trained enough for the piecework the other women did to earn money and that she who had worked the fields and herded goats in Calabria could only do wash in the city.

The street had a life of its own that reminded her of the dusty streets of Castagna when they had sat out and gossiped as they did their work and minded the children. But Castagna was becoming more unreal and insubstantial as time passed, and her memory glossed over past fatigues to fasten on to the present ones. If one had asked her how Castagna was, she would have answered, "Quiet . . . quiet as the woods and the ruined abbey in the valley." And to her mind now, constantly battered by the sounds of the New York streets, it did seem that Castagna was a place where only the wind in the trees or the rush of the stream was heard.

On Bleecker Street, together with the constant roar of the Broadway Elevated, there were the wagons and peddlers, the organ grinder and monkey, and a continual chorus of calls from the vendors: roasted peanuts, *ceci,* chestnuts on a charcoal brazier; baked sweet-potatoes or, in season, watermelon, peaches, and cherries. Even for the poor, abundance flowed through the streets, replenishing afresh the dream that had brought them there.

Yes, it was hard; but how could one doubt? Umbertina watched the color and bustle of everyday life and saw, despite the wretchedness, the look of expectancy on everyone's face that seemed to replace the old look of stolid resignation which was native to Calabria. And then there were the feast days, when the neighborhoods took on a gaudy, brazen look with illuminated arches over the streets, flags, banners, and huge ornate candles, fruits, flowers, and pastries in profusion to honor the old country's saints. They paraded and feasted for *martedì grasso* just before Lent, for Corpus Christi, for Our Lady of Mount Carmel, and then each street had its own special *festa:* the Sicilians for Santa Rosalia, the Neapolitans for San Gennaro, the Calabrians for San Rocco. Processions were formed; the children skipped alongside, bright-eyed with wonder; and everyone joined in.

There was solidarity among the countrymen who stuck together in their neighborhood. None of them strayed out into the alien city, despite Anna Giordani's chidings that things were better uptown, or over on the West Side. They had already been wrenched once from their homes; they could not give up their last comfort—the protective feeling of being together where their language was understood.

Each payday a dime or even a quarter went into the savings Umbertina kept with their countryman Ranucci, who had a bank in his grocery store on the corner. Then, one day, Serafino came home with a message from some new arrivals from Soveria Mannelli.

"Beppino wants us to send some money so he can come over."

Umbertina looked up with a scowl from the table where she was rolling pasta. She looked to see if Serafino—the husband to whom, by custom and Church law, she owed deference and obedience—had taken the correct estimate of this preposterous message from her brother.

"I could take something from what we have at Ranucci's," he said, "and send him a money order." He spoke as if it were the most natural thing in the world.

For the first time in their married life, Umbertina looked at him with anger. He was a man of over forty and she a young woman in her twenties, already thick with childbearing and heavy now with her newest pregnancy.

Her face flushed and she screamed, "Let Beppino make his way as we did! He hasn't a wife or children. He can work." It was the first time she had shown rage at him and her eyes filled with tears at her feelings. "You are a fool!"

Serafino felt the same hurt as a child who is turned upon by someone he loves. He was astounded at her reaction and what he considered her hardheartedness. *"Non hai sentimenti,"* he said chidingly.

"Feelings!" she threw at him in anger. "Why should I have feelings for a grown man like Beppino who lives in his own home while my children live in the land of strangers in this sty," she screamed. "*You* have the sentiment and no brains to go with it!"

For years she had been silent and stoic, bearing everything. But now the time had come for her to take charge, and she would do so whether it meant disrespect to her husband or not.

Serafino was crushed. He did not fight back or give her the blow she deserved. "What do you want from me, *Signore Dio*!" he said in a self-pitying tone.

"I want you to get us out of the city. Now I am having another child and we are still here. Giacomo is eight and Benedetto six . . . maybe they remember what it was to see trees and the sun shining. But this new baby and Paolo—what will it be for them? To live in this room or on the streets? Even the goats in my father's pen were let out into the hills. Are we worse than the animals?"

"We will go, we will go," Serafino muttered in a tired, defeated way. He was already forty-four and he had never recovered all of his strength after his health had broken. Could he be sure to find other work if he left what he had? The work was steady now in New York; he had his *paesani* in the saloon with whom he found pleasure playing cards.

But Umbertina had different ideas: to have a piece of land, to be again in the open air under the sun working the soil—most of all, to use their strength for themselves.

Before the beginning of a third summer was upon them, Umbertina took things into her own hands and had Anna Giordani write to Domenico Saccà in Cato for her. She couldn't send a written message to her relative Giovanni Muzzi directly because he was as illiterate as she. She told Anna Giordani to write Domenico, asking him to find out what work Serafino could have in Cato and to see if Giovanni Muzzi could find them a place to live. Domenico could answer through Anna Giordani.

Umbertina's fourth son came before the answer to her letter. Named Rocco for the saint of the impossible, the child was born in June. Anna Giordani had helped at the birth and then found the wet-nurse for the baby, because Umbertina, having nursed Paolo through his second summer, had no more milk.

Anna had been there to visit Umbertina on the day when Serafino learned that their savings were gone. Ranucci's store hadn't opened one day because he had taken all the money from his bank and gone back to Italy.

Umbertina, already weakened, felt defeated by the news. She resigned herself to sinking like the others into the life of the slums, not making the effort any longer to get out.

There was too much to fight against. Despite the wet-nurse the baby was wasting quickly, and Paolo himself, never strong, was sickly and pale. I have mocked God, Umbertina thought as she watched Rocco whimper and struggle for air. I wanted to change our place in the order of things and to be something more than what God wished. And God is punishing me with these calamities.

But if that is true, her stubbornness told her, what kind of God is He?

∞

Classic and Good

There's really no use calling my mother.

It only starts her off: "What about me?" she says. "What do I do here day after day, night after night, except cater to your father? We sit here not even talking. No conversation. He watches TV and I pick up the dishes. I might as well be you! I say to him, I might as well be a widow like Fran for all the company I get out of you."

Her voice always rises as she recites the familiar decalogue of her woes, as she forgets her having told me to call whenever I had things on my mind to talk over and when I needed someone to listen. Instead, I become the listener even though it's I who put in the call and it's my nickel, so to speak. But life, as our presidents tell us, isn't fair.

On this Saturday night it was raining and I was home alone because Mara, the only daughter left at home, was out baby-sitting when my mother called me.

She was anxious to know if I were still seeing that man named Joe. "You should pray to God," says my mother. "Every night I pray He'll send you a husband while you're still young enough."

I say goodnight to her and think of all the people committed to seeing me with a man in my life. I think of all the advice heaped on me: "See a shrink," some say. "Get into politics, that's where the men are," another adds. Or, says the divorced woman in my exercise class, come along to a Singles Week-End in the Poconos.

How little they know me, all of them. Why a husband? I've had that. Or why religion, therapy, politics, or the Singles Scene?—all things I have always mistrusted and avoided.

But then, no one understands my aloneness, including me, for it's a quirky thing, inconstant like the weather. There are fair and serene days, there are dismal ones; nothing to count on day in and day out. Lately it's been raining continuously and my spirits have drooped. I think of old Sister Marie-Claire, the French nun of my Convent School days. "I feel like zee wetter," she would intone lugubriously in French class impugning the weather, and we there, in our blue serge uniforms, snickering at her. Her stocky little European frame never habituated itself to the bizarre turns of upstate New York weather which could produce a hot spell in February or freeze the apple blossoms on the Convent grounds in late April. It was an unsettling capriciousness of divine order which made her nervous and sad.

Dino, my husband, had a sensitive European frame, too, and he hated our weather. Did he mention it to his Italian classes as Sister Marie-Claire used to? He died, a full professor, of a heart attack at the college where he taught. He left the girls and me and now it's been seven years without him.

Oh, how iffy life is! Everything seemed to go at Dino's death: the big house, our friends, our vacations, my two older daughters, my teeth. I told the girls we could still make a home in the little Victorian cottage I moved to but the eldest said, What are we supposed to be, Little Women and Marmee?

I made a few friends in my new neighborhood. I began working part-time for the paper. I had my hair shaped so that I'd never have to go weekly to a hairdresser and I started working out at the Y where I now can run a mile in laps. I was feeling pretty good about myself when I met Joe Farba.

It was at Jane Bookman's. I knew Jane from years ago when she was a married suburbanite like the rest of us. Then one day she left her husband and children and went west where I lost track of her. I refound her when I heard her by chance on a radio talk show where she was introduced as a successful single woman artist living in Soho. The next day I called her.

"Wow!" she said. "Fran, is that you—it's been so long! You've got to come for dinner. Come meet Eric."

I went to her place on Spring Street, taking a freight elevator up to the sixth floor where the door opened directly into Jane's loft. And there she was, standing at a miniature fridge getting out salad greens. Behind her was the sink and an old-fashioned bathtub on lion paws.

"Welcome to a stately home of Soho!" she laughed, her voice zesty and rich.

I looked around. There were pillow seating arrangements on the floor. Under a Jane-made wire mesh lighting fixture that hung from the pressed tin ceiling was an oak pedestal table with unmatched chairs around it: a Queen Anne piece from a formal dining set, a piano stool, a wicker thing, a swivel chair, etc.

All around us in the huge open space was Jane's work—bright, triumphant, assertive wood sculpture of leaping and prancing abstracted human forms. Everything moving and flowing in rhythms of joy. The place was crammed with her work, with canvases, with skis and bicycles, a motorcycle, concocted lamps and masks made from egg cartons and feather dusters. In the rear was a platform bed under a huge painting of nudes. A door opened out onto a narrow iron balcony lined with plants.

Jane had become pretty, she looked wonderful. Her face was no longer gaunt and frowning, as I remembered her, with hair pulled tight from her scalp and tied in an austere knob on top of her bony head. Now she wore it loose around a fuller face and she kept smiling and laughing, so free from remorse that she made it seem as if it had been her husband and children who left *her*, but she forgave them.

"We were going to barbecue on the balcony but the weather's too drippy," Jane said. "Eric's doing butterfly lamb—it's been steeping two days in garlic and lemon juice. He's a great cook—I should marry him." She made the statement sound hilarious. "But twice is enough!"

"Where is he," I asked.

"Coming, coming . . . and he's bringing a man, a lawyer."

I might have dressed differently if I had known. I'm aware of men now almost in the same way as when I was a teen-ager. Only now it's not that I'm trying to date to be popular, but because a man's company seems as much a part of my life as air and light. The trouble is American men seem not to know how to act anymore, or what the rules are; they've put us all back into adolescence. It's not just the weather that's more predictable in Europe.

Eric, very good looking, and wearing a head-band and jeans, arrived with a tall, solid man of dark complexion and bushy eyebrows who was dressed in a very serious suit and striped tie.

"Everybody, meet Joe Farba," Eric said. "I know Joe from the fish store, he's become one of my best customers."

"You have a fish store?" I asked.

"Not mine, I just work there. It's near City Hall. That's why we get lawyers like Joe for our customers."

"Brain food?" I asked.

Jane laughed in her full-bodied, deeply enjoying way. "Not fish to eat," she said, "fish for tanks—goldfish, tropical fish, and such."

Things went well around talk of fish, the passing of cheese, and pouring of wine. Eric described the demise of a competitor, the schmuck who thought he could get more business by operating with topless salesgirls and charging admission. Instead, his fish store folded and now he worked for Eric's boss, but Eric stayed away from him because he was, said Eric, a Jew with a Nazi heart, one who blamed the Blacks for doing him in.

"He must be the exception to Jews," said Joe from his place in the pillows. "You know, as a kid I always wanted to be Jewish. At City College, when my name was taken for Joe Farber I let it pass so they'd think I was Jewish."

"What are you really?" I asked.

"*Siciliano!*" he answered with a put-on accent.

"Me, too, in part," I said.

"My first wife was Jewish," Joe went on, "so you see I was well on my way to becoming Jewish myself."

"Why did you want to?" Jane asked.

"They were the only ones I could admire as I was growing up in Brooklyn. All my father could say was, what good is an education—you can get a job without going to college. And then that parochial school they sent me to! I had it up to here with being a Catholic and an Italian. I decided I'd go to City College no matter what."

I found this very appealing. By the time we sat down to eat the lamb and thick chunks of fresh crusty bread and salad, we were all into our life stories; all theirs began, "My second husband . . ." or "my first wife . . ."; I was the only one with one marriage.

Leaving, I said to Jane and Eric, "Come out to see me—we'll take a walk in the country and I'll make pasta."

Joe accompanied me to my car and I told him, "I meant for you to come, too, with Jane and Eric. I hope you do."

I thought that anyone who had had two wives and now collected fish might be lonely and it wouldn't have been right to invite Jane and Eric and not include him. Besides, as I notified my mother, I liked him.

A few days later I got a card in the mail in which Charlie Brown is saying to Snoopy, *Per me tu sei la senape in un panino con l'arrosto*. It was from Joe and it came on yet another rainy day. I was like the mustard on his ham sandwich is what it said in Italian. Was he rethinking himself to what he actually was?

The card reminded me of that old-time song, "You're the cream in my coffee . . ." from some movie with Joan Blondell, Ruby Keeler, and Dick Powell where everyone sings and dances and everything always comes out right. It made me feel good.

Inside Joe had written, Let's you and I meet for dinner, the two of us, before we all go walking in the country. On the back of the envelope he had tried to render his name and address in Italian as Joseph the lawyer, on the square of Washington, in the city of Big Apple; it was grammatically wrong and misspelled, but very appealing.

When Mara got home from school I was singing:

You're the cream in my coff-eeee
you're the salt in my stew
you will always be, my nec-ess-i-teee
I'd be lost without you.

You're the starch in my collar
you're the lace in my shoe
you will always be, my nec-ess-i-teee
I'd be lost without you.

She was bemused and said, "You're in good spirits!"

"The sun is shining," I answered.

The night I went into the city to meet Joe for dinner he was wear-ing a greenish suit with wide stripes that was quite terrible and unlike his decorous lawyer outfit. He consulted a clipping torn from a newspa-per and read a blurb about a restaurant. "This sounds good," he said, "we can go there if it's all right with you." Instead it was all wrong.

We went into a long, narrow, noisy, smoky room in which tables for two were jammed together in relentless lines down both walls. "Itsa not so big-uh," Joe said as we were seated.

We ordered and the waitress brought two salads. "Is there garlic in the dressing?" he asked.

She was leaning close as she served and she looked at him in sur-prise. "Well, a bit. It's the house dressing and very good."

"I don't eat garlic or onions," he said firmly.

"Here, have a taste of mine first," I said. "Try it and see—maybe you'll like it."

"No," he told me, and turning to the waitress said, "Just bring me some salad with oil and vinegar on the side."

The waitress hesitated as I pushed my salad plate towards him. "Try it—there's no taste of garlic, it's all blended in to make the dressing better."

"Look, will you do me a favor," he said irritably to the waitress, "bring me some plain salad with the oil and vinegar on the side."

"Sure," said the waitress, shrugging her shoulders.

When he turned back to me, I saw how beetling his eyebrows were, how black his eyes, how dark his skin. He was like the Saracen of folk-lore, the bogeyman kind that plundered Italian shores and raped the women, stole the children.

"I consider that an insult," he said loudly. "When I say I don't want garlic in something why should she insist like that? You know, that's an insult." He was angry, his eyes looked wider and his face bigger.

"She didn't mean it that way," I told him, "and besides it was I who was insisting, not the waitress."

"The way she was hanging over me and everything!" He shook his head, his look still dark and threatening. "Cree-tone-ah!" he muttered in the direction of where the waitress had disappeared.

"*Cretina*," I said automatically, correcting his Italian.

"I've never liked garlic or onions," he went on, "you know, sometimes when I was a kid I'd get up from the table and leave, I was so disgusted. There was my father with this bunch of parsley in his hand, dipping it into a combination of oil, water, salt, pepper and garlic and passing it over everything he ate, sprinkling it everywhere as if he were anointing the stuff."

I smiled at the picture. "Maybe your problem is your father, not the garlic."

He reacted angrily. "You know there's such a thing as individual choice. That's what this country is supposed to be about: freedom of choice."

"Oh, I agree. Choice is fundamental. It's just that there is a classic and good way of preparing some things that's time-tested and so we just accept it, like pasta with cheese, white wine with fish. It's just better that way."

"Well, I disagree. Who says it's better? Just because you like it one way doesn't make it better for me. If I want pasta without cheese and salad without garlic, why shouldn't I?"

I changed the subject to Sacco and Vanzetti. It was the fiftieth anniversary of their execution and I had just finished reading a very moving book about them.

"So you're convinced, now, that they were railroaded," he said.

I felt offended at his taking me for someone who had just then been enlightened.

I tried again. "I should get a sofa, I was looking at some today . . . but everything's so expensive. I guess I should get a better paying job, but it's so hard. . . ." I stopped. Why was I sounding so doleful? Actually I liked the freedom my part-time, though low-paying, job gave me. I liked not having a sofa or drapes or wall-to-wall carpeting anymore. So why the dirge?

He looked at me very deliberately with a half-smile on his lips. "You sound deprived out there in the sticks. You must like the country to live out there."

"If I had my choice, I'd live near the sea, I love the water."

He smiled cunningly.

"What's wrong with that?" I said defensively.

"Freud," he answered.

"What's that supposed to mean?"

"Sex."

"Oh, come on—everything's sex! Being the mustard on a ham sandwich is sex." I tried to say it lightly but somehow it came out as all our conversation had, contentiously.

Things weren't going well. Far from being the perky know-it-all who corrected his Italian and insisted he try my salad because it was the right salad and I knew best, now I was Mrs. Lonelyhearts sitting there woebegone because I didn't have a husband, a sofa, or even the guts to walk out of the awful place.

Joe Farba smiled, in better humor now, ready to be patronizing. "What is your daughter studying?"

"The usual, getting ready for college, but I'm making her take Latin. That's classic and good, too," I smiled.

"Making?"

"Yes. I told her it was part of her Italian heritage, that she should know the beginnings of the language and culture."

"And she didn't want to take it?"

I nodded.

"Well, if I were her, I'd tell you, Fuck off!"

"She did, but it didn't work. And you know something?—she's glad it didn't. Because now she really likes taking Latin only she first had to go through this assertive thing where she pretended to hate it." I looked at him surmisingly and said, "You know how kids are. Do you have any?"

"No," he said. "What are you with all that heritage stuff, a born-again Italian?"

I wondered. I thought of Dino and our times in Italy. I thought of the proud but perverse Nicola Sacco at his trial, goaded beyond endurance by slights and slurs and falling into the trap of defending an Italy which he had left. And by defending Italy, and making himself seem ungrateful to be in America to that New England Wasp jury, poor Sacco did himself in. Just so was this lawyer in his lurid suit luring me into traps and getting me 100% wrong.

It wasn't the garlic that made him mad, it was my Italianness because he hated his and didn't understand mine. He had married one Jewish woman, then another of German background. But they had divorced him because a leopard can't change his spots and what Joe was underneath was a bad-tempered Sicilian not a rational Jewish intellectual.

Leaving he said, "I'm sorry about that garlic argument—we agree on important things, it was silly to squabble about that."

"Don't worry about it."

It was the following day at work that it hit me that Joe Farba had eaten Eric's garlic-marinated lamb and loved it. I was furious. Then I felt remorse because I knew we wouldn't see each other again, and somewhere behind his front there was an appealing person, the person who had been hurt by his parents' fighting, his father's tyranny, and his growing up conflicted.

Free-flow, free-flow. . . . I thought of Jane's marvelous free-flow figures dancing and leaping in joy; let everyone have freedom, let them flow as they will, eat garlic or not.

Joe Farba and I had tried to come together, then had retreated, each of us, to our separate ideas and places in the scheme of things. I thought of how my eldest daughter once said that the men I choose is like pissing in Versailles. She said my dreams of glory crumbled with reality because they were the outward view of Versailles while reality lay behind the magnificent facade where the courtiers pissed in its corridors.

Joe probably bought a new fish for his tank for consolation. I put an ad in the *New York Review of Books:* Good-looking widow, 45, seeks single, smart, sexy man who loves garlic.

And I won't tell my mother when I get a call.

Regina Barreca

My Grandmother,
A Chicken, and Death

The miracle of death I first had the privilege to witness when I was about five years old.

My grandmother and I, along with a dozen other females, had been waiting about six years for a bus to come down Avenue U in Brooklyn, N.Y. We'd been marketing—as people then referred to the process—and now stood in vigilance alongside our string bags lined up next to us on the pavement as if on parade. In addition to the bags of flour, boxes of salt, and cans of olive oil bought for convenience, my grandmother had purchased a live chicken which she held under her arm. This was a Big Deal, this particular purchase. Relatives were coming all the way from New Jersey and the big chicken was a special treat. I had never seen her buy a real live chicken before and although I knew this practice was not actually unusual, I was fascinated by the ritual: the selection process, the holding of the bird, the fact of the creature's vitality.

The bird was in her embrace, nestled in the broad expanse of her black cotton sleeve. It seemed calm enough. Resisting the temptation to ask my grandmother if I could try to hold it, I settled for sneaking looks at its eyes. The bird seemed to look back at me and I rather fancied that we had built up a bit of a friendship. I felt sort of proud of the bird and of my grandmother's ability to control and deal with the creature on this warm morning. Other people waiting on line also looked at it and commented on it, some speaking Italian to my grandmother, and smiling at me.

Finally, the bus arrived. Other people got on first; we waited until they were seated. My grandmother, in her seventies at the time, and a slow mover, took her time. Only after we had dragged our parcels up the few steps to the little entry platform did the driver notice the chicken. "Lady," he said, with some impatience, "you cannot bring a live bird on the bus. Sorry but I gotta ask you to leave."

I stood, ashamed and shocked, not knowing what to do, afraid of what would come next. We were holding up the bus; other people had important places to go, and there we were, bags and bags of food and a big live bird, standing not quite on the bus and not quite off of it. My grandmother had never been questioned to her face before, at least not in my presence. Hers was the last word on anything; she wielded an authority so supreme it went unquestioned. And this bus-driver had the courage to issue a command! What could possibly happen?

Without a word, and without diverting her eyes even for a second from the face of the driver, my grandmother put her right hand into the cleft of her left elbow and deftly twisted the chicken's neck. It took maybe one and a half seconds. The chicken no longer filled her arm with its vitality; it was just another grocery item. Nothing was special about it anymore. Then my grandmother raised her eyebrows, cocking her head towards the man, as if saying "Now is there a problem?" and the driver shook his head "no" while motioning for us to pass through. Nobody on the bus said anything. My hands shaking, I put coins in the metal and glass box for our fares. We sat down. My grandmother put the chicken into one of the larger bags and brushed off her dress. She looked straight ahead, but she also stroked the back of my neck, as if to reassure me. I loved my grandmother but I was far from reassured by the gesture.

Don't think I didn't eat with a full appetite that night—I was as appreciative of a good meal as ever. The relatives from New Jersey were treated like royalty and everybody had a good time. The next day my aunts made chicken-salad sandwiches with the leftovers.

So much for the miracle of death. One minute the chicken is nestling and making eye contact and small noises and the next minute it's just an ordinary chicken for dinner, head flopping to one side and silent. Death was easy, it seemed; one moment and the whole business was completed.

The miracle of birth would be explained to me only much later and treated with far more shame.

Joy Behar

My Life in
Funeral Parlors

Not long ago, I attended the wake of a long-time acquaintance of mine. The deceased had two daughters and one of them was grieving openly, bemoaning the fact that she no longer had a mother. Her aunt, a woman of limited resources, was doing her own brand of grieving, trying out her theory of lost relativity while at the same time ostensibly trying to comfort her niece.

"Yes," she said, "you lost a mother, but I lost a sister. And Nana lost a daughter. And your father lost a wife. And your son lost a grandmother. And Carmine Pecoraro lost a friend." The list went on for what seemed like forever. And the building lost a tenant. And the dentist lost a patient. And the butcher lost a meat lover. Finally, I lost interest and, needless to say, the poor girl was not consoled.

For me, and certainly James Joyce, and now apparently TV programmers, wakes have an odd, almost surreal attraction. From the Princess Diana funeral to the Sonny Bono funeral, there seems to be a tremendous interest in funerals. Italian funerals have yet to be televised. Maybe it's because with so many women throwing themselves into the grave, it's hard to tell who the deceased is. But Italian wakes are incredibly interesting. Where else do you get a horseshoe of gardenias saying SUCCESS except when an Italian dies.

As a child, I was brought to many wakes in my old neighborhood in Brooklyn. It was almost like going to a birthday party, what with me decked out in my Shirley Temple pinafores. On the other hand, most of the other people who attended these wakes wore black or some other subdued color to show respect. But not everyone. I remember one woman who walked into the funeral parlor where the body was laid out, wearing a red outfit with shoes to match and a hat with feathers.

Everyone was stopped cold in their tracks, or as my mother's friend Mary Ricciardi used to say, "We remained." They just "remained" in their horrified state, shocked at the temerity, the audacity, the utter tackiness of the outfit. Or how can I forget Carmine Russo, who shocked my family when he sauntered into my grandmother's wake wearing a T-shirt and displaying a tattoo of the Last Supper. My Aunt Sadie simply remarked that she had no idea that Carmine was that religious.

Initially, these wakes, often given for people who were strangers as far as I was concerned, were kind of scary for me. But as I grew older, they would prove to be a wonderful source of fun. They also provided an unexpected method of altering my mother's mood, which most often matched the predominant color worn at these gatherings: black. On any given day, I'd be likely to find her at the sink listening to a recording of *La Traviata,* streams of tears rolling down her cheeks, relentlessly reliving all the depressing moments of her life. The only way you could cheer her up was to inform her that you were going to a wake. "Oh, yeah?" she'd say, her voice rising gleefully. "Who died?" And suddenly the blood would rush back to her face. Once again, life was worth living.

My Aunt Sadie was another frequent wake attendee. In fact, over the years she attended so many wakes that she should have received frequent flyer mileage. Aunt Sadie didn't have to actually know the deceased. If she passed them on the street once or twice on her way to the sausage store, that was enough of a relationship for her. After all, wakes were often social situations where you ran into old friends and neighbors. If the person in the coffin was old, there usually was a lot of talking, smoking, and general shmoozing in the antechamber. And Aunt Sadie could talk, smoke, and shmooze with the best of them. That there happened to be a dead body in the room seemed at best an ornament, and at worst, irrelevant. Nor did it put a damper on the occasion.

Oh, yes. The deceased. To some an afterthought, but after all, if it weren't for the dear departed, my mother would be sobbing at the sink listening to Italian operas and Aunt Sadie would be talking to herself.

To me, one of the more bizarre traditions coming out of religion is the Christian custom of putting makeup on dead people, dressing them in fancy outfits, and fixing their hair in some sort of coif, all of which inevitably prompts various people to make comments like, "He looks good." Or, "He looks just like himself." (Who else would he look like?—all he got was an embalming, not plastic surgery.) Rarely, however, do you hear, "He never looked better," although in some cases I have seen, this would be a far more accurate observation.

My Aunt Rose often got into trouble at wakes because her voice carried and she was quite capable of making an inappropriate comment that would be heard across the room. Once, a woman she knew from childhood accused her of making fun of her dentures. My aunt claimed that she was not talking about the woman's teeth, but an argument broke out anyway.

Denture Woman: Are you laughing at my teeth?

Aunt Rose: What are you, crazy?

Denture Woman: I saw you. You were staring at my mouth and then you said something to your sister-in-law and then you both laughed.

Aunt Rose: I was not laughing at your teeth. I was laughing at Carmela Mangiapropette. She had toilet paper on her shoe.

Denture Woman: Don't lie, Rose. I know how vicious you can be.

Aunt Rose: Me? And what about you? I heard you call your daughter-in-law a *putana*.

Denture Woman: That's a lie. I never called her a *putana,* even if she was one. And what about that time when you put soap in your mother-in-law's mouth?

Aunt Rose: She deserved it. She was cursing me up and down.

Denture Woman: You're a bitch and you know it.

Aunt Rose: And you're a buck-toothed old hag. I don't think it's a laughing matter when someone pays thousands of dollars on dentures and ends up looking like she's running at Aqueduct.

When my mother died, people were pretty upset. She was one of those people who never made an enemy. She was incapable of hurting anyone's feelings. She never said a mean word to me, or anyone else for that matter. All in all, she was a good mother, despite the occasional fits of melancholia, which she couldn't help. If it were today, she'd be on Prozac and my life would have been a picnic. I don't know if I would have become a comedian, however, since the motivation to save the world from its misery would be missing.

One of my friends, a comedian who has a hideous relationship with his mother, came to my mother's wake to pay his respects. Comedians are a rare breed. First of all, they have trouble with serious situations, and secondly, they say whatever they want, God bless them. So there we were standing in the smoking room with a few people, and suddenly he says to me, "Joy, you are so lucky. You have a boyfriend, you have a career, and now you have a dead mother."

Believe it or not, we had a good laugh over that. My mother would have laughed, too.

Mary Jo Bona

From *Claiming a Tradition:*
Italian American Women Writers

Perhaps the conflict most insistently dramatized in these novels [Italian American novels by women] has to do with a struggle in the family between the Italian belief in *la via vecchia,* "the old way," and the American emphasis on innovation and liberation from old beliefs. The following well-known Italian proverb encapsulates the Italian family's investment in *la via vecchia: Chi lascia la via vecchia per la nuova, sa quel che perde e non sa quel che trova* (Whoever forsakes the old way for the new knows what he is losing but not what he will find). [. . .] Traditionally subordinate to the men in her life—father, brothers, husband—the Italian woman's stake in the old ways perpetuates her inferior status. In certain instances, the female characters interpret the belief in *la via vecchia* through the lens of their status as mothers: responsible for transmitting to their children the moral heritage (for which they were highly valued in Italy), Italian immigrant mothers felt particularly threatened by the public schools of America, which they feared underrated their roles as educators of their children.

Defined through family affiliation, the Italian immigrant mother's role was potentially attenuated in America, especially when she was required by economic or legal necessity to send her children into a strange public world outside the confines of *la casa:* the factory and the classroom. Social historian Elizabeth Ewen believes that maternal authority over children was not weakened in America. Rather, mother and children were intensely involved in adjusting to a new land. [. . .] The novels in the Italian American tradition at times portray mothers as defensive and resentful toward their children's American ways, but in other cases, mothers in fact succeed in maintaining the cultural authority and economic stability of the family.

Novels focusing on second- and third-generation Italian American women tell another story. The inherent struggle resulting from a devotion to *la via vecchia* and an allegiance to the new world is often meliorated by the Italian American writers' inclusion of another feature of *italianità: comparaggio* or *comparatico* (godparenthood). [. . .]

Although godparenting in the religious sense is not emphasized in the novels, the creation of what Micaela di Leonardo calls "non-religious fictive kin" offers a writer like Mari Tomasi the means by which to depict the struggle between immigrant parents and their increasingly Americanized children. The godparent in *Like Lesser Gods* mediates between old and new worlds, aiding in the young Italian American's formulation of an identity that is neither Italian nor American but a combination of both. The Italian family insisted on the privileged status of elders, in accordance with *la via vecchia*. [. . .] That Italian American women writers employ such a figure as a mediator between two contrasting cultures attests to the resiliency of the role itself and the innovative aspect of ethnicity. [. . .]

The code of *omertà*, the cultural injunction to be silent, may very well have originated in the Sicilian countryside where bands of brigands fought against governmental authorities. [. . .] This feature of *italianità*—*omertà*—has peculiar resonance for women of Italian origins and for women who want to write. Perhaps the codes informing the southern Italian family were considered inviolate in Italy, but they were subject to an authority closer to home in America: the wife, the mother, the sister, the daughter. That Italian American writers have chosen to use the family as the focus of their novels, to write of the family and tell its secrets, is a profoundly courageous act of autonomy.

The proverbs and expressions relating to words themselves attest to a tradition of wariness about their function and efficacy. Consider the following proverbs: *La migliore parola è quelle che non si dice* (The best word is that which is not spoken); *A chi dici il tuo secreto, doni la tua libertà* (To whom you tell a secret, you give your freedom). [. . .] The gender of the speaker also affects the putative value of the word. Thus, we have the proverb *Le parole son femmine, e i fatti son maschi* (Words are female; actions are male). When males use words, they are given fuller legitimacy. Italian men are said to use words more sparingly than females, and the words they use are connected with loyalty and *onore*. Hence, we have the expressions *Ti do la mia parola* (I give you my word) and *parola d'onore* (word of honor).

Women's words, on the contrary, are supposedly used for hurtful and useless gossip, revealing their lack of loyalty and inability to form "superior" relationships (that is, male friendships). [. . .]

Coupled with this attitude toward words is the code of *omertà*. Although the imposition of silence may very well have pervaded the psyches of Italian immigrants, it did not necessarily prevent them or their children from using the family as the focus of their writings. One method women use of overcoming inhibitions placed on them implicitly or explicitly by the family is to write through the silence. Italian American writers, like their Asian American and African American sisters, start out from what they know—the family—and tell the secrets. . . .

Italian Americans from southern Italy and Sicily may very well have come from a nonreading, premodern culture in which nearly 62 percent of the men and 74 percent of the women who came to the shores of Ellis Island were illiterate. [. . .] Nonetheless, second-generation writer Pietro di Donato, author of the critically acclaimed novel *Christ in Concrete* (1939), predicted in 1978, a "renaissance" of Italian American writers was inevitable: "Our time is now. I see it because you are no longer *figli di muratori* (children of construction workers) you go to school and you are children with brains." [. . .] Even though he might not have been considering women as part of this rebirth, di Donato's prediction has come to fruition in the past twenty years.

As if in anticipation of Gay Talese's discussion of the Italian's inherent reticence, Jerre Mangione and Ben Morreale, authors of *La Storia: Five Centuries of the Italian American Experience,* explain that Italian American novelists write "with the distinctive advantage of listening to tall stories. [. . .] The least educated immigrant was often naturally endowed with a strong gift of narrative that planted the seeds for [his or her] offspring's form of storytelling." Mangione and Morreale suggest that Italian Americans possess a natural capacity to create stories and explain that, even though the immigrants were illiterate, "they did bring with them a form of literature in their proverbs, their legends, and in the oral tradition of their *cantastorie* (the village storyteller)."

Dorothy Bryant

From *Miss Giardino*

"No sign of Papa?"

"No, Mama."

She sighs, and we do not look at each other. We know where he is.

I try not to think about him. I think about the other end of the road, down the hill, the long house where the thin lady rang the bell to open the school. She taught us all to write our names. I draw my name in great swirls over and over again. Everywhere, with my finger, in the mud outside our cabin, in the dust on the pipe of the wood stove, in the soap suds of Mama's tub of clothes, steaming, always steaming, on the frosted window while I wait for Papa. But the teacher has gone away. No more school till another thin lady comes. But I can read. Somehow I have learned to read. At first I only held, hugged, smelled the books, but now I can read them. I am the only one in the family who reads English. I hold the book the last teacher left with me, but I do not dare to read now. I must watch out the window. Watch for Papa.

Then it is dark, and Mama says not to wait anymore, come and eat.

I am in bed when he stumbles into the cabin. I wake up hearing the muttering, rumbling words, like the growling of the mine guard's dog. I crawl over Alfonsina, over Victorina, out of the bed, and I go to the doorway. Mama sits at the table, a blanket wrapped around her. Her eyes look sleepy but afraid. She stands up, offers Papa some food. He does not answer. She sits. He says she does not want to feed him. She gets up again, gets the plate of food she has kept for him. He pushes it away. "Cold, not fit to eat." He stands over her, over the table. He swells up with anger, and his swelling chokes me. I see the fight coming, the fury. Nothing can stop it. He wants it. He needs it.

Mama is already crying.

"Stupid woman, stupid!"

Now everyone is up. Mike puts on his clothes and goes out, slamming the door. He can do that, he is a boy, almost a man, already working in the mine. He can walk out, go to a friend, even go to the saloon. Alfonsina hugs Mama, they cry together. Victorina yells, "Leave Mama alone! You're drunk again!" She grabs the heavy iron that always sits on the stove waiting to be heated and then pushed across the wash Mama does for the miners. "If you touch Mama, I'll kill you!"

Papa chases Victorina around the kitchen table. She dodges him and laughs when he stumbles and gasps. He cannot move fast without gasping and losing his breath. He grabs a knife from the sink and throws it at her. She ducks. The knife sticks in the wall behind her. Alfonsina and Mama wail. Victorina screams. Papa stands leaning on the cold stove, shaking his fist, at Victorina, then at God, looking up at the ceiling.

I stand in the bedroom doorway, watching. He turns to me, stops and looks at me. His black eyes look into my black eyes. I don't let him see I am afraid. I show him nothing but fierce black eyes like his. I don't believe what Mama and the others say about the Old Country, about how he sang and was happy. I don't believe in that man. I only know this one, this cruel, mean man who sleeps in our cabin, this monster like the giants in the book of fairy tales the last teacher gave me.

"And you! What are you looking at!"

I say nothing.

"The hard one, eh? Hard and skinny, eh? You don't cry!" He almost smiles, to give me a small opening, so I can reach in to touch his anger, make it burst like the bubbles in Mama's wash tub. But I don't move. I make my eyes narrow and fierce, the way I have to do on the first day of new school in each new town, when I stand tall and pretend to be older and stronger than the bullies.

"Answer me!"

I say nothing.

"Won't talk? Talk! Answer me! I'll make you answer!" He comes at me. Mama and Alfonsina scream. Victorina steps between us, swinging the iron. He pushes her, and she crashes against the wall. I stand still, saying over and over in my head, I hate you, I hate you. I know if I stop saying it I will flinch, fall, even cry like Mama. I won't let him make me cry. I will die first.

He stops in front of me, stands over me, then starts to shake and cough. I do not move while he coughs, breathes great sucks of air, the way I did when I almost died of whooping cough. "Answer me, talk. I'll make you talk." But his voice is already softer. He stands with his hand over me, but does not hit me. His hand hangs in the air over my head. My head bends back as far as it can go, so that I can keep looking into his eyes as he looks down at me, coughs down at me. His hand droops. He shakes his shoulders. "This one is too afraid to talk."

"I am not afraid," I say. Quietly. In English. Somehow I know the words in English will hit his eyes like a whip. He blinks. The new language, the language of the people outside the family, outside the cabin. The language of the people who own the mines. It is my language too. I alone in the family speak it without accent, read it, think in it.

I will never, never speak to him again but in English. I will save Italian for Mama. All my life, all her life, I will caress her with the easy, good-humored Piedmontese dialect, the tongue of golden sunsets and sweet oranges, of the place that is forever home to her. But to Papa I will speak only the language of this new country, my country, that promised him a new life but instead brings him to a new kind of death.

After a while he does the same, speaks to me only in broken English, laughing and saying, "You think I am a stupid immigrant, eh, but I speak English too." He stops calling me Anna. To him I am "the skinny one" or "the stick" or, more and more, "the American."

———

"Anna Giardino! Stay after class!"

"Yes, Mr. Ruggles." I sit choking in my chair. The other students turn to look at me. What have I done that is so terrible? It must be the paper I wrote. But it is only the first. If it is so bad, won't I get another chance? Maybe he will tell the principal I can't do high school work, and I will go into the factory with Mama. Papa would like that.

The bell rings. Lunch time. The other students rush out. I go up to Mr. Ruggles' desk. He is stern, gray-haired, the oldest English teacher, and the only *man. Yes, he is holding my paper. Well, I won't cry. No matter what he says I won't cry.*

"Where did you learn to write like this? It's the only literate paper that's come out of the whole freshman class!" His eyes narrow, and he says, almost accusingly, "You read, don't you." He is praising me! Yes, but he still looks angry. He asks me about myself, who I am, where I live, what my parents do. He listens without comment. Then he begins to talk. He talks and talks.

". . . and I've been teaching here for twenty years. When I started, there were five hundred students in the school and not very many of those were real students. Now there are over two thousand, and anything approximating real education is impossible. The compulsory school law crowds every ignorant fool into my classroom!"

I am too shy to say that, but for the compulsory school law, I would not be here listening to him.

"And this new breed of teachers they are hiring! I don't think many of these ladies have ever read a book, or would ever want to!"

I believe that he must have read every book in the world. And he has seen most countries too. But most marvelous of all, he is a poet. Some years ago he published two books of poetry. He shrugs and frowns as he mentions them.

I begin to stay after class almost every day, eating lunch, going over my papers with him, listening to him talk. He talks about his travels, about poetry, about writing, about books. But always he returns to his obsession, the war, the Great War which has just ended.

"I was born too late. I wish I'd died before I saw it. It's the death of everything. The beginning of the end of everything."

I speak up, for I now read the papers. "Oh, now, it was the war to end all wars, President Wilson said. We will have a League of Nations and live in peace. Women will get the vote soon. And poor people will get education and become . . ."

"Don't parrot slogans! Look at what's really happening. We're already on our way to another war!" He sighs and shakes his head at me. "I have started writing again."

"Poems?" I ask, full of awe.

"No. Not poems. A prose work this time. A survival book. Very practical. These are the days for practical books. This book will tell how to survive in the world as a refugee. What to take when you are forced to leave your home. How to handle police interrogations. Physical fitness in a six by eight cell. Education in a prison camp. Escape techniques. Disguises. A very useful book in the days that are coming."

All the years that I know him, until he dies in 1934, he works on this book. When he dies, his wife says she will keep his manuscript, all his notes, but when she dies only a year later, there is no trace of it.

In my second year of high school, I have another English teacher and see less

*of Mr. Ruggles. And there are other changes. The Sterns now own three stores and,
really rich, they move to Pacific Heights. They want me to come with them, but
Papa demands that I move back into the rooms above the store with him and
Mama. I know he does it out of fear that I will escape him, and partly out of pure
spite.*

*My sixteenth birthday is coming. Papa has marked the date on the calendar,
pointing to it and saying that on that day I will cease to be a parasite on him. I
look at the date like a prisoner waiting for execution. I tell David I will have to
leave high school. And I tell Mr. Ruggles.*

*He explodes. He demands to know where I live and walks home with me
after school on that very day. He walks up the steep stairs into the dim room
where Papa sits by the window. It is like an old drama being played again, like
the librarian in Gilroy, like the truant officer. My fairy tale rescuer from the monster, the cruel giant.*

*I watch Mr. Ruggles and Papa confront each other. Mr. Ruggles is an un-
likely looking knight, and Papa is a shrinking giant. For the first time I realize,
amazed, that Mr. Ruggles is older than Papa, and both of them look tired, worn.
But both are angry, passionate.*

*"Your daughter is a very intelligent girl, the best student I have had in years.
She should finish high school, she must finish, and go on to college. If you do not
want to let her do so, there are others who would be glad to take her into their
homes, including my wife and me." He adds some vague phrases about courts and
guardianship of minors. But his empty threats are unnecessary. I know Papa will
collapse. I watch the old fear creep over his face, and I feel ashamed for him. I do
not even enjoy my victory because I understand the fear and shame that make
him so easy to crush. I have my own share of that same fear and shame.*

*David adds his help. As usual, it is more practical than threats. He persuades
his father to hire me to work in his store on Mission Street. Now I bring home
more money than before. My sixteenth birthday passes, and no mention is made
of leaving school.*

*But my last two years at Camino Real High School are gray and dreary ex-
cept for lunches with Mr. Ruggles and Sunday dinners at the Sterns' big house
on Clay Street. Everything else is school, work, homework, with never enough
sleep or food. I cannot sleep through the nights when Papa restlessly moans and
curses, nor can I eat much sitting across from him at the table. Again, I am spending as much time as possible in the library across the street.*

*One morning I start my usual walk to school, up over the hill, past the
Phoenix Street house, now owned by strangers. I walk past the house, pretending
that I am still living there with the Sterns, with David, leaving that lovely house
to walk to school, walking down the hill, crossing through the park, down toward
the school.*

At first I see nothing different. The red brick walls with the long windows are the same. Then I see the people in the street. I wonder why so many students are staying outside the building. As I come closer I see the strangely black look of the windows and the piles of debris on the sidewalks. Then I recognize the damp, smoldering odor that has teased me ever since I woke up this morning, and I know that the high school does not exist anymore, only the shell of it, with nothing inside. My first thought is that Papa has won, and I will be sent to work in the factory with Mama.

Instead I spend the last months of my high school days pleasantly, in tents set up in the park, in the homes of some teachers, Mr. Ruggles for one, who is again my teacher. He has been giving me forms to fill out, and soon after the fire he tells me I have been accepted to the University of California, with a scholarship to pay for books. He has already located a family in Berkeley, friends of his, who will give me room and board for some housework and tutoring their child in English.

Papa makes it easy for me. He calls me a dozen filthy names, accuses me of sleeping with David and with Mr. Ruggles. He says he hopes he will die soon rather than live with the knowledge of such terrible children as he has had. He says he has no children, disowns them all, especially me. He never wants to see me again, and will make sure I never see Mama. With the last bit of strength he has, he pulls my few belongings out of the box beside the couch in the kitchen and throws them out of the window. He watches from the window as I run down and pick up my things. Mama, crying, follows me and helps me pick them up. She pushes them at me, pushes me, and says, "Go." When I try to answer, she shakes her head and repeats, "Go."

I turn and walk away. When I look back, the street is empty. I know Mama must have run upstairs to care for Papa. His anger will have brought on a coughing fit, and he will need her.

Anne Calcagno

⌘

Story of My Weight

Until the other day, I did not know my feet had become so crookedly misshapen and wide. I told myself my socks were unnecessarily thick; the weather too hot; it stood to reason my shoes were squeezing me. That wasn't true. The things I owned or faced hadn't twisted on me: it was me. I had changed without knowing it because I hadn't looked my way for a long time. With my eyes focused away from me, I've lived out my days in an interlude. Because when I suddenly saw the width of my warped feet, my eyes next traveled up the length of my legs, noticing mottled bruises like disheveled leaves rotting on my legs—I have distractedly smashed into things. I moved to cover them, saw the back of my hand, vein-swelled and colorful, too, like a cabbage leaf. In surprise, I touched my face, the skin slack as silk. I was stunned; as if it all happens in one day, the pieces lined up: I am not young.

It feels as if I have always been fat. I married twenty-three years ago, have been overweight for twenty. Over time, I lost all personal perspective, grew overwhelmed in reaction to wide-eyed glances: when you're fat you're a focus. In public places, like the supermarket, they observe you until you can't get away from being your own prisoner. Wheeling my cart around, I peered at as much as I could, before fleeing. I've been an exaggeration of cells, and a reduced woman. My short blond hair curls into squat corkscrews, tips up; sometimes, when the perm is running out, I look bristling. Yet, when the harried supermarket cashier glances up, I'm the one whose eyes roll into her lap. This is how it is to be an anomaly. Yet, the point is: the other day I looked at my feet which are garbled by widening corns and it became terribly clear: like other women, conclusively mortal, I am going by degrees. No one is a constant picture.

My disfigurement was a private affair. I ate and many things became mine. My consumption accumulated, giving me the appearance of having more years than my actual age. For many years, with a lot of effort, I still could have peeled off these layers and reached a young person. But it is too late. Time went ahead and did some real altering. I am forty-one and have come to look like hell. But my feet, the other day, weren't a continuation of this exaggerated flesh that haunts me. They were life and the broad response of time. I don't know why I saw this.

Age is an invisible train charging through the dark, wearing down the rails. Gradually, I'd been feeling in need of repair. I grew to have more bent space inside. I thought: what should I call this? what have I done?

My husband, perhaps two weeks before I looked at my feet, became aware of his own wearing down. He began to feel his life erasing, tried to leap back from the movement of the train, the foreshortening of horizons. He grappled to stop losing things, saw me. He remembered me differently: supple, eighteen, my eyes on the gravel lifting up very quickly to notice he was there. I was like a leaf. He could have picked me up and taken me anywhere, kept me in his pocket, or pressed in a book.

So, a martini in his hand, he said, "You were sweet and your ankles were thin, hon. Now you're close to a heart attack."

"What's happened now?" I asked.

"For Chrissake, Susan, you're wasting your life. Listen, I won't watch you do this anymore. Lose some weight. I'll buy you dresses. We'll make you into a star, the star of my life, Susan. We've waited too long for this."

"Isn't this coming out of the blue?" I ventured.

"Don't you understand what I'm saying?" he replied.

Harry is almost bald and his remaining disconnected hairs stood straight up with the lamplight gleaming behind them. He had finished his drink. He stared at me. We were in the middle of a movie episode and I was a girl in bright dresses, and he was a young dapper ready to love. But he was catching on fire with the lamplight gleaming around his head and shoulders.

Harry invested himself in this rejuvenating idea, and became insistent. He had not talked to me much in a long time, yet now he repeated himself. "You lose some weight. I'll buy you dresses. What about the good old days?" These must have been in the beginning of our marriage. Being a salesman, he started going away. Absence became a pattern. I sought company in food. I grew into a wide plateau; crushing the good old days, he says. I can't remember the good old days.

Five years ago, I started working. The newspaper ad looked for someone "willing to learn." I am a secretary for an escort service, on the top floor of an old undecorated building. They call it a modeling agency. This is the way it's done: hidden and glorified. I believed the disguise for a long time because that's what you see looking up at you in the yellow pages. You have to read the fine print to figure out the code. And I didn't see it. Strangers in town get lonely and greedy. They call my boss, Rose, willing to pay. I file their accounts. An array of girls in tight colorful dresses and hose, with foreign accents or long hair, always in high heels, come to the office dependent and warm, wanting more than they have. I give them applications and they preen themselves in front of me as if I am neutral practice for a man. I watch silent but accustomed. I keep thinking I'm to give them something, but I can't find it. I have come to believe in the heart of every woman there is a secretary; she wants to assist. These women are so different from me in their way of serving; each is a bird full of plumes and her red fingernails hand me back the forms. But she is a secretary. As I am.

I tried to explain this idea to Harry a while back. "Hell, call them something better than secretaries. Can't get help like that from Kelly

Girls!" His hand slapped his knee with gusto. In the beginning, I remember I was happy because of the way he enjoyed his own jokes.

"It's serious," I said. "So many servants in the world."

"We all need to rely on each other, sweet cakes. That's what you forgot when you shut yourself tight as a rock."

When I found out the girls were not models, I was amazed. Thereupon, Harry visited me at the office to peek at photos. "Pretend I'm an important account," he said.

In the meantime he had been having a few salesman's affairs, things in motels of which he lately informed me. He was explaining his decision to help me regain the shape he first met. Upset, he confessed, he could not make love to my shapeless flesh; he pursued women with angles and curves until it bored him. "I can't remember one face," he said. "That's pretty sad."

"Why did you tell me that?"

"You need a confidante, to understand yourself. When you tell someone else your sins, you've got a responsibility to change. Now you'll make me change, hon."

"I never wanted to know everything about you," I said. "Can't you see what I've done to keep myself protected?"

Harry wanted the woman he loved to be so riveting that the envious stares of others around him would, like a magnetic force, keep him gravitated to her. I grew into a monstrosity. Precisely the fact that they stared at me spun him away.

After Harry confessed, I couldn't get rid of what he had told me and how my weight had ruined my life. Two weeks later, on a glazed-flat day, my swollen feet caught my attention. I stared. Minute by minute I grew amazed, because my realization was unprecedented. Looking at my feet, I saw that age had bitten into them with all its crookedness. It didn't appear hesitant to finish its meal. And I don't know why but then I knew that my hands, my eyes, my cartilage—all of me—was tied close to the same sounds and ways of others, held to the globe. I am what always happens in time, and it's so magnanimously unlike my own failings. I know now I am in common. Now, the only thing is: I do not want to become the shape of a woman Harry chased.

If I am ever thin I will not have thrown off dead weight; my husband will have pressed it into a thin red lining right under my skin; that is what memory is like. Harry stormed into our house with yesterday's picture of me in mind, hoping to peel me back out. I am very full but he has decided I could just as well be beginning. No one can be emptied out. Never before has my aloneness been made so clear. There are other fat women like me; I see them in the pastry aisles. But I am in myself alone.

Harry has been out of town, on a job, for three days. At lunchtime, I went to the Red Cross shoe store and selected bright green comfortfit pumps. Their sharp little heels protruded like horns from cocoons. It was me and the geriatric ladies all belonging in the store together, relishing our colorful spoiling of our troubled feet. Things have blown open around me as if I suddenly stepped over the horizon into a rushing wind: it lifts my hem, pulls my hair into disarray, swirls up my sleeves. Walking to work in this pictured disorder I've realized I want someone to talk to, to explain this. I feel newly in existence, terribly sensitive, sick of confinement. What is this? An older woman. Unlike before, I'm impelled to watch myself as a part of everyone.

I know the women Harry slept with were likely to spend an hour getting ready to go out for coffee. He looked for this, having found me incapable of it. It wasn't for him to see that their ardent self-description is an embroidery of hunger. When these women are as young as the escorts I work with, they feel the pulse of their generation clicking in their heels, and they toss and turn looking for something. They stretch into life like branches, to grow. My husband, I am sure, never sensed this feeling in them; instead, felt out his advantage. Their limbs were octopus tentacles he could feast on. And when they were older didn't the women still seem to be looking for an answer? By habit, they allow their men to imagine that they are waiting to be shown life. The men become accustomed mostly to devouring them blind. The women don't ask for change. They don't like change. They want to remain beautiful and wanted. Over the years it takes more and more time.

Today, a girl walked into the office, tallish, in a red coat. Her hair bleached, curling down her shoulders, her nose pointed, her mouth plump and nubile as a rosebud. She reminded me of a picture of the women at Louis XVI's court in France, women in high hair and lace, with red cheeks, women decadent in their life, who at the end of the world said: "Let them eat cake."

I wondered if she knew any of this. "You think women understand the world less than men?" I asked.

She looked at me, her eyes compressing very thin. "Are you kidding? Every one of those men had a mom, and if those moms hadn't been preparing men for the world the men wouldn't be able to handle anything." She looked at her red fingernails. "It takes a woman to know." She leaned close, "I know how to baby men, too."

"Don't do it," I said.

"Shit. I don't have much time. Is this an interview?" She hiked up her hose, tugging at her ankles, clamping her thighs.

"They look at photos before the interview," I said.

"I look good," she replied. Rose called the girl into her office.

I made a sudden collect call to my friend Rema who I've known since childhood. She listens without needing preliminaries, though she lives far away. "Rema, thank God you're home. Can you listen now?"

"Well, tell me."

"It just hit me like a ton of bricks that I haven't given myself a look in years. Who've I been?"

"You've been living, honey," Rema says. "Where did you get the idea you have to stare at yourself all the time, to live? That can hold you up. Plenty of people go nuts like that."

"No. We don't have this idea straight, most of us; you have gold running in your veins, rising up to your heart. If you *see* that, you begin to catch it."

"Some people might feel that way," she says. "Sure, some do. What's been happening?" Her voice is patient as lake water.

"I can't understand myself why everything has changed," I say. "Everything seems on fire. It makes me so nervous." I just looked at my feet.

Rema says, "That's how it is: you can't tell when the next thing is going to happen."

After work, to see the world a little, I walk a few extra blocks to the bus stop. People are so busy running home, I'm not noticed. Today, the yellow leaves were falling and breathing themselves into the wind, mingling up a bitter scent of regret. I've noticed each winter comes by advance of many tantrums; the trees toss their heads, the grasses shake, disheveled, blown up, turned brown. Today, the leaves scurried over, wildly dancing between my feet while an endless blue blanket looked down, self-contained. All at once, something alive darted at my feet. I flung myself back, against a wall. My heart nearly leapt out of my mouth. It was a squirrel, now staring at me, a yard away, flicking its tail, raising itself on its hindquarters. It began to gesture at me by way of masticating though it had nothing in its jaw. Two others ran up and all three performed this communication, chewing a mock meal, under the understanding that I had something to give them. And I do understand hunger. But I had nothing for them. On the bus going home I saw animals in people's faces: a lynx, goats, the flamingo, a saddened spaniel. But these citizens won't show their hunger.

It saddens me to know I walked around for years in trepidation of myself without knowing or remembering this hunger in others. I tried to hide my own but it spoke on my body. I peered out a small window which never opened. Every day circled me like gauze, and I was mummified into the years. My husband called it a disgrace. My heart closed like a little stone. Harry is ravenous for taut flesh yet now age flicks him around in its large jaw, tugging at his skin, decomposing his bones. He is amazed, denying time's hunger.

I never had his brazen confidence to deny life's big appetite, but I never thought I'd understand it either. Yet life and time are always tapping inside your ear to confide in you. Occasionally, I would be startled by sounds like a foreign song; vague, remarkable music. I placed it far away. But chords were rising through me, to describe me. This is how potential approaches you: in no one else's language. If you grasp it, other people sense it. It begins to announce itself. Like a song, you can't exactly say you see it. Mine rose up through my feet.

I looked down at myself and saw the silent onslaught of years, the wide general thing represented in my feet. This isn't my failure. I have a double dimension of weight: one fat made me hide, but this can have grace because it's everyone's mirror.

The night before Harry left on his present trip, he visited the supermarket. Lettuce, trim-fat dinners, broccoli, tomatoes, celery, and crackers returned with him. He looked as happy as an auctioneer. He slapped his hands together, grinned: "Here we go! We're ready, aren't we?"

It is as if a beetle began crawling inside my stomach.

"The thing I want to tell you, honey, is that this isn't just about taking off pounds; it's about building a whole new love. A spic-and-span streamlined one, Susie. I can hardly wait."

I looked him straight on; "I'm concerned with my spirit. And you can't get that with celery. How could you go looking in the supermarket?"

Harry's pupils retracted quick as crabs. "So you're a coward?" he asked. "Are you? Shit, you're the biggest disappointment of my life." He turned to the kitchen sink and spat. He grabbed the porcelain edge as if he was saving it from falling off the wall. "You're going to ruin our life!" he shouted.

I have my age. It climbs around my hips and pulls them down into more and more chairs. All my veins are pulsing fiercely, and this work, through time, has slackened my skin, interspersed it with magnets and marbles. This is an accumulation I must tend to. Life surreptitiously crowded in me. I want to walk through my markings, to pick them up as on a cafeteria line, to have so full a dish I'll be stunned by it. Age is a sort of overeating.

Many of the escorts from my office fear life will pass them by. They fling themselves into the world to be touched. Life has walked through me and, like a town square, I have been mute through the walkings, have been the vessel not the subject. I see that though I did not pay attention to the way life was changing me, I cannot say it passed me by. It passes no one. I must try to tell them this. Age draws itself on the flesh and time becomes palpable. You can tell yourself certain things did not happen and let your mind become a blank slate, but the flesh won't play chameleon. It stabilizes you, and imprints the artifacts of your route; they're yours.

I am rising, heavy and powerful as an old seal, independent in my digestion, awake.

Phyllis Capello

Careless Love: How Women Get to Hell

With some it is circumstantial;
familiar terrain reconfigures, one
misstep, and lives disassemble;
illness manifests, husbands vanish,
children spin wildly off into darkness.
The certainty of loss is bitter
on their tongues as they descend.

Others march there,
fancied up, lusty enough
to kiss the devil; the gate
swings open; destiny
turns the key.

Some marry the devil,
spend lifetimes exchanging
immense effort for small affection,
terrified silence for perilous calm.
They enter meekly, bereft of thought,
empty of notions.

But the young ones,
because they are blind,

or blithe or beautiful,
seem to find the path no matter
which way they turn;
that slippery, golden path,
which takes them, smiling
and unsuspecting, to the brink;
where they stand, pretty toes
pointing down, ready for the push.

Nancy Caronia

From *Macaronis*

My mother was screaming. As usual. Her mouth moving in time with the accusatory stabs of the car keys, held like a sword in her left hand. "I'm really goin' this time," she shouted. Her emaciated frame rigid, a matchstick about to be struck.

I stood on the second-floor landing of our house, my back straight, my face impassive. Only my hands, gripping the black metal railing, betrayed my feelings. I was tanned to a dark brown, but my knuckles were white. I stared past the wave of blue carpeted stairs that reminded me of Christ walking on water. Sometimes when I go to bed at night I'd pretend I *was* Jesus Christ walking on water, but on this day JC was nowhere to be found. I ignored the waves and stared at the blue slate tile shore below where my mother and two sisters were clustered together. They stood in a tight group by the front door, the sun's rays bathing them in a late afternoon reddish amber glow, a reflection of my mother's anger and frustration.

Rosie's chubby hands clutched Mom's back; Louise grabbed the front of her blouse. They reminded me of the statue of Iwo Jima we'd seen in social studies class the week before, though my sisters were soldiers in a losing battle. My mother as thin as the flagpole the Iwo Jima soldiers raised.

When I came out from my room, the one I shared with Louise, I was gonna tell them, "Shut up! I'm tryin' to read." I thought it was just the three of them. I wasn't afraid of my mother. We shouted at each other all the time. That seemed to be our favorite form of communication. My sisters' whining had become so loud, I thought one of them was getting hit. Mom was usually more talk than action, but I wouldn't stand for her hitting them, no matter how much I didn't want my sisters around most of the time.

Once I opened the door and rushed out of the room, I realized what was really going on. My sisters were crying, "Don't go, Mommy! Don't go." Just once, I thought, I'd like to have supper without this kind of cocktail hour. Just once, I looked up at heaven, I'd like to go to the dinner table without an upset stomach.

Babies, I thought, when I saw my sisters clutching at our mother and no one making a move. Big fat babies. They're nuthin' but crybaby whingers. Told them to shut up in my mind. Sent out the vibes to get them to shut their mouths. I wanted her to go. Just leave, I thought, I'll take care of everything. I'll make sure we're okay. We'll all get along fine without you.

My mother jangled the car keys. Set her mouth in a grim straight line. The more my father seemed to ignore her pleas for his attention, the more shrill her voice became during these summer months before I began ninth grade, high school at last. Hallelujah! Only four more years of yelling and fighting and then, I hoped, I'd be free.

"Well?" it was a threat meant for my father, invisible to me behind the wall separating the foyer from the den. Too fat to be included in this picture of family angst, family decrepitude. I didn't know what he was doing for certain, though I could make a pretty good guess. Standing with one hand in the pockets of his faded jeans, the other smoothing his kinky black hair, he was more than likely holding back a grin while she yelled at him. The grin hid his fear the way my mother's shouting masked hers.

When she threw the keys at him, he let go and laughed, his voice hoarse and hard. "Go ahead, Maeve. Nobody's stopping you. The door's always open. You know that. I ain't never told you different." He took a breath. My mother's complexion was the color of taillights. "Where ya gonna go?" he continued. "Huh? Yer afraid to drive on anything bigger than a one-way street. Where the hell do you think yer gonna go?" And his hand, tanned black from the sun, shoved the keys in her splotchy, scarlet face.

She screamed louder than I'd ever heard her. The way Mrs. Catracas let loose in first grade when her husband came to school and told her their oldest son was killed in Vietnam. Her classroom was next to Mrs. Dolan's room, the teacher I had in first grade. Usually, we didn't hear anything through the thick, cinder block walls, but that day was different. It felt like the world stopped as Mrs. Catracas made a sound I'd never heard before. It was more animal than human. It shut everyone up, even Mrs. Dolan and Freddie, the class clown. The air vibrated with loss.

And that was what I felt hearing my mother's voice. Her scream was about losing. She was losing her husband, if she'd ever had him, and she didn't know how to get him back. For my part, I didn't know her lungs could hold that much air, thought her chain-smoking had stolen the space reserved for oxygen. Her usually pale complexion was fire engine red now and her stick figure torso was shaking so fast I was certain her head was gonna explode. "You think this is a joke? You think every-thing's a goddamn joke. I'm kiddin'! That's what you think, right? But I'm not. This time I've had it with you! What'll you do widdout me? What'll ya do? Huh?" There was a pause. Just my sisters' sobs filled the house. "Answer me," she pleaded. "Answer me, dammit!"

The tile floor creaked. The house was still settling. The creak was in answer to my father shifting his body. He turned away from my mother. No big surprise. He hated confrontations. "Go ahead. Leave then. It'll be peaceful widdout yer mouth." His voice shook, betraying the bra-vado of his chosen words, but his step was steady as he walked through the den, his heavy footfalls softened by the orange and yellow shag wall-to-wall carpet. My father slammed the screen of the patio behind him as he entered the backyard. My mother was left standing there, her open mouth an empty cave.

Go ahead, I chanted in my head, just leave. I didn't know why this fight started and I didn't care. They interrupted me while I was reading about David Cassidy in *Teen Beat*. I was pissed. They were fightin' all the time and none of us were immune to their battles.

We didn't move or take a breath until the lawn mower started its drone. Then, my mother looked down and noticed my two sisters for the first time. She pushed them roughly away from her. "Get off a me! Why are you kids always hangin' on me?"

My sisters whimpered. Rosie wiped her chipmunk cheeks with the back of her left hand. She's a lefty. Catholic school has a problem with lefties. The left hand, it's the Devil's hand. Her teachers tried to retrain her to only use her right, but Mom and Dad told the teachers to leave her alone, let her be whatever she was gonna be. Louise couldn't stop sniffling. She was too skinny—same as Mommy. At least she didn't have a fat ass, like Daddy always said I had. She had skinny stick legs and snif-fled all the time. She tried to keep the snot from running down her nose by wiping it on her shoulder. Disgusting, I thought. She is totally dis-gusting. I'm so glad I'm not like her.

Their heads shot up and looked at me like a chorus from a Broad-way musical and I was the star making my grand entrance at the top of the center staircase in the finale. I hadn't given them a cue for that. How did any of them know I was standing there? I didn't want the spotlight.

It would mean trouble, especially after Mom lost another skirmish to Dad. She definitely lost this one. Didn't even bother to yell after him this time. She looked as though my father had pulled the plug on a life raft as he walked away from her.

I stared back at my mother, my two sisters, still clustered in a group by the door, though they no longer touched. Didn't say a word, didn't move a muscle. Mom broke the silence when I wouldn't give her anything to vent on. "I'm goin' for a ride," she announced.

Louise yelled out NO and it reverberated through the foyer. The white walls were bare, the rooms half-furnished. Only the living room, a room we couldn't enter, was complete. Plastic covers protected the emerald-green velvet sofa, love seat, and white velvet chairs we weren't allowed to sit in. It was a museum diorama of suburban furnishings, but it wasn't two hundred years from now, it *was* now. We lived as though we were still in a five-room railroad tenement, though we'd been living in a suburban four-bedroom, one-and-a-half-bath house for two years. Louise's NO played off the emptiness. It felt like an instant replay of the fight, NO calling up the visuals locked in each of our own memory banks.

Mommy shook her head. Tried not to cry. Her face was bright red. "Don't worry. I'll be back. I gotta get outta here fer a little while. Yer father's an asshole." She sighed, "Marie," and looked up at me. She knew I'd seen the whole thing. "Set the table," she said to me. "Put the macaronis on." And without another word she walked out the front door and left us alone.

I knew she'd get me somehow and, bam, there it is. I'm in charge. Of dinner, of cleaning, of these two sniveling babies. My sisters looked up at me expectantly and waited for me to tell them what to do. They hoped I'd run after Mommy to stop her. Louise wanted to do that, I could tell, but she was afraid she'd get hit. Her toothpick legs looked like they were runnin' a marathon without even moving. Her knees were slightly bent as she stood on the balls of her feet, her heels not quite touching the ground. I stared at the two of them for a few minutes. They turned their eyes away from me. I always won staring contests. They stared instead at the blue slate tiles.

We perked our ears up to listen as the Malibu drove away. She started it after only two tries. Usually she flooded the engine. But she was real mad this time, determined to get away.

I didn't want to cook dinner. Again. "Shit," I said out loud. My sisters' heads snapped to attention. Mommy was gone. I was the mommy now. I sighed loudly, stomped to my room and slammed the door. Louise

knew better than to enter our room when I slammed the door that way.
I sat on my bed. Only I couldn't sit for long. I heard Auntie Ida teasing
me, "What's a matter? Ants in yer pants?" "Shut up," I told her and hit
my head with both hands to get her out of there. I walked back and forth
to keep myself from crying. "Yer a real Camille," Daddy always said. I hit
my head again and paced real fast, like I was a father waiting for the baby
to be born. I picked up *Teen Beat,* kissed David Cassidy's picture, wished
my family were like the Partridge Family. Wished my mother was Shirley
Jones. Wished there was no father. I kissed David again and decided to
give in. I didnt want to get in trouble later. I went downstairs.

The two crybabies were standing in the foyer. Still. Sniffling. Still.
I shook my head at them. "C'mon. Let's drink some Hi-C." I put
on a happy face for them. "She'll be back," I yelled when they wouldn't
follow me. "Where's she gonna go? Huh?" I imitated my father's voice,
got right in Rosie's face. Kissed her on the nose. She swatted me away.
Almost smiled.

———

I went to the refrigerator and took out the butter and the grated Locatelli
cheese. That's the only kind of grated cheese my father liked. "Parmi-
gian' and Romano cheese, they're no good. They got funny smells and
they don't taste right," he said once in the Italian grocery when my
mother tried to buy Romano cheese because it was cheaper. I put the
fresh-baked Italian bread from the Italian bakery on the table and then
stood there rubbing my forehead before I finished setting the table.

I wanted to cry. I was tired of being the one who folded my clothes,
helped with the laundry, with dinner, vacuumed the house. I wanted to
run away, but I knew if I didn't do the stuff I did, none of it would get
done. Either way, no one noticed except me. I folded the napkins pretty
and put the forks and knives on top. I went back to the stove and stirred
the sauce and the ziti. It was almost dinnertime and I hoped that
Mommy would come home before dinner was over. I didn't want to
wash the pots myself. She was pushing it asking me to do this again. I
didn't want to have to clean up after everyone for the rest of my life. If
I had to do that, then I wanted some privileges. I wanted my own room
and to stop sharing with Louise. I wanted a car even if I didn't know
how to drive, even if I wasn't old enough to have a license. I wanted an
allowance. I wanted my own charge card. I wanted someone to take me
to the beach. I wanted to watch the programs I wanted to watch for a
change instead of boring bowling and stupid wrestling and dumb soap
operas. I was tired of them telling me Shakespeare was shit and what do

I gotta read all that crap for. I was tired of taking care of all of them and not getting nothing in return. I was tired.

I wanted to yell and scream, "I'M gonna leave! Mommy thinks SHE's got it soooo bad. Well, let's see what would happen if I left. You'd miss me. You'd miss me more. And you'd never find me. Never. I'd hide good. You'd never know where I was until I won an Oscar and when I won I'd say, 'I'd like to NOT thank my parents because they never gave me anything but a goddamn headache.'"

––––––––––

My father shaded his eyes with his left hand so he could see me behind the screen. "Well." He paused. "What kind a macaronis did you make?"

"Ziti." I sighed and stomped back into the kitchen, picked up the phone and dialed Billy Stevens's house, told Millie, Billy's mother, to send Patrick home, that dinner was almost ready. Patrick got on the phone and said he wanted to eat dinner at Billy's house. They were having a pool party and Billy's father was making a barbecue. He'd rather have that than macaronis. I screamed into the phone, "Go ahead. See if I care!" And slammed it down in his ear. Thought, goddamn boy. Always gets whatever he wants.

I held onto my breath and the receiver at the same time. "Damn," I whispered when I realized the ziti could be overdone. I asked Louise and Rosie if they wanted to taste the macaronis with me.

Louise smugly replied, "Rosie was the one who wanted them. Let her test them."

Rosie walked into the kitchen, her stomach sticking out. She looked pregnant, sticking her belly out as far as she could. I blew on one ziti for her to taste and one for me. We sucked them in with one breath. "They're done." I nodded my head and turned off the electric burner, only one of a myriad number of complaints my mother had made about the house my father was determined to purchase, with or without her. "Whad'ya expect," she'd answered my father one night after he complained the food tasted funny soon after we'd moved in. "I'm not a miracle worker. I told ya the food would taste different on an electric stove. But, no, you hadda move. The gas stove in our apartment was just fine, but you hadda get outta where we were comfortable to move to the country." She said the word "country" like it was cancer she was talkin' about.

Rosie spit the ziti out in the sink. "They're too hard. I don't like them like this."

"Too bad," I answered her. "This is the only way Daddy likes them." I emptied the pot into the colander. "Dinner," I yelled, though they knew it already. "Dinner's ready." Louise turned off the TV, Daddy entered through the screen door just as I shouted out. He turned on the radio before he washed his hands in the kitchen sink, where I'd just emptied the macaronis into the colander. I don't know why he never washed his hands in the bathroom like a normal father, but I didn't say anything. It made me not want to eat dinner.

"Where's yer brother?" he asked me as I put the pot of sauce on the table.

"He's eatin' dinner at Billy's," I told him.

"Don't we ever eat like a normal family anymore," he sighed as he grabbed a Piels from the fridge. Louise, Rosie, and I walked to the sink and filled our plates with as many of the macaronis as we wanted. I went back and filled up Daddy's plate. We sat at the table in the same seats as always, even though two of us weren't there. We were like a record that's skipping, only no one took the needle off or pushed it forward to keep the song going.

I like a lot of sauce, I take after my father in that way, but Rosie and Louise used hardly any. Somehow, in spite of that, Rosie's chin was covered with the red stuff before I had a chance to sit down at the table. I moved my chin toward her to let her know she needed to wipe it away. She rolled her eyes at me, gave a quick look at Daddy and Louise to make sure they didn't notice, then grabbed her napkin and rubbed it off. She asked Daddy to pass the cheese. He asked me to pass the butter.

When Daddy got up to get another beer, Louise dropped her fork loudly on her plate, popped from her chair, and said brightly, "I'll get it," as she ran to the fridge. My father rounded his body back over his plate, his elbows on the table, and muttered a thanks as my sister put the beer down.

None of us looked at each other. Silently, we listened to Casey Kasem's countdown, hoping his dedications would drown out the static memories in our heads. We stared at our plates, speared ziti covered in leftover red tomato sauce and cheese and shoved them quietly in our mouths. We waited for something outside of ourselves to change the way things were. We couldn't conceive it was up to us. No one had ever bothered to let us know.

Grace Cavalieri

Grandmother

for Graziella Zoda

What is the purpose of visits to me twice since you've died?

Downstairs near a woodstove I hear you
in motion, always working,
a long silken dress—
tight sleeves at your wrist, soft above the elbow
wide top at your shoulder for free movement.

When we were young you didn't visit—
you never baked a cake that I remember
or babysat or held me in your lap,
you were in the men's part of town running a man's business
calling the world to order,
seven children behind you
raised singlehanded in your large house. You were
moving, always moving.

When I kept losing things like my parents, my children,
   money
my time and health
why did you appear in my room with gifts painted
red, yellow, blue,
brilliant colored toys. What
essential fact did you want me to know,
that the body is the essence of the spirit and so
must be in motion?

Now that I've lost my foothold, my direction, my way,
what is your message, strong spirit,
strong Grandmother,
what is the meaning of your dream-present,
a bright clock shaped like a train—
                    simply that it moves?

Diana Cavallo

From *A Bridge of Leaves*

When my friend and I visited St. Anne de Beaupré, we had detoured on a vacation trip to make this pilgrimage. My waning zeal and Phil's amused superiority led us to that place, dreams of impregnable monastery walls high above the sea, salt rocks below, a view of infinite sea and sky beyond. We saw a minor cathedral, landlocked, not even facing the sea. Where we had imagined black cassocks, even cowls against the damp wind, and fringed shawls on gaunt pilgrim women who moved parched lips to say the rosary, were tourist faces we had left smiling in camera poses in upper Quebec.

The desperate fervor that had erected the first monument at that site was surely absent, as was a roughhewn character, an old-sea-ship look, that grateful Breton sailors would have carved into the stone and worked into the plaster. Once this was a pledge gift to the mother saint who plucked a doomed craft from the sea and tucked it on the shore, Beaupré. Now on that site someone had built this grand cathedral, a collection of small buildings for one enterprise or other, circular, rectangular, flat modern storefront—none the stark tribute of the sailors, with simple, strong lines against the sea.

We wondered how the Old World had, to appearances, survived, while the New World seemed always to obscure her past in rebuilding. The original stones, rock, plaster, spirit seemed to endure centuries of Sinai sand and wind, Roman sun and rain, Gallic seas and wars, whereas the New World swallowed her small history as a guppy gulps her young. Yearly, old churches, houses, relics are devoured by fire, by flood, by civic improvement, and by complete remodeling enterprises. There seemed such little sense of history, such persecution of it to serve the whim of currency, even in Quebec where unseen forces strained to keep the old intact, but slowly failed.

At St. Anne de Beaupré few pilgrims rubbed the dark earth with their knees to ascend the sacred slope. More often they looked about as they had on many another tour, and spent most of their time in the mission shop, in the familiar atmosphere of souvenir corners. The favorite when we visited were tiny bottles for holy water that sold for a small fee.

We would have liked to laugh at our disappointment, and to tell the truth, we made many jokes about the hard, pious faces that entered the cathedral, and came out, seconds later, gleaming for the bargain counter. But with all our jokes, we felt a momentary bleakness that pilgrimages were no longer possible. The priests were too well-fed without enjoying what they ate with that full, hearty appreciation old ribald friars had had. And our modern pilgrims—if they made a pledge or vowed a march, it was such a dreary, trying, vexing thing unless they made of it a touring ground and vacation trip. For if *we* did not believe, we had thought that there was a devotion somewhere that Italian masters had drawn from, and that this spirit was what would last forever, if all the rites were ended and if the paintings cracked into pieces. Where was the sea-spray, and in the grotto of St. Anne, where were the rotted oars? There was neither faith in the pilgrims nor truth in the symbol. Yet we were sure that we could stand a whole day before *one* Michelangelo fresco and know all the grandeur there was in religion and the power that could be faith.

This was how we spoke to each other, Phil and I, as though our impressions were seen as one, as if the intervening wall of our nervous systems had become transparent and the effort of relaying messages, wearying and inaccurate, had been dispensed with. So it was no wonder that several times I stopped myself in midsentence to find we had both spoken at once and were saying very nearly the same things. Only on such occasions it was always Phil who plunged ahead to complete the thought, and I who fell back, for he was under the greater press of a rapid, over-agile mind, and restraint came more easily to me. Other times a bystander, hearing our argument, would have grown bewildered by a logic that skipped stages as ours did, by that unspoken mutual consent that persists in conversations between close friends. But with Phil this was carried further than in most friendships, so even I, an initiate, had sometimes to strain for the connection, catch up, so to speak, in my own mind to where he had thrust the line of argument. I preferred this stretching to the adventure on my part to a retrieving action on his, and, too, it was probably these very unnegotiated terms that made our relationship so satisfactory to him and so beneficial to me.

It was that rare time in friendship when we left ourselves unguarded from each other, so that our impressions and sensations emerged unfiltered, unrefined, with a strength and energy that tapped a reserve of power unsuspected by either of us. Our exchanges generated ideas and subtleties of intellect that had never appeared before, so that each mind sought the other to reach the mountain fastnesses, the recesses, and the headwaters which we separately contained. But most of all we laughed, turning into humor our loneliest thoughts and our truest aspirations.

Our friendship had to be taken out-of-doors and aired a bit, made tougher by the exasperating heat of the sun and the sudden coolness of evening. For, as we drove south from Canada, this was the coastland in summer—that summer and every summer, I suppose—dry and thirsty and happy to abandon itself to extremes of temperature when the punitive sun went down.

Sometimes in our wanderings we kept to the highways, but their unrelieved symmetries became so tiresome that we would welcome any promising offshoots with uneven, tree-tipped roads and a peculiar forest fragrance. There were long stretches of road when there was little to say and few words passed between us, when we were content to muse with the unpeopled farmland that rolled under us or to aspire with the sides of mountains that pushed themselves upward with lonely effort. Other times we became so excited with our talk that we could barely drive on, and many a country curve was taken with arms flailing the air in argument and eyes rapt in the course of discussion.

Once when we saw an opening in the trees, we could sense at once the coolness of the water-soaked air, and knew without a further sign that a mountain stream had wound its way among the giant trees and pressed itself ever more deeply into the yielding forest bed. Hot from the dusty road, we looked in awe at the clear mountain water that still preserved in its chill glitter its former snowflake essence.

With short yelps we pushed ourselves into the water and were revived by the first splash of it into our faces. Our indolent bodies began performing vigorous spirals and effortless arcs through air and water, until the initial mineral spirits subsided and we lolled, half floating on the surface. That immeasurable calm spoken of water lifted us to a horizontal plane, so that we were unsinkable even on the miniature crests that pressed up under us. Without any effort on our part we remained suspended, and it seemed nothing existed but the changeless sky overhead and the cool rippling life that seeped out of us into the eddying stream. Blinking, we turned our eyes from the sky, and saw passing on the bank sudden patches of brown and green, and our joint gaze was arrested a longer moment by a grotto of stone and a black-draped figure with raised fingers—the Black Virgin of the Rocks that Canadian farmers placed everywhere to invoke a blessing—and that looked ineffectual and helpless as she tried in vain to stay the river and to keep us rooted by her side. I turned my head and half of my body to look back at her again, and in so doing I toppled and was suddenly upright in the tugging current, every tree and rock a clear entity bathed in sunlight, and now turning on his stomach in the water was Phil, almost beside me, where he, too, had been carried by the water. I looked at him and saw passing from his eyes the sweet immobility we had felt together, and I knew as our gaze met quietly that we had experienced not only the same moment but almost the same thoughts. The water that lapped against my chest lapped also against Phil, and its transparent touch was broken by the sunlit outline of his flesh as by mine. We had both been held suspended on the face of the water by a bond of oversky and undersea that kept us afloat and bodiless together for a timeless space. It was a thing experienced in common, not he through me, nor I through him; in our separate worlds we had been touched by the same purgative mineral spring that sustained us while we let drop our human form, while it ran down into the chill whiteness and reluctantly returned to restore time and place, vision and thought into that reciprocal gaze by which we recognized each other and saw how closely persons might be joined by their blind nonhuman selves. As I reflected on it, Phil pushed himself forward, and feet up, threw splotches of water on me, breaking the even pattern of the stream into a shimmering and impermanent design.

Thomas Centolella

Ossi Dei Morti

Under the iris of each eye she has that white space
that could signify murder one,
or sex, or ennui, and which the Japanese
take to mean constant sorrow. I never know
what she's going to say next. I'm not sure
she does either. Among the usual pleasantries
she says, "I always fall in love
with the wrong person. I just do."

At the best café in the city, an antidote
for unwise choices: coffee pitch black
as if brewed straight from soil, Florentine
cookies on a gold-rimmed plate.
And in the voice, a remarkable matter-of-
factness. "I just do, that's all."

On our way out, the proprietor and a cop
trading tips on the longshots, she lifts
two *ossi dei morti* from under their noses:

two sticks of candy, silver and jointed,
that a crone with a sweet tooth long ago christened
bones of the dead. "They taste better
when they're stolen." Her face lights up

but her eyes still look like my uncle's
in his final days. Someone usually so at ease
his life had seemed a kind of answer
to those who questioned life . . .
Then cancer of the bone marrow
and precious few choices left.
A self-made man, reduced to the point
of begging strangers for his death.

"Bite into it," she says, "hard,"
the hard candy in her mouth, her even teeth bared
like a skull mask on Mardi Gras
or Halloween. A macabre grin,
worn in celebration.

Some unknown factor elates us
in spite of ourselves. It's a given,
not a choice. It's dark and bittersweet,
this chocolate marrow, this brief time
people call a life. We bite into it
hard. We do this together.
A local cure for sorrow.

Small Acts

Whitman thought he could live with animals, they were
so placid and self-contained, not one of them dissatisfied.
I have lived with animals. They kept me up all night.
Not only tom cats on the prowl, and neurotic rats
behind my baseboards, scratching out a slim existence.
There were cattle next door in the butcher's pen,
great longhorns lowing in the dark. Their numbers had come up
and they knew it. I let their rough tongues lick my sorry palm.
Nothing else I could do for them, or they for me.

Walt can live with the animals. I'll take these vegetables on
    parade:

string-beans and cabbage heads and pea brains, who negotiate
a busy crosswalk and feel brilliant, the smallest act accomplished
no mean feat, each one guiding them to other small acts
that will add up, in time, to something like steady purpose.
They cling to this fate, clutch it along with their brownbag
   lunches:
none of us would choose it, but this is their portion, this
   moment,
then this one, then the next. Little as it is, pitiful as it seems,
this is what they were given, and they don't want to lose it.

The gawky and the slow, the motley and the misshapen . . .
What bliss to be walking in their midst as if I were one of them,
just ride this gentle wave of idiocy, forget those who profess
an interest in my welfare, look passing strangers in the eye
for something we might have in common, and be
   unconcerned if nothing's there.
And now we peek into a dark café, and now we mug at the
   waitress
whose feet are sore, whose smile makes up for the tacky
   carnations
and white uniform makes it easy to mistake her for a nurse,
even makes it necessary, given the state of the world.

And when the giant with three teeth harangues us to hurry up,
what comfort to know he's a friend, what pleasure to be
   agreeable,
small wonders of acquiescence, like obedient pets. Except
   animals
don't have our comic hope, witless as it is. They don't get
to wave madly at the waitress, as though conducting a
   symphony
of ecstatic expectations. If I turned and lived with animals
I'd only be a creature of habit, I'd go to where the food is
and the warmth. But I wouldn't get to say to my troubled friend,
"Your eyes are so beautiful. I could live in them."

John Ciardi

True or False

Real emeralds are worth more than synthetics
but the only way to tell one from the other
is to heat them to a stated temperature,
then tap. When it's done properly
the real one shatters.

     I have no emeralds.
I was told this about them by a woman
who said someone had told her. True or false,
I have held my own palmful of bright breakage
from a truth too late. I know the principle.

Useless Knowledge

To trap a chipmunk put a bait of nuts
in a glass milk bottle and lay it on its side
by a bush or a stone wall you have seen it favor.

The chipmunk will pop through the bottle neck,
fill its cheek pouches as if with Heaven's bounty,
and find there is no escape from the gifts of God.

By creature law, the chipmunk is forbidden
to spit from its mouth the nuts of life, once given,
until they have been brought to holy storage

in the ark of the winter covenant, and rather
than break commandment, this fluff of life will starve
with its pouches full and more food in the bottle.

A Vermonter from the bone-scraped ridges told me
that one starved winter's end he bottled a chipmunk
and filled the bottle with water to force it out,

but the thing drowned. He had to smash the bottle
to boil that ounce. He had no other bottle.
He said he starved through mud-time sick on roots

and curls of fiddler fern. He could have been lying.
Or stretching. But only God knows all His saints.
Something is always fevered by hard intention

for less than the wholly edible. These are notes
for a sermon on the sanctity of survival
to teach that life is not worth dying for.

But have we a choice? I have flown my hot missions
in a flammable bottle when I could have been grounded
on permanent garbage detail.★ What's wrong with garbage?

those fragrant, bursting calories of revulsion
yardbirds can fatten on?—and damn the stripes
that jammed us lockjawed in the bottleneck!

All this may be as relevant as sainthood
inside a cyclotron. I haven't seen
a glass milk bottle since home delivery stopped.

If I could find one in an antique shop,
I could trap a chipmunk I would have no use for
and wouldn't know how to free without some danger

of killing or maiming it when I smashed the bottle.
This feels like something I know too well already.
It is useless knowledge, but what other is there?

The Evil Eye

*The belief in the Evil Eye is a still-surviving superstition among
Italian peasants. One method of detecting its presence is to pour
olive oil on a saucer of holy water. The shapes assumed by the oil
can then be read by the gifted.*

★ In the 73rd Bomb Wing aircrewmen who lost their nerve were no good to their crews and
were allowed to ground themselves, the enlisted men losing their stripes and being put on
permanent garbage detail. In my ten months on Saipan, only two gunners in my squadron
chose to go on the garbage truck. I never knew anyone to mock them. There were times, in
fact, when I envied them the certainty of their stinking survival.

Nona poured oil on the water and saw the eye
  Form on my birth. Zia beat me with bay,
  Fennel, and barley to scourge the devil away.
I doubt I needed so much excuse to cry.

From Sister Maria Immaculata there came
  A crucifix, a vow of nine days' prayer,
  And a scapular stitched with virgin's hair.
The eye glowed on the water all the same.

By Felice, the midwife, I was hung with a tin
  Fish stuffed with garlic and bread crumbs.
  Three holy waters washed the breast for my gums.
Still the eye glared, wide as original sin,

On the deepest pools of women midnight-spoken
  To ward my clamoring soul from the clutch of hell,
  Lest growing I be no comfort and dying swell
More than a grave with horror. Still unbroken

The eye glared through the roosts of all their clucking.
  "Jesu," cried Mother, "why is he deviled so?"
  "Baptism without delay," said Father Cosmo.
"This one is not for sprinkling but for ducking."

So in came meat and wine and the feast was on.
  I wore a palm frond in my lace, and sewn
  To my swaddling band a hoop and three beads of bone
For the Trinity. And they ducked me and called me John.

And ate the meat and drank the wine, and the eye
  Closed on the water. All this fell between
  My first scream and first name in 1916,
The year of the war and the influenza, when I

Was not yet ready for evil or my own name,
Though I had one already and the other came.

In Place of a Curse

At the next vacancy for God, if I am elected,
I shall forgive last the delicately wounded
who, having been slugged no harder than anyone else,

never got up again, neither to fight back,
nor to finger their jaws in painful admiration.

They who are wholly broken, and they in whom
mercy is understanding, I shall embrace at once
and lead to pillows in heaven. But they who are
the meek by trade, baiting the best of their betters
with the extortions of mock-helplessness

I shall take last to love, and never wholly.
Let them all into Heaven—I abolish Hell—
but let it be read over them as they enter:
"Beware the calculations of the meek, who gambled nothing,
gave nothing, and could never receive enough."

On Flunking a Nice Boy
out of School

I wish I could teach you how ugly
decency and humility can be when they are not
the election of a contained mind but only
the defenses of an incompetent. Were you taught
meekness as a weapon? Or did you discover,
by chance maybe, that it worked on mother
and was generally a good thing—
at least when all else failed—to get you over
the worst of what was coming. Is that why you bring
these sheepfaces to Tuesday?
                              They won't do.
It's three months work I want, and I'd sooner have it
from the brassiest lumpkin in pimpledom, but have it,
than all these martyred repentances from you.

Statement

Our fathers, whose art was Heaven,
honored be your names. Our kinship shown,
your need be known on earth
as it were in Heaven. Show us this way

our doubtful breed, and forgive us
our truth's passing as we forgive those
whose truths pass against us.
And example us from evil.
For yours is the kindling, and the pyre, and the storied
endeavor.
      —A man.

Rita Ciresi

Lifelines

The spring I worked in the Dairy Queen I hated everything: school and home and work, my teachers, my manager, my mother, myself. I was always walking toward something, always waiting for something wonderful to happen, waiting for a card or letter from my father, waiting for love to strike. But I bumped into more things than I consciously found, and I lost things habitually. Either I was shedding or I had bad luck. In any case, I lost two sets of house keys that spring, and every other day before I walked to work I lost a quarter in the school Coke machine. I lost so many quarters I went to our principal, Mother Superior, and complained.

"If you lose something, you ought to know what to do," she said, gazing down at me through her silver half-glasses.

"Go look for it?" I said.

"Wrong. Pray to Saint Anthony. He has divine intercession and can find you anything."

My mother snorted when I told her what Mother Superior had said. "Can the great saint find me my lost youth?" she said. "And can he find me a man? That's what I want to know. I'd believe in saints if I could see miracles like that."

My mother was old at thirty-five, and looked worn out. I was seventeen and I didn't believe in saints either. I didn't believe anything lost could ever be found, at least not in its original state. Still, I wanted to grab onto things, seize them, get whatever I could get, even if I couldn't hang on to them.

Wanting steady things to surround me came from moving place to place. My father worked construction, and we moved up and down the coast, following the jobs. For every place we lived I found a special shell on the beach. "Why do you want to carry those broken shells around with you?" my father asked.

"They wouldn't get broken if we didn't move so much," my mother commented before I could even answer.

"If we didn't move so much, she wouldn't have the chance to find them in the first place," my father said.

"If we didn't move so much and everything else wasn't so topsy-turvy, she wouldn't want to collect them," my mother said.

"You think everything's topsy-turvy?" my father shouted. "I'll show you topsy-turvy, my friend."

"Nothing's the way it used to be!" my mother said.

"It's always been the same, no matter where we moved; lousy, lousy, and lousy again."

"If it's so lousy," my mother said, "then get out."

My father got out. My mother chose Port Charlotte, sight unseen, for the name. "It's not a *beach,*" she said scornfully. "It's not a *fort,* it's a port, and it's Port Charlotte. Charlotte, Charlotte—doesn't that name sound good and old-fashioned? Comforting?"

My manager at the Dairy Queen, Bob, said it sounded like the name of a Southern belle withering away on a sagging front porch. "Charlotte sounds like the name of some old maid saving herself up for some Prince Charming. Charlotte's wasting her whole life waiting for the prince to come along when there's somebody else just as good waiting on the front porch next door. She's a dying flower, that Charlotte girl." He winked at me.

I thought about my mother, shuffling around the house until noon on a Saturday in her slippers and thin, see-through nightie. When I told her to get dressed, she said, "I'm not going anywhere, so what's the point?"

Bob was as old as my mother, but he was more like my father. "I'm an enterprising fellow," he said one afternoon as he stood by the chocolate syrup machine. "I don't let anything stand in the way of what I want to get. You look like you're having a little trouble tying on that apron, Mary Ellen."

"I can get it myself," I said.

I didn't tell my mother that Bob and I worked the afternoon shift at the Dairy Queen alone. She would have disapproved. I was always careful to complain just the right amount about my job at home, but awful as it was, I sometimes looked forward to it. Bob and I usually worked without talking for the first hour. We bumped into each other sometimes as we backed away from the counters. The bit of Coke left in the can I finally had coaxed out of the fickle school vending machine tasted warm and flat, but familiar and good, and even though I watched it every day through the tall windows of the Dairy Queen front, there still was mystery in the way the Port Charlotte sky grew dark in the afternoon, and clouded over. Bob and I had made up a game called the Rain Game. Each person tried to predict the exact moment the storm clouds would break and pour down rain. The person who guessed closest to the minute won the right to sit down, while the other person had to serve the winner a miniature hot fudge sundae.

"Four-thirty," Bob predicted.

"Quarter to five, quarter to five," I sang. I felt smug when the hands of the clock edged past four-thirty and the sky turned pitch.

The first clap of thunder shook the building at 4:46, emptying the parking lot and reducing the music on the radio to static. Bob switched it off. He grumbled as he held the plastic dish of ice cream under the chocolate syrup spigot. "You're a smartass," he said, "but you're my best girl. And you know why?" He winked at me. " 'Cause you know who's boss around here."

"And who might that be?" I asked.

"Well, I've heard he's really smart and really good-looking," he said. "His name's B-O-B."

I shrugged. He laughed and handed me my miniature chocolate sundae.

Outside, the rain came sheeting down the tall windows. Bob pulled up a stool beside me. "Your skin's too pale," he said.

"So what."

"So nothing. It just means you probably don't get enough sun and fun. You like to have a little fun, I bet."

"I guess," I said. I kept on eating. The hot fudge was sickly sweet and I dug deep with my white plastic spoon to bring up the vanilla ice cream.

"Like right now," he said. "There aren't any customers, so we ought to have a little fun, Mary Ellen, just you and me."

"What's your idea of fun?"

"What's yours?"

"We could play a guessing game," I said.

"Go on, guessing games."

"They're fun if you try to guess the right things."

"Like what?"

"Like the kind of things you wouldn't find out about people in ordinary conversations. Things that tell you something about the other person, like what they wanted to be when they were little, and stuff like that," I said.

"Who cares about what people wanted to be when they were little?"

"It tells a lot about them as grown-ups."

"Yeah, well, I forgot what I wanted to be," Bob said. "Anyway, I never turned into it." He sighed. He rubbed his hands back and forth over the stains on the thighs of his uniform pants. "Stop looking at me that way," he said.

"I'm not looking at you."

"It isn't the past that counts, anyway. It's the future."

"I guess."

"The Rain Game's enough of guessing games."

The chocolate syrup machine buzzed. The buzz died into a hum. Bob rubbed his hands together. "Time to get serious."

I thought he was going to suggest cleaning the counters. Instead, he examined his thumbnail, then suddenly looked up. "You like to read palms?" he asked.

"Psalms?"

"No, palms, p-a-l-m-s. Tell fortunes."

"I've never done it," I said.

"What do you mean, never? I thought that's what girls do at slumber parties. Sit around in their pajamas, talk about boys, curl their hair, read palms and jazz like that."

"If you're Catholic, telling the future is a sin."

"You gotta be kidding!" he said.

"I'm not."

"But don't they teach you that God's got it all figured out before it happens?"

"Sure."

"So don't you figure you got as much right as God to know what sort of things are going to happen to you?"

"I guess."

"It isn't God who's got to live your life."

"That's true," I said. "It's me."

"Isn't God who's got to get up and go to work every morning. Isn't God who's got to tell customers yessir and no ma'am. So why don't you put that sundae down," he said, taking it out of my hands. I watched him set it on the counter with regret. "Let's do a little palm-reading, a little fortune-telling, while there aren't any customers." He looked at me expectantly. I held out my left hand. He cleared his throat, moved his stool up closer, grinned, and took my hand. Chocolate syrup clogged his short fingernails; a smear of vanilla ice cream crossed the top of his hand. He turned my palm upwards and traced his finger across it. The skin on the top of his finger was rough. Underneath my hand, on his hand, I could feel his callouses.

"This is the Lifeline," he said. "It tells you how long you're going to live."

"Don't tell me," I said. "I'm afraid to die."

He snapped his chewing gum and leaned closer. "Then I'm happy to report you're going to live a long and healthy life. But every break in the Lifeline—here, here, and here, man, you got a lot of them—means something traumatic is going to happen. Something B-I-G that's going to change your whole life. Now you're born here—" He jabbed his finger halfway between my thumb and index finger. "And then here's the first break less than a fourth of the way up your hand. So calculating you're about seventeen or so, I'll bet the first traumatic thing has already happened, might I be right?"

I nodded.

"And it seems to me the way this line moves—" Bob scratched his head. "I don't know, something about it—means it's got something to do with your parents."

I nodded.

"The line kind of splits and breaks off into two here. Your parents divorced?"

"So what?" I said. "Lots of people's parents are."

"Did I say anything moralistic?"

"That isn't a word," I said.

"You got a dictionary in your back pocket, Smartypants?"

"Nope."

He laughed. "You live with your mother?"

I nodded.

"Father left your mother, huh? For some other person, maybe, of the female sexaroo? Some lady friend?"

"What's it to you?" I said.

"It's all in the lines, you see. You see how this stronger line, this masculine line, breaks off? See how it intersections with this weaker line here, while the other, weaker line—meaning of the female sex—just wanders off on its lonesome without intersectioning with anything?"

"Inter*sect*ing."

"Intersecting, intersectioning, what's the difference? Either way your father gets the woman while your mother doesn't get anything."

I tried to pull my hand back, but Bob hung onto it. He looked me straight in the eye. Then he drew his stool closer with his left hand. The rain beat against the windows. Outside, in the parking lot, a palm frond ripped slowly off its trunk and fell like a feather onto the asphalt.

"So then your Lifeline continues," Bob said. "Because even though you thought maybe you would die when your father packed his bags and left you, you kept on living. And your mother, she kept on living too, right?" He cleared his throat, squinted his eyes, and concentrated on my palm. "But enough of that. Now you got yourself a Lifeline, and then, Mary Ellen, you got yourself a Loveline. You consult your Loveline to find out all about the loves of your life and whether or not you're going to win or lose at them. The Loveline, see, starts right up where the Lifeline begins. That means the closest love in your life is the love you got for your parents, and you can't get away from that, ever."

I nodded.

"Okay, so then after that comes the first crack in your Loveline. Quit turning all red there."

"I'm not turning red."

"You know what that means, I guess."

"It doesn't mean anything."

"It means enough to make your face turn red."

I pulled my hand away. One of his nails scraped the length of my pinkie finger. "It doesn't mean anything, because I don't believe in any of it."

"You think I was just making it up as I went along?"

"Yes."

He leaned closer to me and took my hand back. "So what's the matter, you don't admire a guy with a little imagination?"

I shook my head.

He let go of my hand. I turned my head so I didn't have to look at him. Outside, in the rain, a couple pulled up in a red Buick and ran up to the counter, holding hands and laughing. Bob jerked his head toward the counter and headed back to the coat room. "Looks like you have yourself a customer, Mary Ellen," he said.

I stood, and hesitated a little, the way I always hesitated when I stood up from the sand after lying too long in the sun on the beach. The couple knocked on the service window. They knocked again, and I went over and yanked open the glass. Hot, humid air hit my face. The rain splashed down on the asphalt.

They wanted banana splits. They wanted just a little syrup on the ice cream, the bananas cut up teeny-weeny, and heavy on the nuts on top. My hands felt funny. My fingers tingled and went numb. I clutched the dishes too hard and the wax coating flaked off underneath my nails. I was afraid I would drop the dishes.

"Not so much whipped cream," the man called out.

Bob came out of the coat room. "Give the customers what they want," he said.

The whipped cream piled up on the dish. I moved over to the

chocolate syrup spigot. I put too much pressure on it, and syrup pooled up on top.

"Mary Ellen," Bob said. "Hey, Mary Ellen, what the hell are you doing? You heard the customer! Give the customer what he wants!"

He grabbed the dish away from me and threw it in the trash can, where it hit the bottom with a thud. "You're good for nothing," Bob said, making up two more banana splits. "Just goes to show you if you want something done right, do it yourself."

The couple at the window snickered. I turned my face away from the glass so they wouldn't see me.

"And how many times do I have to tell you to close the service window?" Bob hollered, after the customers drove off. "You think we get our AC free?"

I untied my apron fifteen minutes early. Bob followed me into the coat room. "You're taking off before the buzzer?" he asked, his voice apologetic. "Don't forget to punch out before you leave." As I pushed the back door to the parking lot, I heard him calling. "Hey, you're supposed to punch out, company regulation! And besides, your shift ends at six!"

I looked back and saw him standing in the doorway, hands on his hips, towel draped over his wrist. He waved. I walked away.

The rain had stopped abruptly as it had started, but the air was still muggy. The traffic had cleared off Old Washington Road, but the sidewalks were cluttered with soggy pine cones, palm branches downed in the wind, and long, flesh-colored earthworms edging onto the cement off the grass. I gazed into the windows of the shops I passed: Quinlan's Grocery, where the drawers of the cash register were left open to prove to thieves they were empty, Miss Desiree's Salon of Beauty, where the chairs tilted at odd angles away from the mirrors, as if never expecting to be sat upon again.

No lights shone through the windows of the apartment, but because I was in the habit of lifting the top of the mailbox as quietly as if I were stealing something from it, I lifted it just as softly as I would have had my mother been waiting, and listening, on the other side of the door. Nothing inside. My mother was right; I looked in there too often. "So he sent you a birthday card," she told me last week. "You'd be a damn sight better off if he sent the alimony check."

I stood on the outside steps of the apartment, unlocked the door, and reached in to turn on the hall light. I closed my eyes and gave the cockroaches time to climb into the woodwork before I went in. I turned the box fan on high, lit the stove, and shoved some frozen fish filets under the broiler. I changed into a T-shirt and shorts, and combed my long, scraggly hair. I was staring in the hall mirror, thinking *Someone just made a pass at me,* when my mother let the screen door slam.

I turned. But I couldn't look her flush in the face because I was afraid she might know what I had been thinking. She wore her white blouse and red skirt and the red criss-crossed sandals with the bright gold buckles. Her toenails were supposed to be painted to match the sandals, but the polish was too orangey to match the red. She carried a paper bag. "This is for you," she said. "And I'm sorry I couldn't give it to you on your birthday, but I didn't have enough cash to take it off layaway."

The paper bag fell to the linoleum as she pulled out and held up a white blouse which was a slight variation on the one she wore: sleeveless polyester, with a wide collar turned back into a V-neck, the breast pocket cut and stitched to resemble eyelet. I never had liked the blouse she wore, any more than I liked her red criss-crossed sandals, but once or twice I had told her she looked nice in it because I wanted to make her feel pretty. But she wasn't pretty. She wasn't vibrant, like my father's wife, Janine. Janine was my idol. "You're my candle on a dark night," my father once said to her, hugging her. Janine would never wear a sad-sack blouse like that.

"That's just like yours," I told my mother. The disappointment must have seeped into my voice; she dropped her arms and the blouse fell in her hands like a limp rag.

"I can't return it," she said. "I bought it on sale."

I reached out and touched the fabric. "It's really pretty," I forced myself to say. "And yours looks so nice on you."

"Try it on," she said. "See how it fits."

I turned my back to her and pulled my T-shirt over my head.

"Why don't you wear your bra?" she asked.

"It's too hot."

"You'll sag before you're twenty."

I turned around only enough to take the blouse from her. I slipped it over my head. She put her hands on my shoulders as if she were afraid I might bolt away before I looked in the hall mirror. Her hands were so much more gentle than Bob's; they used so much less force, but were still persuasive. But I didn't want to be persuaded. I didn't like Bob or my mother or the blouse, which hung down past my waist, covering my shorts. On the side of the blouse without the pocket, the dark outline of my nipple showed through the thin material. I looked naked.

"You look—very pretty," my mother said. I knew she meant it no more than I had meant it the one or two times I had told her the same thing. I shivered when I felt her warm breath tickling the hairs on my neck.

"Any boys yet?" she asked softly.

I thought of Bob. I thought of my father. "No," I said.

"People don't appreciate," she said. "Nobody appreciates what you have inside. It's all what you look like. It's all how well you can pass off being happy when really you're miserable inside." She sighed. "That Janine," she said. "Janine, Janine—don't that just sound like the name of some slut?"

"It does not."

"Whose side are you on?"

"Nobody's. I'm not on anybody's side."

"You could have fooled me," she said. Her fingers closed tighter around my arm. "Don't ever let me hear about you carrying on with any boys."

"I'm not."

"That's just the kind of thing your father would encourage."

"He would not!"

"They're all after one thing. And then they call you a tease, and worse, if you don't give them what they're after." She let go of my arm and inhaled deeply. "What's that smell?" she asked. She walked into the kitchen. I rubbed my arm. I heard her yank the stove open. I smelled the fish filets crisping.

She came into the doorway. "I tell you time and time again, and still you don't listen. You don't listen—you don't listen! How many times do I have to tell you it's better to slow-cook something in the oven than burn it under the broiler?"

She was sleeping on the couch as I turned off the lights that night. The Lifeline couldn't register the small, horrible things that happened, like hearing your mother snore. It couldn't register the rustle of a cockroach exploring the inside of the paper bag my mother had left lying on the linoleum. Naked in front of the bathroom sink, I scraped my nails across a wet bar of soap, then took a metal nail file and pushed all the soap out. I couldn't get my hands clean enough.

Robert Corrente

Ellis Island

My Dear Mario,

    Two days we are off the boat. We are near, to Jesus I pray this, to be citizens in America. Many things I forget. Today I know these things, starting when you kissed me near the boat and said soon too you will come.

Never in my life there is such a boat ride. We are put in the belly of the boat and do not go up near the sun. Much darkness and noise from the sea around the boat, like noise we know is bad weather from the north. My old ways to make the children not cry are no good. Dusolina cried even sleeping and little Mario kicked a girl from the north. We were all the time close like sheep in the rain side by each. It is a long time in the boat. The children ask what day is outside but we know nothing without light. It is a long time in the boat like a night that I do not sleep. The food I have from you they take from me and they give us all the same and not good food. Little Mario takes milk from Dusolina and more she cried. One mother pulled my hair for bread. It is hard this way to go even to America. I am telling Dusolina there will be Jesus also here when there is shouting and light. It is time and we are all shouting America America.

We all three of us push with others to the light. Dusolina holds little Mario. Little Mario holds me. And I hold the bundle and Dusolina. There is noise more than the sea was. I forget what people said but there also was crying and songs. Here the sun is very much and it hurt in my eyes that I see nothing and hold much on the children. When I can see it is the Statue of Liberty near us. It is big like the Madonna near you and then more. Also green. Soon Dusolina and little Mario cry also to see. They laugh when I hold them to look. Mama see they said you are crying and I do not say it is you my Mario that is not here with us.

Words on the statue I did not read that they were too small. I hear it was America is happy we come here. All the time we look to the green woman and then more shouts for stores and houses big to the sky. When we are looking the boat hits to the side of America near a big house. They run to all places with noise and two women cried to run down in the darkness. I pull Dusolina and little Mario to go off the boat. They look at the sea where we came and say where is Papa when we look. They forget this when we step on America.

There is not time to look even back. Four men in clothes all the same stop and dance near the boat and get pushed to the big house with us. We say our names but they give us these. I am L-23. Dusolina is L-24 and little Mario is L-25. Why no one says. We sit and there are not chairs that the children sit on my legs. One man that danced near the boat said things they must know to his family. All said the names of leaders in America and we were happy still to know things from the book at home and many words. I hope you read much that it will not be hard when you come. They ask us no words but to put pieces of wood in places on a board. In the room one man is crying encora encora and they think he is not there.

There is a long hall and when they shout L-23 L-24 L-25 we go down. A Neapolitano was kind and he went far walking with sticks. Then they take away the sticks and said walk and he can not. They put on his back a big white mark and take him away but not his woman. We pray to Jesus to walk and be good when they feel us. The hands of the blue man are hard and it is not good to be felt this way. how it is with you Mario. Also then I saw Jews who are in love praying with their padre and hugging to be a man and a wife.

In a big room with pictures of America they say where we will go. There is shouting and a man kicked a chair that he does not want to go far away. Soon they say L-23 that we will go to Fall River Mass that is near to where we are at New York. I told your name to them and how you look that they will send you also to Fall River Mass. We go tomorrow and soon also Jesus will give you money to come. If it can be we will all go here to New York to see you from the Statue of Liberty. For you are my love and prayers and soon it will not be hard for us here in America.

God Bless,
Your Linda Susanna

Gregory Corso

Youthful Religious Experiences

When I was five
I saw God in the sky
I was crossing a bridge
on my way to buy salt
and when I looked up
I saw a huge man
with white hair and beard
sitting at a desk of cloud
that had two gigantic books on it
one was black
the other white
Saturday I asked the priest
in the confessional box what it all meant
and he said:
"The black book is for all the bad you do

the white book for all the good
If the black book
at the end of your life
weighs more than the white book
you'll go to hell and burn forever!"
For weeks afterwards I assured myself
that buying salt was nothing bad—

When I was six
I saw a dead cat
I put a cross on it
and said a little prayer
When I told the Sunday school teacher
what I had done
she pulled my ears
and ordered me to go immediately
back to the dead cat
and take the cross off it
I love cats I've always loved cats
"But don't cats go to heaven?" I cried
"Thou shalt not worship false idols!" she replied—
I went back to the dead cat
it was gone
the cross remained
Fittingly so . . . that day the earth had died

When I was seven
I sat in church one Sunday
next to a fat little boy
I'd never seen before
He had a small glass elephant
cupped in his chubby hand
And it was during the raising
of the Eucharist
when he showed it to me
That's when it happened
I remember how fast it happened
He fainted
They carried him away
the glass elephant still in his hand
The part that scared me most
was when the two men who had carried him out
came back and sat beside me

one on each side of me
Was I next? I wondered
I who had seen the glass elephant?
I never saw that boy again
And to this very day
I cannot totally comprehend
what it all meant . . . if it meant anything at all

Peter Covino

Poverty of Language

If a mother were to say: "I pray
to the Virgin you die of AIDS."

You see I'm doing it again,
shutting you out.

"I should have eaten *you* at birth."
This language is wealth,

a red dress,
an injection.

* * *

Father spoke to us
in erudite Italian:

pederasta—pederast,
infangare—to muddy,

to soil
as in ruining one's name.

Mother spoke
in a strange combination

of denial
and southern Italian dialects:

femminiello,
she'd call me

femminiello,
she'd call my sister

femminiello,
my father

femminiello—one-half little girl,
one-half little faggot.

Infidel

At the Wellington Diner, this fine Spring
Day, my life before poetry came to me,
Like an alcoholic's before AA:

How I sat those many years earlier,
On a cloudy Easter morning at another
Diner, alone, at a counter seat, its beiged

Vinyl, the checkered and scuffed linoleum.
I had just outed myself, distanced
Myself from everything I wanted, cast

Away from all the comforts of lamb shank
And relatives, my parents whispering
With the shame of me. Holy week, and no one

To call family, not unholy, but reluctant,
Woozy as a newborn giraffe, crouched there
Beneath the knobby knees of its mother

Who's just delivered, from six feet above,
While standing. And each step, because in this
Life I'm born again, feels like a conversation

In another language. This new, stuttered
Existence, so far from the *Kyries*
And the thirteenth station in the church

Of my youth, named after St. Roch, healer,
Patron saint of the sick, especially
Revered in this Italian neighborhood

(Rocco, a name common as John). It was
There that words first saved me, prayers, to some
Sanctimonious muse. A surrogate

God-mother, I spoke to again today,
When a familiar void filled me—that night
On the edge of twenty and suicide,

When the parish priest, Father Della Rosa,
Came to the house, and commanded in barely
Passable English: "No matter what, God

Loves you." Right about now in Rome, in the
Square of the saint I'm named after, namesake
Also of my grandfather, pilgrims begin

To shuffle in—I can almost touch them
Through the diner window—bus-loads full,
From Uganda, Brazil, Papua New Guinea,

Placards and whistles of tour guides excite
The air. Men, children and women (mostly)
Crossing the threshold of the basilica,

Like entering another world, the long
Journey of a lifetime culminating,
In this one, rapturous moment. Some burst

Into tears, saving waters rushing over,
Some even swoon, needing to be revived,
Slapped back—back, into this forgiving life.

George Cuomo

From *Family Honor: An American Life*

With what was for them an impressive show of patience, the whole
family had been waiting for Meg to have a baby. "It don't take so long
to do it," Serafina would say to Sirola, raising her eyes knowingly, "if
you know how. You know how, eh?" When early that spring Meg
missed two periods and the doctor gave her the good news, she didn't

want a fuss over it. "After all, it's a perfectly normal and reasonable out-come, and not worth spending the next seven months talking about."

"What else do they have to do for the next seven months?"

No one expected Meg to make use of Bella, who hadn't delivered a baby since leaving Italy, but they knew of younger *mammane* in the neighborhood and shook their heads dolefully over Sirola's insistence on putting his little wife in the hands of some strange and heartless doctor. They were even more dismayed to learn that he was actually planning to send her to a hospital.

"You think it's gonna be good for her, breathing in all those medi-cines when there's nothing even wrong with her?" Serafina wanted to know.

Sirola's mother wore her best dress and, with Serafina's help, had done up her hair and tinted out the streaks of gray. Meg and Eva had dressed too, and Sirola and Joe wore their business suits. It was only a neighbor-hood restaurant, and they were the classiest people in sight. Sirola brought two bottles of Chianti in a paper sack and the waitress provided glasses; even his mother tried a sip. But with Manny still in their minds and everyone knowing the purpose of the evening, they didn't make a very cheerful group. Joe seemed annoyed at having to be there, and Eva had never been one to dazzle you with her sparkle.

During the meal, his mother spoke about Manny and Josie. It had been that way after Sirola's father died; funerals were a time for family history, for revelations of important events that, because they were im-portant, had never been brought up before. Speaking gravely, she told them how Josie and Manny had gotten married. It was not something Sirola had given any thought to. They'd always been his aunt and uncle, their marriage something that simply *was*. With his slow, sweet smile and habit of fading away from others, of drifting off into corners, of sidling over to Crotona Park to pass the time with whatever cronies he had, Manny always seemed to be informing people, shyly, that his smile was not meant to bring them close; it was his way of pulling back and edging away, from his wife as much as anyone else. In turn, it was hard to remember Josie ever saying anything to her husband beyond asking where he was going, when he would be back, whether he had shoveled the sidewalk. Whether Manny was present or not, Josie would speak of him as she did of her children, as wayward and exasperating but never mean. She would refer to *them* with a wave of her hand: her husband Manny and her children, Carmella and Little Vinny and Poor Antonio, all lumped together, pleasant but sometimes tiring burdens.

Sirola's mother told them at the restaurant that when Josie was a beautiful girl she had fallen in love with a young man who owned and operated—he had people working for him!—a fashionable millinery shop. He was artistic too, this man, designing his own hats and cutting the material and then supervising the women in the back room who sewed. Josie had gone to work for him not as a back room seamstress but as a saleslady in the salon itself, her poise and beauty being such that she was the perfect person to wait upon the gentry and their elegant ladies.

The milliner quite naturally fell in love with the ravishing Josie and there were coy hints of marriage, then open talk, and finally a date set, plans made, a bridal shower arranged. But it was not to be, his mother said.

Why? Sirola wanted to know, although he dared not interrupt his mother's stately rhythms to ask.

Whatever the reasons, poor Josie was rudely jilted, and the lovely young girl in her salon finery ended up with a broken heart.

"Poor thing," Meg said, almost tearfully, having no trouble envisioning Josie as the magic princess Sirola's mother was describing. "She must have been crushed."

Enter Manny, armed with pushbroom. No one, including Josie, was impressed by his sweet smile, his unassuming gentleness. The gnat in the wake of the eagle. What chance could such a fellow have of winning the hand of this beauty? Every chance in the world, it seemed. Josie had no hopes of ever again meeting the likes of the marvelous hatmaker. Besides, she'd begun to suspect that perhaps, in men, there existed a connection between the dashing qualities that so attracted young girls like herself and the callousness with which these Lotharios treated their victims. Therefore someone who lacked flair and dash could also be assumed to lack hardness of heart. The gnat could not soar, but neither did it have razor-sharp talons.

And what finally was the point, the motive behind his mother's belated revelation of a story she had known for so many years? *Poor Manny,* the point seemed to be. Shy and pliable, smiling while backing away at the same time, demanding nothing, he'd spent his whole life trying to placate a woman who would not be placated, whose wound was too deep for healing. Ah, but it was *Poor Josie* too, for how easy it was for those ignorant of her heartbreaking experience, of her lifelong hurt, to make fun of the unfortunate woman. And it did not stop there. *Poor Serafina,* too; *Poor Bella.* Uprooted and tossed upon the churning ocean, deposited on the alien shores of some faraway country—how easy to make fun of their accents, their superstitions, their gossipy concerns, rather than to imagine, in your own heart, what it must have been like for someone like Bella, famous and revered in her native village for half a century, to have her whole world disappear forever beneath the rim of the ocean. And Serafina, never to marry or have children, never to know a man, never to be held close, her whole life foreordained by the childhood rickets that had softened the bones of her cruelly bent legs. Did people think she was unaware of her losses, that she never dreamed of what might have been? "You never hear her complain," his mother said, "yet she suffers every minute of the day." And then, beyond even that, the real moral of her story: "It is always easy to make fun, to blame, to scold, to turn away, when we do not know what pain people have put up with in their silence."

It was only after a moment that she added quietly, her eyes down, "Paolo too. I cannot bring myself to it yet, but I know it is wrong of me. I know that I must somehow find a way to forgive."

They remained silent. The meal was done; she had been talking almost an hour, probably the longest she'd ever held anyone's attention, and Sirola, finally, was convinced that it must have happened exactly that way. Josie must have been incredibly beautiful. The story had somehow created its own truth; it had made itself real.

His mother sipped her wine and settled back with her hands in her lap: they could go on now to whatever they had come to discuss.

"Okay," Joe said, "we might as well get to it." His impatience showed through, his relief that the long prelude was finally over. After the waitress cleared the table and brought the pot of espresso, Joe placed a notebook on the table, pressing the heel of his hand along the spine to make the pages lie flat. Briskly he ticked off the facts. Manny hadn't been making any kind of money but at least kicked in a third of the rent and kept his wife and kids in food. With him gone, they were left with a two-story house inhabited by one mother, two aunts, one grandmother, and three cousins, without a thin dime coming in from the whole gang put together.

"We could have them draw straws to see who gets taken out and shot," Sirola said.

"C'mon," Joe said.

"You make them sound like a bunch of vultures."

"I'm not making them sound like anything. I'm describing the situation."

"We've been paying a third each on the rent anyhow. We'll up it a bit to half and figure out what it costs to keep—"

"We can't. At least I can't. I get my salary and that's it. I don't have any slush fund to play around with."

"Slush fund?"

"You told me you get an expense account."

"He gets five dollars a week," Meg said, "and spends ten."

"He should learn to handle it better. To tell you the truth, Vinny, I never really understood what they were paying you for in the first place. What do you do all the time? There can't be a strike every day of the year, can there?"

"Strikes aren't that big a part of it. I visit the shops. I run the office. I go to meetings."

"The way I see it, when the boss tries to toss some guy out on his ear you tell him the man's a *boney fidey* union member in good standing and therefore can't be thrown out just because he's a deadbeat who couldn't find first base with a map. All of which you take care of between the street riots and the run-ins with the cops, right?"

"Right."

"Don't talk like that," his mother said to Joe.

"Why kid ourselves? Vinny's not spending his days at Lady Astor's garden party."

"Stop it," his mother said.

———

"What do you think, there's always money everywhere, for everybody who wants it? It's America, eh, so *poof!*—everybody's rich!"

Sirola wasn't all that optimistic himself. Every time the stock market came back a few points the Wall Street crowd whooped it up, only to watch prices fall even lower the next day. Spring, Hoover said: by spring the country would be prosperous again. Sirola would have liked to believe it, that when the snow melted into the sewer drains on Tremont Avenue and the grass came up green in Crotona Park the worst would be over.

All right, Serafina said, for a while life was good. Who knew why? Maybe it was an accident. Maybe the country suddenly needed locomotives and railroad tracks and big buildings, what with the millions of people coming from Italy and all those other places. But no one came anymore, and the railroads already went to all the places there were to go to, and anybody could see that the cities had enough big buildings to last people a lifetime. And so now, no surprise to her, it would be the same here as it had always been in Italy, and probably all those other countries too. After all, Italians weren't poor because they were Italians, but because they were people. The proverb said it: only before you were born could you count on warmth and nourishment. Afterward, expect cold and hunger. Work was a luxury, a gift, a stroke of fortune. If you were like most people, you clawed in the dirt or starved or got rickets as a baby and lived out your life with bent legs. That was the world. It had always been the world. God for His own reasons made it that way, and no one with any sense expected anything different.

It wasn't the hard times that would go away, Serafina insisted, gesturing with touched fingers to show her contempt for those *ottusos* who couldn't see this. The fancy clothes and noisy cars, the dollar bills, the pastries on the plate: *that's* what would go away. "Learn to scrape and pinch," she advised sternly. "Learn to do without."

Little Vinny took it hardest, convinced that it was somehow his fault that Paolo's business had fallen off so much that he no longer needed or could afford a helper.

"Stop worrying about it," Sirola told him. "You worked harder than he did, you did your best. It's time you quit anyhow. Paolo's not the world's greatest boss." And then, suddenly remembering: "Was he still paying you in nickels and dimes?"

"Oh yes," Little Vinny said, wondering why Sirola even asked.

"You should've left sooner," Sirola said.

Every week Sirola's mother took the trolley to Joe's apartment in the afternoon to visit with Eva and the kids for an hour, and then see Joe himself, briefly, when he came home from work.

"He still has the job," his mother said. "But it's different. Everyone there—everyone who is still left—is making less. That was the agreement."

"What agreement?"

"I don't know what agreement. He's still there, that's all he said. He's one of the people still working."

"What about you?" Josie asked. "Are you still working where you are?"

"I'm still working," Sirola said with a laugh.

"What's so funny?"

"Nothing."

"Is it steady?" Josie asked.

"It ain't ever been steady."

"You should be careful then," Serafina said. "When times are hard, it's the one with the big mouth who gets shown the door first."

————

Meg still went to church Sundays, and Sirola generally went with her, without much enthusiasm. Neither of the priests impressed him with what they said or the way they said it. With sin, corruption, and Jesus Christ going for you, a guy should at least be able to keep a crowd breathing. He'd seen speakers generate more excitement explaining the clauses in the Wagner Act. Besides, he didn't much appreciate the general Church attitude toward workers. A few priests seemed to care, but most either kept hands off or sided with the bosses. The archbishops and bishops Sirola met at banquets were even worse. They sounded like Standard Oil stockholders and wrote off unions as hotbeds of Godless communism. Their big pitch was to get workers to accept their lot with Christ-like forbearance. It was the same old story. Cutting wages to beef up your profits wasn't a sin, whereas striking against a wage cut somehow was. The Church even fought the child-labor reforms because a ten-year-old was better off in a spinning mill than idling around all day thinking un-Christian thoughts.

Seeing a priest about their troubles didn't therefore seem too promising. Sirola considered a psychological doctor, but Meg said: "I'm not seeing any more doctors. Any kind of doctors."

She was willing, though, to talk with a priest. In fact, she was the one who suggested it—as long as it was someone from another parish, who she wouldn't have to face every time she went to Mass.

Sirola waited in the dark gloomy sitting room of the rectory while Meg was inside. She came out and said, "He wants to talk to you too."

A stocky, bullet-headed priest sat in a lumpy armchair with his legs apart beneath his cassock and his blunt hands clasped over his knees. He nodded curtly for Sirola to sit. "We had a good talk, your wife and myself. A good talk. She was very honest about her attitudes, her beliefs. I wonder, though, about *your* attitudes—your reasons for bringing her here."

"It's mainly that she's been so depressed and everything lately. I thought—"

"Perhaps like all too many men in public affairs these days you've drifted so far from the teachings of the Church that you fail to recognize the sincerity of another's faith. Your wife is a very humble woman. She asks nothing for herself. That's unfashionable now, isn't it? Everyone's out for himself, for all he can grab, with Roosevelt of course showing the way. We've lost sight of Christian humility and self-denial. I would say that our problem here is that perhaps your own material and physical concerns have kept you from realizing that your wife has finally found in the holy Christ Himself a true inner peace. . . ."

Joseph Cuomo

The First Night of the Wake

I remember my mother, younger than I am now, the meticulous wife in her white apron with the red trim, standing outside in the park, standing on the uneven pavement near the handball courts (where we watched the boys show off), the cobblestones separate as teeth, her sensible shoes at slightly different heights. I remember sensing something odd about her presence there, among us. So odd that my friends, my antic friends, fell instantly silent. It was the suddenness with which she appeared, but it was also the way that she held herself, heels together, arms at her sides, as if she were trying to flatten herself, to occupy only two dimensions. And yet, at the same time, there was such authority in her stance. Like an alarm going off, an alarm in a foreign country, an alarm you have never heard before, but recognize instinctively.

I don't recall being told. I don't think I was told until we got back to the apartment. But I do remember the walk home from the park, the steady, unnatural pace, the unspoken understanding that I shouldn't look at her. The strange light on the street, like the light that follows a summer shower. Cars and stoops and children's toys caught out, luminous. Like idealized facsimiles of themselves.

That night, sleep, when I could get to sleep, was a succession of nightmares. I lay awake, curled in my bed, anticipating them, watching the reflections of streetlamps travel across my ceiling, an occasional car speeding past, marking intervals in the interminable night. When finally, after fits of sobbing, I drifted off, the next thing I knew my eyes were open and I was aware of a disturbance in the lightless room. It was me. My own dreams had startled me out of sleep.

The funeral, the wake the following day, was my first. And my mother, thoughtful in a way I had never known her to be, told me that I didn't have to go up and kiss the body.

"Now when I was a girl," she said, "they put them out in the home. Right in the living room. We didn't have no funeral parlors. In the home they put them, packed with ice. With nickels on the eyes. Oh yes, yes. When my Uncle Tony died, my mother made me go up there." And she gave a solemn nod toward the front of the room, in the general direction of what had once been my father. "I didn't want to go, I didn't want to see or touch. But I guess that's just the way they did things then." And she sighed in a way that seemed to unsettle her.

It was rare to hear this sort of talk from my mother, it was unusual to hear the tone in which she spoke, to hear her say something without turning it into a pronouncement, without presenting it as a matter of actual fact. It was also unusual to see her recoil as she did, even briefly, at the sight of what until that moment I had not fully understood to be a corpse.

This set off in me an unusual response to her, an unusual sense of commiseration, yes, but also a rare protective reflex. I knew that I was grateful to her for speaking to me like that. And yet, at the same time, I wanted to shield her from the very thing she was saying. But I had no idea how to accomplish this.

The rest of our relatives, as a whole, seemed sullen, but not in a way that was wildly out of character, not in a way that was indistinguishable from their ordinary selves. Which perhaps is what made them seem a little unnatural to me, a little unnerving. That day, the first day of the wake, my father's aunt, my great-aunt, Aunt Sophia, was already arguing with the undertaker, the two of them gesticulating beside the bulbous casket. She was short, thick-waisted, stocky, almost geometrical in shape, like a practice sketch that artists make. Though there was nothing tentative or frail about her. Some people wear their age on their face like a piece of paper balled up in your hand, then released. But Aunt Sophia's wrinkled pallor was reminiscent of fissures in the surface of a stone, evidence of what had passed over it, evidence of what remained.

Illiterate in English, barely literate in Italian, she had dominated the family ever since she had worked the hilly fields outside of Naples. Then, in her twenties, with her siblings in her charge (one of whom would become my grandmother, my father's mother), she left behind the only world she had ever known—the peasant town, the farm, the livestock, her parents—left it all, packed what could be carried and set out to conquer the good life in the New World, a life of factory work and piecework, of sixteen-hour days that wrapped around her nights, of overtime paid as straight time, often with only Sundays off—all of it for the better life, if not for her own generation, then for those who would follow, my father's generation, my generation, me.

I can still see the undertaker as he argued with my aunt that night, a thin man beside the sleek, dark casket, gleaming like a new car. I don't remember his face, just the stooped, gaunt form, his gray suit short in the sleeve, exposing too much shirt cuff. And his hands: veined and empty.

It says something about my relatives, their resilience, perhaps, that what happened next would become the stuff of Sunday-dinner conversation, another anecdote, another burlesque interpretation of events. (Sometimes I think every argument in my family is simply a variation on the same theme: whether the world is acceptable or not. With everyone arguing in the affirmative, except me.)

"He should have the smile," said Aunt Sophia, and she actually tucked her thumb and forefinger into her nephew's bluish mouth.

"Smile," she said. "Like this." But the smile did not stay put. "You fix," she said.

You fix.

I am haunted by this, even today, by the sight of those fingers in my dead father's mouth.

The first night of the wake, the room was too crowded, close. Grandma Va, my mother's mother, asked Uncle Sal, her Sal, to take her out for air. He escorted the wiry old lady through the many mourners, out the door and down a hallway hazy with smoke.

I remember my mother standing primly beside me then, I remember the two shades of black, gauzy for her shoulders, satiny for her back, but between this moment and all that followed, there is a gap, an absence, a tiny hole in time, like a film that is missing a few frames. I can see her there, but I can't remember her turning or moving in my direction. I just remember her suddenly upon me, falling on me, her chest heaving against mine. She was wailing, her shrill cries muffled by my own weight. Her face buried in my shoulder, her hands wrestling with my wool dress, tugging at the sleeves, sliding in under the arms, grabbing at the fabric from within it.

Usually, I am good with other people's grief, or at least I try to be. But not then. My back was so rigid it was numb. I couldn't move, wasn't sure I wanted to move, to be there at all. To have her there, wrapped around me, trying to hide inside my clothes.

Things moved quickly after that. Somehow my mother must have been calmed, or taken from me. Somehow my cousin, my ungainly cousin Joey, must have taken me out of that room. (Later, he would catch hell for this, for taking me where he did, for foisting me upon the men.) I don't remember the door we used, where it was. But I remember being led down an open stairwell. From above, I can still see the dark, curly-haired heads, the repetitive bald spots. Uncle Sal, Uncle Emilio, Uncle Augie, Great-uncle Mannie, and the slightly oversized pompadour of Uncle Frank, the first (and, at the time, the only) man in our family to wear a toupee. They were sitting around a small, flesh-colored card table, a bottle of Dewar's on the unsteady surface, pointed paper cups in their calloused hands. Sitting there as they might have sat in my mother's pristine dining room. Except that here they were surrounded by caskets. Several gray, several gold, several black. All of them tipped almost upright, in an uneven line against the wall, as if they had been arranged around the card table and the scotch and the men with their paper cups. Like cabanas on a beach.

It was then, sitting there among my uncles and the caskets, that my own perceptions came to seem almost unreliable, it was then that the world they reflected back to me came to seem unreal.

That night, watching the evening news, the full force of the day's events exploded within me. It had nothing to do with the news, with the dead in the headlines. Though with Vietnam beginning to rage, there was plenty of dead in the headlines. It was the weather.

For a moment, I had felt safe, my aunts shuttling back and forth around me, setting the enormous table, the permanents, the perfume, the flouncy aprons, the skirts down to the shin, my uncles and the red-and-white deck of cards, the sound of the ice in their pungent drinks, shifting, changing shape, the smoke from their filterless cigarettes drifting, shimmering like a mirage, catching the glint of the set in the other room.

Then, out of nowhere, there it was: a certainty, hard, fast, inescapable, a certainty such as I had never suffered before.

The weatherman, I now realized, the weatherman is going to die.

His name was Tex Antoine, and he was as familiar as the furniture in the room. The freckles on his high forehead, the receding hairline, the trim mustache, the smock he wore. The sly smile he offered whenever he spoke the name of Mr. Weatherbee, his cartoon assistant.

There are other things that people would come to associate with Tex Antoine. There was a scandal, as I recall. But I was never able to absorb the details. After that night, I was never able to see him as I had before.

It was as if once he entered my mind in this way, he undid something, unleashed it. A logic I could not muffle or mute. Cruel, absolute. For I saw now that if he was going to die, that meant others would die too. Every person I had ever known was subject to the same indifferent process, every person I had ever known was little more than a shadow, wavering, tenuous. Everyone in my world was being ripped from it, torn from me. And as I sat there, the grim, familiar faces filled the dim living room. Mrs. Kaplan at the candy store, Helmut at the deli, Mrs. Berman who taught chem. Mrs. Antonelli, Mrs. Barone, Mrs. Venezia.

And unspeakably, unthinkably: even my grandmother, my cousins, my uncles, my aunts. Even my mother.

Even me.

That night I dreamed of my mother. I remember it, I remember slowly waking up, that bald, still time between sleep and the returning anxiety of consciousness. I lay there with my home in my head. The cracked photos on the nightstand, the black dresses on the doorframe, the gaping shoes beside the bed. The votive candles on the huge bureau, the wild shadows on the wall, the rising threads of black smoke, quivering, disappearing. I remember watching my mother tip one of the small red cups sideways, the flame sizzling against the glass, the wax running out liquid, dribbling onto my palm. I had expected it to sting, and it did. But I was surprised when it stopped stinging, when the liquid simply cooled, and cooled quickly, the soft wax adhering like a second layer of skin.

Even now, I can see her dipping her fingers into the wax as if it were holy water, bowing her head as if she were in church, genuflecting on the orange carpet. Then, abruptly glancing up at me, her eyes screwed up, tongue dangling, shoulders caved forward, like a child mimicking its own death.

Even now, I can't say if this actually happened. I can't tell you whether I dreamed it, or simply recalled it. But that night, it terrified me, thinking of her like this. And I wallowed in that terror. I courted it, calling up the crucifix above my parents' bed, fixing it there in that room with my mother. The dead Jesus a lurid white in the shallow darkness, the ash-bright arms extended as though frozen in flight.

The more I focused on it, the more unlikely it became, this vivid image of my mother. It was like a child's game, focusing on a word, repeating it again and again, until it lost all sense, all meaning. Only this wasn't a game. I didn't know what it was. And it occurred to me then that perhaps I had dreamed the entire thing. Not just the candles and the wax, but the fingers in my father's mouth, my uncles in the basement with the caskets, my mother in her apron in the park. It seemed possible I had invented it all, imagined it. And this possibility plunged me even further into the chaos of the night, a chaos so cavernous it seemed palpable, it seemed I was lying inside of it, but couldn't touch it, couldn't see the end of it. I was lost in it, but part of it, part of the darkness itself. And it occurred to me then, as I lay there, that even these thoughts, this uncertainty over what had taken place—even this, I now saw, even this could be a dream.

★ ★ ★

It's odd having written what you've just read, it's odd reading it back. It's odd that my father isn't in it. He's barely mentioned. I see that now, I see that I've left out any direct reference to him. The things of his that I found, the emptiness of the apartment, the way he looked in the casket—though it shocked me to see this, it stained my retina. Or so it seemed at fourteen. The afterimage clinging, the way it does when you stare at a flame.

Which is to say, there are still some subjects I avoid at night. There are still some subjects I can't revisit. Even now, even as I write this, some thirty years after the fact, I find myself resisting it, resisting this very sentence itself. And all at once, I am aware of the room around me, the gray slab of the tabletop, the distant ceiling, the relentless clock, the glaring light.

Don DeLillo

From *Underworld*

The Italians. They sat on the stoop with paper fans and orangeades. They made their world. They said, Who's better than me? She could never say that. They knew how to sit there and say that and be happy. Thinking back through the decades. She saw a woman fanning herself with a magazine and it seemed like an encyclopedia of breezes, the book of all the breezes that ever blew. The city drugged with heat. Horses perishing in the streets. Who's better than me?

She heard them talking out there.

He wants me to go to the zoo because the animals are real. I told him these are zoo animals. These are animals that live in the Bronx. On television I can see animals in the rain forest or the desert. So which is real and which is fake, which made him laugh.

It would have been easier to believe she deserved it. He left because she was heartless, foolish, angry, she was a bad housekeeper, a bad mother, a cold woman. But she could not invent a reliable plot for any of these excuses.

But it was the sweetest intimacy, his whispered stories of the gamblers and the police, lying in bed the two of them, his days with the garment bosses and bellhops. He made her laugh, telling these stories late at night, love nights, whispering to her afterward, lying close in bed, and even when he was flat-pocket broke he told her funny screwy stories in the night.

She began to drift into sleep now and said a Hail Mary because this is what she always did before she went to sleep. Except she wasn't always sure anymore whether the last Hail Mary she said was a Hail Mary from last night or from two minutes ago and she said this prayer and said this prayer because she mixed up the time and didn't want to go to sleep without being sure.

She had more material things than most people she knew, thanks to sons who provided. She had nicer furniture, a safer building, doctors left and right. They made her go to a gynecologist, with Janet calling and then Marian calling, women of the world hooray. But she still couldn't say, Who's better than me?

What she knew about the knife grinder was that he came from the same region as Jimmy's people, near a town called Campobasso, in the mountains, where boys were raised to sharpen knives.

It took two hours to bead a sweater. She listened to the radio but not really, you know, letting the voice drift in and out. She guided the needle through the fabric and thought of Jimmy's stories. She used to fight to keep him out of her thoughts but it wasn't possible, was it? He replaced the radio in her mind.

She said, "What happened to the knives?"

There was a long pause in the next room.

He said, "He never came. I never heard the bell."

She said, "He always comes on Tuesday. He never misses a Tuesday. Since we've been here, except if it's Christmas Day, he will be here on a Tuesday."

She waited for a response. She could sense the boy's surrender and resentment, the small crouched shape squeezed in utter stillness.

"Am I wrong or is this a Tuesday?" she said in a final little dig.

She saw the pigeons erupt from the roof across the street, bursting like fireworks, fifty or sixty birds, and then the long pole swaying above the ledge—so long and reedy it bent of its own dimensions.

Mr. Bronzini knocked on the door and Matty let him in.

The Italian women in the building, which almost all of them were, called her Rose. They thought this was her name, or one of them did and the others picked it up, and she never corrected them because—she just didn't.

Never mind hello. They started right in talking about a move, a maneuver from a couple of days before. Mr. Bronzini sometimes forgot to take off his coat before he sat down at the board.

Jimmy used to say carte blank.

The boy who kept the pigeons stood invisible behind the ledge, waving the pole to guide the birds in their flight.

They lapsed into a long pondering silence at the board, then started talking at once, yackety-yak together.

She strung the beads onto the fabric.

She didn't want to be a sob story where people feel sorry for you and you go through life dragging a burden the size of a house.

Jimmy used to say, Here's some money. You have carte blank how you spend it. I don't even want to know, he'd say.

She heard a woman in the hall yelling down to her kid. Her head out the door yelling to the kid who's galloping down the steps.

"I'm making gravy," the woman yelled.

How is it we did so much laughing? How is it people came over with their empty pockets and bad backs and not so good marriages and twenty minutes later we're all laughing?

They started a legend that he memorized every bet. But he didn't. They still tell stories about his memory, how he moved through the loft buildings taking bets from cutters, sweepers and salesmen and recording every figure mentally. But he didn't. He had pieces of paper all over his clothes with bets scribbled down.

She heard the women talk about making gravy, speaking to a husband or child, and Rosemary understood the significance of this. It meant, Don't you dare come home late. It meant, This is serious so pay attention. It was a special summons, a call to family duty. The pleasure, yes, of familiar food, the whole history of food, the history of eating, the garlicky smack and tang. But there was also a duty, a requirement. The family requires the presence of every member tonight. Because the family was an art to these people and the dinner table was the place it found expression.

They said, I'm making gravy.

They said, Who's better than me?

It did not happen violent. This was a thing she would never believe, that they took him away in a car. The man went out for cigarettes and just kept walking.

She didn't want her children to see her dragging, slumping, thinking too much, brooding, angry, empty.

Conceal, conceal. But it was hard.

They told her to change her hair. The women in the building. They told her she had a Mother Hubbard hairdo.

No, she wasn't empty. Just tense much of the time, hearing a voice inside that she'd never heard before, her own voice, only edgy and angry and one-track.

She listened to Mr. Bronzini in the living room. He spoke about the truth of a position. The radio was doing a serial drama called "Bright Horizons" or "Bright Tomorrows" or "Brighter Days" and every position has a truth, he told Matty. A deep truth is what you want, not a shallow truth. You want a position worth defending to the death.

This food, this family meal, this meat sauce simmering in a big pot with sausage and spareribs and onions and garlic, this was their loyalty and bond and well-being, and the aroma was in the halls for Rosemary to smell when she climbed the flights, rolled beef, meatballs, basil, and the savor had an irony that was painful.

He used to come home and get undressed, Jimmy, and pieces of paper would fall out of his clothes, scraps of paper, bets in code, his own scrawled cipher of people's names, horses' names, teams and odds and sums of money.

They said, See what you're gonna do.

How is it she could laugh all night at his stories about a day in the garment district, or a day when he went to Toots Shor's famous restaurant, out of the district, the famous Toots Shor, out of his jurisdiction completely, but Toots Shor met him and liked him and wanted to give him some action and he was a heavy bettor, very, and Jimmy made occasional trips to West 51st Street to take limited bets from Toots Shor, a big lumbering man with a face like a traffic accident, and he told her stories about the well-heeled bums around the big bar drinking until four in the morning.

I'm making gravy, they said.

The wife of Mr. Imperato, the lawyer she worked for in her regular job, called a couple of times a week and said, Tell him I'm making gravy.

She did her beadwork off the books. The pigeons climbed and wheeled and the long pole swayed above the ledge.

Some women have one man in their life and he was the one, that bastard, in hers.

Up on the roofs, the tar beaches, they put suntan oil on their arms and legs and sat on blankets wearing shorts, the girls did, or jeans rolled to the knees, and they oiled their faces and sat listening to a portable radio until the heat was too intense to bear and then they sat a little longer.

They sang the week's top songs along with the radio, down the list from forty, and they got the words, the pauses, the dips and swerves, every intonation point-blank perfect, but only the songs they liked of course.

The tar softened and fumed and the heat beat down and the green gnats stuck to their bodies and across the way the pigeon kid sent his birds into spiral flight with a bamboo pole, and waved a towel at times, and whistled like a traffic cop, and his flock mixed in midair with a rival flock from a roof three blocks away, a hundred-birded tumult and blur, and younger birds flew with the wrong flock and were captured and sometimes killed, dispatched within the rules by the rival flyer of the other roof, and after a while the girls had to leave because the sun was just too smoking hot, singing lyrics as they rolled their blankets up.

I drink aged grappa and listen to jazz. I do the books on the new shelves and stand in the living room and look at the carpets and wall hangings and I know the ghosts are walking the halls. But not these halls and not this house. They're all back there in those railroad rooms at the narrow end of the night and I stand helpless in this desert place looking at the books.

I long for the days of disorder. I want them back, the days when I was alive on the earth, rippling in the quick of my skin, heedless and real. I was dumb-muscled and angry and real. This is what I long for, the breach of peace, the days of disarray when I walked real streets and did things slap-bang and felt angry and ready all the time, a danger to others and a distant mystery to myself.

Lina del Tinto Demarsky

From *Leaven of the Pharisees*

Chuck was not impressed.

"She's bluffing, Connie . . . believe me," he insisted over and over. "Sure . . . she thinks she is sick, but I'd be willing to bet anything that it's strictly psychosomatic. Don't you see? Can't you see that she resorts to her illness only when she can't get her own way? God! Connie, how can you fail to see something so obvious?"

For four days now he had been waging a fierce battle to break down her reluctance and win her to his side.

Connie had been appalled at first, to hear Chuck accuse her mother of using her heart trouble to get her own way, but point by point . . . with the accuracy of a mathematician, he had explored all the facets. His logic was so irrefutable . . . so incontrovertible, she had had to admit finally that such a possibility existed. And yet, they were no nearer to a solution than they had been after that fateful night. Even if such a thing were true, what could she possibly do about it? Connie asked herself.

They had been over the same ground for hours . . . with Chuck asking the same questions . . . she giving the same answers.

"Call it a tantrum . . . call it anything you want," Chuck muttered as he paced up and down his living room, gesturing now and then to illustrate a point, his eyes fiery, intense. "You stop seeing me and she'll be all right, or better yet," he added pointedly gazing at her, "I'll bet if I promised to do what she wants she'd be all right, wouldn't she? Wouldn't she?"

Connie looked away.

"There's just one thing," he added emphatically. "I'm not that interested in finding out."

He turned suddenly, as though appalled by his momentary cruelty, and rushed to where she sat, a small, forlorn figure all but lost on that big couch.

Connie had changed over the last six days. Her eyes were no longer lustrous, alive! Red stains marked the once clear, blue-whites . . . deep circles spoke only too revealingly of sleepless nights. The fine nose, the full lips were the same, her skin still had that pink-white that Chuck found so devastatingly inviting. . . . but she looked older. Her expression, when it changed at all, went from sadness to despair.

"Darling . . . my darling," Chuck whispered hoarsely, kneeling beside her. "For Christ's sake. Connie. It's your life! Why can't you live it? Why don't you leave them all? Isn't it time you cut those strings?"

"Please, Chuck, please," she pleaded wearily, stroking the bright yellow hair. "Don't you suppose I have been over this a hundred times? Don't you suppose I have tried to find a way out? Do you think that I don't want to find a way out? But I am afraid . . . so afraid . . . Suppose we got married in a civil ceremony? Suppose . . . suppose then that something happens . . . What if the next attack would prove fatal? Do you have any idea of the guilt complex I'd be carrying around all my life? Who would release from my mind that I had killed her? What kind of life would I have with that on my conscience?" Her voice was lifeless, colorless, the voice of one who has lost all hope.

"But why should you have a guilt complex about anything?"

Chuck demanded, viciously beating the sofa with his fist. "Look, Connie! She's had you at her beck and call for twenty-six years! Isn't that enough? She's made you an emotional dwarf as it is . . . when are you going to live your own life?"

Connie had no answer. What words could she use to explain to him that in the world she lived in, there was no such thing as "your own life"? She could not make him understand that you did not throw aside your family's traditions and rituals, just because you wanted to. How could she explain to him that in her world you respected your mother and father even if that meant putting aside your own wishes and desires. Sacrifice . . . that was the key word to her life . . . she had lived with it as long as she could remember. One always sacrificed for the love of a mother . . . sacrifice . . . sacrifice . . . sacrifice.

"Honey . . . honey," Chuck was pleading. "Why . . . why can't I make you see reason? In everything you have an open mind . . . but when it comes to your mother and your family. God! I feel so helpless! It's like beating my head against the wall. These damn blind spots of yours, Connie, I . . . I . . . Just can't seem to get through to you. It's depressing."

Connie hid her face in her hands. "Chuck . . . please . . . please . . . Don't take everything away from me . . . I haven't much left."

"I'm sorry to have to be so harsh, Connie, but I've got to make you see reason . . . I can't just let you throw your life away . . . I won't see you sacrifice yourself to the whims of a selfish woman."

"Chuck . . . I . . ."

"Christ, Connie, I admire your loyalty," he went on. "Don't think that I don't . . . but at least, find out what it is that you're being loyal to . . . and how can you expect to do that when you keep on hiding?"

Connie jumped up suddenly. She walked away from him. Presently she turned. "What do you want from me, what do you want from me?" she cried hysterically. "Leave me alone . . . please . . . Leave us alone. What do you want me to do? What can I do? This is the way I've been brought up . . . this is what I've been made to believe . . . it is all I've ever known." She reached for her handkerchief. Damn it, anyway, why was she always crying?

"All right . . . all right," Chuck replied firmly. "But why don't you look and see what it is that you're believing in? Just because you've been brought up on that is no reason for you to accept it. You're not a child . . . you're old enough to make your own choice. You don't have to accept anything just because your parents do . . . their beliefs should not necessarily be sacred to you."

He got up and followed her. He took her in his arms and held her. Gently, he pushed back the dark hair from her forehead.

"Darling . . . darling!" he whispered, "Let's not go on like this . . . I don't give a damn about what you want to believe . . . just marry me . . . that's all I ask." He kissed her gently. He kissed her on the lids . . . the forehead . . . Tenderly he lifted her chin and gazed into her sad eyes . . . "Is what I ask so awful? So terribly hard? Is it so hard to look at the facts, squarely, to call a spade a spade . . . is it so hard, Connie?"

She began to sob. "I . . . I can't I can't," she cried brokenly. "Believe me, Chuck . . . I want to . . . I wish I could . . . don't you think that's what I've been trying to do for weeks . . . to get up enough courage to let go. I . . . can't outgrow my background . . . I can't suddenly disbelieve what I've believed all my life. I can't . . . I just can't, Chuck." Her voice broke off. She clung to him.

They stood for a minute, silently clinging to each other.

"My darling . . . My darling," Chuck murmured, his arms, tightening around her. "You know I can't do it your way, don't you? God, don't you suppose that just for this once, just for this once I wish I could give in? Just for this once, I wish I could compromise and sign that goddamn agreement . . . but I can't . . . Connie . . . I can't . . . I just can't do it . . . can you understand? Can you, Connie?"

Connie looked at him steadily for a moment. He was weakening. Not very much, perhaps . . . but she saw the signs . . . He was protesting too hard.

She knew that by playing on his emotions now, she could still get him to change his mind. A word . . . a gesture . . . a look . . . a sigh, properly placed . . . that would do it. But did she want that? Did she want him on those terms?

She thought of Reds. Had he been through such an ordeal? Had Angela played on his emotions, too? Yes, of course. She must have. Reds would never have agreed otherwise. Not with his temperament. If she could only sway Chuck now would she ever win him back? Would it ever be the same between them? Or would he grow to resent her as Reds now resented his wife and her family? Connie knew how much Reds had come to resent everything that had to do with her Church. He relished the telling and retelling of how he had once thrown a priest out of his house.

Oh, God! She just couldn't bear it if Chuck became as bitter. No! she loved him too much to take advantage of his momentary weakness, but how could she let him go?

Once again, grief, real, deep, overwhelmed her. She started to cry again. Chuck held her close. "Don't . . . don't . . . please, Connie," he murmured tenderly.

But she could not stop. Her reasons for crying were manifold. She cried because a few times during the last few months, she had caught a glimpse of something wonderful. It had been like walking down a dark corridor, and at the very end, she had seen a door open, just enough to let in a sunbeam, a mischievous, laughing sunbeam, beckoning to her, urging her to go on . . . to go on and see what was on the other side of the door. She struggled in the darkness, trying to reach that door and push it open. But there was a powerful evil presence that kept pushing her back . . . back. And with each backward step she took the door closed a little more, until not even a crack was visible. Darkness . . . utter darkness engulfed everything. She cried, above all, because she wanted to hold on to what she had found, yet knowing that she would not force that door to open.

She cried for all the Redses and the Joans and the Connies of the world. She cried because she wanted to stay with the man she loved, yet knowing, . . . knowing all the while that she had to find the courage to let him go. And this realization filled her with sadness. But she knew she must. Her duty was to stand by her mother and her family, but even beyond duty, she knew that a deep-rooted fear paralyzed her, and she knew that this fear would not allow her to break away, no matter how much she wanted to . . .

As she lay in his arms, with a sudden sense of shock she realized that she might never see him again. Never to see Chuck again? No! No! Somehow her numb brain refused to accept it. She couldn't give him up. She wouldn't! Please, God, no . . . no!

She collapsed on the couch. Chuck sat down beside her.

"Darling . . . hold me . . . hold me!" she cried frantically, clinging to him. He kissed her then, not tenderly or gently, but roughly, demandingly. It was not the caress of a lover-friend, but the passionate, burning demand of a man . . .

Connie responded to his every kiss . . . his every move. An overwhelming desire for Chuck possessed her . . . she wouldn't deny herself any longer . . . she wouldn't!

Mary Russo Demetrick

I study Italian

to understand my heritage
why I fly off the handle
at the slightest nuance
the slightest rudeness
why tomatoes and basil
simmer in my blood
why the smell of espresso
brings back memories
too strong to ignore

I study Italian
to understand my family
why silence was understood
but never called omerta
why my mother ran the house
why my father played the mandolin

I study Italian
to understand the words
my grandmother said to me
stai zitto, a chi,
piacere, stai bene

I study Italian
to understand my bond
to roll my tongue around
double consonants
to try out my new-found
Tuscan language
on my mother's Neapolitan ear

I study Italian
to understand who I am
in the world of spongy
white American bread
turkey and mayonnaise

I study Italian
to understand why I crave pasta
on Sunday at noon
the taste of good wine
with dinner
olive oil on my salad

I study Italian
to understand
to come home
to bind with past
to create a future
where my heritage
will not be lost
to my children
to keep alive
all that has gone before
I study Italian

I stash treasures

like my grandmother did
in drawers
in the dining room
buffet   between
paper plates
and tee shirts

She secreted
small things
next to aprons
blessed candles
and hairnets

I put shoe inserts
and coupons
an ankle brace
three small stones
from a beach
in Florida
in with blouses

from Italia
and inflatable
neck pillows
used for traveling

I never understood
her need
to keep these
small things
I wanted
to sort
discard
but knew
it was forbidden
we did not touch
grandma's stuff

Under the lace
dresser scarf
holy cards
from dead relatives
and leaves
from some plant
that struck her fancy
in the park

In her apron pocket
a dime
for eye-sha-schee-ma
as she called
the frozen treat

Saint Anthony watched
from under
his glass dome
vigil candles flickering
lit with a wish
for health

Grandma
always had
what we needed
if we cut ourselves
she found a strip of cloth

in one of her drawers
to bind our wound

If our hair blew
out of control
she found a comb
or bobbi pin

Tina De Rosa

From *Paper Fish*

The mother said that Sabatina was the child of royalty, that she was kid-napped by gypsies who wore golden earrings and stole children. She said she found Sabatina in a basket in the garden, and that Sabatina was a princess who would never do a lump of work in her life. Doria laughed when her mother said this, because in her heart she knew it was true that Sabatina was lazy as the sun and would never amount to anything if she did not wake up soon. It was true that there were gypsies. They roamed the countryside and played music on their dulcimers, they shook tambourines in the dark. The cries of the strings and of the little silver bells enchanted the children. Doria had seen them, the black eyes and black souls of them. The breasts of the women were large, like the udders of cows; they swung under bright red dresses. Their bodies were dressed in golden jewelry; they wore silver combs in their hair. They were beautiful; they were terrifying. They frightened goats in the night so that their milk turned sour; they terrified the chickens so that they went barren. Whenever Doria and Sabatina passed the gypsies on the dirt roads, they crossed themselves and called upon the Madonna for protection from the evil eye. At night the two little girls lay in their white bedroom, on the clean sheets beaten white in the river. Outside the moon was a blue hole in the sky, washing the world blue-black, making the trees black as ash or as death, making the trees stick all out of the world like the broken brooms of witches. Outside the world turned blue from the moon, its enchanted light made the bedroom blue, and the sheets and their toes sticking out from under the sheets turned blue along with the world. It was then that Doria and Sabatina heard the singing of the gypsies, heard the cry of the dulcimers and the strangled chatter of bells, heard the laughter and songs of the gypsies reaching up out of the ground. The gypsies ride black horses, Doria said, and Sabatina curled into her side of the bed, pulled her feet away from the pitiless blue light, hid her face in the pillow. The gypsies ride black horses that once were devils, the devils grew tired of hell and changed themselves into horses. The gypsies find them and ride them, and the horses run faster than the horses made by God. The teeth of the horses are like knives, they can bite through the walls, Doria said. Sabatina buried her pretty brown face in the bedclothes and her legs were stiff. The horses run faster than the wind, faster than the rain, and if a gypsy wanted to catch you, you could never run fast enough, Doria whispered. Outside their windows the trees were black as matchsticks; a gypsy could set them on fire with his curse. Outside the window the trees looked into the bedroom with twisted faces. The voices of the gypsies travel through the ground, Doria said. The gypsies can reach up out of the ground and grab you with their teeth. The devil gave them special power. Sabatina screamed into the pillow and Doria scared herself. The sound of the dulcimer and of the thin tambourines travelled through the night hills. It was magic music, and sad. The gypsies were sad because they had been cursed by God to wander the world; they must live forever in tents, pitched by lonely fires. They sat round the fires dressed in their devil's gold, with gold at their ears and at their breasts, with gold at their waists and in small beautiful rings round their toes. The gypsy women sat with their long black hair and sang out of throats which burned. The men with their hard gypsy muscles listened and wept and grew angry. They revenged themselves. They stole children. They twisted the life of the animals so that goats vomited and chickens gagged. Sabatina rushed to the window, slammed the wooden shutters shut. She slapped out the blue light of the moon and the evil arms of the trees. Under the sheets, she still heard the music and Doria laughed at the way she scared little princess Sabatina. In the dark room, Doria watched the small slip of blue light under the shutters, clean and swift as a fish. She watched the shadows, stuffed like thick milk into the corners. The shadows only seemed to move. When she grew up, Doria would run away to the circus. With her blue eyes and black hair, she saw the circus and loved it. She loved the humped little dwarf with the yellow teeth, she loved the old wagons. There were green babies, flat and floating in bottles. The people of the circus dressed in clothes like jewels; Doria with her laughing blue eyes would be a part of them. The people in all the towns the circus passed would call out, there is Doria run away. Sabatina would grow old and fat; she would be forced to make large dresses to wear; no bracelets would fit her fat arms. But Doria would be beautiful, with slim ankles. She would lead the elephants, smiling.

In their small bedroom, his children were still asleep. Pasquale glanced for a moment at his daughters. He was a rough man. He had learned all he knew at the side of his father now rotting in the graveyard. The skin of his hands was almost as thick as the wood he worked; his eyes and the world they saw were the same. He wrestled with the world and forced it to yield to him all he demanded. He spat in the face of anyone who would steal from him that which was his. Carmella his wife was his; she had been given in proper ceremony. He had taken her properly in bed. She had yielded him two children though neither, curse God, was a son. He hammered and nailed and chiseled the wooden world into place. What would not yield he placed in a vise and then shaved off or sawed off what would not submit. His hands were black from his work; the palms were scarred by small tears in the skin which would not heal and by slivers of wood which were fixed parts of his flesh. His eyes were not the eyes of his brothers the farmers. His eyes were not marked by days spent under the yellow sun. His eyes followed the narrow grain of wood, followed it closely so that it would not deceive him and crack at a vital point. His eyes watched the fine shavings give way to correct proportions. His eyes ran over countless beams, ferreting out failure. The earth and its rooms, its fields and gardens, its houses and sheds, smelled of varnish and turpentine. He had long since lost the smells of his wife's kitchen, of the dishes set before him. Long ago he surrendered the delicate feast of anise in his coffee, the smell of honey in his cakes. The world smelled of turpentine and of sharp black varnish. His hands he had trained to know a slab of wood as a lover's hands know a woman's sex. They were hands fine in their work, and from them came the cabinets, tables and chairs which enabled him to marry Carmella his wife. His work had given him his family and this small house. He would not, like his father, become a broken doll, lose his trained eyes. He had taken care of these his eyes and hands, the tools given him by God to make his way on the earth a man and not a shrivelled worm.

He did not know if his children were beautiful. He knew that they were his. He had made them, he continued making them the way he made a ladder or stool. When he walked into his daughters' bedroom on the morning when the pictures were taken, he noticed only that they were asleep. His eyes were trained to see the joints and pinnings of the world, and not its luster. Behind him, the black hills of Italy were filled with spectacular creatures, with creatures of myth, of legend, of dreams and nightmares, squirming out of the people's minds, leaping out of their souls. The restless people looked up from their cooking, from their seeding, working the pulp of fig against the soft skin of their mouths like squirrels, looked out from their eyes and seduced from the humps of stone images which nourished them as the earth could not. They supplemented what the earth failed them. They provided the mysteries which God in his haste had overlooked. Thus the hills were peopled by bandits who slit human throats with the ease with which mothers slaughtered chickens; who slit open and spilled human life while glancing at the stars. Their taste was for swift and splendid death, their hands were bruised with blood, and they licked them clean. Headless bodies floated in the streams, suspended astonished in the water. The air was rich with the smell of their blood. Travelling through the hills was never an unconscious act. The people's eyes filled with what they expected to see; their irises were moist with the blood they might shed. Waiting, the people believed their bones lacked marrow, like birds. But more than the thieves filled the heavy pockets of the hills. The unborn, the never-seen, populated the trees, the small stone paths, and the stories of these astounded Doria. Creatures which had never existed lurked in the tales of her mother, Carmella, lurked in her words, in the catches of her voice. They peered out of their red eyes at the small child listening. The mother stirred beans in the pot on her stove, shredded the cheese and told Doria of these, the unseen creatures. The mother's face was deeply olive and her eyes sought the truths outside her kitchen window, as she prepared the meal. The souls of the unforgiven dead walked the hills at night. They held their hands before their faces, hiding their rotted features. They marched in a hard blue line and the sight of their faces could shoot you into madness, could spit you into hell. On a hill outside the town they gathered in a blue-black circle and chanted their prayers for forgiveness. They set their faces towards the stars, searching out the fingers of God which would hold them safely once again. They dressed themselves in leaves and danced. In the rain, they turned silver as pond scum, in the rain their secrets were revealed. It was true according to Doria's mother that each man is given a secret when he is born. He is meant by God to protect his secret, to hide it like a jewel throughout life. Each secret is different, and only God knows them all. The telling of secrets is forbidden. They must be held close to the body all through life, because they are the only treasure. Without them, a man is a snail. You must never, Doria, squander the secret. You must, Sabatina, be careful. Do not tell.

Sabatina is one of the faces on the family stone. Her eyes look out from behind her glasses; her smile is quiet on the stone where Carmolina is watering the grave. Her quiet dead eyes smile at her sister Doria. She looks like Doria who is slicing the tomatoes open so that the seeds will spill into her hands, but Sabatina is slimmer, and she is dead. She does not have little whiskers on her chin.

Because Grandma Doria is the only member of the family who has little whiskers on her chin, like a goat. The whiskers float in the air when she talks to Carmolina, Carmolina stares at the whiskers, they are like the antennae of a gentle insect. She laughs from her stomach; Grandma's laugh has a wheeze in it. It is as though she uses up too much breath, laughing, and Carmolina is frightened of the wheeze, let God never take Grandma's breath away. Her skin and her teeth are yellow. When Grandma makes lunch, it is cheese on Italian bread, or tomatoes on Italian bread, or just Italian bread. They sit together at the Formica table in the kitchen, the whole world is burning from the heat of the summer, but coolness is on the table and Carmolina and Grandma talk.

When Great-Grandma Carmella died, she was sick a long time. Then Grandma was just a little girl and she sat with Great-Grandma who was dying, and everyone else was asleep. Deep in the night, Great-Grandma screamed and sat up in bed. Grandma saw a woman dressed in white crawl out from under the bed; she was a skeleton; she was Death; only Grandma saw it. Grandma screamed and ran out of the room; Great-Grandma died instantly. There is a mountain in Italy filled with candles. Some of the candles are tall and white. Some are short and sputter with the blue flame. Each person has his own candle. When he is born, the candle is lit; when the candle goes out, he dies. You can see this mountain, Carmolina, only in your dreams, but God will not let you see your own candle, even in a dream. If there is a mistake, and you see your own candle, you will die. This is how people die in their sleep. Great-Grandma, knock wood, did not die in her sleep.

Grandma keeps food on the back porch. She hangs long red peppers from the line with wooden clothespins. She keeps white lima beans in jars of salted water; she keeps them there until they grow juicy and bloated; then she salts them more and feeds them to Carmolina, who loves them. Grandma keeps trays of seeds from the pumpkin to dry in the window. When they dry, she salts them and cooks them in the oven until they are brown.

Grandma stands by the window on a hot summer day; the air is yellow outside. She is laughing, she is fat in her black cotton dress. The sun makes her little whiskers precise and obvious; they are white. She is smiling at the little girl called Carmolina and lifting the screen from the window. The sill is cement and the birds are nowhere to be seen, but Grandma breaks the day-old bread and places it on the cement sill. The sun is making her face beautiful. It is doing magic to her face, and here, in the corner where Carmolina sits, the shade is gray and peaceful and Grandma is standing in the spotlight of sun that someone is shining on her because she is feeding the birds. The old woman laughs, she throws bread out the window. The little girl Carmolina can not reach, the grandmother picks her up, holds her high against the sun so that she can feed the birds too. The circle of sun shines on the little girl, she is laughing, her grandmother owns the sun and is calling the birds:

In the sun the sand was hot like nothing else could be hot under her feet, so that her body did little jumping motions when she walked and she looked like she was flying, but she wasn't, she was walking on the hot sand that sent her up and jumping into the world. In the shade the sand turned cool. It was gray there and small things grew with quiet rocks and red lady bugs that flew in the air and landed on her skin, and all that made it cool. Carmolina left the land and went walking off into the water, and before the water began, the sand was ripples, it was rippled by the wind and was packed hard, like a bed sheet, and she went walking into the water, which was blue like an egg, which made long soft breaking sounds out there where it struck against the world, and spilled over. Standing in the sand, she could hear the water breaking far away, it sounded like thunder only it was sweet and she wanted to go out into it and she did, she ran out, she ran into the blue water and it was cold around her feet and the water was eating her body up, like a little rock or a fish, and she jumped up and down in it, she put her feet into the bottom of the water and she stood on the world and laughed. When she looked back at the sand, she could not find the blanket with her family on it, she could not see her grandmother with the lunch basket filled with sandwiches, she could not find the right colors in the sand, none of the colors were hers. She splashed her hands in the water and her toes dug themselves into the sand, it was packed hard, with little rocks in it, the rocks bit her feet, they were small mean bites under the water, like angry fish. Then a voice called her from the sand, one of the colors was moving, she watched the color float across the sand, it had no feet, but moved towards the water and was calling a sound like her name. Her toes dug into the water, something was coming to get her. The color came into the water, it was big like a tree, it called her name but she could not find its face and the water no longer was cold, the warm skin lifted down for her, in its hands she was warm, and she was lifted from the water and carried back to the sand. Then she rode the horses of the merry-go-round. The horses were painted red and gold and green and black, they had separate saddles and the reins were real leather, the bit was metal. She climbed up on the horses and she was as far above the ground as she would be on the second level of the monkey bars. The merry-go-round started slowly, it made slow circles of light in the hot summer air, and slowly she moved past her mother and father behind the mesh fences. They were small figures, smiling, and she smiled back at them as the horses moved past. Then they turned into quick little blurs of colors, whisked by air into pure colors which were smiling at her. And her horse rode up and down, it carried her up closer to the top of the merry-go-round where she could see the fantastic iron works which made the horse move, the iron bars pumping steadily up and down, making the horse dance. And the music of the merry-go-round was sad, it was the sound of the ball park where people stood straight and sang to the flag, where the wind was so gentle it was like a hand on your face, and sometimes you saw the moon over the grass until someone moved it and you had to watch the game instead. It was the sound of the men at the ball park whose voices called coke and hot dogs and beer and peanuts, it was the sound of the men running out there. The feel of the wooden horses between her legs was cool like the sand on the beach when the sun is going down and it's time to go home. It was the feeling of the fun house where everything happened and moved and exploded and disappeared in the half-light; it was the sound of her mother calling, calling to her where she drew chalk pictures into the bricks of the alley to come home, because the sun was going down and dinner was ready but she never wanted to leave because she loved it and this was the last day of summer before school started because tomorrow was September. And the music of the merry-go-round slowed down and the funny fat colors turned into her mother and father, and they were smiling because she was laughing so hard on the horses, and when she got off the ride, she couldn't find them for a minute because she was so dizzy and everyone looked like maybe they could be her mother and father and she looked back at the merry-go-round, at the horses, at the man who stood by the lever, the giant metal lever that made the horses move, and he was lighting a cigarette and his face was sweating, he was wearing a dirty t-shirt and one of his front teeth was missing. And the horses were hard like wood, like all the other rides in the amusement park, like the wood of the roller coaster where they strapped you in so you wouldn't fly out and bump into the clouds or blow across the ocean to the other side of the world. And the music of the merry-go-round was the sound of young voices calling at the beach to pick up the blankets and wrap up the sandwiches, to shake the sand out of your clothes and the rocks out of your shoes, to run to the water to wash the sand off, to splash your feet in the water, to watch a bird fly away, to do everything quickly.

Louise DeSalvo

From *Vertigo*

When I meet my future husband, in the summer of my sophomore year in college, my mother tells me to bring him home for dinner. I know she hopes my roving days are over; I know she thinks it's time for me to start looking for a husband, a man who will be a "good match." If I marry well, she tells me—someone with prospects, someone who will have a profession, someone who can support me well—all her sacrifices will have been worthwhile. I tell her not to worry, that I can take care of myself and support myself and that I don't need a man for any of these things. I say that what I want is an equal partner. Someone who wants the same things for me that I want for myself. She's not sure this is possible. But I think that I've found such a man in Ernie.

I don't want to take him home for dinner, though my mother invites him. I'm not stupid. I don't want to fuck up my chances with this guy. We get along. He knows about Sartre, Camus. We play bridge. Go to see foreign films together. He's Italian. He likes pizza. He's sexy. Spent most of his life in an Italian neighborhood in the Bronx like mine in Hoboken. He's going to be a doctor.

My mother persists.

"I'll cook him a nice meal," she tells me. I'm skeptical. I can't wait to see what this will be, what she'll manage. I tell her what not to make. I tell her not to make anything like liver or brains or kidneys or any of the other stuff I hate. She looks at me like she never makes these things, wouldn't think of making them.

"I'll come up with something," she says.

"Just make it good," I plead.

She wants the meal to be a big surprise, for me, too. She likes the sound of this guy I tell her I'm bringing home. He sounds much better to her than the other guys I've brought home, whom she hasn't liked, but whom she has welcomed.

Like the guy I told her was an auto mechanic.

He *wanted* to be an auto mechanic, but, really, he pumped gas. He drove a Ford that was rotting, which he was trying, but failing, to fix up. She told me she was afraid that one day the two of us would drop through the bottom of his car onto the roadway. I knew there was little chance of that happening. We never went anywhere, didn't want to go anywhere. We only drove as far as a deserted street by the railroad tracks in our hometown so we could make out. We had very little to say to one another. No matter. He was sexy, he turned me on, I liked his body, and that was enough.

After we broke up, when I asked my mother why she was so nice to him, though she didn't think he was suitable, she said, "I thought you read *Romeo and Juliet* in high school? If you didn't read it, read it now. If you read it, read it again." I got the message.

Coming between us would have sealed our love, turned it fatal. My mother wanted better for me. By not standing in the way of my loving this boy, my mother was standing in the way of my loving him.

On the night that I bring Ernie DeSalvo to my parents' home for the first time, my mother serves the best meal I've ever eaten in that household.

A lovely consommé for the first course. Little triangles of crisp toast on the side. (Not burnt.)

Broiled lobster tails (lobster tails!) for the main course. Sprinkled with paprika so they have a nice color. Served with double-baked potatoes (potatoes, baked, their insides taken out and mashed with butter and cream, then put back into the potato skins, and baked again) and Le Sueur tender tiny peas (a premium brand my mother has never bought before).

For dessert, Indian pudding with vanilla ice cream (expensive brand). Somehow, my mother has learned it's Ernie's favorite dessert.

At first, I'm happy that my mother has tried to please my new boyfriend. But then I'm not. I'm furious. To me, this now seems an even worse betrayal than if she had served him what I call "the usual garbage."

This is a wonderful dinner, beautifully conceived, executed, and served, at the dining room table, on china, with crystal and silver, on one of my grandmother's crocheted tablecloths.

To me, this meal means that my mother knows what's good, and that she has known what's good all along. She just hasn't cooked what she knows is good for me, though she's willing to cook it for this young man who isn't even one of the family. At least not yet.

I don't know what to do. I want to make a scene. Tell my mother off. Ask her why she doesn't always cook like this. Why, for him, and not for me?

But I know better. I don't want to scare this guy off. I don't want to show him how bitter, mean, and sarcastic I can be. How I try to punish my parents with my sharp tongue. How I try to get back at them. For what? For everything.

I control myself. But clearly I am not happy and my mother, who has tried so hard to cook this excellent meal for me, can't figure out what she's done to get me so upset this time.

Now, if I could travel through time, and do this night all over, I would do it differently.

I would look across the table at my mother. I would see the tremendous effort it took her to cook this dinner. I would remember how afraid she was of knives, of fire, how she was always cutting herself, or burning herself by accident, and how that would make cutting, chopping, cooking so hard for her. I would see how food was a problem.

I would remember how she got herself dressed, how she (who didn't leave the house unless she absolutely had to) got herself out of the house early this morning. How she walked to the market, chose the ingredients, so carefully. How she carried them up the big hill.

I would remember that she spent the day preparing, making sure that everything was perfect. Perfect for the young man she thought might make a suitable husband for her troublesome daughter who had a way of bringing the most unsuitable young men home, men who couldn't or wouldn't give her a good life.

If I could do this night over, I would remember these things and I would look across the table at my mother and say, Thank you. Thank you very, very much.

From *Breathless*

September 30, 1996

When I ask myself who I want to be now, I see myself as a woman who can be free to mourn my sister. I haven't realized that I've never grieved for her. I start to cry for her and can't stop. I think that something about the way my breath catches when I can't take in a breath has to do with how my sister died. She stopped her breath by hanging herself.

I will always wonder what happened to her and what made her kill herself. Perhaps I really have felt guilt these past years for being unable to stop her. My breathing disorder—the mucus that blocks my breath—

might be connected to all those tears I haven't shed for her, all the tears I've held inside.

After she died, I remember living my life as if nothing had happened. But I soon broke out in gigantic hives. And nearly lost my breath, nearly fainted, often.

Jill killed herself about ten years ago. She was almost thirty-seven. And I think the acute stage of my asthma started then, though I am certain that I've had it since I was a girl. I remember being sick in the summers, when it was humid. I remember coughing uncontrollably during the winters, when I breathed in cold air, and having long bouts of what the doctors called "chronic bronchitis" several times a year throughout my life. And, yes, since her death, I have gotten sick each year (though never as severely as this past year), and at the same time of year as she killed herself.

I want to remember her, to remember us together, as children, heads bent over some small task that pleases us both, like cutting out clothes for the paper dolls we kept in shoe boxes covered with shiny gold paper. I want to imagine us breathing together. Effortlessly. In synchrony.

A friend asks, "Do you think your asthma flared after your sister's death as a way of keeping you connected to her?"

My first impulse is to say no, emphatically, no. But I know that if *I* heard my own story, it is the conclusion I would inevitably come to.

My sister and I lived our lives in what was to me an all-too-close proximity. When I was a child, my mother consigned my sister to my care, and, at first, I hovered over her, unsuccessfully trying to keep her out of harm's way. Then later, when I was a teenager, and too old, I thought, to have a shadow sister, I tried to ignore her and deliberately outpaced her as she trotted unhappily after me. At seven, ten, thirteen, fifteen, I felt too young to be someone's mother.

My most complicated memories of Jill are those of sharing a bed with her from when I was seven until I left to marry. Though four years separated us, I often told friends that, in sharing that bed, we became twins, *ex utero.* There was something comforting, and troubling, in her closeness, in our togetherness. I wanted my own bed, my own space; yet I wasn't comfortable unless she was near, couldn't fall off to sleep until after she had.

I made elaborate rules for how she had to behave in bed if I were to continue to tolerate her existence. (In truth, I had no choice. We shared the double bed my mother had bought to save money. No matter how much I protested, there would never be twin beds, and it never occurred to me to sleep on the floor.) She had to sleep with her back to me, so that I wouldn't have to breathe the air she exhaled. She couldn't hog the covers, cross over to my side, or raise her legs (which made air pockets).

So, did my asthma flare as a way of keeping me bound to my sister beyond her death? And, yes, I must answer, to my friend, and to myself, yes, as, in memory, I see myself reach across our bed to pull the covers over my sister's slender shoulders during her fitful sleep, turn my back to her, and try to relax, as I listen to make sure she is still breathing, listen to make sure she is still alive.

Carole DeSanti

From *Ars Longa, Vita brevis?*

One evening in the year 2000, near the beginning of my fourth decade of insistence (despite my name, appearance, and general affinities) that I was *not* of Italian descent; in other words, sticking firm to the story I had been told as a child, my father called with some news. A distant relative had turned up, wanting to regain contact with our family.

"What kind of relative?"

"Let's see, it would be my father's brother from the New York branch of the family."

"Your uncle?"

"No, his son."

"Your cousin, then?"

"That must be why I call him *cugino, campagno.*"

"You do?"

My dad, with his dark, Latin looks and surname terminating in a vowel, had never hesitated to claim an Italian ancestry, if his luck seemed to blow that way, but the circumstance had never before arisen with anyone even remotely related to us. ". . . What New York branch?"

Mine has always been a family of silences; of contradictory anecdotes and gray areas; stock answers lacking in the kind of nuance where truth might lie. Despite my father's occasional theatrics with pasta and pepperoni, his occasional, and sudden, proficiencies in the spinning of spaghetti on a fork, the available evidence was that he had grown up speaking Croatian and eating cabbage and *kolachi;* with relatives dwelling not under Italy's hot blue skies but behind that rainy shroud known during my childhood as "the Iron Curtain."

When I tell the story I have always believed about my ethnic background and my name—that the *c* at the end of the original, "true," and pure Croatian name "Desantic" had somehow been unfastened by a careless clerk at an immigration desk and never retrieved—Italian friends have listened tolerantly, or impatiently, and generally taken me on as one of their own. The missing *c* has resulted in a gentle rain of generous, Italian-friendly acts: leaking pipes fixed over a holiday weekend; a locksmith materializing in the middle of the night; the assuaging of troubles over *calamari fritti* and red wine in Boston's North End. It was an Italian-American friend who set me up for my first job interview out of college and lent me the clothes to wear to it; another, who at a dire time in the New York real estate market and in my personal finances, passed me the name of a particular, *neighborhood* broker: no questions asked; no pay stubs or credit searches—terra firma, at last, in a jewel box Brooklyn apartment.

Favors based on the fiction of my name were pure lagniappe; and certainly a contrast to what seemed to be the fierce estrangements of the Slav clan: an uncle who was not welcome in my grandparents' house; cousins who resented one another; property that was a cause for jealousy between siblings. In the undertones of my relatives' discussions were the Balkan topographies of envy and blame nurtured and handed down through the generations and even imported, whole cloth, to the land of the free. It became clearer, a few years into adult life, why my father occasionally sought sanctuary in an Italian inflection.

A few days after our conversation, a sheaf of computer printouts arrived in the mail: the documents, a work-in-progress compiled by the genealogically inclined cousin, tracing the progress of our ancestral lineage. Pages for recent generations reflected intermarriages between Slavs and Italians, the branching off of surnames ending in *c* or *ch;* but not too far back, I found myself not in the deepest interior of the Balkans, as I'd always assumed—but, instead, having traveled back through time in the geographically opposite direction, in Venice.

"Just think how lucky you are that it's not the other way around," said a Japanese-American friend, a hybrid himself, with his deeply Asian looks and a Norwegian surname. "To think you've been Italian all this time, only to have to accept your true *Croatian* roots. Think: Florentine paper. Shopping for shoes in Rome. The Amalfi Coast. And Venice! What better place to be from than Venice? It's time to get rid of that Balkan chill. That, well, you know, *Croatian* quality."

"Do I have a Balkan chill?"

"It's the . . . *sprezzatura* you need. You need to get out and embrace the Italian side."

My tourist's dictionary didn't list the word.

". . . *Spruzzare,* to spray; *sprizzare,* to spurt, as in to be bursting with health, or *speranza,* hope, or *soppresso,* to suppress, delete, do away with?"

"More like, the Italian *je ne sais quoi.* That *joie de vivre. Whatever.*"

"Rent *The Sopranos,*" another friend advised. "You can get all the back episodes."

It was in the early 1700s, as I learned, that our hybrid ancestry was born. The first known DeSanti—who was a *Dessanti,* Mariano—migrated from Venice across the shallow waters of the Gulf to the Istrian Peninsula. He left the city of Vivaldi and Canaletto; a center of printing and publishing, an astonishing rate of divorce and various exotic social structures—to a life on the wild, bora-swept rocky spine of an Adriatic island. In so doing he did not cross any national border at all, but remained securely within the Republic. Istria and its fringe of islands had been a part of the Venetian lands for centuries, through the Middle Ages and the Renaissance, and at the height of Venice's prosperity as a port, when its trade routes threaded down the Dalmatian coast. The areas were fundamentally linked: the magnificence of Venice's architecture was built on Istrian pine pilings and saltwater sturdy Istrian limestone; my ancestor traveled to a place of ancient Roman bridges, lions rampant, and his own language. But his new world was closely bounded by complicating influences—to the north, the Hapsburg Empire; to the south, the Ottoman. And the peninsula neighbored Croatia, lands inhabited by the Croat people since A.D. 600.

According to my historical atlas, the cusp of land that is Istria, and its islands, changed hands several times over the course of the Dessanti/DeSanti generations—as it was taken sequentially by Napoleon, then by the Hapsburg Empire; acquired by the Kingdom of Italy after the First World War, then ceded to Yugoslavia after the Second. Jan Morris writes, in *Trieste and the Meaning of Nowhere,* "[Istria] has been ruled in its time, in one part or another, by Romans, Byzantines, Franks, Venetians, and Austrians. Bavarian Counts and Aquilean Patriarchs have lorded it there. . . . It has been threatened in its time by Ostrogoths, Lombards,

Genoese, impious Turks and sinister Uskoks from Senj." In other words, in Istria, land of hybrids, the only political constant has been change; although the life of the place—craggy rocks, shipping, olives, and sheep— seems to have remained relatively constant, at least through the early years of the twentieth century.

Five generations after Mariano's relocation, when my grandfather was born, his country was called Austro-Hungary, even though his name was André and he considered himself Italian; because of the Croat migrations to the island, he spoke Croatian as well. Later, in the United States, somewhere under the acrid, steel-orange skies between Pittsburgh and Youngstown, Ohio, he took a pure-blooded Croatian woman as his wife; and it must have seemed a sympathetic union.

"So, Dad, about the Italian side of the family," I began another telephone conversation, still puzzled about the story of the missing *c*. From the available genealogy, it seemed that instead of a *c* at the end of our supposedly Croatian name, the itinerant consonant was, instead, an *s* and the spelling *Dessanti* seemed to carry with it some of the *sprezzatura* of which I was now in pursuit. In fact, I was even considering the idea of reverting to the earlier spelling, a symbolic act that might allow the repatriation of some of my lost Italian qualities, which I had recently come to associate with good luck and *joie de vivre,* among other positives. I was ready to abandon the Croat side of things altogether, in fact. "If the name was originally Venetian, there was never a *c,* and never a mistake—?"

"A mistake?"

"An error at immigration . . . ?"

Whatever the Balkan mysteries of my father's family, I had always suspected that my grandmother's role in them was not benign. But she did not cultivate language or closeness with her grandchildren. If she knew any English, she never allowed a word of it to pass her lips; on our pilgrimages to that house, we took only wrapped diabetic candies; little squares too unappealing even to consider pilfering from the box, and, in return, she set out overboiled chickens and kielbasas on a dining room table—the same dishes, in the same places, every time. Her energies were reserved for long diatribes in her mother tongue, delivered to my father with her back turned toward the room, as she faced the kitchen sink.

. . . But as a younger woman, my father tells me now, his mother was proud and exacting, a posture I can see clearly when I look, now, at her wedding portrait. With her Zagreb education, fiery blue eyes, and tastes that set her apart from her fellow immigrant neighbors, she was the most sophisticated, and the only literate, woman on her block. Conversant in all the Slav dialects, Hungarian, and German, she wrote letters for everyone in the community. But her children were born over the course of the 1920s, and Depression-era Youngstown became a long, hard, broken promise. My grandmother soon realized that what paved the streets of the midwestern United States wasn't gold, but dust from the mills, and what she had to put on the table for a husband and four children was less than she had had growing up as a girl in Prebic, Croatia. And, so, like many women before and after, with nothing within her grasp but the power of narrative, she seized upon the murkiness of history, and initiated the story of the "mistake," the fiction of the missing *c*—a story that suited many conditions, not only her ethnic purity and her Croatian pride, but also the carelessness, the betrayal, of the America for which she had had such great hopes. There, too, the battle lines of my grandparents' marriage were also drawn: the tongue spoken in the household was Croatian; so, too, was the church the family attended. The children, two boys and two girls, would be Croatian-raised on Croatian myths: purity, nationalism, and the Catholic faith. But my grandfather, now dubbed a "Dalmatian" by his wife (a term, to her, of impurity, although to me it carries endearing qualities of spotted-ness), ended it there: for himself, he bought grapes from the back of a truck and kept barrels in the cellar; turned the Croatian priest away at the door, spoke English and Italian, and never allowed the *c* at the end of the name.

Pure Slav defiance and loyalty; language, and fiction, in other words, were my grandmother's refuges in life.

". . . I saw a photograph," says my father, now—mentioning it for the second or third time. His cousin, who had come to Cleveland to visit, and talk DeSanti ancestry, had shown it to him. And he described it: a picture of a man who looked exactly, surprisingly, incredibly, like his own father; who could have been his twin, even down to the thumbs, the ones my dad used to reach up and hang on to, when he was knee-high. And I remember traveling through Italy, once, myself and experiencing the odd, almost bodily sensation of the older men who looked like my own father, and my grandfather—drove like the two of them, with an elbow out the window, head tilted; a kind of style, perhaps a driving *sprezzatura*. "I loved my dad," my father says, now.

The Cleveland to which my own parents migrated after the Second World War, and in which I grew up in the 1960s and 1970s, was divided by East and West, Catholic and Protestant, black and white. The East Side had its rolling lawns, horse farms, private schools, and, later, sprawling malls with marble and fountains. On the West Side were the working-class Poles and Slavs, Greeks and Italians, all bunkered down in discrete neighborhoods amidst roofed shopping strips. Ethnic nuances could be shed, in the right kind of neighborhood; or lost amidst the other tensions of a city split around money, religion, and, especially, race. No road connected Cleveland's two halves, at that time; between East and West was a no-man's-land, an area referred to by my father as the "Gaza Strip," which meant, and not only to him, slums, blacks, riots, and crime. We lived on the West Side, and every other area of the city was forbidden, cordoned off by class, ethnic superstition, or fear. My father adapted himself to Cleveland's multiethnic terrain, using his own hybrid attributes deliberately, opportunistically; but never wholeheartedly. In so doing he did not consider himself "confused," as I once heard a half-Slav, half-Italian describe himself: just adaptive. But the only acceptable journey from our home, for some years, was the weekend trip down a long, gray stretch of highway to visit my grandparents, where life seemed spent out, like boiled cabbage leaves; or bare plaster walls: like a long argument lost by everyone, in the end.

A true American, I have always turned away from what is difficult to look upon. The Yugoslavian wars of my adult years; the feuds of my incomprehensible relatives. The parched, arid terrain of the divided Cleveland of my childhood, and the tensions between my own parents that gradually increased. As I study the genealogical sheets, trace the comings and goings, connections, marriages, flights and resettlings of eight generations, it raises, more than anything else, the question of refuge: where, or to what, we have each turned, to find a safe place.

My distant ancestor, perhaps, sought a retreat from the eroding, carnivalesque Venice of his day on the wild and beautiful Adriatic coast. Built a new home, scratched it from the hills and bred sheep and several generations of daughters and sons. My father's mother, disappointed in her destiny, sought sanctuary in her language, in her "pure" Croatian heritage; in a confirming fiction about her married name. My parents, after the war, looked for their shelter in the suburbs, in the uniformities of the middle class; and in giving their own children an education meant to inoculate against ethnic distress. I, in turn, tried to escape the rifts and difficulties of my family, sought my own refuge in cities far from the one in which I grew up: making my home not in family and ethnicity but in career, friends; what I would consider elected affinities. . . . Only to be brought back, in the years 2000, 2001, to the contradictions of blood, of character, and to my own biases.

A nation of hybrids, our minds and hearts seem not yet up to the task of truly living in the global world we have been so instrumental in creating: even within our own families, we still seem to long for the closed category; to consecrate what is easily identified—easily fearing the "other;" using our biases, often, like truncheons over the backs of what, and whom, we do not understand. Life just seems too short. Too short, even to begin to comprehend the complexities of our own histories, and what they might portend. •

Acknowledgments to Fiorenzo Dessanti for the genealogical information in this piece.

Rachel Guido deVries

From *Tender Warriors*

He never stopped reaching across the bed for Josie. Two years after her death, two years of sleeping alone night after night, he woke in the middle of foggy dreams, or at the light of sunrise, and reached for her. Over the years Dominic had been, in his own way, faithful to his wife. He'd been to bed with other women but always returned home before daylight, always began the day with Josie. He had to admit that after her death the thought that he could now spend the night, all night, with whomever he chose had crossed his mind. But he couldn't.

He had tried to a couple of times, but always, just before falling asleep, he would see Josie. He could see her small and delicate frame sleeping curled slightly in a pale blue nightgown, her hand tucked just under her chin as though she had fallen asleep wondering, her hair mussed and wispy on the pillow. Dominic, when he had these flashes of Josephine, saw them from changing times during their forty-year marriage. Josie on their wedding night honeymooning in New York City, wearing a white silky nightgown, her black hair thick and long and loose against his chest. He remembered her being both timid and bold at once. Josie, when he first saw her months after Rosie was born, falling asleep with the baby held against her breast. Josie getting up at 3:00 a.m. when he'd walk in, fixing him eggs in the middle of the night. Josie, sleepy and complacent, giving him her quiet company despite his wanderings.

Dominic would see his Josie, and a small and tender and decisive tug would win in his chest. It was love. He never felt guilt making him move. If in fact it had been guilt, he probably would have stayed; for he was an impulsive and passionate man who followed always what he knew was true for him, despite the consequences. Always at night what he felt was the tenderest love for Josie, and he longed for the feel of her familiar body next to him. So he had kept his habit, even after her death, of returning to their bed with its blue satin bedspread, to their room, their wedding photographs, and Josie's scented presence. When the kids had come to take her clothes and belongings, Dominic had made them leave the Blue Grass perfume, a couple of her nightgowns, and their photographs. In this way he kept her close to him.

Dominic knew he had not made life easy for Josie and that she stuck by him despite it. The early years of their marriage, before he left for the war, had been tense. There was never enough money, and even then he was running around with other women. They lived with his mother, Filomena, a strong-willed, iron-fisted matriarch, whom Dominic adored. Filomena took to Josephine the way she did to all who were not members of her immediate family: she was intimidating and aloof, and she made Josie more timid than she already was by nature. If she occasionally allowed Josie to cook, she always criticized the results. She never stopped letting Josephine know that it was she, Filomena, who best understood Dominic. Josie did not thrive there, but when she brought it up with Dominic, he would fly into a rage. If she hated his mother, he would say, that was her problem. He was staying. They didn't have enough money for their own place, and no, of course Josie could not work so they could have enough money.

Dominic knew that Josie was right, knew they should move to their own place, but nothing in him was prepared to defy his mother and leave. She was a saint to him. She had raised seven kids as good as alone. His father, Pasquale, had been a rough and lazy man who worked occasionally and used Filomena to vent his outrage and lust. Nothing more. By the time Dominic was in grammar school, Pasquale was almost always drunk and hostile. When he died, Dominic, at seventeen, was relieved. He was the baby of the family, and only one sister, Theresa, was at home. Until he married Josie, his life had been calm and well cared for by his mother and sister. When Josie came into the household, Theresa was married and living with her husband. There sprang up between the two women in his life a tension and competition he was unready for. His solution was to throw up his hands and turn it into a fight with Josie: she had no respect, he'd say. What would she do if her mother were still alive? There was simply no way that Dominic could willfully leave his mother's house.

This situation might have gone on and on, but in November of 1942 Dominic enlisted in the army, the one sure way he could leave his

mother's house and the situation within it without having to choose between his mother and his wife. Josie, of course, had to stay there with
Filomena. Had it not been for Dominic's finally allowing her to get a
job at the telephone company—after all, it was wartime—Josie would
have suffered even more. The problem of moving into their own place
was solved for the moment. Dominic didn't know if he'd come back at
all by the time the whole thing was over.

He returned a few times on leaves, twice in close succession, and
the second of these two visits was to be the last before he was shipped
overseas. It was December 1943, and it was the time of two events that
would change things forever for Dominic and Josie. On their fourth
wedding anniversary, December 12, Josie told Dominic she was pregnant; the baby was due in August. Dominic felt a motion around his
heart, as though a sparrow were fluttering its wings. It was one of his
first sensations of tenderness, and it was directed toward both Josie and
their baby, and even toward himself for his part in this. Josie was proud
and nervous, her olive skin flushed slightly with the news. Dominic had
stared at her, finding it hard to believe that his little Josie, looking skinny
and delicate to him just then, was pregnant, and finding it harder to believe that he would almost certainly not be able to be home when the
baby was born.

He shipped out just after Christmas and was sent first to France and
later to India. He was there when the second event took place: on
March 14, 1944, Filomena died suddenly. Dominic would always remember that he could not be at two of the most important occurrences
in his life. He blamed the army for this, and felt, afterwards, that the
army owed him something for it. In August of that same year, Dominic's
and Josephine's first child was born, and he was still in India flying surveillance missions. He did not learn of Rosie's birth till nearly a month
after it happened. The news came in a letter from Josie with a picture of
the baby. She was a tiny thing with a lot of black hair combed up like a
rooster's and with Josie's large dark eyes looking up at him. Josie had
written across the photo: "To Daddy, from your daughter Rosie. Hurry
home, I love you."

But he did not get home until just after VJ Day, in October 1945.
Rose was fourteen months old, and Dominic was filled with hope and
excitement about his life.

That excitement was soon to include a touch of bitterness, a resentment, small at first but growing. Before the war, Dominic had been
used to having two women cater to him, and now Josie, in charge of the
big house Dominic and his family had grown up in, and a devoted
mother to Rosie, did not always have the time to baby her husband.

Dominic saw this as neglect, as Josie not being as good a wife and mother as his mother had been. He took to throwing this up to her whenever they argued, a fact that brought out the stubbornness in Josie. Powerless in the world beyond her home, and steeped in the role she knew as well as breathing, being the good Italian wife—docile and attentive, mostly silent, understanding and forgiving—she found the one way to rebel against Dominic's tirades. Often she forgot to strain the sauce, knowing the seeds drove him crazy; or she'd iron everything except his handkerchiefs; or she mismatched socks. If she really wanted to get to him, she would leave the bathroom uncleaned for days on end, watching the mold creep up between and around the tiles, insidious, commiserating.

But she was also there, tender and vulnerable to him. That she loved him deeply was clear, even in the passion of their arguments. To Dominic she was the one innocent thing that was only his. Even Rose, he knew, would eventually grow away from them. But Josie was his light. She understood what no one remotely guessed about Dominic De-Marco: his vulnerability, his alarm in and at the world, his defensiveness about being Italian. This from years of being tormented and teased by calls of *greaseball* or *guinea,* accused of being dirty or lazy, and from an acute memory of the time he'd been fired from a job as a stock boy, long before the war. He was sixteen, working at the five and dime—twelve, fourteen, sometimes sixteen hours a day. He worked hard and was honest. After three months he had asked about a promotion, and the manager fired him on the spot, telling him, "You're a *wop,* DeMarco, don't forget it." He hadn't.

To the rest of the world, Dominic DeMarco was a tough guy, a guy who would do anything for you unless you crossed him, a guy who always had his suits tailor-made and flashed money when he had it—or he wasn't around—a guy with a very short fuse and a tendency to fist fight. He worked construction for awhile, booked numbers and horses for years, quit construction to book full time, and quit that a few years after the kids were all out of high school. He had run a small trucking firm ever since with two of his brothers, called ADS Trucking Co., for Anthony, Dominic, and Salvatore. Dominic was pleased with their outfit; for even though he was in his forties when the company was formed, it showed him that Tony and Sal finally accepted him. As the baby of the family, and as his mother's pet, he had always been seen as the kid, in need of protection. Perhaps to change this image, Dominic had taken to fighting as a boy, a taste he never abandoned, and to mouthing off to anyone who came close to rubbing him the wrong way. He was raised to believe that the only way to get respect in the world was to wield power, to be tough *and* smooth. He watched his brothers, practiced, and learned well.

In 1946 Lorraine was born. Josie had been initially upset with the pregnancy. She wanted time, a little time for herself before having another baby, and the months of carrying Lorraine were difficult for her. She didn't feel well. Rose was two and into everything, and Dominic was rarely around. But along Lorraine had come, a baby as unlike her sister as was possible. Rose had slept through the night almost from the start; Lorraine was colicky and awoke several times during the night until she was nearly a year old. And then she became a solitary little girl— reticent, easygoing to a fault. Rose was independent, talked constantly, and as she got older was always in fights, often to protect her kid sister. If Lorraine had been a boy, that might have been it with the DeMarcos, but Dominic wanted a son fiercely, a son to take his part in the household of women, a son who would play football the way Dominic had always wanted to, a son with flash and pizzazz with girls: his son. And in 1954 Josie gave birth to Dominic, Jr., and they called him Sonny.

He was not the son Dominic anticipated, nor the one he wanted. Unable to see Sonny for what he was, Dominic tried relentlessly over the years to change Sonny into a copy of himself. It was not that Dominic didn't love his son. He was simply unable to understand that what he passed on to each of his children was a passion for living life that matched his own, but in a different way in each of them. In short, he wanted himself all over again, particularly in Sonny, a common enough desire in a father, but it became distorted in Dominic. He never let them grow into themselves. He never stopped resenting each of them just a little because they wouldn't live their lives the way *he* thought they should. Anything they did that he opposed he took as a sign of their lack of love and respect. And Sonny's illnesses all through his life, his self-consciousness instead of cockiness, made Dominic nervous. It was unfamiliar to him, and he didn't understand.

When both of the girls left home, Dominic felt the bitterness in him sharpen. Sonny stayed longer than his sisters, but after Josie died, Dominic's need for his son was profound. Unable to express this need, this love (as he had always been unable to express the tenderness in him with anyone except Josie), he turned to riding Sonny's ass about a dozen little things, the way he'd always done. Without Josie to tone Dominic down and stand up for Sonny, Sonny could take no more. He finally lost his temper, a temper he had chewed and swallowed and taken to bed with him for more nights than should have been possible. They had fought plenty before, but in the fight that made Sonny leave home last April, Dominic had raised his hand to strike Sonny, and Sonny, at twenty-six, had at last had enough. He drew back his own fist and punched his father in the mouth, screaming his outrage saved up all these years, screaming in that high-pitched tone his voice took on when he was upset (a detail which infuriated Dominic), screaming and crying and wishing desperately for his mother. His control shot, his head pounding, he had packed a duffle bag of clothes and ran from the house, Dominic screaming all the while: "Get out you miserable son of a bitch. Get out, get out, and don't ever come back." It was the "don't ever come back" that both he and Sonny would remember.

Now it was early November, and Dominic was alone. He woke this morning, a few days before the two-year anniversary of his wife's death, feeling lonely for his Josie and for his kids, pitying himself a bit for how alone he was this day, and thinking hard about his son. For the last couple of weeks he couldn't get the kid off his mind. Sonny had never been away from home before, and Dominic missed him. Lately he had also missed Josie fiercely. He knew that she was angry with him for what had happened between him and Sonny. He rose, thinking, "Okay, Josephine, okay. I'll try to find him. I'll call Rosie. But he can't come home. Unless he says he's sorry. Got no respect."

Pietro di Donato

From *Christ in Concrete*

"Lay brick! Lay brick! Lay brick!" shouted Black Mike while the laborers, carpenters, bricklayers, plumbers and other crafts meowed, booed, made train and boat noises, razzed and shouted "Shuddup Goddem yuh!" Nazone jumped off the scaffold, threatened Yellow-Fever with his trowel, took Paul back up on the scaffold with him; and Yellow-Fever bit both his hands in groaning rage. . . . The Lucy gestured to no one in particular and questioned, "May a gentleman bricklayer learn what is happening here?"

And laying bricks, he reflected aloud, "What imbroglio. What fracas. What a dung-a-fying of the noble Italian blood . . . Pa-poo e' coo-coo."

With how much money will I surprise mother Annunziata . . . how much money will the corporation give me . . . how much am I worth?

One bricklayer said he was worth four dollars a day, another, five, another said four and one-half, and Paul pushed himself into mortar and brick knowing how sweet would be the bread his flesh had earned, how mother and children would glorify with their appetites the good meat and fruit, how dear would be the weekend rest.

Saturday morning.

He could not possibly pause long enough to breathe normally. Job that day would never be forgotten: the day when Job would first give its holy communion of freedom. One-on-two-one-on-two-bend-scoop-swing-spread-tap-clip—and bend on for one-on-two—and now Job was no longer a bewildering corridor which one visited by chance and did not realize. Job was establishing itself in gray of stony joint and red of clayey brick, in smell of men's gray bones and wet red flesh.

Job was becoming a familiar being through aches and hours, plumb and level. Job was a new sense which brought excitement of men and steel and stone. Job was a game, a race, a play in which all were muscular actors serious from whistle to whistle, and he was one of them. It was pay-day, and in a few hours pay-check would sign short-short armistice. It was war for living, and Paul was a soldier. It was not as in marbles where he played for fun, it was men's siege against a hunger that traveled swiftly, against an enemy inherited.

Giovanni Rinaldi mumbled hours and figures, and Black Mike with cemented fingers thumbed dollars and stuck them into envelopes.

Yellow-Fever with stupid down-set lips of importance awkwardly handed out the envelopes. The men did not figure out their hours. They accepted, and hoped Rinaldi had blundered and put in five or ten dollars too much. The men were now smiling like foolish girls, and pleased. There were no more enemies, all were friends and Job a wonderful thing. They had received their money, all but Paul who stood alone with his jumping heart outside the shed.

"Haven't you figured something for Paulie?"

"Who?"

"The boy, Paulie."

"Oh, yes, yes the boy. . . . What are we to do?"

"What value has he? He throws himself well . . ."

"It is not a fact of value. . . . And if we get into trouble?"

"Perhaps a serious complaint—from a trouble-making American, or jealousy-blinded paesan. We must watch ourselves, I say."

"Yes, we have woes of our own in abundance."

Giovanni Rinaldi called Paul in and handed an envelope to Yellow-Fever who handed it to Paul. He said thank you and it sounded as though he had said it in a foreign tongue. Everything seemed rushed and indistinct for he did not know what to do with the envelope clutched in his hand. Behind the shed alone he was afraid to open the envelope. Why was it so light and thin? Why did the corporation, so set and explosive, turn as though hands had pushed their heads down and around from him? When he finally opened the envelope he saw one papery five-dollar bill.

He ran through Job and came out the back way—to walk home alone. *Why why whywhy?* had they given him only five dollars? What could mother Annunziata and the children do with five dollars? What had he failed to do . . . ?

Saturday afternoon and the restless void and flesh of Job momentum that at home feels not at home and longs for the movement of wall and scaffold. Saturday afternoon in the pallsome fast world of Tenement, and Job's bruised rough fingers and crying spine remaining close. Saturday afternoon and Annunziata before the crucifixed Christ, votive light and glassed-in Virgin, kissing in tears the papery envelope. . . . Guard him, my Lord, guard him . . .

Sunday morning Annunziata and Paul visited Luigi. At first sight he looked better than usual, but he was flushed with fever. He followed raptly what Paul recounted of Job, and on hearing that they had given him five dollars he exclaimed, "They have spit into the hands of a boy. The son of the master who taught them the art and gave them the bread of work when there was none to be had, they have maltreated. They have bruted, widow's boy and one's kind. O men men you are cowardly blind and put to shame by children . . ."

Monday morning.

And men's tinged faces of spilled lust and breaths of undigested meat spaghetti wine garlic and sour tobacco lingerings and sleepy acid expression and ungraceful set of disconcerted lips and mean jerking of legs and hunched shoulders and slight smell of abused flesh and silence as pasty chill as morning . . . then . . . whistle and forced stilted push of bone-flesh into red-grays with voices of men and Job organizing out of the cold into action.

On top of the piano and facing the Cripple directly was a large plaster Indian chieftain's head; and in disarray beside it were dirty kewpie dolls with torn spangles, starfish and dusty photographs. Above and behind the Cripple was a lithograph in heavy colors of an Indian maiden atop a mountain peak, her arms upspread toward a dazzling pink heaven. The room was close and musty, and rankly disinfected with chloride. The phonograph stuck and kept repeating:

"Calling you-ooo-hoo—calling you-ooo-hooo"

The Cripple turned it off.

"Lemme have your wedding ring, missus."

When she received it she fitted it onto her left index finger, dropped the rose in her lap and began revolving the ring with the fingers of her right hand. Her hands were round, full, hard, the short thick fingers running off to thin bony ends.

She began straining her entire being and shut her eyes fast. Her face reddened and perspiration formed about her lips. Annunziata and Paul felt uneasy. She stopped rocking and her right hand went up to her forehead.

"There's a voice from the spirit woild . . ."

Annunziata and Paul reached forward.

She rocked once more.

"It's the voice of a woman. An old woman. It seems to me she passed away in the old country—some time ago. She's saying something. And it's in the Eyetalyun language."

The elevated trains went by. She opened her eyes and stared at the anxious and slightly perplexed Annunziata.

"This party reaching out from the spirit woild is on your mother's side."

Paul looked inquiringly to his mother. And Annunziata was pushing herself terribly to understand the difficult American tongue. Who could it be? Why do I not know? Why am I so stupid when the spirit world wishes to communicate with me?

"Wait!" requested the Cripple. She fell back again into the rocker and shut her eyes. She swayed her head about.

"There's interference—there's another party trying to push this old woman—he's trying to force his way through the spirit woild—he's a man—how he pushes!"

She shuddered forcibly. She ceased rocking and leaned forward as though seized with cramps, and clutched her great bulging throat.

"Oh how strong he's comin' in. He's so eager!"

Annunziata and Paul clasped each other's hands and held their breaths.

The Cripple stiffened, choked and writhed.

"My God in Heaven—he's so anxious to break through and embrace you! He must have died not so long ago because he's trying to reach out to you from the spirit woild before his time. . . . The force is grippin' my neck and paralyzin' me! Now tell me, who is this man that passed away not long ago? He must be very dear and lovin' to you. I get a pitcher of him. He's about your age and is Eyetalyun and looks so healthy with dark hair and red cheeks and dark beautiful eyes—" She reeled as though hit. "Oh God, I've gotta use all my strength to receive him—I can't rest—he won't stop . . . He reaches right out from the spirit woild with his arms open wide and a great big smile on his face—and he says—he says . . . He's comin' so strong, I can hardly make it out—"

The door opened and Florine stuck her head into the room.

"Momma, Margie's actin' like a reg'lar bitch, and there's people out here!"

The Cripple, with her eyes shut tight, and straining, waved away in Florine's direction. She shuddered violently, and nodded to some distant realm that she was heeding. Her face broke out in kindly smile and enjoyment.

"He says, I kiss my wife and children—"

Annunziata softly cried: "Geremio!" She reached out from her living world and up to the spirit world.

The Cripple opened her eyes and compassionately permitted Annunziata and Paul to rejoice and weep.

"He stands before me and says to me that he wants to tell me somethin'." With closed eyes she listened and nodded.

"He says for you to be happy 'cause he's livin' in Paradise—"

Annunziata whispered, "The richest treasures of Paradise to Geremio . . ."

". . . He opens his arms and takes you endearing to his breast. He wants for you specially not to weep too much—for I see him holding his chest, and that means it hoits him when you cry."

Annunziata and Paul wiped their tears and smiled.

". . . There, now he takes his hand away from his chest and his face is shining like the sun."

Annunziata wanted to speak from her overflowing heart but the Cripple raised her hand.

"He's not ready for questions—he has a message and if you talk I'll lose the connection with the spirit woild."

For a minute all were silent, and the Cripple listened on to the spirit world, nodding that she understood.

"Oh, what a beautiful message!" And tears came from her eyes. "His face comes through and he's speakin' right over my shoulder and facing' you and your boy. He says that he never left you, and never will. He says he's watchin' you with his endearing love every minute and that he's doin' all in his power from the spirit woild to protect and help you. . . . Now he stands back and wants you to make a wish to yourself; the wish of your heart's desire. Don't let me hear it!"

Annunziata and Paul clasped their hands and closed their eyes. They prayed to God. They forgot themselves and their troubles. They spoke to God and prayed:

O God, our wish is for the peace and happiness of him who is in Paradise, our Geremio, our father and husband who is in Heaven . . .

And while they prayed the Cripple pressed the rose to her lips and aided them.

"He says he heard your wish and blesses you for it, and tells me to tell you that it will be taken care of. Now he says from the spirit woild for you to ask questions before he goes away; for he came in so strong he's worn me out. Now open your heart an' don't be afraid to ask. He's listenin'."

Annunziata molded her comprehension to the Cripple instinctively. She spoke to Paul.

". . . My mama wants to know if papa . . . is happy."

The Cripple shut her eyes, pressed her forehead, and rocked for a moment.

"Yes. He says he's happy and poifectly content. He says there's only one thing he wants—but not now. He wants your mother to join him someday in Paradise. . . . But not now! Someday when all the children grow up, and she is old. . . . Oh yes, he shows me all his children—ah I see—there's around five or more, and they all have his face. He has his arms around them. He says: 'See, these are my children, and I love them.' Yes, he's very extremely happy. Any more questions?"

Paul hesitated, and then wistfully said, "There is one thing I want to ask father more than anything else . . ."

"Don't be afraid to ask, sonny; that's what he wants you to do."

"Missus Nichols," he began, "when the building fell apart and came down . . . when he died . . . did it frighten him terribly—did it hurt him much? . . . What did he think of . . . ? How did he feel . . . ? What did he say?"

She closed her eyes and rocked.

"Sonny, he says he's glad you asked that question. He has his arms out to you and is pleadin' for you to put your mind at rest, for when his time came, he says, he knew he had to go and that God needed him. When the accident happened, he told God he was ready, and just asked Him to take care of his family, and then he went to his Maker just like that!" And she snapped her fingers sharply. "No, sonny, he shakes his

head and says there wasn't a stitch of pain, and that he went to his Lord
God with a clean soul and a smile."

The weight of the world lifted itself from Paul. Tears dropped
soothingly from his eyes.

"That was a wonderful question, sonny," said the Cripple softly.

"Is there anything more you want to ask him?"

"Yes. Will Ci Luigi's leg get better?"

"Your father shows me a man's leg. There's been a lotta trouble. I
see a horspital—I see a big number four. Now, it's not clear, but anyway
it'll be four days or four weeks or maybe four months when this leg
trouble will be cured—if he takes care of himself and prays, your father
says. Anything else you want to know?"

Paul asked slowly, and in low voice, "Ask father if my heart will get
better . . . please."

The Cripple rocked. She stopped.

"Your father says for you not to strain yourself, and all will be well.
I see him putting his strong hand on your shoulder and helping you. I
hear him say proudly: 'This is *my* boy, and while I help him he will be
the champion of my family!' And how wonderful he looks when he says
it! Now ain't there anything else?"

Paul thought. And slight fear passed over his face.

"Missus Nichols, I just thought. I thought about how little money
we have . . . and I was thinking . . . about the children home—will anything happen to them—will they be all right?"

"Hmmnn . . . your father says not to worry. . . . He does say
though, that if one should pass away, it'll be 'cause . . . he was lonely and
wanted one of his dear little children. But don't let that worry you
'cause I don't see anything like that. He does say that he can help and
pray for them only if they try to take care of themselves. Now he's kissing you, missus, and all his children, and says, 'Do not worry, my endearing family, for I am always with you an' have never left you!' . . . Oh
missus, this has been the best communication with the spirit woild I've
had in years! See, now he's left me, and look at me . . . I swear I'm like
a rag."

Annunziata kissed the Cripple's hands. And Paul did likewise in his
heart. When Annunziata timidly asked what she owed, the Cripple
sniffed the rose and studied its petals.

"You an' me's poor people. . . . And I'll only charge you one dollar."

Mother and son thanked her.

"Florine!" cried the Cripple.

Florine stuck her head in.

"Are you ready for the next people, momma?"

"Florine, bring a nice cup of tea for me and the missus here, and her boy."

"But momma, you promised these people two o'clock and now it's past three . . . ?"

"Never mind, Florine, tell them to come tomorrow at eleven, and make a note of it. Got the name?"

"Yes."

"Well, bring us the tea and do as I tell you."

As Florine prepared the tea the Cripple became very amiable with Annunziata. She told of her two sons killed in the War and pointed to the photographs on the piano. She told of the sickness in the family. She told of the police trouble and the bribes they grafted from her because it was against the law to contact the spirit world. "So you see, missus, we all got our troubles. What good's my husband to me? He doesn't bring in a cent, and drinks every dollar I make." Annunziata felt for her, and in return passionately unburdened to her of her Geremio, her Paul, and her children.

Florine brought the tea in thick, soiled cups—the first time they of Geremio had ever tasted tea.

"Momma, Missus Schaefer says it's very important, and she'll wait until you're ready."

The Cripple sucked her tea.

"Is it a matter of life and death?"

"I'll ask her."

"Yes, do that, Florine, 'cause this last communication's worn me out. . . ."

". . . And momma, about Margie—"

"Don't bother us now."

Florine soon limped back from the kitchen.

"Missus Schaefer says for me to tell you, 'You can call it life and death.'"

The Cripple settled back into the rocker.

"Awright, tell her I've gotta have my tea here with the missus and I'll be ready for her in fifteen minutes."

Home. And hours were wings of fantasy to a mother and son. They gathered the children. They told what father had said, and they kissed them. They told of a father who had never left them, a father whose love surmounted the distance of death, a father who held their hands by day and cradled them in the sleeping dark. Never now would living be without Geremio. No force could harm them, no filth could soil nor sicken them, no circumstance could discourage them, and no discord could displace their faith.

That night Geremio was present in the two narrow bedrooms. Wan, happy Paul could not sleep. He lay at the foot of the bed, and spoke to the wavering votive light that hovered from Annunziata's room.

O papa, forgive my tears. . . . For I weep with joy. And papa . . . why can't we all be together? Can't we go up to you, and never separate? Doesn't God need us? We could help . . . And papa, there's something I want to tell you . . . When the job fell down on you I felt every pain. But now that I know you did not feel the wounds, now that you told mama and me that you were not frightened and that you went when you had to go . . . I don't feel the building on you, and me . . .

The votive light burned its delicate fire of devotion beneath the crucifix, and in the dark dust of dreams came a vast pressure to blanket the senses of mother and son; a force coming from afar and stealing their breathing, a sucking breath upon their own. And through their breathless world a consciousness told them that . . . the living do not die.

——————

Nicky came to Paul and told him that the foreman thought Paul was a "dandy little bricklayer" and wanted him to take his tools and come in and work on the particular walls of the stairwells.

He'll put his tools here—no—put them there . . . workers up and down the stairs—then the battery of riveting guns let loose and reverberating the live metal air of Job—whang! whang! resound the ironworkers' sledges . . . hey buddy dump some mortar here—I can't stretch to the other tub—and get me an armful of damn brick in this corner!—put it up!—what's the bond in this angle?—uorrrrhhhhhh sing the hoists—goddamn-damn sonofabastarddd I said brick on the hoist—not tile! Brick you dago screwball! *brick* . . .

Hey Murrphpheeee . . . !

Ratatatatatat—ratatatatatatatattt

Hal-lloooo?

Send up the fourfoot angleirons!

Noise! noise O noise O noise and sounds swelling in from the sea of city life without of pushing scurrying purring motors and horns and bells and cries and sirens and whistles and padded stream of real feet O noise O noise—O noi—se and through Job mouths stretch wide screaming:

I want brick!

I want tile!

I want the scaffolder!

I want mortar!

I want speed I want rush I want haste I want noise I want action

I want you all of you to throw yourselves into job!

With the midday sun the close stairwell became a hotbox, and Paul stripped off his shirt. Just before lunch hour, as Paul was working a wall up along the stairs, someone came slowly down. When the man neared him Paul felt drops plash on his sweated back. He wiped his back and saw his hand covered with blood. He was frightened. He turned and looked up. A Swedish carpenter was coming down slowly and holding up his right hand. It looked like a ghastly dripping rose. The four fingers had been shorn off to the palm and the mangled remains ran red faucets. He walked silently with white face down the stairs. Later, Nicky told Paul that the carpenter was greasing the wheel at the top of the hoist when the cable suddenly ran and caught his hand against the wheel rubbing off his fingers.

"Don't let that bother you, kid," said Nicky.

O my Jesus, guard me. I am not afraid—It's that I am needed . . . and I know O Lord that I shall work on Job unharmed . . . in constant prayer and thanksgiving to Thee—our Jesus.

The scaffolds rose a floor a day. With each floor the height and majesty of skyscraper fascinated him, but he never told mother Annunziata about the danger of falling or being pushed from a swinging scaffold forty or fifty floors above the street. Or of a derrick cable snapping and sending a girder crashing the scaffold to earth. It seemed so daring to lay brick at the edge of a wall that ran down hundreds and hundreds of feet to a toy world below, a wall that leaned out and seemed about to fall away.

This was steel Job where danger was ever present with falling planks and beams and bolts and white-hot molten steel from acetylene torch and breaking cable and unexpected drop of hoist—great dangerous Job who thrilled Paul.

I must win the award! said Dave the only Jew bricklayer—said Frank the Scotchman—said Barney the Irishman—said Tommy the Englishman—said Hans the German—said Grogan the "real" American—said they all.

I must win! prayed Paul.

The men ran away with the job; to the delight of the foremen and the firm. Years of bricklaying sense were amplified to a point of acute accuracy and speed, and a man's spirit was mortified if he was a brick or cross-joint behind the next man. Nothing seemed impossible. Difficult brick cuts were made without spoil or trail—stiff mortar was spread neatly—soupy mortar was spread neatly—one man became two men—perverse twisted vitrified tile blocks were "humored" with darting instinct—while a man's hands sleighted the quick mortar and brick into upping wall his eyes crosshaired plumb and level—he twisted to let laborer go by and let fellowbricklayer do his share—he shouted for material—his feet kicked brick and fallen mortar from scaffold planks—he measured the man's pace—he planned immediately his following moves—man's flesh lent itself completely to the balanced delirium of building.

Night and day they lived with the award and automatically trained to the task. Real men grown men watched their habits and felt they could keep laying brick and sawing wood and bolting steel through eternity without ever pausing. They cared little for lunch or joke or woman; the smell and feel and action of building was their in and out of living. They never mentioned the award and became respectful strangers bearing each other a wholesome terrible hate. Grown men real men fell away to one blind dimension and suffered beauty from their beings so that vision became the constant photography of rising walls from out of their bodies while foreman's morbid pall loomed over shoulders.

. . . And within minute's reach out in the street world passed thousands who never set foot on building Job who never touched a brick nor smelled mortar who never thought of Job and her men. . . .

The day of the award the men worked with unusual tension. Grogan especially was beside himself in endeavor and open smiling to the foremen. At ten o'clock the thin expressionless Mister Ross came along the line of bricklayers working on the parapets. He stopped near Grogan. Grogan smiled wildly and made an anxious move to step out. But Ross tapped Paul and quietly told him to come down to the office. Paul dropped his trowel in the tub and followed him, his head getting light and trembling. The men paused and watched Ross and Paul go into the penthouse door and downstairs.

Dave the fat Jewish bricklayer wiped his forehead and exclaimed:

"Vell, I'm soit'nly glad for Paulie—He's a crackerjack!"

The men slowed and worked like empty shells—the suspense over. They felt slightly bitter, but relieved.

Grogan remained standing. He clenched his trowel-handle and his eyes glittered. Then, urinating against the wall, he cackled: "This is more than the barber kin do to his woik . . . !"

He scooped up some mortar and deliberately dirtied the wall.

The frogface showed its ugliness and spat:

"So they gi'e it to the goddamn li'l Dago!"

At noon the men were summoned to a large space on the second floor. Upon a wooden platform was the committee; the dapper bright-eyed mayor, officials, a stenographer, a few newspapermen, and three richly dressed women. When the workers saw the women they removed their caps and hats. Speeches were made while the men stared at the sheer-silked legs of the three rich women. Speeches were made and Paul gazed in wonder at the beautiful pink cheeks and fine tailoring of the men upon the platform.

Even when his name was called and he was handed a certificate and the men clapped it seemed a revelation that these glaze-skinned, soft, white-fingered men who looked like painted mustached women dressed in tailored men's clothes owned the great building and the city.

That afternoon while laying brick he marveled at the memory of the dainty pink-cheeked perfumed dolls of men who gave out the awards and spoke tired high-class talk.

Could he ever forget that these hot-housealia owned great Job!

W. S. Di Piero

The Depot

When I was young, they taught us not to ask.
Accept what's there. If you want something else,
or more, don't look too shameful wanting it.
They were too right. Bituminous words,
useless rhyme, cadence, dream structures, plots
to turn life's material fact into sound—
such things helped no one, and gave nothing back.
Our mothers scrubbed sidewalks, ironed white shirts
starched upright and sure for school or Mass.
The Infant of Prague balanced his gilded globe
above the T.V. screen. On Saturdays,
we had to sit through two double features.
Between times, our fathers worked in steamy plants,
stamped dies, troweled mortar, mixed paint, broke concrete,

carpooled home to beer and shots at Mike's,
a late supper home in silence, then back to Mike's
for night baseball or cards. Our fathers taught us
we had enough. Brick homes, *Your Show of Shows,*
the mothball fleet and flaring oilworks.

Sabbioneta to Parma

In the corridor outside my compartment,
a washerwoman hooks her elbows on the window,
flipping the landscape between her hands.
A black-haired boy with yellow fingernails
talks to his rooster: *Ma cosa vuoi da me?*
Reading Tasso, the young priest wiggles his lips
while a high-breasted girl studies him,
and the station porters scrubbed our windows
to wipe away smugglers' secret messages.
The slow crabbed vineyards beyond the glass
throb in the plain's unforgiving light,
and cordons of cypress carve out portions
of green sky. Not much depth here,
no counterinsurgency of things
plundering the standard night. The planet
sits or sinks in its nervelessness.
Five months from now snow will braid
the creekbeds and vinestumps,
even while a morning express curves past
just as the porticoes of Sabbioneta
curved away from me, away from life.
I'm one more passionate bystander here.
It seems simple enough. Silence, work,
accident, that's really all there is.
Sunslats keel and slice through poplars,
trunk hacked from soil, spindled crown
a stranger to its branches. If I could see
everything, I'd probably go crazy.
The sun crazes the soil. There's an ox
pulling a man. There's water running in a ditch.

Diane di Prima

From *Recollections of My Life as a Woman*

Of all the wars of those early days, one of the most pernicious, most hidden and far-reaching in its effect on my life, was the war between the Mallozzis and the Di Primas. Between my mother's and my father's families. The battleground of that war was my psyche, that soft and delicate juncture of body and spirit; the dwelling place of the Word. Now wounds to the psyche are invisible, and even harder to find forty or fifty years later than wounds to the flesh or spirit. They dwell out of the light in tiny crevices, the deeply hidden assumptions of our lives.

The problem is compounded when, within the cosmology in which the wounds are inflicted, there is no such thing as the psyche *or* the spirit. Then you search for the invisible in the invisible.

In my childhood home there was no room for the soul. Though lip service was paid to Dante in some begrudging homage to Emma's father, neither soul nor spirit dwelt in the universe. Or so I was given to understand. The world, you see, was packed so close with matter, every crevice filled, that nothing else would fit, neither soul nor spirit, no angels or saints filled my evenings with prayers, no god looked down from the sky. For my grandfather there was the heroic quest for truth, but my parents were two children abandoned at the bottom of a well.

The world was packed so close, every cupboard filled. "Knickknacks" on every shelf. Drawers filled to overflowing with pins, with twine, embroidery thread, bushels of unused corny greeting cards.

Time was filled that way, too: no free ruminating moments. Only the next task: dinner, dishes, sweeping. The laundry, ironing, continual stair-washing. Gardening, canning, sewing, mending. If all else is done you can always plan ahead: fill the freezer with casseroles, crochet a throw for the couch. Never to take a walk with an empty head. Lest something come upon you from the skies.

I remember that when I heard *A Christmas Carol* on holiday radio for the first time, complete with sound effects (I was five or six), I went to bed and hid deep under the covers. Afraid to sleep for the hint of invisible worlds. Ghost of Christmas Past. Ghost of the Past. Afraid to sleep, and needing some reassurance. "No such thing" my mother told me then, "as a spirit". Spirits more palpable in the room than she was. Crowding, filling that air. Dad, a dark spot among ghosts and saints, spirits and angels, upheld her. They left, and I watched the dark.

The Mallozzis, I was given to understand, were everything desirable. (These matters were discussed only by my mother and her sisters, and usually in Neapolitan.) Mallozzis were smarter, thinner, more ambitious. "Upwardly mobile" we might say but there wasn't that term then. All the Mallozzi women had gone to college. The one male Mallozzi sibling had rebelled and refused: but of course, that is different from not being able to, because of lack of money or of brains. Each of the kids in the family was often under discussion: was s/he a Mallozzi or a Di Prima? (I am sure it extended out to my cousins: was s/he a Mallozzi or a Biondi? Mallozzi or a Fregosi? Mallozzi or—oh hated idea!—a Troisi? Rossi?!)

I felt it as a moral imperative. Mallozzi or bust. They were more "northern", too, the Italian snobbery. "Pop"—what the "Mallozzi girls" always called their father, even unto their own deathbeds at eighty or ninety—Pop's blue eyes were often mentioned and with great pride. I remember them for their fierceness myself, a bit like my own stare, but more angry, less distanced and contemptuous than I. Com-passion he had, a fellow feeling I had walled off. In my young life, it probably would have been deadly.

Di Primas, I learned very young, were "like children". (Not a compliment, and frequently used in our hearing.) Except for my father, of course, they were uneducated, got lower-class jobs. Pietro, my father's father, believed in God! Told us stories about Mary and the Baby. They were fat and loud, and going to their houses was like slumming, or so my mother's voice conveyed as we got ready. They tended to be what mom called "laborers": upholsterers, waiters, factory workers.

Di Primas were always being rescued by my father. From something or other, I never knew from what. Probably they needed money, maybe they got into trouble with the Law. He was the oldest son, and seemed to think it natural, as did they. "Frank will take care of it".

Being a Di Prima meant you would come to no particular good, would definitely let mom down. You'd wind up redhaired, with freckles (ugh!) and very white skin. You'd probably be round and not very smart. You might work in a candy factory or a bank. It was almost a threat: If you're not good, you'll turn into a Di Prima! Invitation to unlawful use of the Will. Only ingredient besides Matter in that world.

* * *

Oh built-in Manicheanism, very stuff of the Tao! Of Yin and Yang, though I can't say which was which. All dichotomies in the world were laid out for me, and before my birth: Mallozzis and Di Primas. Cosmology.

I learned I was a Mallozzi early on. My brothers were the Di Primas. But it would change. Frankie remained a Di Prima, but Richie? Was Richie not a Mallozzi after all? Polymorphous creature—could he possibly have "a little of both"?

There was this catch, this small detail that warped the heart. This invisible wound I find today woven throughout the fabric of my life, so that to correct this mistake would be to take my life apart, even unto dissolution. The hands that reach to do this work are formed by these same dichotomies. The secret places of my soul.

There was, I was saying, this catch:

The Di Primas, whoever they were, were loving beings. In their loud and rundown houses you were safe and welcome. As nowhere in all that fine Mallozzi world.

In a Di Prima household (there were six besides ours), the children were valued. *I criaturi.* (The creatures. Were we fauns? satyrs?) We might run wild, knock over a vase, eat things out of the refrigerator, even raise our voices in play. Someone would be overlooking us with a beam of love coming out of each eye. We were the kids.

I grew up thinking the price for this love was poverty, low-class life, the contempt of mom. Maybe more than I could pay. Love was not for me. But thinking it secretly, unbeknown to myself.

To give up schooling and maybe be loud and fat. The price for a lap to sit on was to give up ambition. I paid the price, but didn't take the prize. Thinking perhaps to keep my Mallozzi pride.

Mallozzis had precious things on glass-topped tables. You didn't talk loud or move fast in their houses. A couple of them would hold you on their laps. But it was more tentative, certainly not unconditional. It helped if you looked nice, if you had been "good".

Mallozzis knew what you should look like and what you should want. They knew how you should get it, too, if you'd only listen. Straight A's and neatness were the important things. And with these came a rigid self-respect.

The pleasing of Emma, the destruction of Frank. Though these things were seldom spoken in front of him, and always then in a pseudo-impartial tone: "Does s/he take after his/her *father* or *mother*"?

etc. But everyone knew Sicilians were outré. Still, an impossible position, and surely a part of his rage.

Codependent, we say now, but that doesn't say it all. To be apologist and rescuer of his father; his brothers and sisters. To feel them a handicap, and care for them as duty. Straining to please his wife and her sisters. Caught between.

His genes not okay. I feel that still.

And find, in the hidden corners, a child's suspicion: Maybe Di Primas were bad *because* they loved us kids? We being after all, not all that lovable. Family love, Mallozzis knew, was something you earned. A corollary of respect, not a thing in itself. Not your right, nor the ambiance you grew in.

Division in yourSelf: between your mind and your hair. Eyes, skin, emotions, nose, voice, all part of the battle. Were your feet too wide? Could you change all this by Will? First use of the Magickal Will against yourself. Against the very tissue of your genes.

• • • • •

All through this time, the war raged, internal and external. Raged in Europe as far back as I can remember, a presence in my life from the beginning. Raged in America under a blanket of silence.

At school the nuns had us pray every morning for the children. All the children in the world, they said. The children, they told us, on both sides of the war: did they not have souls? Did they not all belong to God? It was the closest I came to hearing the war news spoken, and I was hungry for speech, for open speech.

At home, the war news in Southern Italian: Neapolitan, Sicilian, sometimes Calabrese, when friends of the family came over. It was assumed that none of us kids understood. I schooled myself not to respond by word or expression. Lived in stealth. A discipline.

War news was mostly worry and despair. What they heard or did not hear from the relatives overseas. Or earlier portents: Mussolini's overtures rebuffed by Roosevelt. Or so I heard. "Italians are good for nothing but a stab in the back", is what they repeated, what they said Roosevelt said. That one phrase in English amid passionate Italian. Roosevelt's refusal to see Mussolini, if that's what in fact it was, felt fiercely as personal insult by one and all. Left him, they said, no choice, but to turn to Hitler.

And 1991, standing outside the corner store, speaking with two Arab grocers, I heard the same words, heard the dilemma from the

1930s. "Hussein", said the older man, "wants to talk. He said he wants to talk. But a man can't talk while he's being insulted". The immigrant's impasse, pain of American arrogance I knew, growing up. Felt again the mute despair "Can't get out of it now". Unbroken bitterness and desperation. Mute pride, fifty years late, the same Mediterranean pride. Arab, Sicilian.

Late war news on the radio. Long after we were in bed. Did I sometimes creep half down the winding stairs, where I could watch, or listen, hidden? As I often did when the air in the house grew tense, to check out the coming storms. My interest in weather forecasts holds to this day.

Or sometimes, a bit of the news on Aunt Ella's lips. Her husband, my Uncle Hugo, stationed in Panama, sending home silver filigree bracelets, long letters with words or paragraphs blacked out. Sometimes she spoke despite my parents' prohibitions. Sharing her fears when she came to share my bed. Her warm, pregnant body beside me in the dark. That was later, after war was "declared".

In Catholic school we learned the United States sank the *Maine* on purpose, started the Spanish American War all on its own. Made it easy to wonder about Pearl Harbor. Made it easy, especially if you were Italian.

If you were Italian, growing up in my house, your father handed you Machiavelli to read. To help you understand history, he told you. One of the only books he had besides Shakespeare and the encyclopedia. He read you *Julius Caesar* to show how Mark Anthony manipulated the crowd. What propaganda was. You never forgot.

The actual War began when I was seven. Amid tears and hysteria, my mother hanging onto us as if we were about to disappear. No school that day. That first day the large wooden radio was never turned off. A few days later, a false air-raid alarm led the school to dismiss us, send us all home. Through what my mother imagined as an air-raid. Kindergartners through eighth graders wandered the Brooklyn streets, wending their ways to homes where someone or no one was waiting. Where they could or couldn't get in. And then at my house the real blackout began: the war news ceased to exist.

There were blackouts in the "real world" too: the black shades drawn, a single lamp or candle. Civil defense personnel rapping at our door: there was a pinhole in our shade, the light was showing through. We played cards by flashlight, did homework, all gathered at one table. My parents angry at the intrusion of the war.

Everything was carefully monitored. None of us kids had a radio in their room, the only phonograph, a windup, was in the living room. Scratchy 78s: "I sit alone in my cozy morris chair / playing solitaire / so unhappy there". Made no sense at all, then or now. No newspapers, no comics, no movies, books chosen by mom. Though I had the wild freedom of the library. Where I found out about Leibniz, but not about what was happening right then. Right under my nose. It's where I'm still at, in some ways: can tell you more about Proclus than about TV. Trained to look away, I do so still.

It was into this silence that the Bomb exploded.

It was 1945, my eleventh birthday. August 6, 1945, and we were waiting the celebration for my father. Inane party hats I disliked even then, cake and melting ice cream. My brothers were noisy and annoying, my mom was excited with a fake excitement I hated. Dad was working late. Or whatever he did in the evenings in those years.

He came in finally with a newspaper in his hand, and I saw that the headlines were huge, more than half the page. I can remember stealing a look at them, something I did on the sly sometimes, but cannot remember what the words were. His face was louring, gloomy, it often was. He often exploded, and no one could say why. He still had his hat on though he was in the house. Something he never did. I noticed that.

My brothers stopped giggling and shoving, and the room grew silent. The cake sat on the table, candles unlit. My mom's apprehensive "What's the matter, dear"? her apotropaic formula, was missing. My father threw the paper, still folded, on a coffee table. He who inveighed against drama was being dramatic.

He said *Well, we lost,* and all hell broke loose. The bitterness in his voice. Everyone spoke at once: How could we lose? What had happened? Was the war over? Mom's hysteria breaking the surface of her voice.

It was the Bomb, though none of us knew what that was. It was Hiroshima, though none of us knew where that was. He said, *Whatever we do now, we've lost.* Breaking the cool of his conservative posture. We had no answer.

We ate melted ice cream, I got stupid dolls. My party proceeded, almost as if nothing had happened.

———

I had hardly been married two months before I knew I had made a mistake—shouldn't have gotten into this at all. Alan was out somewhere partying, hadn't called, of course, to say where or when he'd be back, and I was alone in a dark house in a small clearing, on a dusty and ominous mountain, with no money and almost no food, aware that my mate's benevolent but nutty whims could take us all anytime in any direction.

Part of me wanted to pick up the phone and call my parents. Tell them what was what, ask for their help in getting out of it all. But I was far too proud to let them in on my misgivings, to admit to them, of all people, that I had made a mistake. And a kind of ancient Italian wisdom told me that asking for help might produce many effects, but would not most likely produce the desired one.

They would certainly *not* be sympathetic. Although they were not Catholic, mom and dad definitely believed that marriage was for life. "She made her bed, now let her lie in it" had been a frequently muttered axiom in my childhood home. Besides, Alan was still a hero in their eyes. Had he not married me (read: rescued me from disgrace) even though I had two kids by other men? And one of the kids half Black? Should I be looking a gift horse in the mouth? No, I was in this with no one but myself to rely on. I would have to figure it out.

I remember sitting at the table that night while the kids slept, and staring at the phone in the dimly lit room, and deciding not to use it. Acknowledging that the wall between my parents and me could not be bridged that simply.

John Fante

From *The Brotherhood of the Grape*

I thought my father's funeral would bring out the whole town, but I was mistaken. More people had attended the wake on the previous afternoon than were present at the church service. Most were members of the family, and many were grandchildren who didn't want to be there in the first place, for the circus was in town at the fairgrounds and the kids were annoyed at their grandfather for picking such a lousy time to die. The rest of the mourners were friends and neighbors of my mother and a loyal group from the Café Roma.

Waiting gloomily in their Sunday clothes, the pallbearers shaded themselves under a big elm on that hot, cheerless afternoon. They were Zarlingo, Cavallaro, Antrilli, Mascarini, Benedetti and Rocco Mangone. They were as beautiful as old stones strewn across a patch of hillside. Grief plucked at my throat like the leap of a trout as I looked at them. Now that I had none, I would have taken any one of them for a father. Indeed, any man, or bush, or tree, or stone, if he would have me for a son. I was myself a father. I didn't want the role. I wanted to go back to a time when I was small and my father stood strong and noisy in the house. To hell with fatherhood. I was never born to it. I was born to be a son.

The pallbearers doffed their hats as Harriet and I entered the church. I waved. I wanted to shout: "I love you, I need you, take care of me, you funny old men!"

The family was gathered in the two front pews before the main altar, my mother in the first pew between Virgil and Stella and their families. Mama wore a black veil covering her hair and face. Harriet and I and our sons slipped into the pew behind them, next to Peggy and her kids. Right away I noticed that one of us was missing. I turned to Peggy.

"Where's Mario?"

"In a state of shock. I told him to stay home."

Virgil glanced over his shoulder and sneered:

"With the Giants and Atlanta playing a doubleheader on TV? That's funny, Peggy. Very funny!"

"It's true!" Peggy hissed in a loud whisper. "He cried and cried. He really loved his father. But you were all against him. You alienated him. Why did you pick on him? Why didn't you have a little faith in him? Well, you'll see. You'll be sorry, all of you!"

"God help you, baby," Virgil smirked.

"You fucking bank clerk!" she raged. "You're not fit to clean Mario's shoes!"

"Says who?"

"Says me, you creep."

"Shh!" Mama chided under her black veil. "Please. Papa's dead."

Then the hearse arrived and the pallbearers carried the brown casket down the aisle to the communion rail. The mourners watched the attendants bring funeral wreaths and bouquets of flowers to place around the casket. How small the casket seemed. My father had been a bull of a man, but not tall. Horizontal in that box, he seemed no larger than a boy.

Then an enormous wreath was brought down the aisle, all roses and carnations and ferns, so large that two attendants carried it. They placed it at the foot of the coffin and stood it up on wire brackets. It was six feet tall, a gaudy splendor, very impressive. It bore a strip of white silk upon which a red inscription was embossed. It read: COMPLIMENTS OF CAFÉ ROMA.

The pallbearers gazed at their tribute with pleasure and satisfaction. No question about it, the Café Roma brotherhood had come through with the biggest and the best. My mother, bless her, was so impressed that she turned, raised her veil, and nodded in appreciation. The Roma boys smiled in sympathy.

A bell tinkled and Father Martin emerged from the sacristy behind two altar boys. Beneath the boys' cassocks you could see the green and white stripes of their baseball socks, and you knew that somewhere in the town their teammates were waiting for them.

Father Martin moved down to the casket, blessed it with holy water, and read the Latin rites from a missal. Closing it, he put his fingers together and tried to assemble his thoughts as people waited for him to speak. It must have been a problem, for he was dealing with the life and death of a man who had rarely come to church and who had never performed his Catholic obligations.

"Let us pray for the soul of Nicholas Molise," he began. "A good and simple man, an honest man, a fine craftsman who lived among us for so many years and gave his best for the improvement of the human community. Instead of weeping, let us rejoice that he has come to the end of his toil on this earth, and is now at peace in the arms of his Father in heaven."

That was it, short and sweet, a bull's-eye. The mourners joined him in the recitation of the Lord's Prayer, and he concluded with: "Eternal rest grant unto him, O Lord, and let the perpetual light shine upon him."

The padre returned to the sacristy as the undertakers opened the casket and my mother led the mourners past the body. She raised her veil and kissed her husband on the forehead. Then she laced her white rosary around his stiffened fingers. Virgil led her away as she cried softly. One by one we passed the bier and stared down at Papa, the children startled, horrified, fascinated, the others weeping silently.

I did not weep. I felt rage, disgust. Good God, what had they done to that poor old man! What had they done to that craggy, magnificent Abruzzian face, those lines of pain and toil, the resolute mouth, the cunning knit of his eyebrows, the furrows of triumph and defeat! Gone, gone . . . and in their place the smooth, unlined, cotton-stuffed face, the rouged cheeks. It was a shame, an obscenity, and I was stung with a writer's wickedness, thinking, that's not my old man, that's not old Nick, that's Groucho Marx, and the quicker we bury him the better.

Hail Mary

Hail Mary, full of grace, the Lord is with thee; blessed art thou among women, and blessed is the fruit of thy womb, Jesus. O Holy Mother Mary, I am now in Hollywood, California, on the corner of Franklin and Argyle, in a house where I rent a room at six a week. Remember, O Blessed Virgin, remember the night twenty years ago in Colorado when my father went to the hospital for his operation, and I got all my brothers and sisters down on the floor in our bedroom, and I said: "Now by gosh—pray! Papa's sick, so you kids pray." Ah, boy, we prayed, you Virgin Mary, you Honey, we prayed and my blood sang, and I felt big feelings in my chest, the ripple of electricity, the power of cold faith, and we all got up and walked to different parts of the house. I sat in the kitchen and smirked. They had said at the hospital that Papa was going to die, and nobody knew it but me and Mamma and you, you Honey, but we had prayed and I sat smirking, pooh-poohing at death because we had prayed and I knew we had done our share for Papa, and that he would live.

The rest of them wouldn't go to bed that night, they were afraid Papa would die, and they all waited, and already Grandma planned the funeral, but I smirked and went to bed and slept very happy, with your beads in my fingers, kissing the cross a few times and then dozing off because Papa could not die after *my* prayers, because you were my girl, my queen, and there was no doubt in my heart.

And in the morning there was wild joy to wake me, because Papa had lived and would live some more, a lot of years to come, and there was Mamma back from the hospital, beaming and sticky when she kissed us for joy, and I heard her say to Grandma: "He lived because he has an iron constitution. He is a strong man. You can't kill that man." And when I heard that, I snickered. They didn't know, these people, they didn't know about you and me, you Honey, and I thought of your pale face, your dark hair, your feet on the serpent at the side-altar, and I said, she's wonderful, she's sure wonderful.

Oh, those were the days! Oh, I loved you then! You were the celestial blue, and I looked up at you when I walked to school with books under my arm, and my ecstasy was simple and smashing, crushing and mad and whirling, all these things across my chest, sensations, and you in the blue sky, in my blue shirt, in the covers of my blue-covered book. You were the color blue and I saw you everywhere and then I saw the statue in the church, at the side-altar, with your feet on the serpent, and I said and said a thousand times, I said, oh, you Honey, and I wasn't afraid of anything. . . .

Hail Mary, full of grace, the Lord is with thee; blessed art thou among women, and blessed is the fruit of thy womb, Jesus. O Holy Mother Mary, I want to ask a favor of you, but first I want to remind you of something I once did for you.

You will say that I am bragging again, and that you have heard this story before, but I am proud of it, and my heart is beating wildly and there is the rustle of a bird in my throat, and I could cry, and I am crying because I loved you, oh, I loved you so. That hot flash on my cheek is the course of my tears, and I flick it off with the point of my finger, and the finger comes away warm and wet, and I sit here and I am of the living, I am saying this is a dream.

His name was Willie Cox, and he went to Grover Cleveland. He was always razzing me because I was a Catholic. O you Mary! I have told you this before, I admit the braggadocio, but tonight, one day removed from Christmas Eve, I am in Hollywood, California, on the corner of Franklin and Argyle, and the rent is six a week, and I want to ask you a favor, and I cannot ask until I tell you once more about this Willie Cox.

He chewed tobacco, this Willie Cox. He went to Grover Cleveland, and he chewed tobacco, and I went to St. Catherine's, and we used to pass one another on the corner, and he used to squirt tobacco juice on my shoes and legs and say: "*That* for the Catholics. They stink."

Willie Cox, where are you tonight? I am on the corner of Franklin and Argyle, and this is Hollywood, so it is quite possible that you are two blocks away, but wherever you are, Mr. Willie Cox, I call upon you to bear witness to the truth of my narrative. Willie Cox, I took a hell of a lot of your guff that spring. When you said the priests ate the nuns' babies, and then spat on my shoes, I took it. When you said we had human sacrifices at Mass, and the priest drank the blood of young girls, and you spat across my knees, I took that. The truth is, Willie, and tonight I admit, you scared me. You were very tough, and I decided to do as the martyrs did—to do nothing. To take it.

Hail Mary, full of grace! I was a boy then, and there was no love like my love. And there was no tougher boy than Willie Cox, and I feared him. Ah, but my days were celestial blues and my eyes had only to lift and there was my love, and I was not afraid. And yet, in spite of it all, I was afraid of Willie Cox.

How is your nose today, Willie Cox? Did your front teeth grow out again? He was on his way to Grover Cleveland and I was on my way to

St. Catherine's and it was eight o'clock in the morning. He shifted the wad in his jaw, and I held my breath.

"Hi, Red Neck."

"Hello, Willie."

"What's your hurry, Catholic?"

"Gotta, Willie. I'm late."

"What'sa matter? Scared of the nunnies?"

"Don't, Willie. You're choking me."

"Scared of the nunnies?"

"*Don't,* Willie! I can't hardly breathe!"

"I heard somethin', Red Neck. My old man, he tells me you Catlickers think Jesus was borned without his mother having kids like other people have kids. Is that right?"

"It's the Immaculate Conception. Ouch!"

"Immaculate, crap! I bet she was a whore like all Catlickers."

"Willie Cox, you dirty dog!"

Mr. Thomas Holyoke, you are dead now, you died two years later, but even in death you may speak out tonight and tell what you saw from your window, there on the lawn, fourteen years ago one morning in the spring. You may say what you said to the policeman who ran from the courthouse steps, you may say again:

"I saw the dark lad here struggling to get free. The Cox boy was choking him. I thought he'd hurt the boy, and I was about to intervene. All at once the dark lad here swung his fist, and the Cox boy went sprawling across my new spring lawn. I thought they were playing, until I saw the Cox boy didn't move. When I ran out his nose was bleeding and his front teeth were missing."

Hail Mary, full of grace! Here in Hollywood, on the corner of Franklin and Argyle, I look through my window and gaze and gaze at an unending pattern of celestial blue. I wait and I remember. O you Honey, where are you now? Oh, endless blue, you have not changed!

In her room next to mine, my landlady sits before the radio. Willie Cox, I know now that you are in Hollywood. Willie Cox, you are the woman in the next room playing the radio. You have given up the vulgar habit of chewing tobacco, but, oh, Willie, you had charm in those days, and you were not nearly so monstrous as you are now, slipping little pieces of paper under my door, telling me over and over that I owe you eighteen dollars.

Hail Mary, full of grace! Today when I talked to my agent he said there was a slump in Hollywood, that the condition was serious. I went down the stairs of his office and into the big, late afternoon. Such a blue sky! Such riotous blue in the Santa Monica mountains! I looked every-where above, and I sighed, and I said, well, it won't rain tonight, any-way. That was this afternoon. Willie Cox, you are my landlady and you are a Slump in Hollywood.

Mary in the Sky, what has happened to me? O tall queen standing on the serpent at the side-altar, O sweet girl with waxen fingers, there is a Slump in Hollywood, my landlady slips little pieces of paper under my door, and when I gaze at the sky it is to form an opinion about the weather. This is funny. It is probably goddamn funny to the world and it is funny to me, but this gathering dust in my throat, this quiet in my chest where once there was whirling, this cigarette-clenching mouth that once bore a smirk of faith and joy in destiny—there is no laughter in these things. Willie Cox has got me by the throat again.

Willie Cox, I am not afraid of you. I know that I cannot bloody the nose of a Slump in Hollywood or knock the teeth out of my landlady's mouth, but, Willie Cox, remember that I still look to the sky. Remember that there are nights like these when I pause to listen, to search, to feel, to grope.

Hail Mary, full of grace, the Lord is with thee, and blessed art thou among women. Holy Mary, Mother of God, I was going to ask a favor. I was going to ask boldly about that rent. I see it is not necessary now. I see that you have not deserted me. For in a little while I shall slip this into an envelope and send it off. There is a Slump in Hollywood, and my landlady slips little pieces of paper under my door, and once more I sit in the kitchen of my world, a smirk on my lips. . . .

From *Wait Until Spring, Bandini*

Arturo Bandini was pretty sure that he wouldn't go to Hell when he died. The way to hell was the committing of mortal sin. He had com-mitted many, he believed, but the Confessional had saved him. He al-ways got to Confession on time—that is, before he died. And he knocked on wood whenever he thought of it—he always would get there on time—before he died. So Arturo was pretty sure he wouldn't go to hell when he died. For two reasons. The Confessional, and the fact that he was a fast runner.

But Purgatory, that midway place between Hell and Heaven, dis-turbed him. In explicit terms the Catechism stated the requirements for Heaven: a soul had to be absolutely clean, without the slightest blemish of sin. If the soul at death was not clean enough for Heaven, and not befouled enough for Hell, there remained that middle region, that Purgatory where the soul burned and burned until it was purged of its blemishes.

In Purgatory there was one consolation: soon or late you were a cinch for Heaven. But when Arturo realized that his stay in Purgatory might be seventy million trillion billion years, burning and burning and burning, there was little consolation in ultimate Heaven. After all, a hundred years was a long time. And a hundred and fifty million years was incredible.

No: Arturo was sure he would never go straight to Heaven. Much as he dreaded the prospect, he knew that he was in for a long session in Purgatory. But wasn't there something a man could do to lessen the Purgatory ordeal of fire? In his Catechism he found the answer to this problem.

The way to shorten the awful period in Purgatory, the Catechism stated, was by good works, by prayer, by fasting and abstinence, and by piling up indulgences. Good works were out, as far as he was concerned. He had never visited the sick, because he knew no such people. He had never clothed the naked because he had never seen any naked people. He had never buried the dead because they had undertakers for that. He had never given alms to the poor because he had none to give; besides, 'alms' always sounded to him like a loaf of bread, and where could he get loaves of bread? He had never harbored the injured because—well, he didn't know—it sounded like something people did on seacoast towns, going out and rescuing sailors injured in shipwrecks. He had never instructed the ignorant because after all, he was ignorant himself, otherwise he wouldn't be forced to go to this lousy school. He had never enlightened the darkness because that was a tough one he never did understand. He had never comforted the afflicted because it sounded dangerous and he knew none of them anyway: most cases of measles and smallpox had quarantine signs on the doors.

As for the ten commandments he broke practically all of them, and yet he was sure that not all of these infringements were mortal sins. Sometimes he carried a rabbit's foot, which was superstition, and therefore a sin against the first commandment. But was it a mortal sin? That always bothered him. A mortal sin was a serious offense. A venial sin was a slight offense. Sometimes, playing baseball, he crossed bats with a fellow-player: this was supposed to be a sure way to get a two base hit. And yet he knew it was superstition. Was it a sin? And was it a mortal sin or a venial sin? One Sunday he had deliberately missed mass to listen to the broadcast of the world series, and particularly to hear of his god, Jimmy Foxx of the Athletics. Walking home after the game it suddenly occurred to him that he had broken the first commandment: thou shalt not have strange gods before me. Well, he had committed a mortal sin in missing mass, but was it another mortal sin to prefer Jimmy Foxx to God Almighty during the world series? He gone to Confession, and there the matter grew more complicated. Father Andrew had said, "If you think it's a mortal sin, my son, then it is a mortal sin." Well, heck. At first he had thought it was only a venial sin, but he had to admit that, after considering the offense for three days before Confession, it had indeed become a mortal sin.

The third commandment. It was no use even thinking about that, for Arturo said 'God damn it' on an average of four times a day. Nor was that counting the variations: God damn this and God damn that. And so, going to Confession each week, he was forced to make wide generalizations after a futile examination of his conscience for accuracy. The best he could do was confess to the priest, "I took the name of the Lord in vain about sixty-eight or seventy times." Sixty-eight mortal sins in one week, from the second commandment alone. Wow! Sometimes, kneeling in the cold church awaiting Confessional, he listened in alarm to the beat of his heart, wondering if it would stop and he drop dead before he got those things off his chest. It exasperated him, that wild beating of his heart. It compelled him not to run but often to walk, and very slowly, to Confessional, lest he overdo the organ and drop in the street.

"Honor thy father and thy mother." Of course he honored his father and his mother! Of course. But there was a catch in it: the Catechism went on to say that any disobedience of thy father and thy mother was dishonor. Once more he was out of luck. For though he did indeed honor his mother and father, he was rarely obedient. Venial sins? Mortal sins? The classifications pestered him. The number of sins against that commandment exhausted him; he would count them to the hundreds as he examined his days hour by hour. Finally he came to the conclusion that they were only venial sins, not serious enough to merit Hell. Even so, he was very careful not to analyze this conclusion too deeply.

He had never killed a man, and for a long time he was sure that he would never sin against the fifth commandment. But one day the class in Catechism took up the study of the fifth commandment, and he discovered to his disgust that it was practically impossible to avoid sins against it. Killing a man was not the only thing: the by-products of the commandment included cruelty, injury, fighting, and all forms of viciousness to man, bird, beast, and insect alike.

Goodnight, what was the use? He enjoyed killing blue-bottle flies. He got a big kick out of killing muskrats, and birds. He loved to fight.

He hated those chickens. He had had a lot of dogs in his life, and he had been severe and often harsh with them. And what of the prairie dogs he had killed, the pigeons, the pheasants, the jackrabbits? Well, the only thing to do was to make the best of it. Worse, it was a sin to even think of killing or injuring a human being. That sealed his doom. No matter how he tried, he could not resist expressing the wish of violent death against some people: like Sister Mary Corta, and Craik the grocer, and the freshmen at the university, who beat the kids off with clubs and forbade them to sneak into the big games at the stadium. He realized that, if he wasn't actually a murderer, he was the equivalent in the eyes of God.

One sin against that fifth commandment that always seethed in his conscience was an incident the summer before, when he and Paulie Hood, another Catholic boy, had captured a rat alive and crucified it to a small cross with tacks, and mounted it on an anthill. It was a ghastly and horrible thing that he never forgot. But the awful part of it was, they had done this evil thing on Good Friday, and right after saying the Stations of the Cross! He had confessed that sin shamefully, weeping as he told it, with true contrition, but he knew it had piled up many years in Purgatory, and it was almost six months before he even dared kill another rat.

Thou shalt not commit adultery; thou shalt not think about Rosa Pinelli, Joan Crawford, Norma Shearer, and Clara Bow. Oh gosh, oh Rosa, oh the sins, the sins, the sins. It began when he was four, no sin then because he was ignorant. It began when he sat in a hammock one day when he was four, rocking back and forth, and the next day he came back to the hammock between the plum tree and the apple tree in the back yard, rocking back and forth.

What did he know about adultery, evil thoughts, evil actions? Nothing. It was fun in the hammock. Then he learned to read, and the first of many things he read were the commandments. When he was eight he made his first Confession, and when he was nine he had to take the commandments apart and find out what they meant.

Adultery. They didn't talk about it in the fourth grade Catechism class. Sister Mary Anna skipped it and spent most of the time talking about Honor thy Father and Mother and Thou Shalt Not Steal. And so it was, for vague reasons he never could understand, that to him adultery always has had something to do with bank robbery. From his eighth year to his tenth, examining his conscience before Confession, he would pass over "Thou shalt not commit adultery" because he had never robbed a bank.

The man who told him about adultery wasn't Father Andrew, and it wasn't one of the nuns, but Art Montgomery at the Standard Station on the corner of Arapahoe and Twelfth. From that day on his loins were a thousand angry hornets buzzing in a nest. The nuns never talked about adultery. They only talked about evil thoughts, evil words, evil actions. That Catechism! Every secret of his heart, every sly delight in his mind was already known to that Catechism. He could not beat it, no matter how cautiously he tiptoed through the pinpoints of its code. He couldn't go to the movies anymore because he only went to the movies to see the shapes of his heroines. He liked 'love' pictures. He liked following girls up the stairs. He liked girls' arms, legs, hands, feet, their shoes and stockings and dresses, their smell and their presence. After his twelfth year the only things in life that mattered were baseball and girls, only he called them women. He liked the sound of the word. Women, women, women. He said it over and over because it was a secret sensation. Even at Mass, when there were fifty or a hundred of them around him, he reveled in the secrecy of his delights.

And it was all a sin—the whole thing had the sticky sensation of evil. Even the sound of some words was a sin. Ripple. Supple. Nipple. All sins. Carnal. The flesh. Scarlet. Lips. All sins. When he said the Hail Mary. Hail Mary full of grace, the Lord is with thee and blessed art thou among women, and blessed is the fruit of thy womb. The word shook him like thunder. Fruit of thy womb. Another sin was born.

Every week he staggered into the church of a Saturday afternoon, weighted down by the sins of adultery. Fear drove him there, fear that he would die and then live on forever in eternal torture. He did not dare lie to his confessor. Fear tore his sins out by the roots. He would confess it all fast, gushing with his uncleanliness, trembling to be pure. I committed a bad action I mean two bad actions and I thought about a girl's legs and about touching her in a bad place and I went to the show and thought bad things and I was walking along and a girl was getting out of a car and it was bad and I listened to a bad joke and laughed and a bunch of us kids were watching a couple of dogs and I said something bad, it was my fault, they didn't say anything, I did, I did it all, I made them laugh with a bad idea and I tore a picture out of a magazine and she was naked and I knew it was bad but did it anyway. I thought a bad thing about Sister Mary Agnes; it was bad and I kept on thinking. I also thought bad things about some girls who were laying on the grass and one of them had her dress up high and I kept on looking and knowing it was bad. But I'm sorry. It was my fault, all my fault, and I'm sorry, sorry.

He would leave the Confessional, and say his penance, his teeth gritted, his fist tightened, his neck rigid, vowing with body and soul to be clean forevermore. A sweetness would at last pervade him, a soothing lull him, a breeze cool him, a loveliness caress him. He would walk out of the church in a dream, and in a dream he would walk, and if no one was looking he'd kiss a tree, eat a blade of grass, blow kisses at the sky, touch the cold stones of the church wall with fingers of magic, the peace in his heart like nothing save a chocolate malted, a three-base hit, a shining window to be broken, the hypnosis of that moment that comes before sleep.

No, he wouldn't go to Hell when he died. He was a fast runner, always getting to Confession on time. But Purgatory awaited him. Not for him the direct, pure route to eternal bliss. He would get there the hard way, by detour. That was one reason why Arturo was an Altar Boy. Some piety on this earth was bound to lessen the Purgatory period.

He was an Altar Boy for two other reasons. In the first place, despite his ceaseless howls of protests, his mother insisted on it. In the second place, every Christmas season the girls in the Holy Name Society feted the Altar Boys with a banquet.

Rosa, I love you.

She was in the auditorium with the Holy Name Girls, decorating the tree for the Altar Boy Banquet. He watched from the door, feasting his eyes upon the triumph of her tiptoed loveliness. Rosa: tinfoil and chocolate bars, the smell of a new football, goal posts with bunting, a home run with the bases full. I am an Italian too, Rosa. Look, and my eyes are like yours. Rosa, I love you.

Sister Mary Ethelbert passed.

"Come, come, Arturo. Don't dawdle there."

She was in charge of the Altar Boys. He followed her black flowing robes to the 'little auditorium' where some seventy boys who comprised the male student body awaited her. She mounted the rostrum and clapped her hands for silence.

"All right boys, do take your places."

They lined up, thirty-five couples. The short boys were in front, the tall boys in the rear. Arturo's partner was Wally O'Brien, the kid who sold the Denver Posts in front of the First National Bank. They were twenty-fifth from the front, the tenth from the rear. Arturo detested this fact. For eight years he and Wally had been partners, ever since kindergarten. Each year found them moved back farther, and yet they had never made it, never grown tall enough to make it back to the last three rows where the big guys stood, where the wisecracks came from. Here it was, their last year in this lousy school, and they were still stymied around a bunch of sixth and seventh grade punks. They concealed their humiliation by an exceedingly tough and blasphemous exterior, shocking the sixth grade punks into a grudging and awful respect for their brutal sophistication.

But Wally O'Brien was lucky. He didn't have any kid brothers in the line to bother him. Each year, with increasing alarm, Arturo had watched his brothers August and Federico moving toward him from the front rows. Federico was now tenth from the front. Arturo was relieved to know that this youngest of his brothers would never pass him in the line-up. For next June, thank God, Arturo graduated, to be through forever as an Altar Boy.

But the real menace was the blonde head in front of him, his brother August. Already August suspected his impending triumph. Whenever the line was called to order he seemed to measure off Arturo's height with a contemptuous sneer. For indeed, August was the taller by an eighth of an inch, but Arturo, usually slouched over, always managed to straighten himself enough to pass Sister Mary Ethelbert's supervision. It was an exhausting process. He had to crane his neck and walk on the balls of his feet, his heels a half inch off the floor. Meanwhile he kept August in complete submission by administering smashing kicks with his knee whenever Sister Mary Ethelbert wasn't looking.

They did not wear vestments, for this was only practice. Sister Mary Ethelbert led them out of the little auditorium and down the hall, past the big auditorium, where Arturo caught a glance of Rosa sprinkling tinsel on the Christmas tree. He kicked August and sighed.

Rosa, me and you: a couple of Italians.

They marched down three flights of stairs and across the yard to the front doors of the church. The holy water fonts were frozen hard. In unison, they genuflected; Wally O'Brien's finger spearing the boy's in front of him. For two hours they practiced, mumbling Latin responses, genuflecting, marching in miltary piousness. *Ad deum qui loctificat, juventutem meum.*

At five o'clock, bored and exhausted, they were finished. Sister Mary Ethelbert lined them up for final inspection. Arturo's toes ached from bearing his full weight. In weariness he rested himself on his heels. It was a moment of carelessness for which he paid dearly. Sister Mary Ethelbert's keen eye just then observed a bend in the line, beginning and ending at the top of Arturo Bandini's head. He could read her thoughts, his weary toes rising in vain to the effort. Too late, too late. At her suggestion he and August changed places.

His new partner was a kid named Wilkins, fourth grader who wore celluloid glasses and picked his nose. Behind him, triumphantly sanctified, stood August, his lips sneering implacably, no word coming from him. Wally O'Brien looked at his erstwhile partner in crestfallen sadness, for Wally too had been humiliated by the intrusion of this upstart sixth grader. It was the end for Arturo. Out of the corner of his mouth he whispered to August.

"You dirty—" he said. "Wait'll I get you outside."

Arturo was waiting after practice. They met at the corner. August walked fast, as if he hadn't seen his brother. Arturo quickened his pace.

"What's your hurry, Tall Man?"

"I'm not hurrying, Shorty."

"Yes you are, Tall Man. And how would you like some snow rubbed in your face?"

"I wouldn't like it. And you leave me alone—Shorty."

"I'm not bothering you, Tall Man. I just want to walk home with you."

"Don't you try anything now."

"I wouldn't lay a hand on you, Tall Man. What makes you think I would?"

They approached the alley between the Methodist Church and the Colorado Hotel. Once beyond that alley, August was safe in the view of the loungers at the hotel window. He sprang forward to run, but Arturo's fist seized his sweater.

"What's the hurry, Tall Man?"

"If you touch me, I'll call a cop."

"Oh, I wouldn't do that."

A coupe passed, moving slowly. Arturo followed his brother's sudden open-mouthed stare at the occupants, a man and a woman. The woman was driving, and the man had his arm at her back.

"Look !"

But Arturo had seen. He felt like laughing. It was such a strange thing. Effie Hildegarde drove the car, and the man was Svevo Bandini.

The boys examined one another's faces. So that was why Mamma had asked all those questions about Effie Hildegarde! If Effie Hildegarde was good-looking. If Effie Hildegarde was a 'bad' woman.

Arturo's mouth softened to a laugh. The situation pleased him. That father of his! That Svevo Bandini! Oh boy—and Effie Hildegarde was a swell looking dame too!

"Did they see us?"

Arturo grinned. "No."

"Are you sure?"

"He had his arm around her, didn't he?"

August frowned.

"That's bad. That's going out with another woman. The ninth commandment."

They turned into the alley. It was a short cut. Darkness came fast. Water puddles at their feet were frozen in the growing darkness. They walked along, Arturo smiling. August was bitter.

"It's a sin. Mamma's a swell mother. It's a sin."

"Shut up."

They turned from the alley on Twelfth Street. The Christmas shopping crowd in the business district separated them now and then, but they stayed together, waiting as one another picked his way through the crowd. The street lamps went on.

"Poor Mamma. She's better than that Effie Hildegarde."

"Shut up."

"It's a sin."

"What do you know about it? Shut up."

"Just because Mamma hasn't got good clothes . . ."

"Shut up, August."

"It's a mortal sin."

"You're dumb. You're too little. You don't know anything."

"I know a sin. Mamma wouldn't do that."

The way his father's arm rested on her shoulder. He had seen her many times. She had charge of the girls' activities at the Fourth of July celebration in the Court House Park. He had seen her standing on the Court House steps the summer before, beckoning with her arms, calling the girls together for the big parade. He remembered her teeth, her pretty teeth, her red mouth, her fine plump body. He had left his friends to stand in the shadows and watch as she talked to the girls. Effie Hildegarde. Oh boy, his father was a wonder!

And he was like his father. A day would come when he and Rosa Pinelli would be doing it too. Rosa, let's get into the car and drive out in the country, Rosa. Me and you, out in the country, Rosa. You drive the car and we'll kiss, but you drive, Rosa.

"I bet the whole town knows it," August said.

"Why shouldn't they? You're like everybody else. Just because Papa's poor, just because he's an Italian."

"It's a sin," he said, kicking viciously at frozen chunks of snow. "I don't care what he is—or how poor, either. It's a sin."

"You're dumb. A saphead. You don't savvy anything."

August did not answer him. They took the short path over the trestle bridge that spanned the creek. They walked in single file, heads down, careful of the limitations of the deep path through the snow. They took the trestle bridge on tiptoe, from railroad tie to tie, the frozen creek thirty feet below them. The quiet evening spoke to them, whispering of a man riding in a car somewhere in the same twilight, a woman not his own riding with him. They descended the crest of the railroad line and followed a faint trail which they themselves had made all that winter in the comings and goings to and from school, through the Alzi pasture, with great sweeps of white on either side of the path, untouched for months, deep and glittering in the evening's birth. Home was a quarter of a mile away, only a block beyond the fences of the Alzi pasture. Here in this great pasture they had spent a great part of their lives. It stretched from the backyards of the very last row of houses in the town, weary frozen cottonwoods strangled in the death pose of long winters on one side, and a creek that no longer laughed on the other. Beneath that snow was white sand once very hot and excellent after swimming in the creek. Each tree held memories. Each fence post measured a dream, enclosing it for fulfillment with each new Spring. Beyond that pile of stones, between those two tall cottonwoods, was the graveyard of their dogs and Suzie, a cat who had hated the dogs but lay now beside them. Prince, killed by an automobile; Jerry, who ate the poison meat; Pancho the fighter, who crawled off and died after his last fight. Here they had killed snakes, shot birds, speared frogs, scalped Indians, robbed banks, completed wars, reveled in peace. But in that twilight their father rode with Effie Hildegarde, and the silent white sweep of the pasture land was only a place for walking on a strange road to home.

"I'm going to tell her," August said.

Arturo was ahead of him, three paces away. He turned around quickly. "You keep still," he said. "Mamma's got enough trouble."

"I'll tell her. She'll fix him."

"You shut up about this."

"It's against the ninth commandment. Mamma's our mother, and I'm going to tell."

Arturo spread his legs and blocked the path. August tried to step around him, the snow two feet deep on either side of the path. His head was down, his face set with disgust and pain. Arturo took both lapels of his mackinaw and held him.

"You keep still about this."

August shook himself loose.

"Why should I? He's our father, ain't he? Why does he have to do that?"

"Do you want Mamma to get sick?"

"Then what did he do it for?"

"Shut up! Answer my question. Do you want Mamma to be sick? She will if she hears about it."

"She won't get sick."

"I know she won't—because you're not telling."

"I am too."

The back of his hand caught August across the eyes.

"I said you're not going to tell!"

August's lips quivered like jelly.

"I'm telling."

Arturo's fist tightened under his nose.

"You see this? You get it if you tell."

Why should August want to tell? What if his father *was* with another woman? What difference did it make, so long as his mother didn't know? And besides, this wasn't another woman: this was Effie Hildegarde, one of the richest women in town. Pretty good for his father; pretty swell. She wasn't as good as his mother—no: but that didn't have anything to do with it.

"Go ahead and hit me. I'm telling."

The hard fist pushed into August's cheek. August turned his head away contemptuously. "Go ahead. Hit me. I'm telling."

"Promise not to tell or I'll knock your face in."

"Pooh. Go ahead. I'm telling."

He tilted his chin forward, ready for any blow. It infuriated Arturo. Why did August have to be such a damn fool? He didn't want to hit him. Sometimes he really enjoyed knocking August around, but not now. He opened his fist and clapped his hands on his hips in exasperation.

"But look, August," he argued. "Can't you see that it won't help to tell Mamma? Can't you just see her crying? And right now, at Christmas time too. It'll hurt her. It'll hurt her like hell. You don't want to hurt Mamma, you don't want to hurt your own mother, do you? You mean to tell me you'd go up to your own mother and say something that would hurt the hell out of her? Ain't that a sin, to do that?"

August's cold eyes blinked their conviction. The vapors of his breath flooded Arturo's face as he answered sharply. "But what about him? I suppose he isn't committing a sin. A worse sin than any I commit."

Arturo gritted his teeth. He pulled off his cap and threw it into the snow. He beseeched his brother with both fists. "God damn you! You're not telling."

"I am too."

With one blow he cut August down, a left to the side of his head. The boy staggered backward, lost his balance in the snow, and floundered on his back. Arturo was on him, the two buried in the fluffy snow beneath the hardened crust. His hands encircled August's throat. He squeezed hard.

"You gonna tell?"

The cold eyes were the same.

He lay motionless. Arturo had never known him that way before. What should he do? Hit him? Without relaxing his grip on August's neck he looked off toward the trees beneath which lay his dead dogs. He bit his lip and sought vainly within himself the anger that would make him strike.

Weakly he said, "Please, August. Don't tell."

"I'm telling."

So he swung. It seemed that the blood poured from his brother's nose almost instantly. It horrified him. He sat straddling August, his knees pinning down August's arms. He could not bear the sight of August's face. Beneath the mask of blood and snow August smiled defiantly, the red stream filling his smile.

Arturo knelt beside him. He was crying, sobbing with his head on August's chest, digging his hands into the snow and repeating: "Please August. Please! You can have anything I got. You can sleep on any side of the bed you want. You can have all my picture show money."

August was silent, smiling.

Again he was furious. Again he struck, smashing his fist blindly into the cold eyes. Instantly he regretted it, crawling in the snow around the quiet, limp figure.

Defeated at last, he rose to his feet. He brushed the snow from his clothes, pulled his cap down and sucked his hands to warm them. Still August lay there, blood still pouring from his nose: August the triumphant, stretched out like one dead, yet bleeding, buried in the snow, his cold eyes sparkling their serene victory.

Arturo was too tired. He no longer cared.

"Okay, August."

Still August lay there.

"Get up, August."

Without accepting Arturo's arm he crawled to his feet. He stood quietly in the snow, wiping his face with a handkerchief, fluffing the snow from his blonde hair. It was five minutes before the bleeding stopped. They said nothing. August touched his swollen face gently. Arturo watched him.

"You all right now?"

He did not answer as he stepped into the path and walked toward the row of houses. Arturo followed, shame silencing him: shame and hopelessness. In the moonlight he noticed that August limped. And yet it was not a limp so much as a caricature of one limping, like the pained embarrassed gait of the tenderfoot who had just finished his first ride on a horse. Arturo studied it closely. Where had he seen that before? It seemed so natural to August. Then he remembered: that was the way August used to walk out of the bedroom two years before, on those mornings after he had wet the bed.

"August," he said. "If you tell Mamma, I'll tell everybody that you pee the bed."

He had not expected more than a sneer, but to his surprise August turned around and looked him squarely in the face. It was a look of incredulity, a taint of doubt crossing the once cold eyes. Instantly Arturo sprang to the kill, his senses excited by the impending victory.

"Yes, sir!" he shouted. "I'll tell everybody. I'll tell the whole world. I'll tell every kid in the school. I'll write notes to every kid in the school. I'll tell everybody I see. I'll tell it and tell it to the whole town. I'll tell them August Bandini pees the bed. I'll tell 'em!"

"No!" August choked. "No, Arturo!"

He shouted at the top of his voice.

"Yes sir, all you people of Rocklin, Colorado! Listen to this: August Bandini pees the bed! He's twelve years old and he pees the bed. Did you ever hear of anything like that? Yipee! Everybody listen!"

"Please, Arturo! Don't yell. I won't tell. Honest I won't Arturo. I won't say a word! Only don't yell like that. I don't pee the bed, Arturo. I used to, but I don't now."

"Promise not to tell Mamma?"

August gulped as he crossed his heart and hoped to die.

"Okay," Arturo said. "Okay."

Arturo helped him to his feet and they walked home.

Lawrence Ferlinghetti

The Old Italians Dying

For years the old Italians have been dying
all over America
For years the old Italians in faded felt hats
have been sunning themselves and dying
You have seen them on the benches
in the park in Washington Square
the old Italians in their black high button shoes

the old men in their old felt fedoras
                              with stained hatbands
have been dying and dying
                              day by day
You have seen them
every day in Washington Square San Francisco
the slow bell
tolls in the morning
in the Church of Peter & Paul
in the marzipan church on the plaza
toward ten in the morning the slow bell tolls
in the towers of Peter & Paul
and the old men who are still alive
sit sunning themselves in a row
on the wood benches in the park
and watch the processions in and out
funerals in the morning
weddings in the afternoon
slow bell in the morning Fast bell at noon
In one door out the other
the old men sit there in their hats
and watch the coming & going
You have seen them
the ones who feed the pigeons
                    cutting the stale bread
                          with their thumbs & penknives
the ones with old pocketwatches
the old ones with gnarled hands
                          and wild eyebrows
the ones with the baggy pants
                          with both belt & suspenders
the grappa drinkers with teeth like corn
the Piemontesi the Genovesi the Sicilianos
                    smelling of garlic & pepperonis
the ones who loved Mussolini
the old fascists
the ones who loved Garibaldi
the old anarchists reading *L'Umanita Nova*
the ones who loved Sacco & Vanzetti
They are almost all gone now
They are sitting and waiting their turn
and sunning themselves in front of the church

over the doors of which is inscribed
a phrase which would seem to be unfinished
from Dante's *Paradiso*
about the glory of the One
                   who moves everything . . .
The old men are waiting
for it to be finished
for their glorious sentence on earth
                to be finished
the slow bell tolls & tolls
the pigeons strut about
not even thinking of flying
the air too heavy with heavy tolling
The black hired hearses draw up
the black limousines with black windowshades
shielding the widows
the widows with the long black veils
who will outlive them all
You have seen them
madre di terra, madre di mare
The widows climb out of the limousines
The family mourners step out in stiff suits
The widows walk so slowly
up the steps of the cathedral
fishnet veils drawn down
leaning hard on darkcloth arms
Their faces do not fall apart
They are merely drawn apart
They are still the matriarchs
outliving everyone
the old dagos dying out
in Little Italys all over America
the old dead dagos
hauled out in the morning sun
that does not mourn for anyone
One by one Year by year
they are carried out
The bell
never stops tolling
The old Italians with lapstrake faces
are hauled out of the hearses

by the paid pallbearers
in mafioso mourning coats & dark glasses
The old dead men are hauled out
in their black coffins like small skiffs
They enter the true church
for the first time in many years
in these carved black boats
                    ready to be ferried over
The priests scurry about
                as if to cast off the lines
The other old men
                        still alive on the benches
watch it all with their hats on
You have seen them sitting there
waiting for the bocci ball to stop rolling
waiting for the bell
                    to stop tolling & tolling
for the slow bell
                to be finished tolling
telling the unfinished *Paradiso* story
as seen in an unfinished phrase
                    on the face of a church
as seen in a fisherman's face
in a black boat without sails
making his final haul

Robert Ferro

From *The Family of Max Desir*

Right after Christmas, John took her out to have the tapestry framed;
subsequently it came back edged in dramatic black lacquer with a thin
stripe of gold—a cross between a decree and a funeral announcement,
but smart. Max set up the ladder in the den and took down all the
prints, plaques, needlepoint, photographs, silhouettes and inspirational
sayings from the main wall—the whole pictorial archive of the family,
now summed up in this new piece, the largest and therefore the center

of a new arrangement. John suggested the tapestry be raised a few inches and Marie put her hand to her mouth, not in alarm but conversationally, at the risk Max took in standing at the top of the ladder.

Later when he and Nick left, Marie was quiet and John asked if there was something wrong. She said no and waved away the whole idea, which he interpreted to mean, yes, there was something, but she preferred to withhold it.

Is it the tapestry? he asked, pointing up at the tree. She looked at him, then up at the wall. She lifted her chin in the old way, meaning, What about it?

Well, the lettering, John said, as if she had actually spoken.

She squinted in the direction of the tapestry, meaning it was too far away for her to see distinctly.

You know that Nick's name is on there with Max's, John said, going over to it. Do you know that? He took the tapestry off the wall and brought it over to her.

She looked at it, leaned toward it and peered at the branches. Max Desir and Nick Flynn, she pointed silently to the syllables. She nodded and sat back in her chair.

After a moment John said, Do you think his name should be on there?

Perhaps he had waited too long to ask. Marie looked at him again and frowned. What was he talking about?

The name, John said, something like exasperation in his voice. Nick Flynn's name is on the tree. . . . It's a family tree, Marie.

His impatience made her cross. Again she waved him away, and John leaned the tapestry against the wall.

Marie's younger brother Frank and his second wife Helen walked in the back door. They came Saturdays from Long Island, right after their visit to Dan in the nursing home. Marie had not been to see Dan since before Thanksgiving and whenever Frank arrived she looked at him inquisitively until he said, He's the same, Sis, and then she looked away.

They all watched television. Frank was the first one outside the family to see the tapestry. He said it was beautiful, then he saw Nick's name, read it out loud and said, Why is Nick Flynn's name on here with Max?

In the kitchen John pretended not to hear. How about another drink, Frank? he said, and Frank said, No, we better get started.

Later when Robin came in and noticed the tapestry leaning against the wall, John said, Max put it up today. I took it down.

You took it down . . . why? Robin later repeated this all to Max.

John threw up his hand, immediately angry. I don't want everybody asking me who Nick Flynn is, he said. It's my house. It's my wall. I don't want *My son is a homosexual* written on it.

Oh Dad, come on, Robin said. Who's going to see it?

Well, your uncle Frank was just here and asked me why Nick's name was on there with Max's, dammit. I don't want them looking at that tree and asking me who the hell's Nick Flynn. I want his name off that tree or it won't go up on the wall.

Now wait a minute, Robin said. It's not something you can do just like that. They're . . .

They're not married, he interrupted her.

Do you expect them to be married? she asked. They've been together fifteen years.

Well, what do I say when people ask? he said. You tell *me.*

If you have to say something, say Nick is like a son to us. . . .

So why would he be on the branch with Max? he said. Like a son to us or a wife to Max?

Why are you making such a big deal out of this? She went back a little. Hardly anyone comes in here and it doesn't matter what you say.

I have a board meeting of the Cadets here tomorrow. There will be eleven men here. I don't want every Tom, Dick and Harry asking me about my son and this man.

Later that afternoon John asked Andrea, through the reluctant Robin, to erase Nick's name from the branch, to which Andrea replied that her grandfather could do what he liked with the tapestry, she didn't care, but she wasn't going to erase anything. Then Sunday morning John moved a seascape from another room to the empty space on the den wall and told Robin to put the tapestry away. As she was going out the door she said that removing this symbol of his relationship with two people was the same as removing the people themselves. Did he understand that? She said that the seascape he was hanging in place of the tapestry represented the gulf he was putting between himself and Max and Nick, and that in this case it was filled with purple water.

When Max returned with Nick for dinner that evening, the first thing he did was peek into the den at the new arrangement. He saw the seascape. Where's the tree? he asked.

There's a problem about that, John said. I was going to talk to you about it after dinner, with Nick. But all right, he said, turning and walking into the den, why don't you tell Nick to come in? And Max, immediately wary, said, You tell me about it first and I'll tell Nick. He followed his father into the big room.

I took the tree down, John said, and put his hands in his pockets.

Why did you do that? he asked.

I did it because I didn't want Nick's name on the tree with yours.

You took it down, Max repeated—as if for an official record that now silently and suddenly fell into session around them—you took it down because you don't want Nick's name on the tree with mine.

That's right, his father said. It embarrasses me. I don't know why I have to have it written on my wall that my son is a homosexual.

I'm very surprised, Max said evenly. I thought we had covered this.

Well, we have. But you see—his father was suddenly aggressive—it's when people come in here. He peered across the room as if squinting at the tapestry. Who's Nick Flynn? he said. Is he part of my blood? What am I supposed to say? Why do I have to say it?

Look, Max said. I don't care what you say. But have you thought about our reaction? Did you think about what Nick would think? Don't you care about the way we feel?

Yes, I do, John replied. That's not the point

What is the point? That you won't be embarrassed in front of your friends? Is *bella figura* the point?

What am I supposed to do? John demanded. You can be anything you want, and so can Nick. But not on my wall.

Why do you say it like that?

Why do I have to advertise it?

It sat here for a month, Max said. Why, with everything that's happening in this house—

Let's keep our voices down, his father said. We don't want your mother to hear this.

And what did she say about it? Max asked.

Nothing . . . I don't think she understands.

What the hell do you know? Max said, and they looked at each other across two yards of carpet.

Max, I'm sorry. You're my son and I love you, no matter what.

I'd rather have a little common sense and decency.

What do you mean by that? John said.

If you loved anybody you'd realize what you're doing.

You and Nick—his father began.

Me and Nick are part of this family, Max cut in. Whether you see it that way or not. He just spent the summer taking care of Mom just like everyone else. . . . He was family then and he's family now.

Whoever heard of two men being on a family tree together?

What a hypocrite you are, Max said.

I don't want his name with yours on that tree, John repeated.

But it *is* on the tree. That's the way it is.

Well, I don't have to like it, or advertise it, John said.

No, you don't. It's your house. Do what you want. He turned to leave. His father called him back. A crowd of demons knocked at the door, rang the bell, flicked the window shades, tipped over furniture.

I don't want to talk about it anymore, Max said. I think it stinks. I don't think you know what you're doing.

Yes, I do, John started to say, but Max left the room.

Throughout dinner he thought of things he would like to say to his father but couldn't, not in front of Marie, or Nick, who certainly knew Max was angry about something, but didn't know what it was. John cut Marie's food into tiny pieces. It was clear that Penny, who had arrived just before dinner, knew what had happened. She nervously presided over the meal as if hired for the occasion.

Max told Nick as they were driving back to Manhattan. Nick was surprised, then incredulous and quiet for most of the ride. By the time they reached the bridge he was angry and when they got through the apartment door Nick started to cry. It seemed to mean that no one in the family cared enough to defend him.

What about the others? he said. How could they let him do it? He takes my name down like I don't exist. I can't believe it.

It was surprising even to Max that it mattered so deeply. He called Jack and then Robin to ask what they knew, which was only that each of them had pleaded with John to put the tapestry back on the wall. Robin said she had been very specific, explaining what it meant and what the results were likely to be. Jack had even predicted to his father that he might lose Max, and certainly Nick.

It's very simple, Max said. Either he puts the tapestry back on the wall and apologizes to Nick, or after Mom is gone I'll never see any of you again.

Us? But why penalize us as well? his brother said. We tried to stop him, Max. We tried everything.

You should have stopped him. You should have held him down. You should have stuffed his mouth with rags.

I don't think he knew how strongly you would react, his brother began. In their conversations Jack tended to speak in long sentences and Max tended to interrupt him.

I thought you said you told him that, Max said. Maybe you mean that *you* didn't know how I would react.

It's a horrible thing, Jack said.

What would you do, Max said, if Dad took Mary Kay's name off the tree? What would you do?

It's not the same thing.

Don't give me that shit. It's exactly the same. If you can't see that you're no better than he is.

How can you say that, Max? Your homosexuality means nothing to me one way or the other.

This happened, Max said, because you and Robin and Penny didn't face him together and say it was wrong.

But we did!

Penny didn't say a word, not to him or to me. Not a fucking word. She's too busy being a daughter to be a sister.

You can't blame Penny for this, Jack said.

Why not? I blame everyone. What the hell is this? Am I less than you? Are you better than me? Do you think Nick and I can be erased?

No, of course not.

Either you talk to him now, Max said, or I'll never see you or your wife or your kids or any of you again.

But Max . . .

If Nick and I mean anything to you, you'll say it. You all will. You'll threaten him and convince him he's wrong.

But we tried, Jack said.

Oh fuck, Max said, and hung up.

Camille Lavieri Forman

From *A Perfect Time for Butterflies*

When Grandma Minnelli left Corleto, Mary was about four years old, Rose five or six. My grandfather Giuseppe Nicola Minnelli (or Minelli or Manelli) had arrived in the United States a few years earlier, with the intention of getting a job and then sending back a ticket for his wife and daughter Rose. However, shortly after arriving in the United States, he received news that his family was about to increase. Anna Maria was pregnant with my mother Mary (her full name was Immaculata Maria), so now he had to earn enough to bring all three to join him.

He was proud of the fact that he had been able to earn enough money so that they were not obliged to travel steerage class but had better accommodations. Food was a problem, however, as almost certainly none of them had ever eaten a meal away from home. I recall my grandmother describing her first experience with butter, unknown in the arid countryside they'd come from. "It was something like soap, but you put it on bread, and they tell me it's good for children."

Their third child, a son, Frank, was born in Hartford in 1914. My grandfather told me a few years before he died in 1971 that my grandmother had been pregnant with a fourth child but had a miscarriage when she continued to go to work picking tobacco on a farm in the Connecticut River Valley. My grandfather had wanted her to stop but she chose not to. Was this her way of limiting the size of her family? My grandfather came from a big family, most of whom had lots of children. Indeed, one of his sisters had twenty-three pregnancies, not all of which went to full term, and perhaps my grandmother was haunted by that image.

My grandmother hadn't wanted to leave Italy with such small children, so she kept delaying the departure time until my grandfather in desperation sent her a letter saying that if she didn't leave soon he would find himself "another woman." The story is that she got on the next available boat.

Rocco Fumento

From *Tree of Dark Reflection*

I was enjoying my stay at Albero. After the quickening tempo of the *festa,* the town settled down to its normal, easy pace, and I discovered it was a quiet, peaceful existence that my uncle and his fellow priests led in their boys' school. I was grateful to be allowed to share this existence with them, to rest well, to sleep dreamless sleeps and with an easy conscience, even if for so brief a time. I felt refreshed, invigorated, clean, free of the cumulative tensions of the past few months, especially as concerned my relationship with Madalena, and I even believed quite firmly that I was truly free of her at last.

Only in one respect did I sense a vague dissatisfaction with the progress of my visit. Though I wouldn't admit to myself, and so certainly not to my uncle, [. . .] the main purpose of my trip to Albero was to seek out those events in the past which would lead me to a better understanding of the relationship which evolved between my parents.

I came abruptly upon the Father Superior. He was bent in what seemed deep concentration over a bed of wilted roses, and since I had thought he had not seen me, and to save us both the embarrassment of his cool, constrained greetings, I began quickly to retreat.

"There's no need to flee from me," he called out, and I turned back to him and his eyes met mine enigmatically a moment, as though he hoped to communicate something to me without the necessity of saying it, and then he lowered them again to the flower bed. "A pity. The frost last night has killed the last of them. I had hoped we'd have a few for the altar tonight. These are a breed unique to Albero—long-blooming hardies they are, but thornier than most. I brought them from my home in Sicily. My mother's first love was her husband and children. Her second love was roses. She was known for her roses as far off as Palermo, and even the Mayor of Palermo came to visit once. Well, that's in the past. Do you know anything about roses?"

"No," I said. "I'm not much of a gardener."

"Aren't you? What a pity. To plant, to watch things grow, and to know you've had a hand in it—makes one feel like God a bit." He carefully brushed the earth from his cassock and then came toward me. The corners of his mouth were twitching, as though he were attempting to restrain a nervous laugh. "I haven't been very civil to you, have I?"

"It doesn't matter," I said. "I know it must be difficult. . . . I can understand your feelings."

"Can you?" he said dryly. "I see your busybody uncle has already spoken to you. I wish he hadn't. It's no excuse for my behavior."

"Really, it doesn't matter," I assured him.

"It matters to me! If you knew of the sleepless nights, the many times I . . . Do you believe in sainthood?" he asked abruptly.

"In saints?"

"No, not only in saints, but that every man is a potential saint. That the purpose of life is to attempt to achieve sainthood. No, perhaps not. Or perhaps you've never thought of it. Those in the world don't often think of such things, do they? But that was my goal in life, you know— to achieve sainthood."

He paused, as though simply to speak were a great effort for him now, and I was startled to see that he was trembling, that his eyes shone with an intense, feverish light, and I knew he was making a supreme effort to control himself.

"And why shouldn't I be a saint, I asked myself," he burst out finally in a frightening release of his emotions. "Hadn't I followed the teachings of Christ? Didn't the people love me for my humility, my charity, my understanding, for my submission to the will of God? Inevitably, perhaps I'm already a saint, I said to myself, and I wonder if it was the devil who spoke within me, for it was then I learned my family had been bombed out of existence by the Americans and too soon my flimsy sainthood was to be put to the test. When they came here, forced themselves upon us and turned our boys away, lived under this roof, ate at our table, I already hated them. Finally I knew, and a bitter knowledge it was, that I was not a saint, and so I hated them all the more because they had made me aware that I was not, until, in the end, I hated them not because of my family, not because of my dear mother who grew beautiful roses, but because through them I learned I had loved myself too well. Do you understand? It was because of my pride, only my pride finally, that I hated them—and then you."

"There's no need, Father, no need at all for you to tell me this," I said, embarrassed by his confession, by his abject account of it, and why to me of all people?

"There is a need, a terrible need!" he protested. Then a convulsive sob shook his body, and to my dismay and astonishment he fell to his knees before me and grasped me about the legs.

"What are you doing?" I cried out, wondering if he were perpetrating some monstrous joke upon me. "My God, please get up! What if someone comes?"

"Let them come, let them all come to see me kneeling before you, for my sin weighs too heavily upon me and I know I must humble myself if I am ever to seek forgiveness."

"Seek forgiveness! Of me?"

"Yes, yes. The moment you arrived it was like a sign from God. Here is your salvation, He whispered in my ear, and I haven't been able to sleep since, for I knew this was the way it must be."

"Why me? What harm have you done to me?"

"The others, all whom I detested, have long since gone away, and so who else can I ask forgiveness of? There remains only you—you are the last. Don't you see?"

"No, I don't see, no! Ask forgiveness of God, if you must, not of me!"

"If you do not forgive me, how can I ask forgiveness of God?"

"I forgive you then, only get up," I pleaded, struggling to raise him to his feet, knowing that we must have made a ludicrous sight and uneasily hoping we weren't being observed. "Please, get up."

"You truly forgive me? For all the Americans and for all my hatred?"

"For God's sake, yes."

He grasped my hand and kissed it and allowed me finally to help him to his feet. "Thank you," he whispered, "thank you. May the good Lord look down in favor upon you." Then he smiled at me and asked, as though all the while we'd been holding a polite conversation: "Will you take tea with me this afternoon? Your uncle tells me you're fond of books and I've some rare editions I'd like you to see." I nodded a bewildered assent and he smiled again and walked swiftly into the school.

I was shaken and for a moment I almost doubted that the scene had taken place, doubted my sanity because it was ridiculous and pitiful and incredible that this man, whom I thought so proud, so arrogantly cold, should kneel before me and make me his confessor. I sank down onto one of the garden benches and it was there my uncle found me.

I didn't see him until I felt his hand on my shoulder and I looked up at him in confusion. "Are you ill?" he asked. "Didn't you hear me call?"

I shook my head. "Tell me," I said. "Is your Father Superior a madman?"

"No madder than any of us, I imagine. Have you been sitting in the sun too long?"

"But you should have seen! He fell on his knees, right here, and asked forgiveness of me—for all the Americans, he said, all he hated."

"Is that it?" he smiled. "Well, good, then, good."

"Good!"

"Yes," he nodded. "I think he may indeed become a saint now—really a saint now."

"Is that all you think of in this place?" I said irritably. "Do you all strive for sainthood?"

"Oh no, not all. Not me, for instance. No, I'm not capable of sainthood, not true sainthood. I am what you Americans might call a middle-of-the-roader, incapable of great good or great evil, like most of humanity, I'm afraid. No, sainthood requires a tremendous amount of imagination, the mystical ability to glimpse heaven and hell. I don't have that kind of imagination—only a few have. Your father, I think . . . Perhaps I am wrong, but he may have had the imagination."

"My father!"

"Does that sound too incredible to you? From the expression on your face I imagine it does." He sat next to me on the bench, searching my face intently as though seeking a clue for understanding in it. "I suppose that's why I haven't mentioned him sooner. Oh, I can understand why you haven't—the memories are all bad, perhaps. That's why it's too difficult for me to comprehend and why I haven't been able to speak of him."

"To comprehend what?"

"All the things I've heard. All the things your mother has written to me. Are they true? Really true, Daniele?"

"Do you seriously doubt they're true?"

"Because he was so good, I mean—not only religious, but truly spiritual. Much more so than I was. I was always rather envious of him because I felt he was in direct communication with God and I was not. Oh, many a time I doubted my own vocation—how I doubted—but I never doubted his."

"His vocation?"

"Yes, of course. When we were in the monastery together. It was also a seminary, you understand, for those of us who wished to become priests."

"My father—in a monastery? A seminary?"

"Didn't you know?" he said incredulously.

"I knew nothing," I said. The idea seemed too preposterous and my first impulse was to laugh. My father, who did not believe in God and yet was plagued by the devil, in a monastery? My father studying to be a priest?

"No one told you?" He was flustered suddenly, obviously disturbed by my surprise and just as obviously wondering whether he'd made a revelation he probably shouldn't have.

"No one, Uncle Guido," I assured him. "Yes, I knew some old priest took him away, but to a school, I thought, not to a monastery. Is that where he took him? You must tell me all about it, Uncle."

"What is there to tell?" he said, rising abruptly to his feet and turning his back upon me. "Didn't I already tell you? He was in the monastery with me and that's all."

"And he was studying for the priesthood?"

"But why has no one told you? I don't understand—not at all."

"For God's sake, what difference does it make now?" I said impatiently. "Was he expelled from the monastery? That was it, wasn't it?"

"Expelled! What an incredible notion. We thought he was a saint. Do you understand?"

"Italy, the land of the saints." I smiled sardonically. "Now, please, tell me of my father's sainthood, Uncle."

"Do you hate him so much?"

"I've no reason to love him," I said.

"I suppose not," he sighed. "Well, at least let us walk into the garden where it's cool. I cannot bear this harsh sunlight."

I followed him into the garden. It was unbearably sweet with the scent of laurel and mimosa and we walked silently for some time, beneath the shade of lemon trees and rose arbors while my uncle, apparently, sought to collect his thoughts.

"Yes," he began finally, hesitantly, "an old priest brought him to the monastery—up in the hills it was, overlooking the village of my birth. His mother and father were dead and the old priest brought him to be raised by the brothers. Oh, he was quite young at the time—just a boy and at least several years younger than I."

"And so they attempted to make a priest of him." I smiled.

"Certainly not! They had no intention of making a priest of him and none of us scarcely imagined the priesthood was for him. No, he was too wild a boy—moody, insolent, spiteful, filled with strange passions. Strange to me, at least, for I've never been able to comprehend such passions."

"Yes," I said. "That sounds like my father."

"Does it? Well, it's not the Domenico we came to know and love, some years later. Perhaps he was merely lonely and frightened, I don't know. You must remember, he was quite young. He spoke of an old woman and said he must return to her. She was his mother, he said, and yet we knew his mother was dead. Several times he ran away and each time he was brought back by the Abbot Cossimo. 'Why do you waste your time with him?' the brothers asked the abbot. 'He was left in our care,' the abbot replied. 'Are we to abandon him now?'

"The brothers were willing enough to abandon him, but not the abbot. 'All he needs is taming,' he would say of Domenico, and even made him an altar boy. Domenico an altar boy? Yes, that was a marvelous joke, everyone laughed. And what did Domenico do on the day he first served Mass? He placed a frog in the abbot's chalice. The abbot saw the frog and still drank from the cup. What else could he do? It contained the blood of our Lord. Everyone was appalled at the boy. He was an agent of the devil, they said. It was a monstrous act he committed, a sacrilege, they said, and he must be sent packing immediately."

"So even then he was corrupt," I interrupted. "I knew if I looked deeply enough into the past . . ."

"Corrupt? No, the abbot didn't think so. He had tremendous faith in Domenico, you see, and soon enough his faith was justified, much to the astonishment of us all, of course. Outwardly there was no change in him, however, until the abbot lay dying and Domenico went to him. 'I wish to become a priest,' he said. 'Do you say this to make me well? Ah, Domenico, do not jest with me.' 'I say it because it's what I want. Truly what I want,' he said to the abbot. It was a justified lie, a noble, justified lie, we thought, to bring happiness to the abbot's final moments, and we loved Domenico for it. But it was no lie.

"Ah, to have known him then, after the abbot's death. He was a warm, affectionate person—kind, gentle, selfless, with a humility rare in one so young. He volunteered for the worst duties, scrubbing floors, weeding the gardens—all the work that must be done on one's knees. An old man came to the monastery one day and sought refuge. He was a leper and had been driven from his village. 'A leper in our midst? No, impossible,' the new abbot said. 'The most we can do is to give him some food and send him on his way.' But Domenico couldn't bear to send him away. 'Let me care for him in the ruins of the old church. Then we need not contaminate the monastery,' he said. 'And if you should catch the disease?' the abbot said. 'God will protect me,' he replied, and so what could the abbot do? The leper lived for six months and for six months Domenico cared for him, cleansed his rotting flesh, bathed him, washed his clothes, all in the solitary ruins of the old church, for the abbot would permit none of us to approach this abandoned pair.

"I learned to love him then. We all did. And his intense love for God, his great faith, made me ashamed because mine seemed so weak in comparison. Though he was younger than I, he always plagued the abbot with: 'When may I take my vows?' It wasn't enough to serve man, you see. He couldn't wait to be of service to God as well."

"Am I supposed to believe this charming tale?" I said, not admitting that it had left me a bit shaken and terribly perplexed. "A hypocrite. Wasn't that what he was? Didn't he simply pretend to love God and the leper?"

"To what purpose? And if it were so, could we all be blind to his hypocrisy? Ah, Daniele, why do you persist in being so cynical?"

"Because what you're saying . . . I can't believe . . . it's impossible to believe this was my father."

"I know nothing of your father except from hearsay. I can only tell you of the man I knew."

"Can a man change from devil to saint and back again?"

"If he has the power to glimpse eternity, to witness heaven and hell, yes, why not? Wasn't Mary Magdalene possessed by devils before she achieved sainthood? And St. Francis and St. Augustine and so many others?"

"You compare them with my father? You expect me to believe that he . . . ?"

"I don't expect you to believe anything I say, Daniele. I can only tell you what I know. If you want to listen."

"Yes, I want to listen," I said sullenly. "Tell me what happened then—as you know it."

"There's not very much to tell. Not as much as you expect, perhaps. I myself am not certain what happened—not at all certain." We came to a bench and he sat down. He was subdued now, seemed exhausted, and for the first time since my visit I became poignantly aware of the fact that he was an old man.

"I loved him like a brother," he continued. "Even more. He was what I wanted so desperately to be, and it began, I suppose, when I asked him to come home with me. We were permitted to go home for the holidays—before we took our vows, that is. And so, during the Christmas season it was, I took him home with me. At home he was shy with everyone, even with your grandmother, who made a son or daughter of everyone we brought home. And he seemed actually terrified of your mother—perhaps because she was young and beautiful, I don't know—and when we returned to the monastery, he prayed more fervently than before and was more insistent with the abbot about taking his vows.

"At Easter time I invited him home again. At first he refused. He had been ill—a fever, the doctors said, though they couldn't find the cause—and he was pale and spent and I thought the change would be good for him. When I insisted that he come, he became angry. I had never seen him angry before, not since he was a boy, and his anger frightened and perplexed me, and so I left him. He ran after me when I was just beyond the gates. 'Wait,' he shouted. 'I'm coming with you.' It was then the change occurred. Oh, he returned to the monastery with me, but only to tell the abbot that he wished to leave, wished not to take his final vows. He was to have taken them in another month, you see. Instead he returned to my village and became an apprentice to a carpenter. My mother wrote and said he came often to the house. A few months later he married your mother. That's all I know, Daniele. Nothing more."

"His departure from the monastery," I prompted uneasily. "Did it have anything to do with my mother?"

"I don't understand you," he said.

"Was it because of her? Is that why he left?"

"How can I say? I didn't have access to his heart—or to your mother's."

We were both silent then, for a very long time. His story was too incredible—more than that, ridiculous—and I wanted to laugh, and suddenly I did laugh, softly at first, as though I were enjoying a private joke, and then uncontrollably. "I'm . . . I'm sorry," I stammered finally, attempting to stifle the laughter. "I'm sorry, but I can't help it. It's too fantastic. My father a priest! If your story is true, and how can I doubt it, then why has no one mentioned it before? Not my mother, not my father . . . And what, in God's name, has happened to him since then?"

My uncle seemed frightened by what at best seemed a reaction of levity on my part. "How am I to know," he said, "when I've seen neither him nor your mother in so many years? But listen to me, Daniele. His call to serve God was genuine and strong and beautiful. That I do know. And perhaps . . . well, in leaving the seminary, perhaps he felt he'd refused to answer God's call, do you see? Perhaps he felt he'd turned his back upon Him and so betrayed Him like a Judas or a Lucifer, and slowly a guilt began to fester within him. Guilt, you know, can cause a man to do many terrible things, and maybe that's why he's changed."

Yes, it was an explanation, or a partial explanation, for my father's behavior, but at the time it was impossible for me to accept it. What did I know of vocations and calls to God? One became a priest like one became a dentist, a lawyer, a plumber, I thought, and if one decided to become a dentist rather than a lawyer, did one spend a lifetime in guilty self-recriminations and so destroy himself and others with him?

But my uncle, it seemed, had told me all he knew, or at least all he intended to tell me. However, it wasn't quite enough, I felt, and I knew someday I must seek the other answers from my mother.

That evening I attended midnight Mass at the school chapel. I was embarrassed because the Father Superior announced he was offering it for me, in thanksgiving. In thanksgiving for what he didn't say, but the other priests seemed to know what he meant and smiled warmly, affectionately at me, as though we shared a sublime secret, giving me credit for his salvation, no doubt, and so making me a hypocrite because, of course, I'd done nothing. And because of this, and because of Uncle Guido's revelations and what I chose to interpret as his too benign, too charitable attitude toward my father, which had estranged me from my uncle and now made me uncomfortable in his presence, I wanted to get away as quickly as possible. But I'd promised my uncle I'd stay for Christmas, and so I stayed.

I left the day after Christmas and took the blessings of the priests with me. The Father Superior brought me a present, a small silver tray with a tiny rosebud delicately etched in the center. "It was a wedding gift from my father to my mother," he said. "I found it in the ruins of my home and nothing much else, I'm afraid."

"No, I can't accept it," I said. "Please, Father."

"You must. It was a symbol of my hatred, you know. Now let it be a symbol of my love."

My uncle came to the railroad station with me, though I begged him not to. His eyes were moist as he embraced me and, I suppose, he sensed my discomfort, my disillusionment with him.

"I'm just a foolish old man," he said, "fumbling my way through life. I wanted to show you, to tell you. . . . Well, no matter. You're the last of my people I shall see, and so forgive me my tears . . . my inadequacy. I've always wanted to help others, you know, and I'm afraid I've never been much help."

Then, as I was about to board the train, he grasped my arm. "Try not to hate him too much, Daniele," he said. "At one time many of us loved him. Surely he's not abandoned God completely. I know God has not abandoned him."

He seemed a pathetic, lonely, bewildered figure as I last saw him raising his hand in a final good-by gesture, and I was filled with a sudden remorse for the estrangement I'd imposed upon us during the latter part of my visit. It was I, after all, who had forced him to tell me of my father, and because I was unwilling to accept the implications of my discovery, antagonistic to his attitude toward the man who became my father, was it fair to release my antagonism upon him?

The trip back up north was long and depressing, and by the time I arrived in Trieste, I knew my period of atonement was over and I went to visit Madalena.

Richard Gambino

From *Blood of My Blood:*
The Dilemma of the Italian-Americans

Although I tried to explain the basis of familial devotion, she seemed psychologically incapable of understanding such feelings. Thus the irony, an Americano of Sicilian ancestry explaining the ways of the not so distant past Mezzogiorno to an uncomprehending native Italian, even if a Northern Italian. Little wonder, then, that to most Americans the Chinese character is probably more scrutable than that of millions of their own countrymen who are Italian-Americans.

This background of the *ordine della famiglia* helps illuminate the confused situation of Italian-Americans today. As all of us are confronted with the conflicts of our loyalty to a sovereign state vs. our cosmopolitan aspirations, so the Italian-American has found himself in the dilemma of reconciling the psychological sovereignty of his people with the aspirations and demands of being American.

To the immigrant generation of Italians, the task was clear. Hold to the sovereignty of the old ways and thereby seal out the threats of the new "strangers," the American society that surrounded them. The complicated customs and institutions of la famiglia had been marvelously effective in neutralizing the influence of a succession of aliens in the Mezzogiorno. In the old land, the people survived and developed their own identity over centuries not so much by their periodic violent rebellions, a futile approach because of the small size, exposed location, and limited resources of Southern Italy. Instead they endured and built their culture by sealing out the influence of strangers.

The sealing medium was not military or even physical. It was at once an antisocial mentality and a supremely social psychology, for it formed the very stuff of contadino society. It constituted the foundation and hidden steel beams of a society that historically had been denied the luxury of more accessible (and vulnerable) foundations or superstructure. This is a reason for the contadino's famous pride. L'ordine della famiglia was a system of social attitudes, values, and customs that had proven to be impenetrable to the *sfruttamento* (exploitation) of any stranieri, no matter how powerful their weapons or clever their devices. But like all defenses, this life style had exacted costs in the old land. These were the vexing social and economic problems that Italians still lump together under the terms *problema del Mezzogiorno* or *questione meridionale,* meaning "the Southern problem." The problem became catastrophic after the founding of the Italian nation in 1860–1870. And [. . .] millions of contadini were forced by the specter of starvation to immigrate to other lands.

Because it had worked for so long in the old land in providing them with stability, order, and security, the ordine della famiglia was held to tenaciously by the immigrants in the new country. Thus the immigrants were able to achieve their twofold goals. One, they found bread and work. No matter how dismal and exploitive, it was better than the starvation they fled. And, two, they resisted the encroachments of la via nuova into their own lives. In their terms, their audacious adventure has to be judged a success. But the price in the United States was very high. It included isolation from the larger society.

The immigrants' children, the second generation, faced a challenge more difficult to overcome. They could not maintain the same degree of isolation. Indeed, they had to cope with American institutions, first schools, then a variety of economic, military, and cultural environments.

In so doing, what was a successful social strategy for their parents became a crisis of conflict for them. Circumstances split their personalities into conflicting halves. Despite parental attempts to shelter them from American culture, they attended the schools, learned the language, and confronted the culture.

It was a rending confrontation. The parents of the typical second-generation child ridiculed American institutions and sought to nurture in him la via vecchia. The father nurtured in his children (sons especially) a sense of mistrust and cynicism regarding the outside world. And the mother bound her children (not only daughters) to the home by making any aspirations to go beyond it seem somehow disloyal and shameful. Thus outward mobility was impeded.

The great intrinsic difference between American and Southern Italian ways was experienced as an agonized dichotomy by the second generation in their youth. They lived twisted between two worlds, and the strain was extreme. The school, the media, and the employer taught them, implicitly and sometimes perhaps inadvertently, that Italian ways were inferior, while the immigrant community of their parents constantly sought to reinforce them.

Immigrants used "American" as a word of reproach to their children. For example, take another incident from my childhood. Every Wednesday afternoon, I left P.S. 142 early and went to the local parish church for religious instruction under New York State's Released Time Program. Once I asked one of my religious teachers, an Italian-born nun, a politely phrased but skeptical question about the existence of hell. She flew into a rage, slapped my face, and called me a *piccolo Americano,* a "little American." Thus the process of acculturation for second-generation children was an agonizing affair in which they had not only to "adjust" to two worlds, but to compromise between their irreconcilable demands. This was achieved by a sane path of least resistance.

Most of the second generation accepted the old heritage of devotion to family and sought minimal involvement with the institutions of America. This meant going to school but remaining alienated from it. One then left school at a minimum age and got a job that was "secure" but made no troubling demands on one's personality, or the family life in which it was imbedded.

Another part of the second generation's compromise was the rejection of Italian ways which were not felt vital to the family code. They resisted learning higher Italian culture and becoming literate in the language, and were ill-equipped to teach them to the third generation.

Small numbers of the second generation carried the dual rebellion to one extreme or the other. Some became highly "Americanized," giving their time, energy, and loyalty to schools and companies and becoming estranged from the clan. The price they paid for siding with the American culture in the culture-family conflict was an amorphous but strong sense of guilt and a chronic identity crisis not quite compensated for by the places won in middle-class society. At the other extreme, some rejected American culture totally in favor of lifelong immersion in the old ways, many which through time and circumstance virtually fossilized in their lifetimes, leaving them underdeveloped and forlorn.

The tortured compromise of the second-generation Italian-American left him permanently in lower-middle-class America. He remains in the minds of Americans a stereotype born of their half understanding of him and constantly reinforced by the media. Oliver Wendell Holmes said a page of history is worth a volume of logic. There are few serious studies of Italian-Americans, particularly current ones. It is easy to see why this has left accounts of their past, their present, and their future expressed almost exclusively in the dubious logic of stereotypes.

In the popular image, the second-generation Italian-American is seen as a "good employee," i.e., steady, reliable, but having little "initiative" or "dynamism." He is a good "family man," loyal to his wife, and a loving father vaguely yearning for his children to do better in their lifetimes, but not equipped to guide or push them up the social ladder. Thus, Americans glimpse the compromise solution of this generation's conflict. But the image remains superficial, devoid of depth or nuances.

We come, thus, to the compound dilemma of third- and fourth-generation Italian-Americans, who are now mostly young adults and children with parents who are well into their middle age or older. The difference between the problems of the second generation and those of the third is great—more a quantum jump than a continuity.

Perhaps a glimpse at my own life will serve as an illustration. I was raised simultaneously by my immigrant grandparents and by my parents, who were second generation, notwithstanding my father's boyhood in Italy. So I am at one time both second and third generation. I learned Italian and English from birth, but have lost the ability to speak Italian fluently. In this, my third-generation character has won out, although I remain of two generations, and thus perhaps have an advantage of double perspective.

My grandfather had a little garden in the back yard of the building in which we all lived in Brooklyn. In two senses, it was a distinctly Sicilian garden. First, it was the symbolic fulfillment of every contadino's dream to own his own land. Second, what was grown in the garden was a far cry from the typical American garden. In our garden were plum tomatoes, squash, white grapes on an overhead vine, a prolific peach tree, and a fig tree! As a child, I helped my grandfather tend the fig tree. Because of the inhospitable climate of New York, every autumn the tree had to be carefully wrapped in layers of newspaper. These in turn were covered with waterproof linoleum and tarpaulin. The tree was topped with an inverted, galvanized bucket for final protection. But the figs it produced were well worth the trouble. Picked and washed by my own hand, they were as delicious as anything I have eaten since. And perhaps the difference between second- and third-generation Italian-Americans is that members of the younger group have not tasted those figs. What they inherit from their Italian background has become so distant as to be not only devalued but quite unintelligible to them. It has been abstracted, removing the possibility of their accepting it or rebelling against it in any satisfying way.

I was struck by this recently when one of my students came to my office to talk with me. Her problems are typical of those I have heard from Italian-American college students. Her parents are second-generation Americans. Her father is a fireman and her mother a housewife. Both want her to "get an education" and "do better." Yet both constantly express fears that education will "harm her morals." She is told by her father to be proud of her Italian background, but her consciousness of being Italian is limited to the fact that her last name ends in a vowel. Although she loves her parents and believes they love her, she has no insight into their thoughts, feelings, or values. She is confused by the conflicting signals given to her by them: "Get an education, but don't change"; "go out into the larger world but don't become part of it"; "grow, but remain within the image of the 'house-plant' Sicilian girl." In short, maintain that difficult balance of conflicts which is the second-generation's life style.

When the third-generation person achieves maturity, he finds himself in a peculiar situation. A member of one of the largest minority groups in the country, he feels isolated, with no affiliation with or affinity for other Italian-Americans. This young person often wants and needs to go beyond the minimum security his parents sought in the world. In a word, he is more ambitious. But he has not been given family or cultural guidance upon which this ambition can be defined and pursued. Ironically, this descendant of immigrants despised by the old WASP establishment embodies one of the latter's cherished myths. He rationalizes his identity crisis by attempting to see himself as purely American, a blank slate upon which his individual experiences in American culture will inscribe what are his personality and his destiny.

But it is a myth that is untenable psychologically and sociologically. Although he usually is diligent and highly responsible, the other elements needed for a powerful personality are paralyzed by his pervasive identity crisis. His ability for sustained action with autonomy, initiative, self-confidence and assertiveness is undermined by his yearning for ego integrity. In addition, the third generation's view of itself as a group of atomistic individuals leaves it unorganized, isolated, diffident, and thus powerless in a society of power blocs.

———————

To Italian immigrants and their descendants today, work involves more than questions of economics. Work is regarded as moral training for the young. And among adults, it is regarded as a matter of pride. To work is to show evidence that one has become a man or a woman, a full member of the family. So strong is this ethic that it governs behavior quite apart from considerations of monetary gain. There is a dialect saying I heard among the people of Red Hook that is indicative: *Poveri si, ma perchè lagnusi?* (Poor yes, but why lazy?). I have often since heard Italian-Americans repeat the gist of the saying, even those who no longer remember the old language or who never learned it. It is a moral wrong not to be productively occupied. Even the unemployed should find something to do, something to care for. Like all Italians, the contadino enjoyed relaxation—the feeling of *dolce far niente* internationalized by modern Italy's jet set. But relaxation only in the context of first having pulled one's weight, and preferably more.

The sense of pride for something done by oneself and for one's family, whether building a brick wall, a small business, or making a fine meal, is essential to the Italian-American psychology. It cannot be overlooked if we are to understand the kinds of work done by Italian-Americans, the kinds of work they have avoided, and the types of work in which they have not succeeded. They have avoided work where the product or result is abstracted, removed from the worker. And as a group, they have been conspicuously unsuccessful as corporation executives, as "team men." They have sought a proximate relation between the individual and the end result of his labor, whether it be digging a ditch, running a restaurant, nursing a patient, playing a musical instrument, filling a pharmaceutical prescription, or teaching a child. In short, the pride that comes from seeing and feeling one's efforts and skills mingled with some result. The Italian-American seeks to do something the result of which he can demonstrate to his family. Herein lies another important component of his pride. "With these hands I built *that* wall." "*This* is my restaurant." Etc.

The rewards of modern corporate life are abstract, ambiguous, anonymous, transcending any one individual. Indeed it is because corporate life offers so few basic human satisfactions, and in fact demands service to the company to the exclusion of other personal satisfactions such as family life, that it compensates by offering great monetary rewards. The modern executive, as the sayings go, is "wedded to his company," and his "career is his hobby."

Following their traditional values, Italian-Americans have sought work where the rewards are more palpably human. This involves their sense of dignity, and it has nothing to do with keeping one's fingernails clean or even necessarily in "pride of craftsmanship." In an America where leisure and corporate status are prime values, and where the pride of the craftsman is nostalgically remembered, the Italian-American values instead his sheer labor first and his individual share of it as much as his skills. There is satisfaction felt in swinging a longshoreman's hook, or laying bricks, and feeling the relationship between the ache in one's arms and back after a day's work and the benefits from it to one's family. In work as in all dimensions of life, pride among Italian-Americans is much more visceral and passionate than sublimated and abstract.

The Italians replaced the Irish as the target of anti-Catholic hatred, Americans neither knowing nor caring about the differences in the Catholicism of the two ethnic groups, or that the American Catholic Church was in many regards unfriendly to the Italians. The ways of the Southern Italians were totally incomprehensible to Americans. In the twisted logic of bigotry, they were thus flagrantly "un-American." And Italians replaced all the earlier immigrant groups as targets of resentment about the competition of cheap labor.

The strain between Italians and the huge Know-Nothing sentiment in America came to a climax in a sensationally publicized series of incidents that took place in New Orleans in 1891. Italians were being recruited to labor on the farms of the American South. In particular, they worked in Mississippi and Louisiana during the sugar cane cutting season which Italians called *la zuccarata* after the Italian word for sugar, zucchero. Many of the immigrants settled in New Orleans, some temporarily, others permanently. Because the system of regionalism or companilismo was transplanted to the New World, Italians tended to settle among other Italians from the same regions of Italy. In New Orleans, 93 per cent of the Italians were from Sicily.

In a crime that remains unsolved to this day, New Orleans Police Superintendent David Hennessey was assassinated. Fueled by wild rumors that the clannish Sicilians belonged to a then mysterious secret criminal society called the Mafia, or, as it was then more commonly called, the Black Hand, the city's Sicilians were made scapegoats. Hundreds of them were arrested without cause. They were treated to beatings in and out of jail [. . .].

The die was cast. From the early days of immigration from the Mezzogiorno until today, the nativistic American mentality, born of ignorance and nurtured in malice, has offered Italian-Americans a bigoted choice of two identities somewhat paralleling two imposed on blacks. Indeed, among the oldest epithets hurled against Italian-Americans was "black guinea," or "black dago," etc. Italians were considered an inferior *race,* as were blacks. Racists insist that blacks must be either childlike, laughing, Uncle Tom figures or sullen, incorrigible, violent, knife-wielding criminals. Similarly, the nativists and their descendants, the anti-Italian bigots of today, insist that Italian-Americans be either/or creatures. They must be either spaghetti-twirling, opera-bellowing buffoons in undershirts (as in the TV commercial with its famous line, "That'sa some spicy meatball") or swarthy, sinister hoods in garish suits, shirts, and ties. The criminal image imposed on Italian-Americans is in itself a major issue [. . .]. Even if the image did not exist, however, the "inferior race" slander would alone constitute a major problem for Italian-Americans.

The disposition toward insularity among Italian-Americans was ingrained over centuries of Mezzogiorno history. It has since been reinforced by American bigotry. However condescendingly euphemistic and polite the language of some bigots today, they still regard Italian-Americans as racially inferior "dagos," "wops," "guineas," and "greasers." Those who assume that such insults have disappeared, or only come from the uneducated, should read Glazer and Moynihan. They cite a comment made by a "world famous Yale professor of government." In 1969, upon hearing that an Italian-American had announced his candidacy for the office of mayor of New York City, the professor commented, "If Italians aren't actually an inferior race, they do the best imitation of one I've seen."

Also, we might recall well-known tests used to identify this prejudice. In one classic study, American college students were shown photographs of members of the opposite sex with what purported to be the name of each person on the photograph. The students were asked to evaluate the attractiveness of the person in the photograph. Then, sometime afterward, names were changed and the procedure repeated with the same students. The result was that those people who were regarded as "handsome" or "pretty" when they had names like "Smith" were found not attractive when their names were changed to Italian ones. (The same result was found using names commonly thought of as Jewish.)

The fear of foreign radicalism grew to hysteria. The fear culminated in two of the worst crises of the Italian-American saga—their mass deportation (along with immigrants of other nationalities) in the infamous Palmer raids, and the vicious antiradical, anti-Italian case of Sacco and Vanzetti, an affair that rocked the world and for years overshadowed all other factors in determining the path of Italian-Americans.

Alexander Mitchell Palmer was a political hack who gained power by currying favor with Woodrow Wilson, helping him to become President. In 1919, he was appointed Attorney General of the United States. During his three-year tenure of office, he raised a red scare to mammoth proportions by prosecuting and persecuting aliens, including Italians, as suspicious and dangerous radicals. His most infamous tactic was the Palmer raid. Agents of the Department of Justice would descend upon an immigrant family, or sometimes a whole neighborhood, in the middle of the night, arresting people indiscriminately. In violation of every decent legal ethic and the due process of law itself, those who were not citizens were kept incommunicado by Palmer's witch hunters, and many were summarily deported. Years later, inquiries failed to find any links between those deported and subversion. It was cold consolation to those sent back to the Old World misery they had labored so hard to escape. This insane persecution, equating foreign birth with subversiveness, created panic among all immigrant groups. Among Italians, it strengthened their insularity from the larger society, an old inclination traceable to the maxim of the Mezzogiorno that "the law works against the people."

The shameful red scare and hatred of immigrants had roots in the xenophobia of Know-Nothingism. But it was brought to flower in the twentieth century when very prominent American leaders openly embraced its bigoted positions. In fact, it may be questioned whether it could have reached such damaging proportions if the way had not been laid by some very famous and powerful Americans. Because Italians constituted by far the largest ethnic group immigrating to the United States at the time, they bore the brunt of the outrage. For example, in October 1915, former President Theodore Roosevelt went out of his way to insult all immigrants and their children, and particularly Italian-Americans. In a speech to the Knights of Columbus assembled in New York City's Carnegie Hall and including Italian-Americans, he said, "There is no room in this country for hyphenated Americans. . . . There is no such thing as a hyphenated American who is a good American." Before he became President, he had called the 1891 mob lynching of eleven Sicilians in New Orleans "a rather good thing," and boasted that he had said so at a party where there were what he called "various dago diplomats." In 1915, Woodrow Wilson said that "hyphenated Americans have poured the poison of disloyalty into the very arteries of our national life . . . such creatures of passion, disloyalty and anarchy must be crushed out."

The violent nativists got the message. In 1891, several Italians were lynched in West Virginia. In 1893, several others were murdered in Denver, Colorado. In March 1895, six Italian labor "agitators" were lynched in Colorado. In 1895, six Italians were torn from a jail by a mob in Hahnville, Louisiana. All were beaten, and three hanged. In 1899, a mob dragged three Sicilian shopkeepers from a jail in Tallulah, Louisiana, and caught two others. All five were lynched. Their offense? They had permitted Negroes equal status with whites in their shops. In July 1901, Italians were attacked by a mob in Mississippi. In 1906, a mob in West Virginia killed several Italians and maimed several others. Italians were attacked in Tampa, Florida, in 1910. In that same year an Italian was pulled from a jail in Willisville, Illinois, and shot to death. Another Italian met the same fate in Illinois in 1911.

Perhaps the most rabid of Italian haters was Senator Henry Cabot Lodge of Massachusetts. It is not true that the "Lodges speak only to the Cabots, and the Cabots only to God." Or at least it was not true of Henry. In his five years as a member of the U. S. House of Representatives and during his thirty-one years in the U. S. Senate (1893–1924), he spoke often to the American people about his hatred for Italian-Americans. In 1891, he made a distinction between Northern Italians (whom he termed "Teutonic Italians") and Southern Italians. He labeled the latter inferior, and said the "great Republic should no longer be left unguarded from them." In March 1900, he made a speech in which he alluded to Italian-Americans:

> We have seen a murderous assault by an alien immigrant upon the Chief of Police of a great city [the 1891 incident in New Orleans], not to avenge any personal wrong, but because he represented law and order. Every day we read in the newspapers of savage murders by members of secret societies composed of alien immigrants. Can we doubt, in the presence of such horrible facts as these, the need of stringent laws and rigid enforcement, to exclude the criminals and anarchists of foreign countries from the United States?

Bigoted Americans responded to the incitement of people like Lodge. In August 1920, mobs invaded the Italian neighborhood of West Frankfort, Illinois, dragging people of all ages and both sexes from homes, beating them with weapons and burning whole rows of their homes. The attacks were repeated, and the Italians fought back, turning the small neighborhood into a battleground. It took five hundred state troopers three days to end the fighting. At its end, hundreds of Italian-Americans were left homeless and, with millions of their paesani in the United States, convinced that they were in a hostile country with only themselves to rely upon.

Anti-Italian fever was virulent when on April 15, 1920, five men held up a shoe company in Braintree, Massachusetts, killing an employee and fleeing in a car with fifteen thousand dollars. Witnesses claimed the holdup men "looked like Italians." When two Italians, Nicola Sacco, a factory worker from Puglia in South Italy, and Bartolomeo Vanzetti, a mustached fish peddler from the Northern Italian province of Piedmont, came to claim a car that police had linked with the crime, they were arrested. Circumstances linking them to the crime were questionable. But when it was discovered that they were under surveillance by Palmer's Department of Justice as political anarchists and that they carried firearms, a cry for their heads was raised all over the land. They were tried under conditions that were a mockery of the judicial process and found guilty. The prosecuting attorney appealed to the worst biases of the jury, treating Italian-American witnesses in an outrageously insulting manner. The testimony of eighteen Italian-born witnesses was dismissed out of hand by the court as unreliable. After the trial, the judge who had presided is alleged to have commented to a Dartmouth professor, "Did you see what I did to those anarchistic bastards the other day? I guess that will hold them for a while." The same judge, Webster Thayer, an old immigrant-hating pillar of Back Bay Society, one year before had presided over another trial in which Vanzetti had been accused of a holdup in Plymouth. At the time, the judge had instructed the jury that, "This man, although he may not actually have committed the crime attributed to him, is nevertheless morally culpable, because he is the enemy of our existing institutions. . . . The defendant's ideals are cognate with crime." Despite the testimony of thirty witnesses that Vanzetti was elsewhere at the time of the crime, Vanzetti was convicted of the Plymouth holdup.

During their trial, nine witnesses, including the clerk of the Italian Consulate, swore that Sacco was in Boston at the time of the Braintree robbery. Six witnesses placed Vanzetti in Plymouth making his door-to-door rounds as a peddler during the time of the crime. The two Italians were found guilty, and after seven years of protests and appeals they were executed. On the morning they were to die, Massachusetts' Governor Fuller, when asked if he would intercede to halt the execution, smiled at reporters and said only, "It's a beautiful morning, boys, isn't it?"

A commission headed by Harvard University's president had found nothing wrong in Sacco and Vanzetti's trial, prompting the distinguished reporter Heywood Broun to write sarcastically in the New York *World*:

> What more can the immigrants from Italy expect? It is not every person who has a president of Harvard University throw the switch for him. If this is a lynching, at least the fish-peddler and his friend, the factory hand, may take unction to their souls that they will die at the hands of men in denim jackets or academic gowns. . . .

The last hearing held for the two Italians was presided over, as were all of their hearings, by Judge Thayer. Sacco said to him:

> I never knew, never heard, even read in history anything so cruel as this Court. After seven years prosecuting they still consider us guilty.

Both men protested their innocence until they were killed.

The guilt of the two men remains in controversy. But, guilty or innocent, they received a good deal less than a fair trial. Italian-Americans, divided on the question of their guilt, were all but unanimous about the unfairness of their trial. They felt as one with Vanzetti in the latter part of a statement he made in newly learned English when he last faced Judge Thayer. "I am suffering," he said, "because I am a radical and indeed I am a radical; I have suffered because I was an Italian, and indeed I am an Italian."

Many years later (I was born in 1939, twelve years after their execution), I remember my grandfather and his friends speak with bitterness about *il caso di Sacco-Vanzetti*. Totally indifferent to political ideologies, my grandfather was typical of Italian-Americans who were convinced the two were railroaded into the electric chair in good part because they were Italians. Countless numbers of Italian-Americans contributed to the defense fund of the two men. The outcome of the affair was simply another confirmation of the ancient belief of the Italian immigrants that justice, a very important part of their value system, had little to do with the laws and institutions of the state. The poison of the Sacco-Vanzetti affair was not to be purged from relations between

Italian-Americans and the United States until years later when Italian-Americans faced a new crisis of nationality in World War II, and resolved it with resounding loyalty to the United States—a story for another chapter.

The unequivocal loyalty of Italian-Americans to their country is astonishing when one considers much of their ill treatment at the hands of America.

[Before 1840] there was plenty of room and work for all. [. . . T]hese early immigrants were from the British Isles and Northwestern Europe. They were of the same ethnic group as most of the founders of the country—White "Anglo-Saxon" Protestants. In fact, as late as 1864, despite the already active Know-Nothing movement, then aimed at the Irish, the official policy of the American government as written in a law passed that year was to encourage immigration. In the next decades, however, pressure to exclude immigration rose rapidly as the ethnic composition of the immigrants changed. They were no longer predominantly WASP. By 1899, when the total United States population was fifty million, Protestants were among the minority (18.5 per cent) of immigrants. The majority (52 per cent) were Roman Catholics, and 10.5 per cent were Jews. In the next eleven years 2,300,000 were to arrive from Italy alone, only 400,000 of these from Northern Italy. And by 1925, there were upwards of five million Italian-Americans, a figure the nativists found alarming.

Exclusionary pressure gathered unturnable momentum as such diverse American groups as the American Federation of Labor, the American Legion, and the American Grange lobbied for restriction on immigration. Moreover, the pressure was for selective exclusion of undesirable "races," especially Southern and Eastern Europeans. This sentiment was expressed in a very popular book by Madison Grant published during World War I, called *The Passing of the Great Race*. The great race was the WASP ethnic group, or, as Grant called it, "the Nordics." The thesis of the book was as simple as it was vicious. The immigrants of Eastern and Southern Europe were "storming the Nordic ramparts of the United States and mongrelizing the good old American stock," and threatening to destroy American institutions. Grant singled out Italians as inferiors. In his crackpot explanation, Italians are the inferior descendants of the slaves who survived when ancient Rome died. This at a time when some 10 to 12 per cent of the American Army fighting in World War I were Italian-Americans. Thousands of them died and one hundred were awarded Distinguished Service Crosses fighting for a country Grant and his fellow nativists called "Nordic."

Fred Gardaphé

From *The Italian-American Writer: An Essay and an Annotated Checklist*

What you carry in your head
you don't have to carry on your back.

—*ADVICE FROM AN OLD WORKER*

If there is one thing I've learned about advocating ethnic-American literature, it's that you can't avoid getting personal about the literature that comes from your ancestral culture. And so, this essay is a personal account of my encounter with the literature produced by American writers of Italian descent. Through this development I have come to see my life's reading and writing as entries onto an historical rap sheet of the cultural crimes of breaking into and entering mainstream America.

I grew up in a little-Italy in which not even the contagiously sick were left alone. To be alone is to be sick. The self-isolation that reading requires was rarely possible and considered a dangerous invitation to blindness and insanity. This was evidenced by my being the first American born of the family to need glasses before the age of ten. I would not understand their attitude towards reading for many years. In fact, it wasn't until I came across Jerre Mangione's *An Ethnic at Large* that I realized I wasn't the only one whose reading was treated this way. In Mangione's autobiographical writing he tells of how being Sicilian and American created a double life inside of which he fashioned a third "fantasy life . . . well nourished by the piles of books I brought home from the public library, most of which I read clandestinely in the bathroom or under the bed since my mother believed that too much reading could drive a person insane" (13–14).

There was no space in the home set aside for isolated study. We had one of the larger homes of those in our extended family, and so our house was the place where the women would gather in the basement kitchen after sending their husbands off to work and their kids to school. They'd share coffee, clothes washing, and ironing; they'd collectively make daily bread, and prepare afternoon pastas, and evening pizzas and foccacie. Those without children would spend the entire day there and so we would always return home from school to scenes that most of our classmates only knew on weekends or holidays. We were expected to come home from school, drop our books on the kitchen table and begin our homework. It was difficult to concentrate on work with four children at the table all subjected to countless interruptions from family and friends who passed through the house regularly.

The only books that entered my family's home were those we carried home from school. Reading anything beyond newspapers and the mail required escaping from my family. I would try reading but the noise would be so great that I'd shout out, "Shut up, I'm trying to read," to which my mother would respond, "Who you tellin' to shut up? If you want to read, go to the library." But the library was off limits to any kid who wanted to be tough. I'd leave the house with homework in hand, find a place to park my books and join in on the action in the streets. When the action didn't consist of organized play, it was made up of disorganized troublemaking. Once, while I was being chased by the police for disturbing local merchants so my partners could shoplift, I ran into the public library. I found myself in the juvenile section and grabbed any book to hide my face. Safe from the streets, I spent the rest of the afternoon reading, believing that nobody would ever find me there. So whenever I was being chased, I'd head straight for the library. The library became my asylum, a place where I could go crazy and be myself without my family finding out.

It wasn't long before my reading habit outgrew the dimensions of the library. I had developed a chronic reading problem that identified me as the "'merican" or rebel. My reading betrayed my willingness to enter mainstream American culture, and while my family tolerated this, they did little to make that move an easy one. Sometimes at night I would bring a flashlight to bed and read, but sharing a bed with my two brothers, this often ended up in a fight, as well as a reprimand from my father telling me I was not only keeping my brothers from sleeping, but that I was also teaching them bad habits. In spite of all these obstacles I managed to become quite the bookworm. I read to escape both my home and the streets and in the process entered places in my mind I had never before seen.

While my father encouraged my studies, he wanted me to know what real work was like. So whenever he'd see me reading something that was obviously not homework, he'd put me to work in the family business—a pawnshop as well as the building we owned. Only after I'd clean floors, put away stock and run errands, would I be given some time for myself. There wasn't much to read in the store; the constant flow of customers would not allow for anything longer than a news article at one stretch, but I always managed to get through a newspaper and the Green Sheet, a daily horse racing newsletter. I'd return home and reenter the imaginary worlds others created through words, never thinking there could be a bridge between the two. For a long time it never occurred to me that literature was something that could or even should speak to me of my experience, especially of my ethnicity. The worlds I entered through reading were never confused with the world in which I lived. Reading was a vacation. The books I read were written by others about experiences that were not mine; they took me to places I had never been. This naive notion of reading was shattered the day my father was murdered.

When I read the news accounts, it seemed for the first time that my life had become a subject for writing. Since we share the same name, to see his name in print was to see my own name. It was especially haunting to see that name on his tombstone. I knew that a part of me had been buried with him. From that day on, I began to read in a new way. For many reasons, I began to feel that my life was no longer in control; I began to think that the only way I could regain control of it was to be the one who wrote the stories. I was so shocked by reality that I began to search for a way out, and that way, I thought, would come through reading. Because my father was murdered in the pawnshop, my family wanted me to have nothing to do with the business, but my grandfather needed me more than ever. I returned to the store, now in my father's place, in spite of the fact that I was just a kid.

Since books were non-negotiable items in my community, the giving of them was considered not only impractical but taboo. Sometime, shortly after my father's death, my Uncle Pasquale gave me a copy of Luigi Barzini's *The Italians*. He just handed it to me, without even a word, assuming through his glance that I would know what to do with it. Back then I thought I knew more than enough about being Italian. But all I really knew was that being Italian meant being different from the ones I wanted to be like. The last thing in the world that I wanted at that age was to read about a group with which I no longer wished to be associated. I put the book on a shelf connected to my bed, the only shelf outside our kitchen; there it would lie unread for seven years. From then on I read nothing beyond my school assignments. One day— a day of no special occasion—one of my aunts again broke this book-as-gift taboo by giving my mother a copy of Mario Puzo's *The Godfather*, she told my mother that if her nephew was so intent on reading he might as well read a book about Italians (neither of them had read it of course). The title of the book was quite appropriate since, due to my father's early death, I, at the age of ten, had been made godfather to one of my cousins.

The novel lay unread until I found out that there was an excellent sex scene on page 26. That's where I started reading. I sped through the book, hoping to find more scenes like the one in which Sonny screws the maid-of-honor at his sister's wedding. Along the way I encountered men like Amerigo Bonasera, the undertaker, Luca Brasi, the street thug, and Frankie Fontaine, who were like the regulars I knew in the pawnshop. Some would come in with guns, jewelry and golf clubs to pawn. Men like these formed alliances in order to get things done. Because of its stock of familiar characters, *The Godfather* was the first novel with which I could completely identify. The only problem I had was that this thing called mafia was something with which I was unfamiliar. I was familiar with the word *mafioso,* which I had often heard in reference to poor troublemakers who dressed as though they were rich. But that these guys could have belonged to a master crime organization called The Mafia, was something I could not fathom. In spite of this, the world that Puzo created taught me how to read the world I was living in, not only the world of the streets, but the world within my family; for in spite of the emphasis on crime, Puzo's use of Italian sensibilities made me realize that literature could be made out of my own experiences.

The novel came out the year after my grandfather was killed in a holdup at the pawnshop. With him gone, the business was sold and I was free to find my own way through the world. One of the ways I searched was crime. Throughout my high school years, I was accused of being in the mafia. So during my senior year, I decided to investigate the subject through my semester-long thesis paper that my Irish-Catholic prep school required. One way or another I had been connected to the mafia since I left my Italian neighborhood to attend high school, so I decided it was time to find out what this thing called mafia was. This was the first writing project to excite me. I searched the Barzini book and between him and Puzo, I thought I had it all figured out. When I completed the paper I was certain of an excellent grade. The grading committee decided that the paper, although well written, depended too much on Italian sources, and because I was also Italian my writing had not achieved the necessary objectivity that was essential to all serious scholarship. I read the "C" grade as punishment for my cultural transgression, and decided to stay away from anything but English in my future formal studies.

As soon as I graduated high school, I leapt into the youth culture that had been held at bay by the strict rules of my prep school. But it wasn't enough for me to get some jeans, let my hair grow and smoke some dope. I might become a hippie, but not without finding an historical context by which to explain the culture I was entering. My historical reading pointed to poetry. I started tracing the hippies back in time and came upon the Beatniks, whom I followed back to the American Romantics, like Thoreau and Whitman. That's when I found the poetry of Lawrence Ferlinghetti. That he was Italian American never entered my mind back then. All I knew was that suddenly here was a man whose poetry sang without rhyme and told truths in clear and simple language. I bought up every book of his that I could find. Inspired by Whitman's "Song of the Open Road," I took a year off between my sophomore and junior years in college and hitchhiked out to California with the idea of finding Ferlinghetti. I imagined City Lights Books to be a Mecca that was waiting for punk pilgrims like myself. When I arrived, I browsed the shelves until I got up the nerve to ask the clerk if Ferlinghetti was in. He pointed me to the basement. I approached his office cautiously, rehearsing what I would say. The door was opened just enough to allow me to see the poet's profile; his head was bent slightly, as though he were pondering a half-written poem still in his typewriter. I stood there awhile, staring at him, and decided that this was ridiculous. What could I possibly say to him? How stupid he'd think I was to hitchhike all the way from Chicago. What could I have wanted from him? I ran back up the stairs, bought a book entitled *Six San Francisco Poets*, by David Kherdian, and told myself I'd come back. I never did. Kherdian's book lead me to other Beat writers, like Diane di Prima and Gregory Corso, who were, like Ferlinghetti, coincidentally Italian American, and as I continued hitchhiking around the country I'd pick up their books and read them on roadsides, in hostels, and fleabag hotels. That was 1973. I kept a journal of my trip and returned home with the decision to be a writer.

When I returned to college, I began studying literature and film with the idea of getting a teaching job so that I could make reading and writing my career. After a few years of teaching high school and writing bad poetry, I decided I needed to get away. So I took off to hitchhike through Europe, thinking perhaps I'd stop in Italy.

Now my grandparents had never told me why they left Italy. They never talked of their childhood. I guess they thought it was enough to be in America and that all that had come before no longer made any difference in their new home. After my mother's father died no one seemed to care much about getting together for Sunday dinners. With him were buried many of the Italian traditions our family had followed in his presence. Without his influence, Italians became strangers in a collage of media images: spicy meatball eaters, Godfathers and opera singers. In the late seventies I decided to get as far away from the family as possible. I planned a trip to Europe to visit friends in Denmark and Sweden. As I gathered addresses I thought it might be interesting to visit Italy for a few days, if I had the time. Grandma had maintained only Christmas card contact with the "other family" in Castellana Grotte. She had the address of Grandpa's brother and I wrote him. By the time I left, I had not received a response and wondered if I should bother to stop in Castellana. My trip began in northern Europe and it seemed that the closer I came to Italy, the more emotional I became. On the train from Venice to Bari I began to feel confused. I asked myself many times: "What if my family doesn't recognize me; They have no pictures! What if they can't understand me? I'd only studied Italian for three months and Venice had proven that I could understand it but not speak it well!" But even as I worried, the excitement grew.

As the first of the American family to return to Castellana Grotte, I was welcomed with tears, kisses and strong embraces. I felt like a traveller who had come home after a long voyage. After only a few days I knew I belonged in Castellana. I was able to live as Grandpa did. I even worked ten hours picking beans in the same field that he had worked in when he was young. When I couldn't straighten out my back after picking the fava I understood why he had left Italy. I was able to speak to his brother and sister, and for the first time I knew what his life in Italy had been like. I learned that he, like so many other southern Italians, had left home to find work in America. He would send money back to Castellana Grotte and he promised continually that one day he would return. That one day never came, as soon he had a family of his own to support. Learning all this helped me to regain a part of myself that was lost when he died. I was whole, and now more than ever proud of my Italian heritage.

My pride no longer stemmed from arrogance and ignorance. It was a pride of wisdom and of love for the life that he had lived. I visited the house where Grandpa was born. I spent a long time inside the stone cottage, touching what he had once touched, seeing what at one time I knew he had seen. I was so lost in emotion that I cried without trying to hide my tears. I felt that this place had some kind of power over me. When I left his home, I felt for the first time that I had a history, a history that I had never studied in school, a history that would have been lost if I had not traveled to Castellana Grotte.

When I returned I knew I needed to write about the experience. I had come home a born-again Italian, who took to drinking espresso instead of coffee, taking naps in the afternoon, and hanging out in places where I could continue to speak Italian. I might have been obnoxious, but I was directed. I began writing screenplays and short stories, but felt I needed the direction that might come from a teacher. I left my teaching position in an Uptown Chicago street school, took out major school loans and started a Master's program at the University of Chicago. Under the supervision of Richard Stern, I began a novel. To support myself I assisted an Italian professor's first-year Italian class. Along with my English and American literature courses I took seminars in Italian literature. At this time I renewed my search for and read books by Italian Americans. This was done outside of my formal classes, of course, and I never considered them in the same light as the literature I studied in my graduate courses.

Each novel led me to another. I began with Mario Puzo's earlier work. In his novel *The Fortunate Pilgrim* (1964), I found my widowed mother, who raised four children by herself, to be very much like the protagonist, Lucia Santa, who "makes the family organism stand strong against the blows of time: the growth of children, the death of parents, and all changes of worldly circumstance. She lives through five years in an instant, and behind her trail the great shadowy memories that are life's real substance and the spirit's strength." I was so taken by the novel that I started writing letters to Puzo, none of which were ever acknowledged. I began sending him birthday cards every year, but like the fanatic letters, they too were never acknowledged.

In Pietro di Donato's masterpiece, *Christ in Concrete*, I heard my hod carrier grandfather through Geremio's dreaming aloud while he worked on a construction site: "Laugh, laugh all of you . . . but I tell you that all my kids must be boys so that they someday will be big American builders. And then I'll help them to put the gold away in the basements. . . . But am I not a man, to feed my own with these hands? Ah, but day will end and no boss in the world can then rob me the joy of my home!"

Through John Fante's novels and short stories, I came to see not only my grandparents, but the way their children might have seen them, as through his story, "The Odyssey of a Wop"—where he writes, "I pick up little bits of information about my grandfather. My grandmother tells me of him. She tells me that when he lived he was a good fellow whose goodness evoked not admiration but pity. He was known as a good little Wop." And later on, because of Fante, I understood why my mother used to say, "I'm a dago, you're a wop; I eat spaghetti, you eat slop." "From the beginning," writes Fante, "I hear my mother use the words Wop and Dago with such vigor as to denote violent distaste. She spits them out. They leap from her lips. To her, they contain the essence of poverty, squalor, filth."

I eat up every Fante work I can find. He becomes my Hemingway. Just as Puzo became my Norman Mailer, and di Donato, my James Farrell. All of a sudden, American literature is not something descended from the Pilgrims. I make sense of the drama inside the Catholic Church and understand the sturdy pagan underpinnings of my family's fears of the "Evil Eye" and defiance of literate authorities. These writers transformed my grandparents' broken English from signs of stupidity and sources of embarrassment into beautiful music that I begin recreating in my stories. And when I do, I hear them, as though for the first time; their resurrections keep me sane.

Sandra M. Gilbert

The Tidal Wave

that toppled me
when I was three
was no doubt only

three feet high
but like a white and spiky
ancestor

it hovered over me
a minute as if brooding
What to do with this one?

then struck, then plunged
upon me—pail and all—
and although through

its hissing veil
of blue-green salt
I saw my parents running,

heard, loud and absurd,
their voices calling
Sandra, Sandra,

the muscles of the tide
held me tight,
dragged me up the shore

over rocks, shells, broken glass,
along the beach
to this high seaweedy place

where—schools and inches,
salt and scars and children—
later, I lie by myself,

years out of their reach.

∝∾

Mafioso

Frank Costello eating spaghetti in a cell at San Quentin,
Lucky Luciano mixing up a mess of bullets and
calling for parmesan cheese,
Al Capone baking a sawed-off shotgun into a
huge lasagna—
are you my uncles, my
only uncles?

O Mafiosi,
bad uncles of the barren
cliffs of Sicily—was it only you
that they transported in barrels
like pure olive oil
across the Atlantic?

Was it only you
who got out at Ellis Island with
black scarves on your heads and cheap cigars
and no English and a dozen children?

No carts were waiting, gallant with paint,
no little donkeys plumed like the dreams of peacocks.
Only the evil eyes of a thousand buildings
stared across at the echoing debarkation center,
making it seem so much smaller than a piazza,

only a half dozen Puritan millionaires stood on the wharf,
in the wind colder than the impossible snows of the Abruzzi,
ready with country clubs and dynamos

to grind the organs out of you.

Tailors

for Elliot

my grandfather the tailor sat in his little dark shop
sewing me together
(twice a day my Sicilian grandmother brought him
platefuls of praise like bowls of spaghetti)

my other grandmother the seamstress basted and hemmed
(her needle traced strange Russian characters
on the rough cloth)

your grandfather the tailor lengthened you
imperceptibly
(he lovingly made you a beard and a *tallis*)

and in the sultry sweatshops of the lower East Side
(where summer swelled like a giant cabbage)
hundreds and hundreds of great aunts
hunched over glittering machines
in the heavy weather
crooning and clucking and
weeping and gossiping

and stitching together the sidewalks
that would stitch us together

Maria Mazziotti Gillan

Opening the Door:
19th Street, Paterson

The crumbling cement steps led down to the dark cave of the cellar where the mouse traps waited in the corners and the big, iron coal furnace squatted next to the coal bin. My father used a shovel to scoop the coal out; it made a scraping sound, iron on cement, and the coal rattling. When he opened the little door of the furnace and threw in the coal, the flames rose up, and the heat poured out. In the back of the cellar was a room made out of scrap wood where my father made wine each summer, the cellar reeking of fermenting wine, his arms bulging when he carried in the heavy boxes of purple grapes. I told my brother there was a secret room in the cellar, like the secret rooms in the mansions in Nancy Drew novels, except our house was an old, imitation Victorian house cut up into apartments. In my mind, I could open up the little door behind the furnace, and step into a magic world far removed from the dank ordinary cellar. The life of 19th Street with its factory workers and drunks, the people next door who fought and screamed constantly. The world of my mother's life where she kept us confined to the front porch, but, through that door, everything I was not and wanted to be waited for me, and who knew, who knew to what dangerous, exciting places it would lead?

Secrets

In my family, we never told our secrets, our lives
hidden like the undersides of leaves.
Even today, though I talk to my sister a lot,
though she tells me little facts about her life,
mostly I remain private and hidden and afraid.
I, who can write out every secret in a poem,
never tell anyone anything.

In our family, our pride too great to admit how
        vulnerable we are,
we follow my mother's example.
She demanded that we keep our spines straight,
our feet on the floor, but I remember arguments so loud,
our neighbors would stare at us for days.
My mother always pretended nothing happened.

In our house, I was always afraid
my mother wouldn't approve of me.
So many lies I told to cover up
the things my mother's rules would not allow,
how I wanted to crack out of that cast of rules,
the things a person could and could not do.

So how could I tell the truth about the night
when I slept over at Anne's house?
We went to New York City to see a play
and we missed the last train.
We had to spend the night
in the train station in Hoboken.
The bums who slept there kept asking,
"What are nice girls like you doing here?"
In the morning, after being afraid
to sleep all night, men reeking of alcohol
peering into our faces, we walked at dawn
to the Catholic Church, went to the six o'clock mass,
and then caught the first train to Ridgewood

where Anne's parents were waiting for us,
both of them furious in a stiff, middle-class way,
saying, "Why didn't you call?"
and Anne saying, "I thought you'd be asleep."
"We were up all night," her mother hissed at her.

I wanted to crawl under their dining room table,
only glad that this icy anger was directed at Anne
and not at me, glad that my mother didn't know.

Though I'd come to my mother's house sometimes
when I was a grown woman myself
and sit in her kitchen, sobbing,
unable to stop or explain.

She held me, asking, "What is it?
What is it? Cry. Cry. It will be good
for you. What is it?" and I,
unable to say.

Dana Gioia

Cleared Away

Around the corner there may be a man
who shop by shop, block by ruined block,
still sees the neighborhood which once was here,

who, standing in the empty lot, can hear
the vacancies of brick and broken glass
suddenly come to life again, who feels

the steps materialize beneath his feet
as he ascends the shattered tenement,
which rises with him in the open air—

story by story, out of memory,
filled with the smells of dinners on the stove
and the soft laughter of the assembled dead.

Money

> Money is a kind of poetry.
> —*WALLACE STEVENS*

Money, the long green,
cash, stash, rhino, jack
or just plain dough.

Chock it up, fork it over,
shell it out. Watch it
burn holes through pockets.

To be made of it! To have it
to burn! Greenbacks, double eagles,
megabucks and Ginnie Maes.

It greases the palm, feathers a nest,
holds heads above water,
makes both ends meet.

Money breeds money.
Gathering interest, compounding daily.
Always in circulation.

Money. You don't know where it's been,
but you put it where your mouth is.
And it talks.

Planting a Sequoia

All afternoon my brothers and I have worked in the orchard,
Digging this hole, laying you into it, carefully packing the soil.
Rain blackened the horizon, but cold winds kept it over the
  Pacific,
And the sky above us stayed the dull gray
Of an old year coming to an end.

In Sicily a father plants a tree to celebrate his first son's birth—
An olive or a fig tree—a sign that the earth has one more life
  to bear.
I would have done the same, proudly laying new stock into
  my father's orchard,
A green sapling rising among the twisted apple boughs,
A promise of new fruit in other autumns.

But today we kneel in the cold planting you, our native giant,
Defying the practical custom of our fathers,
Wrapping in your roots a lock of hair, a piece of an infant's
  birth cord,
All that remains above earth of a first-born son,
A few stray atoms brought back to the elements.

We will give you what we can—our labor and our soil,
Water drawn from the earth when the skies fail,

Nights scented with the ocean fog, days softened by the
    circuit of bees.
We plant you in the corner of the grove, bathed in western
    light,
A slender shoot against the sunset.

And when our family is no more, all of his unborn brothers
    dead,
Every niece and nephew scattered, the house torn down,
His mother's beauty ashes in the air,
I want you to stand among strangers, all young and ephemeral
    to you,
Silently keeping the secret of your birth.

Daniela Gioseffi

For Grandma Lucia La Rosa, "Light the Rose"

"You're one of only two or three Italian-American women
    poets in this country. You're a pioneer. There are fewer of
    you known than Black or Puerto Rican women poets."

—*PROFESSOR ERNESTO FALBO, SUNY BUFFALO, N.Y., 1976*

On the crowded subway,
riding to the prison to teach
Black and Puerto Rican inmates how to write,
I think of the fable of the shoemaker
who struggles to make shoes for the oppressed
while his own go barefoot over the stones.

I remember Grandma Lucia, her olive face
wrinkled with resignation,
content just to survive
after giving birth to twenty children,
without orgasmic pleasures or anesthesia.
Grandpa Galileo, immigrant adventurer,
who brought his family
steerage passage to the New World;
his shoemaker shop where he labored

over American factory goods
that made his artisan's craft a useless
anachronism; his Code of Honor
which forced him to starve
accepting not a cent of welfare
from anyone but his sons;
his ironic "Code of Honor"
which condoned jealous rages of wife-beating;
Aunt Elisabetta, Aunt Maria Domenica, Aunt Raffaella,
Aunt Elena, grown women huddled like girls
in their bedroom in Newark, talking in whispers,
not daring to smoke their American cigarettes
in front of *Pa;*
the backyard shrine of the virgin,
somber blue-robed woman,
devoid of sexual passions,
to whom Aunt Elisabetta prayed
daily before dying in childbirth,
trying to have *"a son"*
against doctor's orders, though
she had five healthy daughters already;
Dr. Giuseppe Ferrara, purple heart veteran
of World War II, told he couldn't have a residency
in a big New York hospital because of his Italian
name; the Mafia jokes, the epithets:
"Wop, guinea, dago, grease-ball."
And the stories told by Papa
of Dante, Galileo, Da Vinci, Marconi, Fermi, Caruso
that stung me with pride for Italian *men;*
how I was discouraged from school,
told a woman meant for cooking and bearing
doesn't need education.

I remember
Grandma
got out of bed
in the middle of the night
to fetch her *husband* a glass of water
the day she died,
her body wearied
from giving and giving and giving
food and birth.

American Sonnets for My Father

for Donato Gioseffi 1906–1981
written in Edna St. Vincent Millay's studio
at Steepletop, New York, November, 1981

You died in spring, father, and now the autumn dies.
Bright with ripe youth, dulled by time,
plums of feeling leaked red juices from your eyes,
pools of blood hemorrhaged in your quivering mind.
At forty, I climb Point Pinnacle, today,
thinking of you gone forever from me.
In this russet November woods of Millay,
I wear your old hat, Dear Italian patriarch, to see
if I can think you out of your American grave
to sing your unwritten song with me.
Your poetry, love's value, I carry with your spirit.
I take off your old black hat and sniff at it
to smell the still living vapor of your sweat.

You worked too hard, an oldest child of too many,
a lame thin boy in ragged knickers, you limped
all through the 1920s up city steps, door to door
with your loads of night and daily newspapers, each worth
a cheap labored penny of your family's keep.
You wore your heart and soles sore. At forty,
not climbing autumn hills like me, you lay with lung disease
strapped down with pain and morphine, hearing your breath
rattle in your throat like keys at the gates of hell.
Your body was always a fiend perplexing your masculine will.
You filled me with pride and immigrant tenacity. Slave
to filial duty, weaver of all our dreams, you couldn't be free
to sing. So be it. You are done, unfulfilled by song except in
   me.
If your dreams are mine, live again, breathe in me and be.

You never understood America's scheme.
Your wounded dream, father,
will never heal in me, your spirit mourns forever
from my breath, aches with childhood memory,

sighs for my own mortality in you,
which I, at last accept
more completely than ever when we
laughed together and seemed we'd go on forever—
even though we always knew
you would die much sooner than I
who am your spirit come from you.
Remember, *"a father lost, lost his!"* you told us,
preparing us with Shakespearean quotation
and operatic feeling for your inevitable death.

Good night, go gently, tired immigrant father
full of pride and propriety. We, your
three daughters, all grew
to be healthier, stronger, more American than you.
Sensitive father, I offer you this toast,
no empty boast, "I've never known a man braver!"
The wound that will not heal in me
is the ache of dead beauty.
Once full of history, philosophy, poetry,
physics, astronomy, your bright, high flying psyche
is now dispersed, set free from your tormented body,
but the theme you offered, often forlorn,
sheer luminescent soul, glistened with enough light
to carry us all full grown.

Woman with Tongue
Sculpted in Cheek

There are no rules for sadness—
so much despair rising from the sink drains of evening.
The chairs are empty,
curtains full of wind,
the room silent as a lantern.
Who couldn't go on
spilling pages of wordy histories,
cracking thoughts as shells
from nutmeats of philosophies,
spinning threads from fish eyes.

I lift my breasts waiting for the ceiling
to sprout fingers.
Men do not let women live in their dreams
but dream of women in their lives
as if we could be as good as trees,
as calm as photosynthesis in all our fornication.

Guilty since Eve, I will not be responsible for temptation,
I pull the trap door shut, close my legs against eternity,
build a moat around my uterus,
use my ovaries for amulets,
cease rattling my bracelets,
cut off my nails
and close my lips tight against kisses, new mournings.

My hair was not my own idea;
it grew from his rays and he commanded
that I brush it till it shown as moonbeams
because he was the sun,
he was
everyone:
He was Dr. Kildare, Emmett Kelly, Christ;
Leonardo da Vinci, Albert Einstein, Louis Pasteur;
Charlemagne, Napoleon, Mozart, and Shakespeare;
Mailer, Ginsberg, Plato, and Buddha;
Lincoln, Rembrandt, Donato Gioseffi, and Richard Kearney.

Father, husband, whom I've worshipped all my years.
I've let you commit crimes in my name,
place me on a pedestal of halos,
hide my clitoris as my hips grew wider
and a child squeezed out of my heart,
grew big as a mountain,
swallowed me for dinner,
held me in a sucking grip until I crooned lullabies.

I've washed a thousand bathtubs
and watered a million geraniums
with the fallings of my dreams,
and the knight,
the Knight,
the night,
never comes riding never comes riding

never comes
riding
except to admonish me
for vanity he creates in me
or to drape a heavy blue robe around my shoulders
and rest his crucified body
in my soft and tired lap.

Arturo Giovannitti

Anniversary I

Along the flocks of clouds that browse the firs
The moon goes like a mystic grail of light,
Between the bowed heads of the worshippers.

The branches of the oaks swing with a flight
Of censers and the poplars sing a psalm
Of ancient glory to the holy night.

Peace lies upon our roof, and in my palm
Your hand unclasped lies restful and secure,
And everything is strong and white and calm,

For we are still in love and are still poor.

Edvige Giunta

Litania *for My Mother's Hands*

Sewing the hem of her dress
knitting a sweater
with blue-and-white wool
in a Norwegian pattern for a Sicilian girl
writing a letter to daughters now *Americane*
to the granddaughter they no longer know

washing plates the ones for special occasions
with gold lines
the plates she keeps in the *sparecchiatavola*
(the chairs of the dining room falling apart)

dusting Capodimonte porcelain in the *salotto*
where her youngest practiced endless scales
on the piano she could not touch
the wedding gifts
luscious and preposterous
slicing eggplants for the evening's *parmigiana*
purple skin grace on the open garbage bin
wiping her forehead after spreading the sweet *astratto*
for the ragù reddish condensation of women's sweat

grating fresh pecorino on a steaming plate
(I no longer remember the smell)
spreading *nutella* (always Ferrero) on my brother's bread
thin generous slices of *pane di casa* from the bakery in the
   alley
wiping tears after he fell one story
broken head after dancing with the birds
blood spilling out his ears magnificent fountains

picking oranges and tangerines parsley and basil
grading *dettati di prima elementare*
guiding the hands of first-graders
tracing awkward consonants and vowels on the lines
(how can English vowels be so different?)
paying bills
paying for an Alitalia ticket only to come back
dialing always new numbers zero one one three nine
(but that's what I dial, I don't know her numbers)
carrying her suitcase bus train plane

straightening her dress
fixing clothes fixing rooms fixing their lives
stirring the past simmering its smell
wrapping packed box of almond pastries
for Catania Miami Southampton Schenectady North
   Brunswick
Jersey City
still sending their bounty
without restraint with sorrow

squeezing between sheets of rough brown paper
DO NOT SEND BACK IF UNDELIVERED
wringing the water from a silk Rinascente blouse
wringing sorrow
holding me rough softness on my face
a craving of their touch.

John Glavin

From *MANAYUNK: Growing Up in Philadelphia During and After the War*

I am supported by my grandparents. It is 1945. I am three, or there-abouts. They are pressing me against a window that is almost exactly as tall as I am, and almost as wide as it is high. Though I am very tall even from the beginning, I am certainly not yet three feet. The window's sill is flush with the linoleum floor. My grandparents are crouched or kneeling one on either side of me. It is very dark outside the window. And cold. I am in my nightclothes. We are laughing. They have awakened me so that together we can watch the drunks being tossed out of the saloon across the street.

The stupid, falling-down drunks delight us. They are being thrown out, one by one, from a side door, which is almost opposite our front door, except that our front door is reached by a very high set of steps, while the side door of the saloon seems to be at or near basement level. Also my room is at the very top of the house, four stories above the street. So, in every sense, we look down on this half dozen or so of hapless, helpless drunks.

How stupid they are, big men, to fall down like that, like babies, to slip, and slide, and roll. What pleasure the bouncer takes in tossing them one by one out the door so that they mostly fall on top of each other. And then they try somehow to scramble up and out from the pile before it becomes heavier, higher. But he always gets the next one out first.

I know they are drunks, so this must have happened before, this ritual watching. And drunks have been explained to me, so that I know this is funny and not sad. I know that no one is being hurt. Or maybe I only know the men who are being hurt deserve it. Drunks are stupid, men who have no dignity, who waste themselves. They are unworthy, and they deserve to be laughed at. They have made themselves into nothing but a way to make other people, us, laugh at them.

This is my earliest memory. We are a very happy family up there at the cold, dark window, my grandfather, my grandmother, and I. This remains the best memory of my life before I became an adult.

My grandfather, Giovanni Abbandonato, was born in 1888, and my grandmother, Carolina Consolo, in 1896, in the town of San Donato, in the province of Cosenza, in Calabria. My grandfather was a shepherd. My grandmother, the daughter of the village blacksmith. They married because the blacksmith died young. He left no protector for his widow, her daughter, and her young son in that society of routine and ruthless violence against women. Also because my grandfather had been drafted as a soldier, hated the army, and had come back to San Donato bone-lonely. And in addition my grandmother, at fourteen, had milk-white skin and wine-red hair, there deep within the uniformly olive and brown South. My mother, Rosina, first of their five children, same red hair, was born in San Donato in 1912. In late 1913 the three emigrated to America, to Pennsylvania, where they lived till his death in 1960 and hers in 1970. My grandfather never stopped regretting the decision to leave Italy, never thought of himself as an American, though he became a citizen, never stopped hating the fact that because the man at Ellis Island was pig-stupid, he had to spend the rest of his life being called Mr. Bonder.

My father was Irish. His father referred to my mother as Kon's Little Dago. Happily, my Irish grandfather died a year or so after the marriage, and was missed by no one. He died at Mass, just after he had received Communion. He knelt, put his head in his hands, and never lifted his head again. Which shows how little you can learn from appearances.

Curiously, my Italian grandfather also died at church, but in very different circumstances. He had gotten a job as night watchman on the construction site for our parish church. Some kids started throwing stones at the new windows. As he ran them off, he suffered his final, fatal heart attack, and collapsed on the steps of the convent, supported in his final moments by the praying nuns. He was seventy-two.

Except for the divinity of Jesus, everything my father thought differed entirely from everything my grandparents knew. For example, this is how he explained drunks to me. "Your Uncle Joe," he once told me—Uncle Joe was married to one of my father's four sisters—"people call him a drunk. Actually, Joe was never a drunk. Joe drank. But he was never a drunk. He'd work a full week, till Saturday, when we used to work six days a week, and then Fridays. He never missed a day. Never showed up late on the job. And everybody who ever knew him will tell you he was a great housepainter. Ask anybody. Then, when he finished work, he'd collect his pay, and go to that big taproom that used to be around the corner from Our Mother of Sorrows. Big place. Gone now. He'd divide the pay money in half. Exactly in half. And Joe always made good money. Even in the Depression Joe made good money. Because the builders knew they could count on him. Half the money he'd count off for the bartender to hold for Margaret and the kids. The other half he drank. Sometime the next morning Margaret, or one of the boys when they got older, would come down to the taproom. Joe would be asleep in a booth. They let him sleep there because they knew him. They knew he'd never give them any trouble. The kid would pick up the money for my sister. Round lunchtime Joe would wake up and keep on drinking. Monday morning his half of the money would be gone, but he'd get himself up and go right back to his job. Now you can't call a man who lived like that a drunk. A drunk's a slob who neglects his family, a bum who doesn't support his kids. My sister Margaret, she never had to work. Those kids never went without shoes. Their father was not a drunk."

My mother made it a point of her marriage that my Aunt Margaret, my Uncle Joe, all of my father's family, never visited our house. The first time I can recall meeting them was when they showed up for my grandfather's wake. Without Joe.

The house where I lived with my grandparents is in a part of Philadelphia called Manayunk. It's the last section of Philadelphia that you see when you are driving toward Valley Forge on the Schuylkill Expressway. If you look to your right, you see slip rapidly from sight what looks like an Italian hill town curiously perched above the banks of the river. Even to the big church, Holy Family (or was it Holy Innocents? No, Holy Family), crowning the top. I can't be sure of the name of the church because we never went to it. We went to the Italian church, St. Lucy's. Holy Family was for the Americans.

Manayunk was not where my grandparents came when they arrived in country. In fact, they did not initially come to this country together. After they married, my grandfather emigrated alone, in order to raise the money to buy a later passage for his family. For almost nothing single men could get a hammock someplace in the bowels of virtually any ocean-crossing boat. But he was not one of those people you see in the sepia photographs from the great age of emigration. On the steamer deck, the men collarless but wearing vests and caps, their women in aprons, heads kerchiefed, adults pointing out Miss Liberty to the wee ones, gap-toothed smiles, high on hope. He came not because he wanted to but because he was afraid to stay behind. He had hated being a soldier. Shortly after his marriage, in 1911, Italy, like the other monarchies, began to arm seriously for one of those practice runs at the war that would ultimately undo all but one of them. She decided to conquer and annex Tripoli. My grandfather was warned that veterans would be called up, and sent to the front first. Anything, he felt was better than that, even America. And so he set sail.

His reluctance entirely shaped my early sense of my own Americanness. It wasn't until I got to college that I began to sense that there might be something not second-best about the U.S. That it might be a place with some value of its own, and not just, as my grandparents taught me to believe, the barely better of two bad choices. But until I was almost twenty I took it as an article of faith that everything of real worth was and remained in Europe. In my upbringing "American" was always a term of disparagement.

My grandfather crossed to join a colony of other Italian men working the coal mines in eastern Pennsylvania, to a squat shantytown that called itself New Columbus. While he was gone, my mother was born. By 1913 he had earned enough to return for his daughter and his soon-again pregnant wife. They hated the journey itself as much as they hated the reasons for having to make it. The late autumn seas were stormy. They were at the bottom of the boat below the waterline. They didn't see sky or breathe fresh air the whole of the long crossing. Of course, this was the year after the *Titanic,* so perhaps they had something, unbeknownst, to feel grateful for. They did get here. But when you read that the *Titanic* offered the most comfortable steerage quarters on the Atlantic, and those quarters contained exactly one bathtub for several hundred men, women, and children, you begin to image the squalor they endured. For my grandmother, furiously clean in the manner of all Italian women, this life must have made her feel she had come out on the wrong end of the Last Judgment.

From the beginning, then, it was clear to both of them that coming here had been a disastrous mistake. But they responded differently to that disaster. My grandfather, with the fatalism that would mark, and mar, his entire life, believed they had no choice. He was entirely illiterate, able to read and write neither English nor Italian. He had only his powerful back and massive hands. What else was he fit for, then, but to dig coal? He was lucky he had steady work. My grandmother, however, had been to school, up to the fourth or the fifth grade. She kept her two battered little textbooks all her life, arithmetic and reading, the only thing I ever saw that she kept from her old home. She even taught me basic Italian grammar out of the reader when I was old enough to follow. Why, then, should she accept this mulish impoverishment of her own and, more pressing, her children's futures? Without her knowing how, what had happened to her was beginning to change what happened within her.

Married as a child, at fourteen, to a man eight years her senior, overseen by her needy and frightened mother, she had dutifully followed the old ways in the old place. But in this new place, where all the old ways had fallen not just aside but apart, she refused to continue blindly biddable. She had these children. Why should they be made to lead lives like those she saw around her? Growing up the blacksmith's daughter, she had been a person of status and privilege, such as it was, in her village. Had they made this terrible journey, left behind everyone they knew and everything they loved, to live like this, like people she would not have spoken to crossing their path in the village street?

One night she was alone with the two children, her husband down below the earth on the long night shift. He would not be home until after sunrise. Some sort of terrible noise broke out from below the house, a loud, whining crying like a call for help. It would not stop. It woke the children, my mother, and her eldest brother, who later became my Uncle Jim. Terrified, the toddler and the infant started crying along with whatever it was. My grandmother knew it was a dead soul, released from hell by the miners' incessant pummeling at the earth's bowels, but still trapped, and begging for release. She assured the soul that she would help if only it would let her know where exactly it was. Alternately, when the soul didn't respond, she prayed to Our Lady of Mount Carmel to intervene and save, at least, the babies.

Finally, after hours in which neither prayer was answered, she heard a drunk outside, singing on his way back from the saloon. She hardly needed to explain her terror. Even outside the house he could hear the cries. Fortified with Dutch courage, he crawled under the house. And returned with a trapped nanny goat, who immediately ran off to join her own probably frightened young. Two mothers restored.

When my grandfather got home that morning, she told him they had to move. They couldn't live like this. Nanny goats under the house. They had to go to Philadelphia. That was a real city, with real houses, not shacks like this one.

He told her it was impossible.

She insisted.

He beat her. Something he found himself forced more and more often to do since they had come to this country.

He went to sleep, and at night he went back down into the mine.

When he returned the next day they were gone, his wife, his daughter, his infant son, and so were most of their belongings. No note (he could not have read it in any case), no message left with a friend (they had no friends). Nothing.

Mute, he took one thing that remained, their wedding photograph, and left by train for Philadelphia. He wandered with the picture from Italian neighborhood to Italian neighborhood, asking anyone who looked like a fellow countryman, if he had ever seen there the woman in this picture. She has red hair. And, finally, miraculously—perhaps Our Lady of Mount Carmel, but delayed, in one of the Divine's usually strange ways—he stopped a man who said the equivalent of: "Sure, she's the new cook in my boardinghouse. Come on. I just got off work, I'll show you the way." And there she was, happily cooking for a large boardinghouse, with two rooms for them in the attic (as far from basements, and goats, and indeed from mines, as possible), and the promise of a job where one of the boarders worked as soon as he showed up. Which she knew he would do.

The next day he started his job in the cardboard box factory, where all that was needed were those powerful shoulders and those massive hands, and worked there until the day he retired some thirty-three years later.

He did not stop beating her. Just the reverse. But they both knew he had lost control, the last vestige of the manhood he had begun surrendering on the day he left Italy. He started sleeping with gypsy women, who told fortunes and turned tricks down near the cardboard box factory. I remember as a boy, not a little boy, but still young, hiding behind a parked car with my grandmother, again cold and dark, while we watched him leave his gypsy and start home. Yet, despite his violence, her power continued to grow, like his anger.

A few years after they arrived in Philadelphia, she heard there were houses for sale, the down payments within the range of what she had managed to save. She went to stand outside the real estate office, the only woman in the crowd of men. One by one they advanced toward the door, only one let in at a time. Each man who exited seemed similarly glum. Finally, she stopped one that she knew.

"Don't waste your time in this line, *signora*. The sign says they have houses but when you get inside they say they have sold the last one."

Nevertheless, she stayed and finally got inside the door. At the counter, two men carefully scrutinized her, and then asked: "Are you Italian?"

She got it at once.

"No," she said, managing to make them notice her milk-white skin, her red hair, "I am Dutch." Mrs. John Bonder, it sounded Dutch to them.

She got the house. The house on Fountain Street where I started my life.

She had figured America out. In Italy you pay back. You forget nothing. You exact revenge when you've been slighted. And you never stop obeying your parents, honoring, supporting, maintaining them for your entire life. Nothing, no subsequent connection, emotion, tie, experience, can overrule or outbid the claims of the past. In America you invest in the future, if not in your future then certainly in your children's. The past is what you leave behind, cast behind if required, obviously if that's possible, cannily if it isn't. You have to. Here you can't let the past hold you. Here its grasp is a death grip. That's how my grandmother lived her, and her children's, American life. Forget the past. Make the future you need.

Here's a nice example. When my Aunt Mary, the third child, became engaged, she and her fiancé went down to Philadelphia's City Hall to get the marriage license. No, they were told, we're sorry, but there is no birth certificate registered for a Mary Bonder born on that date in February 1916. Try, she asked them, Mary Abbadonato. Sorry again. Try Maria Abbandonato. Sorry still. But oddly enough, they had a Teresa Bonder born on the same day, same year.

At home, my aunt, distraught, explains that she can't get married because she can't prove she was born. My grandfather fulminates. Only in America. My grandmother takes her daughter aside. "When you were born, your father wanted you named for his sister, Maria. Mary. But I didn't like that name. And I wanted to name you myself. Because he had named your sister after his mother. So I told my friend, who was your godmother, that when the priest asked, she should say your name was Teresa, because that was a name I liked. And that was the name they put on the certificate. I will go down to City Hall with you tomorrow and we will get the marriage certificate."

And they did. But my aunt's marriage was not happy. Perhaps my grandmother should just have stayed still. I asked my aunt why she had married, so young and strikingly beautiful, someone so obviously unsuited to her. "Pop used to beat us. Both us girls. And Mom. With his strap. I took the first offer that would get me out of the house. What did I know?"

Whether or not this had been true of her early life, by her twenties, living in America, my grandmother had lost all respect for any form of earthly authority, my grandfather's, or anyone else's. Never, for instance, she would tell me, never believe the priests. Strange, since she was eager that I become one. Because they had the easiest life, she thought. They never had to work. They made you think that you could only find God in the churches. That was the source of their power. That's why other people worked for them. It was all, everything they said, a lie.

Nor could she be doubted in this, because she had actually seen the Blessed Mother. To be fair, she herself never claimed it was the Blessed Mother. This is what she said. In 1918 she was told by her doctor that she had to have an abdominal operation, a grave operation. If she did not have it she would die. I don't remember being told what the operation was supposed to do. I think that is because she herself did not know. He was a doctor, he didn't have to explain to an illiterate Italian woman the details of his diagnosis.

Of course she consented. On the morning of the operation, after she had been prepared for the surgery, and had said good-bye to my grandfather, she lay waiting in her hospital bed to be wheeled to the operating room. Suddenly, at the foot of her bed, she saw a woman. This woman, what did she look like, people hearing the story would ask. How much they wanted her to be dressed in blue and white, Lourdes, or white and gold, Fatima, to be crowned with roses, or a tiara, to be, clearly, The Virgin, no matter what her own modest silence on the subject might say. But my grandmother would only say that this woman was dressed as a widow.

And this widow said to her, "Caroline, you cannot have this operation."

"Who are you?" my grandmother asked, not unreasonably.

"You know who I am," the widow insisted. At this her listeners would sigh, knowingly. "You must not have this operation."

And she didn't. She called in my grandfather and told him to find her clothes. And when he cursed her and said he would have nothing to do with it she said she would walk out into the streets in her hospital gown. So he got her clothes and they went home.

Many months later, she was pushing her new baby, my Uncle Tony, in his carriage when she encountered the same doctor coming from a neighbor's where he had made a house call. These days, I know, that sounds like the real miracle in this story.

"Mrs. Bonder, I thought you were dead."

"Not only am I not dead, Doctor, I have just had this baby boy."

Now comes the clincher: "Well, let me tell you something, Mrs. Bonder, if I had performed that surgery, you would not have this baby today."

I never learned the truth behind this mysterious disease and diagnosis. I only thought it meant that God was especially interested in my Uncle Tony, which also meant, since he was my godfather, that something special was also waiting in store for me too.

My uncle grew up to be a cop, a narc, having first found being a professional shortstop too lonely. My father always insisted to me that Tony was the only honest cop in Philadelphia. Something I believed completely because my father never said a good word about anyone in my mother's family when my mother wasn't around to hear. But which tested even my credulity since, through one of my uncle's friendships, we never paid a butcher's bill.

————

Except for weddings, funerals, and First Communions, my grandmother never set foot inside a church. My grandfather went to church whenever I, or later my brother, served Mass. Silently, he would wake me with milky coffee, no matter how early the service. And then he'd mutely trudge beside me, no matter what the weather, back and forth over the railroad bridge that led to the parish precincts. But this had nothing to do with worship. It was simply and lovingly the childhood version of his earlier, infantine protection when up at the viaduct I went to watch the trains.

My parents, however, and my brother and I, we went to church constantly. Twice on Sundays, usually two or three other evenings a week, for "devotions." In Advent and in Lent, and often throughout the rest of the year, we attended daily Mass. My mother had become ill in the early 1950s. Every other year some part of her body would be lopped off or carved out. She would go away to convalesce for several months. Then she would return to us, paler, weaker, until the time for cutting came again, until there was nothing left to cut away. We prayed in church for a cure, all the time. She begged not to leave us orphans, which meant leaving us with my father. Nevertheless, she died at fifty-one.

But my grandmother stayed home from church, and cooked. Before we left for midnight Mass, she would feed us slowly the Italian vigil dinner, starting with *baccalà,* salt cod, and smelts, and continuing with crab, shrimp, pasta, and then various courses of the fish available at the A&P. We'd go off, stuffed, while she stayed behind to clean it all away. When we got back, close to 2:00 A.M., there was a freshly set table and plates of just-made *crespelle,* sugar-dusted, fried doughnuts, and *pizzelle,* anise-flavored, paper-thin waffles. The same thing, on a diminished scale, happened after Mass every Sunday. We never came home without finding a hot breakfast waiting, each person provided in those nutritionally macabre days with a half pound of crisp bacon and unlimited fried eggs. You had fasted from midnight if you were going to Communion, which meant that going to and returning from Mass you were ravenous. And of course you took Communion every Sunday, because you had confessed the day before, children in the afternoon, adults in the evening.

In the Church of Ireland, Confession, not Communion, was the central sacrament, because sin, not grace, was its key belief. For us, even though we went out to Mass, Sunday (like every other day) belonged to my grandmother and the Italian religion of the family. Each of her five children, with their spouses and their children, came to see her every Sunday afternoon, most to be fed by her. But Saturday was my father's. On Saturdays his counterrituals, of sin and discipline, for just that once in the week, took over the house.

Mandatory weekly Confession for all, except for my grandfather, who could not say his sins in English, and my grandmother, who would not. For the rest of us, however, at least from the age of seven, it was an unexamined fact of life. "Have you been to Confession yet?" "I can't come over, because I haven't been to Confession yet." "We'll come for coffee after Confession." Outsiders might have thought we were the Borgias, so stained we would have seemed. Except that there were no outsiders. Everyone we knew belonged to the Church of Ireland. Everyone we knew was a member of the parish, Saint Clement, a pontifical Roman saint for an Irish congregation. Everyone we knew sent their children to the parochial school. Which never celebrated his feast day, but always gave a day off for Saint Patrick. And everyone went to Confession. The lines at the confessionals rivaled each week the lines at the local movie houses.

My father not only insisted on the Saturday confessional drill, he elaborated it to make it his especially own. To the confessional drill he added also the inspection of uniform, the only bit of barracks life he had been able to retain from his happy time in the war. Before he left for church, he would have me set my shoes on the basement stair landing, to be spit-shined while he was gone, and inspected the first thing after he got back. After that, still in the basement, the part of his house his mother-in-law allowed him, I had to demonstrate my skills at tying the perfect bow tie. He would each Saturday night select one of his own, sometimes squared off, sometimes butterfly, and watch while, without access to a mirror, I made a perfect knot. Except that it was, of course, never quite a perfect knot.

This ritual absorbed him because it was almost the only thing he controlled in his own house. Sterner, smarter, and infinitely more energetic then he, his mother-in-law emerged the victor in every contest. But she could also be gracious in her superiority. She fed him bountifully. She allowed him his Saturday evenings. And beyond the cellar steps she never interfered with his basement. He made himself content. In his Irish Catholic schools he had been walloped by tough Sisters and pummeled by even tougher Brothers. Together they had taught him to live according to the most onerous possible interpretation of the Ten Commandments. One of those commandments ordered you to honor your father and your mother, which also meant your wife's father and her mother. You weren't meant to like it. In fact, you knew you were doing good when you didn't like it at all. Once my father asked his brother-in-law Jim why he never took his parents with him when he went down the shore in the summer. "Because I want to have a goddamn vacation, Tommy, that's why." My father never got over that answer. "For Chrissake, she's his mother," he'd repeat.

The reason my grandmother didn't need to go to church was because she had a banner of Our Lady of Mount Carmel. It hung over her bed. A gorgeous thing, which had been presented to her in the 1930s for her services as a Grand Venerable of the women's branch of the Sons of Italy. It was a large banner, the kind that is carried in processions in Italy on feast days. Cream satin with heavy, gold bullion fringe. The Virgin in brown satin, crowned with elaborate gold stitchwork, bestows the scapular on a kneeling Saint Simon Stock, the founder of the Carmelites.

Her religious practice radiated from Our Lady of Mount Carmel. Several times a day she would retire to her room, take out a well-worn prayer book, held together by a rubber band and paper clips, and perform her devotions to the banner. This was a strictly private office. I only caught accidental glimpses. It lasted only about fifteen minutes and involved, as far as I could see, a great deal of bowing.

But every year on the feast of Our Lady of Mount Carmel, July 14, I would get to join in. Since she had very limited English, from the time I was about ten, it was my job to escort her by bus from Philadelphia to Flemington, New Jersey, a small town which celebrated the feast in the Italian way with a street fair and grand procession. We would eat sausage and peppers fried at local stands, and inspect booths of religious goods, which she would dismiss as trash. At length the intercessory procession of statues would pass. She would give me the largest bills she had managed to save. Then I would rush into the midst of the procession and pin our bills to the constantly replaced satin streamers attached to the statue of Our Lady for just that purpose. We would not stay for the next and final part of the procession, a priest carrying the golden monstrance with its sacred host. After Our Lady of Mount Carmel had passed by, there was nothing left to see.

Other saints sometimes mattered, all of them, I realize now, female. The most important of them was Saint Thérèse of Lisieux, the Little Flower, the would-be namesake of my miscalled aunt. And it was through the Little Flower that my grandmother provided me with my most vivid religious experience, far more vivid than anything I ever received through the Church of Ireland.

In the early 1950s she and I returned to New Columbus, from which she had so precipitously forced her family's exit. These visits, which we took once a year, were described in the family always as "going upstate." They reversed the annual summer trip to the ocean, always called "going down the shore." Living upstate were my grandmother's sister-in-law, the widow of her younger brother, Luigi, and his many sons, and their families. Luigi had followed my grandfather to the mines, but he had not been able to follow his sister to the city. It was early October, which meant that our visit intersected the feast of Saint Thérèse, marked in that remote, entirely Italian village, in a way that bizarrely interwove Italian and American life.

There was of course the customary procession of life-sized statues supported on long rails shouldered by the village's strongest men and boys. There was the pinning of the bills on the ribbons. But there were also two innovations.

Saint Thérèse is famous among Catholics of all sorts for having promised that she would spend her heaven doing good on earth, metaphorically described as shedding roses. And so at the culminating moment of the procession, we heard first the dull drone of an old plane. Then suddenly it was there above us, as I remember, almost within our grasp, from its color and markings clearly U.S. army surplus. It dove steadily toward the crowd and then, miraculously, from its opened port, showers of roses began to fall, blessed roses, completely covering the processional route.

We ran amok. We scrambled onto the hoods and the trunks of cars. We climbed porch roofs. We scaled trees to grab roses caught in the crotch of branches. How many roses you could grab, what did that mean? How many favors you would receive? Who knew, but we needed to keep grabbing because even as we touched them their petals fell, and we held only stems. They must have already been dead when they were purchased in bulk by this poor parish. But I didn't understand that. My knees were skinned, my palms burning. I was trying to shimmy up a drainpipe above which, I was sure, there were roses intact and immaculate. I had to carry back at least one, one perfect one, for my mother, at least one other, also perfect, for my grandmother. But even as I clambered and slipped, slipped and clambered, the crowds below me began to dissolve. Over the loudspeakers a man was being introduced, who would speak to us from the steps of the church. And as I came to understand who this was, his claim to my attention canceled every frustration.

This was Alessandro Serenelli, the man who had raped and murdered the saint whose name was constantly brought to our attention, the one whose life we were to model ours on. The man who had killed, and thereby created, a saint. A real saint. There were stained-glass windows in her image. There were statues. In Philadelphia there was even a high school named after her. Maria Goretti. She was born in 1890 to a family of peasants near Ancona. She lost her father when she was ten. So that her mother could work to support the family, the child then stayed at home to keep house for her even younger brothers. Serenelli was the hired man. Finding her always alone, he attempted to seduce her. She resisted. Finally he raped, and then killed, her, stabbing her more than forty times. She was twelve. He was twenty-two. Almost the ages of my grandparents when they married. She had been quickly canonized, a blessed in 1947, a saint in 1950, and made a patron of children, with explicit emphasis on her chastity.

Released now from his long prison term, Serenelli was making the rounds of churches in America, publicly repenting his terrible sin. And now here he was among us, upstate. Most of the time I had little idea what he was saying. He spoke in Italian, of course, but in a dialect that frequently lost me. It didn't matter. I only wanted to stare at him. He was the closest thing I had ever seen or known to real history, or for that matter to God, someone who had done something so big, grave, that he had created from it a saint, a cult, a history. If the saint herself had come down to earth in that moment she could hardly have been more interesting. After all, she did nothing, merely said no. But he was the principal agent. And, just as clearly, his role in the procession meant he was a part of her sanctity, its occasion, its instrument, its cause.

In this moment I grasped what it had taken my grandmother many years to get me to understand, but which now stood out clearly: there was no such thing as sin. There was stupidity. There was vulgarity. There was cowardice. None of these were ever forgivable. To show yourself capable of them showed you were not really entitled to be considered a man. For the rest, there was what you had to do to make a life for yourself and those you loved. Nothing else. In this supreme liturgy of my grandmother's church, all merely moral distinctions, like those Ten Commandments on which my father centered his life, seemed to vanish.

The killer-rapist, tears steaming down his face, preached on about his saint, *his saint,* from the steps of the church. He could have been her widower, so deeply moved was he, so deeply did he move us by his story and hers. And all around us lay the severed petals of Saint Thérèse's squandered roses. It was all one.

Barbara Grizzuti Harrison

Godfather II: *Of Families and families*

When my radical friends cottoned to the fact that I was a *Godfather I* junkie, I was quick to anticipate and disarm criticism by arguing that while it was possible for a *lazy* audience to understand from *The Godfather* that Mafiosi went around knocking off only one another in internecine wars, making offers that couldn't be refused only to other pestilential pigs, leaving the rest of the citizenry to go about their God-fearing ways in peace, an *intelligent* audience could easily extrapolate the truth from Coppola's film—which is that the Mafia ruins small lives, destroys innocent grocers as well as rival dope-dealers. *The Godfather,* I said, bore witness to the bitter truth: evil, hydra-headed, renews itself and triumphs in the end; in America, the Corleones win.

To which my radical friends said, *Bullshit:* "Don Corleone and Sonny and Michael were all so damned attractive. They were killers, but one liked them just the same. Their evil was mitigated by their charm." And my brother said, "You liked it because you're Italian." And of course my friends, and my brother, were right. I had not, after all, seen *Godfather I* six times for the pleasure of witnessing the triumph of Evil over Good. I saw it because, in spite of its celebrated violence, it was perversely comforting and warm; it had a uniquely tender, cradling quality. Each time I saw Don Corleone die his rose-garden death, I was set squarely in that fabled place where families honor, respect, support, and protect one another, *touch* one another, forgive one another their sins. Viscerally I understood the Corleones better than, say, the Louds (and I liked them better, too). *The Godfather* nourished the notion that there was someone, some force, who could absolve guilt and make all the hurt go away, someone whose accepted authority could gentle and sustain us.

"Heresy," my feminist friends snorted. "You are talking about patri-archal families who have no remedy for pain, families that smother you, that protect you because you're their property. Step out of line and see what they do for you." My critical intelligence—and my own ex-perience as a third-generation Italian—told me they were right. And yet I returned, as if on a pilgrimage to an atavistic part of my nature, to the courtliness of Don Corleone, to the sanguinity and vivacity of Sonny, to the magnificent reserve of Michael—that eloquent stillness that promised everything, that promised absolution. *Godfather I* created a world analysis could not sour. I felt embraced by the film, and not just because I so rarely see the pungent gestures and rich rituals or hear the rude songs, the lyrical-vulgar dialect of my childhood, reflected in lit-erature or art: I have a vestigial yearning to believe, damn it, that there is a safe, redemptive place, a landscape where everyone knows his or her place, where one follows, with benediction and grace, the yellow brick road to the shrine of approving family gods.

And then Coppola, in his extraordinary sequel to *The Godfather,* did more to challenge my cherished conviction that the family can be a Sal-vation Army than did all the harangues of my radical friends.

Consequently, *Godfather II* gave me an attack of spiritual indiges-tion similar to the heartburn I invariably suffer after Italian weddings. I return, always, from a family wedding blood-warm, warmed by "the blood." I think of the extravagant assurances we have all ritualistically exchanged: "You are our blood," we tell one another, "We will love you whatever you do, we are here for you." And then I think of the work some of those men with whom I've danced the tarantella and ex-changed blood-love do in the world (it's not pretty); and I marvel at my capacity to be seduced by the passion and authority and vigor and charm of men whose work I cannot love. And I think—looking at their wives, who have reaped the traditional rewards of traditional lives—What would have happened to those warm, smiling women if they had chosen separate identities, if their paths had violated the ethic of *la famiglia?* Would, in fact, their men have been there for them? And then I think of my brother, who is a just and generous man, whose author-ity I *do* accept, who can outcharm Sonny any day of the week, who *is* always there for me, who stills my restlessness and makes me feel safe, as no one else in the world can make me feel safe. And I think of my gen-tle father, who has learned painfully to love his maverick daughter, who defends me even when he finds my life incomprehensible. And then I think of a few bitter women, sitting outcast and alone, who are toler-ated merely because they are "the blood," but who are not protected, not loved, because in some way they have violated the sacred rules of this large, lusty family composed of good men and bad men, of strong women and selfless women. I think of the strength of Italian women, of strength perverted and strength preserved. And I am painfully confused. I want all of these people to love me, to comprehend me; I want none of them to constrain or confine me. And I know that what I want is impossible.

I would be surprised if Coppola were not also a victim of the hopelessly ambivalent feelings about family—about the bonds that both heal and mortify—that all second- and third-generation Italians suffer. I think *Godfather II* must have been a painful film for Coppola to have made.

Politically, *Godfather II* is as explicit and forthright as *Godfather I* was elliptical. It bludgeons us with what its predecessor hinted at. It says, with a specificity that leaves little room for a gentler interpretation, that we are one nation under capitalism, and that under capitalism, the Enemy is One—and the enemy includes corporate business, members of the United States Senate, organized labor, and the Mafia. It is, as Pauline Kael has aptly said, "an epic vision of the corruption of America."

Psychologically, *Godfather II* is kaleidoscopic—some have said muddled. But its confusions are *our* confusions, its malaise *our* malaise. *Godfather I* was an almost elegiac film. *Godfather II* is an ice bath. After three and a half hours spent inside the second-generation Corleones' conspiracies and psyches, I felt as if I'd been savaged, betrayed, cheated. I've spoken to Italian friends and they agree: Coppola, who gave us in *Godfather I* the romantic family idyll we all craved, forced us in *Godfather II* to test all our own troubled, troubling feelings about family. What he gave us was not entertainment, not a mythical romance that released us, briefly, from the oppression of our singularity and aloneness, but necessary pain.

There was a kind of golden aura about Brando's Don Corleone, even as he was plotting to destroy half the population of Harlem. He was a luminous goon. There, but for a few wrong turns of fate, one felt, goes a real sweetie pie of an Italian poppa. One could imagine being caressed by his caring; he was the prototypical daddy of our nursery dreams—the powerful man of the world who wipes the tears from the eyes of his babies and acts always, and only, to protect his cherished family. He was, literally, the God/Father. Don Corleone was a rock against whom one might lean. The Michael of *Godfather II* is a defoliator, a glacier. There is, about Michael, everything dark, dank, and pernicious. Charity is inimical to his nature; he feeds on the blood not only of his enemies, but of his family. He kills his dopey older brother Fredo, destroys the womanhood of his sister Connie, and shuts his wife, Kay, out of his heart and his life and robs her of her children. As *Godfather II* ends, he is absolutely powerful and absolutely evil, locked in the solitary confinement of his own corruption, without warmth and without pity.

How well Coppola knows that in Italian families the blood calls to the blood; how devastatingly he deals with the fact that a sister needs, above all things, the approval of her brother to remain whole. When thrice-married Connie approaches Michael (on her knees) and says, with palpable self-loathing, Everything bad I have done to myself I have done to hurt you because you killed my true husband and turned me into a whore, she begs to be allowed to return to the family, *to take care of Michael,* in order to *redeem herself.* Now, for one brief (shameful) moment, I felt my heart leap: the family is back together again! Reunion! Fortunately, I was sitting next to my sister-in-law, who has lived through enough Italian melodramas and vendettas not to be so easily gulled. She introduced a note of raucous sanity into my mindless sentimentality: as Connie groveled and Michael bestowed his icy benediction, my sister-in-law yelled, *"Right? There's always some woman around to pick up the pieces!"*

I would like to have seen a woman like my sister-in-law portrayed in *Godfather II*—a strong Italian woman, that is, with a built-in bullshit detector. I'm sorry that the woman who *named* Michael (who pronounced him evil) was the quintessential WASP Kay. When Kay can no longer pretend to herself or to Michael that she is innocent so long as she is ignorant, when she aborts Michael's dynastic successor, her bitter reproach is couched in words I find unacceptable: "I won't," she says, "be part of your two-hundred-year-old Sicilian thing any longer."

My Calabrian chauvinism notwithstanding, I wish Coppola hadn't allowed Kay to imply that Sicilian families have a particularly bad odor. Clearly *Godfather II* tells us that crime Families stink to heaven. But what about our need for *family?* Coppola's film says brilliantly and unambiguously that the end preexists in the means—that a single small maggot of corruption, given enough filth to feed on, becomes a devouring multiheaded dragon: I gave you Don Corleone, Coppola says, and I permitted you to love him; but you should have been smart enough to know that evil breeds greater evil, and that the end result would be Michael, would be devastation.

But does Coppola not believe that families can heal? My brother and my father—who are good men—inspire me to believe. Does Coppola? I don't know. I don't know because *Godfather II* doesn't tell us. It tells us about a killer Family; its ambiguities spring, I think, from the fact that the bleakness of its vision cannot wholly disguise Coppola's need to believe. But the need to believe is not the same as belief itself. There is a tension between the need and the conviction. *The Godfathers, I* and *II,* reflect that tension, that anguish.

One thing is certain: Coppola understands the terrible hunger of second- and third-generation Italians. Caught in the limbo between the old ways and the new ways, we all want what we are quite sure we cannot have: we want to suckle forever at the family breast. I think he also understands the hunger of all Americans to believe in the goodness of human nature. What Coppola says to that is, Forget it. Bad people are bad people.

What men do in the world resonates in their bedrooms. If one's work in the world is evil, one's "love" for one's family turns into something obscene. The Michael Corleone who has a prostitute butchered to compromise a defiled and defiling senator is incapable of loving *any* woman. The protection the Corleone men offered their women was predicated on the ignorance of those women; and those women, who cultivated blindness, reaped their own destruction. The price they paid for being sheltered was the loss of their souls. I have known women like that. As long as they remain mute and unprotesting—as long as they care more for pasta than for politics—they are happy. As one is happy in a dream. The Corleone men created a dreamworld for their women; they locked them into pink and pretty closets. The closets were roomy— there was space enough for laughter and lust and love and fun. I know those closets; I know that it is possible to stay in them forever. But, for most of us, eventually the world impinges. Mama Corleone, who never questioned, never stepped outside her defined and defended world, died relatively happy in her Skinner-box closet; but even she, at the end, had a glimmer of recognition that her acquiescence had helped to produce that which Kay called "unholy, . . . an affront to God."

If *Godfather II* has a moral, it is that you cannot feed evil men and expect to be nourished by them. Evil men are never "good family men." The myth that Italian-Americans have helped to perpetuate ("Joey Gallo brings his Mama roses every Sunday") an Italian-American has helped to destroy. Americans have found that myth irresistible; in these lean and hungry times, when people huddle together for warmth, when robust folk heroes are the vivid symbols of our weary desires, audiences may find Coppola's iconoclasm unforgivable.

From *An Accidental Autobiography*

Italians' "deep contentment with the accustomed bespeaks an attitude toward a meal that makes of it a daily *festa*" (and not a test), Kate Simon writes; "many of the lovely words that purl out of Italian mouths, you will notice, deal with eating: *'Ha mangiato bene?' 'Sí, mangia bene.' 'Che mangiamo oggi?' 'Dove mangiamo?'* All are invitations to long, animated discussions [and not about calories or fat grams]. Should you be on an Italian excursion bus that takes off at, let us say, 8 A.M., the exchange of greetings and autobiography will last until about 9:00, to be followed— first from one quarter, then another and soon burbling through the bus—by requests for a coffee stop, which will include a nibble of cake [a *cornetto*] or a small sandwich. At 10:30 paper parcels will unfold and chunks of bread, slices of prosciutto and medicine bottles full of wine come into action. From that time on, until the lunch stop at 1:30, lascivious fantasies are exchanged about delicious possibilities: pasta, chicken or veal, salad, fruit and wine, always familiar, always a promise of pleasure. . . . The pace of an authentically Italian meal is distinctly musical. The first movement, the pasta or soup, is a *presto agitato,* fast and eager. The meat is cut, lifted and chewed in a calmer *allegro,* while the fruit introduces a stately *adagio* of slow, careful selection, aristocratic discarding, exquisite peeling with knife and fork, the deliberate, slow jaws returned to serenity. We have now reached the interminable *lento.* Although your bread, wine and first course were brought with the speed that accompanies emergencies—a hungry man is a man in serious trouble—the waiter, having fed you, turns to more urgent matters." The waiter is performing a kind of triage, and catering to another raging hunger.

At this very moment I am daydreaming of a perfect *bollito misto.*

Why am I always looking for the illusive perfect Italian restaurant in New York? I know at least six restaurants in Rome I consider perfect, including one that is in what amounts to a parking lot behind the Pantheon. I love that restaurant so much . . . "You have ordered well, signora," the waiter says, as if choosing perfection from a perfect menu were clever of me; to celebrate my perfection, he brings me a glass of Averna (the *digestivo* that, in perfect Italian fashion—and like coffee, which is said both to stimulate and to pacify—arouses the appetite before the meal and calms the full stomach after the meal). I love that restaurant so much I didn't allow my eye to see that our *al fresco* was be-

ing shared by at least six Vespas and five Cinquecentos. I was happy to
regard the carved wooden doors of the thin houses that leaned toward
us on the narrow cobblestone street, the cheerful pots of flowers. "Barbara," my friend Alice informed me, strands of spaghetti *carbonara* curled
lustrously around her fork, "we're eating in a parking lot!" "Yes, but
such a lovely parking lot," I said, "a *Roman* parking lot"; and Alice
agreed. (And how can one not regard as perfect a restaurant where a
waiter greets you with open arms, asks you where you have been and
how your Uncle Carmine is—after an absence of five years, during
which time you have gained twenty pounds.)

So Kate Simon is right: "The passion for Italian food is less a need
for veal in six styles or chicken in three than a yearning for Italianness.
So, even if your diet forbids you . . . you will eat pasta because you see
it eaten with a total joy, a concentration of pleasure, as if it were a rare
Lucullan dish rather than the habitual staple served at least once a day.
You will plunge and wallow in the manipulating, slurping, moistly shining, sexy happiness, not so much to eat as to share the buoyant Italian
greed for experiencing deeply, everything, from roaring in a winner at
the races to the wash of peach juice in the mouth."

I attribute the "buoyant Italian greed for experiencing deeply, everything," to the fact that Italians know they will one day die, knowledge
bred deep in their bone and marrow, knowledge denied us, in our Puritan zeal for moderation. (Is it any accident that that super-Puritan,
quintessential Calvinist Ralph Nader, when he decided to address himself to food-consumers' issues, began with the hot dogs that vendors sell
at baseball parks? He deluded himself into thinking sports spectators the
continent over would rise up in protest against the unwholesomeness of
stadium franks. Whereas everybody knows that no hot dog in the whole
world ever tastes as good as the one you're eating when your team is
winning on a summer day; and who cares what's in it?)

Body and soul, according to Dominicans and Franciscans, yearn for
each other after death—a pretty fancy. The body, according to Saint
Bonaventure, is a composite of spirit and matter.

But it is by matter that we are most often judged—by others, and
by ourselves.

"With few exceptions," says Sallie Tisdale, "to diet is to put image—*surface*—before kindness, wisdom, and joy. We diet to be thin, not
to be healthy. . . . Hatred of female bodies is deep within us, surely. But

even deeper is a fear of all bodies, of the imperfect and unpredictable flesh itself."

When I walk into a room I absolutely know that the first thing anybody will think about me is: She is fat. How fat she is. Yuuch. This may not be true. I *know* it nonetheless. And I know women who are a perfect size 8, and they know it too—they know that everybody in the room has a kind of radar that will allow them to know they've gained a pound and a half.

One solution to this problem is not to walk into a room unless you have good reason to believe it is one in which you will be perfectly safe and completely loved by all therein. How many rooms does that make available to you?

It is better not to have an opinion—any opinion—if you are fat; it is certainly better not to voice an opinion if you own one. After all, anyone can dispute you: What do you know? they'll say; you're fat. I am not alone (did you think I was?) in this fear. Erica Jong, righteously inveighing against the fact that weight is perceived as *will*, says, "I've even had my weight attacked in purported reviews of my books." What is being judged is not one's metabolism or one's flesh-and-only-one's-flesh; what is being judged is one's character: you are slothful, you are given to instant gratification (Fool! Don't you have any decent long-range goals?); you are acting like low-class trailer trash: SHAPE UP. (As for your wisdom, your generosity, your wit, your kindness, your goodness, do they announce and declare themselves when you walk into a room?)

A famous feminist, svelte, who on occasion could be heard to moan that there was a fat lady in her skinny skinny body hammering to be let out, was once, in my presence, shown a portrait of a gorgeous woman who'd had nine kids: "Yeah," she said, "but what does she look like below the neck?" "*Jesus*, Gloria," I said; whereupon she attacked me for not being understanding of her problem—her problem being invisible fat.

Another Spokesperson, whom I interviewed when I was five or ten pounds overweight and she, an occasional actress and producer, was concentration-camp weight, allowed as how men's perceived superiority resided in their large size: "You, for example," said the fragile (but tough as nails) lady, "could, for instance, knock me over with your weight—with one finger." And how I wish I had.

Well; but anger isn't usually the response to casual cruelty. Hurt is. I'll never know why those kids on the Grand Canal in Venice laughed at me when I passed them by; but I'm willing to bet—even though there is no evidence for it—that it was my girth; and it poisoned a summer day.

Once I was invited to give a speech at a college where a stringy cousin of mine worked. She saw fit not to pass the invitation along, seeing as how it would embarrass her for her colleagues to know she had a relative who wasn't thin.

I have a friend who weighs over three hundred pounds. She is magnificent. She is a gifted teacher of young children. She is funny. She is loyal. She is smart. But she is FAT. And that, so far as the world is concerned, is her only identity. I realized this when she was my guest at a California restaurant. You'd have thought I'd brought a serial killer to dinner. I'd cased the joint ahead of time, and her arrival disturbed no one's arrangements; but people made it appallingly clear that they were repulsed and disgusted—put off their food, poor dieting things—by her weight. She gave every appearance of sailing above it all, so as—kind creature—not to upset me; but of course it hurt. (How do you think it would feel to be obliged to ask for a seat-belt extender on an airplane? For the unfashionably bulgy, life is a series of small humiliations.)

. . . Patricia Neal says to Roddy McDowall, What would you rather be, fat or dead? Dead, says Mr. McDowall; and Ms. Neal agrees. On a TV talk show Cloris Leachman says, "Fat people should kill themselves so the rest of us don't have to see them." Just chitchat, meant-to-be-clever talk, small talk—unless, of course, you happen to be fat. . . . Woody Allen in a Woody Allen movie sees a rotund lady jogging around the Central Park reservoir in a red (bless her) sweat suit; "Jesus," he says, "why doesn't she just put her fat in a little red wagon and pull it behind her?" (And he isn't remotely pretty.)

. . . At the MacDowell Colony, a communal residence for artists, I have unwittingly made an enemy of a young woman in a wheelchair. Her disability is the result of bone cancer; I have, in the course of private conversation, used the word *malignant* to describe someone or something in the news, I forget now what. She spins around to confront me and orders me never ever to use the word *malignant* again, it causes her pain. (Long ago I was bitten by a mad dog, twelve anti-rabies needles in my stomach; I do not as a consequence seek to exorcise the word *rabid* from human speech.) She speechifies all the time, her wheelchair her pulpit; she monitors what we watch on television, judging most of it to be racist, ageist, sexist, -ist, -ist, -ist (Linda Bloodworth Thomason's *Designing Women*). Then, exhausted from speechifying and edifying, she says, "Oh why is it always me? Why do I have to always be the conscience of the group? Why do I always have to raise everybody's consciousness?" "Perhaps you don't," I say. "Why don't you give yourself a vacation, perhaps we can get along without you, think how pleasant that would be for you." She shoots a malignant glance at me. So later she takes her revenge. We are—ten or twelve of us, painters, writers, musicians—in a cabin deep in piny woods; my friend Bill McBrian is playing Cole Porter music on the grand piano; we sing along. The conjunction of sophistication and rural woodsy simplicity amounts to a kind of innocence that delights us all. She has been waiting for her moment. We pause to catch our breath; and, her clear high voice occupying all of space and demanding everyone's attention, "I've always thought," she says, "that fat people were subjected to the most awful unacknowledged oppression." She says this apropos of absolutely nothing; and she folds her thin lips in a little smile, and she sighs, and we are meant to interpret her sigh as one of compassion, which it is not.

———

I went to one meeting of Overeaters Anonymous. Everyone else there was bulimic or anorexic; I was the only one who was fat. I was the only one there whose secret was visible: lazy, overflowing flesh. The meeting was in the basement of a church: lazy flesh *and* spiritual sloth? In *The Sayings of the* [Church] *Fathers* it is written, "As the body waxes fat, the soul grows thin; and as the body grows thin, the soul by so much waxes fat." Muriel Spark, whom I love and adore in spite of it, equates fat with venality and stupidity. She characterizes one of her notorious villains—a woman who disappears when there is no one in a room to see her—as one whose poundage outweighs her intelligence. (Oh. And I am afraid that I am fatter than I am good, fatter than I am smart.) Spark's bête noir is the "English rose," plump and pink and soft and ripe, bullying and vapid.

Here is a *Newsweek* cartoon by Lynda Barry: "What happened to the Women's Movement?" In separate panels, different women answer: "too hairy, radical, lesbian, poor, too many rules; way too p.c.; no jokes; lame music and boring sex; too anti-male, middle-class, caucasian-centric; bad clothes, bad hair, totally anti–breast implant, anti-Republican, fat; anti-baby, anti-housewife, anti-husband; no profit motive; they tricked me!" Which, of all these many pejorative words, is underlined twice, despised twice over? The question answers itself: FAT. There is nothing worse than fat.

———

Food, like God, can be put to many uses.

———

I cannot for the life of me think of another thing I learned in home ec or hygiene. In civics, we learned how to fold and crease the *New York Times* so as to be able to read it on the subway in the rush hour, standing up or sitting down. (All our parents read the *Daily News* . . . and my father, who worked nights in any case, never had trouble securing a seat. He chewed a whole head of garlic before he entered the subway car, nobody wanted to be near him.)

Granary, bin and cellar are village prototypes of library, archive, museum, and vault.

—*LEWIS MUMFORD*

In seventeenth-century France, the words *cabinet, closet,* and *museum* were used for the room in which a collection was displayed, or for the collection itself. (Museums are curio cabinets, some—like the Victoria and Albert—more than others.)

In the Imperial Library in Vienna, large birds—pelicans—were trained to pluck books from the upper shelves (are you giddy with delight?).

I actually like hodgepodgy museums, museums where things are jumbled and not discretely organized and where apparently unrelated objects—swords, carved thimbles, desiccated frogs, jade figurines, snake skins, musical instruments—are gathered capriciously; these museums (which exist in backwater cities of Third World countries) force the mind to unify and tidy and classify all by itself, without the assistance of a curator.

The mind is a curio cabinet made up of cubicles in which there are rare and lovely things and unnatural things, flowers and monsters and moss and voluptuous ruins, pearls of great price, stuff and ideas and colored experiences and animate notions.

Touch them.

Josephine Gattuso Hendin

Who Will Marry You Now?

As soon as the N train screeches to a halt at Grand Avenue and I reach the platform, Astoria envelops me yet again. The dome of St. Demetrios's church rises nearby, stained and enduring in the hot sun, but a fence of corrugated metal now conceals the view that once spread wide from the platform over the row houses and one- or two-story garages. Descending the steep stairs from the El, a low panorama opens up—the liquor store across the street that used to sell mass cards, the bakery on the corner filled with breads—rounds, baguettes, twists, rolls, pouring their irresistible aroma into air thickened with car exhaust. Astoria rises to meet me like that summer smell, an aching hunger tinged with tension, anger, and guilt. There are no easy streets here.

I have not come back to these Queens sidewalks for years, but it feels as though I had never left. The street is thick with the ghosts and the voices of people I knew there and loved. Walking toward the old place where we lived, I pass the Astoria Federal Savings Bank. My mother died there waiting impatiently for it to open so that she could run her errand, a massive heart attack seizing and silencing her calculations in seconds that still reverberate in memory. Across the street younger women sit watching children in a sandbox. At the edge of the little park there are the grandmothers, soft ladies in neat black dresses, their gray hair streaked with black and pulled back from their faces, revealing gold earrings that seemed grown into the pierced lobes that have held them for years. They sit talking to each other, lapsing into an attentive silence, alert to whatever passes before them. Nowadays they are joined by old Indian women in colorful saris. The grocery that used to sell Italian salamis and cheeses is now the Punjab deli.

Looking up Grand Avenue, I can see a line of double-parked cars. These are the people who come back from the suburbs to the cheese store, the fish store, the Terrizzi bakery for gelati and pastries. How can they just double-park and run in to pick up an order phoned in advance? Even when they are distracted inside by temptations of biscotti and sfogliatelli of such unanticipated glory and crispness that they cannot tear themselves away without waiting to buy a few, they turn and run to drive, drive, drive back to the better world of Nassau County. These are the people we used to know who left the old neighborhood for the Promised Land of Long Island and suburban dreams. But for us and for me, the city was what we knew. I am ready to take the whole walk, to cover the neighborhood. Astoria for me is not a place for simple comings and goings, but the place that colors every other place in my life.

I can hear, mingling with the rustling of leaves in the wind and the traffic sounds, my mother's voice telling family stories. In the calls and steps of the mothers and their children outside the fruit store I hear the child I was and the mother I loved. "Send a girl to school and you send her into trouble," she would say her mother had told her whenever she kept her home to help her in the house. "I don't believe in that. Go find me some nice tangerines!" She knew the families of the fruit man, the baker who sold her bread and pastries, the fellow in the fish store from whom she bought eels and flounder; she was utterly at home and in charge of life in this enclave that in my childhood had replicated, more than anyone could have thought possible, an intact village. She had completely mastered that face-to-face world. She had serietà, that authority that comes not only from a considerable intelligence, but also from the composure of knowing your competence for the life around you. She wanted a life for me that was better than the one she knew, but she could not imagine how to find it.

This was the world we both knew: Our Astoria was a Mediterranean village where each group had its appointed role. The Greeks had their beautiful church in honor of St. Demetrios and bakeries that sold baklava drenched in honey, galatoboureko and katemeria with sweetened cottage cheese nestled in crisp phyllo. The Jews had a synagogue on Crescent Street where I went to birthday parties arranged in the basement for my friends and was sometimes asked to their bat mitzvahs. I was sometimes the shabbas goy who turned lights off and on for the rabbi's wife who lived in the building next to ours. She was an ancient lady who always wore a flowered housedress and kept her gray hair pulled back into a neat bun. She was almost indistinguishable to me from the old Italian ladies except for her oddly accented English and failure to trade in her flowered housedress for black. She had a glass dish in her living room filled with strange-tasting hard candies she gave us to say thank-you for turning on her lights. Farther up Crescent Street was Our Lady of Mount Carmel, an elegant simple church in limestone in front with yellow brick in back. Conveniently located across the street was a funeral home where we attended the funerals of all the relatives of all the children in our catechism class.

Despite these monumental churches and temples that housed our differences, separateness unraveled in P. S. 5, Junior High School 126, and Long Island City High School, the district schools that claimed most of us. We lived in an apartment building called The Roman Gardens that stood on Crescent Street opposite two stone churches. Our home was in a large building with four separate "houses" or entrances, each of which led to a six-story walk-up. The entrances were built around a courtyard that boasted two six-foot planters, each in the shape of a caryatid supporting a large birdbath-style bowl in which flowers and trailing ivy, my mother insisted, had once been planted. I never saw anything in the planters, but I believed her rapt descriptions of how the hardened dirt of the "gardens," so packed and so cemented by us children running over it that not even weeds could sprout easily, was once lush with flowering plants and bordered by clipped hedges. All that had long gone along with the landlord who had bought a house facing the water in Bay Ridge.

Now children playing hide-and-seek had no shrubs or hedges to hide in and had to find other places for concealment while yells and warnings to shut up rained down from the windows above the courtyard. These were the cries of women too weary to climb up and down the stairs to join those who spent the day sitting in front of the building. They were our very own noise police. When we played handball they yelled; one reserved a bucket to unleash water on us and invented a new game of dodge-the-water that we loved more than box ball or jump rope.

My father believed we were lucky to be there, living on the ground floor. The packed dirt of the courtyard did not diminish his memory of The Roman Gardens and inspired him to his favorite paraphrase of St. Augustin: "Those things that are corrupted could not have been corrupted had they not once been good!" Our apartment satisfied his spirituality, his determination not to care about possessions and comforts. It was badly laid out and dark. It was shaped like an *L*: there were four rooms reached by walking from the door of the apartment down a narrow fifteen-foot corridor to the first room, a living room about twelve by twelve. Through the room the corridor continued with a bathroom off to the right, two small bedrooms at the foot of the *L*, and a narrow kitchen which finished off the toes of the *L*. My mother was unhappy in the apartment. "It's dark," she would say. "It's on the ground floor," my father would retort, "and you don't have to climb stairs."

From the top-floor front apartments, there was a view of midtown Manhattan in the distance. My mother and I would climb the six flights to the roof with our wet laundry to hang it on the clotheslines we had set up. My mother liked the roof and would point out the buildings whose names she knew: the Chrysler Building and the Empire State, the skyscrapers luminous and bright, haloed by windows reflecting the sunlight. She had tipped the super in the next building to tell her when a four-room apartment became available. That building was called The Whitney Crescent and it had elevators and well-laid-out apartments. The kitchens were large and opened on to roomy dining areas. "The four rooms are really five," my mother pointed out to my father. Those apartments seemed beautiful to me too. One of my friends lived in one in an airy bedroom with two large windows and a view of rooftops and a huge sky. When one just like it became available for not much more than we were paying in rent, my father regarded it as the height of frivolity to move. And so we stayed.

Down the street was a lovely house my mother never tired of describing. It was a gorgeous Victorian, huge with a large porch, on what seemed like an immense lot filled with white hydrangeas, a "private" house that stood alone in its splendor. Next to it was the home of the minister of the Episcopal church. Since his garden adjoined the beautifully tended grounds around the stone church, it created a parklike green swath, a speckled paradise of pink, yellow, and white flowers in the spring. My mother would tell me how my grandfather had once offered to buy the Victorian house with my father. It cost $5,000 at the time. It had a separate entrance and apartment on the side that he wanted to live in. My father had turned that down too as interfering with our independence. My grandfather moved down the block to a small apartment. And so we stayed.

As a child, I spent my time with my mother in our tiny kitchen, where she gave me a series of important jobs I could do sitting at the table while she cooked and told stories and tried to teach me "something I had better learn because I would have to do it all myself someday." My jobs at first consisted of emptying packages of lentils onto a dish and looking through them for stones before she soaked the lentils to make Zuppa di Lenticchie. Or I would break the ends off string beans, careful not to waste much of the bean. Later there would be more complicated work slicing peppers or peeling tomatoes, but both these jobs involved a knife and I had not yet proved myself. While we worked together, she regaled me with stories. She was the best story-teller I ever knew.

Her Astoria was a world of ever kind but ever watchful black-clad widows for whom the world of Magna Graecia was right here, transported in the power of watchful mothers who knew the high price paid by erring daughters, dramas of Demeters and Persephones in which every young girl ran the danger of winding up in hell if she were carried away by the wrong man. It was a world my mother had known from her mother and one she had added to and extended with comparable tales gleaned from the women who worked with her as sewing machine operators in a sweatshop near our apartment. A fine dressmaker, my mother accepted the din and boredom of the work because the shop was near home.

Somehow, the women there accepted the perilous path women followed and their own hard labor with surprising good nature. They did piecework and told stories over the noise of the machines, tales handed down to them from towns where women brought water home from fountains and labored at bitterly exhausting tasks, but could still witness the miraculous—sudden sightings and even conversations with those who had died years before, visits in dreams from those who had been loved and had passed into the next world, but could return to inquire whether their children were heartsick or poor or alone or even, sometimes, just to demand reassurance that they remembered the right recipe for Easter lamb. "What do you think?" my mother would ask me. "Did they really come back?"

I became a writer in that sweatshop. My mother would ask me to meet her there each day after elementary school, always on the excuse that she needed my company while she worked or that she needed my help to make up a shopping list. I didn't believe her, but it never occurred to me to question her. She had a place for me to sit and there I would remain eating an apple, coloring, reading, doing homework, or scribbling until it was time for both of us to go. When I was about ten years old I could no longer escape only through reading and I began to construct selves that were in Astoria but not of it. I began to fill six wide-ruled black-marbled school notebooks with a mystery novel in which a child detective named Maria discovers clues to an unsolved murder in Astoria Park, our close-to-home resort. There we watched the Greek and Italian boys of the neighborhood play soccer. It was there my father taught me to pitch and catch ("If you don't move fast it will hit you in the face and break your nose! Look alive!") and there that I learned to swim in the huge city pool that shimmered in the summer heat. The dazzling views of the river and the mirage of the city from Shore Road somehow captured a way of both being in and dreaming yourself out of Astoria.

As I remember it, my mystery story began with some boys from a local soccer team, the Cypriots, discovering a woman's body in the shrubbery off Shore Road at the base of the Triborough Bridge and calling the police. I had a particular feeling for that spot in the park. It was hilly and from there you could see the dazzling skyline of the city and imagine the green and white beauty of Gracie Mansion and the elegant buildings of East End Avenue my father had regaled me with on one of our walks to the foreign country of "New York." In the honeysuckle bushes climbing the fence surrounding the base of the bridge were clues my child detective discovered—a man's St. Christopher's medal, an address in Manhattan scrawled in a matchbook, and a woman's silver bracelet engraved with "H. R. to J. G.," still in a velvet gift box. Recovered from the scramble of honeysuckle and morning glory vines by my overcurious Maria, they now seem to me artifacts that presaged my future—a residual Italian American brand of Catholicism that would haunt my own fantastic imagination of myself as a voyager protected through any reckless trip; a matchbook suggestion of life in the city that loomed like an incendiary truth, and the not-very-subtle engraving of my own initials on a lovely gift not yet opened.

I can't remember how Maria discovered who killed the unidentified woman, but now I think I know who the dead woman was. I think she is the part of me that I wanted to leave behind in Astoria, along with the turmoil of restlessness and love, loneliness and connection, exasperation and hope. At P. S. 5 we were tested and the principal, Miss Burns, who wore her reading glasses as a headband, told my mother I could be anything I wanted to be and that she should give me the best education possible. My mother decided that she would never keep me home to help her around the house as her own mother had done to her. Her older sister had gone through high school at night; her younger sister was the indulged party girl, but my mother had been her mother's mainstay. She decided that I would be an elementary school teacher because it was not only a profession but also one that could prepare me for motherhood. Not everyone thought that was a good idea.

"You married a diploma," my playgirl aunt had accused her, "and where did it get you?" None of the women in my family had gone to college, so my aunt didn't see the point. She herself went in for makeup and exercise and had become a blonde. She would visit us on Saturdays on one of her bike rides, tanned and toned and filled with vivid stories of tourists to whom she sold replicas of the Empire State Building at a gift shop there. One day she brought me a lipstick and showed me how to put it on. She promised to show me how to put on eye shadow. "There are a lot of things your mother doesn't tell you," she would whisper. My other aunt, who had become a bookkeeper, had little patience with her, and tried to quiet her with "Let her make something of herself." But my playgirl aunt only laughed and explained the benefits of lip gloss.

The things my mother told me had cadences of simplicity and stark drama. Her stories resonated with mythic encounters in urban terms. A little boy went into the boiler room of our building and, between the coal-eating furnace and seething water, he discovered a pathway into the next world! My mother's stories about girls had a sharp, unsentimental realism undercut by her all-forgiving, optimistic compassion. She would not take a chance on letting me out of her sight until I had heard enough cautionary tales to be able to watch out for myself. To be drawn to her stories was to be drawn into a world of large and even costly emotions; it was a world of clear standards and rigorous values governing relations between the sexes. That was where everything mattered, and any misstep meant disaster. How could you tell when disaster would strike? It always came when Mr. Wrong was mistaken for Mr. Right. A girl needed to be able to tell the difference between them.

"How a man treats his mother is how he'll treat his wife," she would declare. That was the way to tell who was Mr. Right. She had chosen one for me, a heavyset, good-natured, bright friend of my older brother who was studying to be a pharmacist and working in a drugstore. She had met my father while he was doing that and so considered it a sign of reliability. She had been engaged to my father for nearly ten years and had known him even longer from the neighborhood where both had lived. No surprises there. My father, "for all his faults," she would say, never drank, or gambled or ran around with other women. Satisfying these three criteria meant a man might be Mr. Right. If he were attached to his mother and treated her well, that clinched it. But Mr. Wrong had many guises and my mother, who seemed to have had no life as a woman apart from my father, nevertheless seemed to know about all of them.

In my novel, *The Right Thing to Do,* the fictional mother, Laura, tells a story to her husband, Nino, that deals with a mother whose daughter has landed in Bellevue because she fell for a man who, having exhausted his mother in caring for his children, has enticed her with promises of marriage to take care of his entire family. When the pressure explodes in her screaming breakdown, he disposes of her in a closed ward. In the novel, the story prefaces the fear that a fate worse than madness is about to befall their daughter, Gina. Nino thinks, "It was one thing to take advantage of somebody's trust to make them take care of a house and children, but another to use a girl for everything, without even marrying her."

The ultimate Mr. Wrong is the seducer. Laura has found a photograph of their daughter Gina and a young man with a blond beard having dinner and shows it to Nino, who appraises it for clues to Gina's life:

"They were not looking into the camera. . . . They were smiling at each other. Nino studied the picture carefully, as though it were a code, complex, but not indecipherable. In a peculiar way the boy was attractive. He was elegant. Amazing what a suit and tie will do for anyone! His hair and beard were so perfectly clipped there wasn't a hair out of place. He was fair; his intensely white skin made the yellow of his hair and beard seem even brighter. Gina's profile was striking—her heavy black lashes, straight nose, and long dark hair were set off by a white silk blouse. . . . Her skin was rosy and olive. They made an interesting pair: his pallor, her darkness. They were, he concluded, a couple. The demure correctness of their clothes couldn't mislead him. Look how casually the boy's arm rests on the back of her chair, his hand brushing her shoulder. Look how easily she remains within his reach, looking up at him, amused. There was an intimacy there, a heat that had been satisfied. What a fool he had been to give her the benefit of the doubt" (69).

Always the stories I heard from my mother attested to the power of male authority, the danger of its misuse and the necessity for women to keep their wits about them. In one Italian story my mother said she heard from her mother, a clever peasant girl succeeds in marrying a prince who, recognizing that she is smarter than he is, makes the marriage conditional on her not interfering in his decisions. When she does, he banishes her, telling her she can take the thing she most values from his court and go back to her poverty. She tricks him into having dinner one last time with her, gets him drunk, and has him carried with her to her father's house. When he wakes up in a hovel confused and demanding to know why he is there, she replies that he was the thing she valued most. He is both flattered and entertained by her wit and her refusal to become enraged over his unfair banishment of her, and he takes her back to the palace. My mother accepted as a given that a woman's life depends on the whim or behavior of a man and she must never express whatever anger she feels directly or forget the necessity of finding a balance between self-protection and amiability. She saw these as simple facts.

My mother had great compassion and no condemnation for the girls who experienced the ultimate disaster and got pregnant "out of wedlock"; she was always kind. But she was absolutely realistic about their prospects in the neighborhood. Beyond Astoria the post-pill paradise may have been flowering its lush and careless blooms. Miniskirts and skin-tight jeans carried the day, but here, sealed in its time capsule, Astoria was the world as it had been when she was young and she assumed nothing would change. I was in high school when I saw a girl I knew but hadn't seen for a while round of belly and sitting on the bench in front of the principal's office. She was weeping racking sobs. "What's wrong?" I asked her, sitting down. "They're throwing me out of school," she said. I was about to ask her what she was going to do when she looked at me with such despair and hopelessness that all I could do was hug her. I never saw her again.

In my grandfather I found a gentleness that was filled with compassion and a love of music that, ironically, reinforced my mother's views. He was a semiretired tailor who had worked for the best men's designers. My mother would send me to him with trays of lasagna, or meatballs, or a pot of lentil soup thick and rich as a stew. I would find Papa Joe at home listening to opera on the radio, sitting by the window and sewing or standing with a suit dummy on which he was carefully making a man's jacket. He rose with the sun and rarely stayed up past sunset in summer. He did not believe in the propriety of paying for electric light, preferring the window to any reading lamp. He would hug me for bringing him my mother's dishes and give me a treat. Usually it was apples sliced in a small bowl with a little red wine. He would tell me about the opera he had on while I munched. His favorite was *Rigoletto.* He could describe with fierce passion the useless efforts of Rigoletto to keep his beautiful daughter safe from the attentions of the philandering, careless duke, a man whose wealth and position had given him an untroubled sense of entitlement. The duke cheerfully despoils Rigoletto's daughter, driving her father to misery and vindictiveness while the noble Gilda, knowing the duke is a worthless betrayer, sacrifices her life for him.

High art and working-class life conspired to send the same message about the central fact of a woman's life. I would bring Papa Joe his lunch to the empty lot two blocks away in which he and his cronies had built bocce courts and planted a garden with a fig tree, sweet basil, and some grapevines. It must have been these old Italians, who began to plant and cultivate empty lots they could never own, who were among the first urban gardeners. They could not bear to see unused land remaining ugly and strewn with debris. There Papa Joe and the other ancient men played bocce and talked. After I left home and was living on the Lower East Side, I went to swim one day at the Carmine Street pool in Greenwich Village and my heart ached when I saw in the green corner at its edge a bocce court and fig tree. Nearby, someone had planted sweet basil, but had not pruned the plants and left them to flower, letting the taste of the leaf go awry, The sight of the little garden rushed me back yet again to Astoria. Plunging into the pool under the cool water could not soothe the bittersweet ache of that return, a deeper plunge into longing and exasperation.

I will probably always be haunted by the tumult of memory—the depth of my feeling for my family and my sense, even in their midst, of isolation. For years I could not escape feelings of suffocation, of being trapped in a world frozen in time without an imagination of anything beyond its own mores. All through junior high and high school I felt buried in a time capsule. I dealt with it by withdrawing into books. As a child, I had discovered the library on Astoria Boulevard. Then it seemed an imposing building built into a green hill, stone steps rising to an entrance of heavy oak doors, shaded by old trees and surrounded by flowering shrubs. As I pass by now, the tawny brick that seemed so soft and sunlit when I was a child is the only thing that hasn't changed. The building is small, the steps are concrete, and the surviving plants lack the towering proportions they seemed to have when I looked up through their leaves as a child. I withdrew into the books I took from it. I read, read, read, better off in imaginary worlds that had never existed than the real one I knew. I read as if each page before me was the fast train out into a larger, more open world.

After leaving the library, I would go to the park with my books. I always followed a route that led through winding streets, aromatic with wisteria in spring and the scent of kitchen gardens filled with rosemary and basil plants. Here and there it was possible to glimpse the Manhattan skyline, mythic and grand on the other side of the river. Why did others belong here or there while I felt at home nowhere? I did not have to ask to know that my father's answer to all such questions would always be: "As the Greeks said, 'A wise man is happy anywhere!'"

Outside of the tiny apartment on Crescent Street, the world of authority seemed to have crumbled. Civil rights protests would give way to race riots, anti-Vietnam protests, and then to feminist activism. But in the neighborhood, girls still seem to get "into trouble" and were forced to marry or accept "ruined" lives. My mother lived by ritual time, not current events. She kept the calendar by the regular flow of holidays, family Sundays, and traditional foods that marked them. Every month on a Sunday my relatives and now and then some old family friends came for conversation and an endless flow of bruschetta, mozzarella di bufala with fresh basil and ripe tomatoes, roast vegetables, lasagna, shellfish or chicken or lamb or braciola, and pastries. My good-looking older brother, who was studying to be a pharmacist (what else!), was the life of his fraternity at college and would try out the more unobjectionable skits he had put together for their parties. He could make even my father laugh with drugstore jokes.

All through high school, I would be shamed into putting on a skirt or a dress for these Sundays. I carried dishes to the table from the kitchen, helped keep the flow of courses moving, and filled the soapy sink basin with plates to be washed. My mother treated such days as sacramental; cooking for God and home began on Saturdays and, if many were coming, on Fridays too. My father looked forward to seeing his nephews with whom he loved to discuss baseball, and his sister who still thought he was fun.

However, one month they couldn't come and only my playgirl aunt arrived. With the years, her flamboyance had grown into a mad and maddening ability to say whatever she wanted. My brother managed to get away. Vivid, insistent, and high-strung, she had been complaining for weeks about her husband, who had refused to take her to Florida and she quickly filled the tiny room with laments.

My father decided to stop her complaint by telling a story he claimed to have heard from his father. He began, lightheartedly, as if he were telling a joke:

"One afternoon there were three devils who sat down to play cards after a day of stoking the fires in hell. Devil Luigi, who worked on those sentenced to dance forever on hot coals, began to complain that there were so many men for whom he had to provide burning coals that he had no time to himself.

"'No one else,' he claimed, 'works that hard.'

"'They are all men, on the coals where you are?' asked Devil Giovanni. Devil Luigi nodded.

"'Did I ever tell you what happened when I went to earth to find out why so many men were ruined?' Devil Giovanni asked. 'The men all complained that it was their wives who doomed them with their demands. Everyone in hell is a liar, so I laughed. But then they offered me a bet. If I would go to Naples and get married and prove them wrong, they would stop their yelling for a day. But if they turned out to be right, I had to cool down the coals for a week.'"

"This is not another of your men-have-all-the-trouble-in-marriage stories, is it?" my playgirl aunt demanded. My mother rolled her eyes and looked to heaven, but help was not forthcoming. I waited for the inevitable. My father ignored us and continued.

"Devil Giovanni found a beautiful woman in Naples. Her skin was white as ricotta, her lips were tomato-red and her eyes were like black olives gleaming with olive oil."

"Are you still hungry?" my mother asked.

"So Devil Giovanni asked her to marry him. He said, 'I will give you everything you want on only one condition: you have to ask me for everything you want before we are married and you can never ask me for anything after our wedding day.'

"'So what are you doing back here?' asked Devil Luigi.

"Devil Giovanni continued: 'We were happy for a year and she was content until one night we went to the opera. She had no interest in the singing. All she could see were the different jewels the other women wore. She had five hundred necklaces, but not one was red like the one the queen wore. She fidgeted and squirmed, but said nothing.

"'What is bothering you?' I asked her.

"'I can't ask you for a ruby necklace, that is what bothers me,' she said. 'From that moment on, she didn't ask me for a ruby necklace every minute of the day until I decided I was better off in hell than married to her! And so I lost my bet'"—my father paused to be sure we all caught his punch line—"'because a woman determined to have what she has been forbidden can bedevil even a devil!'"

My aunt was not impressed. "You don't have to worry about that, my beautiful brother-in-law, because I don't see five hundred necklaces around here! There isn't even a dining room! And no Devil works harder than my sister does. There's a proverb Mama used to say, 'When no money comes in the door, love flies out the window.'"

"Your family was always big on talking real estate," my father said.

She began to sing: "'*C'è la luna mezza mare.* If you marry a fisherman all you'll see is fish!' I want to see something different. I want to go someplace else! I want to see palm trees!"

"Well," said my mother, hoping to quiet her, "it's not a true story."

"I don't know about that," my father said.

"Why don't you let her be!" I said.

"Giuseppina, sweetie," my aunt said to me, "don't pay any attention to him. My sister doesn't. He doesn't know what he's talking about."

My father tried another tactic. "Things were more human in the Depression," he said, "when no one had anything or expected to have anything. I was only a child, but I remember that everyone pulled together then, and had some concern for the other person. They didn't outdo each other with demands to leave just for fun. Now it's all about 'I want! I want! Me, me, me!' Augustine says," and he paused, a paraphrase always at the ready for him, "'Of a forward will was a lust made and lust served became custom, and custom sated became necessity, and by that chain was I enthralled.' You," he said to my aunt accusingly, "have wanderlust!"

My father had none. His urge to travel was entirely satisfied by taking us to the "city," that "New York" where showing my brother and me the old neighborhood, or taking us on the ferry to Staten Island while he talked about Ellis Island and pointed out Miss Liberty, was sea voyage enough. Going back in time for my father was going everywhere that mattered.

"People were not so full of themselves in the Depression," my father continued, nostalgic for his childhood.

"You are the only one I know who has a good word to say about the Depression," my mother said gently. "Remember how miserable people were."

My playgirl aunt agreed. "Even now," she said, "there is so much disappointment."

My father sighed, giving up, for the moment: "We're ready for the pastries." He had no hope for my aunt, who was always desperate to be wherever she was not. When she was eighty and was recovering in a nursing home from a hip operation, she held on to her walker and "ran" away. Although she could barely hobble, she was able to leave the building and get all the way to a bus stop before they caught up with her and brought her back.

My father, on the other hand, had built a moral and social world without exits. He was big on structures of suffering. He had a penitential vision that was more like a penitentiary where no one won redemption or even parole. Driving through Jackson Heights in a blighted neighborhood, we stopped for a light at a corner where an African American man sat miserably on the curb looking grimly at the sewer drain beneath his feet. My father turned to me and said, "We're all damned, you know, white souls and black."

My father had wanted to be a doctor. He had gone to college, bankrolled by a wealthy uncle who had promised to send him to medical school, but who died after my father's first year at Columbia. My father had finished college in the evenings and now worked nights as a pharmacist and days at Catholic Charities as a social worker with what used to be called delinquent boys. He believed in their ultimate goodness and he would receive grateful letters from men whom he had helped years before who credited him with their better lives. He understood the difficulties boys and men experienced and, in his way, he was good to my mother by a definition both accepted completely. He was fluent in Spanish, Greek, and Italian as well as his own Sicilian dialect, and voluble at work or with his friends. By the time he came home, he was exhausted.

An odd but understandable mixture of people were his heroes. Aside from virtually every New York Yankee, and especially the mythic Babe and Joe DiMaggio, there was St. Thomas Aquinas, locked in his castle by his own mother who could not bear for him to join an order of mendicants, Carlo Tresca, and inspirational figures from the Catholic workers' movement. His meager spare time was spent helping in union organizing. He kept telling me to do something useful, but I was never clear on whether he wanted me to be Mother Teresa, Dorothy Day, or the mother of six children.

My father was determined to embed St. Thomas in my bones. What seemed to appeal to him were St. Thomas's writings on the conduct of life. There, after affirming that the goal of life and thought was the understanding of God, St. Thomas used lock-step syllogisms to prove why neither honors, nor glory, nor fame, nor wealth, nor health, nor strength, nor sensuality, nor even moral virtue nor the practice of art constitutes happiness. Adding the creations of art to that list always struck me as particularly unfair. My father would read these negative passages to me or ask me to read them to him. I think what appealed to him was the perfect orderliness of those thought processes, a brilliant architecture perfect in the symmetry that pierced both life and death and left nothing to chance and no way out of its logic.

Eventually I suspected that he used that entrapping logic of Aquinas's writing to let me know indirectly that there are orders of obligation, meaning, authority, and value that no one can escape. I think now that my father was at a loss to deal with me in part because I was not a boy and he was ambivalent about what a woman will do if she has complete autonomy. I did my share of troublemaking by keeping his curiosity about my life at a distance, using a polite and often smiling silence that shut him out. That was how I balanced self-protection and amiability! From time to time in high school, I would catch him picking up my library books to see what I was reading. He never discussed them with me or asked me how I was doing in school and I never volunteered to tell him. I later discovered he had found out independently by checking in with the school principal. At the time, all I could think of was escape from the negative logic and fatalism he embraced as wisdom.

Endlessly loving, wise and cheerful, my mother kept her good nature both expansive and intact. She had a gift for finding pleasure in small things—the smell of tangerines and sweet basil, the sight of my brother or me happy, the stream of friends she helped, the knowledge that she had done the right thing by never keeping me home and always cheering me on. She had a sense of justice that was strong and immediate. When she was old and the policeman son of a woman she knew seized all the flowers in the cart of an unlicensed street vendor and boastingly distributed them to his mother and her friends, my mother was appalled and refused them. She took him aside and told him he should not steal from a poor man who had much less than he did and was only tying to make a living. She became the defender of all the old ladies she knew whose English was still poor and who could not cope with the bureaucracies of pension plans, medical insurance, or housing that plagued them.

My mother was always the most loyal, enthusiastic supporter of my "getting an education," even though she was convinced that reading would ruin my eyes. Next to the Holy Mother, she admired Eleanor Roosevelt and never tired of talking about her speeches and largesse. "She made something wonderful of her life," she would tell me. Mrs. Roosevelt, she insisted, had been inspired by her own mother, who had told her to study to compensate for not being beautiful. My mother believed Mrs. Roosevelt's brilliance and her kindness were marks of her overcoming all obstacles. She would offer this as inspiration for my becoming a teacher to make up for the fact that, despite all her careful instruction, I could not even hem a dress with perfectly even stitches.

I left home right after high school and felt completely free for the first time in my life. My mother was hurt by my living apart from the family. Ever watchful, she did not believe in sleep-away camp, going away to college, or anything that broke the tie to home. She feared the fatal misstep! Whenever I visited, she would complain that I was too thin, my hair was too long, or the neighborhood I lived in was a drug-ridden disaster area. But in her optimistic Neapolitan way, she never stopped trying, never failed to come up with a corrective gift—a provolone, a tray of meatballs, a whistle to blow if I were attacked.

I worked my way through City College, fell in love with American history and literature and the glorious, affirmative, no-limits illogic of Emerson. I never met another Italian American at City College who was involved in English literature, but that never seemed to matter. We were all from immigrant somewheres, all high on our respective rebellions, our infatuation with the American past, and the unruliness of current fiction, film, and painting. I was brought into an honors sequence in history, literature, and philosophy and found an intense conversation about books and ideas that compensated for a past of disciplined silence. Our discussions were so heated that every now and then someone got up and bounced his chair off the floor to emphasize a point.

In those days, when the melting pot metaphor reached its high boil and the multiethnic mosaic had not appeared in its place, CCNY insisted everyone take speech courses, perhaps to erase signs of caste and place. There were basic lessons designed to cleanse us of the accents of Brooklyn, the Bronx, or Queens. "Not bad," I was told at the diagnostic. All I had to practice was "Long Island." It was like a charitable penance of only two "Our Father"s and three "Hail Mary"s. Most speech classes were in debate techniques which honed skill in argumentation. Instead of following the old rhetoricians who argued absurd causes like the benefits of incontinence, our professor employed outrage as a way of sharpening our skills. Sparks of anger and laughter flew as he forced the class Marxist to defend capitalism while the would-be businessman attacked private poverty; hip girls had to argue extreme prolife positions while the orthodox defended abortion, and the biology genius gritted his teeth and argued the benefits of creationism. It was great training, but I began to miss my mother's grace and my father's infuriating, but principled, intelligence.

My parents did not know what to make of me, and I didn't know what to make of myself. My sense of the larger world still came largely from books. Perhaps that was because none of us knew, realistically, what to make of a professional woman's life in the world outside. For my father that lack of knowledge was probably willed, part of his refusal to see. My mother was always interested, although everything I did seemed alien to her. When I graduated from college, my mother wanted to come to commencement ceremonies at Lewisohn Stadium. She was thrilled that, despite my leaving her, I had finished college. "You never told me City College was in Harlem," she reproached me. She survived that surprise and the discovery that I was not going to be an elementary school teacher. My father was sick and unable to be there.

I had won a Woodrow Wilson Fellowship to graduate school in English at Columbia. I progressed rapidly, winning Columbia University President's Fellowships that enabled me to receive my master of arts degree after one year and my doctorate in three. Although I was one of the top graduate students in English and could prevail in the stiff competition for fellowships, that did not dispel an intensifying sense of otherness. Most of the women in my class who were from the East had gone to one of the Seven Sisters or were from the Ivy League and had a very different style. Despite my by now perfect pronunciation of "Long Island," they made friends among themselves. When one of my professors complained to me: "My daughter is as bright as you, but what's the point? She'll marry some man and her education will be wasted," my first thought was "Even here!" Astoria had taught me the power of the quiet smile and an understated response, but it had provided no clear maps to show the route through the covert, competitive strife or inevitable impediments I would come to find and know.

I was in my mid-twenties when I graduated from Columbia, had a contract for my first book, and was going on to a job at Yale. Since my father was well enough to attend, and it made my mother so happy, we all went to commencement. My mother beamed at me in my rented doctoral robes; even my father looked content. "I'm so happy you got this Ph.D.," my mother said. Then, as if struck by a terrible thought, she asked, "But who will marry you now?"

She was devastated that, while I had escaped the misfortune she had dreaded, another might befall me. My father smiled and remained silent as I hugged her. But my mother later gave me a reminder of what I had better focus on by making me a beautiful wardrobe—an exquisite navy cashmere suit with a vest and slightly flared skirt whose tailoring my grandfather would have admired, and three simple, beautifully crafted dresses. She threw in a perfect knockoff of Geoffrey Beene's slinky, halter column dress in black, just in case I didn't get the point about finding a husband.

That summer I began the first college course I ever taught, arming myself with lecture notes and lip gloss. I stood nervously in a classroom in Philosophy Hall at Columbia ready to begin with Anglo-Saxon poetry as the afternoon sun filled the room. Much to my surprise, just as the Angles, Saxons, and Jutes were infiltrating England, my father appeared in the class of about twenty-five students and sat down in the back. When the class was over, and everyone had left, he came up to me. The din of my mother's sewing machine, of storytelling voices echoing over clattering dinner plates, rang in the beat of his footsteps as he came toward me. But all he said was, "So you're here!" He shook my hand, turned and went back to Astoria, leaving me speechlessly behind, knowing that Astoria would always come back for me.

Joanna Clapps Herman

The Discourse of un' Propria Paparone

"You're such a *papon'*."

"What's this new curse you're putting on me?"

"Not a curse. It's a slur on your character."

"What're you calling me now?"

I'm in my Upper West Side kitchen talking to my Jewish husband. I'm protesting, insisting, injecting my ethnicity into the New York Jewish intellectual world I live in. The world I escaped to and by which I am now held hostage.

"Look, a *mammone* was the worst thing you could call someone when I was a kid, anyone who was a *mammone* was a putz, a jerk. But really it means mama's boy," I explain a bit pedantically, as I have learned to do in my life in New York. "*O-n-e* is a suffix for big, so when you add it to the end of a word it changes that word from an ordinary nominative to a noun that is somehow adjectival—the noun, made big, bigged up, remember James [our son] used to say, 'You're going to big them up,' when I borrowed his mittens. Not that my family was ever known to pronounce a vowel at the end of any word. We didn't say *mammone,* we said *mammon'*."

"So if you're a *mammon'*, you're big for your mother—too involved with her."

When Marcello Mastroianni died, the *New York Times* obit referred to him as a sex symbol who was actually a *mammone*. I was stunned, thrilled, a word from my childhood in the *New York Times!*

"You know how I always say 'I'm a *chacciaron*',"—*chaccia* means someone who talks a lot, but I'm a *chacciaron*', a really big talker. Annie's family calls it *chacciarese, e-s-e*, that's from her dialect." My friend's family is from a different town, they use *e-s-e*. It makes me sad that I have to explain these words instead of being able to just use them in a community who knows what I mean, the way my husband does with his friends, all those childhood sounds that convey what no other sounds can—intimacy. Occasionally, I say to my classes, which are made up largely of minority adults, "*Stai zitto*." And because I love them I expect them to understand me. They tolerate my explanation and translation because these are a people who recognize affectionate orality when they hear it.

When I was a kid *mammon*' was the worst insult you could fling at someone. That and *cafon*', which really meant someone with no class, a lowlife. But for me and my cousins a *mammon*' was worse, anyone who wasn't tough, capable of doing whatever, climbing trees, swimming out to the island, staring down somebody in the schoolyard.

"But *you*," I say to my husband Bill, "you're a *papon*'." Bill loves this stuff, at least as much as he loves me. My Italianness. It goes with the circles under my eyes, my dark moments, all the garlic browned in olive oil for almost everything I cook.

But where we live on the Upper West Side of Manhattan it is assumed everyone middle-class is Jewish in reality or by association. And in effect I am Jewish by association. It's where I've found a home, where there is enough of the kind of talk I love, lots of it, too much of it, too intensely full of jokes and condemnation. It's where I found people who care more about reading or music or have some similar attachment that burns in them, that has little to do with what was valued in Waterbury, Connecticut, where I was raised. There people care about food, kids, gardens, fooling around, the loss of which burns in me still. But I had to leave because only my father, who had been an ironworker, had been a serious reader. I am at home here on the Upper West Side of Manhattan. But I hate the fact that it's assumed I will be pleased to have my ethnicity replaced. "You're Jewish—everyone ethnic is Jewish," I've been told many times.

"I'm not Jewish, thank you very much and I'm very happy being Italian," I've found myself saying priggishly. Where I grew up it was a point of honor to declare your ethnicity defiantly. "What're *you?*" we asked the first time we met another kid. Everyone understood the question. We were Italian, Irish, a couple of German kids. Elaine Mann was the only Jewish girl in school. Maybe because I was Italian I still feel funny saying "Italian American."

Just as I feel funny saying my family is "working-class" or "blue collar." These are not words my family would use to describe themselves. They didn't define themselves by their work. That wouldn't occur to them. They worked hard. They were good at whatever they did. They mostly voted Republican. So those labels, although accurate, sound condescending, or, as they say in Waterbury, Connecticut, brass capital of the world, "That sounds stupid." Italian American is a name given to them by people who didn't live in our neighborhood. I feel as if I betray my family every time I use those words.

Another one: "That makes me anxious," instead of "She makes me nervous," or, alternately, "He gives me *agiata*." My husband's brother would say, "Don't get all noyved up." How about replacing "She was so inappropriate" with "I'd like to give her a slap"?

I can feel the sting in my hand when I say it. Is one more articulate than the other? The one with the sensation attached makes more of an impression on my synapses. But my language has changed. I only occasionally use phrases like "Gimme the *mapine*," meaning "Hand me the dishcloth." But these decontextualized phrases have taken on the ring of pretentiousness, because I use these words deliberately now, I'm doing something, not just talking in a world in which I belong. "Get the *scola macaron'*," I say to my son sometimes, because I don't want him growing up not knowing my language, where the phrase "Get the *scola macaron'*" means literally "Get the strain the macaroni."

So now I accuse my husband, "You're such a *papon'*."

"You're saying I'm a papa's boy, right?"

"Aren't you?"

"Just because I'm mourning my father after forty years. I was a kid. I was only eight. I never got over it. My father . . ." He looks off dreamily into the kitchen cupboards. "If my father had lived he'd be one hundred and three."

"*Managga diavole!* Bill, if your father were alive, he'd be dead." I can't help it. I'm irritated this morning, sick of the endless talk about the dead father, who's haunted my married life to Bill. We've walked this hallowed walk at least once a week for our twenty years of marriage. I'm tired of this man I've never met. Bill looks at me, stunned. Then he flings back his head and roars. He's laughing so hard he's crying. "You, *you* kill me." He comes over and throws his large body onto me, grabs me, and holds on while he laughs and laughs.

I never get over this. This is acceptable here, it's expected, you make small deflating remarks and if they hit their target, you're a hero. I always feel sheepish for daring to go after "the father."

New York is my home. This is where I grew into my maturity, where Bill and I have lived our married life together. This is where we've raised our son. James, a large Slavic-looking boy, has his father's fine ear, which is why he wins prizes reciting poetry in the Tuscan version of Italian that my grandparents were unable to speak or understand. This Italian has little to do with the dialect I grew up with and can't speak except for a few scattered defining phrases. "My Russian boy," I call James, when I come upon his large blond presence with surprise again. "My big Slavic boy."

James doesn't seem to be in any way confused by these contradictions. His friends call him half-a-wop. He calls himself a dago-yid production. His girlfriend is the Freaken-Puerta-Rican. Despite the language police, he and his friends use these terms as forms of affection. For them all this is grist for pleasure.

The girlfriend is pleasure for me—she looks like family, she has dark hair. She's small, strong and smart; still she looks at us, her boyfriend's parents, eyes wide, asking us to like her. I do. This is stuff that I understand—a second skin to me.

James's a *papon'* too. "What did Dad say when you told him I won the Italian recitation prize? Was he happy?"

Why is there a dialect word for *mammon'* but not for *papon'*? Why is it bad to be a mama's boy or girl, but not mentioned if you are a papa's boy or girl? Is it that these things are understood, part of the paradigm?

How about *un propria paparona?* Here I've modified in dialect this invented noun to describe the Italian girl obsessed with her Italian father—a real bad *papon'*. That's me.

These are the kinds of questions that I can ask here in New York and the people I'm talking to will pick the question up, look at it, turn it over, and add something to what I've just said. Where I came from that kind of talk is considered silly. Anything that made you self-conscious is embarrassing. To be embarrassed is the worst.

"Can you imagine, he called my sister-in-law for *directions?* So embarrassing, a man asking a woman for *directions!*" My father had shaken his head in disgust and deep shame for his Jewish son-in-law when Bill had asked Aunt Tony for directions to the Cape, a place she drove to often. Where do you begin with something like that?

Especially if you are a *propria paparona*—just like my husband and son—I'm one obsessed with her father. Whom I have always adored, who read Emily Brontë to my sister and me, at least once a year, sitting at the kitchen table in his undershirt and gray work pants, not blue, full of welding holes, that my mother washed and ironed every day.

"Listen to this," he had said and I had, though I never learned how to talk comfortably to him. Because girls don't talk to their fathers, they listen. Anyway, after a while I no longer spoke his language fluently.

He said things like "You know what happened down the street with Cockroach Rhinie?" And this had made me want to ask two questions, "Is Cockroach Rhinie the guy who gets the stolen stuff from the colored kids?" And I wanted to ask, "Is Cockroach Rhinie a typical member of the male environment in the social club setting?" Even thinking the second question was a betrayal of him. Thinking the other was a betrayal to the person I'd become. So sometimes it seemed best to stay in my kitchen among the *paponi* of my own and insult my husband in words I've invented because he knows what I'm saying.

Evan Hunter

From *The Paper Dragon*

He felt alone, utterly and completely alone, he had never felt so isolated in his entire life. He thought it odd that he should have come through thirty-nine years of family togetherness, surrounded by aunts and uncles and cousins and *compares* to find himself here and now, at what was possibly the most important juncture of his life, entirely alone. How do you come through it all, he wondered, and suddenly find yourself standing on the edge of the universe waiting for the waves to crash in, maybe to get washed out to sea, without Aunt Louise telling you every other week that you were "her baby," meaning she had served as midwife when you were delivered to your mother in a coldwater flat on East 118th Street? I could use Aunt Louise now, he thought, silly Aunt Louise who accompanied Italian immigrants when they went for their first papers, who was an active member of the Republican Club, who wrote songs in her spare time and claimed that they were all later stolen by the big band leaders—a family trait?—and who sent Queen Elizabeth a hand-tatted bonnet for young Prince Charles when he was born. "Look, Sonny," she had said, "I got a thank-you note from the Queen's secretary, a *personal* thank-you note," and Arthur had thought to himself it was probably a mimeographed note sent to all the Aunt Louises of the world who tatted bonnets for infant princes. And yet he could use Aunt Louise now, he could use her quiet strength and penetrating eye, God but that woman was a dynamo of energy, what the hell was it she concocted—Aunt Louise's Ointment, did she call it? And wasn't it really and truly sold in drugstores all over Harlem, the indefatigable Louise running around selling her product the way she plugged her terrible songs, she'd have made a great rumrunner, or in recent times an excellent dope pusher.

They called him Sonny when he lived in Harlem. I grew up in Harlem, he always told people, and they looked at him as if wondering whether or not he had traces of Negro blood flowing in his veins, whereupon he always felt compelled to explain that there were *three* Harlems. You see, there is Negro Harlem and there is Italian Harlem and there is Puerto Rican Harlem. They are all very different and they are all identical, they are all bug-ridden and rat-infested, those are the three Harlems. But that of course was a mature judgment, a qualified appraisal by a man who was now thirty-nine years old, and not the way he had seen it as a boy. There were no rats in Harlem for Sonny Constantine—he still did not know why they had called him Sonny, he supposed there was a Sonny in every Italian-American family that ever existed. Or perhaps Al Jolson was hot at the time of his boyhood, perhaps any kid became a Sonny Boy and then a Sonny all because of Al Jolson singing through his goddamn nose like a Harvard man, perhaps that was it. But there were no rats in Harlem—well, once a mouse was in the toilet bowl, but only a mouse. It scared the hell out of his mother, she came running out of the bathroom with her dress raised and her bloomers down, her behind showing, he wanted to look, but didn't dare, yelling to his father that there was a mouse in the bowl. So his father just flushed the toilet, naturally, goodbye mouse, out to sea where all good mice eventually go. His sister was terrified. He had called her a baby and a dope and a silly jerk, and then had listened to her crying in her room, really in his parents' bedroom because that was where she slept on a little cot against the wall near the window that looked down on 118th Street four stories below.

There were no rats in Harlem for him, there were no street gangs, there were no rumbles, there was only a placid ghetto—terrible word— a *neighborhood,* a haven surrounded by relatives, you could not throw a stone without hitting a relative. If your mother wasn't home, you dropped in on Aunt Tessie, and she gave you cookies and milk, or you went around to see Grandpa in the grocery store where he worked for a man he had known in Naples, or maybe you ran into Uncle Mike driving his truck for the furniture company. It was said that Uncle Mike knew gangsters, and that the time the social club was held up and they stole Uncle Danny's ring and Uncle Sal's watch, it was Mike who got on his Neapolitan high horse and went off some place into the mysterious underworld where they talked of Petie Red Shirt and Legs Diamond and got the goddamn jewelry back the very next morning; he was a tough guy Uncle Mike, he could break your head with a glance. His sister loved Uncle Mike, she would almost wet her pants every time he stopped by. There was an argument once, Arthur couldn't even remember what it was all about, Mike taking out some girl from the bakery, and Tessie getting all upset and coming to see her sister, Arthur's mother, and her having a big argument with Mike and calling him everything under the sun while his father stood by and listened patiently and Arthur remembered how simply he had flushed the mouse down the toilet, so very simply, pull, flush, and out to sea without a whimper.

Christmases, they all got together, Christmases *then,* but not anymore, blame it on urban renewal, blame it on the decentralization of the family, the speedier means of communication and transportation, there were no more Christmases once his grandparents died. The family died when they died, it shriveled outward from the center, everybody just disappeared, where the hell were they all now? Dead or living in California, which is the same as being dead. He had dropped in to see Aunt Tessie and Uncle Mike when he was out in Hollywood, and Mike who had known gangsters, Mike who had threatened to break heads unless his brothers'-in-law jewelry was returned at once, immediately if not sooner, Mike was a tired old man, bald, his muscles turned to flab, this was the man who used to move furniture and mountains and fearsome gangs. They sat in the living room of the Tarzana development house and had nothing much to say to each other, how is your mother, tell her to write, did you go to Aunt Louise's funeral, and Arthur had wanted to say, "Don't you remember Christmas at Grandpa's house, don't you remember?" But Uncle Mike was an old man, you see, and Aunt Tessie limped, and there was nothing to say to either of them, there was only strong Italian coffee to sip and pastry to nibble, Italian he had not remembered it as being so sweet. Boy, what his grandfather used to buy for Christmas, boy the way that house sang, that crumby apartment on First Avenue, it *must* have been a crumby apartment and there probably *were* rats in the walls. He certainly could remember cockroaches in his own house whenever they turned on the kitchen light, an army in hurried retreat. "Step on them, Sonny," his mother would yell, "get them, get them!" a game each night, the scurrying mob, and then they would all disappear into cracks and crannies, gone like the mouse flushed out to sea, except they would return again. "Where do they go?" he once asked his father, and his father replied, "Home."

Home.

There was everybody there on Christmas and his grandfather welcomed one and all, not only the family but also everybody he knew from the grocery store, the nice old man who wore thick glasses, Alonzo, Alfonso, something like that, who had the idiot son who would come in alongside his father like a ghost and sit there quietly and perhaps sip a little red wine his grandfather poured. And the men would talk about the old country and about Mussolini and about how beautiful Rome was at Christmastime, and Arthur would listen, standing between his grandfather's knees, with his grandfather's strong hands on his shoulders, and the women would be bustling about in the kitchen, Grandma fretting and fussing, and the girls—her two daughters and later Danny's wife, and then Sal's wife—all would be busy with the preparations in the kitchen, and the Christmas gifts would be piled to the ceiling under the Christmas tree and Grandpa would keep pouring wine for all the relatives and friends who kept dropping in from all over Harlem, all over the world it seemed, *Buon Natale, Buon Natale,* the wine being poured and the smell of tomato sauce in the kitchen. God, there were things to eat, things Grandpa used to get in the grocery store, all imported, great provolone and salami, and fresh macaroni and bread, and Aunt Louise would make the pimientos, she would roast the peppers over the gas jet until they turned black, he always thought she was burning them, but no then she would scrape off all the black part and reveal the sweet orange-red meat, and then she fixed them with oil and garlic, oh God. She sent him pimientos in a jar every month, once a month like clockwork, the last day of the month, until she finally died, always the pimientos in a jar because once he helped her with the grammar in one of her song lyrics, just helped her put it in order, that was all, pimientos for life, a great title.

The meal went on for hours, they would sit at the table and dip cling peaches in wine, allowing the thick golden fruit to soak there for a bit, and then bringing it dripping red to the mouth on a toothpick. His grandfather would say "Sonny, here, have some," and hold out the red-stained toothpick with the rich juicy slice of fruit on its end, tart, strong, sweet, everything. The kids would run through the length of the railroad flat, chasing each other, and his grandmother would yell for them to stop before the people downstairs banged on the ceiling with a broom handle, and they would stop for a little while, collapsing on the big bed in the front room, his head close to his sister's, all of them sweating, all the kids in the family, more kids all the time, all of them giggling and sweating on the bed with the picture of Jesus Christ over it holding his hand above his exposed heart and sunshine spikes radiating from his head. "That's God," his cousin Joey once said. "The Jews killed him." He asked his grandmother about it one time, and she said, "That's right, Sonny, the Jews killed him," and then she told a story about a Jew who went to church one day and received holy communion and then ran out of the church and took the wafer out of his mouth immediately and went home and nailed it to the wall. "And do you know what happened to that holy bread, Sonny? It began to bleed. And it never stopped bleeding. It just kept bleeding all over that Jew's floor."

"What did he do?" Arthur asked.

"What did *who* do?" his grandmother said.

"The Jew. What did he do about all that blood?"

His grandmother had shrugged and gone back to cooking something on the big wood stove in the kitchen, black and monstrous, always pouring heat and steam. "Wiped it up, I guess," she said. "How do *I* know what he did?"

But every time he looked at that picture of Jesus with the heart stuck on his chest as if he had just had surgery and they were showing how easy it was to expose a human heart these days, the drops of blood dripping down from it, and Jesus' hand just a little above it, and his head tilted back with his eyes sort of rolled up in his head like a character in an Eisenstein movie, he always thought of the Jew who nailed the communion wafer to the wall, and he always wondered first why the Jew would want to nail the thing to the wall to begin with, and second what he had done about all the blood. In high school, after he had moved to the Bronx and met Rubin, he realized his grandmother was full of shit, and he never trusted her very much after that, her and her communion nailed to the wall.

His sister Julia broke his head one time, this was about the time he fell in love with Virginia Kelly. Irish girls after that were all premised on Virginia, the sixth grade Virginia with long black hair and green eyes fringed with black lashes and budding little breasts—he hadn't been too aware of those at the time—and a way of tilting her head back to laugh, at *him* most of the time, which was the unfortunate part of it all. But oh how he loved that girl! He would watch her and watch her and notice everything she did or said, and then come home and tell his sister about it, which is why she broke his head one day. She broke his head with a stupid little kid's pocketbook by swinging it at him on its chain and clobbering him with the clasp, and all because he told her she would never be as beautiful as Virginia Kelly, no one in the world would ever be as beautiful as Virginia Kelly, she had clobbered him, wham! Even then she had a lot of spunk, you had to have spunk to live in the same house with a man like his father boy, what a battle *that* had turned out to be years later. Where the hell are you now, Julie, living with your engineer husband and your two Norwegian kids in where the hell, Minnesota? There's no such place as Minnesota, don't kid me, sis. Do you remember breaking my head, and then crying when Mama took me to the druggist, and he examined it—who went to doctors in those days?—and wiped the blood away and said, "You've broken his head, young lady," and then put a strip of plaster on it? It was okay in a week or so, but boy did you cry, I really loved you Julie. You were a really nice sister to have, I hope your Norwegian loves you half as much as I did.

He met Virginia Kelly in the hall one day, he was coming back from the boys' room and he had the wooden pass in his hand, and Virginia stopped him. He was nine years old, and she was ten and big for her age, and she stopped him and said, "Don't look at me anymore, Stupid."

"Who's looking at you?" he said, but his heart was pounding, and he wanted to kiss her, wanted to kiss this quintessence of everything alien to him, the sparkling green eyes and the wild Irish way of tossing her head, all, everything. Years later, when he read *Ulysses,* he knew every barmaid in the book because they were all Virginia Kelly who told him once to stop looking at her, Stupid, and whom he never looked at again from that day forward though it broke his heart.

When he moved to the Bronx, the only person he thought he missed was Virginia Kelly. He would lie awake in bed at night and think of Virginia, and when he learned how to masturbate, he would conjure visions of this laughing Irish girl and ravage her repeatedly until one morning Julie said to him, "Hey, *I* have to make the beds around here, you know," and he pretended he didn't know what she meant, but after that he masturbated secretly in the bathroom and carefully wiped up after him with toilet paper. Somewhere along the line, he switched from raping Virginia Kelly to raping Hedy Lamarr, and he never thought of her again except once or twice when he remembered that there were people in this world who drove in red convertibles with their long black hair blowing in the wind, laughing, wearing silk stockings and loafers, the idealization of everything that seemed to him American, everything that seemed to him non-Harlem and non-Italian. Once, in high school, Rubin said to him in the boys' room, jokingly, "Where else but in America could an Italian and a Jew piss side by side in the same bowl?" and he had laughed because he laughed at everything Rubin said, Rubin was so much smarter and better informed than he, but he didn't really get the joke. He did not by that time see anything funny about being Italian, nor could he understand what Rubin thought was so funny about being Jewish. It never once occurred to him, not then, and not later when he was hobnobbing it around Hollywood with stars and starlets and all that crap, nor even when he laid a famous movie queen who kept calling him Artie, for which he almost busted her in the mouth, except she really was as passionate as she came over on the screen, not in all those years, not ever in his life until perhaps this moment when he felt so terribly alone enmeshed in a law system created by Englishmen, not once did he ever realize how dearly he had loved Harlem, or how much it had meant to him to be Italian.

There was in his world a cluttered brimming external existence, and an interior solitude that balanced each other perfectly and resulted in, he realized, a serene childhood, *even* in the midst of a depression, even though his father was a mysterious government employee known as "a substitute" instead of "a regular," which he gathered was highly more desirable. There was an immutable pattern in his household, the same foods were eaten on the identical night each week, Monday was soup which his mother made herself, he hated soup meat, it was stringy and tasteless. Tuesday night was spaghetti with either meatballs or *bracìòla,* Wednesday night was breaded veal cutlets with spinach and mashed potatoes, his mother once dumped a whole bowl of mashed potatoes on his head because he was trying to catch a fly as a specimen for the microscope he had got for Christmas. He threw a dissecting needle at the fly on the wall and, uncanny luck, pierced the fly, even Errol Flynn couldn't have done better. ("You *got* 'im, Sonny!" Julie shrieked in delight.) But a lot of gooey white glop came out of the fly and he refused to eat his mashed potatoes after that. So his mother, naturally, having inherited a few Neapolitan traits from Grandpa, even though she herself had been born and raised in the garden spot called Harlem, picked up the bowl of potatoes and dumped the whole thing on his head. His father laughed. He hated his father for two months after that. Couldn't he have at least said it wasn't nice to dump a bowl of mashed potatoes all over a kid who was maybe a budding scientist and certainly the best dissecting needle thrower in the United States?

Thursday night was some kind of macaroni, either *rigatoni* or *moitaccioli* or *fusilli,* again with meatballs, or maybe sausage, and Friday night was fish, of course. Oh, how he hated fish. There were three kinds of fish his mother made, and he hated each and every one of them. The first was breaded filet of flounder, dry and white and tasteless. The second was breaded shrimp, she sure had a mania for breading stuff, equally as tasteless, except they seemed to come in bite size. The third was a white halibut which she made with a tomato sauce, fresh tomatoes he remembered because the sauce was always pulpy and sometimes had seeds. This was the best of the lot because it was a little juicier than the two breaded concoctions, but he hated each with a passion and deplored the approach of Friday each week. He did not learn how to eat lobster until he went to Maine with a girl from Barnard one weekend, and had not discovered until just recently that his mother hated fish as much as he did and had only made it every Friday because she was a sort of half-ass Catholic who never went to church or confession, but who nonetheless made fish every Friday night. Breaded.

Saturday was either lambchops or steak. Sunday was Grandpa's house, the biggest feast of the week, the family represented in smaller groups except on the holidays, antipasto, spaghetti, meatballs, roast beef or chicken or turkey, fruit, nuts, pastry—his grandfather always went out to buy *cannoli* and *cassatini, sfogliatelli* and *baba* on his name day, a sort of pilgrimage every year. He would come back flushed with the cold (his name day was in November) carrying two white cartons of Italian pastry, tied with white string, "Did you get them, Papa?" his mother would ask. And Grandpa would nod and smile and then grab Arthur playfully and say, "Sonny, help me cut the string, the string is too strong for me."

Structured, everything structured and ordered, the activity in the streets as patterned as the regularity of meals and holidays, each season bringing its own pursuit, its own hysterical joy to the slum. (Slum? What's that? What's a slum?) Roller skates, and stickball, and pea shooters, and pushos, and hi-li paddles, and baseball cards, and roasting mickeys, and black leather aviator hats with goggles, and rubberband guns, one kid had six of them mounted in tandem like a machine gun, and pigeons on the roof, and stoopball, and boxball, and Skullies (I love you, Virginia Kelly) and Statues, and Johnny-on-a-Pony and Ring-a-Leavio, and little girls skipping rope, or playing that game where they lift their leg over a bouncing ball, skirts flying, "One-two-three-a-nation, I received my confirmation," Virginia Kelly had a plaid skirt, blue plaid, she wore white socks, she once beat up Concetta Esposito for calling her a lousy Irish mick, which after all she was. Patterned, structured, safe, secure, there were no rats in Harlem, there was only a street that was a city, a dozen playmates who populated the world, a million relatives who hugged and kissed and teased and loved him and called him Sonny, a busy universe for a small boy.

And juxtaposed to this, the inner reality of Arthur Constantine, the quiet, thoughtful, solitary child who played with his soldiers on the dining room floor, the big oaken table serving as suicide cliff or soaring skyscraper, the intricacy of its hidden structure becoming a bridge to be blown or a gangplank to be walked, each separate lead soldier—the heads were always breaking off, when that happened, you fixed them with a matchstick, but they never lasted long—each separate soldier or cowboy or Indian assuming an identity of its own. Shorty was the one with the bow legs, he had a lariat in his hand when Arthur bought him for a nickel at the Woolworth's on Third Avenue, but later the lariat got lost. Magua was the Indian, he was made of cast iron rather than lead, and he never broke, he outlasted all the others. Naked to the waist, wearing a breechclout, he was Arthur's favorite, and Arthur always put words of wisdom into his mouth, carefully thought-out Indian sayings that helped the white man in his plight. Magua never turned on anybody, Magua was a good Indian. Red Dance was the bad Indian, he had a bonnet full of feathers. When his head finally broke off because Arthur caused Magua to give him a good punch one day, Arthur never bothered to repair him. Instead, he bought an identical piece and named him Blue Dance, who he supposed was Son of Red Dance, and when Magua knocked *his* head off, too, Arthur switched to a villain named El Mustachio who was a soldier carrying a pack, and who didn't have a mustache at all. He would talk aloud to himself while he played with the tiny metal men, he would construct elaborate conflicts and then put everything to rights with either a wise word from Magua or a sweep of his hand, scattering the pieces all over the floor. If his sister ever tried to enter one of these games, he shrieked at her in fury, and once he shoved her against the wall and made her cry and then went to her afterwards and hugged her and kissed her and said he was very sorry, but he still would not let her into any of the solitary games he played with the metal men. He wondered once, alone in his bed and listening to the sounds of sleep in the room next door, whether he would even have allowed Virginia Kelly to play soldiers with him—and he decided not.

Where do they go, he wondered, all those black-haired girls with the green eyes and the wonderful laugh, when the hell have I ever loved anyone as deeply or as hopelessly as I loved Virginia Kelly? Where does it all go, and how does it happen that I'm alone on this day, with Christmas coming and no Grandpa to ask me to help him break the string on the white carton of pastries, this day, when God knows I could at least use Aunt Louise to tell me she has a friend who knows a magistrate, "Don't worry, Sonny, I'll speak to them at the Club," the Republican Club would set it all straight, or if not, then certainly a dab of Aunt Louise's Ointment would. Where? he thought. Where? I've been invited to orgies in Hollywood (and refused)—"The ideah is to have a few drinks ontil éver'one get on-in-hib-ited, you know whut I mean?"—I've seen my name on motion picture screens and television screens and once on a theater program, Arthur Nelson Constantine, the "Nelson" added by yours truly as a bow to our cousins across the big water, an acknowledgment of my veddy British heritage, Arthur *Nelson* Constantine. ("What?" Aunt Louise would have said. "Don't worry, I know somebody in the Republican Club.") I have gone to bed with young girls, and some not so young, and once I went to bed with *two* girls, and another time I went to bed with a girl and another guy and I think we sent that poor little girl straight from there to an insane asylum, but that was in Malibu where such things happen often, I am told. I have sat at the same table with John Wayne, who offered to buy me a drink and then told a story about shooting *The Quiet Man* in Ireland, and I have been blasted across the sky at five hundred miles an hour while drinking martinis and watching a movie written and directed by a man I knew. And it seems to me now, it seems to me alone in this cold corridor that the most important thing I've ever done in my life was skewer a fly with a dissecting needle from a distance of five feet, shooting from the hip, did I ever tell you *that* story, Duke? And my mother rewarded me by dumping a bowl of lukewarm mashed potatoes on my head. And my father laughed. And the fly dripped its white glop all over the wall.

Where else but in America could a little Italian boy from the slums of Harlem (Well, you see, there are *three* Harlems) sit at the same table with John Wayne and listen to a very inside story about the shooting of *The Quiet Man* in Ireland? Where else, I ask you, indeed. Oh man, I played the Slum Kid bit to the hilt, everybody likes to hear how you can make it in the face of adversity. The mouse that almost bit my mother became over the years a foraging bloodthirsty sea monster with matted hair dripping seaweed and coming up out of the water with its jaws wide ready to swallow her bottom and everything else besides. That apartment on 118th Street became the Black Hole of Calcutta, it's a wonder the swarms of flies did not eat the eyes out of my head as I lay helpless and squirming in the squalor of my pitiful crib, it's a wonder the rats did not tear the flesh from my bones and leave me whimpering helplessly for an undernourished mother to hobble into the room and flail at them ineffectually. I was born and raised in Harlem, you hear that, Duke? Not only was I born and raised in Harlem, but I managed to get out of Harlem, which is no small feat in itself. Moreover, I was educated at Columbia University, which is a pretty snazzy school you will admit, and I managed to become an officer in the Army, came out as a captain don't forget, and then went on to become a very highly paid screen and television writer who this very minute is negotiating, or at least *hoping* to negotiate, with one Hester Miers, you've *got* it, mister, the very same, for the starring role in my new play which will be coming to Broadway shortly. (I'll stand in that lobby on opening night, Virginia Kelly, and when you walk in and recognize me and come over to wish me luck, I'll tell you to go bounce a ball on the sidewalk, one-two-three-a-nation. I'll tell you I've got an apartment of my own now in a very fancy building on East 54th Street, with a doorman *and* an elevator operator, and I'll tell you I date the prettiest girls in New York almost every night of the week and I've been sucked off by more black-haired Irish girls than there are in your entire family or perhaps in the entire city of Dublin. And then I'll ask the usher or perhaps the porter to please show you out of the goddamn theater as you are disturbing my equilibrium.) I was born and raised in Harlem, so look at me. Something, huh? You don't have to be colored to be underprivileged, you know. Look at me, and have pity on the poor skinny slum kid, man, did I play that into the ground.

So here stands the poor skinny slum kid (not so poor, not so skinny, never having come from a slum anyway because it sure as hell wasn't a slum to me, it was the happiest place I've ever known in my life) standing alone in an Anglo-Saxon world being represented by a Jew (Where else but in America can a wop, etc.) and going up against a man named Jonah Willow, who sounds like a Eurasian philosopher, and I'm scared. I'm scared not because there were rats in Harlem, I'm scared not because there were pushers lurking on every street corner, I'm scared not because teenage hoods came at me with tire chains and switch blades, I'm scared because I'm alone.

I'm scared because I've been making it alone ever since I was eighteen and got drafted into the United States Army, I'm scared and I'm tired, and I would like to rest.

From *The Blackboard Jungle*

You put [our students] all together, and you got one big, fat, overflowing garbage can. And you want to know what our job is? Our job is to sit on the lid of the garbage can and see that none of the filth overflows into the streets. That's our job."

"You don't mean that," Rick said, politely, incredulously.

"I don't, huh?" Solly shrugged. "You're new here, so you don't know. I'm telling you it's a garbage can, and you'll find out the minute you get a whiff of the stink. All the waste product, all the crap they can't fit into a general high school, all that stink goes into the garbage can that's the vocational high school system. That's why the system was invented.

"Sure, the books will tell you the vocational high school affords manual training for students who want to work with their hands. That's all so much horse manure. Believe me, there's only one thing these guys want to do with their hands. So some bright bastard figured a way to keep them off the streets. He thought of the vocational high school. Then he hired a bunch of guys with fat asses, a few with college degrees, to sit on the lid of the garbage can. That way, his wife and daughter can walk the streets without getting raped."

"No one would want to rape your wife, Solly," Savoldi said sadly.

"Except me," Solly said. "The point is, you got to keep them off the streets. And this is as good a place as any. We're just combinations of garbage men and cops, that's all."

"I don't think that's true," Rick said slowly. "I mean, there are surely boys here who really want to learn a trade."

"You find me one," Solly said. "Go ahead. Listen, I've been teaching here for twelve years, and only once did I find anything of worth in the garbage. People don't knowingly dump diamonds in with the garbage. They throw crap in the garbage, and that's what you'll find here."

"That's why I want an all-girls' school," Manners said.

"Yeah, sure," Solly said. "The only difference in an all-girls' school is that you'll find perfume along with the crap in the garbage."

"You're just bitter," Savoldi said.

"Sure," Solly said. "I should have been a teacher instead of a garbage man."

"Garbage men get good salaries," Savoldi put in.

"Which is more than teachers get," Solly answered.

"Me," Savoldi said sadly, "I'm very happy here."

"That's because you're stupid," Solly told him.

"No, I'm smart," Savoldi admitted. "I teach Electrical Wiring, and that gives me bread and butter. Outside, I do odd jobs, and that gives me little luxuries."

"I don't see you driving a Caddy."

"I don't want a Caddy. I'm not that ambitious."

"You're not ambitious at all," Solly told him.

"I have one ambition," Savoldi said, nodding his head. "Just one."

"What's that?"

"Someday I'm going to rig an electric chair and bring it to class with me. I'm going to tell the kids it's a circuit tester, and then I'm going to lead the little bastards in one by one and throw the switch on them. That's my ambition."

"And you're happy here," Salty said dryly.

"Sure. I'm happy. I'm like a man in a rainstorm. When the rain is coming down, I put on my raincoat. When I get home, I take off the coat and put it in the closet and forget all about it. That's what I do here. I become Mr. Savoldi the minute I step through the door to the school, and I'm Mr. Savoldi until 3:25 every day. Then I take off the Mr. Savoldi raincoat, and I go home, and I become Lou again until the next morning. No worries that way."

"Except one," Solly said.

"What's that?" Savoldi asked politely.

"That the kids will rig that goddamned electric chair before you do. Then they'll throw the switch and good-by Mr. Savoldi and Lou, too."

"These kids couldn't wire their way into a pay toilet, even if they had a nickel's head start," Savoldi said sadly. He sipped at his tea and added, "You made my tea get cold."

"Maybe the kids just need a chance," Rick said lamely. "Hell, they can't all be bad."

"All right," Solly said, "you give them their chance. But whatever you do, don't turn your back on them."

"I turned my back on them this morning," Rick said. . . .

Do you condemn the elementary schools for sending a kid on to high school without knowing how to read, without knowing how to write his own name on a piece of paper? Do you condemn the masterminds who plot the educational systems of a nation, or a state, or a city?

Do you condemn the kids for not having been blessed with I.Q.'s of 120? *Can* you condemn the kids? Can you condemn anyone? Can you condemn the colleges that give you all you need to pass a board of education examination? Do you condemn the board of education for not making the exams stiffer, for not boosting the requirements, for not raising salaries, for not trying to attract better teachers, for not making sure their teachers are better equipped to teach?

Or do you condemn the meatheads all over the world who drift into the teaching profession, drift into it because it offers a certain amount of paycheck-every-month security, vacation-every-summer luxury, or a certain amount of power, or a certain easy road when the other more difficult roads are so full of ruts?

Oh, he'd seen the meatheads, all right, he'd seen them in every education class he'd ever attended. The simpering female idiots who smiled and agreed with the instructor, who imparted vast knowledge gleaned from profound observations made while sitting at the back of the classroom in some ideal high school in some ideal neighborhood while an ideal teacher taught ideal students.

Or the men, who were perhaps the worst, the men who sometimes seemed a little embarrassed over having chosen the easy road, the road to security, the men who sometimes made a joke about the women, not realizing they themselves were poured from the same steaming cauldron of horse manure. Had Rick been one of these men? He did not believe so.

He had wanted to teach, had honestly wanted to teach. He had not considered the security, or the two-month vacation, or the short hours. He had simply wanted to teach, and he had considered teaching a worthwhile profession. He had, in fact, considered it the worthiest profession. He had held no illusions about his own capabilities. He could not paint, or write, or compose, or sculpt, or philosophize deeply, or design tall buildings. He could contribute nothing to the world creatively, and this had been a disappointment to him until he'd realized he could be a big creator by teaching. For here were minds to be sculptured, here were ideas to be painted, here were lives to shape. To spend his allotted time on earth as a bank teller or an insurance salesman would have seemed an utter waste to Rick. Women, he had reflected, had no such problem. Creation had been given to them as a gift, and a woman was self-sufficient within her own creative shell. A man needed more, which perhaps was one reason why a woman could never understand a man's concern for the job he had to do. So Rick had seized upon teaching, had seized upon it fervently, feeling that if he could take the clay of underdeveloped minds, if he could feel this clay in his hands, could shape this clay into thinking, reacting, responsible citizens, he would be creating. He had given it all his enthusiasm, and he had sometimes felt deeply ashamed of his classmates, often visualizing them in teaching positions, and the thought had made his flesh crawl.

These will teach my children, he had mused. *These.*

And these had sent kids to his classes without knowing how to read. These had taught a total of nothing, but who was to be condemned?

Who, who was to be condemned?

He had a tool now, one tool. A magnificently powerful, overwhelmingly miraculous tool, a tool no one in all his years of preparation had ever thought to tell him about. And worse, his preparation had not even instilled in him the curiosity or common sense to ask about this fantastic tool.

He now knew the average I.Q. of his students.

∞

From *The Kiss*

"I see," Carella said.

"So if we allow this trial to become a name-calling contest . . ."

"Uh-huh."

"One minority group against another . . ."

"Uh-huh."

"An Italian-American victim versus . . ."

"I find *that* word offensive, too," Carella said.

"Which word?"

"Italian-American."

"You do?" Lowell said, surprised. "Why?"

"Because it *is*," Carella said.

He did not think that someone with a name like Lowell would ever understand that *Italian-American* was a valid label only when Carella's great-grandfather first came to this country and acquired his citizenship, but that it stopped being descriptive or even useful the moment his *grand*parents were *born* here. That was when it became *American,* period.

Nor would Lowell ever understand that when we insisted upon calling fourth-generation, native-born sons and daughters of long-ago immigrants "*Italian*-Americans" or "*Polish*-Americans" or "*Spanish*-Americans" or "*Irish*-Americans" or—worst of all—"*African*-Americans," then we were stealing from them their very American-ness, we were telling them that if their forebears came from another nation, they would never be *true* Americans here in this land of the free and home of the brave, they would forever and merely remain wops, polacks, spics, micks, or niggers.

"My father was American," Carella said.

And wondered why the hell he had to say it.

"Exactly my . . ."

"The man who killed him is American, too."

"That's how I'd like to keep it," Lowell said. "Exactly the point I was trying to make."

But Carella still wondered.

Albert Innaurato

From *Ulysses in Traction*

Okay? Listen? I talk too much. I drink too much, too. I know it, you know it. And after a while alcohol interferes with the functioning of the brain. So I am foggy minded some of the time, don't sleep well and I can't get up in the morning. I'm late for class a lot, I don't like this department any more, although I have been here nineteen years, longer than anyone else on the faculty, and should have succeeded Doc when he retired. That's when they brought you in, Steve. I wonder about education, because educated people act like savages, as you have all just done. I really don't believe in educational theatre anymore because I don't believe we are training anybody for anything and just about nobody cares about the theatre as anything, even as entertainment, let alone as an art form. I like women. I am not homosexual, I am not comfortable around homosexuals, but I don't hate homosexuals, and my life as a straight buffoon has been nothing to brag about. I go home now to an empty house because my wife is leaving me, and before that she had a lover unbeknownst to me for five years. I had cheated on her exactly seven times in twenty-five years of marriage, and she cheated on me every hour, every second for five long years, during most of which I thought we were as happy as any other suburban couple who drink too much, and fight twice a week, and I am directing this play. This play is a piece of shit, for which I don't blame the author, living as he is, probably, in sin in New York City. I praise him for it, may his next one be better. I don't blame our department head either, since I know he must put up with a lot just to keep this department together, and maybe he is right that if this play is a success, it will act like a sewer and channel some of the shit away. So I suggest humbly, as an all too fallible, flabby and balding human being, that we please bury this bitterness, and go back to work. Thank you.

Marisa Labozzetta

After Victory

Her husband, Pinky, sulks all morning. Barely touches his soft-boiled egg. Leaves an almost-full cup of coffee. Yet Vicky will let nothing dissuade her.

Vicky spent much of the night awake, planning her attire: a blue linen suit and a white crepe V-neck blouse with a string of pearls. No. It's August—too hot for a suit. Besides, the linen would wrinkle during the ride. She chose a floral two-piece sleeveless dress with a scarf that ties at the throat (to hide her slightly sagging neck) and a blouson top to cover her rear end. It's fuchsia and white, perky and uplifting—not like funeral garb.

"Have some." Vicky hands her daughter Toni a plate of French toast before Toni's second foot crosses the threshold. "I have fresh coffee."

"I thought we'd have lunch in Castleton," Toni says.

"That's a long way from now."

"If I eat this, I won't be hungry later."

"So lunch will cost less."

Toni sits at the kitchen table and eats her French toast while Vicky picks out a cardigan to take along: she hates air-conditioning. She wants to ask Toni's opinion, but doesn't want to make a big deal of it in front of Pinky, who has retired to the den. She selects her white cotton knit and runs into the bathroom to check her hair. She thanks God that she colored it last week. She grabs a compact and dark pink lipstick from the vanity drawer. She wishes she had been able to sleep last night: tiredness is an elderly woman's nemesis.

"You want one?" Vicky now offers Toni an opened jar of cherries soaked in vodka, which she made last summer.

"It's nine in the morning!"

Vicky shrugs her shoulders, indicating the hour is irrelevant. She stabs two cherries with a fork and pops them into her mouth. The juice burns the inside of her cheeks, as she bites down and chews; she swallows and lets the alcohol warm her insides—fortify her. She is on her way to meet Andrew Lingua—her love of fifty years ago.

"We'll be back around three," Vicky calls to Pinky who is watching a rerun of *Bewitched*.

"I think this is absurd," he bellows.

"I don't care what you think," she mutters under her breath.

"You'll probably get lost," he calls after her.

It was around Thanksgiving when Andrew's first call threw Vicky DiBenedetto's life off balance. She was at the kitchen table doing the crossword puzzle. Pinky was in the den, watching *Wheel of Fortune* on TV. Vicky had already washed two dishes, two forks, two knives, and two glasses, scrubbed the pots, and wiped down the table and stove top. Lamb chops. She remembers. She broiled loin lamb chops: $7.99 a pound at the Big Y Supermarket, buy one pound, get another free that week. They had eaten at five o'clock, as they always do. There was a time, however, when they still lived in Brooklyn and they were young, that they ate at seven or seven-thirty. That's what her husband had been used to growing up in Sicily. That was the civilized European hour to dine, he always said; however, Vicky knew Pinky really preferred it because he didn't want too much free time left over before he retired for the evening. After dinner, there was half an hour of television—maybe an hour if *Bonanza* was on—and he was off to bed so that he could rise at four in the morning and set out for the Italian bread bakery that he owned.

In those days, their severely handicapped daughter Susan (who now resides in a nursing home) was already in bed by the time he got home. That was what he counted on. Nevertheless, there were those difficult nights, particularly in her early years, when her wailing disrupted their meal and it sometimes took the two of them to calm her down and get her to bed. There was no TV on those occasions. Pinky would just close the door to their room, strip down to his shorts and undershirt, and go to sleep.

Nowadays, they can hardly wait to eat supper; their entire day revolves around it. From the moment Vicky gets up in the morning, she begins defrosting or frying. Wednesdays are a problem. It's seniors' day at the movies: a ten o'clock show at $2.50 a ticket, free bagels and coffee; then the senior lunch special at the Taipei Garden, all they can eat for $5.00. Around four-thirty, Vicky is beside herself, left with a gaping hole in her schedule. She wants to make dinner, but they are too stuffed to eat. She can't understand Toni, who often stops by as late as five in the evening on her way home from work and still has no idea of what she's preparing for dinner. Sometimes Vicky thinks that Toni wanted her parents to move to Hazzardville so that Vicky would feed Toni and her children.

"Nobody cooking at your house?" Pinky asks Toni. Or "Probably getting a pizza," he utters with disgust after she leaves.

The insinuation is that Toni's husband left her because there was no food, when the truth is, it was really Toni who wanted the divorce. It's no wonder she rarely comes around. Pinky manages to alienate everyone; five years in Massachusetts, and they still have no friends. It was Mr. Personality at the Sons of Italy meetings in the beginning. The invitations abounded. But, before long, they all saw that Mr. Personality was really Mr. Blowhard. At least that's what Vicky surmises, because the invitations eventually stopped. That she never reciprocated didn't help. Face it, she tells herself, they never had real friends as a couple. Before people might have had a chance to uncover the real basis of their marriage, Vicky withdrew. She and Pinky always had their parents, siblings, cousins. They had their daughters. And God knows that was enough.

Her life, however, has finally fallen into a peaceful place. While money had been a struggle throughout their marriage, once they sold the bakery, they found themselves comfortable. They have become set in their ways—used to one another. He has gastrointestinal problems and belches after every few bites. And he farts first thing in the morning. She has hemorrhoids and eats stewed prunes, and she cheats at canasta. They food-shop on Mondays. She can follow him on the dance floor. They are a couple: two people individually wrapped in Saran Wrap, and fastened together with a rubber band.

In this university town, surrounded by hamlets of dairy farms, Vicky is uncomfortable—always assuming every other citizen has been highly educated. So unlike Brooklyn. Even the contractors in this small city are college graduates. Even her plumber, who never gets dirty. Even her hairdresser, who doubles as a psychotherapist. The very name Hazzardville made Vicky reluctant to take up residence here, as though catastrophe lurked behind every corner and would threaten her from the second she touched her toes to the floor in the morning to the moment she safely hid them between the sheets again. But, until now, the only catastrophe had occurred in a hardware store where she purchased a tube of Udder Butter, mistaking the ointment used by farmers to lubricate cow teats for hand cream.

She does like her new home and takes pride in how contemporary she's made it: balloon curtains, white rug, bright floral upholstery, accenting her cherished Chippendale bedroom set and Mediterranean dining room. Still, she keeps it all to herself—hides it from the world like a treasure for no one else to enjoy. She's become like that: savoring gifts Toni gives her in a drawer for so long before she wears them they often go out of style. Toni is unlike her. Even as a little girl she flung off the old for the new. Slept in a new nightgown that very night. Wore a new dress to school the next morning. Relegated what she had enjoyed up to that day to the bottom of her closet or a bag destined for Goodwill. Maybe that's how she got over her second divorce so easily: as soon as husband-number-two was out the door, she was done with him—*finito.* Before long, her landscaper boyfriend Omar (who Pinky calls the Lawnmower Man) was on the scene, and it was as though the father of her two children had never existed.

"Victoria? It's Andy. Andy Lingua." The first call had taken her totally by surprise. Her heart rate sped up. She felt her knees giving way.

"Who?"

"It's me, Andrew. But everybody calls me Andy."

The Andrew she had known never allowed her to call him Andy, and insisted on calling her Victoria even against her wishes. Moreover, her Andrew's voice had been robust: this man's was tinny and fragile.

"Well, everyone calls me Vicky. They always have," she said.

"How *are* you?" he asked.

"Fine." She tried to mask her nervousness. "And you?"

"I hope it's okay."

"What?"

"That I call."

She glanced into the den. Pinky was absorbed in his program.

"How did you find me?" She spoke softly into the receiver.

"Alma."

"My aunt?"

Vicky hadn't seen her mother's younger sister in years. Alma had been a tramp—ran away with Andrew's married brother Albert; didn't even come to her own sister's funeral.

"She showed up at Albert's wake last week."

"Albert's dead?"

"Isn't almost everyone our age?" He tried to joke. She didn't laugh.

"I asked Alma about you. She knew you'd moved to Massachusetts, although she didn't know where. I looked up the gals you used to work with. Helen was the only one I found still in Brooklyn. Her son lives in the old house now, and she's in a nursing home on Long Island. But of course you know all that."

Yes. She knew that. Helen was in the same nursing home as her daughter Susan. The old woman had grown so attached to Susan that when Vicky and Pinky moved to Hazzardville, they decided to leave their daughter there rather than move her to Massachusetts. Vicky visits Susan once a month. Pinky occasionally goes along, but leaves for a good while and visits the old neighborhood in Brooklyn. He likes to check in on the bakery—see how the new owner is doing, and hope the answer is not well.

"Did you speak to Helen?"

"That's how I got your number. How's your sister Giose and her husband? I can't remember his name."

"It's Larry. Both he and my sister are fine. They live on Long Island too. They're great-grandparents. Their son Rudy has two grandchildren."

"Baby Rudy a grandfather!"

"He gave up the *Baby* years ago."

"And your parents?"

"Passed away."

"Mine too. Where *has* all that time gone?" His voice began to quiver and she thought he might burst into tears.

He said that he had married once, to an Irish widow from Boston with six children. That was how he had come to Castleton, a small town south of Boston where he had worked as an accountant. But the new family arrangement had been too much to handle for all of them. The children had abused him, he said, taken advantage of him emotionally and financially. The marriage ended after three years and a hefty settlement.

"Funny, isn't it? Both of us winding up in Massachusetts?" he said.

"Vicky!" Pinky called from the den. "*Jeopardy* is on."

"Coming," she shouted back. "Is this really you, Andrew?" she whispered.

"Yes."

She hung up.

She put her cool hands to her flushed face and waited until her heart stopped pounding. She went into the den.

"Who were you talking to?" Pinky asked.

"An old friend."

"What'd she want?"

"He just wanted to chat."

Pinky's eyes grew large with surprise, his mouth tense with annoyance.

"*He?*"

"I think he's ill. I think he's dying. He's been contacting old friends. You know how it is," she lied.

"And he has to talk to *you?*"

"He's also spoken to Helen."

Vicky made it seem as if it had been more than just to get her number. Besides, she knew the mere mention of her benevolent old friend who looked after Susan would calm him down some.

"Do I know him?"

"Andrew Lingua." She took delight in mumbling nonchalantly, and waited for his reaction.

He knitted his eyebrows, his memory straining to recall the name. Then his expression saddened as though the devil himself had found him out, and she felt sorry for him. She waited for him to say, *Don't get involved.*

"It's nothing. He just needed a friend," she reassured him.

When the phone rang during dinner the following week, she told Andrew that he had the wrong number. But she found herself thinking about him while she prepared meals; at the movie theater on Wednesdays; on the buffet line at the Taipei Garden; while watching *Jeopardy.* He had been so handsome. What would he have looked like now? Maybe he would have become pot-bellied like Pinky. And bald like him too. Maybe his breath would have smelled of rotting yellow teeth, and he would cough up phlegm into a large white linen handkerchief when he laughed, like the old friends of her grandfather's she remembered from her childhood. She pictured Raymond Burr as the young, powerful Perry Mason and his attractive loyal secretary Della. Then she thought of how she had seen them both in a recent made-for-television movie the other night. She shuddered. June Allyson consoled those with leaking bladders in Depends commercials. Jane Powell flashed her false teeth in Polident ads. And they were stars! What would anyone from her past think of *her* now?

At Christmastime, Vicky received a greeting card addressed to both her and Pinky. Inside the card were five photos of Andrew, taken—according to the notations on the back—within the last three years. Taller than she ever remembered him, this lean body towered next to a blue spruce decorated with red and gold bulbs. She held a magnifying glass over the picture and studied him in detail. His hair was gray but thick and wavy like Andrew's had been. There was a mustache, something Andrew had never worn. She could detect creases in his skin, but no hanging flesh, no jowls. Red-eye and glasses made it impossible to see the color of his eyes. An overpowering sadness dominated his expression despite the smile he wore. She hid the photos and left the card out with the rest of the others they'd received. Pinky never noticed it.

She baked a large box of assorted cookies—butter, macaroons, anisette biscuits, sesame—and sneaked them to the post office when Pinky was at the hospital having his monthly blood pressure checkup. Just this, and it would be the end of it. Just this to ease her conscience, to end the correspondence, for he had begun calling her on a regular basis when Pinky was at the barber's or a Sons of Italy meeting. A good deed; a corporal work of mercy. It was Christmastime. They had so much, yet this man who lived in Castleton seemed to have so little.

"You take the Mass Pike, then Four Ninety-five. Vicky smooths the seat of her dress as she sits beside Toni.

"I have a map."

Toni picks up the large veiny representation of Massachusetts spread out on the floor of the car and puts it onto her lap.

"Let me navigate. You can't read while you're driving."

"Ma, please."

"All right. So you know how to travel. But I'm paying for the tolls."

"Fine. Now tell me what's going on," Toni says, pulling out of the driveway.

"Do you remember Andrew Lingua? Of course you don't remember him, but you've heard me talk about him to Aunt Giose."

"Your old boyfriend."

"Right."

"You're going to see your old boyfriend?"

"Don't get excited. It's nothing like that. He suffers from depression. Has since World War II. He tried to commit suicide." Vicky's voice quivers. She bites her lip to hold back tears.

"And how do you know this?"

Vicky is quiet for a few seconds.

"He called me yesterday. I didn't know what to do at first. I tried to talk him out of it—tried not to overreact. I didn't even know if I should take him seriously. After he hung up on me, I phoned the police in Castleton."

"I don't understand. He called you after fifty years to tell you he was committing suicide?"

"We've been in touch. Just by phone. Dad knows. At least he knew about the first time," she says. "It's been going on for a while—nine months," she murmurs.

"Without Dad's knowing?"

"Yes. I don't think it's bad, do you? Andrew needed someone to talk to. And I've liked talking to him. Is it bad to have him as a friend?"

"I think it's fine."

"You do?"

Vicky recognizes what Toni is doing. She remembers well doing that herself with Toni when Toni was a teenager: don't pass judgment; just let her talk; keep the lines of communication open.

Vicky tells the whole story from the first day she and Andrew met to yesterday's phone call. Toni nods and encourages her to go on. During the war, Pinky was still called by his real name—Romeo. When Vicky comes to the part about her intimate night with Pinky while she was engaged to Andrew, she embellishes the relationship with more feeling for Pinky than existed. He had been home on furlough; they had barely known one another. Afterwards, she wrote him overseas, assuring him it had been just that—a tryst. But when he returned with all the fingers on his right hand missing except his pinky, he would not take no for an answer.

Vicky makes excuses for Pinky's having revealed the affair to her parents and Andrew. (Vicky's father overturned the kitchen table, slapped her, and called her *puttana*. A shell-shocked Andrew spurned her.) Pinky told out of frustration: he loved me, she tells her daughter. But he did it out of selfishness: he was vindictive, she believes.

"Do you think I've missed something sleeping with just one man all my life?" Vicky asks Toni.

"That's a random question."

Vicky is glad that Toni remains focused on the road. She can't look her in the eye and talk about this.

"Do you?" Vicky needs to know her daughter's opinion.

"If it was good—no. If it was bad—I guess so."

Vicky sighs. She wishes Andrew and she had slept together.

"You know that photo of the sailor kissing the nurse in Times Square on the day of the Japanese surrender," Toni says.

"The *Life* magazine shot," Vicky recollects.

"I read that they were complete strangers. They just met for the first time in fifty years because of all this end-of-the-war anniversary hoopla."

"And what happened?"

"They introduced themselves and went back to their own lives."

"He was an Italian fellow, you know," Vicky says. "The sailor, I mean."

The hospital is bleak and dirty: brown vinyl floors, smudged glass doors, marked-up yellow walls. Vicky slips into the first ladies' room she sees to pee. She swats her face with some loose powder from her compact and reapplies her lipstick. With a comb, she fluffs up her bangs.

No one seems to be able to tell them where the intensive care unit is. They wander around the entire second floor before they come upon a sign warning them that no one but relatives are permitted through the locked door. Toni grabs the open door while a visitor exits, and tells the first nurse she sees that Mr. Lingua's sister is here to see him.

Intensive Care is a large room with a nurses' station in the center and small, glass-partitioned sections that line the perimeter. The nurses yell when they speak to the patients, who are hooked up to all sorts of machines and dripping liquids. The patients look ancient: already dead.

Toni tells Vicky that she'll wait for her in the lounge. Vicky is relieved to have the first moment alone with Andrew. Before she leaves, Toni picks a stray thread off the shoulder of her mother's dress, and Vicky becomes embarrassed because Toni must hear the pounding of her heart.

"You came just in time. Mr. Lingua is about to be moved," a nurse, whose name tag reads Karen Fulgham, says.

"To another room?" Vicky asks.

"To another hospital. Deaconess in Boston. They have a psychiatric unit."

"Can I see him?"

"I think he'd like that very much."

"Andrew, you have a visitor," Ms. Fulgham calls loudly. "He's heavily sedated," she whispers to Vicky, who steps into the room the nurse has been guarding.

Andrew is lying on a gurney. A blue and white johnny peeks through the neck opening of a red plaid bathrobe. In his hand, he clutches a small wallet-sized photo of Vicky and Andrew taken before he went overseas. Andrew looks up at Vicky: his eyes are thick and dull from too many drugs, yet his face is unlined, and his square jawline hardly rounded out by the years. He is indeed her Andrew. She leans over the gurney and takes his hand. He squeezes it: his grip is remarkably firm.

"I didn't want you to see me like this," he says.

His voice is sluggish. His face is pale and his expression strained. He still seems to be trim, although it is difficult to tell since he is lying on his side.

"You mean old?"

"I mean like this."

"Then you shouldn't have called me."

"I never thought Pinky would let you come."

"Pinky had no choice."

She hesitates, then kisses him on his cheek, which is damp and salty from countless tears. He does not smell like a hospital, rather soapy, like a newborn.

"Andrew, you didn't do this to get me here, did you?" Vicky says sternly, trying to make him at least smile.

"I never wanted you to see me like this," he repeats.

"As though I look grand," she says flippantly.

"You're more beautiful than I remember you."

"Seeing me hasn't broken the spell?"

"I'm more spellbound than ever."

"You're not wearing your glasses."

"Don't cry, dear," he says.

"My daughter is here. She drove me. Would you like to meet her?" Vicky asks Ms. Fulgham to bring in Toni; her own legs will not move from the gurney's side. With her free hand she takes a Kleenex from the nightstand.

"She looks just like you," Andrew says when Toni arrives.

"She has her father's coloring." Vicky wipes her eyes.

"It's nice to meet you," Toni says, taking his other hand.

"Don't ever grow old, dear. It's a terrible thing to grow old," he says, staring up into Toni's dark eyes.

"She's ours, isn't she?" Andrew asks Vicky.

"How could she be?" Vicky says, saddened at the thought that he could possess that notion. Wishing that it was the truth.

"It's time," Karen Fulgham announces.

"So soon?" Vicky looks up.

Andrew tightens his grip on Vicky.

"I used to think you were the weak one. But I was wrong. You're strong. You've always been strong," he says.

"And now *you* need to be strong—for yourself. You need to get well," Vicky tells him.

"Forgive me."

"You've already apologized so many times."

"Only over the phone. I should have married you, Vicky."

"Maybe next time around," she says.

"I'll be waiting for you at the gate."

She wants to kiss him on the lips, but not in front of Toni. An orderly walks in, and it's all over.

"Let's go, old man," the orderly says, wheeling the gurney towards the door.

Vicky swings around to face the young man. Her lips are taut, her hazel eyes on fire.

"Don't you call him that! He's a hero. He flew thirty missions in the Second World War. He received the Flying Cross Medal. Don't you dare call him *old man*."

"I'm sorry, ma'am," the orderly says, his eyes wide with surprise. "A war hero, huh? I'll take good care of him." He wheels Andrew towards the elevator.

"Are you the one who called the police?" Karen Fulgham asks Vicky.

"Yes."

"You saved his life. He'd taken a lot of pills, but they didn't work. They found a knife in his bed. He meant business. You're the lady in the picture, aren't you? He won't let go of that for anything."

"It's been fifty years," Vicky tells her as though she herself has just realized it.

"Come on, Ma." Toni takes Vicky's arm.

"In a minute."

Toni goes out in the hall while Vicky sits down in the black leather armchair that has been expecting her and others like her. The rooms of the IC unit whirl by her like horses on a carousel.

She needs to be still for a moment, it was all too quick for one who seems to have been sitting here, in this chair, waiting, for fifty years. She and Toni had considered stopping for a cup of coffee before they visited Andrew. Vicky can't get over the fact that, but for a few minutes, they would have missed him. Who? Andrew, as she had known him, remembered him, tall and straight and unblemished, is gone: in his place exists an old man now on his way to a locked room in Boston. She is numb. And for a few seconds, she cannot imagine any other life of hers, except this hospital, this IC unit, and this chair.

"He's a handsome man," Toni tells her mother in a booth at Friendly's.

Vicky wishes Toni wouldn't compliment Andrew. It makes her feel as if her life with Pinky has been even more of a waste than she already believes.

"He *was* a beautiful man. A beautiful boy with a beautiful soul."

A whole Andrew might have punched Romeo DiBenedetto in the face upon learning what had gone on between him and Vicky. A whole Andrew might have professed his love for Vicky and claimed her despite her fall from grace. But a broken Andrew, who had spent six months recuperating from battle fatigue in a hospital in Scotland, had merely listened, convinced that the love that had brought him home had been a sham.

"Fucking war. It killed him. It's still killing him. It ruined all of us."

Vicky is more surprised than Toni that she has so easily let *fuck* come rolling out of her mouth.

"I don't understand why you married Dad," Toni says.

Vicky takes time to answer this one. Can she explain what it feels like to be trapped by guilt, so trapped that you would give your life to find a way out? That she did, in a way, give her life to make up for what she felt had destroyed her parents' faith in her and Andrew's love. That she had had to do something then and there; that there had been no waiting for time to heal because the luxury of time never existed back then. That it hadn't been so difficult a task because, like Andrew, shock made her unfeeling. There had been no victory in her unconventional behavior with Pinky. There is never victory when others are made to suffer. Can Toni comprehend a world without choice? One always has a choice, Toni will say. And she is right. Vicky had chosen: once to betray and once again to repent by punishing herself and marrying Pinky. Then God sent her Susan. But it still wasn't enough. She inflicted yet more penance upon herself. She denied herself pleasures she once thought she couldn't live without—poetry, theater, the botanical gardens. One by one, with determination, she stripped them and other things from her life like excessive red tape—like Andrew's memory. Soon almost nothing remained except the boring basics. Then Andrew's phone calls began.

"Times were different then," Vicky tells Toni. "My parents were immigrants. They were strict. They had expectations—pride. Everything was about honor and respect. I was young. It was wartime. I made mistakes. But *everything* wasn't a mistake," she is quick to assure her daughter—"you, your sister."

"Even we didn't make life easy for you."

"Were you uncomfortable today?"

Toni shrugs as if to say *some*.

"A mother's not supposed to do these things—a mother my age."

"I'm glad you went. You saved his life! That took courage."

"I couldn't let him down—again. Are you and Omar going to get married?" Vicky feels more at liberty than usual to ask the very private Toni.

"Probably."

"You love him?"

"I think so."

"Differently than your husband?"

"Not like with my first, if we can all remember back that far. That was all passion. The second time around was intellectual. I was trying to do the right thing, believe it or not—make you and Dad proud of me.

This one is friendship—and attraction—but not crazy mad attraction. You know what I mean?"

Vicky knows exactly what she means. That's how she feels about Andrew this very moment.

"The blessing of menopause. You can see men for what they really are," Vicky says.

Toni laughs and Vicky is delighted. She likes Toni, respects her candidness, envies her for having slept with more than one man.

For the first time, it is Vicky who makes the motion to leave. Toni is relaxed and appears to be able to sit like this with her mother forever, and that seems to have made everything in Vicky's life worthwhile.

"My little grandson will be getting home from camp soon," Vicky says.

"He has a key."

"Thank you for taking me, Toni."

"My pleasure, Mom."

The joy of this sudden intimacy between them is almost too much for Vicky, who chooses to destroy it rather than experience the pain of Toni or anyone else beating her to it.

"Finish your sandwich." Vicky points to a quarter of a Reuben lying on Toni's plate. "You never finish anything."

"That's not true. Besides, I'm full. I ate the French toast, remember?"

"At least eat the corned beef. It's—"

"Protein."

"I'm paying for lunch," Vicky says.

On the ride home Vicky's thoughts turn to Pinky. She has never really been afraid of him and his rages the way she used to be of her father. Except for one time, when Pinky stabbed an employee at the bakery for stealing and making a fool out of him. The wound was superficial. They settled their differences without the police, since they both would have been arrested: one for theft, the other for assault and battery with a deadly weapon. Yet, she kept the kitchen knives out of sight for years and held her breath whenever he became frustrated carving the turkey on Thanksgiving Day.

"Don't come in," Vicky tells Toni when they pull up to the house.

Vicky finds Pinky sitting in the den. The television turned off. There is no newspaper on his lap. He comes to life when he sees her.

"It went okay?" he asks.

"Yes."

"He's all right?"

"He's in a psychiatric hospital."
"Did you get lost?"
"No."

Wally Lamb

Food and Fatalism

When I was a kid growing up in Norwich, Connecticut, my family and I were on the road for Christmas—not over the river and through the woods but across town to Nonna's two-story tenement, stucco façade, Pepto-Bismol pink.

In preparation for the two-mile trek, my father, a self-described "swamp Yankee," would stand before the trunk of our army-green Hudson, enacting the creative geometry by which dozens of presents were wedged and cajoled into an insufficient number of cubic feet. Once the trunk was loaded and slammed, we men would get in the car and wait for the women. The smoke from Daddy's perpetual Marlboro would float around our heads and he'd tap his fingers against the steering wheel, mumbling rhetorical questions like "Christ Almighty, what's she *doin'* in there?" I'd be in back, focused on the platter of pizelles resting against my knees. This was closure of a sort: my guardianship of those fragile confections. Each Christmas Eve, I'd supervise the alchemy by which my mother poured runny yellow batter into her special iron to sizzle and emerge as crisp golden snowflakes, aromatic with anise. "Hope she gets out here before New Year's," Daddy would grumble. "Yeah," I'd agree, and poke through the plastic wrap, drag a licked finger in the powdered sugar that had drifted from pizelles to plate bottom, extract it, and suck. Ah, sweet Christmas!

At last, the side door would bang open and out would come the Corningware caravan: my oven-mitted mother and sisters, as purposeful as Magi, bearing hot side dishes for the midday feast at Nonna's. They'd get in, the car windows would fog up before we left the driveway, the defrosters would roar. Over his shoulder, Daddy would threaten to clobber anyone caught autographing the condensation, Christmas or no Christmas.

Nonna lived on Norwich's East Side, an enclave of Sicilians and

Calabrians who had crossed the Atlantic between the 1890s and 1920s, moved north from New York, and settled in this southern New England mill town at the juncture of the Yantic, Thames, and Shetucket rivers. Once the fishing and hunting grounds of the Pequot and Mohegan tribes, the town had been transformed by industry during the second half of the nineteenth century and revitalized by the influx of Canadian and European immigrants hired to labor at the huge factories: Ponemah Cotton Mills, Chelsea Paper, American Woolen, Norwich Bleaching, Dyeing and Printing.

The mills counted Italians amongst their workers, of course, but many Siciliani and Calabrese were hesitant to put their fate in the hands of impersonal companies run by rich 'Mericanos. They hailed from a region which, from the Middle Ages to the nineteenth century, had been vulnerable to and vanquished by powerful strangers, and a self-preserving skepticism had leached into their bones. Many of these Southern Italian immigrants chose to avoid the mills and, instead, operate small, family-run businesses. The East Side became home to tradesmen and tailors, barbers and bricklayers, grocers and roofers and restaurateurs. They served one another and the city at large.

Norwich boasted two Southern Italian strongholds in those days. On the town's more ethnically diverse West Side, transplanted Siciliani lived and worked alongside African Americans, Russians, Poles, Germans, Armenians, and Irish. The East Side, under the leadership of my grandfather, Bruno Pedace, was more uniformly Calabrian. But "East Siders" and "West Siders" were more alike than different. In relocating from the "Old Country," they had lugged, along with their trunks and cardboard suitcases, their fear-based superstitions ("*Spit in the sky and you'll get it back*"), their fatalistic outlook on life ("*Only in the womb are you free from hunger and cold!*"), their cynical humor ("*If your rear end had money, people would call it* Sir *Rear!*"), and, most famously, their deep love of family and food.

At Nonna's, Christmas dinner was served to a packed house: eleven children, eight sons- and daughters-in-law, nineteen grandchildren, and a flotilla of cousins, neighbors, and friends *di famiglia*. The adults ate at the dining room table. The kids were squeezed into the parlor at a series of abutting card tables draped with a single white tablecloth, liberally stained from Christmases past. Grace came first, then the *festa banchetto!* Peaches in homemade wine, antipasto and Italian bread, pasta, turkey with all the fixings. After a breather, a belt-loosening, maybe, there were cream cakes, cookies, pies, the pizelles.

Chaos reigned at the kids' table. Elbows flew, milk capsized, dinner rolls arrived airmail from the other end of the room. More than once, my cousins' antics turned my laughter into choking, sending prickly orange soda coursing through the double drainpipes of my nostrils and onto my mashed potatoes. In these tight quarters, a trip to the bathroom meant sliding off your chair and under the table, crawling on hands and knees through a forest of cousins' legs, and receiving a friendly kick in the *culo* from one or two wise-guy older cousins. You'd reach the clearing, do your business, and then reverse the steps until you were back at your seat for a little more dessert and mischief.

After dinner, the women did the dishes and gabbed, the men played pitch, and the kids caroused unsupervised in Nonna's cavernous cellar, a hands-on museum of costumes, 78-rpm records, a conga drum, Charles Atlas barbells, a pinball machine, and other artifacts left behind by the sons and daughters who had left Nonna's nest. Sometimes we cousins would raid the steamer trunk at the dark, damp canning closet end of the cellar; the trunk, which had come all the way from Italy, was a coffin of sorts for old curtains, worn blankets, and outdated clothes. With her quick reflexes and love of the limelight, my cousin Sandy was usually the first to snatch from the trunk the medal-bedecked, red satin sash that our mysterious, deceased grandfather had worn as *Il Presidente* of the *Società di Mutuo Soccorso di Norwich, Connecticut*—the Society of Mutual Benefits, an Italian social club. With Grandpa's sash across her chest and a yardstick for a baton, Sandy would lead the parade, the rest of us clomping up the cellar stairs behind her. We'd snake our way through the house, playing imaginary band instruments. We were motley, raucous, out of step, off-key. But like most Italian families, mine indulged its children. As we paraded past the adults, their talking, dish-drying, and card-playing would cease. They'd laugh, wave, hoot, beam. We were loved—*speciale*—simply by virtue of having been born their kids.

As Christmas afternoon turned into Christmas evening, out would come roasted nuts, dried fruits, anisette, espresso—and the tins, cigar boxes, and scrapbooks filled with family pictures. Here were seventy-year-old Uncle Jimmy in a bowl cut and knickers, my mom as a scowling third-grader in a burlap dress, Nonna and Grandpa on their wedding day. In the latter photo, the groom looks dapper in his three-piece suit and waxed mustache; the bride looks pretty, too young to marry, and scared to death.

Sometime during this jovial picture-passing, Nonna would disappear back into her kitchen to assemble a tower of turkey and *melanzana* sandwiches. She'd turn a deaf ear to the chorus of protests that everyone was still stuffed and serve the sandwiches with reheated leftovers, cold pizza, and soggy antipasto salad. After this new round of food had been devoured, Nonna would sit in her parlor chair and fall asleep, her mouth open, her stockings rolled down to her ankles. "Look at poor Mama," one of my aunts would remark. "She's dead to the world." Nonna died for good in 1966.

As a kid, I was crazy about Nonna, who, old as she was, could be deliciously silly. I still have the Instamatic picture I snapped one Easter in which she poses, deadpan, arms akimbo, in a flowered bonnet with fuzzy rabbit ears protruding from the brim. She had a sense of play, my grandmother, and could be coaxed away from the stove to play one of the games she liked—Cootie, or Bingo, or "Hot Potato." She was a trickster, too. On April Fool's Day, she'd glue a nickel to the kitchen floor and hide in the pantry, giggling and waiting for victims. Or she'd call you up and tell you to look outside quickly—there was a kangaroo in your yard! One evening when the extended family gathered for Sunday-night supper, Nonna's son Joe returned from a fishing trip with a bucket of mackerel. Later that evening, while the rest of the family sat in the parlor watching *Ed Sullivan,* Nonna snuck into the back bedroom that served as a repository for visitors' coats and stuck mackerel into the coat pockets of her sons-in-law.

"The Mighty Midget," our family nicknamed Nonna, a nod to the fact that at four feet, ten inches and ninety pounds, she was a woman of strength and will—a power to be reckoned with. She lived at the East Main Street house with Uncle Dom, Uncle Bruno, and Aunt Pal, the three of her eleven children who had never married and, therefore, had never left home. Nonna's son Bill ran the luncheonette next door. Her daughter Marion lived in the upstairs apartment with her husband and son. If Nonna wanted Aunt Marion, she'd ignore the telephone and use the broom handle instead. *Bang, bang, bang* on the kitchen ceiling, and Aunt Marion would fly down the back stairs to see what her mother wanted. "Go next door and tell Bill I need three eggs," Nonna might order me during a Saturday-afternoon visit. I'd run out the door and through the back room of the store to deliver the message. Uncle Bill might have six burgers on the grill, a couple of milkshakes spinning on the machine, and a line of customers waiting at the register. Didn't matter. Everything else waited until Nonna got her eggs. Uncle Dom, a bachelor, liked to visit the ladies up at the Jewett City Hotel and gamble on the horses at the Narragansett Race Track. Nonna disapproved of both hobbies. "Eh, *stupido,* where do you think *you're* going?" she asked him one drizzly Saturday as he was leaving for the weekend. I was visiting that afternoon and witnessed the exchange. Uncle Dom froze, his hand on the doorknob. There was a long pause—a showdown of sorts. Then Nonna pointed to the pile of galoshes by the back door. "It's wet out there. Put on your rubbers." Uncle Dom nodded, sat, did what he was told. I was seven or eight at the time. By my calculation, my uncle was fifty-one or fifty-two.

Nonna couldn't read but she sure could cook: pasta and meatballs, soups and stews, pepper and egg sandwiches, pasta "fazoole." Sometimes her sons would ask their wives to cook a dish the way "Mama" did. Nonna's daughters-in-law would quiz her as to ingredients and proportions. They'd ask for recipes. "Oh, you know," she'd say. "A littla this, a littla that." My aunts' subsequent efforts would be fine, but never as good as Mama's. I used to like to watch Nonna in the kitchen. She'd measure with her hands, not with spoons or calibrated cups; she'd gauge cooking time not by the stove timer but by checking, stirring, and poking at whatever was frying, baking, or bubbling. "Here. Watch out, it's hot," she'd say, and hand me a small plate on which sat a fat fried meatball redolent of onion and garlic. "Have a taste," she'd say, and rip the heel off a loaf of Italian bread, inviting me to dip it into her simmering sauce. As a kid, I had an ongoing "discussion" with my mother on the subject of strawberry gelatin. "Don't be ridiculous," Ma would insist. "Jell-O is Jell-O!" But I'd hold fast to my position that Nonna's Jell-O tasted better than hers.

A quietly devout woman, my grandmother attended Mass each week. And like most Southern Italians, she believed as wholeheartedly in the Devil as she did in God. She was never a slave to the superstitious fear of *il malocchio*—the evil eye—but she avoided unnecessary risks. If the sun shifted while she was walking downtown to the market, she crossed from the shady to the sunny side of the street. When she came upon neighbors rumored capable of casting spells or causing harm, she averted her eyes. She pinned charms to the diapers of her babies as an antidote to illness. If she woke to a middle-of-the-night thunderstorm, she hoisted herself out of bed, grabbed her sprinkle-top bottle of holy water from the kitchen, and tiptoed from bedroom to bedroom, safeguarding her slumbering loved ones by dousing their bare feet. One night, instead of holy water, Nonna grabbed from the laundry shelf her bottle of bluing, the cleaning agent she used to keep white sheets from yellowing. The following morning, her family woke up wondering why their feet had turned blue.

She liked TV: Westerns in the evening, her "stories" at midday. Her favorites were Paladin, the gunslinger-for-hire on *Have Gun, Will Travel,* and Joanne Tate, the matriarch of daytime's *Search for Tomorrow.* One memorable Friday afternoon, Nonna and I were watching *Search for Tomorrow* when a crazy intruder broke into Joanne Tate's home, pulled a gun, and shot her. The episode ended as a cliffhanger, of course—the gunshot, followed by a close-up of a quavering Joanne. Faithful viewers would have to tune in on Monday to learn the heroine's fate. When I looked from the TV screen over at Nonna, I saw that she was visibly shaken. "It's not real," I assured her. She seemed not to hear me. "Nonna? It's all make-believe. It's *fake*." But the assault had so upset her that for the rest of the afternoon, she was nervous and distracted. She spent part of that weekend sick in bed, rallying the following Monday when she learned that the bullet had only grazed Joanne and she was okay.

Like most grandchildren, I failed to consider while Nonna was in my midst that she might have had stories to tell—that she might have been someone beyond the tiny, good-natured old woman *I* knew. She cooked; she came from Italy; she wore her gray braids coiled neatly at the nape of her neck and a flowery apron that snapped up the sides. What more was there to know?

Born in 1881 in the tiny mountain village of Giuliana, Sicily, Vita LaRussa left her family at the age of thirteen and traveled alone to America. She did so not because of an adventurous spirit, but because she had no choice. Her mother had died of diphtheria the year before and her stepfather had declared that it was all he could do to provide for his and his deceased wife's *own* children, Vita's half-siblings. An older brother who had relocated to Brooklyn, New York, agreed to finance Vita's voyage and sponsor her immigration.

In Sicily, she had led the sheltered life of a peasant girl and the difficult trip to the seaport in Palermo and then the harrowing and lonely three-week journey across the Atlantic traumatized young Vita. Appalled by the filthy conditions of steerage, frightened by much of the interaction she witnessed, and haunted by the shipboard death of a woman and her subsequent burial at sea, Vita vowed when she landed at Ellis Island that she would never go home again because she would not be able to survive a second trip. For the rest of her life, she kept her promise.

She lived with relatives in Brooklyn for a while and, at the age of sixteen, was matched to Bruno Pedace, a cobbler who had emigrated from Calabria. Vita and Bruno married and moved north to Norwich, where my grandfather set up his shoe repair shop and established himself as an organizer and adviser for newly arrived Italians, particularly his fellow Calabrese. *Paisani* sought his counsel on business deals, family problems, political affiliations, and pregnancies. When the wife of a *gumbare* reached her seventh or eighth month, she'd be taken to Bruno Pedace's shop. My grandfather would halt his hammering of a heel or sole, or his backroom pinochle game with Peter Barber and Louie Iacoi, and, with great seriousness of purpose, remove himself to the front sidewalk. The mother-to-be would walk down the street and back again under Bruno's scrutiny. Then he would make his prediction: girl or boy. According to one of my uncles who kept track, my grandfather's average was only about .500, but his so-so stats apparently mattered less than the ritual itself.

Ritual, tradition, loyalty to one's own, preservation of the "old way": these things *mattered* to transplanted Italians in this strange New World with its inverse value system—its glorification of restless go-getters and rugged individualists instead of stable, self-sacrificing family men. Southern Italians clung as best they could to *la via vecchia,* weaving a safety net from social convention, religious ritual, festivals and street fairs, and family loyalty. Their trust was systematic: they put faith in blood relatives first, relatives by marriage second, then neighbors and the godparents of their children, then fellow villagers. Whoever or whatever operated beyond these concentric circles—the government, the Church of Rome, the educational system, non-Italians—were to be regarded with a healthy measure of suspicion. You smiled warmly in the midst of non-*paisani*—exhibited charm, graciousness, a pleasant disposition. But you trusted only your own, never the world at large. It was unwise, for instance, to allow your sons and daughters to be educated beyond the level which you yourself had achieved. If your children became successful in the world at large, they would become lost to that world, and separation from their family would beget their spiritual deaths.

At both his cobbler's shop and the meeting hall of the *Società di Mutuo Soccorso di Norwich,* my grandfather preached the gospel of group affiliation, death benefits for the widows of *paisani,* not becoming too big for your britches, and the primacy of *famiglia.* With regard to the latter, Papa Pedace practiced what he preached. Bruno and Vita's children—Vincenzo, Bill, Dom, Marianna, Vincenzia, Bruno, Palmina, Anna, Joe, Beatricia, and Johnny—were born over a twenty-five-year span, from 1901 to 1926, with numerous miscarriages interspersed. My mother's cousin, Florence Buonanno, recalls that whenever her own mother was missing at breakfast, the family figured she was over at "Auntie's," midwifing the newest arrival. Nonna birthed her first ten children on the kitchen table and her last in the hospital. She stayed there for a week. It was the closest she ever came to a vacation.

Under their father's strict rule and their mother's loving care, the first generation of American-born Pedaces assimilated and thrived. Vincenzo became Jimmy; Palmina (born on Palm Sunday) became Pal; Marianna was now Marion; Beatricia was Bea. The "boys" became sailors, boxing managers, and haberdashers; there was a state politician, a newspaper editor, a dentist, a *Fortune* 500 CEO. Four of the girls became homemakers and stay-at-home mothers like their mother. The fifth, a self-described "old maid," worked in finance at City Hall. The Pedace children both heeded and ignored their father's message about loyalty to family and *paisani*. Only one moved beyond the boundaries of Norwich; only one went to college. But of the eight who took wives and husbands, only one Pedace married a fellow Italian. The others were betrothed to French-American women and Polish-American men, Protestant-born sailors from California and Georgia, and, in my mother's case, a third-generation "swamp Yankee" of Lutheran faith.

My father, a friend and teammate of my mother's brothers, had been hanging around the Pedace house for a couple of years before he mustered the courage to ask my mother for a date. She said yes. But when Walter arrived at the pink stucco house to pick up Anna, he was met at the door by her mother.

"She can't go," Mrs. Pedace told him.

"Why not?" my father asked.

"Because she's too young." Walter pointed out that *he* was two years younger than Anna. My grandmother shrugged. "She's too young," she repeated. "Her mouth still smells of mother's milk."

Walter gave up that day but persisted nonetheless. He borrowed his boss's Ford roadster and arranged to take Anna to Misquamicut Beach. This time she *could* go. And this time, it was her father who answered the door, dressed for a day of fun in the sun. Walter drove, Mr. Pedace sat up front in the passenger's seat, and Anna traveled, wind-tossed, in the rumble seat. It was a beautiful beach day, my father remembers; Mr. Pedace had a wonderful time. He must have, because a while later, when Dad went to the shoe shop to ask for my mother's hand in marriage, he braced himself for the kind of grueling two-hour torture session my grandfather had inflicted on Glenn Adams, the skinny sailor from Pavo, Georgia, who, the month before, had asked to marry my mother's sister, Jennie. But Walter was in and out of the back room in record time, and with a $20 bill in his pocket to boot, to be spent on the couple's first grocery order once they were husband and wife.

From the start, my parents' marriage was tempered by my mother's "Italianness," particularly her devotion to her family and the Catholic Church. Father Donahue, the Irish pastor of St. Mary's, would not perform "mixed" marriages inside the church, so the nuptials took place next door at the rectory. My father was obliged to sign a promise that his children would be brought up in the Roman Catholic, not the Protestant, faith.

The war was on and money was tight, but Walter surprised his bride with a lavish Manhattan honeymoon. Their itinerary: dining, dancing, a couple of Broadway shows, a few nights of getting-to-know-you *amore*. But as they checked into the Edison Hotel, the newlyweds bumped into Antonio Longo, a friend of the Pedace family and the father-in-law of Anna's brother, Bill. Delighted by the chance encounter with the newlyweds, Mr. Longo invited the couple to dine with him. Walter had been imagining a more private evening, but as he was opening his mouth to decline the invitation, Anna accepted. It wouldn't do to insult Mr. Longo by refusing, she explained later. The Longos and the Pedaces were practically *family*. Her father might get *mad*. So off to supper the threesome went. Mr. Longo ordered a nice bottle of Chianti, and then another, and then a third. At evening's end, Walter's assignment was to get his inebriated host to Grand Central Station and onto a train back home. With much difficulty, he accomplished his mission and hurried back to his bride at the Edison Hotel. But Anna had fallen fast asleep. The following morning, her husband held up a front page: *500 Perish in Boston Blaze*. The famed Coconut Grove nightclub had, the night before, gone up in flames. "Gee, I almost planned a Boston honeymoon," Walter mused. "Lucky I changed my mind."

"Oh, that wasn't you," Anna informed him. "That was God."

Like her mother, Anna believed that destiny was in the hands of the Almighty. You stayed on God's good side by doing your best during the week and attending Mass on Sunday. My father, the lapsed Lutheran, would have loved to stay in bed on weekend mornings, but he got up each Sunday to drive my mother to church. One icy Sunday morning, he awoke, looked out the window, and announced, "Well, no church *this* morning." He pulled up the covers and closed his eyes.

"Why not?" Anna asked.

His eyes opened again. "Too slippery to drive. We'd have an accident."

Anna got up, got washed and dressed, put on her hat and coat. "Well," she sighed. "If you won't drive me, I guess I'll have to walk."

Walter groaned and surrendered. He was inching his Oldsmobile down the steepest part of Spruce Street when the car started to slide. He had two choices. He could steer into a steep rock ledge or crash into the bridge railing. If the railing failed to hold, he, Anna, and the Oldsmobile would tumble into the Shetucket river. Walter chose the ledge. There was a scream, a crash, then silence. Walter turned to his wife. "Well, are you happy now?" he asked.

"We'd be dead if we weren't on our way to church," Anna replied.

A few months later, there was a test of the couple's commitment—a showdown between American initiative and Italian solidarity. A dyer at the American Woolen Company, Walter was called to his boss's office one afternoon and congratulated on being a go-getter and a guy who thought "on his feet." The company had decided to promote him to a foreman's position and give him a substantial raise in pay. But there was a catch: Walter would have to relocate to a sister plant in Maine. Excited about his chance for advancement, he lobbied Anna for a week. There was discussion, argument; there were late-night tears. But, in the end, Walter declined his promotion, quit his job at the mill, and went to work shoveling coal at the Norwich Public Utilities. He did so because his wife couldn't bear to leave her family.

But if there was sacrifice for Walter, there were rewards, too. Now a Pedace *affine,* he'd been taken inside the family circle via its feasts and pitch games and practical jokes. And so my father, too, embraced the culture of *famiglia,* exchanging career advancement for this powerful sense of belonging. For the rest of his working life, he was employed by the Norwich Department of Public Utilities, where he rose slowly through the ranks to a superintendent's position. His leisure time was spent largely at the big pink house at 504 East Main Street and his social circle consisted, primarily, of Pedaces. I saw my dad cry twice when I was a kid: the day JFK was assassinated and the day his mother-in-law died.

I was fifteen when Nonna took to her sickbed with what was to be the last of her "spells." My family was summoned by Aunt Pal, Nonna's stay-at-home daughter and now her principal caregiver. My visits to my grandmother's house had, by then, petered out, replaced by the hubbub of high school life. Nonna had had any number of spells before this one, close calls from which she'd always rebounded. I argued with my mother that I couldn't go. I had a test to study for, a rehearsal for the talent show. No, I *had* to go, Ma said.

We entered the house through the door to the kitchen. Dr. Quintiliani, the family physician, was just leaving. I saw from the consoling way he touched my mother's arm that Nonna was bad. My parents went in first; my sisters and I waited at the threshold. Then Aunt Pal nodded for us to enter, too. We tiptoed into Nonna's room with its ornate mahogany furniture, its spooky painting of the Virgin Mary's Assumption into Heaven, and its marble-top bureau with the tall, three-sided mirror before which I had once knelt with a roll of Necco wafers, dispensing Eucharist after pastel candy Eucharist to my triplicate self in a frenzy of greed and piety.

Beneath the covers in her high double bed, Nonna looked tinier than ever. She was wearing a white embroidered nightgown; her gray braids, knitting needle–skinny, were unpinned and resting against the pillow. Her breathing was labored, her smile weak. I kissed her, told her I loved her. "Good night, God bless you," she whispered. She reached for my hand, gave it a limp squeeze. Then in a stronger, more commanding voice, the Mighty Midget addressed my mother, her daughter, Anna. "There's leftover chicken cacciatore in the refrigerator," she said. "Take it home for the kids."

The next morning Ma sat on my bed and watched me wake up. There was a sad smile on her face, but she was dry-eyed. "Mama died," she said. I was speechless, unable to croak out even a few syllables of comfort. My mother took my hand and squeezed it. "She went quick, just like she wanted to," she said. "When my time comes, I hope I go just like Mama."

There's an old Sicilian saying that advises, *I più gran dolori sono muti*—very great griefs are silent. But if Nonna's assimilated sons and daughters were once removed from the rules of the Old Country, their children, in turn, were twice removed. And so, at Nonna's funeral, it was my teenage cousin April who spilled the Pedace family secret—a confidence so troubling that repeating it now, revealing it in print to strangers, makes me feel like a betrayer of my family and my Southern Italian heritage.

My deceased grandfather had been an enigma to me when I was a child. There were few photographs of him, few mentions of him in the family's comical anecdotes. The most tangible evidence of Grandpa was his satin *Il Presidente* sash that lived in the trunk in the cellar. Whenever I asked my mother about her father, she'd say there wasn't much to tell: he'd come from Italy, he was a cobbler, he was strict, he died before I was born. But April divulged that Grandpa had *not* predeceased me but had died the year I was four, eight years into his locked-down life in the forensic unit of the Norwich State Hospital. He had been committed there for having tried to kill his wife.

The details I have about Grandpa's committal and the violent act that preceded it are sketchy and gap-ridden. Over the years, I have assembled in imperfect mosaic of recollection and information, none of it from the people who knew best: Vita and Bruno's children. Bred to the code of *silenzio*—the Sicilian rule that the greatest griefs are silent—my mother and her siblings simply did not talk about what had happened.

What I know is this. Grandpa had been acting strangely for a week or so. He'd always had a temper, but now he was arguing irrationally with Nonna and frightening his grown daughters and sons to the point that they stopped bringing the grandchildren to the house to visit. In the middle of a violent quarrel, he had thrown Nonna to the floor and attacked her with a kitchen knife. She was cut deeply along the neck and left to bleed. I am not clear about what happened next, or where Grandpa went, or which of Nonna's children found her. Whoever it was arrived in time. An ambulance came. Vita survived and, the next day, signed the papers that committed Bruno to the sprawling hospital campus on Norwich's perimeter—Connecticut's largest asylum for the mentally ill.

The Pedaces closed ranks. Just as Bruno had been a leader in the Italian community, several of his sons were now men of influence in town. Strings were pulled, favors called in. A criminal arrest was circumvented because of Bruno's hospitalization and the story was kept out of the newspaper. But news of the assault and Bruno Pedace's sequestration "down below" spread quickly, first through the East Side and then beyond. Cars slowed down as they passed the Pedace house. People pointed and whispered.

I am told my grandfather begged Nonna to visit him, to forgive him, to sign the papers that would set him free. She refused. He sent word that he wanted to see his sons. When they visited, their once-proud father begged them to plead his cause to their mother. They would not. The Italian patriarchs of Norwich, Bruno's brother Frank among them, stopped by at the East Main Street house with bribes of bread and cheese, homemade wine and sausage. They urged Nonna to stop being so stubborn. It was a wife's duty to *serve* her husband, not to *imprison* him, the *paisani* argued. But Nonna would not relent.

The war ended, the housing and baby booms began, and life went on. East Siders turned their attention to other families' trials and scandals; their daughters and sons built ranch houses on the outskirts of town; their grandchildren went off to college. In 1954, Bruno Pedace died quietly and alone at the state hospital, having been edited out of the family stories and banished from scrapbooks and picture frames. On the subject of their father, his children kept their silence and kept their own kids in the dark—"protected" them from the terrible family truth. Only a few of the family patriarch's artifacts survived: his *Il Presidente* sash, a black-and-white photo of him presiding at a Columbus Day parade, and his death certificate, which lists "cause of death" as cancer of the brain.

In 1960, the year I was a fourth-grader, I received my one and only perfect report card. That same day, my friend Herman Ogulnick told me that *his* parents rewarded him for good grades: a quarter for a B, fifty cents for an A, a whole dollar for an A+. I calculated my report card's net worth and ran home to my mother. "Here!" I said, shoving the card at her. She read it with a worried look. "This is really good," she said. "But don't get too smart."

I was disappointed by my mother's reaction to my perfect report—her failure to reach for her pocketbook or even smile. I was confused, too. I had no understanding that she was being Sicilian—trying to shelter me from a world that valued success and good grades but could not necessarily be trusted. If I got too smart for my britches, I might move away, lose my connection to my family. And such a loss would result in my spiritual death.

In 1968, I graduated from the same high school that my parents had. I enrolled at the University of Connecticut, just seventeen miles up the road. At UConn, fellow students would ask me what town I came from. When I told them, they'd say things like "Norwich? That's where my mother used to threaten to drop me off when I was acting goofy." The city's Chamber of Commerce refers to Norwich as "the Rose of New England," but for many in Connecticut, the town and the "crazy hospital" were synonymous.

The four years I spent at UConn were turbulent and seductive ones—an era in which the world *did* call out to join the party, and the fight. The sexual revolution had arrived. Marijuana smoke perfumed the dormitory corridors. The Vietnam War and the civil rights battle intensified, as did protests, love-ins, the cinema, the stage. *Join* the world? Shit, man, we were going to *fix* it! And so I wore tie-dye and love beads, shoulder-length hair, an American flag sewn to the butt of my jeans. But at the end of that wild four-year ride, instead of launching myself into the fray, I took a U-turn, returning to Norwich to teach at the high school from which I'd graduated. I remained there for twenty-five years.

I was a good and dutiful Italian American son. I visited my parents once or twice a week, dropped in on my aunts and uncles, attended family picnics, served as a pallbearer at Pedace family funerals. Along the way, I fell in love with and married a pretty young woman of Italian and Polish blood—a friend from high school whose family, the Pingalores, had lived on the East Side, diagonally across the street from the Pedaces. The first of our sons, a blue-eyed blond, was born in 1981, the centennial year of Nonna's birth. Our second, born four years later, has brown eyes and brown hair—Italian looks.

I was thirty when I wrote my first short story and have been writing fiction now for twenty years. In retrospect, I realize that my work has been, in part, a search for my Italian ancestors. It was unintentional at first, entirely unplanned. But as my commitment to storytelling deepened, I found myself listening hungrily to the stories of elderly aunts and uncles and laboring to place them into a broader context. I read books about the history and geopolitics of Sicily and Southern Italy. I borrowed the old family pictures, fanned them out across my worktable, and stared into the eyes of long-dead relatives. Some seemed to stare back—seemed, in some inexplicable way, to call across the years. And so I began more deliberately to imagine, make assumptions, and tell lies large and small about my relatives' lives. "A fiction writer must be truthful," the writer Grace Paley once said. "A story is a big lie. And in the middle of this big lie, you're telling the truth."

But here's what I had *not* expected: that by building stories from facts and untruths, I would generate the by-product of a better understanding of myself. Of *why* I am the way I am. Why, for instance, when I cook, my impulse is to disobey the recipe. Why I've never lived farther than twenty miles from my hometown. Why, when I'm upset but in the company of others, I smile. Why, when my books climbed the bestseller lists, I kept apologizing. *Don't get too big for your britches,* the Italian in me kept whispering. *Don't get too smart.*

I was just a few months into the writing of my second novel—a story of identical twin brothers, one mentally ill, one not—when I was awakened in the middle of the night by an eerie dream. In the dream, I am walking across a frozen pond when I see, at my feet beneath the ice, Nonna's face. She's alive, looking at me directly, pleadingly. I don't know what she wants. At the time I had this dream, Nonna had been dead for twenty-eight years, Grandpa for almost forty.

The following morning, at my writing table, I lent my dream to my novel's protagonist, Dominick Birdsey, to see what might happen—hoping the dream might help me discover Dominick's unplanned and unplotted story. This triggered something strange and unexpected. Before the morning was over, I was writing in the voice of Dominick's grandfather, a prideful and arrogant Sicilian immigrant. Reason should have told me to stop—to research, plot, plan. But the voice of Domenico Tempesta would not be denied and the writing kept coming fast and furiously. And this was a first for me. Normally, my writing style is slow and laborious: write a sentence, alter it six times, write the next, revise repeatedly, go back and rework the first sentence, the pair. But suddenly, inexplicably, my Bic pen was flying across the page. Domenico kept talking; I kept writing. I'd glance up at the clock, then return to the page. Assuming an hour or so had gone by, I'd look up again. *Four* hours would have passed; I'd notice the pile of pages around me. I'd reenter Domenico's life and time would warp again. When I next looked up, night would have come.

A week later, I had two hundred or so loose-leaf pages on which, front and back, was scrawled in rough form the life story of Domenico

Tempesta, my protagonist's troubled and troublesome forebear. And embedded within the text were clues and leads about the rest of the story—the connection between present and past. I made my way down to Ellis Island and replicated the step-by-step process by which my twenty-year-old grandfather and later his thirteen-year-old wife-to-be were herded, examined, interrogated, and granted entrance to America. I drove through the old East Side neighborhoods and then to the defunct Norwich State Hospital. I parked, walked its ghostly grounds, and wept.

What had happened during that feverish rush of storytelling that resulted in old Domenico's story? Had I dived into the deep waters of the collective unconscious? Unearthed a buried longing to know a withheld grandfather, or, since I couldn't know him, to invent him in the vacuum? Had I been channeled? To this day, it's a mystery to me. But for the next six years' worth of discovering and revising the story of my troubled twins—of learning where my novel was going and what it meant—I had in my possession the story's center, its beating heart: an old Italian immigrant's reflection on his life, his failed attempts to love, to use power ethically, to forget, to forgive.

"You have your lunch yet?" my mother would ask whenever I stopped in after a day of teaching, or with my wife and kids.

"Yeah, Ma, I already ate."

My answer was irrelevant She'd move toward her fridge, wallpapered on three sides with holy pictures, yellowed newspaper clippings of various relatives' victories, and photos of her children, grandchildren, nieces and nephews, their children, their children's children. ("Ma," I'd say. "Put the tape on the *back* of the picture. You ever want to take these off, you'll rip the faces." But it was a moot point. Once your visage had been affixed to the refrigerator gallery, you were there to stay, compliments of Anna and 3-M.) The door would open and out would come a leftover roast, homemade bread and butter pickles, a green salad, a couple of covered saucepans.

"Ma, I said I *ate*."

She'd clunk the pans onto the stove. "I made chicken soup yesterday," she'd tell you. "It's always better the next day. Let me warm up a little of that pasta we had on Sunday. You want a tomato for your salad?" And she'd grab a knife and cut up the tomato, and my dad and I would exchange smiles, and I'd give in and eat. And always, at the end of those drop-in visits, you left with leftovers: the rest of the chicken soup, chocolate chip cookies for the kids, *basilico* from the garden, and Ma's signature pizelles, all of it shrouded in waxed paper, then Reynolds-wrapped, then put in a plastic Stop & Shop bag and tied with string.

Once you got the goodies back home, you nearly had to engage the services of a safecracker.

Often through the years, I heard Ma repeat what she had told me the morning after her own mother died: "When my time comes, I hope I go quick, like Mama did." But she did not get her wish. Her hearing was the first to go and she suffered the kind of deafness that audiologists couldn't help. A restaurant outing became a shouting match. "MA, THE WAITRESS WANTS TO KNOW IF YOU WANT BLEU CHEESE, THOUSAND ISLAND, OR ITALIAN DRESSING ON YOUR SALAD?" you'd bellow, disturbing the peace of other diners.

"No, thanks," she'd answer. "Wine makes me tipsy."

Like her mother, she had a sense of humor and we often joked about these aural mix-ups. But one day when I teased her, she failed to laugh. "People don't realize I'm deaf," she said. "They just think I'm stupid."

Ma was stricken with a heart attack in 1985, after a hot summer afternoon of blueberry picking. I gathered up her grandchildren and photographed them holding placards with giant letters. In the poster I assembled and stuck to her hospital room wall, a parade of her favorite kids spells out "NONNA, GET WELL, SOON!" As she recovered, she fretted about all those blueberries going to waste, all those jars of jam that wouldn't be put up and given away come Christmastime. She had her first stroke in 1994 but bounced back well. A dozen or more TIAs—"ministrokes"—followed. Each one took a little more from her, but it was a subtle game of subtraction. If she said or did something slightly off-kilter, she'd catch herself and chuckle at her mistake. Today, I wonder about the connection between my mother's TIAs and my grandmother's numerous "spells."

Ma's second major stroke cast a long shadow over the Christmas season of 1997. One minute I was braving the crowds at the mall, armed with my sons' wish lists; the next, I was back in the emergency room, holding Ma's hand and listening to my father's account of how he'd awakened that morning to find his befuddled wife of fifty-five years sitting at the side of their bed, attempting to stretch her stockings over her arm instead of her legs. In the ER, Ma's eyes fixed on mine. *What's happened to me?* they seemed to ask, but what came out of her crippled mouth was gibberish.

She was a trouper about rehab. The parade of physical, recreational, and occupational therapists who worked with her learned to shout, rather than speak, their instructions and Ma, in turn, relearned how to walk, talk, and swallow the thickened coffee and pulverized gray food that was now her diet. "TUCK YOUR CHIN DOWN, ANNA! TUCK YOUR CHIN TO YOUR CHEST AND *THEN* SWAL-

LOW!" the rehabilitators would shout, and my mother would make a face, sigh, and do what she was told.

On the morning of our curtailed Christmas of 1997, my wife, our sons, my dad, and I attended church, opened presents, ate our midday holiday meal. While the others cleared the table, I fed turkey, stuffing, mashed potatoes, and peas into the food processor, converting Christmas dinner into the oozy tan mush that Ma could swallow. I felt sorry for myself and my parents, but sorriest for my sons, who had never known the pleasure of an East Side Christmas at Nonna's. We piled into the car and embarked on the one-hour drive to the gloomy rehab center. No one complained, but no one was happy, either. But in the center's dingy rec room, as I spoon-fed my bibbed and diapered mother her Christmas mush, I saw in her eyes not self-pity but pure joy. I followed her gaze to my boys, slumped in their chairs, lost in the brand-new nylon winter jackets that, in a week or so, would memorize their bodies and fit them. Ma opened her mouth for another bite. Even in this bleak and foreign setting, under these impossible circumstances, she had retained her appreciation of food, family, and *festività*.

Over the next three years, Ma's dementia arrived in earnest. One evening, while I was visiting, she insisted that I was her son but that we had had the same father. After a few foolish moments of trying to straighten her out, I gave up, content to be simultaneously myself and her brother, Bruno. Another time, I arrived to find her addressing the envelope of her birthday card for my youngest son, Teddy. "She's been working on that damn thing all afternoon," my exasperated father told me. When at last she handed me the envelope, it was covered front and back with cross-outs, failed tries, and, in the bottom corner, the inscription she'd finally settled on. I brought the card home and handed it to Teddy. "Mr. Peanut?" he asked.

Throughout her long ordeal, Ma remained the dry-eyed Sicilian stoic whose greatest griefs were silent. But on the February evening in 1999, when I told her she'd be leaving her home, she broke out in tears. My father had fallen the month before and broken his hip. There'd been complications, a second emergency surgery; there was a long and difficult convalescence to face. I had just delivered my mother the news that she'd be relocating to St. Joseph's, the Catholic nursing home where my father was recuperating. "I can't go," she kept saying, shaking her head and sobbing. "I'd like to help you out, but I can't leave my house." The home-health-care worker and I exchanged desperate looks. I drove home, paced, waited out the sleepless night. But the next morning, Ma was packed and ready. I walked her slowly to the car, helped her in, buckled her seat belt. She shook her finger in front of my face and spoke in her stroke-broken speech. "All right, I'm going," she said. "But you better bring me my washer and dryer. *And* my refrigerator."

At St. Joseph's, parakeets chirped from patients' rooms, house cats strolled the corridors, and God was everywhere. Ma's room had been decorated with posters and banners, courtesy of the grandkids. Her roommate was her ailing husband, Walter. She was, once again, able to walk to Mass each morning, taking the twenty or thirty assisted steps down the hall to the chapel. And if her appetite was in serious decline, she remained hungry for the Eucharist, the body of Christ, now delivered with a chaser of applesauce for easier swallowing.

Ma's third stroke stole her ability to speak, but not her ability to communicate. When something was funny, she howled, often dropping her teeth. When her family joined her at Mass, she bellowed with delight. When she'd had enough of Walter, she stuck out her tongue. One afternoon I walked into my parents' room and found them pouting at each other. The TV was on: sexy models were prancing in their Victoria's Secret underwear. "What's the matter?" I asked Dad.

"She's mad because I won't change the channel," he said. "I told her, 'You're not disgusted. You're just jealous.'"

My mother's fourth stroke was the catastrophic one that killed her; I last saw her conscious the night before its descent. She was seated in front of her tray, poking a fork at her supper: a half-sandwich, a sad little scoop of pasta salad. She kept trying to tell me something and I kept not getting it.

"Here," I finally said. "Write it down." She made several attempts, worked at her communiqué for ten minutes or more, and then handed me the pad. It was littered with cross-outs and her looping, still-recognizable, backwards-slanting penmanship. *Have you had your supper yet?* it said.

"NO," I shouted. "WHAT ARE YOU COOKING FOR ME, MA?"

She spoke her reply, which was decipherable. "What do you want?"

"PASTA FAZOOLE!" I shouted. The two of us laughed out loud.

Today, the Pequot and Mohegan tribes have risen from the ashes to reclaim the Norwich area. Streams of cars with out-of-state license plates, traveling Route 2 to the mammoth Foxwoods and Mohegan Sun casinos, pass through the diminished and decaying East Side. My sons have only a passing curiosity about their Italian heritage. Their concept of Italian food is the Domino's guy arriving at the doorstep with a boxed pizza in a zippered vinyl bag and a side order of Cheezy Bread. They may or may not ever understand the link between their ethnicity and the way they are.

Most of the East Side's Italian "old-timers" lie buried now in the Catholic cemetery on Boswell Avenue. My mother joined her parents and siblings there in October of 2000. She was the eighth of Vita and Bruno's eleven to be born and is the eighth to have passed. Sometimes when I drive to Norwich to visit her grave, I stop by first at D'Elia's bakery for a Genoa salami grinder. At the graveyard, I weed around Ma's stone, blow away the dirt that's settled in the engraved letters of her name. Then I sit beside her stone and devour my sandwich so that she can see I'm still eating.

Garibaldi M. Lapolla

From *The Grand Gennaro*

Gennaro Accuci had made America, and he was not the type to soft-pedal the expression. He pounded his sturdy small chest with his rough-knuckled small hand, having first thrust his heavy short-stemmed pipe between his teeth, and declared mightily, as best he could between closed lips, "I, I made America, and made it quick." And then, removing his pipe and allowing a slight interval to elapse, he would laugh and exclaim with a toss of the head that made his matted black curls move perceptibly, "And what's more, without kow-towing to anybody, see, no, by Saint Jerome, not a bit. I kept my earrings in my ears where my father pierced them through and I'll keep them unless the President in Washington sends me a telegram."

Seven years before, without so much as a by-your-leave to priest or mayor, to both of whom he owed money, he had slipped out of his mountain village and taken ship at Reggio for New York. He had not even told his plans to his wife. She was left with two boys, ten and two years old, and a girl of three weeks—others had mercifully died in between. She would manage somehow to keep up the farm, already overburdened with mortgages and taxes, and stave off starvation from herself and the children. The night before he had boarded *La Sicilia* he had gone to confession. But before going to confession he had knelt at the feet of Sant' Elena in the old church near the docks and, pounding his breast very hard, but only once, he cried in prayer:

"I am leaving behind those I love, especially my oldest Domenico who should grow up and clear the farm of taxes and what I owe on it.

It's the wars that eat up our substance. And I am leaving behind those to whom I owe money, but they shall never get it back from me. They take advantage of the poor, and they have the soldiers now everywhere and we cannot run off into the mountains with our women and raid the towns and hold the big folk for ransom and so regain what they steal from us. I shall keep it all even when I make it to pay back, for such a day will come in America where I shall pray to you and keep your statue in a niche day and night with a lamp beneath. And especially I pray you, now that you know, to keep my son Domenico and make him strong and capable with his hands to be a help and an honor to me, and to be good to my wife and the other two children, Emilio the black-haired one, and Elena, named after you. And I promise you now to go to confession and lay bare my heart and do proper penance for my misdeeds, but do you speak for me before the Most High, our God and our Savior, and I shall be good in your eyes and pray to you and keep a lamp burning night and day under your statue, Sant' Elena, the blessed one."

Then he rose and looked about the church for the confessional. He had a mind to pull his pipe out of his pocket but contented himself with stroking his mustache with the back of his hand and stumping determinedly into the booth. He smiled as he came out, looked about him with the air of one who has completed a given task to his satisfaction, and thrusting his pipe into his mouth hurried out of the church.

Gennaro had never gone to school—in the village of Capomonte there were no schools—and the village priest had never got round to instructing him either in the writing of his name or the doing of simple sums on paper. Don Vito was much too old and there were so many children and the farms were none too close, and besides, what did it matter? One need not write his name before entering heaven. So Gennaro at the age of thirty-two had not learned to write or read, but he knew what was what and he made sure that his passport was in good order.

———

Once in New York, he had found his way among the Calabrese already settled in Harlem. Most of them had gone into the small business of pushing a cart with an assortment of bells strung aloft and obtaining for nothing or a few pennies old clothes and rags. They lived like gypsies—in the basements of tenement houses disgracefully overcrowded, in old stores, in shacks in the backyards, some in improvised shanties knocked together out of old lumber and tar-paper and erected against the walls of houses adjacent to empty lots. Their dirty, bare-legged children overran the cobbled streets like the goats their families kept; the older ones made a business of petty thieving from the nearby wholesale markets, or collected, like their fathers but in less formal ways, old tins and coppers and lengths of lead-pipes, all of which they sold to junk-shops that lined the avenue.

Zia Nuora was a person of considerable height, with a large bosom and slender legs. Possibly because of her size, she had obtained the title of Zia, or possibly because her rooming house was a haven for lonely men and her manner put them at their ease. The five rooms that ran the length of the old tenement were always crowded, three, four men to a room. They came and went, but the place was always filled. The rooms were furnished no better than Rocco's and Gennaro's—several cots, crude chairs or stools, the image of the Virgin or San Rocco, San Biagio or San Antonio with a lamp burning under it, the trunks with the men's clothing and effects, and nothing else. The floors were old and the boards gaped but they were always scrubbed clean.

The room overlooking the street was a large one and afforded Zia Nuora some opportunity for artistic effects. An old white mantelpiece held a wooden clock that could be heard over the talk and the noise of forks and spoons when the men crowded around the huge table in the center of the room for their one meal of the day. There were half curtains at the windows, and on the walls lithographs of King Humbert and his father, Garibaldi, and an immense one of the battle of Solferino. In the corners stood earthenware spittoons.

She made the beds for all the men, she saw to their simple washing, cooked the meals, swept up, even wrote the letters, for she was one of the few women who had gone to school in the old country. She presided alone at the table, filling up the plates of the hungry boarders without any reservation, expressed genuine offense if they failed to come back for more, joked with them, gave them nicknames and joined even in the coarse fun that went about the table. Her husband worked out of town and came on a visit once a month or sometimes at rarer intervals. The men joked about it with her.

"What an arrangement! If my wife was within reach. . . ."

"Come, there, Luigi the boaster, what would you do? You're here to make money and you'd make it anywhere."

"Hey, man does not live for money alone, not a woman for that matter."

Beyond such bantering they never got.

He was simply and decisively minded upon building up a fortune for the church.

The church might do a great deal of good. It would bring the straying back into the fold. He talked it over with Don Anselmo.

"It's something in here, padre."

He pounded his chest.

"It tells me, 'Gennaro, you build a church. Gennaro, you do the good deeds now. You help your neighbors.'"

Struzzo offered objections to Gennaro's new activities.

"You'll go broke, old man. You're not the kind to do this sort of thing. Only a millionaire . . . like Martin."

Gennaro turned on him quietly, but nevertheless with a pleading look in his eyes.

"What'll I do, Struzzo? Tell me that."

"Rosaria's death has got you now. I know. But time, man, time . . . that'll make it all right."

"Sure, it's got me. Don't I know? It's opened my eyes. It's like I see where I am going, but not altogether, not clear and straight. Who am I, after all? A clod-hopper from the mountains of Calabria! What have I done? Piled up the money, so soaked it into houses, strung up a big business . . . well, what of it? What'll I do now? See what I mean? What's left? So I build the church, and when I build that, there maybe will be nothing left. Maybe then heaven . . . maybe . . ."

He shrugged his shoulders, and pulled long and thoughtfully on his pipe.

"Sure, Struzzo. I look in the glass. I see my face. Wrinkles getting there now, and gray in my hair, and I say 'You're different now . . . your face, just a twist of wrinkles . . . Only your earrings. They don't change. They shine . . . like they shined on your grandfather.'"

"It doesn't make sense to me," Struzzo persisted. "Sounds like you're just milling around trying to find your way out of something."

"But it does make sense. You see, they say to me what you got with all your money, what's the good? And so I answer watch those piles of granite . . . watch them getting piled up . . . high into the air. That'll show them. Gennaro isn't just snuffing around like a pig in the money-heaps . . . doing nothing good."

"Stop talking like a church-going fool."

Gennaro stood up. His face was pale.

"Maybe, Struzzo, I am an old fool. There are fools get wise things done."

"You're in business. There's where you belong."

"And I'll stay in business. But I'll do more than that. Watch. I'll show them. A *caffone* with earrings I may be . . . but I'll show them, I'll show them."

Salvatore La Puma

Wear It in Good Health

He stuffed his pillow under his belly and the pain napped a little, but returning from his failed bathroom visit he groaned, waking his mother, Philomena, who said from the other bedroom, "You sick, Joey?"

"No," he lied.

She came to his room which he shared with his brother, Gino, who was asleep, and when she switched on the lamp she was frightened. Joey was doubled up, and she thought of her Uncle Guy's false heart attack that turned out to be his burst appendix in the autopsy.

"We have Alka-Seltzer?" said Joey.

"It has the aspirin. Not good for the stomach."

"What's better? Hanging camphor balls around my neck?" Joey's voice was serrated with pain.

"It turns away the polio. In the sack I sew myself. I get the Brioschi. For eating too much. Maybe it helps."

No one should be awake at four in the morning, thought Joey, least of all his mother, who sewed little girl's dresses for fifty cents each in the steamy and dusty factory across the street on 18th Avenue. After downing the foamy remedy, he yawned and, to ease his conscience if not his cramp, pretended to feel better, and convinced her to go back to bed.

When her husband, Enrico, left for work that next morning in 1943, Philomena went down to call Dr. Pilo from the corner pharmacy since they had no phone of their own. In the meantime Joey went to the bathroom to light a cigarette as a possible cure, but it didn't help. To ventilate the smoke, he moved the top and bottom halves of the obscure glass window to the middle, giving him a glimpse of the second-story tiny court on which opened the bathroom and kitchen windows of the four apartments. Seeing nothing of interest out the window, Joey, sixteen, stood in his bare feet on the toilet seat cover to look again at the top this time. In the bathroom diagonally across the court, its window opened from the top, was Mrs. Pita, just recently married. She was washing with her cloth the back of her neck under her long dark hair, the dark hair under her arms, and her small pointed breasts. That was the limit of Joey's view. In those minutes he completely forgot that he was sick. Then he heard his mother coming upstairs.

He went back to his room to be sick again, wondering if the pain were self-induced to avoid his physics final. Up to now his scores were nearly perfect, and he might be a physicist himself someday, but the final exam, which made up a third of his grade, scared him to death. Maybe he wasn't as good as he hoped. He got in bed again to worry about that.

"The doctor's at the hospital," said Philomena. Coming in behind her was another woman, old, narrow, and dried up like a pepperoni in her red dress. Joey flinched at her red dress, since most Sicilian women favored black and other serious colors. Only the young ones at weddings advertised themselves in rose and lilac to attract the bees to the flowers. "Joey, this is Signora Strega. I call her. So we could do something. Before the doctor comes."

"Who's she?"

"When you had the tapeworm. You don't remember? She put the garlic on your belly. Under the teacup. Then it comes out," said his mother.

"That's baloney, Ma. You're smart. You don't believe in hocus-pocus. Magic doesn't work."

"Be quiet now, Joey. And listen. And lie down."

"I have to take a leak."

"Later. And watch your tongue."

The witch bared Joey's belly while keeping his modesty. With two stalks of celery from her brown paper bag, she constructed a flat cross, locating its center on his belly button. "Soon you feel better," said her wrinkled mouth. "No speak. And not your mother. Only me."

Joey pleaded with his eyes for his mother to release him from this witchcraft. Philomena was sitting on his brother's now vacated bed, and wasn't in charge for the first time in her life. "This lady's doing something funny here," he said.

Signora Strega, in red down to her stockings and shoes, with long ears that seemed to be melting on her head, sat in the chair and said, "*Silènzio,*" and sprinkled on his chest and belly the dry herb whose smell Joey recognized as basil for tomato sauce.

"I feel better," he said, faking.

"Go away, pain. Go away, devil. Go away, sickness," said Signora Strega, her tattered eyes closed, her head bent as if in her cupped hands the universe waited to obey her commands "Joey, be strong, be healthy, be a fine boy. *È eccellente. È stupendo. È magnifico.*"

The flat of her hand touched his chest, then his belly, and then under his pajamas his thighs, just brushing by his penis, which he was afraid she might grab and put in her purse. Then her voice dropped to husky mutterings that Joey couldn't make out, and he listened instead to the buses clearing their throats outside his window, and to the honking cars, and he thought the test would have been easier to endure than this crap.

"True? You feel better?" said Philomena, unable to restrain herself.

The pain really was going away. Joey refused to believe that the witch had anything to do with it. Still, he forced himself to be truthful for his mother's sake. "Yes. I feel better."

"Signora Strega is a saint," said his mother.

"It ain't her," said Joey. "Sooner or later a bellyache gets better."

"Now I make the circles," said the witch. "One for each year. When I make the number sixteen, you get up. Then no more pain. Now I make the number one." She joined her thumbs and her palms floated in a tiny circle over his belly. Then her hands flew in enlarging circles until the last circle sailed on the waves of his hair, skipped on the windowsill, tickled his toes, and brushed at the tip of Philomena's strong nose.

Whether it was because Signora Strega commanded him to do it or whether he just wanted to be rid of her, Joey himself wasn't sure as he sat up in bed. Then he went to his chest of drawers for clean underwear and socks.

"Now you kiss the signora," said his mother.

"Do I have to?"

"You must."

The old woman's chin was growing a few black hairs, but, anyway, he kissed her red-painted cheek smelling like dried flowers. To swap what he thought was her bitter taste for a sweet taste, he kissed his mother's cheek too. Then he went to dress in the bathroom, smoking another cigarette stolen earlier from his father's pack. By then Mrs. Pita was gone from her sink.

A few streets away Joey's grandmother, Lillian, in her robe and slippers, was indecisively leaving her bedroom. Finally she descended the narrow stairs in her old house to prepare the breakfast tray quickly so as to limit her minutes away from her ailing husband. In that brief time she thought his thoughts, as if two minds became one from lying together so long in the same bed, and his thoughts chilled her bones. The knife in her hand, as she sliced her own baked bread, was the devil inviting her on a journey, but at her age, and forever toughened by steerage, she cursed the blade and, as if with disrespect, she put the knife away uncleaned.

In their bed upstairs Giuseppe Irprino was getting ready to die. Not that he felt sick enough to die. His pneumonia affected him only with high temperatures and slightly diminished breathing, but otherwise he wasn't uncomfortable. Up to this point he had been as durable as the boat hulls he built in the Brooklyn Navy Yard, of wood in his early years, and then of steel plates as strength took the place of grace. Never seriously ill before, he saw himself now as a burden for his young man within as well as for his off-center leathery old body, and without too much regret he looked forward to a very long night's sleep.

At eighty-eight Giuseppe was weary from doing the same things over again, weary from the same quarrels of his children with their spouses and their children, weary from the same summer heat and the same winter snow, and weary from eating and eliminating.

His one regret would be to leave Lillian. He would miss her, and would tell her that when she came back with his morning coffee. He would also say that his wine press was to go to his namesake, Joey Irprino. His grandson had cranked down the press the last few years when they made muscatel together and, unspokenly, they came to know each other.

They were men from different centuries, different countries and different educations, one exhausted and the other insatiable, but they met at the midpoint between them as if they were one and the same man, past, present, and future. He would miss Joey too, and Joey would mourn and forget him, as young people can forget even their own faces and be surprised by the mirror. But would Lillian forget? Could he leave her? Was it fair?

Then the hand of God reached up from his stomach to squeeze his chest, not with force nor malice, unsuitable to Him, but in the way Lillian could suddenly take his hand as she denied by her grip that they could ever part. And now, without thinking to call her, he did. "Lillian. Lillian."

His voice lacked urgency, but in the kitchen the cup fell from her hand as she grabbed her robe's skirt to drive her knobby legs up to their bedroom. There she threw off her clothes, and in bed took her husband in her wrinkled arms, and his breath rose like their canary to the top of the cage, and then dropped as if to the paper, and rose again.

Worrying that her embrace restricted his breathing, she backed off, but then his face soured, so she held him again. He knew she was holding him, and he had time only to say her name once more, and then he was dead.

Giuseppe was sorry he was dead. Lillian was still holding him, but he couldn't feel her nakedness now, he couldn't feel anything, yet he seemed to know everything there was to know. He knew that God played the mandolin, that Mary was a prude, that tomato sauce in heaven was cooked without garlic, and though the angels had dimples and nice legs they wouldn't dance with an old Sicilian. He wanted his old wife again, having lived with her for so long it was as if they were born on the same day. He saw in her face now all her ages from her birth to this minute, and he was lonely for her even though he was allowed to remain with her now. And Lillian held him all that day until evening when Joey's father came to visit *his* father. And then Enrico had to separate his parents, had to separate the living from the dead.

Joey thought he could buy his own suit for the funeral. "I wouldn't pick out purple," he said to his mother.

"But who sees it fits? It looks good? The salesman? You think he says the truth? Are you his son? He doesn't care if you go out in the laundry bag," said Philomena.

So the next day Joey and his mother hurried to the stores on 86th Street while his grandfather was laid out on the marble slab and embalmed, bathed, shaved, and dressed, to be returned in his mahogany casket to the parlor in his house for the next three days.

"Not a heavy one this time," said Joey, remembering that his confirmation suit was advertised never to wear out.

"We see," said his mother.

"How about Steubbin's?" he said.

"We look. But I don't like them. They don't give you a bargain."

"They have fixed prices, Ma. Like the A&P."

"They should want my business," she said.

"Suppose I also get a sports jacket? Leone has a sports jacket. We're going to New York for jobs in the summer. We don't want to look like hoods from Bensonhurst."

"We don't show off. Be like your father."

The salesman said, "You have broad shoulders. Try this on for size."

"Only black," said Philomena.

"We have a worsted navy in single-breasted."

"I don't like it," she said.

"It's almost black," said Joey.

"What size is the waist?" said Philomena.

"Thirty-two," said the salesman.

"You want to take in two and a half inches? Kill the whole shape?"

"We'll have the tailor take a look," he said.

"I don't need your tailor. I sew myself."

"I have a nice plaid," said the salesman, as they were going out, but they crossed the street to Kaufman's.

Philomena went to the rack herself and thumbed through the suits and found a black one. She held it up for Joey to look at, but he just dropped in the chair as if the fight that hadn't been fought was already lost.

"Mrs. Irprino," said Mr. Kaufman.

"You sold us the suit for my husband. But we paid too much."

"Even you should go downtown to Abraham & Straus you won't find a better bargain than here."

"We see. This suit. How much?"

"Double-breasted isn't for him. He's a young man. And not so tall. You have to keep up with the times. In black he'll be a gangster."

"The men in my family wear black," said Philomena. "Double-breasted."

"You can have it. But first, let me try something. Just see this. What I'm doing." Mr. Kaufman whipped out a jacket, dark blue and single-breasted, and put it on Joey's back. "It was made just for you." Before allowing for contradictions from anyone, or allowing Joey to see himself in the mirror, he danced Joey by his shoulders to his mother, and she was the first to say whether she liked it.

"How much is it?" she said.

"Twenty-three ninety-five."

"It's made out of gold?"

"One hundred percent virgin wool," he said, now dancing Joey to the mirror. "Some handsome devil. God should have mercy on the girls when they see you in this suit."

"It's a little loose," said Joey, liking Mr. Kaufman even though he was pushy, since he was on his side.

"Go put on the pants," said Mr. Kaufman.

When Joey returned, the tailor was waiting with his chalk and pincushion. "You have the face that could be Jewish," he said. The small tailor was like an old baby, hairless and a little paunchy.

"Can you tighten it here?" said Joey.

"So see. I'll mark it with the chalk. To move the buttons. Then you'll be a darling boy. Your mother should give you such a hug. Now let me see the pants. You should do me the favor. Step on the stool. So I should see the cuffs. How they look. Since I'm not such a big person either. You know what I do? Look. No cuffs. They make you shorter. It's better not to have them. For me. One way or the other. It doesn't matter."

"Okay. No cuffs," said Joey.

"He's not short," said his mother. "He should have the cuffs. Like his father."

When Joey thought it was agreed that this was his suit, that it fit good, and that his mother had retreated from her objection to the color, she went to the rack again and took out another suit, black, but this time single-breasted.

"It's reprocessed wool," said Mr. Kaufman. "That's why it's a few dollars less. With the war on. You don't find too much virgin wool. It goes in the Army."

"You should make a better deal, Mr. Kaufman."

"So what's a better deal?" he said.

Now Joey understood the real reason his mother was here: to do the bargaining. She was never satisfied until the price came down. Now Mr. Kaufman looked at the label inside the jacket which was still on Joey's back, and then at the ticket on its sleeve.

"So five months. We have this suit in stock. So we bought it a little cheaper. So I'll give you the benefit. I'll give it to you the same price. As the reprocessed wool. Twenty-one ninety-five. You want a bargain? So that's a bargain."

"It's made cheap," said Philomena, pushing and pulling the fabric so that Joey inside felt like kneaded dough, shaking her head over the lining, breaking off a few threads hanging from the seams, and frowning in despair over the mess she inferred the jacket was in.

"It's a beautiful piece of goods," said Mr. Kaufman.

"Joey, take it off. We go someplace else. Down the street. To what's his name? H&M. Now *they* have suits. I know Hyman there."

Joey whispered in his mother's ear, "I'll pay the two extra dollars myself."

"It's the point," she said. "We should get our money's worth. It wouldn't be fair to pay his price. Mr. Kaufman expects it. It makes him happy to bargain."

"My last offer," he said. "I don't know why I'm doing it. Please, you shouldn't tell my partner. Give me $20. Take the suit."

"It's still too much, Mr. Kaufman." Now she pointed her finger at Joey. "I said take off the suit."

"You're making a mistake," said Mr. Kaufman. "It's made for your boy. Makes him look like a mensch, a man, God bless him. He should have lots of sons."

When Joey came out of the dressing room, two stone faces were waiting.

"Put it aside," she said. "Maybe we come back. If we don't find something. And thank you very much." Then she was walking to the door and Joey followed like an unwilling donkey and Mr. Kaufman followed him.

When she crossed the threshold, Mr. Kaufman, seemingly going down for the third time and short of breath, said, "So what do you think you should pay?"

"I give you $18. The waist fits. So you save on the alterations."

Mr. Kaufman took his pencil from his inside pocket and did math on the back of his business card while Philomena looked calmly at other suits on display, and then she brushed nonexisitent dandruff from Joey's collar.

"So what's what?" she said, acting exhausted.

"The best I could do. This is my last price. If you don't want it, that's fine. Go to H&M. It's nineteen-fifty."

"Go write it up," said Philomena. "But absolutely, we must have it tonight. My father-in-law's coming home from the funeral parlor. Joey has to see him. He has to dress nice."

"Boy, I really want that suit," said Joey, relieved the bargaining was over.

"You should wear it in good health," said his mother, touching his face.

Joey was sick of dead people and had secretly made a promise to himself not to look another one in the face again, but his grandfather had been kind so he had to break his promise. All the other dead bodies had also been dressed up in their caskets in their parlors—his mother's father, two uncles, one aunt, a great-uncle, the landlord, his father's boss, his own friend, Frankie, who was killed on his motorcycle, three other related people he didn't know, and the first one, his playmate and cousin, Marguerite, with golden curls like Shirley Temple's, who at seven was laid out in her communion dress and looked like a plaster doll in her white box lined with white silk.

When he was going up the outside stairs he heard his aunts, and they made him pale and gave him gooseflesh. In the parlor his aunts, his grandmother, and his girl cousins over sixteen were all in black dresses, and the older women were screaming and throwing themselves on the body in the casket to hug the dead man who ignored them all. That was the way his grandfather was, he was moved only by what was inside of him, not by what others tried to heap on him.

The air was sweet from the carnations, roses, and gardenias in the shapes of crosses, hearts, and wreaths, all in a semicircle around the casket, which was on the stand against one wall. And the candle in the red glass in the man-size brass candlestick burned at the head of the casket as the prayer to the God who was getting back one worn-out soul and a handful of dust.

Giuseppe's leathery hands were folded over rosary beads, which hadn't happened when he was alive, since his religion at his nearly antique age had come down to his wife. He had always loved her, he told Joey that once, but had neglected her when there were other things to do—his work, his friends, his children, his wine, his garden, and his money—but then none of that mattered, and his wife, who was always there and had pained him in only the smallest ways, and had endured for him like the sun, was the one person he hadn't tired of, and now her grief rattled the walls and stung Joey's ears.

Since Joey's family was the last to arrive, his mother took her turn at throwing herself on the body in the casket to kiss Giuseppe's face, and the casket wobbled, so two uncles went to steady it. Then Joey's father said to him, "You the first son. So go to your mother. Don't cry." For a moment Joey wondered who was going to help him since his mother's screaming froze his soul, but his father's hand on his shoulder unfroze it. The women were doing the mourning for everyone—themselves, the men, not allowed to cry, the children, and even for their dead ancestors who would grieve for Giuseppe if they themselves were still alive. In the far corner was his grandfather's mongrel dog, Garibaldi, who understood only Sicilian and thought English was cat talk, and he was whimpering for himself.

With his aunts behind him, sobbing into the hollow of oblivion that had won out over life again, Joey, in his navy blue suit, went to take his turn at the bier, kneeling to say his *arrivederci* to his grandfather. The corpse didn't scare Joey since it wasn't dangerous or evil or smelly, but was still and harmless. It was the same old man for whom tools performed, to whom women spoke with courtesy, and who could keep quiet when talking was noise.

Taught the physical laws of the universe, Joey wanted to believe now that in death the conservation of energy principle might also apply, as it did when trees became coal and coal turned into heat and heat was absorbed by other living things. Then his grandfather might be changed from an old Sicilian into bare earth, and earth into a tree, not just his molecules but also his spirit.

He was allowed to be alone at the bier with Giuseppe at this moment, while his many cousins were whispering and fidgeting and the uncles in their suits were standing along the sides of the parlor like silent shadows, perhaps preparing for the day when each would lie quietly in his own ruffled casket. So Joey's first words were prayers to speed his grandfather's soul to its heavenly reward, as always were said at the bier, but Our Fathers were insufficient now. Something more should be required of him in gratitude for his name, for the shared secrets of wine making, and for the press itself, his first grown-up possession.

Even his thoughts seemed inadequate, and because he had learned the art of swallowing his own tears before they could fall, crying too was a gift he couldn't give. Anyway, how did a guy speak to his dead grandfather? As though he could answer back? As though he were just a slain marionette up on its strings again in another performance?

"I'll go to the bay to catch your crabs," said Joey, inaudibly. "But I don't remember when to bottle the wine. You should've written it down. Or I should've. But you didn't say you were going. It's what good-byes are for. But I guess you had your reasons."

The room was suffocating from the closeness and heat, noises and scents, from too many sources, bodies and souls, flowers and candles, clothing and chairs. The light flickered unsurely, and the sunlight was unwelcome and held back by heavy drapes. In that cauldron, Joey could believe that his grandfather seemed to stir in his casket, as if the old man were amused at all the fuss, or had an itch he couldn't scratch with women watching.

Joey studied the powdered face, rouged cheeks, and blue lips and was convinced his grandfather's wicked smile was just under his skin, as when he had taken from his backyard coop a noisy rooster and twisted its neck in his bony hands for a Sunday dinner, and said that a man had to do hard things, had to kill the chicken to have its meat on the table. While Joey himself never expected to wring a chicken's neck with his own bare hands, he understood the lesson, but didn't know in what way he'd ever use it, and hoped that being a man was easier than that. But now his grandfather didn't speak, and soon Joey would have to surrender his place to his brother, Gino.

Finding no solace in religion in which he half-believed, nor in science which he loved, he could kneel there and generously despise death for its thievery. Then, hearing his father's throat cleared at the back of the room, perhaps as a signal, he stood up for the final kiss that he was required to give, placing it on the cold, smooth forehead that could have been a tin can.

Before turning away, Joey impulsively joined his two hands at the thumbs. He made the smallest circle over his grandfather's middle, and then successively wider circles over the body, until the last circle crossed the dead man's corrugated brow, and on the other end, his shined black shoes. In that room where hysteria was the air they all breathed, no one thought him any crazier than the others. Joey wasn't surprised, after the last circle, that his grandfather's soul was climbing out of the casket. His soul was clearly visible to Joey, who could see in his mind even such principles of physics as electromagnetism. Then grandfather and grandson were going out of the room together, side by side, one bent, the other with his ear cocked. Mackerel heads and beef trimmings would catch the most blue crabs in the square wire traps dropped in Gravesend Bay, the old man was saying, and at their heels was Garibaldi.

First Cousins

Aunt Gabriella was taken away in a straitjacket. She was taken to the madhouse. It was what my mother called it then. It was actually Kings County Hospital. Left behind were Uncle Julian and three kids. Their eldest kid had the same name as I did—Philip—both of us named after our grandfather. To tell us apart, relatives knew him as Phil the First, and me as Phil the Second. After Phil the First came Ada, his sister, then Eddie, the youngest. Ada had the face of the angel in the big oil painting in St. Finbar's. She had big brown eyes and long wavy chestnut hair. Ada, at thirteen, before going to school in the morning, and after school in the afternoon, then became a child-mother to Phil the First and to Eddie, until Uncle Julian came home at night from work. I was twelve then and held hands with Ada in the movies, and kissed her in the park.

When it seemed one afternoon there was nothing more for us to talk about, we closed the brocade drapes in the parlor and took off all our clothes. Our webs of immature pubic hair like cobwebs in the neglected parlor were stared at by both of us. Then we embraced. Our clothes, after a few minutes, were put on again. Nothing else happened. Later, after my wild women outside army posts, after my daring women at universities, after two broken marriages, after two broken live-ins, I still remembered myself at twelve with Ada at thirteen when in her parlor nothing much happened. A simple love hadn't asked for a thing. Ada grew into a beauty, and over her one guy tried to hang himself, and another tried to stab her. The guy with the knife was caught by other guys on her street who felt protective of her and they stabbed that guy with his own knife.

Ada, at thirteen, was also a whiz in math and grammar. So I asked her father if she could tutor me in math and grammar—to establish an acceptable reason to see her at her house. Four times a week we met at her house, and most days we also met after school and sometimes on secret dates. Her grammar skills were inherited, my mother said, from her crazy mother, who wrote beautiful poetry in college. And her A's in algebra were inherited from her father, an accountant at a local bank.

Unlike most men in our neighborhood, Uncle Julian didn't do backbreaking physical work. The men in our neighborhood early in life were usually worn down by their work. And Uncle Julian early in life was also worn down, not by his work, but by the absence of his wife from his bed and their home.

It was said of the Italian men of Bensonhurst, and of Little Italy too, that they were the builders of New York's skyscrapers. They were the masons, bricklayers, sheetmetal workers, electricians, plasterers, plumbers, carpenters, and contractors. And took satisfaction from that. Uncle Julian, however, had a degree. And it didn't worry him that he did paperwork instead like some of the women. And when he then became a mother hen to his motherless kids, that didn't worry him either. And it didn't worry him when at night without his wife beside him in bed he even wept like a woman. How he wept soon became known, from Ada to me, from me to my father. When Uncle Julian went to Kings County Hospital to visit his wife in a mental ward, he also smuggled in their kids to be held in the crazy woman's arms. The kids brought home-cooked dishes, new dresses Ada shopped for, and novels Uncle Julian knew she'd like. A year later Aunt Gabriella seemed much improved. So he convinced her doctor to let her out. It would soon be summer and their kids needed to be with their mother when they were home from school.

Aunt Gabriella and my own mother had gone to St. Joseph's College in Brooklyn at a time most of the other girls there were Irish. My aunt and mother were from the same neighborhood, were Italian, and soon became best friends. It was then my mother told her brother Julian how beautiful and bright Gabriella was, and introduced them. It was love at first sight. But he had to promise, before he could marry her, that their kids would go to parochial schools. My mother said that her brother to marry Gabriella then would have promised even murder.

Most Bensonhurst Italians, despite the urging of priests, didn't send their kids to parochial schools like the Irish did. Italians worried that their boys might lose their balls. And their girls might enter a convent and lose their lives. So most Italian kids were sent instead to public schools. For the neighborhood women, Mass on Sunday mornings was often religion enough. And for the men, even Mass on Sunday mornings was too much, and was generally avoided altogether. But that summer my mother went to St. Finbar's Church a few times a week to pray for Gabriella to be restored in all her splendor to Julian and their children. If she had to be taken back to the madhouse, if she couldn't stay there at home where she was loved and wanted, then a horrible tragedy, my mother worried, awaited the entire family.

My own family lived a few blocks away. But I was more often to be found at their house. And I was there the afternoon in June when she came home from the hospital.

"I think, Phil the Second, you're possibly in love with my Ada," Aunt Gabriella said, matter-of-factly, to me the first day she was home. For a year she hadn't seen us together. For the last twenty minutes she had watched us in their backyard poring over a magazine. Then we came inside for lemonade. "It's all right," my aunt said to us, and fondly patted our faces, while mine, I was sure, turned Irish white. "Up to a point it's all right. But you are first cousins, so it shouldn't ever become serious. I'm sure you understand."

I didn't at the time understand. The truth about my feelings for Ada—feelings I'd deny to any adult—spoken openly by her mother took my speech away. So I just nodded as if I did understand. But Ada was angry with her mother. Perhaps Ada, too, had feelings she'd deny to any adult. "Mother, he isn't in love with me," she blurted out. "I help him with grammar, and he helps me with history. How would you know anyway? You've been in the crazy house."

Aunt Gabriella wept like the mother she was. And Ada, so self-contained during the year she'd behaved like a mother, also wept like the girl she was. They held each other and wept for a loss I had only a vague idea about. So I got out of there. And that afternoon our innocent kisses came to an abrupt end. But for years in my imagination I still kissed her.

That summer Aunt Gabriella at home was doing just fine. She was no crazier than other mothers with mischievous young children underfoot all day. Then Uncle Julian lost his job due to hard times in general, and when he wasn't looking for work, he stayed home to enjoy the presence of his wife in their home, and they were a happy family. A nighttime job as a bartender at the 19th Hole Bar then became available, the only job he could find quickly in the neighborhood to be close to home if needed. So he took the job, with his wife at home to mind their sleeping kids at night. In college his good tenor voice, and long fingers at the keyboard, earned him applause and party invitations. But he threw over his show-business ambitions as unsuitable for a family man, which he wanted to be. Those talents again came in handy as he now played the piano and sang for half-soused bar patrons who often overappreciated his performance. He was really now pretty awful. But he again earned enough to buy groceries and pay the mortgage.

One night while Uncle Julian was at work, Aunt Gabriella tried to burn the house down. Smoke reached Ada's alert little nose, and she ran out of her room and drove her brothers out of their room and phoned the fire department. But she couldn't convince her mother to leave the parlor, where the drapes and velvet sofa smoldered without flaring up. Sirens shook up the neighborhood. Neighbors poured out of their houses to witness, first, the arrival of two red fire trucks and the fire captain's sedan, then two burly firemen carrying Aunt Gabriella out of the house between them in a saddle under her made by their joined hands.

In the years that followed, Aunt Gabriella often came home from the hospital on Uncle Julian's arm for a weekend, a birthday party, or a holiday. In still later years, her children also brought her to their own homes, where she got to know her grandchildren. Her visits were usually short visits. Long visits always confirmed that she had to live out her life in a mental ward.

When Phil the First, Ada, and Eddie were still young, my mother would offer a hand in their household. And Julian would accept a hand if it wasn't too much of a hand. If it was too much, as when Mom wanted to wash all their windows, her brother would say, "Gabriella wouldn't like another woman cleaning her house. Any day now, she'll be coming home."

My mother thought that her brother's broken heart was at least partly her fault because she had made the match. That mistake could be corrected, she thought, as she tried to engineer other matches between Uncle Julian and other good and attractive women. The other women, he agreed, were indeed good and attractive. But he didn't want them. He wanted Gabriella. Those women hoped to have in their own lives a man so devoted as he was to one woman alone. Of course, if he chose one of them, that same woman wouldn't any longer consider him so desirable as a one-woman man. Uncle Julian, my father said, was a little crazy himself, because he was so devoted to his wife, even though she was locked away and couldn't give him any pleasure.

After an interval of about two years, after we found others in high school to kiss, Ada and I became friends again. And again I went to her house, to talk with Phil the First about Dodger games, but really to see Ada, to have a word or two with her. Not for long would she linger with me, and yet, during our brief exchanges, when I ached before her beauty, the core of me broken into little pieces, we both were carried away by memories of earlier days. And I went away filled up for days, until I was sweaty to see her again, and had to go back again. It was impossible to let go of her. And sometimes when I first arrived or when I was about to leave, Ada took my hand and we held hands. It wasn't much, yet it was as exciting as the adult love I made in my senior year with another girl in her basement while her mother did the weekly food shopping.

After Brooklyn College, Kathy Kelly was the girl I married. A High Mass and a big wedding were attended by hundreds of our relatives and friends, and even Aunt Gabriella came out of the hospital on Uncle Julian's arm. While she danced at the reception with her son Phil the First, I said to Uncle Julian, "She's more beautiful than ever. Is she getting any better?"

"Much, much better. She asked me to have the house painted, inside and outside, so everything will be fresh, so we'll begin fresh again." He paused to watch his wife on the dance floor. "Monday morning I'm going to see her doctor. And Monday morning the painters are coming."

"How long," I said, "has she been in there?"

"Nine years," he said.

"And," I said, "you still love her?"

"Still do," he said. "She's my wife."

I then looked over at Kathy as she waved to me from the dance floor where my father waltzed her around. Her Irish nose was so deliciously pert, her usually white cheeks were so radiant. Then I caught sight of Ada in a clutch of women relatives, and went to her and said, "How about a dance with the bridegroom, cousin?"

"I believed," she said, coming into my arms, "You'd never marry anyone but me."

"You're kidding," I said.

"Of course I am," she said. "Kathy's lovely."

Kathy was a year behind me at Brooklyn College and so graduated a year after we were married when we were already at each other's throat. It turned out we were both more in love with our studies than with each other. At a movie, in our joined hands there wasn't enough heat to suggest we had much passion for each other either. Regardless of my wish to have a child, Kathy, instead, enrolled in graduate studies at NYU, where I was too. She declared that she really didn't want to be a mother, that she, too, wanted to be a historian. Soon after, it was over for good.

Two years later I married Helen Kirschman. At the beginning it was understood that we both wanted a passel of kids. It wasn't understood by me, however, that she wanted them to be raised as Jews, that kids born of a Jewish mother and a Gentile father were considered by Jews to be Jews (while kids born of a Gentile mother and a Jewish father weren't Jews). The news that my child would be a Jew was presented to me together with the news of her pregnancy when Helen greeted me one evening with a candlelight supper. At that time I flat out didn't believe in the existence of God, and worse yet, the history of oppression all religions were guilty of made me decide that my kid wouldn't be a Jew, a Catholic, or a Muslim. He or she could choose later what, if anything, to be. So we, too, were at each other's throat for what we wanted differently. Not surprisingly, I suppose, as we sometimes slapped and kicked each other, and drank too much, and threw things, Helen miscarried. And I much later believed the universe and life were pointless without a God, so God had to exist, but God wasn't a Jew, a Catholic, or a Muslim, and didn't go to church either.

Stella, my present wife, was a former university student of mine. We have a boy eight, and a girl five, and they find their mother waiting for them at home in the afternoon after school. Mornings Stella is an editor at our university press. And evenings she helps me with grammar for my third book, about the 1861 Unification of Italy. We both now have what we want: some work for her, children for us, and teaching for me. We have, I think, a marriage which might last.

Two years ago in May my father died unexpectedly. "So he wouldn't," my mother said, "have to go with me to Denmark." We were at the funeral parlor, and instead of mourning, Mom was furious that Pop had died. "Even after he bought the tickets," she said, "I knew that somehow, at the last minute, he'd get out of it."

Pop had once loved to travel with Mom. They had visited much of Western Europe. This trip was to be to the Scandinavian countries, where they hadn't yet been, where Mom, oblivious of Pop's protest that he no longer wanted to travel, insisted was where they had to travel. In his later years, Pop had grown weary of travel, and he was done with it. He was done with Mom too, but not in any formal way, just done with her without a fuss, while he still went to bed with her every night. In his last years he wasn't really withdrawn if ignored were those contemplative silences, his thoughts pulling at a knotty problem, before he would come out of himself to laugh out loud when a contemporary of his died unexpectedly. "You know what he wanted to do all his life," Pop would say, "and never even tried to do? He wanted to go skiing once." Or "He wanted to have a beautiful young woman once." Or "He wanted to build a barbecue in his back yard." Pop remembered the unfulfilled aspirations of others and thought it was a big joke that life played on all of us, that the small things that make a life always remained unfinished.

At the funeral parlor Uncle Julian said, "Your Aunt Gabriella, she's come home now, at last."

"That's wonderful," I said.

"Her health isn't so good, but those doctors, they don't know anything," he said. "I told them, I'll take care of her myself, and she'll get better."

"I'm sure she will," I said.

"This morning, when I brushed her hair," Uncle Julian said, "you should've seen how it shined up."

"Say hello to her for me," I said.

"I will," he said. "She makes these long lists for me." He took out and studied a sheet of yellow paper. "I can certainly buy some of these things."

Ada came by and offered her condolences to my mother, then to me. I noticed that her gold wedding band wasn't on her left hand now, as she took my hand. She spoke to me softly. But her presence confused me, so I couldn't focus on what she was saying. Then she drew me to her, so I got up and went with her, the heat in her hand passing into my hand. She led me out of the room and down a hallway, unsure herself where we were going, but certain that she wanted a private place. The first two doors she tried were locked. The third opened into the display room of empty caskets with their lids propped open and their silk interiors covered by transparent plastic to keep the dust off. Ada closed the door. Her arms went around me. My arms then went around her too. We kissed long and deep, our bodies straining to connect. But we were fully dressed and the fabric between us was like the moral stricture which would always be between us.

Maria Laurino

From *Words*

All the pieces of my life considered to be "Italian"—the food, the dialect, the dark hair—I kept distinct from the American side, forgetting about the hyphen, about that in-between place where a new culture takes form.

I had typed a list of dialect words for the professor, and I cautiously began with my favorite.

Stunade, I wrote, a bad transcription because the sound is closer to *stunod*.

He stared at the word, looking quizzical.

Stew-nod, I pronounced carefully, allowing him to examine what my American tongue had done to his dialect.

"*Si, Si, Si,*" he responded. "*Stonato. Fuori da testa.*"

"Yes!" I restrained myself from pounding the desk in my enthusiasm. I had found a wizard who made my words real.

Out of one's mind. In dialect, *stonato* means a person who can't understand anything because he is senile or doddering, and is used to describe anyone who acts a little out of it. In Tuscan or standard Italian, the professor explained, the word *stonato* exists, but its meaning changes. *Stonato* is a person who sings off-key, the opposite of *intonato.*

As the intimacies of language bridged the gap between native and foreigner, professor and student, De Blasi became my linguistic confidant. I handed him my list of household dialect words and he began to decipher my connections to the south of Italy. I stated each word, and he repeated it, sometimes several times, listening to the sound, shifting the stress until he was able to recognize its source in the original dialect of my grandparents.

I learned that one reason why my northern friends didn't understand my southern dialect is that many of these words, which all have Latin roots, exist in standard Italian but without the perjorative connotations found in the south. Mentioning a word like *stunod* to my Roman friends, I was asking them to find the link between a person who is mentally confused and one who sings badly. The same problem exists with *citrulo* (pronounced "chee-trool-oh"), southern dialect for the standard Italian *cetriolo,* cucumber. In the north, the word has no metaphorical meaning, but in the south, where its impossible to separate the people from the land they cultivate, *citrulo* describes a person whose brain is as fleshy and watery as a cucumber.

The Italian-American version of this southern word, in which the *ci* sound changes to a soft *g,* is *gedrool* (as in my friend's childhood game "Follow the big *gedrool,*" or "Follow the big cucumber head"). Anyone who has ever listened to that 1950s Anglo-Saxon paean to Italian-American culture, "Mambo Italiano," which continually creeps into contemporary movie sound tracks, would have encountered the *gedrool.* As Rosemary Clooney swooned in her fake Italian-American accent: "Hey *gedrool,* you donnuh have to go to school. / Just make it with a big bambino. It's like a vino / Kid you're good-ah lookin. But you donnuh know what's cookin."

Other vegetable words, like deep purple eggplant, in dialect *mulignan',* describes black people; and fennel, *finucch* in dialect, is used for gays. I often heard *gedrool* growing up, but I was unaware of the figurative meaning of these other two words. My brother Bob, who is an assistant prosecutor in Newark, New Jersey, tells a favorite office story about the importance of understanding the metaphoric meaning of dialect. An old Italian-American man who spoke broken English went to the police station to file a complaint that he had been attacked by a big *mulignan'*. The officer took down the story verbatim and later asked a colleague, "What is *mulignan'*?" The final report read that the man had been assaulted by a large eggplant.

With the professor's help, I was discovering a set of rules that enabled me to link my hand-me-down words to a real language. For example, the standard Italian word *cafone* (cah-fone-ay), meaning an ignorant person, is pronounced "cah-fone" in the south, where the final vowel, always used in standard Italian, trails off. In the Italian-American pronunciation, the hard *c* changes to a hard *g,* and becomes another one of my favorite dialect words, *gavone.*

Understanding this pattern, I discovered why we called the pie my mother made the night before Easter *pizza gain.* I remember how my mother would chide herself all day if she had mistakenly tasted its prosciutto filling on the meatless Good Friday, and how we voraciously ate thick slices of *pizza gain* after returning from Saturday night confession. My dislike of confession compared to my love of this pie could not be measured with worldly cups and tablespoons, but it was worth any penance to commune with this mixture of mozzarella, parmigiano, and ricotta cheese, egg, peppery salami, and prosciutto baked in a crunchy bread shell. The words *pizza gain* made no sense to the American ear, so the dish remained nameless to outsiders, added to the list of family culinary secrets. Fortunately, when I was in high school quiche Lorraine came into fashion, allowing me to serve *pizza gain* to my friends as "a kind of Italian quiche."

In southern dialect, the *pi* (pee) sound in standard Italian often changes to *chi* (key). So the word *piena,* meaning full, becomes *chiena.* *Pizza chiena,* stuffed full of good things, sounds like *pizza gain* to the Italian-American ear. Northern Italians would describe a similar type of pie as *pizza imbottita.*

De Blasi went on translating with blooming vigor, as if he were rediscovering the ties between southern Italians like himself and his transplanted countrymen. I learned that when my mother called me *mooshamoosh,* she was using the dialect *muscia* in its superlative form, *muscia muscia,* meaning a woman who is weak and slow in doing something.

(In standard Italian, similar words are *floscia,* meaning soft, and *mogia,* downcast and dejected.) On really lethargic days, I was *mezzamaught,* derived from the dialect *mezzo morta,* or half dead.

Gabbadotz comes from the dialect expression *capa tosta,* literally, having a hard head (*testa dura* in standard Italian). Another frequently used word, *gabbafresch,* which captured my mom's jealousy of carefree women, was probably derived from *capa* (head) and *fresca* (cool or fresh in standard Italian, but which in dialect can mean a woman who chatters aimlessly and works idly).

The reference to snotty-nosed *squistamod* kids is from the dialect *scostumato,* meaning poorly raised and educated. My inclination to act like a *mortitavahm* when gobbling down free food comes from *morto di fame,* literally dying of hunger and used to describe someone disgraced by poverty. And *bijanzee* seems to be derived from *pazienza,* patience, meaning a problem that requires a lot of it.

What about her much repeated *footitah?*

"*Brutta parola,*" said Professor De Blasi, shaking his head.

I tensed watching his expression. Had I just unwittingly handed the professor of philology a curse word?

De Blasi explained that *footitah* is derived from the dialect verb *fottere,* which means "go to the devil." My mother was using the second-person imperative form of the verb. My make-believe words not only had real meaning but were branches of a fiery grammatical tree: *futtiti,* or "you go to hell." Yet I could tell from De Blasi's reaction that *footitah* exerted more force than merely going to hell in a handbasket. I later mentioned *footitah* to Alessandra, our Milanese friend who grew up in the south, and she tittered upon hearing the word. *Futtiti,* she explained, is interpreted as "fuck you" (as opposed to *fanculo,* or go fuck yourself).

Fuck you? My mother only spelled out the F-word: "He said ef-you-see-kay" was the construction we heard throughout our childhood. Yet under the veil of dialect, *footitah* hit the air several times a day.

Dialect must have been a relief, a kind of escape for my mother. After many exhausting years of trying to fit into American culture, she could return to the comfortable language of childhood, when life is as plain as your parents' voice. To be raised by the sturdy hands and ancient customs of people from a primitive culture creates an adulthood of confused aspirations and conflicting values. What a simple luxury, especially in moments of frustration, to slip into one's peasant tongue, allowing language to transport you to the cozy safety of the past.

When I use a dialect word, I am repeating the sounds of my grandparents—perhaps the closest contact I could have with them. I am now their young grandchild, uttering playful words, oblivious to the meaning of what I am saying. How could I have understood all those years ago, innocently mixing my own batch of sounds, that dialect brought their faraway culture to our little white house, making us, in some tiny way, carriers of their abandoned way of life?

Early each morning, when my father left for work, my mother said he had to "go *zappa*," to put the food on the table. I always sensed that the word had more power than plain work. Decades later, finding a dictionary of the dialect of Picerno, I saw that *zappá* was a dialect form of the standard Italian verb *zappare,* meaning to hoe.

To hoe? My father, like the rest of the commuter dads, took the train to downtown New York to work as a manager of international shipping for the Allied Chemical Corporation. I don't think he knew how to use a hoe. But he had to go *zappa,* literally to labor in the fields, the exacting ritual of rural mountain people. If my mother had said "got to go work in the fields," we would have questioned her grasp of reality. But *zappa* made sense, good sense. My mother's word choice, her interpretation of the meaning of work, unconsciously restored the lost culture of her parents.

Other dialect words are etched permanently into my brain, ensuring that when I react intensely to a situation, with the kind of raw, unfiltered feelings I am embarrassed to possess, dialect, not English, surfaces. If I see a woman who is well taken care of, doesn't work, and wants round-the-clock help to care for her children, clean the house, and cook the meals, I think, "What a *bubidabetz!*" A pampered woman. This is my mother and grandmother and, I'm certain, my great-grandmother talking, and I pinch myself trying to summon up tolerance but can't: I am conditioned to think that a woman who doesn't work hard is a *bubidabetz*. Of course, my ancestors would consider me a *bubidabetz* if they compared my American life to the one they led. I know of no male equivalent of the *bubidabetz,* perhaps because Italian men were supposed to be pampered, and if they weren't, a woman wasn't doing her job properly.

Bubidabetz. Saying the word is fun; it's like blowing bubbles, as I am puffing the aspirated *b,* which sounds like a *p,* sending forth the foamy anger into the air, an ephemeral burst of envy. I'm in a nether region of language, taking words from a nineteenth-century foreign land which have been passed on orally, using them to judge contemporary American culture.

The word *bubidabetz* stumped Professor De Blasi, and he wondered if it might be derived from the name of a character in an Italian folktale. I think, however, I found the origin of *bubidabetz* after meeting my mother's cousins in southern Italy. I also gave them my list of words, and they couldn't stop laughing, surprised at the curious spellings and the thought that remnants of the family's Italian past existed in America.

BOO-bid-ah-betz. I pronounced the word several times.

"Ah," said cousin Franco, listening carefully. *"Pupa di pezza."* A *pupa di pezza* is dialect for a doll with a head and body of stuffed rags and arms made of rags or corn husks. This cheap doll is what poor people give to their children. In a pejorative usage, a woman who is a *pupa di pezza* squanders what has been given to her; she doesn't understand the value of anything.

As I decipher the meanings of my childhood language, I'm bombarded with relentless negativity, notes of jealousy, belittling quips; these are no Hallmark card messages for a warm and fuzzy day. The culture of southern Italy, in which hope was as elusive as fertile land, may have created a special place in language for expressions that let judgment and envy free. De Blasi joked that dialect descriptions are often derogatory because if you thought highly of someone, there was no need to say anything at all.

Not a bad code for exploited, exhausted peasants to live by. Which suggests another interpretation. The words are sharp, funny, distinctly Italian, absent the self-righteous quest for moral perfection found in nineteenth-century American life, and yet filled with a belief in the ultimate worth of human beings. The opposite of the *citrulo* is the self-examining mind. The *pupa di pezza* corrupts industry; the *scostumato* debases communal values; the *morto di fame* maximizes self-pity. Like a diptych, the well-lived life hangs on the opposite hinge, a knowledge so implicit that no words are necessary; honor lives in silence. Isaac Bashevis Singer noted in his eloquent homage to Yiddish that one can find "a gratitude for every day of life, every crumb of success, each encounter of love." The same can be said for the dialects of southern Italy.

Jay Leno, with Bill Zehme

From *Leading with My Chin*

I was never one to respond well to being yelled at. Fortunately, there wasn't that much yelling in our house. My father would raise his voice, but because he was partially deaf, I figured he just wanted me to *understand* him more clearly. The one time I truly infuriated him was just a few weeks after I'd gotten my driver's license. I had been out driving my mom's '64 Ford Falcon and I turned a corner at a ridiculously high speed. Suddenly, the car rolled over, crushed the roof, then rolled back over onto all four wheels. I was okay, but the headroom was now approximately four inches. I still managed to drive the car home, then went inside and sheepishly told my dad, "Oh, I, uh, had a little accident with the car."

He was very calm. "All right," he said, "let's take a look." He was expecting maybe a broken taillight or a little ding on the fender. We stepped outside and—

"WHAT THE HELL HAPPENED HERE?!"

When you're a kid, you try to diminish your crimes. So I just said, "Uh, the car fell over."

"WHAT DO YOU MEAN IT FELL OVER?! HOW THE HELL DOES A CAR FALL OVER? IT'S SITTING THERE AND THEN IT FELL OVER? IS THAT WHAT YOU'RE TELLING ME?"

"Well, it was slippery and I was on a corner—"

"THE CAR ROLLED OVER ON THE ROOF! THAT IS NOT A DENT!"

And, of course, my mother, who knew nothing about cars, came out and said, "Maybe the car did just fall over . . ."

"IT DIDN'T FALL OVER! THE BOY WAS SPEEDING!"

"Well," Mom said, "it *could* have fallen over."

That was the angriest I ever made my father. And it didn't help that he developed a slight stoop from driving it in to the body shop.

As I've mentioned, my brother, Pat, is ten years older than me. When I was in high school, he was drafted into the army and sent to Vietnam. We all wanted to keep his spirits up over there, but nobody in the family was much of a letter writer. So my father had the idea to get a tape recorder and ship him voice messages. We went to the electronics store and got one of the new miniature reel-to-reel machines that barely pre-dated cassettes. My father said to the clerk, "My boy is over in Vietnam and we want to send him taped greetings from the family!"

The clerk asked, "How long a tape do you want—fifteen minutes?"

"*Fifteen minutes!* We wouldn't even finish saying hello in fifteen minutes! What's your *longest* tape?"

"Ninety minutes."

"That's more like it! Give me four of those!"

So we brought home the recorder and the tapes and a year's supply of batteries. My father set up everything on the kitchen table and called my mom and me into the room. Very excitedly, he announced, "Okay, now we're all gonna talk to Pat!" He pressed the start button and, in his own inimitable way, began:

"HELLO, PAT! EVERYTHING HERE IS GOOD! I'M FINE! YOUR MOTHER'S FINE! HERE'S YOUR BROTHER! JAMIE, TALK TO PAT!"

I stepped forward: "Hey, Pat! How you doing? Hope you're okay! Be careful over there! Here's Mom!"

Mom bent over the machine and said, "Hello, Pat! Take care of yourself now! Don't do anything silly!"

Then my dad came back: "HEY, WHERE'S BRUCE THE DOG? BRING BRUCE OVER HERE AND MAKE HIM BARK FOR PAT!"

Bruce barked: "Roof roof! Roof roof!"

Then, of course, my father had to point out, "THAT'S THE DOG THERE, PAT! THAT'S BRUCE THE DOG! ALL RIGHT! LET'S PLAY IT BACK!"

We listened to all of about three minutes we put on this ninety minute tape. The next day, the same thing: "PAT, EVERYTHING IS GOOD! NOT MUCH ELSE IS GOING ON! HERE'S THE DOG!"

"Roof roof! Roof roof!"

After a few weeks, there was no more than nine minutes of tape filled and it was mostly the dog barking. Finally, my father said, "Oh, let's just send the tape! What the hell!" So we shipped the whole contraption off to my brother. Thinking back, I have a feeling he might have preferred a few letters.

Having a brother in Vietnam was, of course, a very frightening experience, as many families know. All you can do is hope that no bad news comes. I remember watching television with my mom and dad one Sunday night when we heard a car pull into our driveway. Then we heard the car door open and footsteps coming up the walk. Next our screen door opened and it sounded like something had been thrown into the house. This was all very ominous. My father went to check and came back holding a telegram. Without opening it, he laid the telegram on the dining room table and just stared at it. My mother and I saw this and, slowly, we all sat down around the table, looking at the telegram. Nobody said anything for ten minutes. We just sat there, feeling kind of sick and very scared. Finally, my father reached for the telegram and slit it open. He cleared his throat and began to read aloud:

"Dear Mr. Leno: You are invited to Wentworth Chevrolet to view the exciting new Caprice Classic!"

My father was furious! He never drove a Chevrolet again for the rest of his life.

Oklahoma! Where the comic came sweepin' down the plain! So many unforgettable images to recall:

Going through Oklahoma City, I asked somebody for a restaurant recommendation. He said, "Hey, aren't you Eye-talian? We've got one of the best Eye-talian restaurants here! In fact, the owner's from Iowa!" I went there and saw the red-checked tablecloths and wine bottles along the wall. All of which looked promising. I ordered spaghetti and meatballs. Then the waiter asked, "You want fries with that? It comes with fries, you know." So I got the fries, plus three slices of Wonder Bread for sopping marinara. As they say, "When in Oklahoma City, do as the Romans do!"

(This, by the way, was vastly preferable to a place in West Virginia, where the menu listed something called a Wop Salad. The waiter there explained that it was a regular salad made with Italian dressing. I said, "Oh, of course! How foolish of me not to know that!" Then there was the old diner in Des Moines that hung signs boasting: PIZZA—THE NEWEST TASTE TREAT! YOU CAN EAT IT WITH YOUR HANDS!)

Frank Lentricchia

From *Sitdown at the Heartland Hotel*

He was probably already starting to die from a brain tumor, he'd be dead in a year, when he came to Heartland City to attend his niece's wedding. Outside his hotel room door, a big man sat, who must have gone 400 pounds, on a burnished chair he sat smoldering, and let Tommy and me in without a word.

In the room, alone: Gaetano Lucchese, most powerful and reticent of the New York Mafia dons, also known as Thomas (Three-Finger Brown) Lucchese, five feet tall and skinny, morosely watching the *Arthur Godfrey Show* and awaiting the appearance of Arthur's special guest, the stunning Phyllis McGuire, lead singer of The McGuire Sisters. Three-Finger in a multi-colored robe, in yellow slippers, his feet barely reaching the floor, and we're in there with him! Tommy Lucchesi, my college pal, and me, the groom-to-be. Lucchese and Lucchesi, together at last, thanks to me, Geoffrey Gilbert, the innocent bystander. My pal was a solid six-footer. Picture him next to Three-Finger, face to face, because eventually you're going to have to.

In the robe and slippers Three-Finger was like a character they called in Shakespearean times a fantastic, more or less a foppish person, who was more or less a homosexual. I doubt that Three-Finger was homosexual, but he was certainly fantastic, a walking hallucination. He had a wife, if that counts for anything. Tommy was an English major who wrote stories full of violence in a poetic style. Three-Finger, who actually did violence, had a dizzy spell watching the Godfrey show. Claimed it was Phyllis McGuire who gave him the spell, though now I conclude that it was the tumor in all likelihood, not Phyllis, who Three-Finger was deeply in love with.

"The eviscerations of friendship."

"The ice-pick of conversation."

"The blood-gouts of time."

A few phrases, that's what I remember of what Tommy read to me from his work, not the plots or characters, if there were any. "The meathook of love." I like that one. Lucchese, Lucchesi.

Tommy knew everything there was to know about Three-Finger Brown, except one big thing. When I told him who my wife-to-be was related to, he said that he had to meet him, that he had always felt related to Three-Finger, that he was confident Lucchese and Lucchesi were indistinguishable, "from the genealogical point of view," that what he called the "blood values" of his writing had a genetic basis, and Three-Finger was none other than his "hidden muse."

By the way, he never said "my stories," it was always "my writing." He said, "In this world, Geoffrey Gilbert, talking falls far beneath writing." The way he generally talked, Tommy sounded like his writing. A little forced.

"The lacerations of family" was another one of his beauties. His parents were crazy for him, so why did he write "the lacerations of family" is what I'd like to ask him, but I never did, because he didn't enjoy being questioned about "my writing." Tommy was unnatural, a fantastic himself.

We approached the meeting with Three-Finger, which Tommy said we should call a "sitdown," exactly the way you'd expect two serious college boys would. We researched the topic. I knew that Three-Finger's nickname had something to do with an old-time baseball player, so I went into that, while Tommy did the library work on Three-Finger's biography. We memorized our stack of 3 by 5 notecards, but it turned out that our knowledge was useless, because Three-Finger gave me a glare when I mentioned Mordecai "Three Finger" Brown, one of the greatest pitchers who ever lived, who was big in Three-Finger's adolescence. I had no interest after the glare in going further into Mordecai's heroic American story and how he turned his handicap into a terrific asset, throwing the meanest sinker in history. As for what Tommy had accumulated: What was he going to do with the fact that Three-Finger had done 32 murders by the time he was 35? Could he bring up the notorious names of Lucky Luciano or Dutch Schultz? Three-Finger, he learned, referred to himself as a "successful Italian dress manufacturer in a tough Jew environment," so how could Tommy bring up Our Thing, or The Commission, or Murder Incorporated? In the end, knowing all we knew and not being able to discuss it, in an impersonal and therefore objective manner with Three-Finger, was like being forced to swallow a nauseating meal and not being able to puke it up. With Three-Finger, we could have no *discourse.*

I thought he hated his nickname because he was self-conscious about the frankly sickening sight that his left hand presented to the public. The fingernails were too long for a man. It wasn't the hand of a dress manufacturer in any environment. It looked like the foot of a vulture, which went well with the severe aquiline beak, the high forehead, the thick white hair brushed back tight. Try to imagine him with that terrible hand in an intimate relationship, which I had to, I had no choice, after he slipped it a couple of times for extended periods under the robe, awaiting as he was the appearance of the stunning Phyllis McGuire, who that pain in the ass Godfrey was holding back until the end of the show.

Three-Finger stood when we came in, said nothing, and then sat down to watch Godfrey. Ten minutes later Tommy sneezed, I said "God bless you," and Three-Finger broke his silence: "Did someone say God?" I said, "I didn't mean anything by it, sir." Three-Finger said, "Did you say sir? What's your deep implication?" I couldn't reply, and we returned to the silence.

Then Godfrey welcomed Julius La Rosa to the show and Three-Finger perked up a little: "What an excellent country this is. An Italian boy with a Jew first name. In my organization, I brought in the Jews and the Irish, even though some of my associates disagreed, including one who said, 'Over my fucking dead body!' Shortly thereafter, this particular party was called home by the Father."

Arthur started talking to Julius and Three-Finger started talking to us. You would think that the Thomas Lucchese/Thomas Lucchesi matter would have been a subject right off the bat. That would be a normal thought. But not a word from the two fantastics. Instead, Three-Finger wanted to know about what he called Tommy's "plans for life," and Tommy replied, "I want to be a writer." To which Three-Finger responded, "I do a little writing in my domain, so I sympathize with what you have to go through. I can't imagine it on a daily basis. The torture must be tremendous. Who do you like as a writer? Who do you idolize?" Then they had more or less the following exchange, starting with my pal:

"John Keats."

"I'm a little hard of hearing."

"John Keats."

"I heard of him, but we never met."

"John (The Lung) Keats."

"The Lung?"

"The Lung."

"They call a writer The Lung?"

"He died of tuberculosis."

"This is not the Keats I was referring to. The Keats I was referring to won't die of tuberculosis because he's a Jew cocksucker."

"As far as I know, Keats the writer sucked no—"

"You getting snotty with me?"

"No, Mr. Lucchese. I was merely indicating that Keats the writer was no doubt a heterosexual, apparently."

A big silence.

Tommy says again, "A heterosexual."

Three-Finger says to me, "He was merely indicating. How often do you merely indicate, Geoffrey Gilbert?"

I say nothing.

Three-Finger says, "An associate of mine once told me that art and sucking cock go hand in hand."

Tommy laughs, Three-Finger doesn't.

Three-Finger says, "Geoffrey Gilbert, why did you have to bring me this? Why do I have to come all the way out here in the middle of nowhere to have my balls broken for my lovely niece's wedding by this?"

Then he looked at Tommy and screamed, "You got a mouse?" To my total amazement, Tommy screamed back, without hesitation, "Yes!" Then Three-Finger got up and walked over to Tommy and leaned over and screamed even louder: "Is it a parakeet? Is your mouse a parakeet?" Tommy screams, "Fucking A!" Julius La Rosa was singing "That's Amore." Three-Finger returned to his chair and started to sob. La Rosa was singing badly, but that wasn't the reason for the sobbing. Three-

Finger says, very sadly, "Momo has the mouse I want, and she is a heav-enly parakeet, as you will see in a few minutes."

When we left the Heartland Hotel that night, I learned how well Tommy'd done his homework. He explained that in Mafia code "mouse" meant your girlfriend and a "parakeet" was a pretty woman. I said, "So you lied, Tommy. You don't have your mouse either, who is definitely a parakeet." Tommy had a tragic crush on a beautiful girl who lived a few houses away, who never gave him the time of day. I don't be-lieve they exchanged two words, though she knew he had a thing for her, everyone in the neighborhood did. I said, "Why did you lie, Tommy?" He said, "I needed to get close to him." And then he told me the story. Momo was the beast, Sam Giancana, the Chicago mob boss, and the beauty, Phyllis McGuire, was his girlfriend, his "traveling com-panion," as Tommy put it. And Three-Finger was hopelessly in love from afar. I asked the obvious question: "Why didn't you tell Three-Finger that your love for your parakeet was hopeless? That would have made the bond between you." Tommy answered, "I didn't want that kind of bond. I wanted to see his nature at the edge of action, directed at me, in the same room. I wanted the experience but not the conse-quences. He pulled back. They always pull back on civilians." I said, "For your writing? As inspiration for the blood-gouts of time?" For a second he didn't know how to take me. Then he answered, "You need to ask? Of all people, you?" I said, "I feared for you. After the Godfrey show ended, I thought you were finished. The aftermath of the God-frey show was a nightmare I'm still trying to awake from." He said, "I don't appreciate the tone that you just deployed when you said the blood-gouts of time. Do I detect a satiric intention? Geoffrey Gilbert? You cocksucker!" Then we both laughed, but I didn't believe his laugh. A few days later I knew why.

Just before Phyllis came on, Giselle MacKenzie, the cute Canadian redhead, sang "My Funny Valentine." While she was singing the part about you're not good looking by any standard but I love you anyway, Three-Finger looks at Tommy and Tommy doesn't look away. Finally, Phyllis, who glows. Three-Finger says to Phyllis, "Sing 'Sincerely' all by yourself." But Phyllis doesn't sing without her sisters. She just talks to Arthur. Every once in a while Three-Finger would pipe up: "She's so willowy." "She's so willowy." When the show ends, he just says, "Phyl-lis, I'm dizzy." Then Tommy starts with: "She is the parakeet of para-keets, far above." As if that weren't enough, he adds: "And this, then, is the meathook of love. This is love's meathook, Mr. *Brown*."

Three-Finger walks to the door and opens it. The big man comes in. Three-Finger says, "Tell these boys how much you weigh." The big man says, "547 pounds." Then Three-Finger says in a mocking tone to Tommy, "And this, then, is Frank The Whale." He says, "Frank, there is an undercurrent in this room. There is too much undercurrent coming from this boy." He's pointing at Tommy. He says to Tommy, "Stand up." Tommy stands and Three-Finger walks up to him, as close as possible, kissing distance, and says, "Frank squeezes the shit out of people. Young man, your shit comes from your throat. Frank, would you like to stand on this youngster's throat?" Nobody says anything. Then Three-Finger reaches into Tommy's groin with the left hand that's like a claw. In Italian, it's called *la mano sinistra*. Squeezing just hard enough to paralyze him, saying "You interested in me? You interested?" Tommy's in such pain he can't reply, but what could he have said to those questions? If he were honest, he would say yes. Three-Finger then says to the big man, "Tell him why I hate the nickname they gave me against my wishes." The Whale says, "When he was young, he used the hand as a persuasion device. He turned his handicap into what the boys called an asset. But he hasn't done it in years." Then The Whale takes Tommy's pants down and orders him to bend over, which he does. The Whale says to Tommy, "You think this is a clambake?" Three-Finger from behind, up close, says, "And then I put my asset up their ass and dig around in there for the truth. That's where my nickname came from, boys. Three-Finger Brown." I try to break the ice. I say, "Mr. Lucchese, he's noted for it, his undercurrent. Tommy The Undercurrent." I force a laugh. The Whale laughs. Three-Finger says, "Did you say noted, Mr. Geoffrey Gilbert? Did you use the word noted?" What could I say except, "I'm sorry, sir." Then I realize I said sir. Then I say, "Oh my God." Then I realize I said God. I'm shaking all over. Three-Finger, thank God, laughs. Three-Finger says, "Pull your pants up, because you disgust me. The two of you disgust me."

Two days later I received a letter from my friend:

Dear Geoffrey,

You ask me why I didn't seem humiliated and shattered by what happened. I was, but not by that. It became clear, as we walked to the car, that you have cold feelings for me. In your mind you deride me. It all became clear when I heard you say the blood-gouts of time with that tone. I was deeply hurt. How can we be friends if you don't love my writing? It's over.

I ran into Tommy the day after I received the letter. He cut me dead, and we never spoke again.

Jerre Mangione

From *Mount Allegro*

Outside the house she expected us to speak English, and often took pride in the fact that we spoke English so well that almost none of our relatives could understand it. Any English we spoke at home, however, was either by accident or on the sly. My sister Maria, who often talked in her sleep, conducted her monologues in English, but my mother forgave her on the ground that she could not be responsible for her subconscious thoughts.

My mother's insistence that we speak only Italian at home drew a sharp line between our existence there and our life in the world outside. We gradually acquired the notion that we were Italian at home and American (whatever that was) elsewhere. Instinctively, we all sensed the necessity of adapting ourselves to two different worlds. We began to notice that there were several marked differences between those worlds, differences that made Americans and my relatives each think of the other as foreigners.

The difference that pained me most was that of language, probably because I was aware of it most often. Child that I was, I would feel terribly embarrassed whenever my mother called to me in Italian while I was playing on the street, with all my playmates there to listen; or when she was buying clothes for me and would wrangle in broken English with the salesmen about the price.

My mother took no notice of such childish snobbery. As long as I remained under her jurisdiction, she continued to cling to her policy of restricting the family language to Italian. "I might as well not have my children if I can't talk with them," she argued. She considered it sinful for relatives to permit their children to speak a language which the entire family could not speak fluently, and claimed that if she were to cast aside Italian, the language of her forefathers, it would be like renouncing her own flesh and blood.

There was only one possible retort to these arguments but no one dared use it: the language we called Italian and spoke at home was not Italian. It was a Sicilian dialect which only Sicilians could understand. I seldom heard proper Italian spoken, except when my Uncle Nino made speeches or when one of my relatives would meet an Italian or another Sicilian for the first time. Proper Italian sounded like the melody of church bells and it was fresh and delicate compared to the earthy sounds of the dialect we spoke. Yet it was hard to understand how two persons could carry on an honest conversation in a language so fancy.

My Uncle Nino claimed that Italian was "feminine" and Sicilian "masculine." He also said that the only reason Sicilians ever addressed each other in proper Italian was to show off their schooling and prove to each other that they were not peasants. He probably was right, for I noticed that the ostentation of speaking proper Italian was dropped as soon as two Sicilians had known each other for an evening and showed any desire to be friends. Anyone who persisted in speaking Italian after that was considered a prig or, at least, a socialist.

But if my relatives were under the impression that they were speaking the same dialect they brought with them from Sicily, they were mistaken. After a few years of hearing American, Yiddish, Polish, and Italian dialects other than their own, their language gathered words which no one in Sicily could possibly understand. The most amazing of these were garbled American words dressed up with Sicilian suffixes—strange concoctions which, in later years, that non-Sicilian pundit, H. L. Mencken, was to include in his book, *The American Language.*

Mr. Mencken's collection of Italian-American words is a good indication of what happened to the vocabulary of my relatives. Such words as *minuto* for minute, *ponte* for pound, *storo* for store, *barra* for bar, *giobba* for job were constantly used as Sicilian words.

One word that Mr. Mencken should include in the next edition of his book is *baccauso,* which has been in my relatives' vocabulary as far back as I can remember. My parents probably picked it up from other American Sicilians when they first arrived in Rochester. Certainly, the word had no relation to their current mode of city life. It was used when referring to "toilet" and was obviously derived from the American "backhouse" that flourished in earlier and more rural America. Not until a few years ago when I first visited Italy, a nation without backhouses, and mystified Sicilians there by using the word, did I become aware of its Chic Sale derivation. Yet I had been using *baccauso* for a lifetime, always under the impression it was an authentic Sicilian word.

While the gradual effect of such bastard words was to break down the differences between the dialects my relatives spoke, there were enough differences of accent and vocabulary left to lend the various dialects their own peculiarities. Usually, the more distant the relative the greater was the difference between the dialect he spoke and the one we used at home. The relatives who came from towns on the sea (like my father) still talked as though they were hurling words against the wind or through the fog, in a piercing singing accent. Those from towns far inland talked as though they had never heard gay music, and their speech was heavy with mournful and burly sounds.

I gathered that every Italian town left its individual stamp on the language of its people. My Uncle Luigi liked to tell the story of the American priest who spoke perfect schoolroom Italian. When he went to Italy for the first time, the priest decided that the best way of seeing the country and meeting its people was to travel the whole length of the nation, listening to confessions as he went from town to town. He got along famously in northern Italy. Although he found the confessions rather dull, he had no trouble understanding the sins described to him.

Below Rome he began to have difficulties. The confessions were more interesting but the dialects he heard were harder to understand, and on several occasions, he suspected that the penance he imposed on sinners was entirely out of proportion to the sins they had committed. "It must have been very annoying when he got to Naples," my uncle said, "for Neapolitans are some of the most fascinating sinners in the world."

When the priest reached Sicily, he was at a complete loss. He could not understand a word of the dialects he heard and was obliged to conduct all his confessions in sign language.

When anyone who had not heard the story was gullible enough to ask Uncle Luigi how that was possible, he would gleefully grab the opportunity to show off his histrionic talents and act out a sin or two in pantomime. Invariably, of course, they were sins of the flesh.

There was never any effort made to keep any Sicilian words secret from us, no matter how heretical or bawdy. Yet my parents would be shocked whenever we repeated a word they did not consider proper. Once I horrified my parents with a word which my father often used in his speech. The experience taught me to regard every Sicilian idiom thereafter with a wary eye.

One evening my Aunt Giovanna gave a party for some of the women who worked with her at the tailor factory. She invited my family but, since my parents were expecting visitors that evening, they begged off and sent me, the oldest son, to represent them. Like so many women gathered together away from their husbands, my aunt's guests were inclined to be boisterous.

I was the only male present, but I was only eleven years old and did not inhibit them at all. They were all very attentive to me. My aunt let me drink a glass of wine, and when no one was looking, the buxom woman sitting next to me gave me more. After dinner, I pumped the player-piano while the women danced the schottische and the polka. By the time I was ready to leave, I felt quite stimulated by the gaiety of the evening.

I came into the house, my face radiant with the wine and the crisp wintry air. After introducing me to the guests, my mother asked about her sister's health.

"Aunt Giovanna is fine," I said. "Her *risotto* was good—and I had wine and nuts," I rattled on enthusiastically.

"Did you drink much of the wine?" my father asked with a sly smile.

I avoided the question. "There were lots of people there and I played the piano for them." Without stopping to catch my breath I continued, "The ladies danced and made a lot of noise and it all sounded like a *bordello.*"

My father's face suddenly went grim. My mother gasped, and one of the visitors giggled. My father said: "Hold your tongue and go to bed at once. You've said enough."

"But Papa," I protested, "it did sound like a *bordello.*"

"Stop using that word!" he thundered. "Go to bed!"

I went upstairs and brooded. *Bordello* was a word I often heard my father use when he complained about noise. Why should he object to my using it? Downstairs I heard the visitors departing; one of them was telling my mother that boys will be boys and not to worry about me. There was an ominous silence after they left. I heard my mother puttering around the kitchen, and my father angrily creaking his rocking-chair.

It was all too much for me. I decided that I had probably committed some hideous and mysterious crime. My father had once told me the legend of a man who could destroy the world by uttering a single word, secret to everyone but himself. As I cried myself to sleep, I was sure that *bordello* was the word.

The next morning my mother said: "You used a bad word last night. It is a word that only grownups are allowed to use."

"But Papa uses it all the time."

"Yes, but he's a grownup, my little squash."

"What does the word mean?"

"The word wouldn't have any meaning for you now. I'll tell you when you get older. Now hurry to school or you'll be late."

· My mother would never explain adult words to me, though she saw no harm in exposing me to them. Her theory seemed to be that if her children went to church regularly, they would surely develop an instinct that would teach them to tell the difference between good and bad. So far as vocabulary was concerned, the theory worked out pretty well. I had a secret vocabulary of dozens of words I would never dare use at home, even though I had heard many of them there originally. Most of them were terrifying curses involving God, the Virgin Mary, and various kinds of barnyard animals. They frightened me, so much so that I used them only when it seemed necessary to impress new playmates with my bravery.

He may have realized it, but he would never admit that Catholicism was so much a part of his relatives that it was futile to argue with them about it. You might as well have tried to persuade a confirmed teetotaler that strong drink was good for him.

Their Catholicism, like their lives, was enveloped in a heavy blanket of fatalism. In the last analysis, both were impervious to rational argument. Thinking was all right for professional persons, like doctors, lawyers, and teachers, but for laymen it was considered a superfluous and overestimated process.

If you wanted to keep your full senses, you accepted whatever happened to you in life with a full assurance that it was bound to happen. What was the use of thinking about it?

There might be a great deal of noisy emotionalism among my relatives over a misfortune, like a death or the loss of a job, but eventually it was laid on the doorstep of Destiny. *"E u Destino."* That single phrase explained everything. "The good Lord has decided in advance what is going to happen to all of us. You can't fight Destiny," my mother would often say to me.

All this hardly jibed with the philosophy of the Horatio Alger novels I devoured, nor did it fit in with what we heard in school. There we were taught in English, French, and Latin that every man is the architect of his own fortune, that anyone who works hard and has plenty of ambition can achieve anything he wants, that Abe Lincoln got to be President of the United States and so can you and you.

When I repeated some of this learning at home, my father smiled and said, "Sure. Sure. America is a wonderful country," but in his heart he found all this too much to swallow and, whenever he became angry with us, he complained that our school-teachers taught us fairy tales instead of manners.

His belief in Destiny could not be shed in his lifetime. For centuries his ancestors had been relying on the alibi of Destiny, for how else could they have become resigned to the obstacles that stood between them and a decent living? Their priests had talked about Destiny; so had their employers. They came to believe its power and to respect it. They heard nothing else.

Here in America, my father and his relatives, huddled together as they were in one neighborhood, heard the same thing, except from their children who brought home their school-learning. The only real connection they had with their new land was their children, but they had never heard of Sicilian parents learning from their children and they did not listen to them closely. They continued to talk about Destiny in the same vague but dogmatic way people have of talking about life or about depressions.

But life eventually ends and a depression is eventually conquered. Not so with Destiny. It had no beginning and no ending and no one could possibly cope with it. It was *Destino* that decreed my father should never earn enough money, never save any, and yet have a generous spirit that only a rich man could afford. It was *Destino* that kept sending my mother to hospitals for a series of operations that nearly killed her, and finally it was *Destino* that made it possible for her to survive.

To my parents *Destino* was the magic in the map drawn by God which charted the course of every human being. To us *Destino* never seemed to have any connection with God. Hell appeared like a more likely place for it. It hung over our thoughts like an unassailable dragon who somehow had become the final authority in determining the outcome of all important happenings in our lives, regardless of what our teachers and the Horatio Alger novels said to the contrary.

———

On one hand, my relatives were cynical about *Americani:* they had no manners; they licked their fingers after a meal and they chewed gum and then played with it as though it were a rubber band. Also, *Americani* were *superbi* (snobs) and looked down on people who didn't speak their language fluently. On the other hand, they feared and respected *Americani* and there were times when they emulated them.

If a Sicilian began to behave like an *Americano,* they said he was putting on airs but, actually, they had great admiration for anyone who achieved any degree of Americanization. After all, to be an *Americano* was a sign that you were getting on in the world. The bosses were Americans. The police were Americans. In fact, nearly anyone who had plenty of money or a good steady job was either an American or was living like one.

You had only to look at the example set by the sons of poor Italians who became doctors or lawyers in the community. As soon as they had established themselves, they married blonde American girls and moved as far as possible from their former neighborhoods. Some of them dropped the vowels from the end of their names, so that people would think they had always been American. They stopped associating with their relatives. Their wives got their pictures in society pages and, instead of having a raft of children, they bought wire-haired terriers and walked them around the block, like many other prosperous Americans. The only times they liked dealing with Italians was when it meant money in their pockets.

In spite of the fact that the word *Americano* was usually preceded by the Sicilian word *fissa,* meaning stupid, Americans were suspected of miraculous shrewdness and dishonesty. Yet once an *Americano* had shown his friendliness to a Sicilian in any way, however trivial, he could expect to be smothered with hospitality and love—never, of course, the love that one Sicilian relative has for another, but enough love to make an American regard his own relatives as so many cold fish for the rest of his life.

My relatives conceded that there were good and bad Americans, just as there were good and bad Sicilians, but they suspected that most of them were inclined to take advantage of a foreigner who could not speak their own tongue. Even before coming to the United States, Sicilians were educated to be suspicious of Americans. From their relatives in America, they received long pathetic accounts of how they had been robbed and cheated. Those who were planning to migrate were warned to beware of Americans from the moment they set foot off the boat.

The first supposedly English word many of my relatives learned even before they landed in America was *girarihir,* meaning "Get out of here." Immigrants were solemnly advised to yell this word at any stranger in America who approached them, for it was emphasized that if a Sicilian was identified as a *greenhorno,* some American would surely try to rob him of his money or belongings.

Jerre Mangione and Ben Morreale

From *La Storia: Five Centuries of the Italian American Experience*

The most autobiographical of his novels, *The Fortunate Pilgrim,* according to Puzo, was intended to express his childhood dread of "growing up to be like the adults around me." Into the years of his adolescence he was contemptuous of adults and looked down at them for their willingness to settle for very little in life. "And so," he writes "with my father gone, my mother the family chief, I, like all the children in the ghettos of America, became locked in a bitter struggle with the adults responsible for me. It was inevitable that my mother and I became enemies." One of Puzo's complaints was that his mother's highest ambition for him was to become a railroad clerk.

Puzo, however, matured into an adult with a sense of perspective and compassion. He was still bitter about his Italian relatives when he began writing *The Fortunate Pilgrim,* and had every intention of portraying himself as "the sensitive, misunderstood hero, much put upon by his parent and family"; but to his astonishment, his mother soon took over the novel and became its heroine. Moreover, the Italians of his youth whom he had regarded with contempt "turned out to be heroes." What struck Puzo most, in retrospect, was their courage. "How," he asks, "did they ever get the balls to get married, have kids, go out to earn a living in a strange land, with no skills, not even knowing the language? . . . Heroes all around me. I never saw them. But how could I?"

If this admission smacks of sentimentality, there is almost a complete lack of it in *The Fortunate Pilgrim.*

The central character is Lucia Santa, a tough-minded, indomitable matriarch who, through force of circumstances, is burdened with the responsibility of raising six children. Puzo has explained that Lucia Santa bears a close resemblance to his own mother who, at the age of eighty-two, was "positively indignant that death dares approach her." Like Puzo's mother, Lucia Santa comes from an impoverished and illiterate family from the hills around Naples. So poor are they that when she reaches the age of seventeen, she is informed by her father that because there is no money and many debts she cannot hope for a dowry—sentencing her, in effect, to spinsterhood for the rest of her life. In a spirit of rebellion, Lucia marries by proxy an immigrant in America whom she can barely remember as a childhood playmate. By traveling 3,000 miles to a strange country and a strange people, she follows the example set by the American pioneers, even though, as Puzo says, "they never walked an American plain. Actually, the immigrants moved in a sadder wilderness, where the language was also strange, where their children became members of a different race. It was a price that had to be paid."

The price that Lucia Santa has to pay would have defeated a less courageous woman. Besides her two unfortunate marriages, there is the task of dealing with the disparate temperaments of her six children, who are exposed to the turbulence and pitfalls of an Italian American enclave on Tenth Avenue. Their activities constitute the main thrust of the narrative as Lucia Santa's Old World standards come into conflict with the standards of the New World of her children. Puzo's artistry interweaves their actions with those of Lucia Santa against the background of a Little Italy during the hard times of the Depression, justifying Puzo's own contention that *The Fortunate Pilgrim* is the best of his novels.

Mary Ann Mannino

Your Children Are Your Children,
but Your Wife Is Just a Good Cigar

Palmina had been in America exactly six days. Because it was Thursday, the day on which she always baked the week's bread, she had risen early. She wanted to claim for her own this crisp American kitchen with its starched curtains, and its porcelain table, that rang like a bell when she set a kettle on it. By making her bread in that kitchen she thought she would knead out the room's stiffness, and take charge of it, banishing the nauseating smell of new paint with the nourishing aroma of bread.

She tiptoed out of the bedroom, noting that her shoes made no sound at all on the stairs, which were the first she had ever seen covered with a rug. On the kitchen linoleum her heals tapped like rain in a barrel. She took the *lievito* from the cabinet where her sister-in-law had stored it when she explained that in America women did not keep a piece of the dough from the previous week's bread to add to the new dough to make it rise. Instead, Marion had said, they bought a packet of *lievito,* yeast, which had to be mixed with warm water and then blended with the flour. Marion had added that making bread was unnecessary because on Wakefield Street there was a bakery that sold hard-crusted loaves warm from the oven every morning.

Palmina opened the cupboard and a dozen new yellow cups beamed at her from shiny gold hooks. Just as she reached up for one, the still-unfamiliar roar of the toilet flushing on the second floor startled her, and she nearly dropped the cup. The sound meant Peppino, her husband, would soon be coming down for his American coffee. She left the yellow cup on the counter and began to prepare the weak coffee that her husband had grown to love in the twelve years when she had been home in Castille Franchi, and he had been in America. He had come a week after her fourth child's birth to work for a year and return with money for more land, but had gotten trapped by the war.

Scooping the coffee into the pot, she knew that something was troubling her. Something about Peppino was disturbing. She could not say what it was, but thinking back she decided her feeling that something was just not right had begun the night she had arrived in America.

"Your children are your children, but your wife is just a good cigar." Those were her brother Ralphalooch's exact words the previous Friday, at his table, the very night she had arrived with her twelve-year-old daughter, Elena, and her bundles of gifts, lace borders for the sheets of her sisters-in-law, cheeses filled with butter for her brothers. Everyone had eaten the salad, the bread, the salami, and the cheese. They had filled their glasses many times with her brother's own wine, and then Ralphalooch, father of eight living children, had made his joke, pinching the cheek of his wife, Rosina. The wives at the table had smiled and lowered their eyes, but the men had laughed, even Peppino. His laughter had been more explosive than the others, like the opening of a bottle of American ginger ale, and the extravagant oozing of its foam down the glass sides. She saw no reason for him to laugh. She did not think of herself as indistinguishable, like a cigar, exchangeable, like a coin. She had turned her eyes on his face and saw him rein in his smile, distorting his mouth so that he bit his lip. The incident had been small, but she believed that his easy laugh and its sudden halt was a hidden message that was important for her to understand.

Palmina turned the bright silver spigot labeled *H* to the right and instantly warm water gushed into the porcelain sink. She knew this would happen, but she couldn't resist the magic of it, watching it heat until a loop of steam, like one of Peppino's smoke rings, curled toward the ceiling. In America he had learned to smoke Camel cigarettes, cuddling them protectively with his thumb like the American soldiers had done. She memorized things like that as though in knowing his new habits she would be able to read his thoughts. She filled the pot with water and coffee and put it on the stove. Then she turned the gas on, and instantly without having to light a match the flame was heating the water.

She put the cups on the table, the sugar and the milk, and a bowl of fruit. From the bread keeper she took the rest of a loaf of bread and began to slice it.

Since that moment that first night she had wanted to ask, "Peppino, why did you laugh at my brother's thoughtless joke, and why did you stop, like a person guilty of something, the minute you saw me stare at you?" There had been no good time to speak so directly to a man who was both her husband and a stranger. Ralphalooch drove the four of them to their house very late, and then Elena had to be settled in the flat American bed that did not sink with the body's weight but remained rigid and hard like a table. When she was alone, holding Peppino for the first time, she could not say words that would suggest she questioned the behavior of her husband. Such a thing would show that she lacked respect. Nevertheless, with each passing day the importance of the incident grew.

Peppino walked into the kitchen. Sniffing the air, he lowered the flame under the coffeepot.

"The coffee smells good."

He patted her behind as he passed her, then he sat down at the table, and turned the dial on the American radio. While some man's voice rose and fell in English phrases, none of which Palmina could understand, Peppino began to peel an apple.

She watched the way he absently pierced the skin with just the tip of his knife, and then glided it over the fruit, slowly removing the red covering in one unbroken peel.

She had first watched him do that from her father's window when she was fifteen and he was a soldier home from the front visiting her brother Pasquale. She had liked the way he controlled the knife, the way he never let it get away from him, while at the same time he appeared to pay no attention at all to what he was doing. While the red peel grew long enough to drag in the dirt under the rock on which he was sitting, he called out the numbers for the game of fingers Pasquale and Ralphalooch were playing. A year later, when he asked her to marry him, she had said yes because her parents had chosen him for her, a respectable man who had a small farm as his inheritance, but she had loved him because of the arrogant way he peeled apples.

Palmina was no longer fifteen; she was fifty-three, and no longer found his skill with a knife a sufficient reason to love him. She wondered about his time in America. Twelve years was a long time for a man to be alone. She wanted to tell him about the war. To say, "Do you see it, like I do, as an intruder who woke you up?" She wanted to say, "The day it ended I stuffed my mouth with all the American chocolate bars that the soldiers threw at us from their trucks until my tongue was black with the sweetness, and then I vomited all night. For the first time I was alive. Do you understand this?"

"Nina, pour the coffee."

He hold out his cup. She began to fill it.

"Basta."

She watched him fill the top third of the cup with milk and then dip a slice of the bread into his cup.

She had never spoken to him about dangerous things that a woman should not feel. But it was not until the war, when life seemed to exist as a spiderweb in the hedge, so easily pulled down, that she had felt them. She had never asked him about what he did the other times he had come to America and worked for a year or two; it was not her place. But this time she wanted to know.

"Peppe, I . . ."

He hold up his left hand to silence her, pointing to the talking box with his bread.

"Not now."

She poured herself a cup of the coffee, and sipped it black, looking at his hands around the yellow cup.

She wanted to know if there had been other women. Even she could have been tempted by the gentleness of Carmen Garmandi, who had brought her his last chicken to make soup when Elena had pneumonia, but she had her four children and the paesans to think about. What was a disgrace in a woman was to be expected in a man.

She reached for a slice of the bread, and buttered it. She began to eat.

She knew she was not fat, but her breasts sagged, and her hair had long streaks of gray. Her face had fine lines. She wondered if he wished she had died in the war like Carmen's wife so that he could find a younger woman.

Abruptly she got up and went to the sink. She filled a cup half full of the warm water and then she dropped a cake of yeast into it.

"Nina, sit and eat."

"I want to start the bread."

"You don't have to make bread. The bakery on Wakefield Street—"

"Makes hard-crusted loaves that can be bought warm every morning, I know."

He looked at her, and she knew he thought she had not shown respect.

"Peppe, why pay money for bread when I can make it?"

"Because in America there are bakeries where the bread is fresh every day."

She wanted to say, "In America this. In America that. I never wanted to come to this damn America!"

She cleared half the table of the fruit and dishes. Then wiped the porcelain surface with a dishrag. He took another apple and placed it on his dish.

She thought, There is no place in this wonderful American kitchen to make bread. There is no wooden sink to mix the dough. No place but this table that rings like a bell.

She poured several handfuls of flour onto the table and then poured the yeast and water into the well she made. She began blending the water and flour together with her hands.

She had written to him as soon as she was allowed after the armistice. She had told him the four children had survived, although their oldest son, Joe, had been captured by the British and was in North Africa. The Germans had eaten all the chickens, the American soldiers had bought the pig, the house had been saved from the bombing by Maria Santissima del Socorso, but the tree in the front yard by the road had been hit. She had told him to send money so that she could buy seeds for the spring planting, and more baby chickens. She told him to come home as soon as possible.

He had written back that he had placed her name and the names of the two youngest children on the list to emigrate to America. In the United States life was better. There was more food, comfortable houses with furnaces in the cellar for heat. He had earned enough money to own such a house with indoor plumbing, a telephone, and even a radio.

She had responded that she had lived through the war in her home and would not leave it. He had built it for her the year he left. It still had the best brick oven in the paese. He should come immediately and see his youngest daughter before she became a woman.

His reply had been short. He was never coming back to Italy. She could do as she chose.

She had weighed the matter. She could continue to raise her two children the way she had done, alone in her house near her married daughter and her sister in the town where she had been born, or she could leave everything that was familiar and travel to a place where no one spoke her language and begin again with a man who would surely not be the same one who had left. She who had never been farther from her house than she could walk would have to take a train to Naples and then a ship to America. She wrote Peppino that she had decided to stay in Italy. She bought the seed and planted the field.

It was her son, Pierino, the young one who had eaten the chocolate with the American soldiers, who would not stay. At sixteen, when his name came up, he had left to live with his father. A year later she and Elena had followed. She had known there was no going back when she locked the door to her house, looked at the spot on the plaster wall where she had painted "Viva il Duce!" one year and then covered the words with white paint the next. She had given the key to Carmen Garmandi to keep for her daughter.

"Nina, more coffee."

He held out the cup. She wiped her hand on the apron she had sewn by hand and brought with her, then she filled his cup.

He turned off the radio, put sugar and milk in his coffee and began to drink.

"Peppe, what is her name?"

"Whose name?"

She began punching the dough with the heel of her hand to smooth out the lumps.

"The name of the woman."

"What woman?"

She looked up from the dough into his face.

"The woman. The one responsible for all this." She waved her arm around the kitchen. "The one who bought the new dishes and all the fancy knives."

He looked down. He picked up his knife and began to casually peel his apple.

"I did it myself," he said easing his knife under the skin.

"Who picked out this paper on the walls?"

He kept his eyes on the apple, and the peel began to grow.

"I did it."

"And the sheets? Who picked out the sheets for my bed so that the color matches the towels in the bathroom?"

"Me."

He pointed to himself with the knife, then continued peeling the apple.

"Who ironed the curtains?"

His knife slipped and he cut the apple skin, which fell in a heap on his plate.

"You are crazy," he said, standing up.

She looked at the apple peel curled like a hair ribbon.

"The war has left you mad." He tapped the side of his head.

"The war has given me a voice. I want to know who has shared your bed."

At first he said nothing, did nothing. He stared at her, incredulous, and she knew that she had acted in a way that she would never have done before the war. But she did not feel shame. She wanted to know.

"What is her name?"

Peppino did not touch her. He lifted the side of the porcelain table, sending the apple and the knife, the dish, the radio, the sugar, the milk, and the bread dough crashing to the floor under the table that rang as loudly as the church bell at home.

"In America we buy the bread," he said.

He walked to the closet; took his hat and coat from the hook, came back in the kitchen, and leaned forward to kiss her.

Palmina did not lower her head but looked into his eyes. He did not kiss her, but walked out the door, quietly closing it behind him.

Palmina righted the table, set the radio on it, and began to sweep the food and broken dishes into the shining new dustpan.

"Mama, what happened?"

Elena stood in the doorway in her nightgown.

"I heard the noise." She ran across the floor and picked up the ball of dough.

"Leave it."

"We can save the bread dough."

"Leave it."

"I'll just brush it off."

"No, Elena," she said, taking the ball of dough from her daughter. "Your American father doesn't want my bread. He likes his bread from the Wakefield Street bakery."

Paul Mariani

Duet

Noon: the Jones Beach causeway
shimmering in the August haze,
the hoods of overheated Fords
& Packards, Depression black, and by
the thousands, stalled in traffic.
My brother, sister & myself in back,
my mother with the baby on her lap
up front, my father inching forward
as if still testing Shermans
for the Army. She tried to salvage
things by turning up the radio
to sing, my mother, for she sang
beautifully, and she was beautiful
and young. She kept coaxing him
to sing along with her, her bell-bright
voice & his in harmony. A duet.
Bass & alto. The male & female of it.
But there he was, my father, leaning
on his horn as someone tried
to inch around him. Then that someone
shouting through my father's window,
my mother pleading, my father out
the door, then back & vindicated. . . .

Forty years, forty years, and still
I see her, her lips pale and shaken
in the rearview mirror as we sat there
stunned & silent. By then the music
on the radio was gone. Gone too
whatever song she had been singing,
ground down again first to a sound
like bearings scraping, then tears,
then after that to nothing.

∽

Show & Tell

This poem is for you, Miss Birnbaum, my once-upon-
a-time 4th-grade teacher, whom I shall never
never forget. Back in the fall of '49,
while the invincible Yankees, golden as ever,

were beating the worthy (but vincible) Red Sox
on the greensward enclosure which the late Bart
Giamatti used to call our New World paradise,
back when the Russians had just ended the short-

lived U.S. hegemony created by those twin
phoenixes rising sublimely over Hiroshima
& Nagasaki, ending *our* invincibility by detonating
their own version of an H-bomb, and that a monster,

at that very moment, Levittown, Long Island
(that ex-potato-farm & homemade muddy eden
for all those GIs like my father, as well as other
huddled masses living in New York's superheated

flats & tenements) was still so new, it didn't
even have a school which at that particular instant
it could call its own. Those one-storied brick
& plastic wonders still lay in the "not-too-distant

& forseeable future," like our wonder malls.
The answer was to bus us kids across the tracks,
over to your four-storied ancient redbrick school
in picturesque Old Bethpage, replete with its oaks

& maples out of Norman Rockwell. The leaves
then were in their autumn beauty, flame red
& flame gold. My imitation leather shoes squeaked
with every step I took across your sun-bled

dusty wooden floor. And when my sad pants
at last split up the back, you gathered three other
teachers, ladies like yourself, and made me
bend over in the courtyard, amid a smother

of giggles, to pick up stones for you,
my backside showing through the tear, much, ah!
much to your delight, Miss B, until one woman
had the decency to call the torture

to a halt. And now that I am twice the age
you were back then, Miss B, now, before the bell
dismisses both of us for good, I want to thank you,
especially for the morning ritual of Show & Tell.

Everyone did Show & Tell, you reassured me.
Everyone. Tomorrow it would be *my* turn, you said,
to do my Show & Tell. I worked hard that night,
sweating cold sweat to try & make a card.

Scissors, ribbon, old crayons, a piece of pretty paper,
except at home we had no tape or glue & I knew
we had no money, then, for sure, for either
tape or glue. I even tried to make a home brew

of flour mixed with water, but the batter
wouldn't stick. Nothing stuck. Finally, I sewed
the goddamn thing together & made my card for you:
a red heart rampant on a piece of yellowed board,

which, Miss B, I remember you holding at arm's length
between your thumb and forefinger, away from you
and, before that class of strangers, asking why,
instead of sewing it, I hadn't simply glued

the thing together, the way any of the other
children would have done. I said nothing then,
or when I had to take the others' jeers
down on the playing field that noon, or even when

I got back home and hid, or at anytime since then,
except, Miss Birnbaum, the kid grew up the way
kids do. Eventually, the boy from the other side
of town even learned to read & write & say

things properlike, and make a proper bow.
And now, Miss B, though you may already be in hell
& I left speaking to a ghost, I have come back to try
and get it right this time. This is my Show & Tell.

∞

The Old Men Are Dying

After the three days' watch, after the flowers
are tossed into a heap, after the last mourner,
feeling the coming on of the autumn squall, turns
and leaves, the crew comes to seal the boxes, caulking them,

screwing the tops down tight, to make them seaworthy
for the last long voyage. The little boats tug
against their moorings until they pull free at last
and begin moving toward the north, a north

more north than any the dead pilots have ever
sailed before. Two uncles gone in three short
months. How the four remaining brothers huddle
closer now for warmth against the coming cold.

Twice my brother and myself had to make the trip
south from western Massachusetts to New York to pay
our last respects. And what was there to say? That
the old men were dying? First Victor, my father's

dead sister's husband. Short-order cook and journeyman
mechanic, his family from Milan. Bertazzo lopped
to Bert. Strokes broke him until he listed badly.
One more and I will not come back, he said, and meant it.

When that one hit him, he turned to face the wall,
turned north those last six weeks, until the dark snows
swept him up and he was gone, without a word, the way he was
in life. Then John, the burly one, his whole life lived

on the same mean street. Mayor of Sixty-first
and First, the neighbors came to call him, as his
Little Italy turned to swinging singles' paradise
around him. In the old photos I can see how strong

he must have been, so that I do not doubt the tales
my father told me of his brother and, for what
they're worth, I have passed on to my sons. How
he pinned two men to a barroom table by their throats,

one with his huge left paw, one with his right. How
for years he lifted kegs of prohibition booze
and lugged ice boxes five flights down to the old Ford
van. How he raised the back end of a Packard

while a buddy fixed a flat. It ate him slow, the cancer,
ate his stomach first, then the rest. Leaving
his last room late, I walked down five flights
of empty waking rooms, saw the unattended open coffins,

each with its still pilot waiting to set sail north.
And what was there to say? All sorts were there
to bid their last goodbyes: those who'd made their mark
and those who'd missed. With the greatgrandchildren

all family looks are lost. The blood gets too thinned out,
the young enter a world we never knew. Julia
and Giuseppi: left Compiano some ninety years ago.
Settled in New York with a million others like them.

Their first: run down outside their flat at sixteen
by a drunken iceman who jumped the curb and splattered him.
Siciliano, those from the north of Italy shrugged,
then turned away. For what was there to do? Once

my father sat on his sister's pineslab coffin, roped
to the flat back of the horsedrawn wagon as his family
began the long procession across the 59th Street bridge,
headed for Calvary. Too young then to understand,

he smiled into the camera. Now even he must feel
the cold. You see it when the four brothers gather
at family picnics, then turn, each one alone, to watch
the ducks drifting in the stagnant pond. They stare

at the water in the last light of Long Island summer
and, though they never talk of it, brace themselves
for the time when their little boats will be cut
loose and, dressed in their best navyblue two-piece suits,

their leathery browned hands folded stiffly
right over left with the polished black beads
between them, they begin to drift out through the once
familiar channels for the last trip north.

Carole Maso

The Lion's Head

Sheridan Square is still here. The statue of General Sheridan, still standing. The Lion's Head is still here, 59 Christopher Street. I walk down the steps into the bar and watch the legs go by the window.

"We often went to the Lion's Head in those days. And the White Horse."

Still there. It's comforting to picture my young parents in the White Horse Tavern. Or the Lion's Head.

"But no, Caroline," he says whispering, shaking his head. "Those were not the good old days.

"My God, what do you think it was like for her? Everyone around her seeing and hearing and feeling, or she thinking they were. What must it have really been like? Painters, writers, composers, all working—all *engaged* in things. Artists drinking all night, discussing pure form, twelve tones, God knows what. Journalists yacking away into the wee hours about politics, the left, baseball, I don't know what else, singing songs."

A boyfriend and I used to come here sometimes, Max. There is something about the light here, late afternoon, amber drinks, an early snow—it made us say things we never meant before and would never mean again, but we meant them at that moment at the Lion's Head.

"Yes, Caroline, I understand that."

The head of a lion. The floating hands of that boyfriend. I see things in pieces, in parts. A black shoe with a bow where the foot arches. A delicate ankle. A table separates that foot from the rest of the woman. Why do I see so many things in fragments? A whole person bisected by a table. It becomes something too hideous. I look away.

Was it always so bad for her, Max?

"Well, no. It was actually OK for a while. She got worse as she got older, as she entered her late twenties. Or perhaps it was just that after a while I could better see it. Once I got past the bone structure, the elegance of her movements, the dark hair, the sheer perfection of her, she was an all-consuming feast for the eye. Her ever-changing face in those days."

"Something to eat?" the waiter asks me.

"The food was always inedible in those days."

"No," I tell him, "just another drink."

"At the age I began losing interest in 'death,' your mother's interest seemed to escalate. But no, that's sarcasm talking, bitterness. It wasn't like that. I don't think she ever really thought about killing herself. It never actually occurred to her, I'm quite sure. Even that night in the street. 'The people who have walked in darkness have seen a great light.' she kept whispering. My God, how ghastly, the damn streetlight shining on her extraordinary face."

"But the day she finally died, what made that day different? Surely she suffered many, many days."

"She simply couldn't go on. If nothing else, I'm quite sure of that."

"Why did she do it, Max?"

"She simply couldn't go on."

"Couldn't you have stopped her?"

"What do you think, Caroline?"

"But she was a devout Catholic. You yourself have said."

"She was devout enough to believe He'd forgive her."

"Will He forgive her, Max?"

My father laughs loud, as if he's still alive. "I wouldn't count on it."

Friend

I look at my friend hooked up to a huge machine. It should be possible to say something, to do something with words. But all I can manage is "I love you." I hold his hand lightly, watch the liquid drop from its bag into the tube and into his arm. The nurse comes in, but sees me and turns. I realize I could be his sister perhaps, and, it is true, I could be his mother. He's that young all of a sudden today. "I'm just like a pioneer," he sputters, lying there. He opens his childish eyes. Stares at the poster that hangs across from him. Closes them again. "It looks like a carnival," he says, "a carnival on a hot summer night." A ferris wheel—he rode it into fever.

He is sleeping, this pioneer, and I am grateful for that. I watch him sleep for a long time. No one seems to mind. It's visiting hours, after all.

Max, I don't understand any of it.

I am not mother or sister, wife or lover. Remember how we used to dream of having children together, Steven?

I am your friend.

He's sleeping so soundly. On his night table, *The Vampire Lestat, The Face* magazine, *Mr. Palomar,* his Walkman, his Rolodex.

Men with masks and gloves come in. I move my fingers to my lips to say, Quiet, my friend is asleep. They are young men and even in masks I can tell they are good-looking. Like my friend.

Steven opens his eyes. He looks at them as they remove the red plastic bags that are full and replace them. He's thinking, Oh, those cute orderlies, or, Didn't I meet you once at the Paladium? or—I don't know what he's thinking. He turns his palm over. I put my finger lightly in his hand and he folds his finger around mine. He's thinking so many things lying there. He opens his mouth slightly, like a baby bird. It should be possible to do something with words.

"Caroline," he whispers, "I love you too."

Sometimes it is best not to go directly home after a visit to the hospital. Sometimes it is best to go sit in a cafe for a while. Espresso and an anisette biscuit. Lean against some column, some faux marble.

I feel the toll that suffering takes. You are my friend and you are suffering. High fevers, chills. Tests, a bronchoscopy, a spinal tap.

"My brother had a spinal tap once," I tell him. "He said it wasn't too bad."

You are sarcastic with suffering, and then not. When you are not, you sit up in bed, you clip things from newspapers, looking for shapes. You make out bills. You send me the latest fashions in an envelope. You type me little notes.

Then you're doubtful. We find it difficult to talk about the future. All talk of galleries stops. Shows. You are sarcastic with suffering. What gallery would want you with your machines, your chills, your death sentence? You are not old enough to die. This I know for sure.

These things are true about yourself, Caroline:

Sometimes you need to sit in a cafe after a visit to the hospital. You like to watch the people around you, pretend it's the whole world. You sit, even now, with a pen in your hand. You hold it like a paintbrush sometimes. Sometimes like a staff. Sometimes like a weapon. Now and then you still think of Maggie and Alison, of Candace and Henry.

You push your hair to one side of your head, capable of arranging, if nothing else, the way your hair falls.

You are perceived as aloof, sad, a little strange.

"Another espresso, please. Something strong, with a kick."

We used to joke about having children.

"I had a dream that I was making love with my doctor and all of her friends on this enormous bed."

"You were making love with your woman doctor?"

"And all her friends," you add. "All women."

They were saving your life, I thought, biting into the anisette biscuit.

"I called my parents this morning at about six o'clock and told them how much I loved them, how much I appreciated all they'd done, how wonderful they've been. They called back an hour later. They thought I was going to kill myself. End it right here. They thought I was saying good-bye."

Put the ashtray in the center of the table. The little vase with the flower and baby's breath slightly to the left. The sugar in its glass pot to the other side.

The woman at the next table has four cigarettes left in her pack.

My house is about four minutes from here.

Let me amend what I have always thought. I love not things that are certain, but simply things in themselves.

Four cigarettes on a table in a cafe. I love not the future. Not the fact that she will surely smoke them, but that they are here right now. Four of them, in a brightly colored package.

What he was saying was thank you.

What they thought he was saying was good-bye.

Christine Palamidessi Moore

From *The Virgin's Nose*
(or Picking Up a Piece of the Pietà)

Papa had told Carlo there was so much beauty in Rome that a hole twisted through the sky connecting it to heaven. The center of the hole was the dome of the Vatican. Papa suggested Carlo go there and pray for success in a career as an Italian lawyer. "You'll have a direct line to God," he said. But the first time Carlo had been in Rome, he hadn't gone to St. Peter's, having found the Americans filming *Ben-Hur* instead. But this time, Carlo decided, St. Peter's was where he would go. He might find a thread of Mama's soul, or Papa's, and he wanted to say goodbye. Carlo wasn't convinced heaven existed, but he was open-minded.

Inside the cool Basilica, hundreds of saints huddled above Carlo, painted on the dome of the ceiling. "The chosen," he mumbled. "Thank God I never believed I could be one of them."

He crumpled the twenty-dollar bill he had planned to put into the copper alms box and passed a wall of candles flickering in red cups. "God wouldn't end up with my money anyway," he said to himself. "The pope will buy a case of spaghetti for the cardinals, or the janitor will sweep it into his own wallet."

Carlo followed a group of tourists into the adjoining vestibule. They paused in front of a statue that was exhibited on a raised platform roped off from an altar area.

"This is the *Pietà*," the thin tour director announced. "Michelangelo's only signed sculpture."

At first, Carlo stood still, allowing the presence of the statue to sweep over him. He thought about how heavy it must be and how hardness penetrated through it from surface to surface. The image of two people, one grieving, the other dead had been carved from one huge chunk of stone. The artist must have lived inside the stone, feeling its grain and knowing its weak spots, making what was imperfect perfect. He shook his head. A dead son draped across the lap of a virgin was an image of complete suffering, and a curse Carlo refused to carry. Life wasn't as bad as the *Pietà*, he told himself. Mothers and sons were cocreators. Sons die. Mothers die. It was natural. Carlo decided Michelangelo must have been commissioned to show death and denial, otherwise he would have carved something less painful from the beautiful rock.

Carlo glanced to his right and left. The men and women standing next to him were as serious as the statue, seeming to believe in its suffering. Their breathing compressed to a hiss. Carlo wished he had chocolates or chewing gum to hand out to them. Better yet, he wanted to stand on the platform himself, to topple it down and say, "Hey, I'm Carlo. In America, In God We Trust—we don't fear Him. When you visit Boston, find me on the Freedom Trail."

But Carlo didn't move. He had come to St. Peter's for a revelation. He waited for a beam of light, or a song, to relieve the explosion in his brain. Too many voices screamed behind his forehead. His Mama had died, he hadn't seen her to her grave—or Papa—and his sister Alicia hated him. Carlo could hear them arguing inside him, taking away the peace of his own thoughts. It all would have been okay if his sister had embraced him, and asked to depend on him now that she had no one else. He had come as soon as he could. He was a generous man. She had pushed him away from herself, their own mother, and the soil he had first stood on. Carlo looked up at the *Pietà* again and felt as if he were the Virgin holding on to his dying self. It wasn't the revelation he wanted.

Just then, a skinny man with stringy red hair scaled the balustrade to the right of the statue. His eyes frightened Carlo. He might have a gun. No one moved.

The man didn't pull a gun from his baggy trousers, but a huge iron hammer, and he began pounding the Virgin's face.

"I am Jesus Christ," he shouted, pausing to whack his own chest before continuing to hammer away at the statue.

The crowd screamed and held their hands over their hearts, but not Carlo. It was an opportunity, perhaps the revelation he was waiting for. He pushed to the front of the crowd and knelt on one knee, lifted a flash camera, which he had hidden under his gray jacket, and snapped pictures of the man destroying the Virgin's head. Carlo advanced the film and pressed the shutter as quickly as his short fingers could move.

A guard blew a whistle. "Quick!" he shouted. "Somebody get him!"

The red-headed man stood on the platform, at Christ's bare feet.

Chunks of marble fell to the floor, and tour groups from other rooms pushed into the vestibule where they could hear the pitch of metal hitting stone. The crowd pressed shoulder to shoulder, a mass of uplifted heads mimicking the faces painted on the dome above them. They watched the man with clenched teeth hammer the Virgin's face.

A piece of marble landed near Carlo's foot. He picked it up.

A young guard scaled the statue's balustrade and seized the criminal's arm. The hammer dropped.

"No one leaves this room!" the guard commanded.

Another guard blasted three short screams on his whistle.

Carlo hid his camera under his clothes.

The crowd hovered under the damaged *Pietà*. "It's ruined. She's ruined," one person wailed. "It will never be the same," someone else said. Strangers held on to one another. "God help us! *Mamma mia.*"

In the rage of the event, Carlo slipped out of the Basilica into the spilling Rome sun.

In his hotel room, he turned on the television. Laszlo Toth's act was already news.

The Hungarian had cleaved the nose off the Virgin, gouged her left eyelid, her forehead, and veil. His hammer strokes had broken her left arm at the elbow, and when her hand hit the floor, the fingers snapped off.

"This has been the world's first act of violence against a work of art," the TV journalist reported.

The station ran a dramatic reenactment of the event.

"Why didn't the madman hit Christ?" the journalist asked. She pointed out that Christ's face had been an easier target than the Virgin's.

The pope and his entourage appeared on the television screen.

"This has been a terrible act," the pope said. He pinched the crucifix around his neck. He asked that all pieces of the Virgin be returned to the Vatican. "Her fragments are not to be considered souvenirs," he said. The camera zoomed in on the pope's well-scrubbed face. "Please. Return her to us, to your church, to Italy. Don't let her leave this country. We have already lost too many of our precious possessions."

The pope blessed the TV audience before reciting the twenty-four-hour telephone number set up by the Vatican to receive calls regarding the Virgin's missing pieces. Eight-one-seven six-two-two-oh.

The journalist continued her report: "Already the Vatican is receiving bids from artists who want to repair Michelangelo's statue. Some say it will take years, others says only a few weeks. If all the bits of marble are returned, one woman, the daughter of artist Domenica Sica, guarantees she can fix the Virgin in three days by using a tough glue containing an Italian cheese."

Next, Giovanni Urbani, president of Rome's Restoration Institute, appeared on the screen. He spoke from his woodpaneled office. "Let's leave the statue as it is," he said. "Think of Venus de Milo. Why not let the *Pietà* be fragmentary? Why hide damage? One must, at a certain point, accept an accomplished fact of this sort. If not, there is a risk of falsification, an offense to the work of art."

Another group, academics, began to discuss whether or not works of art had lives of their own.

Carlo switched off the television. He lay belly down on the yellow bedspread. He had the Virgin's nose. Though he had been holding it for more than forty minutes, the marble was still cool in his hand.

He slid the top of his little finger around the delicate wings of a nostril. Touching the marble, Carlo enjoyed its sheer slickness and the energy within the rock. The pulse of Michelangelo's hands still vibrated a pressure on its surface, making it perfect. He rolled onto his back, pressed the cracked tip of the Virgin's nose against his own nose and imagined looking into Michelangelo's eyes.

Carlo saw the face of his creator, the person who had turned the dark center of the universe inside out for him. Michelangelo's eyes would be green, he decided, and as humble and invincible as his own. But his eyebrows would be bushy, his forehead more deeply lined, his mouth smaller, and Michelangelo would say "so long" when he was finished and simply walk away. Then Carlo closed his own eyes and imagined what it might be like to be the statue, and be admired by hundreds of millions of people.

With his stone nose, Carlo sniffed what had already passed. A vapor of joy, so unlike the sensation of being carved from a chunk of marble, filled his heart. If he were a statue, he would never die, he said to himself. Then, a fragile but persistent floral odor, which faded as quickly as he consumed the smell, drifted into his nostrils. It came from the fragmented side of the nose, not the nose's smooth finished surface. As he inhaled the scent, Carlo desperately wanted to have something that he could hold on to. He thought of Jassy. He wanted her forever. Was that possible?

He kept the Virgin overnight, placing her nose on the pillow next to his own, and he pulled the covers up to where her chin would be. He skipped dinner and sat in the stuffed green chair next to the nose, thinking about his own children who weren't born yet and who would never know his mother—or his sister. There was nothing in Italy that he belonged to anymore. He was like the nose, cut off from the rest of the statue.

I turned my head when Carlo wept. I was ashamed that I had told my brother to drop dead and disappear. What did I expect to gain by sending him away, besides an inheritance, the land, and my own stubbornness? I thought I should give him a second chance. Carlo had grown to be a sensitive man. It had been a mistake to send him away.

At midnight, Carlo crawled into bed with the nose. I watched how careful he was. He didn't dare to touch the Virgin's waist or face. She was a grown woman, not a child, and she was his sister, he told himself. I was ashamed when I realized it was me he was farewelling. Carlo heard my mean voice: "We share only clouds of childhood. *Fuori!*"

Carlo fell asleep, dreaming about my cloud moving away from his and how he wanted his cloud to become thinner so it could stretch across the sky. But it got too thin, and disappeared like a scent.

I wanted to change my words and his dream. I hadn't yet realized that getting involved in other people's dreams got you nowhere.

The next day, after he had showered, Carlo called the Vatican. He wanted to return the nose. When he peered out of his hotel window, to check for the official black car that was to pick him up at ten, he saw me instead. He didn't know what to think, since he had already made peace with my decision to cut him from my life.

I stood on the sidewalk and lifted my black grieving veil, blew him a kiss, pointed to my valise, and lifted my thumb into the sky. I had decided to go to America with him.

Carlo nodded and indicated for me to wait on the sidewalk until he came down. I feared he would send me back home. I was pushing and pulling on him. "So what?" I said out loud to myself. "My mother has just died." I knew Carlo was thinking I was a woman who couldn't make up her mind and that I wasn't as determined, or clearheaded, as Jassy. But I was his sister and had certain rights.

Carlo rushed out of the hotel to me. "I have a meeting with the pope," he said, as if the meeting were not anything unusual. Then I remembered Carlo had always assumed he was as important as anyone else. He was freshly shaved, his golden skin glistened, and he had doused his cheeks with pine-scented aftershave.

"Oh?" I said, expecting Carlo would tell me to wait in his room.

"Come with me," he said.

A black car pulled under the hotel canopy. At the moment, I suspected he was inviting me because there was no time to do anything else. But later he explained my face had looked so frightened and unsure, he was certain if he left me alone I would change my mind and go back to Subiaco.

A man in a red cassock motioned us into the car. A black-frocked priest—whom I would know more intimately in the future—took my suitcase and put it in the trunk of the car. I sat in the middle of the backseat, between the holy man and my brother. The priest drove.

"*È sua moglie?* Your wife?" the cardinal asked Carlo, eyeing me somewhat critically. I admit I was very unattractive.

"*Mia sorella,*" Carlo answered. "Our mother died two days ago," he said, explaining my black dress.

"I will say a prayer for your mother," the cardinal said. Then Cardinal Ulbaldini rolled back his sleeves and introduced himself. He was Direct Counsel to the Holy See, Ultimate Venerator Supreme of the Vatican Museum Collection, Head of the Limbo Society, and the Official Terra-Firma Father of the International Benevolent Society. I squirmed, wanting to tell the cardinal I worked for the Benevolents in Subiaco, but I said nothing.

"Where is the nose?" the cardinal asked.

Carlo gave it to him, passing the marble piece over my lap.

The cardinal wiped the marble nose with a cloth handkerchief before dropping it into a gold box. He was a fiery-looking older man, with black curly hair and pulsing gray eyes.

"Now, do you want to make a confession?" he asked, leaning forward to bless Carlo, behaving as if his holy grace dared not land on me. It was uncomfortable to be treated as if I were impure—compared to Carlo I was a saint.

"Confession? Me? Never," Carlo laughed. "I don't need it."

"Do you have the camera?" The cardinal became businesslike.

So did my brother. He patted under his arm. "Sure do." Carlo had strapped the camera to his body as if it were a gun.

"We'll be wanting that, too." Ulbaldini held open a leather sack into which Carlo was supposed to drop the camera.

"Wait a minute." Carlo put up his hands. "I speak Italian like a native, but I'm an American. I have individual rights. Here's my passport." He pushed the cardinal's sack aside. "I want you to know I also called the television station. They're going to meet us at the Vatican. They know I have the nose and pictures of Laszlo Toth. Your people said they didn't want pictures."

"It's against rules to take pictures inside St. Peter's. Flash bulbs ruin the frescoes. Didn't you read the signs?" The cardinal rubbed his cleft chin. "I'll give you five thousand dollars for the camera."

Carlo laughed. The cardinal was offering him money. I nudged my brother's knee, urging him to take it. Carlo had planned on giving the pictures away for nothing.

"Not enough? How about ten then?" The cardinal shifted his legs.

"Don't joke." Carlo reached under his tweed sport coat. He had no way of knowing if the pictures were any good. It was a cheap camera—$7.50 off the rack in his drugstore. "I wonder how much the press would pay for the film," he wondered out loud.

The limousine sped through the bright morning, over the bridge, and past ancient townhouses along the Tiber.

"We don't want the pictures to go to the press. Fifteen, then." The cardinal removed a checkbook from the rear glove compartment. "Look," he said. "It's already signed. By the pope himself." The cardinal touched his lips.

If I had wanted to speak, I couldn't. My mouth and throat had frozen. Fifteen thousand dollars from the pope! The money was blessed.

The signature was fancy. Carlo held the blue check between his fingers. The paper was soft as a wave. Carlo shook his head no. "Sorry, I only deal in cash," he said. "Checks have to clear through banks. There's taxes. Half the money will go out the window." Carlo waved his wide hands. I stepped on his foot.

"You're a businessman, aren't you?" The cardinal leaned over my lap to get closer to Carlo. "Don't you have a Swiss bank account?" he whispered.

"That's for the big players, not me. Fifteen thousand is small change. They'd laugh at me." Carlo scratched his sideburns, which I noticed had a few sprouts of gray.

"Thirty, then," the cardinal said.

For a moment neither of the men said anything. Carlo was dizzy; so was I. The limousine stopped at a red light near a garden rimmed with palm trees and a lush blossoming orange tree.

"Listen, Mr. Barzini, let's make a deal. How about I open an account for you and send you the number? Write down your name and address." The cardinal handed Carlo a sheet of white Vatican paper and a fountain pen. "Go on, write."

Carlo hesitated.

"Forty-five," the cardinal said.

Carlo laughed. He was sweating. "How can I trust you? Just because you wear a robe, should I pretend we are like bread and cheese?"

We never made it to the Vatican. The cardinal didn't want to run into representatives from the television stations. "Let's stop at this cafe," he said. The young priest slid the limousine into a parking spot.

The men got out. I stayed behind them. They sat at a table for two. I sat at a table for one. The driver—the priest in black—stood by the car, watching. Without more words from Carlo, other than his ordering a double espresso, the cardinal's offer went up to fifty thousand.

Carlo grabbed Cardinal Ulbaldini's hand. "Stop there, please," he said, laughing. "And if my pictures aren't good, forget the deal."

The cardinal relaxed. "It's been a pleasure," he said.

They continued to shake hands, and they embraced. Both men enjoyed finding their own kind, other men who appreciated the intoxication of deal making. It was that simple. It didn't matter that Carlo got what he didn't expect, and Ulbaldini gave more than he had allotted. Carlo and the cardinal had made something happen.

I was crazy with fury. Why wasn't I born lucky? Why not me? Carlo had no heartaches and earned rewards without bending his back. I struggled and prayed. He saw only the polished side of life. I saw the suffering.

Carlo talked like a rocket, telling Ulbaldini about the North End of Boston, Hanover Street, and his stores. "Cardinal Ulbaldini, you must visit us," he said. "Being there is just like not leaving Italy but better. You can leave," he laughed. "Look at me! I am here."

Ben Morreale

From *The Loss of the Miraculous*

Chris had a small soft mouth whose lips, just before she began speaking, opened up like a flower to pose a curled tongue each time she said such words as *look, lick* or *luck.*

Chris found Brian among his women, routed him out. She slept with men as easily as he slept with women, making sure to tell him—casually. She once had been a nun and had left the convent to marry an older man who had died soon after they both came to our town. Now at age thirty-four she had the air of a suffering widow so appealing to Brian. It made him feel as if he cuckolded the very dead and reaffirmed his own life. But you take everything of a woman to bed with you. And with Chris, Brian took her inherited wealth and her gracious home, with soft lighting and a toilet broad and low that flushed so quietly that one was hypnotized by the swirling silent waters. He took her frenzy to bed with him.

She outplayed him with the madness that lay beneath her sweet smile, and encouraged his panic when he realized that she was equal to him, that she was outplaying him. His panic often burst out in rage and anger against my friend William or me.

It didn't happen often, usually when Chris called him from someone else's bed. A day or two later after Chris told him, casually, all the details of her fucking, he would be gentle and kind to Chris and to all of us, hardly aware of her voluptuous use of jealousy to tie him to her.

In my Mediterranean town they would have said she was possessed of the Demons—*incubus* and *sucubus*—that her evil was not banal. It was an obsession. Her ability to make love to both men and women was proof of that. Her own inability to feel jealousy at anything Brian did would seen unnatural.

In my Mediterranean town they would have noticed her small sharp teeth, her body that seemed to have no bones—only a back bone.

She left her teeth marks on the shoulders of everyone she made love to. Two such women could kill any man or woman. A school of such demons would leave only the bare bones.

Among William's papers there was a letter headed, *To Jeanne.* I don't know if he ever sent it. Much of what it said made me feel that I hardly knew them.

> *You are born with some things and into others; your temperament, your father's gestures, your mother's nuances. Accept these things because you can't do anything about them. Above all, don't fight them. They love a fight and feed on it.*
>
> *Love and life are the same; if they lasted forever, they would not be as sweet.*
>
> *If you have the choice between doing something stupid or doing nothing, do nothing. Most stupidities are done out of boredom or loneliness.*
>
> *Learn to live quietly with yourself. Then living with others will be a dividend.*
>
> *Don't pay too big a price for fraternity; o, n men have lost their freedom in exchange for fraternity.*
>
> *If mindless love should overwhelm you, co ummate it, that is, live in close proximity until it is burned out. Othe vise its possibilities will haunt you the rest of your life and you will mo e from one phantom to another.*
>
> *Explanations are to be found in the future as answers are found in solutions—the reason for our love was to be found in our life together. Anxieties are in the future, not in the past. It must be so, because we know we learn nothing from the past in things that really matter. If it were not so, we'd be much happier. You and me.*

George Panetta

From *We Ride a White Donkey*

"Powicy?" Papa said. "You say before powicy?"

Papa couldn't read and write when he came off the boat, but in those days it was just as it is now in America, and the first thing Papa did was go in business. He opened a big dress factory on Lafayette Street, and I remember when I was twelve and just about getting tired with ring o'leevio, I used to go to Papa's shop and pat all the dress dummies on the behind. Papa had about nine dummies all over the shop, and when you were twelve you couldn't know there was no difference between them and the real girls. Anyway, Papa opened this shop and was making money like an Irishman, and it even looked as if he was smarter than the Irishmen, because although they were making money too, they were always breaking their heads or falling off scaffolds or forgetting to come out of a hole before the backfill. And besides, there was more dignity to what Papa was doing, and once in a while he wore a clean shirt.

But as Papa made the money, Mama spent it by having one of us every year and by lending Helen to Uncle George in Italy, so that after that Mama could make three trips to Italy to see if she couldn't get Helen back. Papa couldn't get over all the money he was making, and for years he had Mama write letters to everybody in Italy, telling them to come quick because the gold was in the streets. . . . In 1926, . . . Papa was ruined.

———

"What happen, Enrico?" Uncle Louie asked him.

"Who know?" said Papa. "Bank she craze."

"You sure you got money, Enrico?"

"Louie, shutupa you too."

"Maybe you no got, Enrico. I'm no say sure, buts could be."

"First time Bank no send," Papa said.

"Fix up with bookkeep, Enrico."

"Fix nothing. Bank send tomorrow."

"Fix up with bookkeep, Enrico. Make sure."

"Louie, shutupa! Go home!"

"Make sure, Enrico. Remember, I say make sure."

"Make sure go home."

Uncle Louie went home, and as he was going home the first thing he wanted to do was move away where relations had to take the train if they wanted to come and borrow money. He knew Papa was broke; he was a little smarter than Papa, had learned to shoot pool, and had become a citizen when his wife explained the widow's pension they give you in this country. He was even smart enough to get in the Army in the first war, become a cook, and get shot in the behind when his company was retreating. He could figure it all out how Papa was broke, and as he was going home he kept saying it over to himself:

The wife three time Italy . . . coupla thousan; coupla thousan just kids gets born, and twenn thousan just kids eats, sleeps, dress him up like somebody. The summer come . . . country . . . Souths Beach. Gotta go country? No, too much, say twenn thousan just country. Gotta go? Jeesa, how can have money! And thena the doctor, Jeesa! The small one get the convulsh, call doctor; the fat one fall swamp Souths Beach, call doctor; gotta call doctor? Say five thousan just call lousa doctor. And the biga one? the girl? gotta go college? What the hell for send college, you know? Gonna marry get kids good-bye college tomorrow. What the hell for send? Thats coupla thousan more. And factory? Jeesa, how can save money? Fifty dollar bookkeep, make check, telephone, hello, good-bye, fifty dollar. . . .

Uncle Louie kept talking to himself all the way home, and by the time he was home he figured that Papa had spent two hundred thousand dollars since he had come to America.

"Jeesa," Uncle Louie said, "how can have money my brother?"

The next day Papa went to the Bank, first thing.

"Whats matter no money?" Papa said.

"Your checking account is overdrawn," said the Bank. "You owe us a dollar and sixty-two cents."

"I own you?" Papa said.

"You mustn't forget, Mr. Caparuta, that you haven't made a deposit in two months."

"I no want know deposits," Papa said. "When I get money pay people?"

"You don't understand, Mr. Caparuta."

"I understan all about," Papa said. "I put put put. Now I take out."

The Bank looked at Papa as if it were almost human, as if it were sorry for all these humans who were mad.

"Isa right?" Papa asked, looking right back.

"But, Mr. Caparuta, you must check your account."

"Demma who know this account. Twenn years I look book? I see whats this? No. Whats got to do book? The people want money; they work, no? Can say go home people, no money. Twenn years Rico Caparuta no do this thing. Now you say account account. Whats got to do account?"

"I'm sorry, Mr. Caparuta, the check is no good with your account in its present condition."

Papa looked at the Bank right in the eye, like all Italians do when they're going to kill you and never do. Then in Italian Papa told the Bank first of all to go to hell, then he said it was no wonder we had bank robbers and that he hoped they would come around that night with sacks and take everything, even the pennies, and that now he knew what they were, crooks, big crooks, taking in money all the time, and once when you really needed it, you couldn't get it.

"Never gen I put," Papa said.

"I'm sorry, Mr. Caparuta."

"Never gen. I swear my seven childra. Put put put, and demma when you wants you get? You gots nothing. Thats good way do business. Fine!"

Papa went out of the bank, back to the factory, and right into the poor bookkeeper's face.

"Why you no tell me?" Papa said.

"I told you a dozen times, Mr. Caparuta," said the bookkeeper.

"You tell me?" said Papa. "When you tell me?"

"A dozen times, Mr. Caparuta."

"You tell me? You lie now too?"

"Even when I was writing out the check, I told you there was no money."

"You craze too, Antonette? You tell me?"

"Yes, Mr. Caparuta. Maybe you weren't listening."

"Whats matter everybody? Go craze?"

It wasn't Papa's fault. When he came off the boat he couldn't read and write, but he opened this factory and got in the habit of making money. Every time he put his cross on the check, they sent the money. Now all of a sudden they didn't send it. And even if the bookkeeper did tell him, it wasn't his fault. Could you believe a thing like that after twenty years? Would you pay any attention to it if somebody should speak about it? After twenty years somebody comes to you and says Mr. Caparuta, no more money, good-bye.

How could be?

It wasn't Papa's fault. And when Uncle Louie came over one night and talked about putting fire to the factory, that wasn't Papa's fault either.

"Enrico, thats we do," Uncle Louie said.

"But you sure money come?"

"Sure, Enrico. Sure."

It wasn't Uncle Louie's fault either. How could he know that Papa's factory wasn't insured.

One night Uncle Louie forgot his cigar between forty yards of black cloth. He came running home to Papa that the factory was on fire.

Together they stood on the corner of Broome and Lafayette looking at the fire.

"You do good," Papa said.

"Better like this, Enrico. No worry no more."

"You sure get money, no, Louie?"

"Sure, Enrico. Sure."

Uncle Louie had done a good job with his cigar, and after that Papa began sitting around the house waiting for Them to send the check. They didn't send the check right away, so Mama started buying everything on credit. It was the beginning of our credit system and the way we got to know everybody. Up to that time we had never had to pay anybody for anything we owed them because we never owed anybody anything; and because we had always been able to pay what we owed, everybody thought it was a good policy to give us all the credit we wanted. It was sound economics. So Mama started with the poor grocer on the corner of Mulberry. At first Mama used to go down herself, but after a week the grocer was looking at her as if he was wondering and Mama decided she had too much cooking and cleaning to do and began sending Aly down. It had to be Aly. It couldn't be Betty because she was going to college and was getting intelligent enough to be ashamed. It couldn't be Helen because she had just come back from Italy with a bald head and it was better to keep her in the house and protect her. And Jenny was twelve and just starting in with the piano and learning to faint any time anybody asked her to do anything. And none of the other boys could go because P.J. could fight me and I could fight Aldo and Aldo could fight Aly. It had to be Aly.

He used to go down every day with four or five of Mama's lists, written on both sides of a paper bag, with a promise on the bottom of each, don't worry as soon as the check comes Mama will be down. The grocer didn't mind at first, because now that Papa was out of work we were spending five or six dollars more every day; but after a few weeks he began to shake his head, scratch out items like provolone and salami, and send notes back to Mama. Then Mama would speak to Papa.

"This check when come, Enrico?"

"She come, shutupa."

"Enrico, the grocer want money. Maybe you work, no Enrico?"

"Shutupa. Do you cook."

But Mama really believed the check was coming, and kept buying everything on credit, groceries, meat, ice, milk and, after a while, bedsheets. One day the grocer sent Aly back with nothing, and Mama sent Aly right back with a long letter written by Betty, in which she used two of the words she learned at college.

"This is what?" the grocer asked.

Aly never talked in those days.

The grocer's name was Max, but he had been in the neighborhood so long, nobody hit him when the people walked along Kenmare Street on Halloween to get to Delancey. He spoke Italian, all dialects; had forgotten Jewish because it was useless and couldn't sell anything in that language. He ate macaroni like the Italians, had as many children, and the only reason he wasn't a Christian was because nobody really wanted to know.

"Who understands this?" he said. "Here take, take. I should worry."

After all, why should he worry? People owed him, he owed the people. If people bought more retail, he bought more wholesale. If the people had no money for him, he had no money for the other people. So he had a little bookkeeping? So?

He shrugged and filled the bags up for Aly. "Here, take the salami, too."

Aly came up with the stuff that day, smiling for the first time since he had the convulsions. Mama smiled too, and I think if it wasn't for Max giving us all that food and showing Mama how easy it was to get everything for nothing, we would have starved many times all the while Papa was waiting for the check. It taught Mama the economics of small business, just as later I learned the economics of big business and was able to get the chicken farm for Uncle Pete and the house for my brother-in-law Frank. We kept eating just as if Papa still had the factory, but at the end of the month the landlord kept coming every day to the door.

It was a new kind of economics, so Mama hid in one of the bedrooms. One day Papa got out of the chair in which he was waiting for the check and answered the door.

The landlord was a small man with spats who should've been dead ten years.

"The rent, Mr. Caparuta?"

Papa wanted to kill him.

"How long I here?"

"Twenty years," the landlord said.

"How long I pay you?"

"You always pay before."

"Well, watch you want?"

"But this is a new month. I've got taxes to pay."

"Figure watch I pay you twenn years," Papa said.

"That has nothing to do with it. This is another month."

"Go head, figure. Twenn years. Figure how much this."

At thirty-five dollars a month it came to about eight or nine thousand dollars, and it was hard to understand you didn't own the rooms, even if you weren't Papa, who had come off the boat without knowing how to read and write.

"That has nothing to do with it, Mr. Caparuta. I must have the rent."

"Get out my house," Papa said. "Come back I throw you down-stairs."

The landlord went down the stairs walking, and stayed away for two months. Mama came out of the bedroom.

"Enrico, who we do?"

"We do nothing. We wait check."

"But you sure check come?"

"Whatthehellwhatsmatter with you? Sure check come. Go cook and shutupa."

The check never came, but Papa was patient and waited another month for it. When it came, Papa was going to go to Boston to see "what's going be," and Mama was going to get a new bed for her bed-room. She kept telling Papa she had had the bed for twenty years, and had the seven children in it, but one of these days the bed bugs were go-ing to come out of it, wait and see.

"All right, all right," Papa said, "the bed. All right."

Mama was going to get the bed, and Betty was going to get her money for college, and then we were going to see if we couldn't get a doctor who could put the hair back on Helen's head. Meanwhile, Mama was learning how to get more and more on credit, and there was a little old man named Blau who was beginning to come around every Monday for six petticoats that Mama had bought for the girls. This was in 1926 and Mama started with a bill of twelve dollars, but in 1936 Mama owed him 362 dollars and poor Blau came every week (this was in Brooklyn) and each time he came Mama was hiding in the bathroom. Jenny had to go to the door to tell Blau to come back next week, and old Blau would say nothing, just look up at the ceiling, shrug his shoul-ders, and go. One week he didn't come, and then he never came any more. If he died, I suppose he thought he was better off. But he never came back and Mama was angry and even a little insulted and began blaming Jenny for scaring Blau away, and when Jenny began to com-plain that she had no panties, Mama stuck out her tongue and told Jenny to go and see if she could get them cash some place.

Blau disappeared in 1936, and after that Mama got Mr. Klide, and the first two dollars Mama spent with Mr. Klide was cash; but now, in 1943, Mama owes him 348 dollars and thirty-two cents, and she has forgotten all about Blau.

Still, when Papa got the check Mama was going to pay everybody, even Max the grocer, although when the check never came, she realized she never had to. But in 1926, when she was first starting, Mama worried a little; and one night she got after Papa about the check, and they had one of those fights Grandma used to tell us about, as if Mama was going to tell Papa she was pregnant again.

"Enrico, I no think check come," Mama started.

"Shutupa," Papa said, right off.

"Shutupa, you, Enrico."

"Go sleep," said Papa.

"Go sleep, you."

Papa looked at her, Calabrese style.

Mama said: "Check no come thats why."

"The check come. Nuncha I want tell you gen!"

"Who this check I like know," said Mama.

"Nothing. No you business. Go sleep."

"I want know Enrico."

"You want know? Go sleep you know better."

"You lie thats why. Check no come. No tell me."

Papa gave her another one of those looks, and if it wasn't that Mama gave him the same sort of look, she would have fallen three flights down on Kenmare Street.

"H'ime no scare, Enrico. I want know. I want know now. Who this check? Who give you? I want know."

"No you business," Papa said.

Mama shook her head almost as far down as her chest. "Thats why. I know. You no get check no nothing. You like sit down all day smoke smoke smoke; you no get check. No tell me. You laze, Enrico. You big laze."

Papa got up for the second time since the factory burned down. He grabbed Mama by the hair and pulled at it, and if Mama didn't scream we would have had another bald head around the house.

The boys and girls all got up—the boys in their underwear and socks, to keep them warm and save time in the morning; the girls in those evening clothes they used to call nightgowns, and one of them in a baldhead, about which she had just sent up a prayer.

"What's the matter?" P.J. said, the big boy, eighteen, five feet three.

"Ooooo," said Mama.

Papa still held her by the hair.

"Stop that," P.J. said.

Papa banged him on the head with one of the pots on the stove.

"Papa, Papa," said Betty. "Stop, Papa, please."

Betty was Papa's favorite in 1926, just as Aldo, the blue-eyed one, was in the days before he failed as a movie actor. And when Betty pleaded with Papa, Papa let go Mama's head, cleaned his hands, and told us all to go to bed, before he threw us all out the window.

The next day P.J. had a lump he didn't get catching without a mask. And that night Papa put on the shoes he had taken off on the night of the fire and went out to see Uncle Louie, who lived around the corner on Broome Street.

"Louie," Papa said, "when hell check come?"

"Check no come, Enrico?"

"Come nothing," Papa said.

Aunt Angie, Uncle Louie's big wife, was in the kitchen, moving around like a giant. They had a big house too, and if Aunt Angie fell over straight, she would fall on Uncle Louie talking with Papa in the living room.

"Why no come?" said Uncle Louie.

"Who, know?" said Papa. "Thats you tell me."

Uncle Louie scratched his head. "You send policy, all right, Enrico?"

"Powicy?" Papa said.

"The policy for fire," said Uncle Louie.

"Whatthehell powicy?" said Papa.

"The policy for fire, Enrico."

"You say before powicy. Who powicy?"

"Insurance policy, Enrico. You know."

Papa knew nothing. He looked at Uncle Louie as if Uncle Louie was lying in a coffin.

"You say before powicy!" Papa shouted.

Aunt Angie came into the room and stood quietly between them.

"How you get check without policy?" Uncle Louie wanted to know.

"Dope," Papa said. "Whatthehell you say powicy!"

"Isa insurance, Enrico. You no get check without policy."

"Dope, lousa," Papa cried, putting out a hand to strangle Uncle Louie. "You say that when burn factory? I tell you burn? I break you head!"

Uncle Louie moved away and Papa couldn't go after him without running into Aunt Angie. But then Aunt Angie started after poor Uncle Louie.

"What's this," she said, "you put fire to Enrico's shop?"

"Was cigar, Angie," Uncle Louie said.

"What cigar?" said Aunt Angie.

"Cigar in goods," said Uncle Louie. "Was accident."

"No him accident," said Papa. "Lousa, no you say, Enrico, go head, burn factory, no worry. No you say that? No you say check come? You see check?"

"No policy," said Uncle Louie.

"Say again powicy I break you head."

"Did you burn the shop?" Aunt Angie asked Uncle Louie.

"Was cigar in goods." All Uncle Louie's kids were out or in bed, and if Aunt Angie went for him now, it would be like knowing he was going to die. "How I know is going be fire."

"Lousa big lie," Papa yelled.

"Quiet," said Aunt Angie.

"Angie," said Papa, "this better no fooling. Louie burn factory. I want pay."

Aunt Angie put out her arm and caught Uncle Louie's right ear. She began twisting it in the opposite direction that the shape of the ear seems to be going. Uncle Louie hollered blue murder.

"Was cigar, Angie, stop! Was cigar in goods. I swear Bless Virgin."

"This true?" Aunt Angie was saying, still twisting.

"I swear on God," Uncle Louie cried.

"Big lousa lie," Papa said.

"I swear on God," Uncle Louie cried, kicking his legs from the pain in the ear. "I swear, swear, swear . . ."

Aunt Angie let go the ear. "Go home, Enrico," she said to Papa. "I believe my husband."

"I want pay, Angie. Nuncha use break ear. I want pay. Thats lie first class you husband."

"I believe Louie," said Aunt Angie. "Next time get insurance."

"Go head, no pay," said Papa.

"Good night," said Aunt Angie.

"No pay, you see, Angie. I tell you."

Papa left, leaving another one of those looks that meant Uncle Louie would be dead the first time Papa caught him in one of the pool rooms. But Uncle Louie was happy that his wife was convinced he had told the truth about the cigar, and Uncle Louie began to talk to Aunt Angie in a kind way, but Aunt Angie didn't answer him and later, when Uncle Louie happened to turn around, he got a boot in the behind he didn't know what for.

Papa waited for Uncle Louie to pay. He sat around all day talking to himself about breaking Uncle Louie's head tomorrow if he didn't come with the money.

But Uncle Louie had nothing, only the nine children, and they ate like horses. He was dying to shoot a game of pool, but he had to sacrifice for the five months more we lived on Kenmare Street.

"He pay," Papa said to himself. "He got money. He get Angie's father."

Angie's father was Uncle Louie's father-in-law and because he worked steady as a pants maker, Papa figured he had a lot of money. When the old man died in 1934 Uncle Louie had to pay for half the funeral.

"I break Louie's head," Papa used to say. "I catch. Wait."

Once, while he was waiting, Papa got up to chase the landlord up on the roof, and that scared him for four more months, but outside of that Papa earned nothing any more. Mama keeps saying that Papa never wanted to work after the fire, but it wasn't Papa's fault. He waited all that time for the fire check and then for Uncle Louie to pay up, and that kept him worried almost all of 1926. Then from 1926 to about 1931, when we began moving all over Brooklyn with the piano, Papa was borrowing from all the friends he had invited to America, and you couldn't expect him to look for work while he had to pay them back and had that on his mind all the time. And after 1931, when nobody had money any more, Papa spent most of his time learning to sign his name because he didn't want to take chances with the relief checks the way he did with the factory; and while he was doing this and getting the relief checks, you couldn't expect him to look for work and make it seem that he was putting something over on the Government. And in 1935, when Mama got a new refrigerator on her credit, and the Government thought it was the same as money and stopped the relief checks, didn't it look as if Papa was all set to go to work? Didn't he ask somebody if somebody was building a building somewhere because he was thinking of being a watchman? And wasn't he getting more active, leaving his chair every five or ten minutes, surprising everybody? It wasn't Papa's fault that it happened to be diabetes.

From *Viva Madison Avenue!*

Me and Joe worked in a big advertising agency, and after we worked there a couple of years, they found out we were worse than Italians: we were Italians who were never going to move to Westchester or Connecticut no matter what happened, and from that time on it was us against the Anglo-Saxons. There were other Italians in the Agency, like the Stag, Pete Moreno, but he was only Italian when he was with us;

then he would tell us all about the stags he went to, not only in the simple words that me and Joe were brought up on, but with gestures and things, so that we could almost feel what he felt and what we would have felt if we only wised up and left our wives for ten or twelve hours. But when the Stag wasn't with us, he was what he was supposed to be, Pencil Buyer for the Agency. He made lunch dates with salesmen, and he talked in a different language altogether, slowly, with periods and commas, and me and Joe always figured that as soon as he got seventy-five hundred a year he would be lost to the Italian race.

Then there was Toro. Toro was the Business Manager; he made so much money he went around telling people he was part Indian. He lived in Greenwich. He called the president Prexy.

Toro wanted to be a vice-president.

He was an Italian, born anyway, and here and there there were some other Italians, a couple of hot-eyed girls, whom the Anglo-Saxons didn't know they couldn't take to bed because they didn't know what kind of fathers these girls had, and what kind of religion. And there was Frankie, the shoeshine man, and though he wasn't an employee of Lowell & Lynch, you could consider him practically an employee after the twenty years he had been shining shoes in the building. But even Frankie was going over to the Anglo-Saxons; he shined the shoes of the president and all the vice-presidents, and he heard a lot of secrets, but instead of telling me and Joe like a good Italian should, he went around with a happy look in his eye, as if an inkwell fell on his head.

We could have used some Italians in our fights with the Anglo-Saxons. Frankie, for instance. When we had our big fight with Jim Leary, Frankie could have helped us by shining one of his shoes black and one brown, or, if that was too obvious, he could have got some polish on Leary's argyle socks. Leary liked to dress, and since he was made a vice-president because he knew how to dress, who knows what would have happened if Frankie put some polish on his socks? He was our worst enemy and the only thing he had against us was that we were stupid; that, and the fact that Ed Noone called us his little children. Noone was the man in charge of the television department, and there was something very unusual about him: he was the only vice-president who felt someday he was going to die. But Leary was an immortal vice-president, and in nineteen forty-eight, when Dewey was going to be president, Leary tried to keep me and Joe from using our expense accounts. What happened was this: Dewey was going to be president, and *Moment Magazine,* who was neutral, decided to cover the election from all the Republican headquarters in New York and five or six surrounding states. Leary was in charge of the *Moment* account, so he was in charge of the television coverage. He held a big meeting. Me and Joe weren't there because somebody told us (probably one of Leary's friends) that there was a very good Italian movie playing in a theater on Fifty-second Street. We got back just as the meeting ended and everybody came out smiling, mostly because Dewey was going to be president, but also because they were going to this hotel or that hotel with expense accounts (although Anglo-Saxons don't rob), and when Joe found out that we were going to no hotel, with no expense account, and no girls in the hotel we would've gone to, he began to blame me for the Italian movie.

"Bastard!" Joe said.

"Who?"

"Him."

"Sure, he's a bastard. He framed us."

"He doesn't like us."

"We're Italians."

We went to our offices, checked in, checked out. We went to the men's room; there were a lot of Anglo-Saxons in there, men who called it the "john." We didn't talk to them.

We went home.

We walked down Madison Avenue.

Have you ever been on Madison Avenue? It's the street of the Anglo-Saxons, the great ad men, and sometime you should sit on the curb and watch them. They look like humans, but take a long look and you'll know they're different; they're something better. They walk with their heads in the sky, not looking at anybody, just up and ahead. There's a reason for the way they walk: they do their thinking that way. These are the great thinkers of our age; they think of headlines, of slogans, of money.

This is a special kind of thinking, and you can't think it on an ordinary street; not on Fifth Avenue, which is a block west of Madison, nor even on Park Avenue, which is a block to the east. Madison starts downtown, in an ordinary way, with maybe an old lady selling pretzels on it, and when it gets way uptown, it is lost in Harlem. But from Thirtieth Street to the Fifties, Madison Avenue is rich with the radiance of the Anglo-Saxons, their manner of walking in the air, their manner of clothes, their manner of telling the world that they have discovered the Great Secret.

Me and Joe never knew what the hell the Great Secret was, but we walked on Madison Avenue just the same, and now we were all the way to where it begins, on Twenty-third Street and Madison Square Park.

"They don't like us."

"They make believe they like us."

"When do they make believe they like us?" That was Joe.

"Well . . ."

"They don't like us, and they don't make believe they like us."

"You're right."

"And that's why they use Italian names for the murderer every time."

I was lost for a moment. "What murderer?"

"*The* murderer. The murderer in all those goddamn mysteries on the air."

"Oh."

"They hate us, that's all."

"Maybe we shouldn't have gone to the movies. . . ."

"Please, don't make excuses for them."

"You think they would've left us out if we were at the meeting?"

"Yeah, I think they would've left us out."

"I guess you're right."

We came out of the park, got back on Madison Avenue. We turned on Twenty-third, went to Fourth Avenue.

"You notice anytime anything important comes up we're left out?"

"Yeah."

"Why?"

"Italians!"

"Yeah, Italians. But what the hell makes them so much better?" Joe was louder now. "Tell me, what makes them so much better?"

"Well, they speak better."

"That's right," said Joe. "They speak better." And then, very very loud, "But they don't think better!"

People were turning around and looking at us now. They always did when we had the miseries—even girls, who, if we were looking at them, would have been afraid to look.

"And it's never gonna change," said Joe.

"We'll always be Italians."

"You know who I blame?" said Joe.

"Who?"

"Toro."

"Yeah," I said.

"It's people like him. An Italian too good to be an Italian any more."

"And the Stag."

"He's another stupid bastard!"

We walked quietly for a long while. Joe was a director and I was a commercial writer, but it would have been better if we took bananas off a boat. It would have looked better too. We were small and dark, and even though we changed our socks and underwear every day (a concession to our wives, not the Anglo-Saxons) nobody would have noticed us among the bananas. But at Lowell & Lynch everybody noticed us, looking like we looked and being what we were, and it annoyed them because they couldn't believe what they saw.

We came to Union Square, and there, without saying any more to one another, we took the subway and went home, Joe down to the Village, and me all the way to Brooklyn.

We couldn't sleep that night, and when we couldn't sleep, we called each other up. Joe usually called me because he had more freedom with the Nut than I had with my wife. The Nut was what Joe called his wife. She was afraid of closets, elevators, subways—everything but department stores. My wife wasn't afraid of anything; that's why I couldn't call her a nice name like the Nut. Whenever I came home late, my wife would blame Joe for it, and then she'd feel sorry for the Nut. Then she'd know why the Nut was afraid of closets: Joe! I don't know how the Nut felt about my wife; Joe didn't ever see the Nut long enough to tell her anything about my wife. She was afraid to cook, so she ate at her mother's, and Joe ate at Hurley's Bar. They would meet home around midnight, six or seven of the Nut's family taking her home, and nobody taking Joe home, though he was the one who was drunk.

He called me around two in the morning: "I couldn't sleep."

"Me too."

"I'm worried that they don't trust us."

"No," I said, "it's the money we're gonna lose."

"The money, right."

"I couldn't sleep thinking about it."

"Expense account two days, another city, a hotel. You know how much we're losing?"

"I figured three, four hundred."

"I figure five or six."

"With the railroad fare?"

"Without."

"You can get five hundred out of it?"

"I can get five hundred. Don't forget, you're not entertaining actors and announcers. You're entertaining senators, congressmen, newspapermen."

"Yeah," I said.

"Figure three meals a day, sixty dollars every meal, how much is that for two days?"

"Three sixty," I said.

"There's three sixty without what you spend in the hotel, or railroad fare, or other expenses—incidentals."

"I guess you can reach five."

"Five or six," said Joe. There was a pause. "Look," said Joe. "Why don't we go up to Ed and tell him we quit?"

"Quit? You mean if we don't go—"

"We don't tell him that. We just tell him we quit, we're hurt."

"Then what?"

"Then he'll get Leary to send us someplace."

"Do we have to tell him we quit?"

"You know Ed. If we just ask to go, he'll say see Leary. But if we tell him we want to quit, we're hurt, then he'll *tell* Leary what to do."

"You sure?"

"What d'you mean, I'm sure?"

"Ed Noone's a funny guy. Sometimes I think he likes us, but sometimes I feel he wants us out."

"You're crazy. He likes us. If we tell him we wanna quit, he'll die."

"I hope you're right."

"Don't worry—Ed's all right. We'll see him first thing tomorrow."

"Okay," I said, and hung up.

So our trip was a success, but the next day they tried to make more trouble for us. Toro, the Business Manager, saw our expense accounts and went screaming into Noone's office as if somebody shot him. You'd think he'd come and tell us about it first, being an Italian, but no; he's the Business Manager now, lives in Westchester now! You could hear him screaming all over the office; that was his Italian blood, but because he went around telling people he was Indian, nobody realized that it was his blood and they thought maybe he had some reason to scream.

Paul Paolicelli

From *Dances with Luigi*

"I have one document—a marriage certificate which has the date my grandparents, Francesco and Caterine, were married and the names of the town and church where the ceremony occurred. My father said the family was from Potenza, but the church is in a village miles away. That's all I have."

"Southerners," said Luigi, pronouncing the word almost like a curse. "All of the people with any skill left the South."

It was a theme I had heard much about since arriving in Italy—an enormous rift between the upper and lower peninsula. A political party was forming in the rich, industrial North with the stated intention of breaking completely with the poorer, agricultural South, forming two separate nations. Everyone defined my family as "Southerners." I was starting to get a complex.

"I guess they were from the South, if Potenza is in the South."

"You didn't know your family was Southern?" Luigi seemed surprised.

"It was never an issue."

By anyone's standards, we had been the typical American family, living happily in post–World War Two suburbia. We didn't think of our heritage as historical or Old World. History began for our generation in phrases like, "after the war your father and I . . ." or, "back in the Depression . . ." We never had to ask which war or what depression. We knew.

Our society was American and that society began when our grandparents or great-grandparents had arrived in the United States. *Our* history began at the same place and at the same time. This, despite the fact that my grandparents and a goodly portion of my friends' grandparents, especially in our hometown of Pittsburgh, spoke with richly accented speech and many dressed with a peculiar and individual sense of fashion.

Our parents used the Italian language only when they needed to communicate something we weren't meant to hear. They'd utter a phrase to one another, then laugh uproariously. We'd fruitlessly beg to be let in on the joke. The Italian language, for our generation, became the language of suggestive jokes or to be used only with some greenhorn fresh off the boat. Americans spoke English.

And for my father, at least, I suspect the language was a source of shame. His family spoke a dialect that even other Italians couldn't understand or thought uneducated. He recalled his mother referring to other countrymen as snobs. *"Alti Italiani,"* she called them; people on high looking down. Now that I had learned the family was Southern, I realized she was probably referring to the Northerners.

I wondered how much this had affected my father, who showed up at school his first day surprised that the other kids spoke another language. It didn't seem to have hurt him. He obviously learned English very quickly—he was promoted by the public school in Clairton, Pennsylvania, to the third grade without having to attend the second.

Dad had no real interest in going to Italy. He had heard stories from friends who had been there, they pleased him, but he never stated any desire to go or to see the place where his parents had been born.

Would my travels and questions uncover something uncomfortable? Would I find ghosts? Would I stumble across something my grandparents didn't want to remember or were happy to leave in the past? Did my father's sense of shame over his Southern dialect run deeper than self-consciousness of grammatical structure and pronunciation?

I prayed I would find nothing to harm or embarrass him, and hoped to eliminate his Italian sense of inferiority.

"So, what's your plan?" Luigi demanded.

"To go to the South and visit the villages I have references for, once I feel comfortable in this language. To ask stupid questions in bad Italian and hope to find some answers."

Luigi sipped his water.

"What particular answers do you need to know?"

"Anything I can learn about Francesco, Dad's dad. Anything at all. Where he was born, why he left, what kind of family he had. I'm curious. And why Pietro, Mom's dad, wouldn't talk about the war. How did he hook up with Mussolini? What was that all about? There's more to the story than I know."

"Maybe he didn't want you to know. Most old and unknown family stories are best left to the past," Luigi said, ominously.

"Perhaps," I said. "We'll see. But what about *your* family? Is your family's history better left in the past?"

"We are from Umbria," he said. "My town is Foligno. My mother and sister are still there. I came to Rome in my military service and stayed."

"Your father?"

"My father was a barber. He was made a *Cavaliere* by the government. He died young. That means I will, too."

Laura came through the door with a tiny pot of fresh espresso that she poured in my small cup. "Ugh, Foligno," she said, wrinkling her nose. "Papa, stop talking about dying." She disappeared back into the shaded apartment.

"She hates my town," said Luigi. "It is too provincial for a university woman of Rome whose mother is from Boston."

"Why was he made a *Cavaliere?*"

"Because he survived the war. He kept his business. He wasn't political. Only the survivors get medals. In the end, only the nonpolitical are trusted by the politicians."

"And his family? Your mother's family?"

"I never learned very much. I never really thought much about it. We've been from Umbria forever. Maybe we're Etruscan? I can't say. What does it matter?"

"Aren't you curious about your ancestors? Don't you want to know more than just the region where you were born?"

"You Americans have such a short-term sense of history. You want to know everything in your own lifetime."

"The Italians don't?"

"I think we have a much longer view of things. It seems to me that the Americans think you have to accomplish everything for yourself during your own lifetime. Here it's different—if we can't get to it during our lives, we believe our children will continue on. We don't need to know everything about the past. We are more content to let the future take care of itself."

He sipped his water. "It doesn't matter at all to me about a hundred or two hundred or a thousand years ago. It matters to Americans because you have such a new country."

I thought about what he said. What happened a hundred years ago *did* matter to me. I didn't know if that was American or not, but I believed it was important.

"Well, let's just say then, I want to see if what they say about the South is true," I replied.

He shot me the Luigi-eye.

Joseph Papaleo

The Shylock's Wedding

When Marie Anne Moretti and her boyfriend John Russo decided to get married, they drove over to the Moretti house in North Yonkers to tell the family.

Anna Moretti was home alone watching TV and when she heard the kids already planning the wedding, she asked them to wait for her husband, Al, who would want a say.

Al got home late from a union meeting at AGFK where he was floor manager; the kids had gone out again because they were too excited to wait. It was better for Anna, who wanted to talk about Mrs. Russo's club, which rented out its ballroom in the off-season for affairs.

Al Moretti knew that the Russos expected a big affair, but he was uncomfortable about using their club because he was not a member; nor did he have any club of his own.

"*Now* how I wish I had joined that place in New Rochelle," he said.

"They were all Jews, they told us."

"Who cares what they are. The facilities are there, and the price was right."

"I only meant we wouldn't *know* anybody."

"Sometimes I think Jews are the last Italians left. But who gives a damn. I need a club right now."

"What's wrong then with the Russos'?"

Al went to the kitchen for his night milk and cookies. Anna sat watching him. "Oh those meetings," he said. "It's a lot of fucking talk that don't mean anything anymore. Who needs a union at AGFK? There's more benefits coming out of management than *we* can think up. Only it didn't do nothing yet to clear my headaches."

"I been meaning to ask you, you in that profit-sharing plan?"

"Yes, I'm in that. But I got to have some money left from the paycheck to buy shares, Anna, the money is flying like feathers, I put myself in hock to do the patio because we *had* to have one right now."

"Don't talk to me like that. You're the one who said I *live* for those Saturday night barbecues. That *was* you."

"All right, all right. So I'm overextended. I bought some more insurance, then Bobbie needed a new jalopy to get to college, and I still didn't finish paying off that stupid power motor. Why the hell I went and bought such a fucky thing—"

"I told you he was taking you for a sucker, just because it was a small down payment. Look how long you been paying for that monster."

"If I had a buck for every guy that borrowed it I wouldn't owe."

"You're the jerk who lets it out." Anna shook her head like an old lady. "Don't look at me," she said.

"I will look at you. We got a wedding reception to make and pay for."

"I'll call Mrs. Russo. She really said it's cheap off-season. The club does it to make a few dollars."

Al was up, carrying his plate to rinse in the sink, then the milk bottle to the refrigerator. "Let's go up," he said, and Anna followed him upstairs to the bedroom.

"What's in savings?" she said.

"Dust." Al walked to the bureau and took out his plastic file. "We haven't paid off two loans, in case you forgot. There's the home improvement and the other one, almost finished. They won't lend anymore right now, though."

"Didn't you say you were due for a bonus this year? That was in the wind, wasn't it?"

"What bonus? Mastercharge *owns* me. That's what's in the wind. Now it means, *now,* I got to borrow."

"From who?"

"From privates. Ralph has a friend who lends money six for five. A shylock, but clean cut. We can get it just before the reception, and I'll have it paid back with the Vig in two months."

"You're sure? You know those people are no good."

"I wouldn't do it if I wasn't sure. Anna, please have a little faith in me for once, just *once* in your life."

"I am only *asking* you. I'm only thinking of you. Last year you had to take that night work."

"I know it, I know it. I had numbers coming out my head."

Al was taking off his clothes like some form of his skin that disgusted him now after a day of use. First he threw the clothes on the silk chair, the walnut clothes rack, and Anna's tubular cosmetic table. But quickly his habits made his neck blush, and he collected all the pieces and hung them behind the sliding doors. Anna didn't speak, knowing that the movements were his nerves coming out: he threw to get it out of his system, and in the morning she was oftened wakened by his moving around, picking up, straightening the room until she had to tell him to stop and go down for some juice.

She watched him go into the bathroom to wash and brush his teeth and come back in his pajamas. He caught her face. "Don't worry, kid, we'll get it all. Because I want to give Marie a nice affair. She's our first one." He sat on the bed with his back to her. "The first one is always special." He was quiet for a minute or so, then turned around to face his wife. "You agree with that?"

"Yes I do," Anna said, and started getting ready for bed. Then she went downstairs to lock the doors and windows because Al had fallen asleep suddenly.

When she was back upstairs, she remembered they had not agreed on Mrs. Russos club. Next morning, as he was ending his breakfast, she turned from the stove and asked him slowly, "You want me to ask the Russos if their club rents?"

"Sure. Go ahead and ask." Al was up. "I'll be seeing Ralph tonight and see about the shylock."

That night Al was back early, "No supper for me. I'm picking up

Ralph and we talk to the shylock at the Adventurer's. What do they call it now? Nathan's? I can pick up a bite there."

Al backed the Electra out and drove to the Minute Wash before starting up Central Avenue to get Ralph. The showroom was just closing, and Ralph had his hat on and came out and got into the car. "Oh how those damn lights get me by night." He was rubbing his eyes. "It's the neon, you know what I mean. It tightens up your pupils. After an hour, you squint and you have to look down at the floor the rest of the night."

"How's business?"

"The volume remains tremendous, I swear." Ralph turned to look out his window as the car rolled out of the parking lot. "I don't know what they're doing with these cars. Storing them in cellars? Dumping them in rivers? And all of them bitching a little bit about the price of bread. They got it good."

"Maybe I ought to sell cars?"

"Not sell for others," Ralph said. "But get a dealership."

"That's a good one."

"Listen, you got a steady thing. Pensions, vacations, the profit sharing. I wouldn't leave it for a job that goes up and down, with no benefits like what you know is benefits."

Al was quiet and pleased. When he saw the lights of the Inn, he began again. "Is this guy we're seeing a broken nose type? Some *cafon?*"

"No! Where you been? Al, this is 1969. This man has clean money. This man is a bank. I don't think he even ever seen a gun in his life. I bet you can't pick him out."

"Well, where's his supply, then?"

"They say some doctor is backing him."

"Then he's safe."

"Well, if you don't pay, I'm sure he knows some telephone numbers, too. He'll get some leg-breakers like anybody else if he gets welched. The man's in business, after all."

"But he's no Mafia guy?"

"Come on with that Mafia crap. Not you, too. What paper do you read in that place of yours? Rosey is a nice person."

They were in the parking lot and parked. "What's his name?" Al said.

"I'm not sure, but he's not Italian. Could be Jewish."

"He's Jewish?"

"You thought it was only the *paisans?*"

Al laughed as he got out. "Jewish sounds better to me, 'cause then most likely he won't be no nut."

"That's what I thought once myself. He's an honest guy. But they're all the same, I assure you."

"Yeah," Al's voice hit the sound with the old heaviness of the Bronx. He heard his own tone and went on with it: "Because they all got the same sucker."

The tone had allowed him to expose to himself what they all felt inside and knew to be true. It was a kind of truth like a pain in the private parts; it was embarrassing, yet it was something you as the sucker wanted to brag about and make jokes about. You were caught like a fish on the hook and still it was a badge of honor: borrowing showed you had made something of yourself but also that you would never come up for air, never get off that hook, never find anything good for the depressions except a new model of next year's car.

"You want to change your mind?" Ralph had been looking at Al, who had stopped like a statue. "Al? You hear me? You want to pull out, it's OK. I know how it is when you get to this point. I'll just meet him myself and tell him we'll call him later, you're not ready right now. He's used to things like this."

Al walked to the door and went right in, to the cafeteria line where he took a tray. He ordered sandwiches for himself and Ralph, more than they could eat, and they carried the stuff to the glass porch. When they were finished, a good-looking, tall man wearing a blue single breasted came along the tables and stopped. Ralph stood up. "Rosey, this here is my friend Al Moretti."

The man shook hands, then sat down. "Ralph says you need a little money."

"About five thousand." Al looked at him, reluctant to mention his reason, the wedding, in front of this man. But the face was not hard, only curious, like a person met at a party. "It's for my daughter's wedding," Al said. "She's my firstborn." The phrase stopped him.

But the shylock had lowered his head, looking down at the trays on the table, "That's very nice," he said, and began to eat from the plate of pickles. "I'm only thinking this. You sure you have some way to pay back? You don't want to get yourself hung up."

"My idea is this." Al cleared his throat automatically; it was like any business deal. He was setting himself to talk right, make a proper presentation. "In about two months I'll have to pay the caterer, the hall, all that. Then I'll start to pay the Vig for a little while; then by that time a piece of property I have will be free to sell, and then I'll have the money."

"You sure about the property? Nothing that will get hung up in the courts?"

"It's over on White Plains Road. Very desirable land. Right next to a Safeway."

"All right." The shylock looked up and turned his face to the side, to look out through the glass; he had a hooked nose that did not show when he looked at you. Al was startled by it. He looked stronger with it, maybe a little ugly, surely something that frightened Al inside.

"I'm giving you a number to call." The shylock was talking to him, writing on a slip of paper torn from a little five and ten cent pad. "Give me two days before you call. Then I'll need a list of your assets, unless Ralph is backing."

"No, he's not. I'll make you the list."

The shylock was up. "Invite me to the wedding," he said, and shook Al's hand.

"Sure, you're invited. I mean it." Al was relieved, and he thought that the shylock had done it, had brought something of himself to the departure. Maybe it was his good suit, the hair so well done.

"OK, then." The shylock was looking at Ralph. "See you around, Ralphie. Tell your friend about too much hock."

Al watched him walk along the tables and push himself out the sliding doors to the lot.

"He doesn't like it too much," Ralph said.

"What?"

"I could hear it in his voice. He doesn't like the deal too much. See, he usually, he likes to see a clear line for the return. Like business men. They'll borrow to meet a payroll, but then they'll sell the season's line and pay right off. Yours is a little fishy. Not fishy, maybe. Just not tight. Once he told me he was getting sick of these guys going into hock to buy a patio."

"What do you mean, *patio?*"

"I am only repeating what he said. Examples. Like guys up here in Westchester, always improving their homes. They don't know what to put on next."

Ralph stood up. "Al, I really had a long day under those lights. Are you driving me to the subway?"

"What subway? I am takin' you to the door."

"No. Just to the Lexington, I'll take it down to Gun Hill Road. It's only four or five stops."

They left and drove slowly to the city line, then over to the Elevated tracks that marked the start of the Bronx. The streets were thinning out, but there were knots of boys at the corner stores. "Why don't you move like everybody else?" Al said. "It stinks over here now. Everything closing down. Come to Yonkers and get some grass under your feet. Look at this shit. The same guys rotting on the same corners and now so many black ones mixed in you know they're going to be here for life."

Ralph patted Al's shoulder. "I just like the neighborhood, still. It's comfortable to me, you know what I mean. The kids still play stickball. So now you even hear the Spanish. I think it's better than what happens there in Westchester."

"You mean *my* kids, for instance? What's wrong with them?"

"You dumb *strunz*. There's nothing wrong with your kids. I just don't like the way kids act up there. They all split up and they go around in circles. And drugs, just as much. I don't know what to tell you. I just don't like Westchester kids. Little empty things, they don't do things. You get these kids come in to pick up their family cars. Nice looking, they got money. They know how to drive. I like the way they dress. But I want to tell you, they're like people with heads three feet off their bodies. They're made of air."

The car had stopped at the station steps. "I know what you mean," Al said. "They're like they are not your own kids."

Ralph was out of the car and moving up the train steps. Al waved and made a slow U-turn and drove back slowly through Mount Vernon before cutting across to Yonkers.

He could not catch his thought until he began to laugh aloud, the noise of his voice bringing it to him. He had been talking inside himself, saying sit down and make a deal. Life was a deal a day. You sat, you made the deal, all for the good that came later. To him success came sitting in a chair, in his office, in the cafeteria, on planes.

Deals were riding his clocks; back and forth he was in the car, out; his week was a sweat to reach Saturday, then to meet with the guys, have steaks on the grill and talk and laughter. Which was getting harder, somebody backing out each week, Charlie Baker telling him he had depressions and didn't go out some weekends at all. Angelo's first son was being sent overseas. Danny, head of the Knights, was going crazy over his drug addict kid. Bill Conroy was on special duty in Harlem and slept in the city at the precinct and told them he had to go to the riots and the order was to not touch them. He was ready to resign. Anna's brother Bob, who had never been right after serving in Korea, was in the Vets' hospital again. They had been told to get him to a psychiatrist, but the family had all been afraid.

When Al got home, the rooms were quiet, and he sat in the darkness on the couch. After a while he heard Anna call from upstairs. He went up and said, "Get some sleep. I'm coming right in." He went for his pills and water. She saw him from the bedroom door. "You getting the pains again?"

"I didn't eat much today so it's not strong. Tomorrow, we have to start the planning."

The next day they made the phone calls and for two weeks the ordering went on—cards, cars, church, food, visiting and setting up the club's big room. Al was anxious to have a good-looking affair, and by now he owed so many cousins, business friends, he decided to put it all together; he even sent an invitation to the shylock in Ralph's envelope and asked Ralph to pass it on.

When the wedding day came, they were ready for almost anything. Al drove over to the club in the early afternoon, and went through the timing with the caterer: three tiers were set up with desserts, two foot round lime pies with lights behind them making the green shine, ricotta cheesecakes for the old folks, and rows of cherry and apple pies interspersed with pastries, petits fours and chocolate layers. On the top was a disc that revolved and would turn the wedding cake when it was brought in. On the sides of the table, two large butcher block tables had been set up, from where men in gay nineties waiter dress would carve the roasts, roast beef to all.

The room had been built around these tables and people would be able to walk along the boards in front of them and look at everything.

Al drove back and took Marie Anne to church with Anna and the other kids. The wedding was very soft, somehow. The music in church seemed so light, the crowd later on the steps smiling and airy, all of them laughing at the back of the church and then walking out into the sun, all of them around the bride and groom, talking about memories, years ago. The dead ones who would have loved to see this day, how these kids turned out, how pretty she was. Johnny's nephews, babies, stood on the lower steps and threw rice.

Al forgot everything unpleasant until he reached the reception and found Ralph and the others ready to shake his hand. And behind Ralph the shylock was half-smiling.

Al was sweating; he had been shaking hands for an hour, was flushed from the laughs, the running to the cars, carrying things, ushering people in. He shook the shylock's hand and led him inside. "You're table twenty-one," he told Ralph. "Where's your people?"

"They're inside going around already." Ralph was looking at people entering, faces from ten years ago, seen only at ceremonies.

The band had begun when Al raised his right arm and now, from behind them the bride and groom, in white and black, came pushing through the brown swinging doors, followed by the three ushers and the three bridesmaids in pink satin. Al and Ralph and the shylock moved to one side and the parade went to the dance floor and stood while the people clapped. The band switched to "Let Me Call You Sweetheart," and the bride and groom danced. Marie Anne lifting her long gown and holding it in her left hand, as if she wore gowns every day.

"How much'd the dress cost?"

Al heard the shylock's voice through the noise but had to ask him to repeat the word in order to understand. "You mean the bridal gown?" The shylock was nodding with a small gesture of the face, as if only his chin could move. "About six hundred," Al said.

"I'll get you a C and a half for it, maybe two."

Al was about to answer, but he kept his words. Marie Anne might want to keep it, in which case there could be no sale. He began to move forward as the music stopped, his head still circled by his thoughts, and the shylock was at his side. "Let's sit down with my people," Al said.

"I'll look around first," the shylock said. He seemed worried. Al went to the family; there were cousins, aunts, people from the office who were not Italian and who were beginning to look at the antipasto squid with question. Al went from table to table explaining what the antipasto was and what was in the minestrone and the lasagna to come.

He met the shylock again near the door to the kitchen; the shylock had been talking with one of the headwaiters of the caterer's staff. "I know these people," the shylock said. "What'd they set you back for?" Al told him, and he placed a hand on his shoulder. "Let me talk to them," the shylock said. "We'll get a rake off."

"Don't you want to sit down now?" Al said. "And meet my people?"

"Come on," the shylock said, and walked with Al to the table.

It was clear that everybody thought the shylock was an executive from Al's firm. He had what Al had called, years before, the blue-suit look, his shoulders square, the shirt always white or white on white, his tie silvery in the light, the black leather shoes that never suggested feet inside, his hands soft and long, the finger rings big and brasslike, but really gold worn for a long time, his suit just-pressed, with trouser creases pointing out, like something stiffer than fabric.

Marie Anne began to talk with him, then Anna started him tasting everything while Al stood behind them because there were no more chairs.

Since he couldn't get into the conversation, Al walked the tables again, ending up near the band where Lou Di Santo, the leader and Al's old friend from Laconia Avenue, was smoking a cigarette.

"What is it?" Al said. He knew Lou was pissed off about something. Lou said, "Didn't we talk about how much the band was costing?"

"Sure we did. I'll give you a check right now if you need it."

"Not that. Why did you send that guy to bug me?"

Al knew he meant the shylock. "What did he say?"

"He asked me what I was getting, so I told him; so he counts the band and he says ten bucks a head. Now you know that comes to less than we agreed on. Guys can't work for that. I never even mentioned 802 scale. It was for friends."

"He's only trying to help me," Al said. "He didn't know we were friends. But our deal is our deal."

"That's what I told him."

"So?"

"Well, not that he threatened me or anything. He only kept saying I better not *putz* around with the price, if you know what I mean."

"Just forget it. He was trying to help out."

Lou did not answer right away. "As long as he's not you that's saying this."

"What I'm saying to you, Lou, is we agreed on a price, and I still agree on that price, and that guy doesn't enter here."

Lou took Al's shoulder and squeezed it. "We better go play a while or I'll start getting drunk with the rest of them."

Al went back to the table and sat down in somebody's chair. "They're all out there dancing," his Aunt Tessie said. "Anna's dancing with your friend."

Al followed her hand and saw the dance floor, with dancers under the revolving lights, finally making out Anna with the shylock when the band changed rhythm to a tango. Anna and the shylock began to do it, movements he hadn't seen since the thirties, and the shylock, he realized, looked like George Raft.

Al turned to the front again because of his stiff tux collar and looked at Tessie. "Is he your boss at the place?" she said. "He's such a *nice* man. He's gonna get me one of those new Italian leather bags. He knows a man."

"He knows a man," Al said.

"What'd you say?"

"I said what you said. He knows a man."

"Do you know those people, too? You never told me."

"No, that's not what I'm saying. What else did he say?"

"What else? He told us a lot of jokes. He goes to Las Vegas all the time. Did you hear the one about the first Italian astronaut?"

"No, what is it?"

"Let him tell you. He's a scream."

"Where's Anna?" Al turned around again.

"She just went outside with him."

"Out? Where'd they go?"

"How should I know. To look at the club rooms? To look around."

Al got up and went to the door, but there were a crowd of guys standing there, his old buddies, all having left their women at the table they were standing, smiling, at the entranceway as they used to do at the candy store.

"Even here you hang out," Al said. "Even here you come to shoot the shit on the outside. Why don't you go dance?"

They all laughed, and Johnny Pacetta came up and said very loud, "We danced, we ate, we smoked, we drank. Now there's only one thing we didn't do yet." And the guys started laughing.

Al went past them shaking his hand at them, finding the outside corridor that led up to white stone steps. A new light covered the gardens ahead as he stepped out. He opened the glass door which was silent: the night was full of cool blue air and empty of people.

He walked between the cut shrubbery and found himself getting closer to a white stone fence ahead: he could see it was the end of the land and that there was water below. He quickened his steps at the excitement of the water.

But as he reached the stone railing and saw the water, his mind was shaken by the cool freshness. He remembered this coast, the Glen Island casino, when portable radios were a new thing and Orchard Beach was liveable and City Island was a place for sailboats: he used to help Joe Paterno in the boat yard each spring. The days left you alone to follow the freshness.

He turned from the water as if it were not permitted: he should also go back and see if people were having the right time.

Down below the moonlight struck something white, a dress with jewels like pins of light. There, below, less than ten feet away, against some bushes, his wife was hugging and kissing the shylock.

He felt the blood rush up and thought he had already lowered his head to charge them. His arms went up, his hands getting ready to grab and kill.

But he did not move. The thoughts went faster and faster. The shylock would have to be killed; if only wounded, he would call hoods.

And Anna. He was surprised she had this jazz in her and shocked that he was surprised by her. He saw her too often in housecoats, in curlers, looking gray and greasy, competing with him for the post of chief family slave. The more Al worked, the more Anna was dressed in a draggy housedress when he came home, pale and exhausted, as if she had been chopping rocks in Sing Sing.

Well, she was out of the housedress now. She was forty-one; her legs were getting puffy and blue. Couldn't she have one sneaky night?

Al backed away from the railing and started back to the glass door. This would surely affect the Vig, he thought, and bring it down. So say Anna was doing her bit for the family budget. Protecting the family treasury in her own way. It was good to have some help for a change.

Jay Parini

Grandmother in Heaven

In a plume-field, white above the blue,
she's pulling up a hoard of rootcrops
planted in a former life and left to ripen:
soft gold carrots, beets, bright gourds.
There's coffee in the wind, tobacco smoke
and garlic, olive oil and lemon.
Fires burn coolly through the day,
the water boils at zero heat.
It's always almost time for Sunday dinner,
with the boys all home: dark Nello,
who became his cancer and refused to breathe;
her little Gino, who went down the mines
and whom they had to dig all week to find;
that willow, Tony, who became so thin
he blew away; then Julius and Leo,
who survived the others by their wits alone
but found no reason, after all was said,
for hanging on. They'll take their places
in the sun today at her high table,
as the antique beams light up the plates,
the faces that have lately come to shine.

1913

"Guarda, Ida, la còsta!"
She imagined, as she had for weeks,
a dun shore breaking through the fog,

a stand of larkspur, houses
on the curling bay.

As wind broke over the gunwales,
a fine low humming.

It was sudden when she came
to rest, the *Santa Vincenta*, thudding
into dock. The tar-faced lackeys
lowered the chains, seals
popped open, and the ship disgorged
its spindly crates, dark trunks
and children with their weepy frowns.
There were goats and chickens,
litters and a score of coffins
on the wharf at once.

Cold, wet, standing by herself
in the lines of custom
under some grey dome, rain falling
through the broken glass above her,
she could think of nothing
but the hills she knew:
the copper grasses, olives
dropping in the dirt, furze
with its yellow tongues of flower.

The Miner's Wake

in memoriam: E.P.

The small ones squirmed in suits and dresses,
wrapped their rosaries round the chair legs,
tapped the walls with squeaky shoes.

But their widowed mother, at thirty-four,
had mastered every pose of mourning,
plodding the sadness like an ox through mud.

Her mind ran well ahead of her heart,
making calculations of the years without him
that stretched before her like a humid summer.

The walnut coffin honeyed in sunlight;
calla lilies bloomed over silk and satin.
Nuns cried heaven into their hands

while I, a nephew with my lesser grief,
sat by a window, watching pigeons
settle onto slag like summer snow.

Ida Parini (1890–1976)

A drowning was the one thing she remembered
from the other side,
how the roiling sea gave up a girl
one morning on the beach
in old Liguria, where she was born.

The body was like alabaster, cool;
the hair was dandled by the lurid waters,
to and fro. She'd known the girl
"not very well."

                    If pressed, she'd say
Liguria was full of shaggy rats; her father
shot them with a long-nosed pistol.
It was not so hard to leave all this.

The crossing she remembered wave by wave.
The maggoty old meat, the swampy water,
how her cousin died of fever
on the mid-Atlantic,
though she suffered "less than one might think."

Her parents left her lonely at the docks
with someone twice her age or more.
He had golden cuff-links, ivory teeth.
They married in Manhattan
as her parents sailed to Argentina,
where an earthquake swallowed their last days.
"It was not as if I really knew them."

She was left alone in Pennsylvania
with her five small sons.

She did not complain, though once or twice
I found her sitting by the swollen river
near her house, her long hair down.
When I would ask her what was wrong
she would say she'd lost so many people
she had scarcely known.
It was "not as bad as I imagined,
but you sometimes wonder what was meant."

From *The Apprentice Lover*

Though not wealthy, I had enough in my reserves to tide me over rather comfortably. My grandfather was bankrolling me to the hilt. Nonno and I had always been close, and when he heard I wanted to live in Italy, he opened his substantial wallet like an accordian. "Alessandro," he said, lowering his voice to an ethnic rumble, "I'm behind you all the way. You're smarter than Nicky ever was, *il povero*. Brains like you got don't come on a platter." He put four thousand into an account for me, saying another four would be lodged there whenever I signaled. "After that," he warned, with a kiss on my forehead, "you are on your own, *figlio mio*."

What he said was only partially true. I was smarter than Nicky in one way: I hadn't got myself killed in Vietnam. Apart from that, I wasn't sure what smart meant, apart from an ability to suck up to teachers and get the necessary grades. But I took Nonno's money. If this was what "family" meant to an Italian American grandfather, so be it. I was indeed part of the family, and partook of its good fortune. The arrangement suited me fine. Had his name been Jones or Smith instead of Massolini, I'd have probably gotten a fond farewell shake and a kick in my skinny ass.

I promised Nonno that when I became a successful writer I would pay him back, but he just waved his hand, a familiar gesture that had waved off endless attempts at gratitude over the years. "I don't want your money," he said. "You can sign your book for me, *basta*." Then he said, "And it better be a good book if it's got my name on the cover." We shared a name, more or less: Alessandro Massolini. But I was Alex Massolini. More American than Italian—that had been the intention of my parents. "You can't get ahead in this country with a handle like Alessandro," my father said. "Even DiMaggio was Joe, not Giuseppe.

Marilyn Monroe would never have married a guy called Giuseppe." But Alex Massolini was close enough for Nonno. So the book had better be a good one.

———

I lay awake that night, thinking about a letter from Nicky, written within a week of his arrival in Saigon.

Dear Asshole,

Arrived Saigon. Not what I expected, but what the hell can anybody expect anywhere?

You'd never know there was a war on. Taxi cabs running up and down the streets, lots of restaurants, people sitting on the sidewalks, drinking beer, making jokes. Looks kind of happy to me. And if it weren't for the occasional Army jeep, you'd say, shit, this is vacationland.

Just waiting and watching, scratching and snoring. That's the problem with this war, they tell me. Gotta make it happen, so says my friend Eddie Sloane, another asshole like you (he dropped out of a college somewhere in Iowa). I better do something before I lose my fucking mind.

Lots of girls and cheap, too, I'm told. Beautiful, in their weird yellow way, with long legs and skinny necks. Fuck like bunnies. If you're lucky your dick won't swell up like one of Dad's big zucchinis and drop off. (Remember those zucchinis? Big motherfuckers, weren't they? He used to come into the kitchen with them in September and scare the shit out of Mom, waving a big one around. "Put that goddamn thing away," she'd say.)

Dad isn't the kind of guy who normally waves his club. You aren't either. Nice and quiet types. Peaceful and easy. Mom likes that, huh? I guess I scare her, since I'm never nice and not very quiet, except when stoned. Booze still sends me screaming through the streets, so I got to be careful. Pot is more peaceful, right? I mean, you don't feel like killing somebody after a good joint. You don't mind so much if they take you down. We all gotta die sometime.

Excuse my rambling. If I don't sound exceptionally intelligent, blame the weather. I've got a good excuse, believe me. It's so fucking hot day and night, your brain gets like a piece of chocolate left on the dashboard in mid-August. Like a wet piece of shit. So you say things you wouldn't say to anybody back home, and you talk bullshit all night because you can't sleep and don't want to, in case you don't wake up. Eddie and I talk all the time. Iowa is nowhere, I tell him. Back in Pennsylvania we pronounce it O-hi-o.

We tell stories when we can't sleep, trading them like you and I used to trade baseball cards. He knew everything there was in just a few nights about all of us. About Mom's fat ass and Dad's big empty tasteless zucchini and your humongous fucking classical brain and literary presumptions. Is that the word? I'm no fucking writer, but I know what I like.

PFC Fucking Massolini. Who's that? I got another month or so here, they tell me, in Saigon. Then up country we go, over the river and through the woods. Can't wait. Proud to serve. Mr. Rawhide himself, with my M-16, gas-operated, ready to rock. Got twenty rounds in the magazine. Thing weighs 8.2, not including the strap. And not including the fucking grenade launchers they're hoping to teach me to launch, which means you're also stuck with ten or so extra rounds of ammo. A lot to hump and haul through mosquito swamps and elephant grass when you've got jungle rot and wanna scratch and dust your balls with DDT.

Eddie's part Indian, he claims, so they made him the medicine man. (We call him Sitting Bullshit.) Bastard's gonna haul bandages, iodine, plasma, morphine, tape, hypodermics, all that glassy, gooey, spooky shit. Save your fucking life in the right (or wrong) situation, so he's got to haul it. The walking drugstore.

Speaking of humping, you still got your cherry? I hear those girls in the Ivy League are pretty damn tight-assed, all talk and no action. A hand-job in the library stacks if you're lucky. Come out here, and get laid in style. There's a whole street in Saigon, Ding Dong Avenue, they call it. Stopped by last night. You'd love it, man—regular shopping mall for tits and ass. Take your pick, honey. You stand in the lobby and point, then the Momma unites you in the elevator, till death do you part. The bitch takes you upstairs, saying things with a shit-eating grin like "Americans big money" and "U.S. soldier good man in bed." Nice bathtubs, where she scrubs your nuts and prick. Big beds, mirrors on the ceiling so if you're into that kind of kinky shit you can watch yourself hump (if you're on your back). Or maybe she can watch you hump. They seem to like it, the fucking, though you can't tell shit from their Shinola. I can't anyway, but what did I ever know?

Dad got all emotional and told me the night I left that he learned something in The War, but he never said what. Started to say something about Italy. About Salerno. But the words didn't come easy and he just quit talking. Like whatever he learned over there wasn't worth saying or was too deep to spit it out. I don't honestly think I'll learn a fucking thing in Nam. Don't believe there's anything much to pick up here except the crabs.

"Is there a God?" Eddie keeps asking me—it's like the biggest question in Iowa, he claims. "If so, how did he think up all this shit? How did he come up with Nam?" Maybe he's a demonic genius, I said to him.

Maybe he's bored. This whole fucking mess happened because there's nothing on TV up there in heaven, and you can't lay an angel.

I told Eddie he should ask you the biggies, and that there's more to you than meets the eye. Underneath it all, you got some balls. I believe that. You come on quiet at first, but then somebody bangs up against your wall, and you squeal.

By the way, if Uncle Sam Wants You, take my advice. Give Uncle the big finger. No good is coming out of this war, that's for sure. Whatever Dad says, he's wrong. He's "so proud of me," he writes. Mom writes nothing, though she sends clippings from the Wilkes-Barre Record. Just the sort of info I really want to know, like who in my high school class got knocked up and had to ring the wedding bells. Not me, I tell you. I'm not going home, not to Luzerne County. That's history. It's funny how clear you can see things from a distance. I recommend it, though you might think of Paris, not Saigon, as about the right sort of distance. You think about home in ways you never could when it's right around the corner, or in your face.

I could have chucked it, the war thing. Gone to Canada like Buzz Mooney or shattered my pinkie toe with a jackhammar like Benny Dixon's cousin from Nanticoke. Some days I think I should have pinched the doctor's butt at the physical or just walked into the exam with a real hard-on and started jerking off on the spot. Guys do that kind of shit, and it works. But I made a decision. Just do it. Go to the fucking war.

Sometimes you just got to do something. Whatever it is, you got to make it happen, goddamn it. Make it happen. You do what you got to do, Asshole. And you do it well.

Hey, enough philosophy for one letter. War turns you philosophical, they say. Eddie claims there is more philosophy in this platoon per square inch than at Harvard and Yale, and I swear he's right. You should hear some of this shit. If you're lucky, maybe I'll pass along some of the good stuff, and maybe some day it will mean something to you. Then again, maybe it won't.

So write me, Asshole, when you can take a minute off from slapping your dick around. I don't know why I'd like to hear from you, since you're a prick and always were, but I would.

> *Your Big Bro in Lotus Land,*
> *Nicky*

Gianna Patriarca

Someday I Will Read "Dover Beach"

Mr. Bowman wore a bow tie
for the three years i knew him
he had three suits
one gray, one green, one blue
the blue one he favoured
was thinning at the ass
by the time i graduated grade thirteen
but his shirts were always impeccable
i think he had the same love affair
with bleach that my mother has

Mr. Bowman was a proud English teacher
he was even more proud of his profound
knowledge of Chaucer, Milton and Donne
Mr. Bowman wanted all of us to be English too

One year i reluctantly showed him some poems
hoping he would choose one for our year book
and when he called me into his office
i had a grin you could stuff with a loaf of bread
and then with his perfect accent he inquired
"Giovanna, have you ever read 'Dover Beach'?"
and i, in my young, cocky semi-delinquent style,
answered, "no, sir, but i think i've heard of him"

Mr. Bowman was satisfied
he flashed his confident style
by pulling at his bow tie
"Giovanna," he said
"if you cannot write
like Matthew Arnold then
you really shouldn't write at all"

so i didn't
for a very long time

Perfect Love

He left me for a girl
who drove a beige Subaru

he left me for a girl
whose breasts didn't need a bra

he left me for a girl
whose smooth white thighs
opened without guilt

he left me for a girl
who didn't need confession
who didn't hang rosary beads
on bedroom walls

he left me for a girl
whose blood was bluer than her eyes

he left me for a girl
whose accent was charmingly English

he left me for a love
that wouldn't confuse him
a love that was perfect

she left him
for someone with a
bigger car.

Sadie Penzato

From *The Movies*

It was Saturday night. Late in the afternoon, I had begun ironing my
brothers' white dress shirts so they would have them to wear to go out
that night. After working hard on the farm, seven days a week, all of us,

Benny, Caroline, Frankie, Joey, and I always looked forward with great pleasure to Saturday night. That was the night Papa gave us money to go to the movies.

Admission was a quarter, 15 cents if you were twelve years old or younger. At a nearby candy store, one could "fill up" for the movies. Nothing in the way of refreshments was sold at the old New Paltz Cinema. At the store, they charged a nickel for a Baby Ruth, Milky Way, or a chocolate bar. For a penny apiece, there was an enormous assortment of loose candy: banana cremes, rootbeer barrels, Tootsie rolls, bubble gum, tiny sugar "dots" stuck to paper, and many, many others. Neither soda nor popcorn was available at either place.

There was usually a double feature. The second feature was always a "B" picture, often a cowboy film. They usually starred Hopalong Cassidy or Gene Autry. I was crazy about Hopalong but thought Gene Autry was a real "drip" (dumb and really "square"). The "movies" included a cartoon and a newsreel. Sometimes, there was also a "film short" and the main feature played twice (this was called a "double feature").

Everybody went to the movies. They were my favorite thing to do and I felt about them sort of how I felt about fairy tales. It was mostly make-believe and was only sometimes like the real world. Movies were "there" and they were enjoyable. Sometimes, they made you feel bad and sometimes they made you feel good. You laughed or cried. But, as you watched movies (or read fairy tales), you were aware at all times that they were eons away from the world that you were experiencing.

I did believe that perhaps somewhere, someplace women did dress in exquisite, expensive clothes and that some people did live in gorgeous homes with maids. Perhaps somewhere children were so squeaky clean they fairly sparkled. The lucky "movie" kids had tons of toys and were often taken to circuses and parties. Above all, they were spoiled, loved, and pampered!

Yet, in other movies, just the opposite would occur. Some, or all, of the characters depicted lived in such misery and squalor and faced so many insurmountable problems that it broke your heart to watch. They too were unbelievable. Nobody could have that many problems or live in such horrible places! Sure, maybe some of those things happened somewhere on earth, but not to me and not where I lived or to the people I knew. And even when I grew up, which seemed so far off in the future at the time that I thought it would never happen, I saw the farm as the only place that I would ever live. I imagined myself there forever, a drudge, always under the hawk-like watchfulness of Papa. Because he was so "old fashioned," I was certain that never in my life would he ever allow me to do many of the things the other kids in school were allowed to do. Stoically, I accepted it as my lot. The fact that Papa permitted me to go to the movies every week made me feel grateful to him for being so benevolent. He really could just order all of us to stay home if he wanted to. It sure would have saved him some of his precious money if he ever did.

As I ironed, my mind was full of what I would wear to the movies that night. Now almost nine years old, I had recently developed an even stronger awareness than before that clothes could do a bit more than cover a body and keep it warm. I had also become a little more aware of personal grooming and of trying to look pretty. At the same time, I had noticed that subtle changes were beginning to take place in my body.

Lately there had been a feeling of tenderness and soreness on my chest all around the area of my nipples. Curiously, the area beneath my nipples had begun to swell, ever so slightly. Slightly or not, it seems that others had noticed enough so that I no longer felt comfortable running about in hot weather with my top off. Gradually I came to the realization that, someday, I would have a bosom just like "big girls." I looked forward to it with mixed emotions of both embarrassment and glee.

What made me cover my chest and be especially aware of the changes taking place in my body happened one day as I walked up the driveway wearing only shorts. One of the young, male boarders, named Sal, was walking toward me. He was very handsome and he came from Brooklyn. I had a big crush on him, but he never noticed me. I realized that to him, I was just a little girl. On that day, however, as I passed by, he was grinning devilishly, staring rudely and intently at my bare chest.

"Hey, Sadie! Are those little tits I see?" he remarked laughingly as he sauntered by.

I felt my face get all hot and knew it was probably a bright red. So embarrassed and insulted by his use of words, I wanted to run after him and punch him as hard as I could! Angrily, I thought to myself, "If I told my brother, Benny, what Sal just said, Benny would probably kill him. Yeah! Even Frankie or Joey would beat him to a pulp. Yes, and if Caroline heard him, she would break his neck! And Papa! Papa would shoot him!" Then, too late to hit him or to make some quick retort, I threw his departing figure my most angry "look." It did no good however, since his back was turned and he didn't see it. Too bad!

You see, being the youngest and smallest in the family I was powerless. However, at an early age I had learned that there was a sort of "power" in my dark brown eyes. They were almost black, like Papa's eyes. I guess my eyes must have been pretty expressive because whenever

I was anywhere near the boarder ladies, they would take note of me, swish their hands back and forth at right angles to their wrists and remark out loud,

"Tallia! Tallia l'occhi, ti parlanu." (Look! Look at those eyes, they speak to you.)

Thus, I made the strange discovery, at a rather early age, that by looking at someone, while strongly and deeply feeling an emotion, I could somehow convey to the other person my feelings toward them; anger, sorrow, or pain . . . joy, affection, or pleasure. Soon, I found that I was using my "look" to convey disapproval, anger, or dislike.

To my great satisfaction and surprise, my "look" became a useful tool. Most of all, I was amazed to find that a "look" could actually intimidate others. Why, sometimes even grownups, if they said something stupid, would respond to the "look" with an embarrassed grimace. The "look" could make other kids look away or try to look back. But their "looks" seldom worked, for a really "dirty look" took a certain sensitivity and a firm belief in one's strength of purpose.

The first time I realized the power of a "look" took place at the dinner table when I was about eight years old. Benny, my oldest brother, used to take strange delight in a small ritual. While passing by my chair, he would stop, spread his fingers and reach under to where my hair grew at the nape of my neck. Beginning there at the hairline at the back of my head, he would slowly push his hand up through my long black hair. As his fingers, gliding upward, caught on the tangles of the hair and pulled on them, I, in an effort to lessen the pain, would rise up in my chair at about the same speed that his hand traveled upward. My brothers and sister would then roar with laughter at the comical sight of me, slowly rising from my chair, like a puppet on a string. I suppose the look of surprise, pained fury, and frustrated anger registering on my face, all at the same time, looked amusing.

As Benny's hand and hair-entangled fingers continued slowly upward, I would continue rising until I was on tiptoe and screeching in pain, at which point he would smile fondly at me and drop his hand, gently disentangling it from my hair. I am certain that in his own quiet, clumsy way he adored me and meant no harm. He just liked to tease me and get me angry. He would then whistle innocently and continue on his way to his own chair. All of this would take place in the space of only a few seconds. Although he had performed this little "ritual" many other times, this time, for whatever reason, I reacted! Up until that time, when I was the butt of family laughter, I would slump in my chair, look down, chin on chest and hide my anger. Seething, afterward, I would talk out loud to myself in my room, helplessly fuming with frustration, furious that I was not big enough nor strong enough to fight back. I would even fantasize that I was Superman or Wonderwoman and able to beat up everybody and get away with it! But this time, I did not lower my head. Not this time! I was so angry! As Benny seated himself, I stood up and pushed my chair back. Then I glared defiantly, for a long moment, at each one of my siblings one at a time. There was an anger from within and I willed my eyes to glow and grow glassy with rage. I stared at Benny for a longer time than the others and said not a word. A hush fell over the table and my brother Joey said, in quiet awe and with a weak smile, "If looks could kill!"

For a moment longer, I continued to glare at everyone seated at the table who had laughed at me. Suddenly, strangely, I felt stronger, bigger, and wiser than all of them. Suddenly, I sensed in myself a new feeling, like some sort of electrical charge. Probably for the first time in my entire life, for a few moments, I was in control.

It quickly occurred to me that I could stare coldly and meanly at those in my family (but not Papa, never Papa, I would never *dare* do it to him) and "get away with it." I could pour all the pain, hurt, anger, venom, and dislike in a look and no one could really "do" anything about it. Recalling cuffs and slaps, some gentle, some hard, delivered when I misbehaved or did not move fast enough, a thought crossed my mind, "I mean, they can't really hit me just because I *look* at them, could they?" Imagine my sense of triumph when I discovered that they did not. I had challenged them with my eyes and nobody did anything to me. Wow! My head held high, I turned away from the table and marched quietly and with dignity out of the room. As I did so, Papa chuckled quietly to himself.

That incident and my ever-swelling bosom, made me feel less like a child than before. Life seemed to be changing. It was obvious to me, in my ninth year, that new and different things were taking place. That each day, each incident which occurred, instituted metamorphoses which brought me closer and closer to what I imagined being grownup was all about. After a while, as more changes took place, I wasn't so sure I wanted to grow up at all! For even though my brothers and sister were sometimes unfair or pains in the neck, other times it felt good just to be the "kid sister" and to be taken care of and loved.

Lucia Perillo

Canticle from the Book of Bob

We hired the men to carry the coffin,
we hired a woman to sing in our stead.
We hired a limo, we hired a driver,
we hired each lily to stand with its head

held up and held open while Scripture was read.
We hired a dustpan, we hired a broom
to sweep up the pollen that fell in the room
where we'd hired some air

to draw out the stale chord
from the organ we hired.
And we hired some tears because our own eyes were tired.

The pulpit we hired, we hired the priest
to say a few words about the deceased,

and money changed hands
and the process was brief.
We said, "Body of Christ."
Then we hired our grief.

We hired some young men to carry the coffin,
we hired a woman to sing for his soul—
we hired the limo, we hired the driver,
then we hired the ground and we hired the hole.

∞

Lost Innocence of the Potato Givers

> They're just a passing phase. All are symptoms of our times
> and the confusion around us.
>
> —*REVEREND BILLY GRAHAM ON*
> *THE BEATLES*

At first we culled our winnings from the offering of fists—
one potato, two potato—until we realized that such random
  calibration
was no real test of love. So we cultivated pain: hunkering on
  the macadam
sun-baked for hours in the schoolyard, our panties bunched
  beneath our skirts.
The girl who could sit there longest would gain title to the
  most handsome Beatle, Paul.
John George Ringo—the rest were divvied according to
  whose buttocks were most scarlet.
And when our fourth-grade teacher asked why we wore such
  tortured looks through long division,
we shrugged, scritching our pencils over fleshy shapes of
  hearts and flowers.

Ed Sullivan started it, his chiseled and skeletal stub of a head,
  his big shoe
stomping our loyalties to the man-boys Dion and Presley.
Even priggish neighbor Emily said I had to kneel before the
  TV as though praying.
Then the pixels assembled the audience's exploding like a
  carcass when it's knifed,
and I copied the pose assumed on-screen: hands pressed
  against sides of my skull
like the bald dwarf who stands goggle-eyed on a jetty in
  Munch's painting, and screams.
My mother rushed to the basement, a dishrag dripping from
  her soaped hand.
What's wrong? she yelled. *Are you hurt? What in godsname is all*
  this screaming?

February 1964: Johnson's choppers were whopping up the
 sky over the Gulf of Tonkin.
Despite the tacit code of silence about the war, somehow
 they must have known:
on television, girls were brawling drunkenly and raking
 fingernails across their cheeks,
ripping their own hair in vicious chunks, as though beauty
 were suddenly indulgent or profane.
That night in Saigon's Capital Kinh-Do Theatre, three GIs
 got blown up during a strip show.
But of course I didn't know that. I couldn't have even found
 Saigon on a map.
Girls were going limp in the arms of riot-geared policemen,
 who carried them off like the dead,
and my mother was stunned when she saw I'd torn my shirt
 over my not-yet-breasts.

After that, I kept everything a secret, the self-inflicted burns
 and scars and nicks.
I was doing it for love love love: the stones in my shoes, the
 burrs in my shirt,
the mother-of-pearl penknife I used for cutting grooves in my
 thumb or palm
whenever I needed to swear some blood pact with another
 disenthralled potato giver.
We spent recess practicing how to stick our tongues in Paul's
 imaginary mouth,
letting everything drain out until we were limp, nothing,
 sucked right into the earth.
Then we would mash our bodies against the schoolyard's
 wide and gray-barked beech,
which was cruel and strong and unrelenting, smooth and
 cold, the way we hoped our husbands would be.

Long Time Too Long

A long time, too long, since we have done—this:
abandoned our tools while the sun's still high
and retraced our trail up the attic steps.

The grass still wants mowing as the quilts sigh
back over the bed; the nightshade tendril
winds another turn round the tomato.
But this is work too, this letting clothes fall
in such harsh yellow light that what to do
with what lies underneath them must all be
relearned. Let the vines choke our one good rose,
let the spade stand, the Mason jars empty:
we're sweating enough at each other's lips.
Leave the fallen plums to the white-faced wasps,
beating their drunk wings against the windows.

Mario Puzo

From *The Godfather*

"Tom," Michael Corleone said, "I'm driving down to the city with Kay tomorrow. There's something important I want to tell the old man before Christmas. Will he be home tomorrow night?"

"Sure," Hagen said. "He's not going out of town until after Christmas. Anything I can do for you?"

Michael was as closemouthed as his father. "No," he said. "I guess I'll see you Christmas, everybody is going to be out at Long Beach, right?"

"Right," Hagen said. He was amused when Mike hung up on him without any small talk.

He told his secretary to call his wife and tell her he would be home a little late but to have some supper for him. Outside the building he walked briskly downtown toward Macy's. Someone stepped in his way. To his surprise he saw it was Sollozzo.

Sollozzo took him by the arm and said quietly, "Don't be frightened. I just want to talk to you." A car parked at the curb suddenly had its door open. Sollozzo said urgently, "Get in, I want to talk to you."

Hagen pulled his arm loose. He was still not alarmed, just irritated. "I haven't got time," he said. At that moment two men came up behind him. Hagen felt a sudden weakness in his legs. Sollozzo said softly, "Get in the car. If I wanted to kill you you'd be dead now. Trust me."

Without a shred of trust Hagen got into the car.

★ ★ ★

Michael Corleone had lied to Hagen. He was already in New York, and he had called from a room in the Hotel Pennsylvania less than ten blocks away. When he hung up the phone, Kay Adams put out her cigarette and said, "Mike, what a good fibber you are."

Michael sat down beside her on the bed. "All for you, honey; if I told my family we were in town we'd have to go there right away. Then we couldn't go out to dinner, we couldn't go to the theater, and we couldn't sleep together tonight. Not in my father's house, not when we're not married." He put his arms around her and kissed her gently on the lips. Her mouth was sweet and he gently pulled her down on the bed. She closed her eyes, waiting for him to make love to her and Michael felt an enormous happiness. He had spent the war years fighting in the Pacific, and on those bloody islands he had dreamed of a girl like Kay Adams. Of a beauty like hers. A fair and fragile body, milky-skinned and electrified by passion. She opened her eyes and then pulled his head down to kiss him. They made love until it was time for dinner and the theater.

After dinner they walked past the brightly lit department stores full of holiday shoppers and Michael said to her, "What shall I get you for Christmas?"

She pressed against him. "Just you," she said. "Do you think your father will approve of me?"

Michael said gently, "That's not really the question. Will your parents approve of me?"

Kay shrugged. "I don't care," she said.

Michael said, "I even thought of changing my name, legally, but if something happened, that wouldn't really help. You sure you want to be a Corleone?" He said it only half-jokingly.

"Yes," she said without smiling. They pressed against each other. They had decided to get married during Christmas week, a quiet civil ceremony at City Hall with just two friends as witnesses. But Michael had insisted he must tell his father. He had explained that his father would not object in any way as long as it was not done in secrecy. Kay was doubtful. She said she could not tell her parents until after the marriage. "Of course they'll think I'm pregnant," she said. Michael grinned. "So will my parents," he said.

What neither of them mentioned was the fact that Michael would have to cut his close ties with his family. They both understood that Michael had already done so to some extent and yet they both felt guilty about this fact. They planned to finish college, seeing each other weekends and living together during summer vacations. It seemed like a happy life.

The play was a musical called *Carousel* and its sentimental story of a braggart thief made them smile at each other with amusement. When they came out of the theater it had turned cold. Kay snuggled up to him and said, "After we're married, will you beat me and then steal a star for a present?"

Michael laughed. "I'm going to be a mathematics professor," he said. Then he asked, "Do you want something to eat before we go to the hotel?"

Kay shook her head. She looked up at him meaningfully. As always he was touched by her eagerness to make love. He smiled down at her, and they kissed in the cold street. Michael felt hungry, and he decided to order sandwiches sent up to the room.

In the hotel lobby Michael pushed Kay toward the newsstand and said, "Get the papers while I get the key." He had to wait in a small line; the hotel was still short of help despite the end of the war. Michael got his room key and looked around impatiently for Kay. She was standing by the newsstand, staring down at a newspaper she held in her hand. He walked toward her. She looked up at him. Her eyes were filled with tears. "Oh, Mike," she said, "oh, Mike." He took the paper from her hands. The first thing he saw was a photo of his father lying in the street, his head in a pool of blood. A man was sitting on the curb weeping like a child. It was his brother Freddie. Michael Corleone felt his body turning to ice. There was no grief, no fear, just cold rage. He said to Kay, "Go up to the room." But he had to take her by the arm and lead her into the elevator. They rode up together in silence. In their room, Michael sat down on the bed and opened the paper. The headlines said, VITO CORLEONE SHOT. ALLEGED RACKET CHIEF CRITICALLY WOUNDED. OPERATED ON UNDER HEAVY POLICE GUARD. BLOODY MOB WAR FEARED.

Michael felt the weakness in his legs. He said to Kay, "He's not dead, the bastards didn't kill him." He read the story again. His father had been shot at five in the afternoon. That meant that while he had been making love to Kay, having dinner, enjoying the theater, his father was near death. Michael felt sick with guilt.

Kay said, "Shall we go down to the hospital now?"

Michael shook his head. "Let me call the house first. The people who did this are crazy and now that the old man's still alive they'll be desperate. Who the hell knows what they'll pull next."

Both phones in the Long Beach house were busy and it was almost twenty minutes before Michael could get through. He heard Sonny's voice saying, "Yeah."

"Sonny, it's me," Michael said.

He could hear the relief in Sonny's voice. "Jesus, kid, you had us worried. Where the hell are you? I've sent people to that hick town of yours to see what happened."

"How's the old man?" Michael said. "How bad is he hurt?"

"Pretty bad," Sonny said. "They shot him five times. But he's tough." Sonny's voice was proud. "The doctors said he'll pull through. Listen, kid, I'm busy, I can't talk, where are you?"

"In New York," Michael said. "Didn't Tom tell you I was coming down?"

Sonny's voice dropped a little. "They've snatched Tom. That's why I was worried about you. His wife is here. She don't know and neither do the cops. I don't want them to know. The bastards who pulled this must be crazy. I want you to get out here right away and keep your mouth shut. OK?"

"OK," Mike said, "do you know who did it?"

"Sure," Sonny said. "And as soon as Luca Brasi checks in they're gonna be dead meat. We still have all the horses."

"I'll be out in a hour," Mike said. "In a cab." He hung up. The papers had been on the streets for over three hours. There must have been radio news reports. It was almost impossible that Luca hadn't heard the news. Thoughtfully Michael pondered the question. Where was Luca Brasi? It was the same question that Hagen was asking himself at that moment. It was the same question that was worrying Sonny Corleone out in Long Beach.

———

Across the table, Sonny's wife Sandra noticed that her husband's face had gone red with flushing blood. His eyes were glazed over. She whispered, "What's the matter?" He waved at her impatiently to shut up, swung his body away so that his back was toward her and said into the phone, "You sure he's alive?"

"Yeah, I'm sure," the detective said. "A lot of blood but I think maybe he's not as bad as he looks."

"Thanks," Sonny said. "Be home tomorrow morning eight sharp. You got a grand coming."

Sonny cradled the phone. He forced himself to sit still. He knew that his greatest weakness was his anger and this was one time when anger could be fatal. The first thing to do was get Tom Hagen. But before he could pick up the phone, it rang. The call was from the bookmaker licensed by the Family to operate in the district of the Don's office. The bookmaker had called to tell him that the Don had been killed, shot dead in the street. After a few questions to make sure that the bookmaker's informant had not been close to the body, Sonny dismissed the information as incorrect. Phillips' dope would be more accurate. The phone rang almost immediately a third time. It was a reporter from the *Daily News*. As soon as he identified himself, Sonny Corleone hung up.

He dialed Hagen's house and asked Hagen's wife, "Did Tom come home yet?" She said, "No," that he was not due for another twenty minutes but she expected him home for supper, "Have him call me," Sonny said.

He tried to think things out. He tried to imagine how his father would react in a like situation. He had known immediately that this was an attack by Sollozzo, but Sollozzo would never have dared to eliminate so high-ranking a leader as the Don unless he was backed by other powerful people. The phone, ringing for the fourth time, interrupted his thoughts. The voice on the other end was very soft, very gentle. "Santino Corleone?" it asked.

"Yeah," Sonny said.

"We have Tom Hagen," the voice said. "In about three hours he'll be released with our proposition. Don't do anything rash until you've heard what he has to say. You can only cause a lot of trouble. What's done is done. Everybody has to be sensible now. Don't lose that famous temper of yours." The voice was slightly mocking. Sonny couldn't be sure, but it sounded like Sollozzo. He made his voice sound muted, depressed. "I'll wait," he said. He heard the receiver on the other end click. He looked at his heavy gold-banded wristwatch and noted the exact time of the call and jotted it down on the tablecloth.

He sat at the kitchen table, frowning. His wife asked, "Sonny, what is it?" He told her calmly, "They shot the old man." When he saw the shock on her face he said roughly, "Don't worry, he's not dead. And nothing else is going to happen." He did not tell her about Hagen. And then the phone rang for the fifth time.

It was Clemenza. The fat man's voice came wheezing over the phone in gruntlike gasps. "You hear about your father?" he asked.

"Yeah," Sonny said. "But he's not dead." There was a long pause over the phone and then Clemenza's voice came packed with emotion, "Thank God, thank God." Then anxiously, "You sure? I got word he was dead in the street."

"He's alive," Sonny said. He was listening intently to every intonation in Clemenza's voice. The emotion had seemed genuine but it was part of the fat man's profession to be a good actor.

"You'll have to carry the ball, Sonny," Clemenza said. "What do you want me to do?"

"Get over to my father's house," Sonny said. "Bring Paulie Gatto."

"That's all?" Clemenza asked. "Don't you want me to send some people to the hospital and your place?"

"No, I just want you and Paulie Gatto," Sonny said. There was a long pause. Clemenza was getting the message. To make it a little more natural, Sonny asked, "Where the hell was Paulie anyway? What the hell was he doing?"

There was no longer any wheezing on the other end of the line. Clemenza's voice was guarded. "Paulie was sick, he had a cold, so he stayed home. He's been a little sick all winter."

Sonny was instantly alert. "How many times did he stay home the last couple of months?"

"Maybe three or four times," Clemenza said. "I always asked Freddie if he wanted another guy but he said no. There's been no cause, the last ten years things been smooth, you know."

"Yeah," Sonny said. "I'll see you at my father's house. Be sure you bring Paulie. Pick him up on your way over. I don't care how sick he is. You got that?" He slammed down the phone without waiting for an answer.

His wife was weeping silently. He stared at her for a moment, then said in a harsh voice, "Any of our people call, tell them to get me in my father's house on his special phone. Anybody else call, you don't know nothing. If Tom's wife calls, tell her that Tom won't be home for a while, he's on business."

He pondered for a moment. "A couple of our people will come to stay here." He saw her look of fright and said impatiently, "You don't have to be scared, I just want them here. Do whatever they tell you to do. If you wanta talk to me, get me on Pop's special phone but don't call me unless it's really important. And don't worry." He went out of the house.

Darkness had fallen and the December wind whipped through the mall. Sonny had no fear about stepping out into the night. All eight houses were owned by Don Corleone. At the mouth of the mall the two houses on either side were rented by family retainers with their own families and star boarders, single men who lived in the basement apartments. Of the remaining six houses that formed the rest of the half circle, one was inhabited by Tom Hagen and his family, his own, and the smallest and least ostentatious by the Don himself. The other three houses were given rent-free to retired friends of the Don with the understanding that they would be vacated whenever he requested. The harmless-looking mall was an impregnable fortress.

Michael was not tall or heavily built but his presence seemed to radiate danger. In that moment he was a reincarnation of Don Corleone himself. His eyes had gone a pale tan and his face was bleached of color. He seemed at any moment about to fling himself on his older and stronger brother. There was no doubt that if he had had a weapon in his hands Sonny would have been in danger. Sonny stopped laughing, and Michael said to him in a cold deadly voice, "Don't you think I can do it, you son of a bitch?"

Sonny had got over his laughing fit. "I know you can do it," he said. "I wasn't laughing at what you said. I was just laughing at how funny things turn out. I always said you were the toughest one in the Family, tougher than the Don himself. You were the only one who could stand off the old man. I remember you when you were a kid. What a temper you had then. Hell, you even used to fight me and I was a lot older than you. And Freddie had to beat the shit out of you at least once a week. And now Sollozzo has you figured for the soft touch in the Family because you let McCluskey hit you without fighting back and you wouldn't get mixed up in the Family fights. He figures he got nothing to worry about if he meets you head to head. And McCluskey too, he's got you figured for a yellow guinea." Sonny paused and then said softly, "But you're a Corleone after all, you son of a bitch. And I was the only one who knew it. I've been sitting here waiting for the last three days, ever since the old man got shot, waiting for you to crack out of that Ivy League, war hero bullshit character you've been wearing. I've been waiting for you to become my right arm so we can kill those fucks that are trying to destroy our father and our Family. And all it took was a sock on the jaw. How do you like that?" Sonny made a comical gesture, a punch, and repeated, "How do you like that?"

The tension had relaxed in the room. Mike shook his head. "Sonny, I'm doing it because it's the only thing to do. I can't give Sollozzo another crack at the old man. I seem to be the only one who can get close enough to him. And I figured it out. I don't think you can get anybody else to knock off a police captain. Maybe you would do it, Sonny, but you have a wife and kids and you have to run the Family business until the old man is in shape. So that leaves me and Freddie. Freddie is in shock and out of action. Finally that leaves just me. It's all logic. The sock on the jaw had nothing to do with it."

Sonny came over and embraced him. "I don't give a damn what your reasons are, just so long as you're with us now. And I'll tell you another thing, you're right all the way. Tom, what's your say?"

Hagen shrugged. "The reasoning is solid. What makes it so is that I don't think the Turk is sincere about a deal. I think he'll still try to get

at the Don. Anyway on his past performance that's how we have to figure him. So we try to get Sollozzo. We get him even if we have to get
the police captain. But whoever does the job is going to get an awful lot
of heat. Does it have to be Mike?"

Sonny said softly, "I could do it."

Hagen shook his head impatiently. "Sollozzo wouldn't let you get
within a mile of him if he had ten police captains. And besides you're
the acting head of the Family. You can't be risked." Hagen paused and
said to Clemenza and Tessio, "Do either one of you have a top button
man, someone really special, who would take on this job? He wouldn't
have to worry about money for the rest of his life."

Clemenza spoke first. "Nobody that Sollozzo wouldn't know, he'd
catch on right away. He'd catch on if me or Tessio went too."

Hagen said, "What about somebody really tough who hasn't made
his rep yet, a good rookie?"

Both *caporegimes* shook their heads. Tessio smiled to take the sting
out of his words and said, "That's like bringing a guy up from the minors to pitch the World Series."

Sonny broke in curtly, "It has to be Mike. For a million different
reasons. Most important they got him down as faggy. And he can do the
job, I guarantee that, and that's important because this is the only shot
we'll get at that sneaky bastard Turk. So now we have to figure out the
best way to back him up. Tom, Clemenza, Tessio, find out where Sollozzo will take him for the conference, I don't care how much it costs.
When we find that out we can figure out how we can get a weapon into
his hands. Clemenza, I want you to get him a really 'safe' gun out of
your collection, the 'coldest' one you got. Impossible to trace. Try to
make it short barrel with a lot of blasting power. It doesn't have to be
accurate. He'll be right on top of them when he uses it. Mike, as soon
as you've used the gun, drop it on the floor. Don't be caught with it on
you. Clemenza, tape the barrel and the trigger with that special stuff
you got so he won't leave prints. Remember, Mike, we can square
everything, witnesses, and so forth, but if they catch you with the gun
on you we can't square that. We'll have transportation and protection
and then we'll make you disappear for a nice long vacation until the heat
wears off. You'll be gone a long time, Mike, but I don't want you saying
good-bye to your girl friend or even calling her. After it's all over and
you're out of the country I'll send her word that you're OK. Those are
orders." Sonny smiled at his brother. "Now stick with Clemenza and get
used to handling the gun he picks out for you. Maybe even practice a
little. We'll take care of everything else. Everything. OK, kid?"

Again Michael Corleone felt that delicious refreshing chilliness all over his body. He said to his brother, "You didn't have to give me that crap about not talking to my girl friend about something like this. What the hell did you think I was going to do, call her up to say good-bye?"

Sonny said hastily, "OK, but you're still a rookie so I spell things out. Forget it."

Michael said with a grin, "What the hell do you mean, a rookie? I listened to the old man just as hard as you did. How do you think I got so smart?" They both laughed.

Hagen poured drinks for everyone. He looked a little glum. The statesman forced to go to war, the lawyer forced to go to law. "Well, anyway now we know what we're going to do," he said.

———————

Hagen said gently, "It's not too late to back out, Mike, we can get somebody else, we can go back over our alternatives. Maybe it's not necessary to get rid of Sollozzo."

Michael laughed. "We can talk ourselves into any viewpoint," he said. "But we figured it right the first time. I've been riding the gravy train all my life, it's about time I paid my dues."

"You shouldn't let that broken jaw influence you," Hagen said, "McCluskey is a stupid man and it was business, not personal."

For the second time he saw Michael Corleone's face freeze into a mask that resembled uncannily the Don's. "Tom, don't let anybody kid you. It's all personal, every bit of business. Every piece of shit every man has to eat every day of his life is personal. They call it business. OK. But it's personal as hell. You know where I learned that from? The Don. My old man. The Godfather. If a bolt of lightning hit a friend of his the old man would take it personal. He took my going into the Marines personal. That's what makes him great. The Great Don. He takes everything personal. Like God. He knows every feather that falls from the tail of a sparrow or however the hell it goes. Right? And you know something? Accidents don't happen to people who take accidents as a personal insult. So I came late, OK, but I'm coming all the way. Damn right, I take that broken jaw personal, damn right, I take Sollozzo trying to kill my father personal." He laughed. "Tell the old man I learned it all from him and that I'm glad I had this chance to pay him back for all he did for me. He was a good father." He paused and then he said thoughtfully to Hagen, "You know, I can never remember him hitting me. Or Sonny. Or Freddie. And of course Connie, he wouldn't even yell at her. And tell me the truth, Tom, how many men do you figure the Don killed or had killed."

Tom Hagen turned away. "I'll tell you one thing you didn't learn from him: talking the way you're talking now. There are things that have to be done and you do them and you never talk about them. You don't try to justify them. They can't be justified. You just do them. Then you forget it."

Michael Corleone frowned. He said quietly, "As the *Consigliori,* you agree that it's dangerous to the Don and our Family to let Sollozzo live?"

"Yes," Hagen said.

"OK," Michael said. "Then I have to kill him."

Michael Corleone stood in front of Jack Dempsey's restaurant on Broadway and waited for his pickup. He looked at his watch. It said five minutes to eight. Sollozzo was going to be punctual. Michael had made sure he was there in plenty of time. He had been waiting fifteen minutes.

All during the ride from Long Beach into the city he had been trying to forget what he had said to Hagen. For if he believed what he said, then his life was set on an irrevocable course. And yet, could it be otherwise after tonight? He might be dead after tonight if he didn't stop all this crap, Michael thought grimly. He had to keep his mind on the business at hand. Sollozzo was no dummy and McCluskey was a very tough egg. He felt the ache in his wired jaw and welcomed the pain, it would keep him alert.

———

The Great Depression increased the power of Vito Corleone. And indeed it was about that time he came to be called Don Corleone. Everywhere in the city, honest men begged for honest work in vain. Proud men demeaned themselves and their families to accept official charity from a contemptuous officialdom. But the men of Don Corleone walked the streets with their heads held high, their pockets stuffed with silver and paper money. With no fear of losing their jobs. And even Don Corleone, that most modest of men, could not help feeling a sense of pride. He was taking care of his world, his people. He had not failed those who depended on him and gave him the sweat of their brows, risked their freedom and their lives in his service. And when an employee of his was arrested and sent to prison by some mischance, that unfortunate man's family received a living allowance; and not a miserly, beggarly, begrudging pittance but the same amount the man earned when free.

This of course was not pure Christian charity. Not his best friends would have called Don Corleone a saint from heaven. There was some self-interest in this generosity. An employee sent to prison knew he had only to keep his mouth shut and his wife and children would be cared for. He knew that if he did not inform to the police a warm welcome would be his when he left prison. There would be a party waiting in his home, the best of food, homemade ravioli, wine, pastries, with all his friends and relatives gathered to rejoice in his freedom. And sometime during the night the *Consigliori,* Genco Abbandando, or perhaps even the Don himself, would drop by to pay his respects to such a stalwart, take a glass of wine in his honor, and leave a handsome present of money so that he could enjoy a week or two of leisure with his family before returning to his daily toil. Such was the infinite sympathy and understanding of Don Corleone.

It was at this time that the Don got the idea that he ran his world far better than his enemies ran the greater world which continually obstructed his path. And this feeling was nurtured by the poor people of the neighborhood who constantly came to him for help. To get on the home relief, to get a young boy a job or out of jail, to borrow a small sum of money desperately needed, to intervene with landlords who against all reason demanded rent from jobless tenants.

Don Vito Corleone helped them all. Not only that, he helped them with goodwill, with encouraging words to take the bitter sting out of the charity he gave them. It was only natural then that when these Italians were puzzled and confused on who to vote for to represent them in the state legislature, in the city offices, in the Congress, they should ask the advice of their friend Don Corleone, their Godfather. And so he became a political power to be consulted by practical party chiefs. He consolidated this power with a far-seeing statesmanlike intelligence; by helping brilliant boys from poor Italian families through college, boys who would later become lawyers, assistant district attorneys, and even judges. He planned for the future of his empire with all the foresight of a great national leader.

The repeal of Prohibition dealt this empire a crippling blow but again he had taken his precautions. In 1933 he sent emissaries to the man who controlled all the gambling activities of Manhattan, the crap games on the docks, the shylocking that went with it as hot dogs go with baseball games, the bookmaking on sports and horses, the illicit gambling houses that ran poker games, the policy or numbers racket of Harlem. This man's name was Salvatore Maranzano and he was one of the acknowledged *pezzonovante,* .90 calibers, or big shots of the New York underworld. The Corleone emissaries proposed to Maranzano an equal partnership beneficial to both parties. Vito Corleone with his organization, his police and political contacts, could give the Maranzano operations a stout umbrella and the new strength to expand into Brooklyn and the Bronx. But Maranzano was a short-sighted man and spurned the Corleone offer with contempt. The great Al Capone was Maranzano's friend and he had his own organization, his own men, plus a huge war chest. He would not brook this upstart whose reputation was more that of a Parliamentary debator than a true *Mafioso*. Maranzano's refusal touched off the great war of 1933 which was to change the whole structure of the underworld in New York City.

Sonny said defiantly, "I saw you kill Fanucci."

The Don said, "Ahhh" and sank back in his chair. He waited.

Sonny said, "When Fanucci left the building, Mama said I could go up to the house. I saw you go up the roof and I followed you. I saw everything you did. I stayed up there and I saw you throw away the wallet and the gun."

The Don sighed. "Well, then I can't talk to you about how you should behave. Don't you want to finish school, don't you want to be a lawyer? Lawyers can steal more money with a briefcase than a thousand men with guns and masks."

Sonny grinned at him and said slyly, "I want to enter the family business." When he saw that the Don's face remained impassive, that he did not laugh at the joke, he added hastily, "I can learn how to sell olive oil."

Still the Don did not answer. Finally he shrugged. "Every man has one destiny," he said. He did not add that the witnessing of Fanucci's murder had decided that of his son. He merely turned away and added quietly, "Come in tomorrow morning at nine o'clock. Genco will show you what to do."

Early in his career the then-young Nazorine, only a baker's helper planning to get married, had come to him for assistance. He and his future bride, a good Italian girl, had saved their money and had paid the enormous sum of three hundred dollars to a wholesaler of furniture recommended to them. This wholesaler had let them pick out everything they wanted to furnish their tenement apartment. A fine sturdy bedroom set with two bureaus and lamps. Also the living room set of heavy stuffed sofa and stuffed armchairs, all covered with rich gold-threaded fabric. Nazorine and his fiancée had spent a happy day picking out what they wanted from the huge warehouse crowded with furniture. The wholesaler took their money, their three hundred dollars wrung from the sweat of their blood, and pocketed it and promised the furniture to be delivered within the week to the already rented flat.

The very next week, however, the firm had gone into bankruptcy. The great warehouse stocked with furniture had been sealed shut and attached for payment of creditors. The wholesaler had disappeared to give other creditors time to unleash their anger on the empty air. Nazorine, one of these, went to his lawyer, who told him nothing could be done until the case was settled in court and all creditors satisfied. This might take three years and Nazorine would be lucky to get back ten cents on the dollar.

Vito Corleone listened to this story with amused disbelief. It was not possible that the law could allow such thievery. The wholesaler owned his own palatial home, an estate in Long Island, a luxurious automobile, and was sending his children to college. How could he keep the three hundred dollars of the poor baker Nazorine and not give him the furniture he had paid for? But, to make sure, Vito Corleone had Genco Abbandando check it out with the lawyers who represented the *Genco Pura* company.

They verified the story of Nazorine. The wholesaler had all his personal wealth in his wife's name. His furniture business was incorporated and he was not personally liable. True, he had shown bad faith by taking the money of Nazorine when he knew he was going to file bankruptcy but this was a common practice. Under law there was nothing to be done.

Of course the matter was easily adjusted. Don Corleone sent his *Consigliori,* Genco Abbandando, to speak to the wholesaler, and as was to be expected, that wide-awake businessman caught the drift immediately and arranged for Nazorine to get his furniture. But it was an interesting lesson for the young Vito Corleone.

Don Corleone gave the speech that would be long remembered, and that reaffirmed his position as the most far-seeing statesman among them, so full of common sense, so direct from the heart; and to the heart of the matter. In it he coined a phrase that was to become as famous in its way as Churchill's Iron Curtain, though not public knowledge until more than ten years later.

For the first time he stood up to address the council. He was short and a little thin from his "illness," perhaps his sixty years showed a bit more but there was no question that he had regained all his former strength, and had all his wits.

"What manner of men are we then, if we do not have our reason," he said. "We are all no better than beasts in a jungle if that were the case. But we have reason, we can reason with each other and we can reason with ourselves. To what purpose would I start all these troubles again, the violence and the turmoil? My son is dead and that is a misfortune and I must bear it, not make the innocent world around me suffer with me. And so I say, I give my honor, that I will never seek vengeance, I will never seek knowledge of the deeds that have been done in the past. I will leave here with a pure heart.

"Let me say that we must always look to our interests. We are all men who have refused to be fools, who have refused to be puppets dancing on a string pulled by the men on high. We have been fortunate here in this country. Already most of our children have found a better life. Some of you have sons who are professors, scientists, musicians, and you are fortunate. Perhaps your grandchildren will become the new *pezzonovanti*. None of us here want to see our children follow in our footsteps, it's too hard a life. They can be as others, their position and security won by our courage. I have grandchildren now and I hope their children may someday, who knows, be a governor, a President, nothing's impossible here in America. But we have to progress with the times. The time is past for guns and killings and massacres. We have to be cunning like the business people, there's more money in it and it's better for our children and our grandchildren.

"As for our own deeds, we are not responsible to the .90 calibers, the *pezzonovantis* who take it upon themselves to decide what we shall do with our lives, who declare wars they wish us to fight in to protect what they own. Who is to say we should obey the laws they make for their own interest and to our hurt? And who are they then to meddle when we look after our own interests? *Sonna cosa nostra*," Don Corleone said, "these are our own affairs. We will manage our world for ourselves because it is our world, *cosa nostra*. And so we have to stick together to guard against outside meddlers. Otherwise they will put the ring in our nose as they have put the ring in the nose of all the millions of Neapolitans and other Italians in this country.

"For this reason I forgo my vengeance for my dead son, for the common good. I swear now that as long as I am responsible for the actions of my Family there will not be one finger lifted against any man here without just cause and utmost provocation. I am willing to sacrifice my commercial interests for the common good. This is my word, this is my honor, there are those of you here who know I have never betrayed either.

"But I have a selfish interest. My youngest son had to flee, accused of Sollozzo's murder and that of a police captain. I must now make arrangements so that he can come home with safety, cleared of all those false charges. That is my affair and I will make those arrangements. I must find the real culprits perhaps, or perhaps I must convince the authorities of his innocence, perhaps the witnesses and informants will recant their lies. But again I say that this is my affair and I believe I will be able to bring my son home.

"But let me say this. I am a superstitious man, a ridiculous failing but I must confess it here. And so if some unlucky accident should befall my youngest son, if some police officer should accidentally shoot him, if he should hang himself in his cell, if new witnesses appear to testify to his guilt, my superstition will make me feel that it was the result of the ill will still borne me by some people here. Let me go further. If my son is struck by a bolt of lightning I will blame some of the people here. If his plane should fall into the sea or his ship sink beneath the waves of the ocean, if he should catch a mortal fever, if his automobile should be struck by a train, such is my superstition that I would blame the ill will felt by people here. Gentlemen, that ill will, that bad luck, I could never forgive. But aside from that let me swear by the souls of my grandchildren that I will never break the peace we have made. After all, are we or are we not better men than those *pezzonovanti* who have killed countless millions of men in our lifetimes?"

———

Kay shook her head. "How can you want to marry me, how can you hint that you love me, you never say the word but you just now said you loved your father, you never said you loved me, how could you if you distrust me so much you can't tell me about the most important things in your life? How can you want to have a wife you can't trust? Your father trusts your mother. I know that."

"Sure," Michael said. "But that doesn't mean he tells her everything. And, you know, he has reason to trust her. Not because they got married and she's his wife. But she bore him four children in times when it was not that safe to bear children. She nursed and guarded him when people shot him. She believed in him. He was always her first loyalty for forty years. After you do that maybe I'll tell you a few things you really don't want to hear."

"Will we have to live in the mall?" Kay asked.

Michael nodded. "We'll have our own house, it won't be so bad. My parents don't meddle. Our lives will be our own. But until everything gets straightened out, I have to live in the mall."

"Because it's dangerous for you to live outside it," Kay said.

For the first time since she had come to know him, she saw Michael angry. It was cold chilling anger that was not externalized in any gesture or change in voice. It was a coldness that came off him like death and Kay knew that it was this coldness that would make her decide not to marry him if she so decided.

"The trouble is all that damn trash in the movies and the newspapers," Michael said. "You've got the wrong idea of my father and the Corleone Family. I'll make a final explanation and this one will be really final. My father is a businessman trying to provide for his wife and children and those friends he might need someday in a time of trouble. He doesn't accept the rules of the society we live in because those rules would have condemned him to a life not suitable to a man like himself, a man of extraordinary force and character. What you have to understand is that he considers himself the equal of all those great men like Presidents and Prime Ministers and Supreme Court Justices and Governors of the States. He refuses to live by rules set up by others, rules which condemn him to a defeated life. But his ultimate aim is to enter that society with a certain power since society doesn't really protect its members who do not have their own individual power. In the meantime he operates on a code of ethics he considers far superior to the legal structures of society."

Kay was looking at him incredulously. "But that's ridiculous," she said. "What if everybody felt the same way? How could society ever function, we'd be back in the times of the cavemen. Mike, you don't believe what you're saying, do you?"

Michael grinned at her. "I'm just telling you what my father believes. I just want you to understand that whatever else he is, he's not irresponsible, or at least not in the society which he has created. He's not a crazy machine-gunning mobster as you seem to think. He's a responsible man in his own way."

"And what do you believe?" Kay asked quietly.

Michael shrugged. "I believe in my family," he said. "I believe in you and the family we may have. I don't trust society to protect us, I have no intention of placing my fate in the hands of men whose only qualification is that they managed to con a block of people to vote for them. But that's for now. My father's time is done. The things he did can no longer be done except with a great deal of risk. Whether we like it or not the Corleone Family has to join that society. But when they do I'd like us to join it with plenty of our own power; that is, money and ownership of other valuables. I'd like to make my children as secure as possible before they join that general destiny."

"But you volunteered to fight for your country, you were a war hero," Kay said. "What happened to make you change?"

Michael said, "This is really getting us no place. But maybe I'm just one of those real old-fashioned conservatives they grow up in your hometown. I take care of myself, individual. Governments really don't do much for their people, that's what it comes down to, but that's not it really. All I can say, I have to help my father, I have to be on his side. And you have to make your decision about being on my side." He smiled at her. "I guess getting married was a bad idea."

Kay patted the bed. "I don't know about marrying, but I've gone without a man for two years and I'm not letting you off so easy now. Come on in here."

When they were in bed together, the light out, she whispered to him, "Do you believe me about not having a man since you left?"

"I believe you," Michael said.

"Did you?" she whispered in a softer voice.

"Yes," Michael said. He felt her stiffen a little. "But not in the last six months." It was true. Kay was the first woman he had made love to since the death of Apollonia.

From *The Fortunate Pilgrim*

Preface

I consider my second book, *The Fortunate Pilgrim,* my best novel and my most personal one. It proved also to be my most interesting book because it was full of surprises.

When I began, the plan was to make myself the hero. It was supposed to be the story of a struggling writer, poorest of the poor, whose mother, sister, and brothers were enemies of his art, and how, in the end, he succeeded in spite of them. It was written to show my rejection of my Italian heritage and my callow disdain of those illiterate peasants from which I sprang.

But what a surprise it was when I discovered that my mother turned out to be the hero of the book. And that my sister was more honest, trustworthy, and braver than me. Through the writing, those immigrant Italians who worked twelve hours a day in gray, sweat-soaked fedoras, wearing great handlebar mustaches, had the dignity of heroes. How it happened, I never knew.

All young writers dream of immortality—that hundreds of years in the future the new generations will read their books and find their lives changed, as my life was after reading *The Brothers Karamazov* at the age of fifteen. I vowed I would never write a word that was not absolutely true to myself. And I felt I had achieved that in *The Fortunate Pilgrim*. I assumed that such a writer would automatically become rich and famous.

I received marvelous reviews. But then came the next surprise: Nothing happened. I didn't become rich and famous. In fact, I was poorer than before; I had to work two jobs instead of one.

I was furious, but only at myself. I rethought my whole life. Why should the public care that I put so much of myself into that book, so much care into each sentence? Why should my family care about my writing when it didn't earn my daily bread? Why should they indulge my eccentricity? And the public, why should they care about tragedies that didn't reflect their own experience? I concluded that I had worked ten years of my life in sheer self-indulgence. I thought myself that most despised figure in Italian culture, a "chooch"—that is, a man who could not earn a living for himself or his family.

But then came another surprise. In reaction to my disappointment, and to feed my family, I decided to write a bestseller. And to use some stories that my mother—who is *Pilgrim*'s heroine, Lucia Santa—told us as we were growing up. That book was *The Godfather*. It took me four years to write, still working two jobs. But it accomplished my aim. It was a bestseller, and this time I became rich and famous. I had done the right thing.

But there were more surprises to come. Whenever the Godfather opened his mouth, in my own mind I heard the voice of my mother. I heard her wisdom, her ruthlessness, and her unconquerable love for her family and for life itself, qualities not valued in women at the time. The Don's courage and loyalty came from her; his humanity came from her. Through my characters, I heard the voices of my sisters and brothers, with their tolerance of human frailty. And so, I know now, without Lucia Santa, I could not have written *The Godfather*.

It is thirty years since I wrote *The Fortunate Pilgrim*. The changes in the culture, and the change in women's roles, as well as the growing interest in ethnic subjects, have made this book in many ways contemporary. The human experience, I hope, is timeless.

I am immensely flattered that Random House is republishing it after all this time. That it still holds its power, maybe more now than then.

I've reread the book and I still love it, and most of all I love my mother and hold her in true reverence. She lived a life of tragedy and still embraced life. She is, I can see from this vantage point, in every one of the books I have written. And I know now I am not the hero of my life, she is. All these years later, her tragedies still make me weep. And the book cries out, "Behold how she was wronged."

Mario Puzo
November 1996

————

Each tenement was a village square; each had its group of women, all in black, sitting on stools and boxes and doing more than gossip. They recalled ancient history, argued morals and social law, always taking their precedents from the mountain village in southern Italy they had escaped, fled from many years ago. And with what relish their favorite imaginings! Now: What if their stern fathers were transported by some miracle to face the problems *they* faced every day? Or their mothers of the quick and heavy hands? What shrieks if *they* as daughters had dared as these American children dared? If *they* had presumed.

The women talked of their children as they would of strangers. It was a favorite topic, the corruption of the innocent by the new land. Now: Felicia, who lived around the corner of 31st Street. What type of daughter was she who did not cut short her honeymoon on news of her godmother's illness, the summons issued by her own mother? A real whore. No no, they did not mince words. Felicia's mother herself told the story. And a son, poor man, who could not wait another year to marry when his father so commanded? Ahhh, the disrespect. *Figlio disgraziato.* Never could this pass in Italy. The father would kill his arrogant son; yes, kill him. And the daughter? In Italy—Felicia's mother swore in a voice still trembling with passion, though this had all happened three years ago, the godmother recovered, the grandchildren the light of her life—ah, in Italy the mother would pull the whore out of her bridal chamber, drag her to the hospital bed by the hair of her head. Ah, Italia, Italia; how the world changed and for the worse. What madness was it that made them leave such a land? Where fathers commanded and mothers were treated with respect by their children.

Each in turn told a story of insolence and defiance, themselves heroic, long-suffering, the children spitting Lucifers saved by an application of Italian discipline—the razor strop or the *Tackeril*. And at the end of each story each woman recited her requiem. *Mannaggia America!*—Damn America. But in the hot summer night their voices were filled with hope, with a vigor never sounded in their homeland. Here now was money in the bank, children who could read and write, grandchildren who would be professors if all went well. They spoke with guilty loyalty of customs they had themselves trampled into dust.

The truth: These country women from the mountain farms of Italy, whose fathers and grandfathers had died in the same rooms in which they were born, these women loved the clashing steel and stone of the great city, the thunder of trains in the railroad yards across the street, the lights above the Palisades far across the Hudson. As children they had lived in solitude, on land so poor that people scattered themselves singly along the mountain slopes to search out a living.

Audacity had liberated them. They were pioneers, though they never walked an American plain and never felt real soil beneath their feet. They moved in a sadder wilderness, where the language was strange, where their children became members of a different race. It was a price that must be paid.

In all this Lucia Santa was silent. She waited for her friend and ally, Zia Louche. She rested, gathering up her strength for the long hours of happy quarreling that lay ahead. It was still early evening, and they would not return to their homes before midnight. The rooms would not be cool before then. She folded her hands in her lap and turned her face to the gentle breeze that blew from the river below Twelfth Avenue.

A small, round, handsome woman, Lucia Santa stood at the height of her powers in health, mental and physical; courageous and without fear of life and its dangers. But not foolhardy, not reckless. She was strong, experienced, wary and alert, well-equipped for the great responsibility of bringing a large family to adulthood and freedom. Her only weakness was a lack of that natural cunning and shrewdness which does so much more for people than virtue.

When she was only seventeen, over twenty years ago, Lucia Santa had left her home in Italy. She traveled the three thousand miles of dark ocean to a strange country and a strange people and began a life with a man she had known only when they had played together as innocent children.

Shaking her head at her own madness, yet with pride, she often told the story.

There had come a time when her father, with stern pity, told her, his favorite daughter, that she could not hope for bridal linen. The farm was too poor. There were debts. Life promised to be even harder. There it was. There could be found only a husband witless with love.

In that moment she had lost all respect for her father, for her home, for her country. A bride without linen was shameful, shameful as a bride rising from an unbloodied nuptial bed; worse, for there could be no recourse to slyness, no timing of the bridal night near the period of flood. And even that men had forgiven. But what man would take a woman with the stigma of hopeless poverty?

Only the poor can understand the shame of poverty, greater than the shame of the greatest sinner. For the sinner, vanquished by his own other self, is in one sense the victor. But the poor are truly vanquished: by their world, by their *padrones,* by fortune and by time. They are beggars always in need of charity. To the poor who have been poor for centuries, the nobility of honest toil is a legend. Their virtues lead them to humiliation and shame.

But Lucia Santa was helpless, though her sulky, adolescent rage endured. Then a letter from America; a boy from the neighboring farm, her companion when they were both little children, wrote and asked her to join him in a new land. It was all done correctly through both fathers. Lucia Santa tried to remember the boy's face.

And so one sunny Italian day Lucia Santa and two other village maidens were escorted to the town hall and then to the church by their weeping parents, aunts, and sisters. The three girls went on board ship, brides by proxy, sailing from Naples to New York, by law Americans.

In a dream Lucia Santa entered a land of stone and steel, bedded that same night with a stranger who was her legal husband, bore that stranger two children, and was pregnant with the third when he carelessly let himself be killed in one of those accidents that were part of the building of the new continent. She accepted all this without self-pity. She lamented, true, but that was not the same thing; she only begged fate for mercy.

So then, a pregnant widow, still young, with no one to turn to, she never succumbed to terror, despair. She had an enormous strength, not unusual in women, to bear adversity. But she was not a stone. Fate did not make her bitter; that was left to friends and neighbors—these very neighbors who so intimately shared the summer night.

Ahh, the young wives, the young mothers, all the other young Italian women in a strange land. What cronies they were. How they ran to each other's apartments, up and down the stairs, into the adjoining tenements. "*Cara* Lucia Santa, taste this special dish"—a platter of new sausage, Easter pie with wheat germ and clotted cheese and a crust glazed with eggs, or plump ravioli for a family saint's day, with a special meat and tomato sauce. What flutters, what compliments and cups of coffee and confidences and promises to be godmother to the yet-to-be-born infant. But after the tragedy, after the initial pity and condolences, the true face of the world showed itself to Lucia Santa.

Greetings were cold, doors were shut, prospective godmothers disappeared. Who wished to be friendly with a young, full-blooded widow? Husbands were weak, there would be calls for assistance. In the tenements life was close; a young woman without a man was dangerous. She could draw off money and goods as the leech draws blood. They were not malicious, they showed only the prudence of the poor, so easy to mock when there is no understanding of the fear which is its root.

One friend stood fast, Zia Louche, an old, childless widow, who came to help, stood godmother when the fatherless Vincenzo was born and bought her godson a beautiful gold watch when he was confirmed so that Lucia Santa could hold up her head! for such a magnificent present was a mark of respect and faith. But Zia Louche was the only one, and when mourning time had passed Lucia Santa saw the world with new and wiser eyes.

Time healed the wounds and now they were all friends again. Perhaps—who knows?—the young widow had been too harsh in her judgment, for these same neighbors, true, in their own self-interest, helped her find a second husband who would feed and clothe her children. There was a marriage in church. These same neighbors gave her a glorious wedding-night feast. But Lucia Santa never let the world deceive her again.

And so on this heavy summer night, with her first batch of children grown and safe, her second batch of children no longer infants except for Lena, and with some money in the post office; now, after twenty years of struggle and a fair share of suffering, Lucia Santa Angeluzzi-Corbo stood on that little knoll of prosperity that the poor reach, reach with such effort that they believe the struggle is won and that with ordinary care their lives are safe. She had already lived a lifetime; the story was over.

Enough. Here came Zia Louche, completing the circle. Lucia Santa paid attention, prepared to enter the torrent of gossip. But she saw her daughter Octavia coming from the corner of 30th Street, past the *Panettiere* and his red glass box of pizza and pale tin cans of lemon ice. Then Lucia Santa lost sight of her daughter; for one blinding moment her eyes were filled by the *Panettiere's* wooden tub, brimming with red coppers and gleaming silver fishes of dimes and nickels. She felt a quick, hot surge of passionate anger that she could never possess such treasure and that the ugly baker should find fortune so kind. Then she saw the *Panettiere's* wife—old, mustached, no longer able to bear children—guarding that wooden tub of copper and silver, her wrinkled shell-lidded dragon eyes flashing fire in the summer light.

Lucia Santa felt Octavia sitting beside her on the backless chair; their hips and thighs touched. This always irritated the mother, but her daughter would be offended if she moved, so she accepted it. Seeing her daughter so oddly handsome, dressed in the American style, she gave the old crony Zia Louche a smile that showed both her pride and a hint of derisive irony. Octavia, dutifully silent and attentive, saw that smile and understood it, yet she was bewildered once again by her mother's nature.

As if her mother could understand that Octavia wanted to be everything these women were not! With the foolish and transparent cleverness of the young, she wore a powder-blue suit that hid her bust and squared the roundness of her hips. She wore white gloves, as her high school teacher had done. Her eyebrows were heavy and black, honestly unplucked. Hopelessly she compressed the full red lips to an imaginary sternness, her eyes quietly grave—and all to hide the drowning sensuality that had been the undoing of the women around her. For Octavia reasoned that satisfying the terrible dark need stilled all other needs and she felt a frightened pity for these women enchanted into dreamless slavery by children and the unknown pleasures of a marriage bed.

This would not be *her* fate. She sat with bowed head, listening, Judas-like; pretending to be one of the faithful, she planned treason and escape.

Now with only women around her, Octavia took off her jacket; the white blouse with its tiny red-ribboned tie was more seductive than she could ever know. No disguise could hide the full roundness of her bust. The sensual face, crown of blue-black curls and ringlets, great liquid eyes, all mocked the staidness of her dress. With malice she could not have made herself more provocative than she did in her innocence.

Lucia Santa took the jacket and folded it over her arm, an act of love that was maternal, that meant possession and dominance. But above all an act of reconciliation, for earlier that evening mother and daughter had quarreled.

Octavia wanted to go to night school, study to become a teacher. Lucia Santa refused permission. No; she would become ill working and going to school. "Why? Why?" the mother asked. "You, such a beautiful dressmaker, you earn good money." The mother objected out of superstition. This course was known. Life was unlucky, you followed a new path at your peril. You put yourself at the mercy of fate. Her daughter was too young to understand.

Unexpectedly, shamefacedly, Octavia had said, "I want to be happy," and the older woman became a raging fury, contemptuous—the mother, who had always defended her daughter's toity ways, her reading of books, her tailored suits that were as affected as a lorgnette. The mother had mimicked Octavia in the perfect English of a shallow girl,

"You want to be happy." And then in Italian, with deadly seriousness, "Thank God you are alive."

––––––––––

They were on Tenth Avenue going downtown. Larry stared out the window at the railroad yard. It was almost as if he were changing second by second, each drop of blood, each bit of flesh, into someone else. He would never go back to work in the railroad yards, he would never be afraid as he had been in that station house. The whole majesty of law had crumbled before his eyes with that handshake between Mr. di Lucca and the detective; his swift rescue and the admiration that marked his freedom. He thought of the baker's blood, of the baker's arms outstretched to bar his escape, of the mad staring eyes above that smashed pulpy face, and he felt a little sick.

Larry had to speak the truth. He said, "Mr. di Lucca, I can't go around beating guys up for the money. I don't mind collecting, but I'm not a gangster."

Mr. di Lucca patted him soothingly on the shoulder. "No, no; who does these things for pleasure? Am I a gangster? Don't I have children and grandchildren? Am I not godfather to the children of my friends? But do you know what it is to be born in Italy? You are a dog and you scratch in the earth like a dog to find a dirty bone for supper. You give eggs to the priest to save your soul, you slip the town clerk a bottle of wine merely to bandy words. When the *padrone,* the landowner, comes to spend the summer at his estate, all the village girls go to clean his house and fill it with fresh flowers. He pays them with a smile, and ungloves his knuckles for a kiss. And then a miracle. America. It was enough to make one believe in Jesus Christ.

"In Italy they were stronger than me. If I took an olive from the *padrone,* a carrot, or, God forbid, a loaf of bread, I must flee, hide in Africa to escape his vengeance. But here, this is democracy and the *padrone* is not so strong. Here it is possible to escape your fate. But you must pay.

"Who is this German, this baker, that he can earn his living, bake his bread without paying? The world is a dangerous place. By what right does he bake bread on that corner, in that street? The law? Poor people cannot live by all the laws. There would not be one alive. Only the *padroni* would be left.

"Now this man, this German, you feel sorry for him. Don't. You see how nice the police treat you? Sure, you're my friend, but this baker, right around the corner from the police, he doesn't even send coffee and buns over to make friends. How do you like that? The man on the beat, the baker makes him pay for his Coffee An. What kind of a person is this?"

Mr. di Lucca paused, and on his face came a look of almost unbelieving, finicky disgust.

"This is a man who thinks because he works hard, is honest, never breaks the law, nothing can happen to him. He is a fool. Now listen to me."

Mr. di Lucca paused again. In a quiet, sympathetic voice, he went on, "Think of yourself. You worked hard, you were honest, you never broke the law. Worked hard? Look at your arms, like a gorilla from hard work.

"But there is no work. Nobody comes and gives you a pay envelope because you are honest. You don't break no law and they don't put you in jail. That's something, but will it feed your wife and children? So what do people like ourselves do? We say, *Good*. There is no work. We have no pay. We cannot break the law, and we cannot steal because we are honest; so we will all starve, me, my children, and my wife. Right?" He waited for Larry to laugh.

Larry kept his eyes on Mr. di Lucca, expecting something more. Mr. di Lucca noticed this and said gravely, "It will not always be like this, living by a strong arm. Enough. Do you still work for me? One hundred dollars a week and a better territory. Agreed?"

Larry said quietly, "Thanks, Mr. di Lucca, it's OK with me."

Mr. di Lucca raised a finger paternally. "Don't pay no more dues for nobody."

Larry smiled. "I won't," he said.

When Mr. di Lucca dropped him off on Tenth Avenue, Larry walked along the railroad yards for a while. He realized that you couldn't always be nice to people and expect them to do what you wanted, not with money, anyway. You had to be mean. What puzzled him was the admiration people had for a man who did something cruel. He remembered the kraut's face all smashed and wondered at Mr. di Lucca's exultation over it. Because of this he would make money, his wife and child would live like people who owned a business, he would help his mother and brothers and sisters. And honestly, he didn't hit the kraut because of the money. Hadn't he paid the guy's dues all the time?

Rose Quiello

*Dedicated to an Old Friend
Whose Kindness I Shall
Never Forget*

"It's nearly ten o'clock, and the band and Mary Magdalene should be here any time now," my mother would say. "Do you have your dollar bill?" The Saint, firmly planted on the shoulders of the young men of the parish specially chosen for the occasion, was paraded throughout the neighborhood, and we would rush to the corner once we heard the band playing, and eagerly await our chance to pin our dollar on The Saint. Children, too short to reach, would be lifted into the air by the adults with the hope that the children would be doubly blessed. The patriarchs of the Saint Mary Magdalene Society would march in front of The Saint, proudly displaying a banner with the name "Society of Mary Magdalene" emblazoned on it. Just behind The Saint would be the band, a coterie of unfamiliar faces that always seemed to play off-key. The street was astir with great fanfare. That evening would be the long-awaited Festa at the end of the street. Each food stand announced its specialty, sausage and sweet peppers, fried calamari, Italian ice, and one's stomach could not eat everything it wished to try.

I am dressed in white. I look like a bride. I am a bride and, as I walk down the aisle, I am thinking: "Maybe I will die before I am asked to say 'I do.'" But I didn't die. I lived as a dutiful wife for almost four years—a slow death. My fear of marriage had always surpassed my fear of being alone, yet I was too timid to say that I did not wish to marry. At least not yet. I had learned early on that Italian women tend to love everything else more than they love themselves: their children, their husbands, their extended families, and their homes. My grandfather, set in his ways like plaster, issued repeatedly this dictum with absolute authority: "You skirts are all alike." I did not know exactly what he meant, but this I had learned: women were always giving, giving, giving. This is not what my grandfather meant, but it was the truth I knew. I felt myself knotted into a hard coil. But like Penelope, undoing the tapestry, thread by thread, while Ulysses was gone, I finally managed to unravel my marriage until there was nothing left.

The Sunday-morning gatherings of the Italian men in the local "athletic club," which was adjacent to our apartment, were like a book group gone bad. They waved their prejudices like medals. Misunderstandings given new life by unnecessary comments from those onlookers on the sidelines, misunderstandings that could have been cleared up in minutes lingered for years. Otherwise joyful moments would become impossibly ripe and tense with the raise of an eyebrow. How could men be the best kind of neighbors and relatives, generous and kind, and yet the worst kind of human beings, I wondered. Still, villains have hearts and heroes have flaws. I knew men who would be no more disturbed by violence—in fact would celebrate it—than they would be by the starting of a car. They would set up equations but not factor in the consequences of their actions. They didn't know that they were living on the edge of a precipice because they never looked down. Gambling and "booking" numbers were pervasive, but were never considered to be against the law where I grew up. In one place such behavior would be considered illegal, even crazy; in my neighborhood, not only sane but as respectable as any human activity can be. The "bookies," a name given to those who received the bets placed by the gamblers, not the voracious "readers" of the clan, situated themselves outside the laws of legality. "I made a lot of illegal money," I remember a relative, well practiced in the arts of duplicity and self-deception, once telling me when I was just a child, "but I never made a dishonest dollar." This sort of non sequitur, repeated enough, soon calcified into received opinion without his ever troubling to think about what was actually being said. Loosely translated, this meant that he had paid off all "bets" to the gamblers who "booked" numbers with him. Nothing was quite as it was represented. As long as something wasn't named a crime, it would mean that it wasn't really happening, leaving us children with an indigestible lump of confusion and sadness inside, a sticky lump of criminal residue that would choke us for a long time. Like the viewer of a large Impressionist painting, standing farther back and farther back to see all those dabs of color come into focus, I can now see the damage that such faulty logic can do to the lives of others. The pure idea of family really has nothing at all to do with blood. But children can read people, even though they do not always understand the language, and we soon would come to learn that the unbreakable and unshakable belief in blood is vastly overrated.

We ate meatballs as if they were lollipops, and since tasting is half the fun in an Italian kitchen, dipping a piece of crusty, fresh-baked Italian bread into my mom's sauce falls just short of heaven. That pleasure is surely compounded when Dean Martin is singing "That's Amore" in the background, a common occurrence growing up in our home. My grandmother would croon over every scrap of meat on a sparerib like a medieval relic hunter musing on the knucklebone of a saint. We dined mostly on pasta. Macaroni meals figured importantly in the family diet: pasta with clams, pasta with peas, pasta with meatballs and sausage, pasta with calamari, pasta with beans, pasta with potatoes. Completely impervious to the modern ground rules of balanced nutrition, carbohydrates often clashed with carbohydrates at the dinner table, and meat was usually reserved for Saturday night. While my dad seemed to cherish his Saturday-night steak, for my grandfather, in particular, a pot roast or a steak dinner was a penance, a measure of atonement, something to be endured until the following evening when pasta would be once again reinstated. Two consecutive nights without pasta was unimaginable. Food became the antidote for feelings of guilt, sadness, and anger. After a recent family tragedy my brother, Michael, feverishly walked every inch of the kitchen floor, shaking his head as a startled horse shakes his mane. We could barely speak as we looked at each other, but we laughed aloud when at the moment of the climax our mother said: "Would either of you like an eggplant sandwich?" Food is a resolution to controversy; food is rescue. We ate and talked and cried and laughed in the kitchen and ate again. This was about more than just food. It was about our mom making connections the best she could and in the way she knew best across the kitchen table, across time and across sadness.

Giose Rimanelli

From *Benedetta in Guysterland: A Liquid Novel*

I may be a whore, Joe. But I love you. You sang for me, and I am what I am because of you.

There are so many things about you to make you dear to me. Things that I will always remember. I love your *voce da orso* and your laughter which always sounds as if you had heard a dirty joke. Maybe I should call it a sexy roar. And next to your voice I love your mouth. The curve of your upper lip and your smile, your laurel cane which so dearly embraced me deep. If I met you years from now I think my first impulse would be to want to bite your lips gently.

But these are the smaller things that I love about you, Joe. Even if your mother's name is Venerea. Dear Joe, dear Joe. I shall continue to ache for you when Zip and the band drag me away from here, looking for another place to perform or to hide. Because you have made me vibrate with excitement, a thing which I had never done before.

Zip just told us about his days in Paliermu, and about two sisters who made him happy with love. One of them was only eleven, and knew a lot. I guess Sicilians are old, old people, older than the Romans, older than the Pyramids, while my people came here with the Mayflower. We have no experience, then. But I have to tell you, Joe, my story too. And I have to tell you that, whether I like it or not, my roots are in the soil of the small town of New Wye, Appalachia, U.S.A., the town of many shady streets where I first learned to love and to hate. I am fleeing that town in a hopeless flight, running and yet ripping out my very core as I run, for I am bound there by the simple fact that I was born and grew up there.

My first memories are Nabokov County memories: . . . the smell of sweet rotting apples in the fall, the smell of the greenfresh leaves of spring, and placed strangely among this fertility, dry dusty and narrow roads symbolic of the people who lived around me.

My first real love was the boy I called the Sandboy because he and I would walk in silence under the moon on the sand of the ocean. Our love was beautiful and subtle, for we could make love for hours at a time with our eyes. Our eyes were exactly alike and I always felt as though I were looking into a mirror when I looked into his eyes . . . dark eyes, deep eyes, neverending depth eyes. But he was too gentle with soft, doelike lips and long pleading artistic hands which move the mute spell of our too short dream together. We covered the dust roads of Appalachia with black velvet and lay down there to listen quietly to the fast tum tum of each other's hearts. But he lay there too long with his eyes closed and a sweet girlish smile on his face. He grew selfish and slow in his enjoyment, afraid to touch me too much as he might scare me. Little did he know that I was waiting impatiently for his hand, or his leg pressed hard against mine. 'Jargon,' I said one night. 'I won't be able to stand this any longer. I am waiting for you when it should be the opposite.' He grew tense and explained to me that he didn't yet know the meaning of love. We sat together all night by the side of a dust road as the moon went down and dawn came, he silent and I waiting. Finally he took my hand and softly rubbed it, saying too slowly and too stiffly, 'Yes, I love you.'

That summer tasted of salt spray, tarred ropes and the wild taste of a wind-tossed land, unspoiled and perfect. Many times I still think that I am waiting for him to come back, to use his beautiful eyes, to seduce me, to conquer me and then be proud of his conquest. But while he is still a boy, he would only be ashamed to wake up the next morning and see me beside him . . . good to him, my Jargon.

———————

(I must be crazy. Am I crazy?)

The way to become an alcoholic is to listen to jazz alone all night. I begin to think of the days when we used to have boyfriends at the age of ten and eleven or twelve, and the time when I told a little boy from New Wye, twelve years old, about a girl becoming a woman when she got her period.

He laughed at me then, and I was so angry that later I showed him my legs to prove to him that what I had said was true.

He was so impressed that he asked me to be my boyfriend on Sundays. From then on, my Sunday afternoons were spent in an old, abandoned house in the woods of New Wye. He bit my body as we lay on an old, lumpy hard mattress between cracked crumbling walls. He with his still soft boy body and I barely curved like a Modigliani nude. Together we learned to laugh at dirty jokes, and drew pictures of crude naked figures.

And I think of my country.

Appalachia is the land where people peer from under their shaggy, winter fur toward a short spring of the mind. They wait calmly as their cows in the March mud for a fleeting glance at green grass, and then they settle back to wait for the snow and the bitter cold when they will again become shadows bent under their loads of firewood.

A man is roughhewn wood or slabs or metal melted in an irregular pattern to resemble a human being. A woman is calico, crazy stern-eyed patchwork, but harder than a nut to crack.

Words are useless there, as useless as speaking to a tree. People grunt yes and no, rarely smile and never use their hands to emphasize the meaning of their words. A man's words are in his feet, in his hands or in the straight, steady stare of his eyes, but never in his mouth unless he is choking on a piece of meat. Then and only then does an outsider know that a man has a mouth rather than a thin, closed slit of pink flesh, yes.

The only forms of passion allowed to him are those of great hunger and that which produces the masses of squirming, dirty children that become any rich man's property after their birth.

The real Appalachia lies below the rich man's Christmas tree with its flickering lights and short-lived tinsel and its sawed-off base that oozes sap until it dies. The real land lies under the roots of spruce forest. It is the land of darkness within the thick needles; the land where people are too poor to provide light for themselves; the land where the eyes of men are made to look across the pastures to count the cows coming home with their bells ringing clear in the fading light. These eyes were not made for squinting at the printed words unless the word is about a new tractor for sale 'or about the fall fair in the next county. Only then does the eye become a practiced reader and convey the words to the brain. And only then does the brain quicken the heartbeat of that almost dead man, yes.

(Yes, I am crazy!)

We think too long in terms of what to be. Yet I lived with deep roots once. And now I wish them awake. Because sometimes I think I'm several.

No, I'm crazy. And divided. Have I got panty hose for you? It's sheer to here. The panty is just a little bitty thing, which is why Burlington calls it Brief Top. But as far as marriage, ah, better dead than wed, at least at the moment. Well, where did I see that? New Woman magazine? It would be O.K. if you didn't have to sign a paper that says forever. No. Femininity is just the enshrinement of cheap labor. And it is in this relation that now I think of my father, a strong man under his quietness which would seem to the stranger a curtain of shyness. My father the Keeper, made of heavy tweed and the smell of pipe tobacco blending with the sweet perfume of a wood fire that burns in the fireplace in his study during the winter evenings. My father the big Man, although now only his hands and feet show his size as his body is beginning to shrink in the eternal cold. My father with the long ears of an Easter Island Aku-Aku statue, in his domain, a room filled with books, papers, the smell of a wood fire and tobacco smoke. My father and his feet. I see his polished, mahogany-colored shoes winking and gleaming under the table as we sit for long hours, silently and intently bent over the chessboard, father against daughter in a contest more involved than that of a game. I play with him to win, and yet if I won, I would try to get him to play another game and make a quick mistake so he would beat me. But I can never beat him at his own game of thinking for the tiny wooden pieces glowing golden-white and ebony in the late evening firelight. With him the great, old clock ticks slowly and steadily on the mantelpiece, the hands travel over the worn face calmly, time and time again, and the fire crackles in the grate. He moves his shoe with a quick, irritated motion and then moves his queen. There are no words spoken during the defeat. Which is for both of us, at the very end, leaving me with a strong desire for physical contact without sex. Yes. He talks to himself gently as he sits alone in a pool of lamplight correcting old English compositions, and nervously bites the end of his pipe as he sweats out the clumsy mistakes of his students, meticulously dotting the grubby papers with a red pencil. The strange, nervous man bent slightly from so much desk work, and squinting slightly from so much reading, does his work because he knows that it is right, and he will only live by the right things. And this is Appalachia about him. He personifies the land of the meek and accepting, the silent and the tired. Now Death has made him sweet but also has shown him that life is too short and that he must accomplish many things before he dies. He belongs in the background of the tall, white wooden steeples of the churches that dot the countryside, for he is a religious man and lives by the iron rod although he does not impose his way of life on anyone. He is too modest. He will talk about himself only when asked and even then will fall silent after a few minutes, perhaps embarrassed. My father, the Lamb, ah! And so the nerves raw a bit.

Well, then, I say: 'Call off the dogs. Am I older than you, father?'

I languished there, as everywhere. Everybody's gone. But I wept there, alone.

————

Zounds! I was never so bethump'd . . . Between the moment when I ordered dinner and when it was rolled in like a corpse on a rubber-wheeled table, I lost interest in it. Zip, however, is eating Oysters Rockefeller and sipping cold white wine. He talks about our strange life, mostly ritualistic—'archetypal' he says. And he smiles.

'You smile,' I say.

'The earth smiles,' he says.

'But this is a smile in the heart of matter. Does it matter? Does anything . . . matter?'

'Go into the stone and find out.'

His tongue seems coated with rum and molasses as it darts in and out of his mouth, licking at his moustache like a pink lizard. His hands flutter like dying birds in an abandoned aviary. And I'm thinking that at the age of fifty the world's most famous guyster stands precariously on the ledge of vulnerability, fighting like a jaguar and talking like a philosopher.

'Go into the stone and find out,' he repeats. 'I did . . . and I fou ʾ out . . . yes, I matter . . . In the very heart of creatio ʾ

————

Anabasis?

Yes, a place where vast expanses of time bea steady roll of a snare drum. It is easy to feel los among the everchanging, evermoving collages of leaf shadows, patterned on lighter green grass. The college is a place of extremes . . . of passions and hatred fashioned from close relationships of teacher to student and student to student. There, there are very live people and dead, sleepwalkers trying to appear a typical 'Anabasis girl' with long, black, stringy hair, great dark eyes, pools of black mascara, and slinky black, theatrical clothes.

Among guys' colleges, Anabasis is known for its artsy-craftsy girls, immersed in painting, sculpture, anthropology and the theater. There is a lot of talent and a lot of fraud. Some of the creatures that walk around the campus are shells, well-dressed and beautiful, but the long cigarette holder is in their mouths because they have nothing to say to anyone. There is a lot of hiding and small talk around the tables in the cavernous, hideous dining room. Anabasis has perhaps the largest collection of unhappy, misunderstood students, the misfits, of any college in the U.S.A. Many of the girls are qualified for their degrees in the mastery of magic depression and the art of making themselves killers by sitting alone for hours in their rooms, in the haze of smoke and thoughts. I remember once hearing a heated discussion between five girls on whose family life was the most unhappy. Each girl in turn discussed her hatred for her mother who had divorced her father and then married after that several times. Each girl picked away the flesh of her innumerable stepfathers and stepmothers and stepbrothers and stepsisters. They took pride in finally awarding the prize to the most unhappy, mixed up girl, and she accepted it as an honor, smiled and nodded her pleasure. They all went off singing 'We're Lucky to Be Us', and ended up at a bar in town.

Behind dark glasses and mass of long, black hair, there are often sad, troubled eyes of children who will never know childhood, who were raised practically from the cradle right to their first martini. Anabasis will not help those who don't help themselves.

Most of the teachers, even though they are kind, are caught like fish in the nets of their own problems or their own creations. The college can sometimes be the most personal place and at other times a cruel, cold home for little wanderers, where faces hide behind an indifferent expression of 'I don't want to get involved with you.' Face upon face, stony reflections multiplied many times in the fog. Individuals all and individuals none.

The college holds in its palms the wild abandon that I love, a freedom from my parents; it captures and holds the wild beat of bongo-n hearts and the isolated pluck of a guitar string, played in the dark hadows by a moth that only flies by night. All forgotten dreams come down from Beowulf's grave up in the woods of another city. But at night the college lives, and especially on the warm spring nights when the trees turn sensual with grazing, tickling leafy fingers and the sap pulsating in the dark. Windows open, lights are lowered and the college breathes freely. Then the fields are secretly crowded with madly clenching couples; half of the beds in the dormitory are empty and it is then that the ugly one realizes that she is sitting as she sits tortured over her books. It is then that the slow ones are left behind in the wake, the scornful exhaust of a Thunderbird or an MG just big enough for two.

The college prepares anyone for the world and its oddities. It is a shocking place for the freshmen who come starry-eyed and eager to learn about life and how to be wicked. A year in an exploratory computer class will teach them how to handle the teacher who gently and consistently massages his cigarette to the point of unnerving the whole world.

The campus can look sterile in the fall, puritanical in the winter whiteness and very much alive in the spring. Anabasis itself, as a college, is an unbelievable myth. It is boring and yet exciting, loved and hated, for it throws back to each one who spends any time there a truthful reflection of their worth, which reflections some spit on with disgust and others embrace with relief.

Ray Romano

From *Everything and a Kite*

To be honest, Italian and Jewish families in my neighborhood were very similar. Especially the mothers.

The mother whose world revolved around food. Who believed any problem could be solved with food. The mother who could never accept that you were actually full.

Even now, when I visit, it's the same story. I get up from the table, put on my jacket, and start heading out, and she still won't stop. She'll wrap the food up to go.

And they're quick, these mothers. They'll beat you to the front door. They're wrap-up ninjas.

"Take it with you!"

"Mom, please . . . I'm just putting out your garbage."

"Take it anyway! Look how far away the cans are. You'll get hungry."

As far back as I can remember, she was like this. The only way I could have friends eat at my house was to brief them before they came over.

"Look. This is going to be like nothing you've ever experienced."

"Ray, don't worry, I'm really hungry. It's gonna be fine."

"Shut up, you fool! Listen to me and listen good. When you're done with the meal, if you want a little more, it's going to get very tricky. Don't tell my mother you want a little more, because then she'll serve you a whole new meal. If you want a little more, tell her you don't want *any* more. Come right out and say, 'Boy, I'm full, I couldn't eat anything else. Please, no more for me.'"

That was what you had to do. Stay one step ahead of her.

You want a little? Tell her you want *no* more.

You want a lot more? Tell her you want a little.

You don't want *any* more? You have to shoot her.

That's right, I said it! You have to shoot the woman. Or at least threaten.

Whatever you do, do it quick. Don't hesitate. As soon as you feel you've had enough to eat, just stand up and announce, "I'm done." Then pull a gun out of your vest pocket.

"Put it back in the bowl, Mrs. Romano . . . *nice and easy*. Now hand the spoon to Ray. That's it, thaaaaaat's it . . . Keep your hands where I can see them . . ."

"SHE'S GOT A CANNOLI IN HER APRON!"

Shoot her! You have to shoot her. And land one. Don't graze her, that'll just piss her off.

She'll take a bullet and keep coming. There's no quit in her. She won't just go down, she'll pass the food off to my aunt. There's always a fat aunt backing her up.

"Take this, Maria—he's a runner! Feed him without me!"

Of course, the upside to Mom's obsession was the amount of food I would get to take to school in my lunch bag. I brought a lot to the table when it came to the old grammar school lunch trading market. I had quantity, I had quality, and to top it off, I had Murray Goldberg as my broker.

"Ray, for half that chicken Parmesan, I can get you a tuna salad, a Yoohoo, and an ice cream to be named later. But we gotta go *now*."*

I used to love the bag lunch. And Mom knew she did a good job. She was proud of her work, and it never wavered. It was always the same size

*Italian women have mustaches. OK, we're even.

brown bag, top folded down three times, and it wasn't complete until she whipped out the Magic Marker and wrote, on both sides of the bag:

RAY

Everybody knew whose lunch that was.

It didn't stop at school, either. I lived at home until I was twenty-nine, doing many different things. I was a college student, a bank teller, a truck driver. Through it all, the one constant was Mom's bag lunch.

Boy, I loved that lunch.

When my mother reads this, I'm sure she'll be flattered, but she'll probably scold me for mentioning that I was a truck driver. She thinks that if people know I worked a blue-collar job, they'll assume I'm un-educated.

"Why don't you ever tell the people how you studied accounting?"

Look, I drove a mattress truck in Manhattan, and I'm proud of it. I was a good truck driver. Never got a moving violation.

I did come close once. A police officer pulled me over. I guess he thought the light was red, I thought it was yellow, who's to say? As he walked toward my truck, I reached for my license and realized that I had left my wallet at home.

I remained fairly calm and explained to him my situation. No wallet.

It was when he got this indignant look on his face that my imagi-nation got the best of me. All I could think of was where was I going to hide a paper clip on my body so I could jimmy the handcuffs open like they do in those prison movies.

I started sweating a little, and he said, "Listen, sir, I need some kind of identification. I don't know who you are."

And it was a reflex. I wasn't trying to be funny. But with one mo-tion I grabbed my bag lunch and held it up to his face.

"I'm

RAY!"

Showed him the other side.

RAY

I didn't get a ticket. I'm not going to explain further. All you need to know is that for the rest of the day that officer's breath smelled like chicken Parmesan.

★ ★ ★

I lived in the typical Italian home.

The plastic furniture you couldn't sit on. Bathroom towels you weren't allowed to touch. China that no one's ever going to use.

It was a museum.

Everything in my mother's house is for a special occasion that hasn't happened *yet*.

My mother's waiting for the Pope to show up for dinner to break out the good stuff. Or Tony Danza.

Growing up, I had to attend thousands of Italian social events. These included the dreaded Italian wedding. Now, as a little kid, this wasn't so bad. Lots of food, and usually you could give the adults the slip and go break something.

But today I get the shivers when my wife and I are invited to one. I'm not antisocial. But I do have a few simple gripes against those big Italian weddings.

For starters, if I have to chicken-dance again, I'm going to kill somebody.

Listen, I'm not against *dancing* at weddings. It's a celebration, and of course people should dance if they want to.

But what's the reason it's always got to be a *stupid* dance? The Chicken. The Hokey-Pokey. The Slide. And my personal dance enemy, The Train.

I'm always getting sucked into that conga line of idiots. They sneak up on you. They blindside you. You don't even see them coming. You get up from your chair, take two steps, next thing you know, some stranger's got his hands around your hips.

"No, no . . . I'm just going to the men's room . . . no, no . . . ohhhhhhh, come on!"

You're in. It's over. Forget it. You better have a strong bladder, because you're going to be cha-cha-ing until the song is done. Sometimes until the end of the reception. There's no getting away. You can't disengage. You let go of the guy in front of you and try to walk away, and now you're the conductor for whoever is attached to you.

Now there's *two* trains shimmying around the room. The train is like an earthworm: cut it in half and both sides are still moving. Your only hope is to try to run them into each other.

Otherwise they're going to hang on and follow you right into the men's room.

"Hey, where's the train leader taking us? What's he doing? Wait, he stopped, the train stopped. Oh . . . um . . . *shake*, everybody, he's *shaking!*"

★ ★ ★

Of course, the only thing that bothers me more than dancing at a wedding is my *mother* dancing at a wedding.

And let me tell you something. I know there are many ways to describe your emotions, but I think as a people we need to come up with another one for what you feel when you see your mother do The Electric Slide. We don't have a word for it yet, but it's a combination of shame, panic, revulsion, and, oddly enough, pride.

Could someone please name that? How about "plunkish"? As in, "Honey, your mom's dancing. Now, don't get all *plunkish* on us."

Of course, now that I live 2,500 miles away, I miss Mom. I miss the worrying, the meals, the Vicks VapoRub. I even miss the way she never quite learned how to use the VCR.

Oh, our VCR. She was actually afraid of it. VCRs were like Kryptonite to my mother. Whenever she was yelling at me for something, I'd just pick it up and scare her out of the room.

"Back it up, Ma . . . look what I got!"

I can laugh now, but I can't tell you how frustrating it was when I had to call her up on the phone because I left the house without setting the VCR.

"Listen, Ma, the game's on, and I need you to set the VCR for me. What? . . . No, you don't need your rosary beads! It'll be all right. I'll talk you through it. Look at the button on the left. What's it say? 'Snooze alarm'? OK, go downstairs, Ma."

Don't worry, I still talk to her on the phone a couple times a week. But let me say this about using the telephone to keep in touch with your mother:

America, can we please find a better system?

You know what I'm talking about. Once a mother reaches a certain age, there's something about the phone that makes her forget that time exists at all.

Don't get me wrong. I'm a good son. I don't mind talking with Mom, even though my half of the conversation is a half hour of "uh-huh" and the occasional "you don't say." (For those of you in the South, that's "reckon so" and "y'all are kiddin'.")

But how do you politely end it? That's the problem. Again, I love talking to her, but what the world needs is some kind of nice way to let someone know that it's time to end a phone call.

And I may have figured something out.

Last year I cohosted the People's Choice Awards. I'm not bragging, but let's just say I got to meet Regis Philbin.

Stay with me.

All the award recipients had an allotment of forty-five seconds to make an acceptance speech. Now, I'm sure you've seen what I'm about to describe on an awards show at one time or another.

If a person went over their time, the band would start to play a little something in the background. Nothing loud, usually just some tinkling on the piano to let them know it was time to wrap things up. The speaker would hastily finish his speech and leave the stage.

Bingooooooooo!

There it is! AT&T, wake up and smell your redial!

How great would that be? Right there, next to "mute" and "flash." The "wrap-it-up" button.

You're talking to Mom. It's getting late.

"... sounds like a great buffet ... uh-huh ... you don't say ... yes, Mom, I've had big shrimp."

One push of a button: *Tinkle, tinkle . . .*

"Oh, they're playing you off, Mom."

"Oh, OK. Well, I know I'm going to forget people, but I want to thank everyone involved, especially your dad, who drove me to the wedding in the first place. Love you, bye. Put on a sweater!"

Click.

Phone companies, please get this feature.

I don't want to have to buy a piano.

Agnes Rossi

From *The Quick*

I was drawn to Phyllis that summer. Her grief seemed stark and genuine; I moved toward it. My own life had more or less fallen in on itself. Nothing was working.

The job at Meyer Brothers was ground zero for me. I had graduated from college in May then taught second grade for eight days. It was after four o'clock on a Friday afternoon and the principal had his raincoat on when I went in to tell him I was never coming back. "Think of the children, Miss Russo," he said, a ruined weekend taking shape in his eyes.

I had been thinking of the children, all twenty-three of them, their primary color clothes, the sleep in their eyes. In more generous moments I felt sorry for my class because their teacher was not the smiling, patient lady they deserved. Their teacher chatted with them one minute, ordered them around the next. By the end of the first week, they were wary of me, slow to smile.

Everything about grammar school made me feel murky and sad. The down-sized desks, the forced wholesomeness, the construction-paper autumn leaves on the windows. If I stayed, I thought, I'd become one of those truly bizarre teachers who tear around the school, nursing private, paranoid agendas, railing at their classes behind closed doors. "I'm so sorry," I said, pushing my resignation letter across the principal's desk.

After a few weeks of feigned job-hunting in Boston—read the classifieds, walked the streets, never once applied anywhere—I ran out of money and decided there was nothing for me to do but go back to East Paterson. More than a lack of money sent me home. In May a boy I'd been in love with and wanted to marry told me to forget it, just forget the whole thing. I'd given him the summer to come around. In August he moved, a disconnected phone, a new name on the mailbox.

I went home because I'd botched everything up. I'd been away long enough to dream up a romantic notion of home as a safe place where I'd be able to get my bearings. At least that's what I told myself at the time. Now I wonder. I had to know my failure as a teacher would hit my father hard. Maybe I wanted to feel the force of his disappointment firsthand.

My roommate in Boston, a nurse, got a big charge out of the idea that we were two career women in the city, high-spirited, ripe for adventure. Then I started walking around the apartment all day in my robe, licking peanut butter off my index finger. I didn't want to tell her I was leaving because I knew she'd be relieved. While she was at work I packed my clothes, left a note on the kitchen table promising to send money for my share of September's bills—I never did and this has always pleased me. I drove to New Jersey as if I were on a leisurely car trip, stopping often for hamburgers and chewing gum.

When I got home, my mother, father, and seventeen-year-old brother were eating supper. I took my place at the table, looked into my lap, told them I'd quit my job. Everybody was quiet for a moment and then my father started to yell. Was I crazy? What the hell had he sent me to college for? Did I think a teaching job was a joke, something to try for a week, and then throw away?

My mother glared at me and shook her head. It didn't matter to her that I'd quit my job. Things that didn't directly involve her didn't engage her one bit. But she took her cues from my father and since he was furious she acted furious too.

Only Chris was glad to see me. He leaned against the counter and smiled every time he caught my eye.

I cried and knew I was crying because my boyfriend didn't love me, because I'd been so inept as a teacher, because I was back home. There is nothing like the sound of a parent shouting at you. The worst of the voices in your head bombards you from the outside.

My father looked out the window and spotted my car, the brand-new Ford Fairlane the down payment on which had been his graduation present to me. He'd pulled up in front of the house flashing the lights and blowing the horn. Then, embarrassed by his own enthusiasm, he was all business when he stepped out. He made me sit behind the wheel while he explained the terms of the loan.

"Just how do you plan to keep up the payments on that?" he asked.

I admitted September's payment was already overdue.

"The car goes back to the dealer tomorrow. You want to act like a twelve-year-old, you get treated like one. Twelve-year-olds don't drive brand-new cars. They walk anyplace they want to go and you can god-damn walk."

I ran up to my room, my old room, but didn't have the nerve to slam the door. I sat on the bed and listened to him lecture my mother about what form their response would take. I could hear his tone but not his words. It was managerial: we'll do this but not that. Every so often I'd hear my mother's voice and knew she was saying yes, Lou, right, of course, of course not.

Later that night he pounded on my door but told me not to open it. "Stay where you are. Do not open this door. Are you listening to me?"

"Yes," I said, feeling stupid, my hand on the doorknob.

"If you think you're going to sit on your ass, goddamn lady of leisure, you're wrong. Until you find a full-time job, you are to do all your mother's housework. Vacuuming, washing floors, everything. See how you like working as a maid." He gave my door another punch, the period at the end of his sentence, then pounded off to his room.

I barely slept; the night became surreal. I felt large, seemed to take up every inch of available space in my twin bed. I thought of Bill C., one of my erstwhile second graders. He'd been left back, a tall eight-year-old among seven-year-olds. When it was Bill's turn to drink at the midget water fountain, he'd lean way over as if he were bowing. I thought about Marty, the boy who'd rejected me and started me on this downward spiral. I was starving but afraid I'd run into my father if I ventured out of my room for something to eat.

I considered my punishment gingerly. It was too humiliating to face head-on, which was, of course, the whole point. To my father, my actions had been self-indulgent, theatrical. His response was designed to cut me down, make me understand that life was not about addressing every unhappiness that presented itself. Life was about work and shouldering responsibility no matter how shitty you felt inside. The punishment was engineered to deflate whatever sense I had of myself as earnestly negotiating with the world. His reading me so accurately infuriated me. I'd get my revenge, I decided, by being a good maid, making him think I planned to be his domestic for the rest of my life.

Our house was small, so I couldn't actually clean all day. Most of the time I walked around town aimlessly or lay on my bed but I made it my business to be doing some intrusive chore, washing windows or ironing in the parlor, by the time my father got home in the afternoon. He tried to ignore me but a couple of times I caught him staring at me mournfully from the end of the hallway or foot of the stairs.

One day I slept past noon and woke up to an empty house. My mother was out and I was alone. I savored the quiet, walked around drinking cold orange juice and waking up slowly.

When my father came in, I was still in my robe, just sitting down to a roast beef sandwich and a big glass of milk. To make matters worse, I'd found goblets of chocolate pudding, my father's favorite, in the refrigerator and had one out so I wouldn't have to get up after I finished my sandwich. My father made himself a Spartan cup of tea, sat opposite me, sipped it noisily. He looked at me and said, "I never thought you'd be the one to disappoint me." I steeled myself against his words, ate my sandwich, put the pudding back untouched.

The next morning I read the classifieds in earnest, called the employment office at Meyer Brothers, was told I could come in that afternoon. My mother softened when she saw me in a dress and stockings. "Marie," she said, "you're wearing lipstick!" I ignored her, went around her.

At Meyer Brothers I was given a tour and introduced to Saul and Phyllis. I liked both of them immediately, his manic energy and rapidly blinking eyes, her steadiness. She looked at him with a combination of disparagement and affection. "Don't pay any attention to him," she said when Saul had gone upstairs. "It's not a bad place, really. We do our work, nobody bothers us."

Mary Jo Salter

Video Blues

My husband has a crush on Myrna Loy,
and likes to rent her movies, for a treat.
It makes some evenings harder to enjoy.

The list of actresses who might employ
him as their slave is too long to repeat.
(My husband has a crush on Myrna Loy,

Carole Lombard, Paulette Goddard, coy
Jean Arthur with that voice as dry as wheat . . .)
It makes some evenings harder to enjoy.

Does he confess all this just to annoy
a loyal spouse? I know I can't compete.
My husband has a crush on Myrna Loy.

And can't a woman have her dreamboats? Boy,
I wouldn't say my life is incomplete,
but some evening I could certainly enjoy

two hours with Cary Grant as *my* own toy.
I guess, though, we were destined not to meet.
My husband has a crush on Myrna Loy,
which makes some evenings harder to enjoy.

Mary Saracino

From *Ravioli and Rage*

When my mother fell in love with the Irish-German priest, I immediately recognized in the lilt of her voice, the curve of her lips, the sparkle in her eyes, that something essential had shifted. When she looked at him, her face beamed as it had done only on ravioli days. Gone was the dejected mother and I rejoiced, longing to slay the evil twin that haunted our lives. Instead, I hung back, afraid to intervene, afraid that any movement toward her grinning mouth would break the spell causing the jubilant princess to succumb to the misery of heartbreak. I hovered at the edges of her joy, just as I had habitually hung back in my aunt's kitchen, not making a peep, admonished by the ravioli-making Ada and Ida to stay out of the way.

My mother had fallen for the taboo. She was bound by the laws of Holy Mother Church. To leave my father was to risk excommunication. And, for a time at least, the threat of such an ominous sentence surely made her stay put. Trapped, she clung to us children as if we were the cure for her misery. Somehow she mustered enough energy to go through the motions of mothering. She fed us, clothed us, wiped away our tears when we ran to her with real or imagined injuries, but beneath each kiss, each hug, lurked a murkier motivation. Our very existence provided her with evidence that her living had value; bearing children and raising them to adulthood could count as much as the life she had miscarried. We children could give her a reason to get up each morning and stare down the dull eyes, the astonished face she encountered in her bathroom mirror. If we repaid her affections with the same fierce intensity, we could satisfy her unquenchable ache. In loving her back, loving her even more than we loved ourselves, we could give her what she most needed. In our devoted smiles she could conjure a vision of the woman she so desperately wanted to be, the woman she was not capable of creating on her own.

I became the adoring daughter who reflected only good, only love, only acceptance. I loved the things my mother loved, hated the things she hated, needed only the things she needed. I had no words for this unholy burden; still I felt the full weight of my mother's disconsolate life on my bony shoulders. It surfaced in undue worry and fear, in stomachaches, bed-wetting, and extreme shyness. I often woke in the middle of the night to phantom footfalls on the stairs outside my bedroom. There were no goblins in the hallway, just the ever-present anguish of sorrow and the panic that I would never be released from the terror of my life inside the walls of my mother's house. What was coming to claim me? No ghoul, real or imagined, could be as fierce as the rage I was learning to swallow, the grief I was learning to squelch.

I hoped always to transform my mother into a blissful Holy Mother of Ravioli, a goddess free of worries and woes. In my deepest heart I believed that the Good Daughter would prevail. My tenacious heart would eventually triumph, as it did on ravioli days. Though banished to the sidelines in my aunt's kitchen, I knew that if I did what was expected of me I would ultimately be rewarded. Through the long afternoon I would stand patiently beside my mother, sensing that before long the joy she exuded on those afternoons with her sisters would be enough to burn through her haze of self-absorption. In due time, she would notice me standing at the edge of the table, waiting, hoping, praying, *please, please, please hand me the fork.* Oh, how I wanted her to invite me to pinch shut the ravioli edges and dance that dance with her and her sisters. When at last the sheets of pasta were stuffed and folded, my aunts would reach for their utensils and get to work. My mother would pause a moment, smile to herself, wink at me, then place her fork in the palm of my outstretched hand. I would balance it between my small fingers, press its tines gently into the dough and enter, finally enter, their holy trinity.

Holiday ravioli-making allowed my mother and me to touch something beyond the hardness of days and the disappointments of living, if only for a brief afternoon. In that rarefied communal effort we found a way to begin to love and understand one another. This sojourn was not to last. As my mother fell deeper and deeper into her extramarital affair, others learned of it. My aunts turned from her. My mother had brought dishonor upon her blood. She would pay with silence and with exile. As rumors spread throughout our small town, Ida and Ada entombed their hearts behind thick walls of judgment and shame. The sisters' joint pasta-making ventures ended.

In the world outside my home there was little respite. People knew. People talked. My mother's private secret was now our public disgrace. I was reluctant to participate in school, unwilling to venture beyond my small circle of childhood friends or engage in conversation with adults. I could not scale the wall of my mother's considerable angst without a guide and none was forthcoming. No aunt or uncle, no teacher or neighbor, swooped in to salvage me as I spiraled into an abyss of shame. Self-loathing became my second skin.

I longed for an end to my inconsolable gloom, but I could barely let myself hope that somehow, some way, some day, my heavy heart would lighten. How could I desert my mother, dare to escape the heat of her dishonor without bringing her with me? Was I not, in some small way, responsible for her infamy? Hadn't I known all along about her illicit affair? Hadn't I kept her secret? Didn't that make my ten-year-old's soul culpable? I could not begin to imagine that I was blameless, a child powerless to affect her mother's choices. I could not envision a life distinct and apart from hers, one in which the daughter is absolved of her mother's transgressions. She had not raised me to occupy my own possibilities, foster my own talents, embrace my own desires. I did not know that a world separate and apart awaited me. It would be decades before I would realize that I possessed the wherewithal to forge a worthy and worthwhile life for myself. The world had been cruel to my mother, first denying her meaning and fulfillment, then shunning her. Why would it treat me otherwise?

As the rumors spread, I worried about my mother. A lot. With the grave necessity of a desperate child, I tried to smooth the tense lips of her angry mouth, quiet the impatience that flared in her sad eyes, calm the ferocious beating of her stifled rage. I told her jokes, held her hand when she cried, listened when she talked of missing her priest boyfriend. All my attempts to ease her pain failed miserably.

Amid the despairing days were delicate moments. Sometimes my mother would sing to me as I helped with the after-supper dishes. *I love you, a bushel and a peck. Beautiful, beautiful brown eyes / I'll never love blue eyes again. But it was Mary, Mary, plain as any name can be.* I would catch a glimmer of how high her unencumbered heart could fly. It would make me fight harder to resuscitate her lost soul. Those times of reprieve freed me to momentarily imagine her dancing all the way to a starring role on Broadway with me tagging along as her adoring understudy. Her light-heartedness never lasted and, so, neither did mine. My parents would fight about my mother's refusal to stop seeing her boyfriend. Her friends and sisters would refuse to return her calls or come over for coffee. The tired, bitter lines would resurface in my mother's face. She would sit in the kitchen, alone at night, puffing too many cigarettes, clogging the room with worries.

These were lonely, hard times for my mother. And for me. I rarely saw my aunts, except for the occasional Sunday afternoon when my father would take us children to visit them. My mother was no longer welcome in the homes of her sisters and brothers and even though we children were, it was never the same again. When my aunts and uncles spoke of her, their hushed tones revealed contempt, their tight jaws and even tighter frowns screamed condemnation. As my parents' marriage unraveled, each of my mother's siblings sided with my father. He was wronged, they had insisted. They disowned her. Dishonor was thicker than blood.

Familial rejection did not stop my mother. When her boyfriend was transferred to a parish sixty miles from our hometown, she kept seeing him. She diverted attention from their weekly rendezvous by hauling my two younger sisters and me with her. Every Friday we would meet her lover at a coffee shop thirty miles from our home. There, as we ate hamburgers and French fries, they would talk about running off together, just the five of us. By then my mother had given birth to her seventh, and last, child who, unbeknownst to me, was the priest's biological daughter. He wanted to raise my youngest sister, be a real father to her, live with her and my mother. My other sister and I were part of the package deal. My mother refused to leave us behind.

As my mother and her boyfriend plotted and planned over coffee and dessert, I listened and prayed. I also worried. They told us not to tell anyone about this new life they were planning. I was too young to understand the lasting consequences. In the beginning, I imagined that my four brothers and my father were somehow included in this fantasy. I was nine at the time. What did I know of love? By the time I was eleven, I came to understand that my father was not invited.

My mother and her boyfriend were persuasive. They enticed my sisters and me, telling us that we could eat ice cream for supper every night in our new home if we wanted. We could zoom down tree-lined boulevards on shiny new bicycles and sleep in canopied beds. Life would be grand in this new town. Maybe in some unfamiliar place we could start over again. Beneath a bluer sky my mother's life could be salvaged and I could be freed from the burden of her.

During those Friday-night coffee shop visits I was lured by the undiluted happiness I witnessed in my mother, an uncomplicated emotion that I imagined was the natural outcome of their coffee-coated dreams, the hope behind the hype. Something loosened in my bones then, something hard and gnarled unraveled into a shimmering wish. *Maybe I could be happy, too.*

In the years before leaving, when leaving was always on my mother's mind, she and I made ravioli without my aunts. I had grown to cherish my status as her confidante. As we measured the semolina and flour, added the eggs and water, mixed the dough to the right consistency, I reaffirmed my vow to keep her secrets. "We're a family," she assured me. "We'll be happy together." I prayed she was right.

Ours was a treacherous alliance. My mother rolled the dough, cut it into long strips of pasta, then scooped the meat filling in place. I followed behind, assuming the role my aunts had once fulfilled, folding the top of the sheet until it kissed the bottom, taking care to gently pat between the mounds. My mother took a paring knife and liberated the ravioli from its obligation of connection. I pinched the edges tightly with a fork, then placed the pasta rounds on the floured board to dry. An unnamed sadness washed over me, for by then I knew beyond a doubt that we would soon be leaving my father and my brothers. Our ritual of ravioli-making would not be enough to shield us from our dangerous future.

Maybe the burst of crimson in the maple tree outside our kitchen window quickened my mother's resolve to leave my father, maybe a chill in the autumn air shook her out of melancholy into action. All I know for certain is that one September afternoon in 1967, when I was home from school for lunch, she packed my younger sisters and me into the car and drove away. We were to meet her boyfriend in a parking lot outside of town, transfer our few belongings into his car and drive away with him. Before we left, my mother scribbled a note for my older brothers and left it on our kitchen table, propped against a salt shaker. *I'm sorry. I'll send for you later. I love you.*

I was almost thirteen. My mother and her boyfriend took us fifteen hundred miles from my hometown. I would not see my father and my brothers again until I was fifteen and then only for a two-week visit during the summer. My mother would not permit a longer stay or more frequent contact. In time, after she was certain that my father would not try to prevent us from returning to her, she acquiesced to yearly summer trips.

In our new home, I felt the absence of my father and my brothers every day but I swallowed the loss and longing. To unmask my grief would only serve to remind my mother of her dreadful error, for by then she had come to realize that leaving my brothers had been a horrid, irreversible mistake. My two oldest brothers were college students by then. The other two were still in high school and they did not join us as my mother had assumed they would. It could not have been easy to choose between Dad and Mom, between the man who ultimately could not prevent the dissolution of their family and the woman who had abandoned them. In the aftermath, my mother's guilt and grief were palpable.

Unarticulated animosity danced between my mother and me as I grew into adulthood. The unspoken bond we had shared as we made ravioli together weakened as I entered my twenties. I began to feel the ache that my mother had carelessly sown inside of me. From the time I was seven years old, my mother had handed the reins of her anguished life to my unsteady hands. I was not sturdy enough to carry her wounds and her worries. I had my own.

In my thirties, I avoided my mother's invitations to breakfast or Sunday suppers. I cringed at her reaction when I said I would not be coming for Thanksgiving. "I'm the only mother you have," she admonished. "You'll be sorry when I am gone." I knew I would rue the lost opportunities to make ravioli, share dinner, invite conversation. But I could not give in to her hunger.

I dove into the muck that had mired me to my mother all those long years. In my forties, I tasted the raw fury full and bitter in my mouth. I learned to shout out my name, tell the truth, and guard the gates to my own soul. Forgiveness is not simple or easy, but in excavating my emotions I was able to uncover the vestiges of a path that led to absolution.

Through the turmoil and the trials of my adult relationship with my mother, I made ravioli. In my own kitchen, miles from my mother's home, in the kitchens of my friends, worlds away from my mother's heart, and an ocean away from my maternal grandmother's Castelnuovo di Garfagnana kitchen, I rolled the dough, sometimes in spite of my mother. I filled the pasta pouches and pinched the edges, searching for a way to love her.

My mother and I may never fully bridge the gulf that separates us, but when language fails us, as it too often does, we can tie our aprons around our waists and signal a temporary truce. We can knead the dough, season the sauce, and recognize ourselves in each other's semolina-dusted faces. One mother, one daughter; related by ravioli and rage.

Jeanne Schinto

From *Huddle Fever:*
Living in the Immigrant City

People who know the insularity of such places must be wondering how I had the nerve to take on the subject of Lawrence. Even if I had decided to live there for the rest of my life, I would always have been an outsider, because I'm not a native—"a lifelong resident of Lawrence," as they say. I don't even pronounce Lawrence correctly ("Lahhhrence," through the nose). And yet everywhere I went in that city, I found myself being recognized for what, in Lawrence's eyes at least, I truly am.

"You Italian?" the clerk behind the counter at the Lawrence Public Library asked me out of the blue one day not long after I had moved there. She is dark-haired, delicate-looking, possibly (probably?) Italian herself.

What did her question mean? It couldn't have had anything to do with the books I had chosen to check out. I hadn't given her my library card yet, so she wasn't going by my name. She had obviously asked her question simply, solely, because of how I look. Was her curiosity supposed to be a compliment?

I told her, Yes, I am Italian, and she smiled, happy to have her hunch confirmed. And I, suddenly, was pleased to have my ethnic heritage acknowledged. In Washington, D.C., where I was a member of a much broader human category—white—and where there was only one large ethnic group—African-Americans—the question would never have been asked of me. In Greenwich, it wouldn't have been asked, either, because the answer wouldn't have been considered important information.

"What part of It-lee did your grandparents come from?" my next-door neighbor John asked me the day we met. "A suburb of Naples," I said, using a line of my father's. But John, born in Lawrence in 1906 to parents who had just arrived from the outskirts of Naples themselves, wasn't amused. He really wanted to know.

So I told him what I had heard in conversations when I was a child, about the two peasant villages—Castel Grande and Castel Franco (names I've seen on a very detailed map, using a powerful magnifying glass)—within the borders of a mountainous place called Benevento. Many families from that region, those villages, had settled in Greenwich together and had remained provincially rivalrous, in work, in play, for decades.

In the late fifties, driving in backcountry Greenwich with my mother, I remember seeing old Italian ladies who wouldn't have looked at all strange in Benevento looking strange indeed in my posh town. They were in a field, bent over, rumps high in the air as they moved along, pulling something from the earth and putting it into brown paper grocery bags. "Awk, that's so Italian," said Mom, clicking her tongue. They were gathering dandelions for salad, she explained. We never ate them at our table—I still haven't tasted them—and yet, pulling the jagged leaves out of my garden, I recall that day in Greenwich and think, I should be eating these for dinner instead.

It was John who pointed out to me another edible weed—a type of *broccoli di rape*—that grew on feathery stalks outside our back doors in Lawrence, sending seeds to lodge everywhere, cracks in the sidewalk included. I could tell he was miffed at my ignorance: what kind of Italian was I never to have heard of it before? (Afterward, I started to notice that the greens are sold in bunches at Italian grocery stores in Lawrence and elsewhere, and that there are recipes for it in Italian cookbooks I've owned for years.)

"Greenwich, Connecticut!" she sneered: No sociopath
could emerge from there. "Were you a debutante too?"

—SUSANNA KAYSEN,
GIRL, INTERRUPTED

When I tell people where I was born, I often add the phrase, "But I was
poor." Of course, I exaggerate for effect. Growing up in Greenwich, I
sometimes did feel "underprivileged," especially since our backyard
ended at the border of an exclusive area called Millbrook—a private association of faux Tudor houses, graced with its own country club (to
which we certainly did not belong) and guarded by its own police force.
But our house, on the other side of the fence (literally), wasn't "huddled" by any means. I never overheard our neighbors' conversations
there. All we ever heard was "Fore!" from the Millbrook golf course.

My parents often debate whether to sell that house my father built
and live in Florida year-round. They're most inclined when they get
their local tax bill, which tripled in 1994; but they say they couldn't
bear to cut ties with their well-heeled hometown forever, and who can
blame them? Besides, where would they go during the summer months,
when Florida's weather is unpleasant? "We don't want to be gypsies," my
father says. "Visit Janet, visit me," I suggest, now with more confidence
that they would pay me an extended visit since I no longer live in
Lawrence, where, in the summertime when the windows were open,
the noise of barking dogs and car alarms and sirens kept them awake.

Whenever they complained, however, I gently scolded them, saying they should consider themselves lucky that their parents didn't hear
Billy Wood's call to Lawrence; or heard it, and didn't heed it. They
should be thankful, I tell them, that they ended up where they did.

I don't mean to imply that, by living in Greenwich, my family escaped hard work—or even hard luck. Nor did they escape hard feelings. I
remember how, as a child, riding in the car on backcountry roads of
Greenwich on a Sunday afternoon, I used to gape at the mansions we
passed, and dream. Occasionally, we—my family and I—used to have a
look inside them, if an estate sale was going on: a family's possessions
tagged to be sold right there on the premises, out of the dozens of rooms.
Chintz-covered couches and chaise lounges, a polished dining table as big
as a swimming pool, a grand piano draped in a Spanish scarf, cases of dusty
books, highboys and lowboys and china in stacks—a rich family's life was
laid out for everybody to see, even people as lowly as I thought us to be.

On one of those outings, my father told me to remember that nobody ever came completely honorably by the shovelfuls of money it took to run such households. I guess that was my father's equivalent of the advice Nick Carraway says he got from *his* father in *The Great Gatsby.* And just like Nick, when I got out into the real world, I discovered for my skeptical self how much of what my father had said was useful and true.

My mother admits she once asked a friend to snap her picture in the pillared doorway of a grand Greenwich manor, pretending it was her family's home and not the house of strangers, who surely would have shooed her off their property if they had discovered her. But that was in Mom's adolescence, a dreamy time by definition. Soon enough, she grew up and married Dad, and they, like legions of other children of immigrants, were content to aspire to the much more modest goal of middle-class life, and in relatively short order, they achieved it.

It's also true that, like many people who have risen in the world, my mother reinvented her family's history. She never went so far as to deny her roots completely, as Billy Wood did, but I remember her telling me more than once that she was descended from kings and queens who'd lost all their money, jewels included, in a skirmish—or something—back in Italy. Yes, she was descended from them and so, therefore, was I. I know she meant it as a soothing fairy tale, but at least for a while I believed it. Even now I can picture the palace that figured in that fantasy. It looks a lot like those backcountry Greenwich estates I used to glimpse through the parted curtains of trees.

As we've seen, however, Billy Wood did more than reinvent his past as a soothing salve for his psyche, and that is why I have cast him (not the Essex Company) as the chief villain in my story of Lawrence's rise and fall: for isn't there an extra hot place in hell for those who would disavow their own kind even as they ruthlessly exploit them? Just because the man embodies that other American dream, the rags-to-riches one in the Horatio Alger tales (as my parents embody the middle-class one), doesn't make what he did to Lawrence—and to Lawrencians—any less ignoble. Nor does it make the sorry state of the city today any easier to bear.

And I do lay a lot of the blame for Lawrence's predicament upon Wood, for his legacy of mammoth mill complexes, more gigantic than any built anywhere before—not to mention the tenements built simultaneously to house his workers—has generated many of the most intractable problems the city currently faces.

More to the point, Wood's architectural bequest killed any hope that Lawrence would continue to be the kind of place where the poor could rationally pursue the middle-class dream *within the city limits.*

After Wood was done with Lawrence, the life we still believe it is the right of all Americans to pursue, no matter where they live, would have to be pursued, for the most part, elsewhere.

Chris Mellie Sherman

How to Marry an
Italian-American Man

If you are a woman planning to marry an Italian-American man, and you yourself are not Italian-American, there are a few things you should know:

1. There will be yelling. Italians yell. It doesn't mean anything. It is just their way of communicating. They are an emotional lot, and they hold nothing back. This is a positive attribute to bring to a marriage. Your Italian-American husband will always let you know how he feels. He'll yell when he is happy, he'll yell when he's mad. You will never be left in the dark to wonder if your relationship is working. When he stops yelling, it's time for you to start worrying.

Tip: Yell back. You want him to feel at home in his own house. Your mother-in-law will be the first to tell you, he's expecting it and he'll respect you more for it.

2. You will live in the same house or neighborhood as your spouse's entire extended family. Your new family will get to know you very quickly. They'll know when you are coming and they'll know when you are going. They'll know when you have a fight and they'll know when you make up. They will know, from the aromas wafting down the hall, what you are having for breakfast, lunch, and dinner. They'll know when you are sleeping, they'll know when you're awake, they'll know if you've been bad or good so . . . well, you get the idea. Also, expect your in-laws' children to be coming around. Once you are married, these children will not be able to tell the difference between you and your husband and their own mother and father. The will think you are all the same people. They will walk right in your house, open your refrigerator, make themselves a provolone sandwich, and go sit down and watch TV. Just ignore them. Go about your business. They don't expect anything from you in the way of communication. Just keep the refrigerator stocked and everyone will get along just fine.

Tip: Keep your door unlocked. If you are planning to lock your door, it would be a sign of respect to call each family member individually to tell them so. It would be seen as a lack of respect if they were standing behind a locked door knocking like strangers when they know darn well you are home.

3. You must always have cake in the house. Because of rule #2, you must always have cake or some kind pastry around the house. When your in-laws inevitably "drop in," they will be expecting coffee. With cake. And you will be seen in a very bad light if you cannot produce some kind of cake to go with it. You will be seen as inhospitable and non-nurturing, two unacceptable traits in a wife. They can (and will) sit at your kitchen table for hours talking and yelling. An empty pot of coffee is no deterrent. They will simply expect you to make another. Even after you've excused yourself and come back into the kitchen in your pajamas, they will not get up. They will only leave when they are ready to leave and not a moment sooner. Usually, they're gone by the time you get up in the morning.

4. You're only as good as your last pot of sauce. In an Italian family, the worth of a person is not dependent upon money or good deeds. The worth of a person is judged solely upon the deliciousness of their spaghetti sauce. In fact, go to any Italian wake of any Italian woman and you'll hear, "What a woman. Made sauce very Sunday for seventy-five years. The best in the neighborhood. She even made the sauce for Little Petey's wedding. Drove the caterer nuts." Now don't panic. Your mother-in-law already knows you can't make sauce yet, and she is ready and eager to teach you to make it for her sonny-boy. BUT SHE WANTS YOU TO ASK HER. She does not want to approach you on this matter. That would be interfering. Here is what you say, "Mom, Sonny tells me he loves your sauce so much he can't live without it. (This inflates her ego and makes her like you, even though you're not Italian.) I just can't seem to get it right. (Here you have admitted you are not Italian. You realize the shortcomings in your cooking that she has suspected all along. You show humility. Her heart will go out to you.) Do you think you could teach me?" (This last statement empowers her. She will feel heady and full of pride. She will be over in five minutes.) A word of caution: She will not give you the entire recipe. She will withhold an ingredient or two. Your sauce will never taste exactly the same as hers. Try not to hate her for this. She does this out of insecurity. She is afraid her sonny-boy will start to prefer your sauce over hers and she will lose her special place in his heart. What you need now is patience. If you really want the exact recipe, try to catch her on her deathbed.

Tip: After visiting one of your husband's aunts or uncles, be sure to give your mother-in-law a call and tell her how you like her sauce much better.

5. Once an Italian man is seated at the table, he will not get up. Italian men are accustomed to being served by their mothers and their sisters and will expect the same from their wives. Now, you can go two ways with this. You can either try to break him of this need to be served, assert your liberated, non-Italian-American self, or you can succumb to this cultural phenomenon and learn to serve in silence. If you choose the former, you must be willing to be patient. (There's that word again.) You must walk your Italian husband around the kitchen and show him where everything is. Take him to the cabinet where you keep the salt and pepper. Point out to him that there are things in the refrigerator behind what he just sees up front. Not seeing the grated cheese is not the same thing as not actually having any grated cheese. Show him where he can easily get a napkin for himself and where he can get a cold glass of water. You may even have to label a few cabinets in the beginning, but after a while he'll get the hang of it. Remember, Italians are among the most intelligent people in the world. Da Vinci, Galileo, Sinatra, were all quick learners, and chances are your Italian-American man is too. Now, if you choose the latter, to serve in silence, then it would be best for you to observe a functioning Italian family to see how it's done. You will no doubt see something like the man sitting down at the table, the wife rushing over with the plate of food, him asking for things such as "Where's the salt?" or "Got anything to drink?" The woman will be totally unfazed by any of this and once he's just about finished his meal, she will sit down and eat her dinner.

Tip: When having your extended family over for a meal, always serve the men first, or it will be looked upon as a disgrace.

Felix Stefanile

The Veteran

Four hundred poems ago
my time off was a conspiracy
to undermine the Muse's citadel;
I worked bombs at my desk.

Now, thoughts of winding down by noon-time,
my beer like a bubble bath . . .

thoughts of the sunny garden,
that new book on ancient Greece,
and our tilted sundial casting its shadow
towards the grackles, who don't care.

Unbudgeable, and full of light,
the hollow hackberry stump by the fence
grins like a mouth;
there are vines at the base trailing upward.
For a moment I recall
the trappings of Dionysus,
the god in the tree.

Nobody has to tell me
poems are of the earth,
craft trains the vine.

For that reason I keep worry away
in a doze, in a dream
of Apollonian summer,
my torch doused in the sun.

In a city as out of date
as Edna St. Vincent Millay
a young poet once burned his candle at both ends,
and starved himself for a book.

Look at him now, smiling,
paunch-happy
like that old Tabby, no leopard cub,
sniffing at the tree stump
before him.
The poet's wife, no maenad,
brings him another beer.
Fame be damned.

Gay Talese

From *Unto the Sons*

As usual, my first plate was spaghetti with clam sauce—and my usual way of consuming this was with a fork and a round tablespoon which I held like a catcher's mitt to scoop up the fallen bits of clam and to stabilize my fork as I attempted to twirl the spaghetti strands into a tight and tidy mouthful.

My father, I'd noticed, never ate spaghetti in this fashion. He used only the fork, with which he masterfully twirled the strands without letting any of them dangle as he lifted them to his mouth. But on this occasion, after my plate had arrived and I had begun in my customary style with the spoon, he sat watching with an almost pained look on his face. Then he said, patiently:

"You know, I think you're old enough now to learn how to do it right."

"To do what right?"

"To eat spaghetti right," he said. "Without the spoon. Only people without manners eat spaghetti that way—or people who are ignorant; or those Italians who are *cafoni* [country bumpkins]. But in Italy the *refined* Italians would never be seen in public using the spoon."

Putting aside the spoon, I tried three or four times to spin the spaghetti around the fork, but each time the strands either slipped off and splashed into the sauce, or skipped off the plate and fell onto the floor.

"Forget it," my father said finally. "Forget it for today—but from now on, practice. One day you'll learn to get it right."

Soon the second course arrived, then dessert and the black coffee in the small cup that my father drank. My parents talked business, and my sister and I shifted restlessly.

My wandering attention was drawn to a large table near the bar, around which a festive crowd of middle-aged men and women were laughing and applauding, raising their wineglasses toward a young soldier who was with them. The soldier sat very tall in his khaki uniform. His hair was shiny black and precisely parted. His shoulders were huge, his long face lean and hard, and his brown eyes were alert. He seemed to be fully aware of how special he was.

The people around him could hardly stop watching him, or touching him, or patting him gently on the back as he bent forward to eat. Only *he* was eating. The others ignored their plates to concentrate on watching him, applauding and toasting his every move with his knife and fork.

As the waiter arrived with our check, I held his sleeve before he left, and asked: "Who's that soldier over there?"

The waiter's eyebrows rose with a slight flutter, and he leaned into my ear and replied: *"That's Joe DiMaggio!"*

Bolting to my feet, I stared at the tall soldier who continued to eat, and I imagined in the distance the solid sound of the bat, the roar of the crowd, the spirited rhythm of Les Brown's band.

I tapped my father's shoulder and said: *"That's Joe DiMaggio!"*

My father looked up from the check he had been scrutinizing for any sign of error and glanced casually at the big table. Then he turned back to me and replied: "So?"

Ignoring my father, I remained standing, in prolonged appreciation. And before we left the restaurant I took a final look, closer this time, and noticed that on the table in front of my hero was a steaming plate of spaghetti. Then his head leaned forward, his mouth opened, and everybody around him smiled—including me—as he twirled his fork unabashedly against a large silver spoon.

———

I climbed the steps to my father's balcony office and seated myself behind a potted palm that provided camouflage. Now I could eavesdrop on the scene below and see spread out on the counter between my father and the lady a red silk cocktail dress. All at once I recognized this dress from having seen it during the previous week, when this same woman had brought it in to have it cleaned, and had made a point of requesting quick service because she wished to wear it to a party on Monday night, which was this evening. I remember that the counter clerk had taken the dress back to my father in the workroom, to ask if it could be properly cleaned in the allotted time. When he examined the dress my father noticed a small spot on the bodice, which was perhaps a stain that would require special, time-consuming treatment. For this reason he was reluctant to accept the dress, and I remember that he himself had walked out to the main room of the store to explain the problem to the woman.

"I'm sorry," I had heard my father say, "but I doubt we can get this back to you by Monday. This spot might be a liquor stain that can't be removed by dry-cleaning, and if we try washing it there's a good chance the dress will shrink. . . ."

"But can't you at least try?" she had pleaded; to which my father had said, "We can try, but we cannot guarantee it. I definitely wouldn't wash this dress, and yet if we dry-clean it—without taking the extra time to analyze that spot and have it specially treated—you'll only get the dress back on Monday looking no better than it does now."

"Oh, just do the best you can," the woman had said, shrugging her shoulders. And as she left the dress and walked toward the door, she said: "I'll see you on Monday."

Now she was back, and it seemed obvious that the cleaning of the red silk dress had brought happiness neither to the woman nor to my father. As they stood practically nose to nose across the counter, with the dress spread out on white tissue paper between them, I heard my father saying over and over, "I told you, I told you, but you wouldn't listen. . . ."

"I *was* listening," she replied, "but I didn't expect you people to make the dress worse."

"How did we make it worse?"

"You made the spot bigger!"

"Look, madam," my father said, sharply, "I've been in business in this town for more than twenty years, and I didn't stay in business that long by making spots bigger!"

"You not only made it bigger," she insisted, "but there is a spot in the back that wasn't there when I left it."

"*Now* you're saying that we not only make spots bigger, but we add spots also, is that right?" His face was taut with tension, anger.

"What I *am* saying," she replied firmly, "is what I said at the beginning. You have *ruined* my dress!"

"*You ruined your own dress!*" My father was now shouting. "You spilled liquor on it, and—"

"I want a *new* dress," she interrupted. "You've ruined my dress, and I want it replaced. . . ."

Suddenly my father slammed his fist against the counter and shouted: "I want you out of my store!"

"Not until we settle this," she replied; but then my mother, who had been watching all this time silently, undoubtedly embarrassed in front of her customers, walked over and said, "*Please,* can't we discuss this quietly. Perhaps tomorrow . . ."

"I have a party to go to tonight, and I want to settle this now!"

"*Out!*" my father said, pointing to the door. "I want you out of here, or I'm calling the cops."

"Well, you can call the cops," she said, glaring at him. "I'm getting my husband, and I'll be right back!"

Watching from behind the palms, my hands perspiring, I saw the woman stride out of the store, leaving the door open. My mother placed a hand on my father's arm, whispering something into his ear, but he began to shake his head. Across the room I could see the salesladies and their customers standing along the dress counters, speaking quietly among themselves. Everyone was waiting; and within a few moments, the husband appeared—a large man in a brown hat and a tan camel's-hair coat, smoking a cigar.

Heading straight for my father, he bellowed: "So you're the man who just insulted my wife!"

"I did *not* insult your wife," my father replied, in a steady voice. "I told her to get out of my store. And now I'm telling *you* to get out of my store!"

"Who do you think *you* are?" the man asked, getting closer to my father, who, standing behind the counter, now quickly took off his steel-rimmed glasses and handed them to my startled mother. Then the man paused and said something in a softer tone, so soft that I am not sure I heard it precisely; but my father surely heard it, because he suddenly left my mother's side, went back into the workroom while everybody in the store stood frozen in position as my mother called out, "Joe . . . Joe . . ."

Perhaps what the man had said—I *may* have heard it—was "dago." There was no other explanation for the fury that now possessed my father as he reappeared, a transformed figure carrying a long, heavy pair of scissors that were customarily used for cutting thick material or fur skin.

"Out!" he said, in a voice now coldly calm. *"Out!"* he repeated, as the man in the camel's-hair coat retreated, walking backward, not taking his eyes off my father, who repeated the word "Out!" as he walked, until the man had pushed the door open and stumbled into the wintry air. But before he left, he took one final look at my father and said: "You haven't seen the last of me yet! You'll soon be hearing from me again—with my *lawyer.* And we'll sue you for every dime you have. . . ."

My father showed no reaction, except the scissors in his right hand began to shake. My mother gently took the scissors and handed it to the white-haired seventy-seven-year-old tailor, who during the commotion had followed my father out of the workroom. Behind this tailor stood Jet and another presser from the workroom, shaking their heads. I left my hiding place behind the palm and walked down the steps to join the others. The salesladies and the two customers still left in the store slowly turned and began to look over some of the new dresses hung along the racks.

With my mother speaking to him softly, my father seemed to have regained his composure. But then, as he turned toward the dry-cleaning counter, the fury flared once more within him. There, on the counter, was the red dress. The couple had forgotten it, perhaps intentionally. Without saying a word, my father grabbed the silk dress, crumpled it into a ball, and quickly headed out the door.

"Follow him," my mother urged me; and I did, trailing a few paces behind as my father looked along the sidewalk for the couple, who were nowhere to be seen on the avenue crowded with Christmas shoppers. But then, near the corner, my father saw the man in the camel's-hair coat, climbing into a car. He ran in that direction, and I followed; but before my father could reach the car, it had pulled away from the curb. I could see that the man behind the wheel turned his head and spotted my father—and, perhaps thinking that he still carried the scissors, had accelerated into the lane, with my father in swift pursuit.

When my father realized that he could not catch up and perhaps wrap the dress around the car's aerial, as I suspect was his intention, I saw him tighten his grip around the balled-up dress, cock his arm, and aim the dress toward the taillights of the moving car. And in that awkward pitching motion, he rocked back and heaved the garment with all his might; and I watched as it sailed through the air, suddenly catching a gust of ocean breeze that swept across the avenue—a breeze that took the dress higher into space and blew it in the direction of an oncoming trolley.

Then, like a magnet, the sparkling overhead wires and prongs atop the trolley seemed to suck the dress into the spinning wheel on the roof; and as my father and I watched, breathlessly, the dress was transformed into a flapping, torn flag and began its long, windy ride across the bay toward Atlantic City.

———

"An apprentice should know his job," Domenico began, in a stern and solemn voice, "and should never defy the rules that wiser men have made. And yet you have defied those rules. And you have disappointed me very much. You, for whom I had high expectations, have shown signs of recklessness, stupidity, and, worse, insubordination. . . ."

As Domenico paused for a second, Joseph began to tremble. He feared that the next words out of his grandfather's mouth would spell out the punishment he most dreaded—banishment to the farm with Sebastian. Before Domenico could continue, Joseph looked up and interrupted. "Grandfather," he pleaded, "it was a *mistake!* It was the first serious mistake I ever made! I was *not* insubordinate. I just did not see that the trousers were hidden under the cloth I was cutting. It was my first mistake after doing many good things that you've never given me credit for." Speaking louder now, though aware that he had never before been so direct toward his grandfather, Joseph added, despairingly, "I can *never* please you! Nothing I ever do is good enough in your eyes. You are always strict with me, harsh with me." Sobbing now, Joseph said, "You just don't love me. . . ."

His grandfather remained silent. He waited several minutes until Joseph had stopped crying. And when Domenico did speak, it was in a voice that was quite unfamiliar.

"I do love you," he said, in the most sympathetic tone Joseph had ever heard. "But you are not yet old enough to understand this love. You confuse criticism with a lack of love. But the opposite is true. People who criticize you *care* about you. They want to see you improve. People who do *not* care about you hold no high expectations for you. They accept you as you are. They allow you to relax. They make you feel contented.

"People who do *not* love you," he concluded, "make you laugh. People who love you make you cry."

———

Lobianco had long aspired to become a *padrone,* which was a somewhat exalted title given to those opportunistic Italian immigrants who functioned as ethnic middlemen during the first years of the mass movement of Italian workers into America. The *padrone* was enriched both by the American employer, to whom he delivered cheap labor and by the laborers themselves, who surrendered to him a percentage of their salaries. In addition to providing jobs and shelter, the *padrone* in the beginning was the guiding influence, if not the outright enforcer, of all that the newcomer did during almost every hour of every day into the night. Lacking a family or friends in America, and not speaking the language, the average worker was totally dependent on his *padrone.* Since at least half of the workers were illiterate even in their own language, the *padrone* handled all their postal correspondence between Italy and America. Having never before been away from home, these workers were now involved for the first time with composing letters, including love letters, which were not only written but sometimes embellished by *padroni* with florid prose styles. Much of the exaggerated operatic longing expressed in some of these letters was more indicative of the *padrone*'s amorous fantasies, or his devil-may-care roguishness, than of what actually existed within the heart of the worker. In their helpless state of dependence on *padroni* many workers remained nonetheless aware that a single sentence of overstated affection in a letter to a village maiden might be interpreted by her—and also by her family, who were never remiss in learning the content of such letters—as a vow of eternal love, and an irrevocable proposal of marriage. But marriage was far from the minds of most of these pioneer Italian workers, who could as yet ill afford the expense of bringing over a bride. And most of these workers themselves did not intend to stay forever in America. More than fifty percent of this first wave of workers were not settlers but sojourners, birds of passage, young bachelors who intended to toil hard for two or three years, and also sow some wild oats while sweating for American dollars in ditches and tunnels, and then to return to Italy— richer, wiser, and no longer dependent on the *padrone.*

But for those Italian laborers who did settle down in America, or who returned home temporarily and then came back with a bride (the groom in some instances ensnared by the effusions of his ghostwriter), the *padrone* continued to play a significant role; and by the early 1880s, when Lobianco began as a *padrone* under the aegis of Keasbey & Mattison Company, several *padroni* were already prominent and powerful in New York City and Philadelphia, in New Haven, Syracuse, Utica, and in other eastern industrial cities and towns where large numbers of Italians had been assembled. Thus long before there were Mafia "godfathers" coining money in America—this did not commence until the 1920s, when gangsters from Sicily and southern Italy began to thrive in the bootlegging trade inspired by Prohibition—there was a syndicate of *padroni* who were prospering legally, if at times exploitatively, as business agents and personal advisers to their usually less astute, less educated countrymen.

Perhaps the most eminent *padrone* in the United States at this time lived in New York City, which had the largest collection of Italian immigrants in the nation. His name was Luigi Fugazy; he was a diminutive man with a professorial air who dwelled in baronial style in a large house on Bleecker Street in the Little Italy section of Manhattan's Greenwich Village. Born into a well-to-do northern Italian family in Piedmont, where his father was a teacher, Luigi Fugazy served as an officer in the Piedmontese royal army during the Risorgimento and briefly had been assigned to a unit commanded by Garibaldi. After sailing to New York in 1869 with a knowledge of English and a substantial inheritance from his father—whose surname, Fugazzi, Luigi later changed to Fugazy, justifying it as a gesture toward assimilation—he promptly increased his net worth by becoming a travel agent for a steamship company, a labor negotiator for Italian employees, and also the owner of a neighborhood bank and a service company that issued loans, provided translators and letter-writers, and notarized immigrants' mortgages, licenses, wills, and other documents. Luigi Fugazy also founded several Italian fraternal organizations, social clubs, and mutual aid societies.

A second New York *padrone,* while not as prominent as Fugazy, was nonetheless very influential because he used part of his earnings as an Italian neighborhood banker and landlord to found the nation's largest Italian-language newspaper, *Il Progresso Italo-Americano.* His name was Carlo Barsotti; and, like Fugazy, he had been reared in privileged circumstances in northern Italy. Barsotti had been born and reared in Pisa. The activity for which he would become most identified in the United States, which he achieved through his newspaper's editorial campaign, would be the inauguration of the commemoration of Columbus Day, beginning in 1892—the four-hundredth anniversary of the discovery of America. Funds were raised for the erection of a statue to Columbus in New York, and this was also done in several other cities that had large gatherings of Italians and persuasive *padroni* who could influence them.

In New Haven such a man was Paolo Russo, a grocer, banker, and attorney (the first Italian-American graduate of Yale Law School, in 1893); in Syracuse, the leading *padrone* was Thomas Marnell (born Marinelli in Naples), who began as a railroad laborer and became a banker; and in Philadelphia, the most prominent *padrone* was a mortician named Charles C. Baldi, a virtuoso consoler of mourning families who also presided over a coal business, a travel agency, a real estate brokerage, and the Italian-language newspaper *L'Opinione.*

The *padroni* who guided the Italian workers in the less industrial sections of the country—in the rural South, the Central Plains, and along the Rockies toward the Pacific—were less wealthy than their eastern counterparts partly because most of the immigrants, being predominantly southern Italian escapees from the farmlands of their fathers, resisted settling in the isolated hinterlands of America. They had seen enough of isolation in their own country, and they not only lacked the money to invest in farm equipment and land, but also were unprepared, linguistically and temperamentally, to venture out into the wide open spaces that had already been homesteaded largely by Irish, Germans, and Swedes, and, of course, by native-born American frontiersmen and gunslingers who had little fondness for foreigners in general. The Italians preferred the protective insularity of ghettos, where their dialect could be understood, where they could buy imported Italian sausage and olive oil at the corner grocery store owned by their *padrone.* And when the imports from Italy included women, they began to nurture their families in towering crowded tenements that in a strange way evoked the mountain village atmosphere that had surrounded them from birth. The fact that few trees lined these city streets was considered a blessing by the women—who, accustomed as they were to the age-old daily habit of sitting at their windows in Italy for hours and spying down on their neighbors, would have become frustrated in America if their view of street life was obscured by leaves casting dark shadows.

And to these city-dwelling Italians there came always enough tales of horror and woe about life in the provinces to convince them that they were better off where they were. One such story concerned a gang of workers who had been escorted by their *padrone* into the Deep South to pick cotton on a Mississippi plantation: When they visited the town they were treated as miserably as the blacks, and sometimes confronted along the roads at night by men with burning crosses. The small Italian restaurant that had been opened near the plantation by the *padrone* was destroyed after an Italian cook served a black man. Another tale involved Italians who organized an agricultural commune in Arkansas, enduring not only droughts and tornadoes, but also the attacks of nativists baiting them as "dagos." The Italians who had been sent into the midwestern wilderness to labor for the Chicago & North Western Railway had been unable to find housing throughout the winter. When they sought shelter and warmth within the haystacks of cattle cars in the railyards, they were awakened by holdup men who stole whatever money the Italians had saved from their nine-dollar-a-week salaries. Many Italians who had been recruited to work in the copper mines of Colorado during a work stoppage were nearly clubbed to death by mobs of laid-off unionists who cursed them as strikebreakers. In Louisiana, after a New Orleans police chief had been killed while investigating reports of extortion and violence among rival gangs of Italian dockworkers, eleven Italians were arrested on charges of murder—but none was found guilty. Outraged by what was regarded as excessive courtroom leniency, a citizens' group of vigilantes raided the New Orleans prison, captured the Italians who had stood trial, and lynched every one of them.

But such atrocities that made headlines in the American press, and also in the newspapers back in Italy—bringing satisfaction to some Italian landowners burdened by the labor shortage caused by emigration—represented only a partial and often distorted picture of Italian immigrant life as it was being experienced outside the ghettos and mill towns of the Northeast at the turn of the century. Equally relevant, if insufficiently dramatic to warrant circulation through journalism or ghetto gossip, was the slowly evolving yet persevering assimilation of the Italians who generally coexisted peacefully with non-Italians throughout the South, the Midwest, and the Far West, and whose next generation often grew up speaking English with a Dixie drawl or a Texas twang, and learned to recite the Pledge of Allegiance in such places as the fraternal hall of the Italian Society of Victor Emmanuel III in Waukesha, Wisconsin.

The Ogden, Utah, native son of an Italian father and a Mormon mother would become a leading American essayist, Bernard De Voto. At Fort Huachuca, Arizona, growing up among soldiers, Indians, and bronco riders, was the adolescent son of an Italian-born U.S. Army bandmaster and a Jewish mother from Trieste; he would one day be elected mayor of New York—Fiorello La Guardia. There was a cowboy born in Texas of an Italian father and an Irish mother who would write best-selling westerns under the name Charles A. Siringo; and an Italian immigrant who ran a small hotel in San Jose, California, had a son, Amadeo Pietro Giannini, who would one day found the Bank of Italy in San Francisco, which would later become the Bank of America, one of the largest private banks in the world.

It is true, the Italians who put down roots west of the Mississippi constituted barely twenty percent of all the Italians who entered the United States before, and slightly after, the turn of the century. But this twenty percent probably arrived at "feeling American" far sooner than did the eighty percent who lived more sheltered lives in industrial towns and ethnic neighborhoods east of the Mississippi, and who continued to rely on a *padrone* as their primary liaison with the American mainstream. In California, where Italians were quick in gaining social acceptance and material success, there were hardly any *padroni*.

It was also true, however, that the Italians who moved into California were predominantly of northern Italian stock; and being the beneficiaries of a higher level of education than the southerners, and from less impoverished circumstances, they came better equipped to function in America on their own. Less than twelve percent of the northern arrivals were illiterate, as compared with more than fifty percent of the southerners. While southerners had been held back for centuries by the oppressive, anti-intellectual traditions of the Spanish Bourbon crown and the Catholic Church, the northerners' heritage had been more worldly, if no less spiritual, as they interacted, and intermarried, through the ages with diverse groups of Europeans who dwelled along or near Italy's northern borders—the French, the Swiss, the Germans, the Austrians: citizens of foreign nations with which Italian authorities had often quarreled, but with whose language and customs many Italian people were at least familiar, and whose religious differences, when such existed, were tolerated in ways that would have been unacceptable to a Bourbon bishop in Naples. The northern Italian heroes who sparked the Risorgimento—King Victor Emmanuel II,

Count Cavour, Mazzini, and Garibaldi—all were lapsed Catholics; and while there was never evidence to indicate that northern Italians were less God-fearing than southern Italians, the northern Italian immigrants in America (unlike their southern compatriots) were not so readily perceived by America's Protestant majority as peons of the Pope and dregs of the earth.

Their physical appearance alone helped northern Italian immigrants blend in better than southerners. Their body structure and skin tone were closer to that of the angular, ruddy Anglo-Nordic European Protestant colonists, pioneers, and arrivistes who most frequently represented, in physique and physiognomy, the American prototype. Northern Italians tended to be taller and less swarthy than most southerners, often having light-colored hair and eyes and, according to the writer William Dean Howells, United States consul at Venice during the 1860s, a "lightness of temper." Not only were northerners more formally educated than southerners, and more inclined to master the English language, but they were as a rule more outgoing personally, less guarded around strangers, more entrepreneurial. They were also fortunate in having a significant number of their northern countrymen arriving in the bustling San Francisco Bay area almost simultaneously with most of the native-born settlers, at the time of the 1849 gold rush, when the tenor and tempo of the region were characterized by a mobile, not yet socially stratified, materialist group of individuals with whom the Italians proved to be quite compatible. Among the early prospering Italians of this period was Domenico Ghirardelli, who traveled through California's mining towns peddling chocolates and harder candy, *caramelle.* Out of his energies would emerge a sweets and syrups factory that would flourish in San Francisco long after his death.

A contemporary of Ghirardelli's, and among the first of many Italians to prosper as a vintner of California wines, was Andrea Sbarbaro, a Genoese banker who founded ItalianSwiss Colony in California's Sonoma Valley. In the waters of San Francisco Bay and beyond, competing with the Chinese fishermen sailing their junks, were immigrant Italian fishermen, mostly from Genoa. But later, in the 1880s, as the Genoese began to advance themselves to more remunerative livelihoods along the shore and in the town, many sold their deep-water feluccas and small crab boats and nets to the most recently arrived Italian fishermen, several of them Sicilian. Among the Sicilians to arrive at the turn of the century was a fisherman born in Isola delle Femmine, an islet off Palermo, where his forebears had earned their living on the sea for generations. His name was DiMaggio. In America he would have five sons, the two oldest of whom would become fishermen. The three younger sons lacked the discipline and temperament for sea life, and as small boys they would often wander away from Fisherman's Wharf and stroll toward the sandlots, swinging broken oars that they pretended were baseball bats.

Not only in northern California but in the Los Angeles and San Diego areas as well, Italian immigrants would in time contribute significantly to the state's economic development, some as vintners, others as large-scale vegetable and fruit growers. Almost everything that could be grown in Italy could be grown in the fertile soil and mild climate of California, which of all the American states most resembled the peninsula of Italy. The transported Italians who capitalized most on the California climate were, to be sure, those immigrants born in Italy's more industrial north, men who eschewed the other side of the country, with its smoky factory towns and ghettos, for a better place in the sun. Ironically, the Italian southerners, who had been toppled by northern invaders during the Risorgimento, in America found themselves still in an inferior position to their northern countrymen—and still ruled by opportunistic men from the north, their *padroni*.

With few exceptions, the *padroni* who governed the lives of Italian manual laborers in America were natives of northern Italy. An exception was the protégé of Dr. Mattison in Philadelphia. Carmine Lobianco's canniness had been cultivated during his youth along the scheming waterfront of Naples, and, as a provider of laborers for Keasbey & Mattison Company of Ambler, he soon attained the prosperity that had been his primary ambition.

But by the mid-1880s there began to appear much negative publicity about *padroni* in the big-city American newspapers, and there were hints that United States immigration authorities were recommending legislation that would ban many practices of *padroni* that were deemed exploitative and devious. Many *padroni* were accused of dishonest dealings with the American employers who advanced the immigrants' passage fares to the *padroni:* the latter would exaggerate the actual cost that the steamship company charged to bring laborers from Italy to the United States (pocketing the difference), and then record the higher passage figure on the list of debts that the laborers were later obliged to repay out of their wages.

On payday, some unfortunate workers discovered that they were penniless after they had reimbursed their *padrone* what he claimed was owed for lodging, food, transportation to and from the job site; such personal services as letter-writing, translating, and notarization; and the interest rates charged on personal loans. Some workers unable to repay the loans were forced to forfeit their small plots of farmland in Italy that the *padrone* had held as collateral. The loss of such land caused deep bitterness among the workers in America and their kinfolk in Italy; and the resultant protests against these and similar situations brought the whole *padrone* system under scrutiny by American lawmakers and the press in the mid-1880s, and tarnished the image of many *padroni* who had long and justifiably enjoyed reputations for being gentlemen of humanity and integrity. Such a gentleman, however, was not Carmine Lobianco.

In the latter part of 1888, Lobianco had gradually drifted into voluntary semi-retirement. With the intensified campaigns waged by American immigration authorities Lobianco became haunted by thoughts of imprisonment. He was now wealthier than he knew he had any right to be; and while this did not plague his conscience—he had achieved affluence, after all, in a manner not dissimilar from that of the barons of his native land, and of such American *prominenti* as his patron, the eminent mixer of potions and a fellow profiteer in the market of cheap labor—Lobianco now wished to devote more time to his diversified business interests. From his profits after six years as a *padrone*, Lobianco owned in the Italian district of South Philadelphia two red-brick rental properties, a neighborhood bank, a travel agency, and a grocery store. He also owned two rambling boardinghouses in the outskirts of Ambler, where work was proceeding on Dr. Mattison's Gothic community and asbestos-manufacturing center. Supervising the boardinghouse was Carmine Lobianco's wife, the sister of an anarchist from Naples who, like him, had been slipped into the country illegally.

Living in the boardinghouses, and sleeping on cornhusk mattresses, four bunks to a room, were many Keasbey & Mattison laborers. At dawn each morning they were led by Lobianco's foreman up the dirt road into the stone quarry to dynamite and haul more rock uphill, to continue building the more than four hundred residences and factory structures that would make up the industrial community in Ambler.

During his years as a *padrone*, Lobianco had been responsible for shuttling more than five hundred men between Naples and Ambler. But in this period of adverse publicity, the countless responsibilities of that position—greeting the arriving boatloads of workers, escorting them onto trains, lodging and feeding them, tending to their varied needs and requirements, serving as their daily guardian and social consort, and all the other thankless tasks—were no longer worth the aggravation and money to Lobianco. He would subcontract most of the customary chores to his cousins and friends from Naples, while he moved back to Philadelphia to spend more time in less demanding circumstances.

The last boatload of workers for which he was directly responsible arrived in late April 1888. On board were forty-three men, all of them bachelors. All of them had jobs awaiting them with Keasbey & Mattison Company, either in the quarry or as apprentices to the stonemasons and artisans who had already completed dozens of Gothic buildings that Dr. Mattison himself had redesigned after expressing displeasure with the original plans submitted by his architects.

The forty-three newcomers did not have written contracts with Lobianco specifying the terms of employment—this practice had been banned by American immigration authorities under pressure from the unions; but Lobianco had been assured by his recruiter colleagues in Naples that each and every man had pledged to remain in the United States, under the guidance of the *padrone,* for no less than two years.

One of the workers who had agreed to these terms was Gaetano Talese.

Mari Tomasi

From *Like Lesser Gods*

Petra and Vetch enjoyed these fall evenings of grappa making. Outside was the chill night. Inside rose a steamy, racy warmth that nipped their noses. To blind the curious eyes of passers-by, Pietro drew the kitchen shades close to the sills saying that the government did not approve of grappa making. And Petra wondered why the government should care if Papa poured a little grappa into his morning coffee to warm himself these cool mornings, and to make his breakfast taste better. For he said it did. Petra heard her father invite Ronato—"Come up tonight, Ronato. You and Lucia. We will sit at the kitchen table for a game of *briscola.* I am making grappa tonight."

Petra knew that if she breathed the racy grappa steam for a long time, it gave her body a pleasing sensation. Tingling, light, gay. Her mother would make a clucking sound and say, "Look at the child's flushed cheeks. *Dio,* almost *inebriata* she is." And she would allow neither her nor Gabriella to sleep in the little room over the kitchen where the steam rose through the pipe hole in the floor. No, on grappa-making nights the two girls slept in the upper hall where doors were kept tightly closed.

Lewis Turco

Failed Fathers

On a theme by,
and with apologies to, Greg Pape

Where do all the failed fathers
go? To Albuquerque? Cleveland?
After the slow slide down the drain,
where do they go? After the last
lay-off, the class reunion where they're shown

kissing the matronly Queen
of the Prom, where do they go. Where
do they go, these old young men, these
paunchy guys with the eyes that squint
into the lens at the family picnic,

the fishing expedition
near the falls, the baseball game where
they played second? After the fights,
the money fights, the brief affair,
after the spree and the morning after,

where do the failed fathers go?
Is there a bar where they gather,
is there a bus they all take,
is there a line at the Bureau
where they talk over their sons and daughters,

their Old Ladies turning cold,
the milkmen they caught spending time
drinking coffee in their kitchens?
Is there a motel in Cleveland
full of fathers playing poker,

smoking cigarettes, squinting
at their hands, drinking beer? Is there,

down in Albuquerque, some street
full of walk-up rooms full of dreams
of mowing lawns, of paneling basements,

    propping children on their bikes,
walking down the aisles of markets
pushing shopping carts? Of course, we
know what happens to our mothers,
but where oh where do the failed fathers go?

Anthony Valerio

The Widows

"I want to go home, Johnny. That is, I want to make a home with a woman I love. My home doesn't have to be in Brooklyn or Queens or on Staten Island. It could be anywhere on the face of the earth, and I'll buy nice things and learn to care for them. Cook and in my garden grow broccoli-rappé and arugula. Despite my age, I'm even thinking of having children. Tell me what to do."

He uncrosses his legs and straightens up enough for his right hand to sail into his pants pocket. He withdraws a wad of cash.

"No, Johnny, please. Not between us—money must not pass between us."

He pauses, conceding I may be right, but then simultaneously his eyes open wide and his sharply defined lips begin to mouth a word. For emphasis, I suspect, for highlighting the word's importance. From its first harsh consonant, I know what the word is and immediately I feel all its lethal implications. I blanch, cringe low on the sofa. My heart pounds in terrifying anticipation. Johnny's lips together with his taut mouth take on the shape of a long bow which shoots the word directly into my heart: *"Job."*

While my heart bleeds, a handyman carries in a telephone, one of those outsize antique telephones, ornate and bright. He holds out the receiver for Johnny—the desired party is already on the line.

Though Johnny is only nine feet away and I can see he's talking, his lips are moving, I cannot make out a word. His lips stop. He holds up the receiver like a torch. His eyes slowly turn on me, and he says peremptorily, "Maître d' at the Club Elegante. Ocean Parkway, Brooklyn. You start tomorrow night, six o'clock."

I die, and then, suddenly, everything grows calm and I see it all. A slight smile comes over my pale visage, and with eyes aglow from the celestial light I thank Johnny from the bottom of my wounded heart. "But it won't work," I go on to tell him. "Oh, I'd wear a fine tuxedo and every night a fresh carnation. Come eight o'clock my face would beam, as it beams now, and I'd stand tall and straight and glide amid the tables and chairs. But do you know what would happen? I'd pick out the widows. I'd pick them out and devote all my attention to them. They'd arrive in groups, at least in pairs, accompanied by their brothers and their brothers' wives, by old married friends of their deceased husbands. I'd know the young widows by their dates, small-time hoods, burly, adorned with gold, thin mustaches, short. The widows, their hair would be done up in silver, and they'd wear sack-like dresses glittering with sequins to deflect the eye from the thick set of their bodies. Atop their heads I'd see the nimbus of love left behind by grief. No amount of make-up and fragrance and show of fun would hide the pain in their faces, their cried-out eyes. I'd see the trace of tears. The purple color around their eyes. *I'd* cry. I'd place my arm around their shoulders and, while ushering them to tables surrounding the dance floor, I'd manage to say softly that they could talk to me of their grief. Throughout the night, I'd pull up a loose chair and sit beside them. We'd talk of other things: children, volunteer work, getting in shape, the value of sweet memories, the prospect of new love. Whenever the band struck up a slow dance, I'd approach smiling, arm extended. Silent, in a light embrace, the widows and I would dance the evenings away."

Song of the Castrato

I'm reluctant to tell Johnny any more about my girlfriend because as soon as I open my mouth about her, I lose all control. My neck rolls as do my eyes. I hyperventilate. My lungs cannot keep pace with the feelings in my heart. My voice changes. Lefty says that I talk the way Frank Sinatra sings, but she doesn't hear me talk about her, doesn't hear my mellifluous baritone transform to a castrato, an impassioned castrato who, after he sings his aria of unrequited love, is so overwrought that all that remains to him are tears in his eyes, pain in his heart, utter exhaustion. He cannot remember the words. They are not meant for now. They are meant for a millennium from now and a different place, one where there are no mountains to echo, just a vast, desolate plain, and every year or so, about fifty feet in the air all across the plain, the words play calm and clear, soothing reminder of one man's ancient love for a woman.

But maybe Johnny will understand. He has loved. He loves his wife so much he'd kill for her. And so, after hearing me, he'll seek to contain my exultation in the here and now. He'll smile slightly, rise from his chair and come over to me, tap my cheek and say, "After all you've said about your girlfriend, she sounds wonderful and I'd like to meet her."

"Oh, definitely," I'd have to say, and then the next Monday, Wednesday or Friday afternoon I'd tell her first thing, excited, "Johnny wants to meet you."

"No problem," she's likely to respond, or "Don't make appointments for me."

In the latter case, what do I do? Cancel the appointment? Coax her into going, stating unequivocally that among Italians one must always consummate the promise, that my very life may hinge upon it because with a man like Johnny, you never know what trips his trigger?

She will remain true to her feelings and mood, one reason I love her more than my life. She knows this and will acquiesce and, if it turns out that she doesn't take to him, she will not say, "I don't like you— you're a bum!" She will, instead, say very little. Nothing, in fact. She will sit demurely in her thigh-length, leopard-skin skirt and halter cut at the midriff, black-stockinged legs crossed, an attentive, intelligent, unreadable look on her face, which for an Italian male is worse than a show of hostility.

Johnny will grow nervous and look to me for an explanation. It's not polite to bring the unfriendly into the parlor. I'll raise my brows, shrug my shoulders, and right there make apologies in the past tense, as if she had died and we were doing the autopsy.

"A new book was coming out and she was under a lot of pressure—reviews, book parties, readings."

"She was just about to get her period, and one of her PMS's was suicide."

"What could a Jewish girl from Long Island know about Italians from Brooklyn? She married a half-Irish, half-Italian from Jersey, who on his wedding day bought a newspaper and a pack of gum, went home and read and chewed, then went to sleep."

L. D. Ventura and S. Shevitch

From *Misfits and Remnants*

They called him Beppo, and her Rita. And seldom, indeed, did it happen that the one was mentioned without the other; for if ever there were bosom friends in the world, Beppo and Rita were such.

Who were their parents? Who can say? They themselves were least able to give a satisfactory answer to this question. All they could remember was that they had found themselves one day side by side basking in the sun and scrambling about among the sands and pebbles of the shore at Naples, that since that day that shore had become their home, and that they had always remained together. Thrice a day Zio Antonio (Uncle Antonio) took them to his hut and gave them macaroni and *frutti di mare*. When night came, if Rita felt chilly, they knocked at Antonio's door and huddled together among his nets and fishing-tackle. But mostly they remained lying on the sand, looking at the bright stars overhead, chattering and laughing until the great sea lulled its children to sleep with its deep, soft murmur.

Beppo was somewhat older than Rita, and she looked up to him as to her natural and powerful protector. He was proudly conscious of this, and would have sprung into a lion's jaws to shield her from harm.

So they grew up, like all that is alive in Nature grows up in those blessed climes,—children of the rich, burning soil on which they lay, of the blue sea which like a mother sang them to sleep.

Beppo was about fourteen, and Rita perhaps two years younger, when Zio Antonio announced to them that in future they had no more macaroni to expect from him, for he was going away—far, far away—to a land called America. Things looked bad in Naples, he said, *molta gente e poco danaro* (many people and little money); and so he preferred work in foreign lands to starvation at home.

The poor children cried bitterly in taking leave of the old man. He was the only human being who had ever cared for them, and now they were all alone in the world. It was not for his macaroni alone that they cried; as long as there was a fisherman on the shore they had no fear of hunger. But the macaroni is, after all, not everything in life, even to a Neapolitan *lazzarone*. After Zio Antonio had left them, Beppo grew daily more restless and thoughtful. He would sit for hours in the sand, his dark, sparkling eyes fixed with a longing look on the blue space of open sea between Capri and Ischia; and when Rita crept up to him, and, nestling on his lap, asked what he thought about, he answered: "Zio Antonio and that foreign land he has gone to."

One day, as they were thus sitting together, a man dressed like a sailor approached them, and, tapping Beppo on the shoulder, said,—

"Cheer up, my lad; I have good news for you from Zio Antonio. I have seen the old man on the other side; he is doing very well, and is fast becoming rich. Would you like to go to him? That ship, the captain of which is a friend of mine, starts to-morrow. He will give you a free passage for Antonio's sake."

Beppo sprang up in delight.

"Of course we will go," he exclaimed; "won't we, Rita?"

"As you will, Beppo," she answered, simply.

And the pair started, hand in hand, preceded by the sailor. The same night they were brought on board the ship, where the captain, a burly, coarse-looking, red-haired fellow, met them.

"Hallo, Domenico," he cried, "are you bringing me some more? We are pretty full already."

"Only two more," answered the man. "Squeeze them up a bit."

Then the captain and the man who brought the children drew aside and held a whispered conference. Some money passed from hand to hand, and then the sailor jumped into his boat and rowed back to the shore.

"What are you staring at?" cried the captain to the children, who stood on deck side by side, bewildered, amazed by all they had seen and heard. "Go down and sleep." Saying which, he seized them roughly by the shoulder and pushed them down a steep ladder into an utterly dark and narrow hole. Groping their way through the darkness, the children stumbled at each step they made on prostrate human forms. Cries and groans arose, and chilled their hearts with nameless terror. Beppo, with Rita half fainting in his arms, rushed back to the ladder; but it had already been drawn up. He screamed aloud; nobody answered him. He shook his fists and stamped on the floor in impotent rage; all in vain. They were locked up, buried alive. With difficulty Beppo succeeded in finding an empty space on the floor. He took Rita in his arms, and, pressed closely against each other, both children cried themselves to sleep.

When they awoke, the broad daylight streamed in through the hatchway. In the narrow and close space forming a part of the steerage a dozen or more ragged children of all ages, from ten to sixteen, were crowded together, lying on the bare floor, with no other bedding than their own miserable rags. One by one the poor wretches awoke, crying bitterly. The ship had heaved her anchor during the night and had already gained the open sea.

"What does this mean? What is going to become of us?" asked Beppo of his neighbor, a little chap of scarcely ten years of age, who cried as if his heart would break.

"We are sold," cried the little one, sobbing, "sold to wild people over the seas, who will roast us and eat us."

The whole passage, which lasted nearly two months, was an uninterrupted series of suffering for the children. Not one soul on board cared for them in any way. Their food was brought to them twice a day in a trough, and consisted for the most part of sea-biscuit soaked in water. Most of the children dwindled to skeletons before they reached New York. Two of them died, and the corpses were thrown overboard without further ceremony.

But of all these hardships and sufferings Beppo felt little; his attention was too intensely absorbed by the care he had to bestow on poor Rita, who was sick nearly the whole time. The lad nursed her with a touching, untiring devotion; and when at length he heard that New York was in sight, his heart leaped with joy. He forgot all the uncertainty of their future doom in the joy of the one feeling that Rita would feel well again.

The next day after the ship had come to anchor in the North River, two uncommonly mean and brutal looking Italians came on board, and were received by the captain with unusual honors. After indulging in a copious libation in the captain's cabin, the three worthies proceeded on deck and ordered the children to be brought out. The little ones flocked out, shivering in the chilly atmosphere of a November morning. Every one of them was minutely scrutinized by both visitors. Half of the party remained on board; the rest, five in number, among them Rita and Beppo, were packed into the boat and brought on shore. On landing, the *padroni* separated,—the one taking, with three children, an easterly direction, and the other driving Beppo and Rita before him like a yoke of oxen in the direction of Baxter Street.

While walking, the Italian explained to Beppo that his name was Matteo, and that they were going to live together.

"And where is Zio Antonio?" asked the lad in despair.

"What do I know about your Zio Antonio?" rejoined the *padrone* gruffly. "You have no business to know anybody but me."

They walked on in silence. With each step through the busy, roaring streets the poor children became more frightened and bewildered by the bustle which surrounded them. A feeling of utter despair and helplessness seized Beppo as he became conscious of the impossibility of finding Zio Antonio amid the waves of this human ocean.

"Here we are," said Matteo, stopping in the doorway of one of the loftiest and most dingy tenement-houses in Baxter Street; "follow me." He stepped into the dark hall. The children followed, trembling with an indefinable horror. The walls of the hall were damp and clammy, the air foul with stenches and emanations of all kinds. The poor *lazzaroni,* used to the balmy, invigorating breezes of the Mediterranean, felt nearly choked in this atmosphere. At the end of a long corridor they descended a few steps into what seemed to be an entirely dark cellar. Matteo opened a door in a narrow, badly lighted basement-room, in which, besides a rough bedstead in the corner, they could distinguish only a great heap of nondescript rags, peanuts, egg-shells, and rubbish of every kind. In the middle of the room there stood a small decapitated iron stove, which had evidently not yet been used during that season, for the air in the room was damp and cold.

"There is your bed," said Matteo, pointing to a heap of rags in the corner. "There is always enough of that rubbish about for you to lie on. Now come along; I will show you your business."

"But Rita cannot walk," exclaimed Beppo indignantly. "She has been sick all the way. Give her something to eat before going."

"Time enough for that," rejoined Matteo, grinning. "Well, the girl may remain at home for this once." Matteo led the boy through a labyrinth of narrow streets to one of the busiest and noisiest corners of that noisy neighborhood. There the worthy *padrone* possessed a thriving peanut-stand, which he intended to trust to Beppo, himself desiring to embrace a new and more lucrative career.

From that day a weary, miserable life began for the poor children. It was not the wretched food and cruel treatment on the part of Matteo which pained them the most; it was first of all the dreadful house, the abominable underground hole in which they lived, the feeling of dependence, almost of slavery, which was hard to bear for these children of Nature. Many a sleepless night did they spend sitting on their heap of rags and talking in a whisper about Santa Lucia and the nights on the coast and Zio Antonio.

Sometimes Rita accompanied Beppo to his peanut-stand. But mostly she remained at home, or was sent out by Matteo to sell evening papers, the names of which he had taught her. One bitter cold night, as Beppo returned home a little earlier than usual, he heard on approaching the door of their room the angry voice of Matteo swearing and scolding, while Rita cried and moaned in an agony of pain. Beppo rushed into the room and saw Matteo holding the girl by the hair with one hand, while with the other he lashed her naked back with a whip. Beside himself with rage, Beppo sprang at Matteo's throat and clung to it with such a firm grip that the man was obliged to release poor Rita. Of course he turned all his fury against the boy. He whipped him until the blood sprang out of his scars; then, opening the door, he threw the senseless body of the lad out into the inner yard of the house. Rita ran after him, and Matteo locked both out, saying,—

"Freeze there all night, you curs!"

The cold air revived Beppo very soon. On recovering his senses, his first question was after Rita. She was kneeling by his side, crying bitterly.

"Why has the rascal whipped you?" he asked.

"He wanted to teach me how to draw a handkerchief out of his pocket so that he should not feel it; and I could not, and then he beat me," answered the girl, sobbing.

Beppo said nothing; but he clenched his fists, and his eyes flashed like those of a wild beast. Rita was shivering with cold. The boy got up and rapped at Matteo's window. An oath and an order to keep quiet was all the answer he could get. With every hour the night became colder. An icy wind came sweeping over the city, and, descending into the deep court-yard in Baxter Street, kept whirling and whirling around, chilling the poor Italian children to their very hearts. Beppo took off his coat and waistcoat to keep Rita as warm as possible, and feeling his limbs stiffening in the frost, leaned against the door and drew the girl close to his bosom. Thus they lay as they had so often lain, locked in a close embrace on the sand of their native coast. Sleep, the great friend of childhood, for whom there are no rich and no poor, who with equal love and mercy extends his soothing hand over the palace and the hut, closed their eyelids with a gentle touch, and sent his sunniest dreams to soothe and to cheer them. A smile of happiness hovered about their pale faces; they saw once more before them the Bay of Naples glittering in the rays of their native sun, they felt the warm breeze caressing their cheeks. The smile on their lips grew brighter and happier.

"Beppo!" whispered the girl.

He heard her in his sleep, and drew her still closer to him.

And then all was still. The smiling friend of childhood had fled, and in his place a graver angel looked down upon the poor sleeping waifs and took them in his arms. The sunshine grew brighter and brighter in their dreams, the breeze warmer and balmier, their smile more radiant. Thus they lay through all that long cold night. And when the morning came at last, and all that giant house awoke to its day's misery and crime, the two lifeless forms were found lying in close embrace, with the same blissful smile illumining their faces.

What became of Matteo? Nothing, of course. He easily proved that he had always been a "respectable" man, that he knew nothing about what had become of the children on that night, and that by "honest work" he had collected a few paltry dollars, of which he would readily give a share to any friends who would help him out of that scrape. It is hardly necessary to add that he found such friends easily.

Robert Viscusi

From *Astoria*

—A lady poisoned her sister for a cameo.

—Two cousins fought over their mother's deathbed for a hat.

—One day my mother's cousin stole her father-in-law's pocket watch after he died.

—My grandmother's mother loved her chickens. One day she left my grandmother, then six years old, to watch the baby. She rocked the baby to sleep, but one chicken kept waking the baby up. Chickens are stupid and willful and will not always listen when you tell them to shut up. She shook the chicken. It made more noise, the baby started crying. She shook its head. It squawked louder. The baby screamed. She wrung the chicken's neck and killed it. *Ah, che maledetto!* She threw the chicken over the cliff at the side of the house, two hundred feet into the ravine where the river carried it away. The baby slept. Her mother came home. Where is my favorite chicken? I don't know, the little girl replied, shrugging her innocent shoulders. Her mother decided that the neighbor, a witch who had put the evil eye on her baby son who had died of fever, had stolen the chicken out of envy. She went and accused her. The neighbor, naturally, denied it and, naturally, counterattacked. They never spoke again. A year later, my grandmother, thinking the chicken so long dead it would be safe now to unburden her conscience, explained the whole truth to her mother who listened to the entire story and then beat the little girl for an hour with a wooden spoon, screaming and cursing and chasing her up and down the picturesque streets of the medieval hill town with its simple Romanesque church so charming to tourists.

—My father's mother said to my mother, 'You do a hundred good things, I no can remember. But you do one bad thing, I no can forget.'

—My father's father worked six days a week twelve hours a day in the G.E. factory in Schenectady. The seventh day he played cards and got drunk.

—We have a *paisan* in Florida who retired in 1969. There was a sale on fluorescent lightbulbs. He has not yet used a third of the ones he bought. He also owns four thousand rolls of toilet paper.

As I write these things, I keep feeling I'm doing something very wrong, putting down in black and white these ordinary stories of ordinary life lived, after all, in broad daylight. There is a Terror in this too. I frighten them by telling these stories. They frighten me by saying, as I write, in my secret ear, 'Why tell these things to strangers? Traitor!'

Octavia Waldo

From *A Cup of the Sun*

Love was the sun that afternoon—a yellow, consuming globe that melted down everything, giving off a blinding glare and a scent of rose petals heated to ash. Love was lazy time and time to do nothing but let the sun seep into flesh, thrilling it with its heat. Love was a bed covered white upon which a man and woman lay apart, beneath an anguished wooden Christ, their fingers alone stretching across the sheet to touch, tip to tip.

"It's too hot today," the woman's lips, full and yielding, but pleading too, murmured softly. "Not today, no."

"Come here. Don't be so distant."

"But how foolish you are! Not now, I say. We'd be like glue upon each other."

"Come here." The man sighed. "Here. Now, Lovely." The mouth coming closer, tempting. The flesh coaxing, erect with its own heat that knew nothing but wanting, knew neither the warmth within itself nor the blazing sun outside.

"But the door," Mrs. Bartoli whispered. "The children."

Mr. Bartoli rose to the door and creaked it closed with his weight against it. In an instant he was back again with his wife, molding her body with his hands as if she were made of clay and he were her creator.

But she resisted. She always resisted—all the twenty years of their love-making. It was part of their game for her to resist until she had lured him to that triumphant minute when their arms and legs knew the oneness of what they were about. Then her touch was all giving and her smile was all pleasure, and her breath, all warmth.

"Don't ever grow tired of this," he had told her when they had just married.

List of Contributors

Flavia Alaya is a writer, scholar, and social activist. She has been a professor of literature at Ramapo College in New Jersey since 1971 and has been awarded Guggenheim and National Endowment for the Humanities fellowships. *Under the Rose* (1999) is a memoir; Alaya has also published a number of scholarly works.

Carol Bonomo Albright is editor of *Italian Americana* and teaches Italian American studies at Harvard University Extension School. She has published articles and book reviews in numerous anthologies and journals, including *Social Pluralism* and *Journal of American Ethnic History*.

George Anastasia, the grandson of Sicilian immigrants, is a reporter for *The Philadelphia Inquirer* and has been nominated twice for a Pulitzer Prize. His books include *Blood and Honor* (1991), *Mob Father* (1993), *Summer Wind* (2000), and *The Goodfella Tapes* (1998).

Tony Ardizzone is the author of six books of fiction, most recently the novel *In the Garden of Papa Santuzzo* (1999) and *Taking It Home: Stories from the Neighborhood* (1996). He is the director of the creative writing program at Indiana University, Bloomington.

David Baldacci is an internationally best-selling author whose works include *Last Man Standing* (2001), *Wish You Well* (2000), and *Absolute Power* (1996). Baldacci also has written several screenplays, published widely in various magazines and newspapers, and made numerous TV and radio appearances. He was born in Virginia.

Helen Barolini has written several novels, including *Umbertina* (1979), and over fifty stories and essays, one of which appears in *Best American Essays 1998*. *The Dream Book* (1985), an anthology of Italian

American women writers, won the National Book Award. Barolini grew up in an Italian American family in Syracuse, New York.

Hugo Barreca received his J.D. from Fordham University and his M.B.A. from New York University. He has recently completed (with Julia K. O'Neill) *The Entrepreneur's Internet Handbook*. Currently consulting publisher of *Doubletake* magazine, he lives in Brooklyn, N.Y.

Regina Barreca is a writer and scholar whose works include *They Used to Call Me Snow White . . . But I Drifted* (1991), *Perfect Husbands (And Other Fairy Tales)* (1993), and *Sweet Revenge: The Wicked Delights of Getting Even* (1995).

Joy Behar, an acclaimed comedian, is the author of *Joy Shtick: Or What Is the Existential Vacuum and Does It Come with Attachments?* (1999). Behar has made countless appearances on radio and television, as well as in several films and plays; she is the co-host of television's *The View*. Born in Brooklyn in 1943, she still lives in New York City.

Mary Jo Bona is the author or editor of several books on Italian American literature, with an emphasis on women writers. She is professor of Italian American studies at SUNY Stony Brook. *Claiming a Tradition: Italian American Women Writers* (1999) is a study of several lesser-known novels.

Dorothy Bryant has written twelve novels, two works of nonfiction, and four plays. She has received several awards, including the American Book Award in 1987 for her acclaimed novel *Confessions of Madame Psyche*. Bryant lives in the San Francisco Bay Area.

Anne Calcagno was raised in Italy; the award-winning *Pray for Yourself and Other Stories* (1993), a collection of short stories, is set in both Italy and the United States. Calcagno's travel writing has appeared in the *New York Times* and elsewhere, and she is the editor of *Travelers' Tales Italy: True Stories* (1998). She teaches English at DePaul University.

Phyllis Capello has forged an innovative career as a writer, musician, and story teller. Her fiction and poetry have received numerous awards. Her work has appeared in *Voices in Italian Americana, The Paterson Review,* and *The Dream Book: An Anthology of Writings by Italian American Women*.

Nancy Caronia is a writer and the co-founder, in 1997, of Girl-Speak, a reading series. Her award-winning work has appeared in *Foot-work, The Paterson Literary Review,* and *phati'tude Literary Magazine.* Caronia lives in New York City, where she grew up.

Grace Cavalieri is the award-winning author of eleven books of poetry, including *Trenton* (1992), *Swan Research* (1979), and, most recently, *Sit Down, Says Love* (1999). She has also written extensively for the stage and screen. For twenty years she hosted *The Poet and the Poem,* a weekly radio show. Cavalieri lives in West Virginia.

Diana Cavallo has written fiction and nonfiction, plays and short stories. Her best-known work is the novel *A Bridge of Leaves,* published in 1961. She is also the author of *The Lower East Side: A Portrait in Time* (1971). Cavallo teaches in the creative writing program at the University of Pennsylvania.

Thomas Centolella, a poet and American Book Award winner, is the author of *Lights and Mysteries* (1997), *Terra Firma* (1990), and *Views from Along the Middle Way* (2002). Born and raised in Upstate New York, Centolella now lives in San Francisco.

John Ciardi, a poet, critic, editor, teacher, and translator, published more than thirty books. *Homeward to America* (1940), *I Marry You: A Sheaf of Love Poems* (1958), *This Strangest Everything* (1966), and *The Birds of Pompeii* (1986) are just a few of his works. Ciardi was born in Boston in 1916 and died in 1986.

Rita Ciresi is the author of *Sometimes I Dream in Italian* (2000), a collection of short stories. An earlier collection, *Mother Rocket* (1993), won the Flannery O'Connor Award for Short Fiction. Other works include the novels *Blue Italian* (1996) and *Pink Slip* (1998). Ciresi teaches at the University of South Florida.

Robert Corrente is an attorney in Providence, Rhode Island, specializing in litigation. He holds degrees from Dartmouth College and New York University.

Gregory Corso, well known as one of the Beat poets, was born in New York City. He published his first book of poetry, *The Vestal Lady on Brattle,* in 1955. *The Happy Birthday of Death* (1960), *The American*

Express (1961), *Elegiac Feelings American* (1970), and *Mindfield* (1991) are just a few of his many works. Corso died in January 2001.

Peter Covino's poetry has appeared in numerous publications, including *The Paris Review, The Ohio Review, Verse,* and *VIA: Voices in Italian Americana.* Born and educated in Italy, he earned a master's degree in social work from Columbia University and an M.A. from the City College of New York in 2001.

George Cuomo is an award-winning poet and novelist best known for his legal fiction. His works include *Jack Be Nimble* (1963), *Among Thieves* (1968), *Family Honor: An American Life* (1983), and a poetry collection, *Geronimo and the Girl Next Door* (1973). He was born in New York City in 1929 and taught at the University of Massachusetts.

Joseph Cuomo is a New York writer; "The First Night of the Wake" is an excerpt from his novel-in-progress. In 1976 he founded the influential Queens College Evening Reading Series.

Don DeLillo is among the most acclaimed contemporary American novelists. The Jerusalem Prize, the National Book Award, and the Pen/Faulkner Award are just a few of the many awards he has received. *The Body Artist* (2001) is his most recent novel; among his earlier works are *Underworld* (1997), *Mao II* (1991), and *White Noise* (1985). DeLillo grew up in the Bronx.

Lina del Tinto Demarsky published her first novel, *Leaven of the Pharisees: The Dark Side of Italian-American Life,* in 1991. She produces the television show *The Italian American Experience,* which seeks to improve the image of Italian Americans and their impact on American culture. Born in Italy, Demarsky now lives in New York City.

Mary Russo Demetrick is the owner of Hale Mary Press and the author of a number of poetry collections, including *Word of Mouth* (1990), *First Pressing* (1994), *Hey!* (1997), and *Malachite and Agate* (1997). She grew up in Syracuse, New York, where she still lives and works.

Tina De Rosa is the author of *Paper Fish,* set in an Italian American neighborhood in Chicago in the 1940s and 1950s. Published in a limited edition in 1980, the book was later revived by scholars and republished to acclaim and a wider readership. De Rosa also wrote *Bishop John Baptist Scalabrini, Father to the Migrant* (1986).

Louise DeSalvo is the author of a number of books, including *Casting Off: A Novel* (1988) and *Vertigo: A Memoir* (1996), as well as a groundbreaking biographer of Virginia Woolf. She grew up in Jersey City and holds a named chair as a professor of English and women's studies at Hunter College.

Carole DeSanti is editor-at-large at Penguin Putnum, where she has worked closely with such authors as Terry McMillan, Dorothy Allison, and Ruth Ozeki.

Rachel Guido deVries is a poet and fiction writer. *How to Sing to a Dago and Other Canzonetti* (1996) is a collection of poetry; *Tender Warriors* (1986) is a novel. DeVries teaches creative writing at the Humanistic Studies Center of Syracuse University.

Pietro di Donato published the highly acclaimed and tremendously successful novel *Christ in Concrete* in 1939. His later works include the novels *This Woman* (1958) and *Three Circles of Light* (1960). Born in 1911, Pietro Di Donato died in 1992.

Elvira Di Fabio has published a number of translations, book reviews, and articles. She has a Ph.D. from Harvard University, where she directs Italian language instruction and teaches advanced courses in language and culture. She also teaches Italian studies at the Harvard University Extension School.

W. S. Di Piero has published six books of poetry, the most recent of which is *Skirts and Slacks* (2001); *Shadows Burning* (1995) and *The Restorers* (1992) are among his earlier works. He also has published several collections of essays. A former Guggenheim Fellow, he lives in San Francisco and teaches at Stanford University.

Diane di Prima is a poet, playwright, cultural activist, and editor. A few of her many works are *This Kind of Bird Flies Backward* (1958), *Dinners and Nightmares* (1961), *Earthsong* (1968), *Memoirs of a Beatnik* (1969), and *Seminary Poems* (1991). She was born in Brooklyn in 1934.

John Fante was born in Colorado in 1909. His short stories appeared in such publications as *The Atlantic Monthly, The American Mercury,* and *Esquire.* He published several novels, including *Wait Until Spring, Bandini* (1938) and *Ask the Dust* (1939), and also wrote a number of screenplays. Fante died in 1983.

Lawrence Ferlinghetti, a poet and playwright, is considered one of the founders of the Beat poetry movement of the 1950s, along with Allen Ginsberg and Jack Kerouac. His works include *A Coney Island of the Mind* (1958), *Where Is Vietnam?* (1965), *Wild Dreams of a New Beginning* (1988), and *How to Paint Sunlight: Lyric Poems and Others* (1997–2000).

Robert Ferro is the author of several well-received novels, including *The Family of Max Desir* (1983) and *The Others* (1977). He wrote *Atlantic: The Autobiography of a Search* (1970) with Michael Grumley. His last novel, *Second Son,* was published in 1988, not long before Ferro's death from AIDS. He was born in 1941.

Camille Lavieri Forman is the author of *A Perfect Time for Butterflies,* a memoir and family history. Forman's parents were from southern Italy; she grew up in an Italian American neighborhood in Hartford, Connecticut.

Rocco Fumento is a novelist. *Tree of Dark Reflection* was published in 1962; *Devil By the Tail,* about a boy growing up in an Italian American neighborhood in Massachusetts, appeared in 1954. He continues to live in Massachusetts.

Richard Gambino is a professor emeritus and former director of Italian American studies at Queens College, CUNY. He is the author of the influential *Blood of My Blood: The Dilemma of the Italian-Americans* (1974), along with a number of other works, including *Bread and Roses* (1981). He co-founded the magazine *Italian Americana* in 1974.

Fred Gardaphé has published a number of influential studies; he is the author of *Dagoes Read: Tradition and the Italian American Writer* (1995) and editor of *Italian American Ways, From the Margin: Writings in Italian Americana* (1991), among other works. Born in Chicago, Gardaphé is now a professor of Italian American studies at SUNY Stony Brook.

Sandra M. Gilbert is the acclaimed author of several books of poetry, the most recent of which is *Kissing the Bread: New and Selected Poems, 1969–1999.* She is also a major literary critic, and the author, with Susan Gubar, of the influential *The Madwoman in the Attic: The Woman Writer and the Nineteenth-Century Imagination* (1979). She teaches at the University of California, Davis.

Maria Mazziotti Gillan has published seven books of poetry, including *Things My Mother Told Me* (1999), *The Weather of Old Seasons* (1991), and *Winter Light* (1985). She is the co-editor, with her daughter, of the award-winning *Identity Lessons: Contemporary Writing About Learning to be American* (1999).

Dana Gioia's collections of poetry include *Daily Horoscope* (1986), *The Gods of Winter* (1991), and *Interrogations at Noon* (2001). He is also the author of two collections of essays and an opera libretto, among other works. Gioia grew up in Los Angeles.

Daniela Gioseffi's books of poetry include *Word Wounds and Water Flowers* (1995) and *Going On* (2000). She won an American Book Award for *Women on War: International Voices* (1990) and a World Peace Award for *On Prejudice: A Global Perspective* (1993). She has lived in Brooklyn Heights for many years.

Arturo Giovannitti emigrated from Italy at the turn of the century. He was a poet and well-known labor activist. *Arrows in the Gale,* his first poetry collection, appeared in 1914; *The Collected Poems of Arturo Giovannitti* was published in 1975. Giovannitti died in 1959.

Edvige Giunta teaches English at New Jersey City University. She is the editor of a special issue of *VIA: Voices in Italian Americana* on Italian American women writers and the co-editor with Louise DeSalvo of *The Milk of Almonds.* She is also the author of influential afterwords to Tina De Rosa's *Paper Fish* and Helen Barolini's *Umbertina.*

John Glavin is a professor of English at Georgetown University. He has an M.A. from Georgetown and a Ph.D. from Bryn Mawr. He is the author of *After Dickens: Reading, Adaptations and Performance* (1999), as well as numerous articles and plays, and the editor of a book on Dickens and film.

Barbara Grizzuti Harrison, raised in Brooklyn, was an award-winning travel writer and essayist. Her works include *Italian Days* (1990), *An Accidental Autobiography* (1996), and *Visions of Glory: A History and a Memory of the Jehovah's Witnesses* (1978). She died in 2002.

Josephine Gattuso Hendin is the author of *The World of Flannery O'Connor* (1970) and a contributor to *Vulnerable People: A View of*

American Literature Since 1945; she has also served as fiction editor of *Savvy.* Born in New York City, Hendin has taught at Yale University, the New School for Social Research, and New York University, and is Tiro a Segno Foundation Professor of Italian American Studies.

Joanna Clapps Herman is a writer whose works have appeared in such publications as *Calliope, Massachusetts Review, Critic, Voices in Italian Americana, Woman's Day,* and the *Crescent Review.* She teaches at CUNY's Center for Worker Education.

Evan Hunter is the prolific author of such works as *The Blackboard Jungle* (1954) and *Strangers When We Meet* (1958). As Ed McBain, his numerous books include *The Big Fix* (1952) and the well-known Eighty-seventh Precinct novels. He has also written a number of short stories, plays, screenplays, and television scripts. He was born in New York City in 1924.

Albert Innaurato is a renowned playwright, and the recipient of a 1975 Guggenheim Fellowship. Among his works are *Gemini* (1977), *Coming of Age in Soho* (1985), and *The Transfiguration of Benno Blimpie* (1977).

Marisa Labozzetta is a writer of fiction who lives in Massachusetts. Her first novel, *Stay With Me, Lella,* was published in 1999, and she has taught at Smith College and elsewhere.

Wally Lamb is a former teacher and the best-selling author of *She's Come Undone* (1992) and *I Know This Much Is True* (1998). He has published fiction and nonfiction in the *New York Times Magazine* and the *Missouri Review,* along with numerous other publications. Lamb lives in Connecticut.

Garibaldi M. Lapolla was the author of several influential early works of Italian American fiction. His novels include *The Fire in the Flesh* (1931), *Miss Rollins in Love* (1932), and *The Grand Gennaro* (1935), which is set in the Italian American Harlem of the 1890s. Lapolla died in New York City in 1954.

Salvatore La Puma is a writer raised in Brooklyn. His works include *The Boys of Bensonhurst* (1987), winner of the Flannery O'Connor Award for short fiction, *A Time for Wedding Cake* (1991), and *Teaching Angels to Fly* (1992).

Maria Laurino is a New York essayist and journalist. The author of the acclaimed *Were You Always an Italian?: Ancestors and Other Icons of Italian America* (2000), her work has also appeared in such publications as the *New York Times* and the *Village Voice*. Laurino grew up in New Jersey.

Jay Leno is a stand-up comedian and host of the award-winning *The Tonight Show*. He is the author, with **Bill Zehme**, of the autobiography *Leading with My Chin* (1996). Leno grew up in Andover, Massachusetts, and now lives in Los Angeles.

Frank Lentricchia is an influential literary critic who, since turning away from literary theory in 1996, has published three novels and a memoir. His many works include *Lucchesi and the Whale* (2001), *The Music of the Inferno* (1999), and *Criticism and Social Change* (1983). He is a professor of English at Duke University.

Jerre Mangione's works include *Mount Allegro* (1943), *Reunion in Sicily* (1968), and *The Dream and the Deal: The Federal Writers' Project 1935–43* (1972). He is the co-author of the acclaimed *La Storia: Five Centuries of the Italian American Experience* (1992). The son of Sicilian immigrants, Mangione grew up in Rochester, New York.

Mary Ann Mannino is the author of *Revisionary Identities: Strategies of Empowerment in the Writing of Italian American Women* (2000). A visiting professor at Temple University, she has also published short stories, poems, and essays in many journals.

Paul Mariani, an award-winning poet and biographer, teaches at Boston College. His collections of poetry include *The Great Wheel* (1996), *Salvage Operations* (1990), and *Timing Devices* (1979). *William Carlos Williams: A New World Naked* (1981) and *Lost Puritan: A Life of Robert Lowell* (1995) are among his biographies.

Carole Maso, an award-winning writer who grew up in Paterson, New Jersey, is the author of such works as *Defiance* (1998), *Ghost Dance* (1996), *The Art Lover* (1990), and *The Room Lit by Roses: A Journal of Pregnancy and Birth* (2000).

Christine Palamidessi Moore, formerly a New York City journalist, now writes fiction and teaches writing at Boston University. The excerpt "The Virgin's Nose" reclaims the original title of her novel *The Virgin Knows* (1995).

Ben Morreale's novels include *The Seventh Saracen* (1958), *A Few Virtuous Men* (1973), and *The Loss of the Miraculous* (1997). He is the co-author of *La Storia: Five Centuries of the Italian American Experience* (1992). His parents were Sicilian immigrants; Morreale was born in New York City.

George Panetta, known for his portrayals of Italian American life in New York, is the author of *We Ride a White Donkey* (1944), *Jimmy Potts Gets a Haircut* (1947), *Viva Madison Avenue!* (1957), and *The Sea Beach Express* (1966).

Paul Paolicelli, a television journalist and producer, is also the author of *Dances with Luigi: A Grandson's Determined Quest to Comprehend Italy and the Italians* (2000). He grew up in Pittsburgh.

Joseph Papaleo's works include *All the Comforts* (1967) and *Out of Place* (1970). Born in 1925 and raised in the Bronx, Papaleo taught English at Sarah Lawrence for thirty years and now lives in Florida.

Jay Parini is a poet, novelist, and biographer; among his works are two books of poetry, *Anthracite Country* (1982) and *House of Days* (1998), and several novels, including *The Last Station* (1990), *Benjamin's Crossing* (1997), and *The Apprentice Lover* (2001). He teaches English and directs the writing program at Middlebury College.

Gianna Patriarca, a poet, was born in Italy and emigrated to Canada as a child. She is the author of two books, *Italian Women and Other Tragedies* (1995) and *Daughters for Sale* (1997), and her work has appeared in numerous publications. She teaches elementary school.

Sadie Penzato, a first-generation Sicilian American, taught art for twenty years and now writes and paints in Highland, New York. *Growing Up Sicilian and Female* (1991) is her first book.

Lucia Perillo is an award-winning poet whose books include *Dangerous Life* (1989), *The Body Mutinies* (1997), and *The Oldest Map with the Name America: New and Selected Poems* (1999). She grew up in a small Hudson River town.

Mario Puzo, born in New York City in 1920, is the popular author of such novels as *The Fortunate Pilgrim* (1965), *The Godfather* (1969), *Fools Die* (1978), and *The Fourth K* (1991). He also wrote a number of screenplays, including the entire *Godfather* trilogy. Puzo died in 1999.

Rose Quiello holds a Ph.D. in literature and currently teaches at Albertus Magnus College in New Haven. She has published articles on such writers as Anne Tyler, Fay Weldon, Kate O'Brien, and John Milton.

Giose Rimanelli, professor emeritus at SUNY Albany, has published fiction, poetry, literary criticism, and journalism. His works include *Accademia* (1997), *Jazzymood,* and *Benedetta in Guysterland: A Liquid Novel* (1993), winner of the American Book Award.

Ray Romano is a comedian and star of the hit sitcom *Everybody Loves Raymond. Everything and a Kite* (1998) is his first book. Romano grew up in Forest Hills, Long Island.

Agnes Rossi is the author of *The Quick* (1992) and *Athletes and Artists* (1987), both collections of short stories, along with two novels, *Split Skirt* (1994) and the acclaimed *The Houseguest* (2000). She lives and teaches in New Jersey.

Mary Jo Salter's collections of poems include *A Kiss in Space* (1999), *Henry Purcell in Japan* (1985), *Unfinished Painting* (1989), and *Sunday Skaters* (1994). She grew up in Detroit and Baltimore, and now teaches at Mount Holyoke College.

Mary Saracino is the award-winning author of *Voices of the Soft-Bellied Warrior* (2001), *Finding Grace* (1999), and *No Matter What* (1994). Her work has appeared in a number of other publications, including *Voices in Italian Americana.*

Jeanne Schinto is the author of *Huddle Fever: Living in the Immigrant City* (1995), a history of Lawrence, Massachusetts. She also has written *Children of Men* (1991), a novel, and *Shadow Bands* (1988), a collection of stories. She is the editor of several anthologies of short stories.

Chris Mellie Sherman is an Italian American freelance writer and a weekly columnist for the *Daily News* of Newburyport, in Massachusetts.

S. Shevitch is the co-author of *Misfits and Remnants* (1886), considered possibly the first collection of Italian American fiction. He also published "Russian Novels and Novelists of the Day," in the *North American Review* (1879), which compares the works of Tolstoy and Turgenev, and debated widely on social and economic reform.

Felix Stefanile was born to Italian immigrants in New York City in 1920 and taught for many years at Purdue University. He is the award-winning author of such works as *The Country of Absence* (1999), *The Dance at St. Gabriel's* (1995), and *In That Far Country* (1982). With his wife, he founded the influential poetry magazine *Sparrow.*

Gay Talese is an acclaimed nonfiction writer. His works include *The Bridge* (1964), *The Kingdom and Power* (1969), *Thy Neighbor's Wife* (1980), *Unto the Sons* (1992), and *Origins of a Nonfiction Writer* (1996). He was born in 1932 in Ocean City, New Jersey, where he spent his childhood.

Mari Tomasi is the author of *Deep Grow the Roots* (1940) and *Like Lesser Gods* (1949), a fictional account of the hardships of immigrant quarry workers in Vermont in the first half of the twentieth century.

Lewis Turco is an acclaimed writer and scholar whose works include *A Book of Fears* (1998), *Shaking the Family Tree, A Remembrance* (1998), *The Shifting Web* (1989), and *The Book of Forms: A Handbook of Poetics,* 3rd edition (2000).

Anthony Valerio is the author of *The Mediterranean Runs Through Brooklyn* (1982), *Valentino and the Great Italians* (1986), and *Conversation with Johnny* (1997), among other works. He lives in Connecticut and New Jersey.

L. D. Ventura was the author of *Peppino* (1885), a fictional account of the early immigrant experience, and the co-author of *Misfits and Remnants* (1886), considered perhaps the first collection of Italian American fiction.

Robert Viscusi is the author of *An Oration Upon the Most Recent Death of Christopher Columbus* (1993), *Max Beerbohm, or the Dandy Dante: Rereading with Mirrors* (1986), and *Astoria* (1995), a novel. Viscusi grew up in Astoria, Queens, and now teaches at Brooklyn College.

Octavia Waldo, whose full name is Octavia Capuzzi Waldo Locke, is a writer and artist best known for her 1961 novel, *A Cup of the Sun.*

Credits

"Poverty of Language" and "Infidel" by Peter Covino. Used with permission of the author.

Excerpts from *Family Honor: An American Life* by George Cuomo. Copyright © 1983 by George Cuomo. Used by permission of Doubleday, a division of Random House, Inc.

Excerpts from *Underworld* by Don DeLillo. Copyright © 1997 by Don DeLillo. Excerpted with permission of the author and Scribner, a Division of Simon & Schuster, Inc.

Excerpt from *Leaven of the Pharisees: The Dark Side of Italian-American Life* by Lina del Tinto Demarsky (Bedford Press, 1991). Used by permission of the author.

"I study Italian" from *La Festa della Donna: First Pressing* by Mary Russo Demetrick (Hale Mary Press, 1994). "I stash treasures" from *Italian Notebook* by Mary Russo Demetrick (Hale Mary Press, 1994). Used by permission of the author.

Excerpt from *Paper Fish* by Tina De Rosa. Copyright © 1980 by Antoinette De Rosa. Reprinted by permission of the author and The Feminist Press at the City University of New York (www.feministpress.org).

Excerpt from *Vertigo* by Louise DeSalvo. Copyright © 1996 by Louise DeSalvo. Reprinted by permission of The Feminist Press at the City University of New York (www.feministpress.org). Excerpt from *Breathless* by Louise DeSalvo (Beacon Press). Copyright © 1997 by Louise A. DeSalvo. Used by permission of the author.

Excerpt from *Tender Warriors* by Rachel Guido deVries. Used by permission of Firebrand Books, Milford, Connecticut.

Excerpts from *Christ in Concrete* by Pietro di Donato. Copyright Bobbs-Merrill Co., 1939. Copyright renewed Pietro di Donato, 1967. Used by permission of Signet, a member of Penguin Putnam Inc.

"The Depot" from *Shadows Burning* by W. S. Di Piero. Copyright © 1995 by W. S. Di Piero. All rights reserved. Reprinted with permission of Northwestern University Press. "Sabbioneta to Parma" from *The Dog Star* by W. S. Di Piero. Copyright © 1990 by W. S. Di Piero. Reprinted with permission of the University of Massachusetts Press.

FOR THE BEST IN PAPERBACKS, LOOK FOR THE

In every corner of the world, on every subject under the sun, Penguin represents quality and variety—the very best in publishing today.

For complete information about books available from Penguin—including Puffins, Penguin Classics, and Compass—and how to order them, write to us at the appropriate address below. Please note that for copyright reasons the selection of books varies from country to country.

In the United Kingdom: Please write to *Dept. EP, Penguin Books Ltd, Bath Road, Harmondsworth, West Drayton, Middlesex UB7 0DA.*

In the United States: Please write to *Penguin Putnam Inc., P.O. Box 12289 Dept. B, Newark, New Jersey 07101-5289* or call 1-800-788-6262.

In Canada: Please write to *Penguin Books Canada Ltd, 10 Alcorn Avenue, Suite 300, Toronto, Ontario M4V 3B2.*

In Australia: Please write to *Penguin Books Australia Ltd, P.O. Box 257, Ringwood, Victoria 3134.*

In New Zealand: Please write to *Penguin Books (NZ) Ltd, Private Bag 102902, North Shore Mail Centre, Auckland 10.*

In India: Please write to *Penguin Books India Pvt Ltd, 11 Panchsheel Shopping Centre, Panchsheel Park, New Delhi 110 017.*

In the Netherlands: Please write to *Penguin Books Netherlands bv, Postbus 3507, NL-1001 AH Amsterdam.*

In Germany: Please write to *Penguin Books Deutschland GmbH, Metzlerstrasse 26, 60594 Frankfurt am Main.*

In Spain: Please write to *Penguin Books S. A., Bravo Murillo 19, 1° B, 28015 Madrid.*

In Italy: Please write to *Penguin Italia s.r.l., Via Benedetto Croce 2, 20094 Corsico, Milano.*

In France: Please write to *Penguin France, Le Carré Wilson, 62 rue Benjamin Baillaud, 31500 Toulouse.*

In Japan: Please write to *Penguin Books Japan Ltd, Kaneko Building, 2-3-25 Koraku, Bunkyo-Ku, Tokyo 112.*

In South Africa: Please write to *Penguin Books South Africa (Pty) Ltd, Private Bag X14, Parkview, 2122 Johannesburg.*